Some Major
ARCHAEOLOGICAL SITES
of the
SOUTHWEST

THE ARCHAEOLOGY
OF ARIZONA

PAUL S. MARTIN · FRED PLOG

THE ARCHAEOLOGY OF ARIZONA

A STUDY OF
THE SOUTHWEST REGION

PUBLISHED FOR

THE AMERICAN MUSEUM OF NATURAL HISTORY

DOUBLEDAY/NATURAL HISTORY PRESS, GARDEN CITY, NEW YORK

1973

ISBN: 0–385–07075–6
Library of Congress Catalog Card Number 72–76192

To W.A.L. and P.L.S.

CONTENTS

LIST OF ILLUSTRATIONS

ACKNOWLEDGMENTS

No matter the type of book, every one has many authors. For the sake of convenience, this book credits only two authors; but this does not blind us to the fact that many people have contributed to our efforts. Some we can name for conspicuous help; others remain anonymous, not because of willful omission but because we cannot always recall whence came many of our ideas. It is generally true, we think, that almost all of our teachers, colleagues, friends, and acquaintances have helped us with the book by presenting us with impressions, images, inspirations, or concepts, parts of which we have freely taken and have interwoven with our own notions. To these unnamed friends we owe a great debt and one that we gladly acknowledge.

The other colleagues-associates are easier to list and to remember because they were constantly at our elbows and orbiting in our galaxy, nudging us and assisting us by reading, criticizing, suggesting, editing, rewriting, and ministering to our needs in many ways.

Before mentioning them, however, we must speak of a unique kind of help given to us by Mr. and Mrs. James Carter of Snowflake, Arizona. They made available to us their immense ranch on which there are hundreds of sites spanning several millennia, any one of which was ours for unrestricted study and unlimited types of digging. This vast laboratory, Hay Hollow Valley, is rich beyond description—rich with data that served to test our many hypotheses all generated in the light of this fruitful research area. Over this vast domain we were free to roam to search for whatever data we required. We owe the Carters great and unceasing thanks for their gifts.

For gracious and good-hearted help, all thanks be to:

Katherine Bartlett, for assistance in using the library of the Museum of Northern Arizona.

Daniel Bowman, for reading, criticizing, and polishing clumsy sentences and mediocre reasoning.

Ellen Bowman, for typing the final versions of the senior author's chapters and the bibliography.

Edward B. Danson, for making available the resources of the Museum of Northern Arizona.

Glen DeGarmo, for helpful suggestions on organizing the material concerning Arizona environments.

Charles Di Peso, for supplying Xerox copies of unavailable data and for supplemental information on the Hohokam.

Mrs. Agnes McNary Fennell, for typing the first drafts from the senior author's longhand versions, and for retyping a second and third draft of many chapters.

Edwin N. Ferdon, Jr., for loaning the senior author books not available to him.

Donald C. Fiero, for data on late, large pueblos.

John M. Fritz, for reading and correcting the chapter on hunters and gatherers.

Cheryl Garrett, for contributing substantially to the discussion of prehistoric water control systems.

Frederick J. Gorman, for special help on the chapter on Anasazi settlement patterns and subsistence, and for creative suggestions concerning late Anasazi culture.

David A. Gregory, for help and criticism of many chapters and in particular for co-writing (through six drafts) the final chapter in the book.

John A. Hanson, for pointing out inconsistencies and for general help.

Alexander J. Lindsay, Jr., for presenting us with a copy of his doctoral dissertation, for the loan of books, and for supplying the senior author with unpublished data from the Kayenta area.

William A. Longacre III, for ideas, for supplying unpublished data about Grasshopper Ruin, for guiding the senior author into undertaking his share of this book, for broadening his philosophy, and for converting him to an anthropologist.

Thomas A. Murray, for spending endless library hours hunting up names and accomplishments of early archaeologists and for compiling the list given at the end of chapter I.

Gayle Plog, for typing preliminary and final versions of some chapters and for endless hours of discussion with and encouragement to the junior author.

Daniel Schecter, for supplying data (with Fiero) on late pueblos.

Michael B. Schiffer, for many suggestions concerning the flow and recycling of cultural elements.

Earl H. Swanson, Jr., for reading and criticizing the chapter on hunters and gatherers and for supplying the senior author with unpublished data.

R. Gwinn Vivian, for sending the senior author Xerox copies of data that his father collected and for unpublished data on irrigation systems in Chaco Canyon, New Mexico.

Tamsin Willard, for reading and correcting first drafts and for making bibliographic cards.

Ezra B. W. Zubrow, for long talks held on morning walks with the senior author at Vernon, for suggestions and inspirations, for critical readings of "sticky" portions, and for creative ideas concerning depletion of resources and the economics of land uses.

Without the support of the Directors of the Field Museum of Natural History—Mr. Stephen Simms, Colonel C. C. Gregg, and, presently, Mr. E. Leland Webber—and the financial backing that the Trustees of the Museum have made available to the senior author for over forty years, this book would not have been possible. By permitting him to concentrate on the Southwest and to investigate any problem of his choosing, the senior author has been able to expand his horizons and to change goals as new perspectives loomed on the archaeological horizon. When his status changed from that of Chairman of the Department of Anthropology to that of Emeritus, financial and moral help continued unabated. That his stance has altered over the past forty years will be clear to readers of this book. In great part this has been due to student-colleagues with whom he has worked, for the reason that they are blessed with a fresh, questioning outlook and are not satisfied with the status quo. Their creative minds are restless and energetic, and these traits led to experimentation. Thus, a certain youthfulness has been maintained in the senior author by this spiritual and intellectual skepticism, by this kind of defiance of the traditional, and by a facile communication.

Dr. Donald Collier, present Chief Curator, has supported our research with great enthusiasm, and for his aid we are grateful.

In addition to financial help provided by the Museum, our funds have been augmented by generous gifts from Mr. Ed Alexander, Mr. C. E. Gurley, Mr. and Mrs. Maxwell Hahn, Dr. Charles W. Keney, Mr. Judd Sackheim, and Mrs. Marjorie Kelly Webster.

The great bulk of financial support during the last decade has come from the National Science Foundation (Research Grants G 13039, G 16006, G 22028, GS 245, GS 984, GS 2381; and Undergraduate Research Participation Program Grants GE 8210, GY 97, GY 2944, GY 4601, and GY 7225). The aid generously given our projects is proudly cited. We have accepted it as a mark of esteem and confidence in our ventures. We hope this book will please the administrators of the Foundation and that they will take it as a tangible token of results and of our gratefulness.

Paul S. Martin
Chairman Emeritus
Department of Anthropology
Field Museum of Natural History

Fred T. Plog
Associate Professor of Anthropology
State University of New York, Binghamton

GENERAL INTRODUCTION
TO THE ARCHAEOLOGY OF ARIZONA

The science of archaeology is undergoing a revolution. New and more rigorous analytic techniques and new explanatory hypotheses are being acquired and used. We are directing our attention less to artifacts and more to the cultural processes represented in archaeological sites by the patterned distributions of artifacts. We are proposing explanations that explain (in the sense of prediction) rather than simply describe. In short, the task of being an archaeologist today is very different from what it was ten years ago.

Most of these changes have been applied at the level of a single site, or at most at the level of a limited geographical region (cf. Martin *et al.*, 1964, 1967; Hargrave, 1931; MacNeish, 1962). To date, no archaeologist has sought to apply these same techniques to even a single whole culture. This book attempts such an analysis not only for a single culture but for the many cultures that existed and coexisted in prehistoric Arizona.

In a sense, Arizona is an ideal subject for such a treatment. It has been continuously occupied since at least 10,000 B.C. All of the major cultures of the prehistoric Southwest—Clovis, Folsom, Desert culture, Anasazi, Mogollon, Hohokam—as well as some lesser ones—Patayan, Cohonina, Sinagua—find representatives in this state. Within its boundaries lies as complete an archaeological record as is available anywhere in the world. The cultural processes about which we can learn in studying prehistoric Arizona are essentially the same as those about which we could learn if the entire Southwest were our subject, or any other part of the world.

A. The treatment that we have chosen for the prehistory of this state seeks to blend analyses that are the Southwestern archaeologists' stock in trade with those that are innovations of the last few years. For this reason, we have begun with two chapters dealing with analytic devices. We consider our tools from two viewpoints: as we use them in the present to discover the past, and as they have developed through constant use by archaeologists who have studied the prehistory of Arizona.

B. Most of the analyses of Southwestern prehistory to date have been almost in their entirety a consideration of the spatial and temporal distribution of cultures. Certainly, spatial and temporal distributions provide the basic data from which an archaeologist proceeds. But, they are hardly the whole picture. Thus, we have chosen to treat cultures in their spatial and temporal aspects in a few chapters rather than in an entire work. Clovis, Folsom, Desert culture, Early Agriculture, Agricultural, and Regressive adaptations to the state are defined. When these levels of organization must be split into distinctive adaptations to a particular area—Hohokam to the deserts, Mogollon to the mountains—we do so. Changes in the spatial and temporal loci of the major prehistoric cultures of Arizona are discussed. But, our major attempt is to go beyond these descriptions and to understand what happened and why it happened when the cultures existed and when they ceased to exist.

C. Our most general level of focus, that of *patterns of change* in prehistoric Arizona, is an adaptational one. We have taken the three major environmental zones—the Southern Desert, the Mountains, and the Colorado Plateau—and traced changes in the cultures that were adapted to each at different moments in Southwestern prehistory. We are interested in the resources that were being exploited in different times and at different places and in the organization patterns and the tools that were being used in the exploitation. We attempt to show how and why later adaptations to each of these zones differ from earlier ones.

D. From this general adaptational approach, we have selected two topics for additional attention. First, we consider the tools that were being used in the exploitation of the environment. To date most Southwestern archaeologists have viewed changes in tools as random or at best chronological or stylistic changes. We try to show that whether one is considering a handheld scraping tool or whether one is considering a tool as complex as an irrigation system, change in the direction of increasingly efficient exploitation of ecological niches lies at the basis of the artifact changes.

E. Second, we focus on changes in the patterns of social organization. This concern is at once the youngest and oldest of Southwestern archaeologists. Our justification for being anthropologists has always rested on the assumption that we are interested in "the Indian behind the artifact." Yet, only recently have we developed tech-

niques that allow us to use our data for inferring patterns of social organization. While for many parts of the state the evidence is still scanty, we believe that it is possible to present a coherent picture of what the social organization in prehistoric Arizona looked like.

F. This background, then, provides a setting for a brief but dramatic delineation of the Great Events that have occurred and those that led to the final abandonment of about 90 percent of the area.

G. Finally, we have tried to draw all of the threads of evidence and inference together into an explanation of why prehistoric Arizona changed and grew in the manner that it did. First, we trace patterns of diffusion. The information that can be gleaned from this approach is presented, but its ultimate inadequacy for explaining is stressed. We then go to the more satisfactory evolutionary view of prehistoric Arizona. The archaeological record is viewed as an integrated set of relationships between social, demographic, ecological, economic, and technological variables. The unmistakable similarity between the developmental sequences in prehistoric Arizona and those that have characterized other areas of the world at other times is discussed.

A final chapter is an attempt to put our money where our archaeological mouth is. For many years, archaeologists have stressed their concern with examining the past as a means of understanding the present. Can we really learn something about the contemporary world from looking at prehistoric Arizona? Can the explanation of past cultural changes be relevant to contemporary problems? We believe the answer to these questions to be an affirmative one and we offer our archaeological insights as a means of explaining how this knowledge can be effective.

PART ONE

TOOLS USED IN RECOVERING ARIZONA PREHISTORY

I History of Archaeological Surveys in Arizona— 1880 to Present

The heading of this section, "Tools Used in Recovering Arizona Prehistory," might be construed as meaning stone tools, bone tools, or stone axes; or picks, shovels, and trowels. The sense in which we employ the term here is an extension of the idea that *tools are implements* but signifies a broader interpretation of the word.

Herein, we refer to a *tool* as an instrumentality or an agency for tracing the course of the prehistory of Arizona. A tool in this sense is a means to an end. The term suggests a strategy that is used in fulfilling our purpose—namely, to present, in this section, a history of the past cultures of Arizona.

Obviously, there are many roads to Rome. We regard archaeological surveys, excavations, techniques for dating sites, and the analyses of past environments and climates as well-established procedures for finding out what has happened in Arizona and neighboring areas for the last ten thousand years.

METHODS OF SURVEYS: THEN AND NOW

An archaeological survey is an important tool in carrying out archaeological research and is a carefully planned operation whose purpose is to find and record all sites from surface observations without excavation within a given region. A site is any place formerly occupied or utilized by a prehistoric group; it might be a place where stone tools were manufactured, or where butchering was done, a camp site, a village made up of several semisubterranean houses (pit houses), a stone-walled contiguous room block built on the surface of the ground (a pueblo), a midden or refuse pile, a burial mound or mounds, a temple, a palace, or an irrigation system.

Before an archaeologist can work profitably in an area, he must acquire certain basic information—the form, position, number, extent, nature, and density of the archaeological remains in his region. In other words, he needs to know as much as possible about the entire "population" of his area. He needs to have "control" of available data in order to have an idea of prehistoric demography, settlement patterns, water resources, vegetation, and topography.

The time spent on an area will vary with the area to be covered—a week, a month, or several seasons, and the sites may be searched for on foot or on horseback. Aerial photos are also used to locate indications of sites, actual sites, and traces of former canal routes, as well as other cultural and geographic features.

In conducting a survey a given area is completely traversed in order to miss nothing. If every square yard of a region cannot be traversed, a carefully selected random sample should be employed, the accuracy of which can be predicted.

This is a far cry from the earliest archaeological surveys of the Southwest which were carried out by detachments of the U. S. Army, railroad surveyors, Indian scouts, geologists, prospectors, and curious laymen. The ruins that they reported were often simply "stumbled on," certainly not found by careful planning. The *purposes* of these earliest American explorations were primarily to gain general geographic and geologic knowledge of the newly acquired territory, to find possible railroad routes, to trade with the Indians, to locate sources of mineral wealth, and to find pots. Usually search for prehistoric ruins was incidental to other projects. The members of the exploration parties did encounter Indians en route and did see large standing ruins and many of these facts were recorded in reports, diaries, letters, and magazine articles.

These kinds of explorations made valuable contributions to general archaeological knowledge. They kindled an interest in Southwestern prehistory and hence are invaluable sources of original information on a vast area that was as yet untouched and unspoiled. But these explorations were, from our point of view, haphazard.

After 1880, however, matters changed somewhat for the better. Due to the explorations referred to above, professional men—geologists and natural scientists, many of whom were employed by the newly organized (1879) U. S. Bureau of American Ethnology, Smithsonian Institution—recognized that the southwestern United States constituted a vast, untouched, valuable "laboratory" in which researches could be conducted in social systems, linguistics, prehistory, religion, and the art of American Indians.

Actually, archaeological surveys from the 1880s down to and including some contemporary ones were unstructured and interested mainly in (1) origins and development of cultures in the Southwest; (2) relationships of one group to another; (3) chronological questions, such as dating of sites, dating the earliest evidence of man's appearance in the area, and dating abandonment of certain regions; (4) securing a catalog of sites; (5) obtaining data in order to reconstruct the human history of a region; and (6) providing information for selecting a site for excavation.

One of the chief characteristics of these types of surveys is that they usually do not conform to the rules for statistical sampling and that the sample does not represent a universe or a totality of phenomena in a given area or province. They record only the conspicuous ruins.

EVOLUTION OF ARCHAEOLOGICAL SURVEYS

Among the earliest career personnel were the brothers Mindeleff, Cosmos and Victor.

With the help of Mrs. Margaret C. Blaker, Anthropological Archivist at Smithsonian Institution, Washington, D.C., we were able to obtain a little information about these two brothers.

Victor Mindeleff, 1861–1948, was an architect and a Fellow of the American Institute of Architects. In his early days he may have been a member (1870s) of the territorial surveys of the United States Geological Survey. Certainly he was in the Southwest and made many significant contributions to our knowledge of the area.

We have been unable to turn up any

biographical data on the other brother, Cosmos. We know he too was in the Southwest in the early days, but beyond that, we have not yet been able to give him his due.

Between them they covered an area extending from the Hopi reservation in northeastern Arizona and the Zuni country (western part of New Mexico) westward to the Verde River Valley, Arizona, down to Casa Grande some thirty miles south of Phoenix, Arizona.

In 1890 Cosmos Mindeleff conducted a survey in the valley of the Verde River (in and about Prescott, Arizona) that still stands as a great achievement. It was one of the first major attempts to collect comprehensive data concerning ruins of all types in that valley as well as descriptions, photos, and sketches of irrigation canals. He discovered, partially excavated, mapped, and photographed, on this one survey alone, over eighty sites of all types—pueblos in river bottoms, defensive sites, cave dwellings, boulder-marked sites (agricultural terraces, or check dams?), and the canals mentioned above. He must have traveled hundreds of miles on foot, horseback, or by wagon in the Verde Valley area alone, in the span of a few months. Even today, with good roads and automotive transportation, this would be a prodigious feat.

Not only did he note details concerning the types of masonry, door openings, fire pits, but he provided ground plans of some of the larger ruins. Even more remarkable was his observation that the sites of the Verde Valley lie near the Southwestern limit of the ancient "pueblo" territory and occupied an intermediate position between the area in which are the large, adobe-walled "houses" of the Gila and Salt River Valleys in southern Arizona and those in the northeastern part of the state. The

marked differences between the northern and southern house types, building materials, village plans, and external and internal differences he ascribed to differing environments. Although he quickly rejected this hypothesis as being too simple, he offered no substitute.

The differences that Mindeleff noted between the culture of northeastern Arizona and that of southern Arizona were significant and are now distinguished by two names, Anasazi and Hohokam, respectively.

He concluded that the ruins of the Verde Valley represent a late period in the history of the Pueblo Indians, that the occupancy of any one site was never long, and that the population for the largest ruin of about 300 rooms was approximately 450 people.

An omission in Mindeleff's report was singular. Fragments of pottery were found but no description nor any illustrations were presented. Perhaps he thought fragments of broken pottery were not significant.

The Mindeleff brothers were followed by a host of other professional archaeologists who later became famous for their discoveries and contributions to general archaeological knowledge of the Southwest. To list these early workers here would make tedious reading, but to omit them from this book would constitute a gross affront. At the end of this chapter we have recorded their names alphabetically with approximate dates of their greatest activities and a few of their momentous finds.

Since this book is not a compendium of archaeological knowledge, further examples of archaeological surveys before the 1930s will not be cited. Most of them only differed slightly in methods and goals from the Mindeleff survey. Other parts of the Southwest were naturally exploited, although some archaeologists have retraced the steps of their predecessors in order to verify or expand their results. It is fairly conservative to estimate that about 50 to 75 percent of the major areas of the Southwest (Arizona, Utah—Salt Lake area and southward, New Mexico, southern Colorado, and the northern portion of Mexico) have been searched and prospected for ruins in at least a cursory manner. Some localities or districts have been examined in careful detail.

If all the data from all the surveys were published, we would have a firm foundation for creating and testing ideas concerning social changes or at the minimum we would know where to carry on archaeological researches. Unfortunately, the bulk of survey data is not published or even collected and deposited in a central repository. Publishing data from a survey is expensive and tedious; thus, it is understandable why so little is available. Excellent survey records are filed at several Arizona institutions, notably, the University of Arizona and the Museum of Northern Arizona, Flagstaff.

Changes in methods and goals came slowly, but in the 1920s and early 1930s a noticeable shift took place.

In 1916 Dr. Harold S. Colton, then Professor of Zoology at the University of Pennsylvania, began the first systematic survey of the area near Flagstaff, Arizona. Since the founding of the Northern Arizona Society of Science and Art and of the Museum of Northern Arizona in 1928, the survey of archaeological sites has been continued and the scope extended to include the whole northern part of the state. As a result, this institution has recorded well over ten thousand sites of various types and sizes—not including those found during the enormous Glen Canyon project.

In 1928 Mr. and Mrs. Harold S. Gladwin founded a research institution near Globe, Arizona, and called it Gila Pueblo. The building was designed to resemble a three-story pueblo with terraces or step-backs and ladders for access to upper stories and was indeed built over or on top of an actual Indian pueblo (abandoned in the late 1400s) that the Gladwins had excavated. The first research efforts were directed almost entirely toward archaeological survey on a large and intensive scale.

Mr. Gladwin was interested in establishing the "boundaries" of the various ancient subcultures (Anasazi or Pueblo, Hohokam, Patayan, and so on), but especially the Hohokam, and how much intermingling, trading, and migrating had occurred. He was also concerned with the origins of the various subcultures, what had become of the Indians responsible for the subcultures and why they abandoned their homelands.

Searching for sites, Gladwin and a corps of assistants, several of whom were to become distinguished anthropologists—notably Dr. Emil W. Haury and Mr. E. B. Sayles—combed great areas of Arizona, Utah, Colorado, and New Mexico. It was the most extensive and intensive archaeological survey ever accomplished. The number of sites discovered, accurately recorded on comprehensive forms, and from which a representative collection of sherds—broken fragments of pottery—was taken numbered well over five thousand. Some of the data were published and all were carefully preserved.

This formidable and celebrated example of what a survey could accomplish and could contribute to general archaeological knowledge spurred others to improve and enrich their survey methods. My impression is that until 1950 no one or no institution surpassed this achievement of Gila Pueblo.

The work done under the direction of Dr. H. P. Mera in 1928 at the Laboratory of Anthropology at Santa Fe, New Mexico, and the work done under the direction of

Dr. Reginald Fisher in 1929 at the University of New Mexico resulted in outstanding early systematic archaeological surveys.

The efforts of the Museum of Northern Arizona and of the Laboratory of Anthropology have been continuous or almost continuous (with short breaks occurring because of World War II and/or for administrative reasons) for about fifty years and forty years, respectively. The work of Gila Pueblo was slowed down because of the war and then terminated when Gila Pueblo was dissolved as such and collections turned over to the University of Arizona in 1950. Since that time the Archaeological Salvage Projects of the Arizona State Museum of the University of Arizona have continued survey work coupled with excavations.

For about ten years the Department of Anthropology of the University of Utah and the Museum of Northern Arizona directed their attention, research energy, and manpower to a meritorious project of gargantuan proportions. In 1956, after the Federal Government decided to build another dam on the Colorado River—the recently completed Glen Canyon Dam—these two institutions joined forces to search for all of the sites or ruins that would be flooded, destroyed, or covered by the waters of Lake Powell—the lake that would be created by the impounding of the waters of the Colorado River. Not only did they plan to search for sites and to record in great detail salient attributes of each one (location, size, type of structure, number of rooms, pottery types present and their frequencies, probable date and other information) but they also planned to excavate strategically placed sites, rare types of sites, and both large and small sites.

Thus came into being the Glen Canyon Salvage Project that required about nine years of intensive work and the efforts of over three hundred people to complete the field aspects alone. Three thousand sites were found and recorded. The laboratory work—analyzing, tabulating, checking—continues, and publications based on project data will continue to appear for perhaps another decade. Glen Canyon area is the best known archaeological area of comparable size in the Southwest (Canyon Lands section of Colorado Plateau contains 150,000 square miles).

Until the 1965 Mesa Verde Project, the Glen Canyon Salvage Project stood alone as the largest Southwest survey ever attempted. In fact, since 1965 individual archaeologists have tended to restrict their concerns and requirements to relatively small localities or districts. Aside from some continuing salvage projects in New Mexico and Arizona, there is no necessity for undertaking anything on such a grand scale. This change of tempo has been induced by lack of funds and by changes in goals and research designs.

CHANGES RESULTING FROM FIELD MUSEUM NSF SURVEYS

The survey done by members of the Southwest Archaeological Expedition of Field Museum is a good example of a contemporary project. The senior author and his colleagues Bowman, Gregory, Longacre, Hill, Fritz, Plog and Leone, White, and Zubrow have been carrying on archaeological research for several seasons in east-central Arizona in a portion of a valley known as Hay Hollow. An intermittent stream flows through the valley from the White Mountains to the south and runs northward to drain into the Little Colorado River. The valley and adjacent country belongs to a local rancher, James Carter.

Searching for sites is one of the usual preoccupations of men engaged in conducting a survey, as was stated earlier. In addition, one might use a survey to obtain data for deriving population estimates, to provide us with the number and range of sites in a limited area, and to gather data of a quantitative sort in order to allow us to make inferences about the cultural history of the valley.

Perhaps the most important development of contemporary survey work is that instead of regarding the survey as just a site selector we now consider it an important source of a set of separate, distinct, unrelated, or discrete facts that may be used in a variety of ways. Our experience convinces us that if one conducts the survey in a technically sound way, the data thus derived can be manipulated in such a way as to provide as rich a set of anthropological generalizations as could the excavation of sites.

The important new dimension that this innovative view of archaeological surveys provides is this:

A *properly planned* survey, the data from which are analyzed by the rigorous logic of inquiry common to all sciences, can be employed as the basis for formulating and testing hypotheses relevant to environmental, ecological, and sociological aspects of man's past behavioral patterns and methods of adapting to an ever-changing setting. This type of survey deals with more complex questions than mere delineation of historical events. Hence, it must be more comprehensive in order properly to test these questions.

This newly defined characteristic of archaeological surveys adds greatly to the value, depth, and scope of surveys and brings them into line with other recent innovations in methodology, theory, and practice (see Part Eight).

An example from our recent (1967–68) work in Hay Hollow Valley will perhaps make the whole idea clearer. An area of

eight square miles in the center of the valley floor was selected for the study area. This was plotted on our topographic map and aerial photographs. A team of eight people walked back and forth over small segments of this area, the segments being plotted each morning before going to the field. The map was taken to the field each day so that sites could be marked on it without delay. To insure regularity, each segment of the study area was staked out with stakes ten feet apart at the north and south ends of the grid segment. Compasses were used to keep the surveyors on a true course. Thus each worker was ten feet from the next worker and as they walked they followed parallel courses. When a "site" was observed in the path of the surveyor, he stopped and collected all necessary data: notes and description of the site, vegetation, land marks; a number was assigned the site, and a complete collection of *all* sherds, stone tools, stone flakes, and debris was made and placed in a paper sack numbered to correspond to the site number.

In this arduous manner, nearly every square foot of that eight-square-mile sector was traversed and scrutinized. A total of 250 sites (some as small as 1 meter square) of all sizes, kinds, varieties, and time periods was recorded.

In order to extend our area of sampling and to include tops and sides of the mountain of lava and the floor of the valley on the other side of the mountain (about twenty additional square miles), we decided to use a technique that would save both time and money. We also felt sure that it would give comparable results with a high degree of probability. This different technique is called a "stratified, systematic, unaligned sample."

We felt assured of good results because this sampling technique was based on the intensive survey mentioned above. Using the previous survey as a test case, we determined that we would have reached the same conclusions concerning the valley if we had taken only a 25 percent sample of the eight square miles. We used that figure as our new sampling proportion. On our topographic map, we laid out alternate discontinuous quadrangles and thoroughly searched about every other block or grid area. In all, about twenty square miles was sampled and this netted a total of 125 new sites. Instead of starting our survey with merely the intent to find and record all possible sites, we began with a number of hypotheses some of which can be tested by acquiring the proper data, by analyzing the data statistically, and then by retesting our original hypotheses.

For example, archaeologists have long assumed that villages had to be near a source of water—a seep, a spring; or a stream. One hypothesis, then, might run as follows:

In an arid area, where rainfall is infrequent, nearness to a water source is a prime requisite for the location of a village.

Following this hypothesis our survey then proceeded to collect data from all possible sites in our study area, including a record of the water source probably utilized by the ancient inhabitants of each site. As the data began to flow in, we first placed each site into chronological categories—e.g., A.D. 500–700 or A.D. 700–900. We then placed each site into one of several categories that indicated the topographic situation in our study area:

1. Flats in and near a river valley
2. Hills and low alluvial fans in the valley
3. Mesa and mountain tops
4. Caves

We also noted the water source nearest each site. These sources might be categorized as follows:

1. A river
2. Small stream
3. Springs
4. Seeps
5. Lake
6. Ancient irrigation ditch

And last, we measured the distance from each site to its nearest contemporary neighbor.

Several statistical tests were applied to these data (derived from surveys by Rinaldo and Longacre) (chi-square, coefficient of variability, and nearest neighbor).

With the results of these three tests in hand, we found that in the period of time between A.D. 700 and 900, a major change in the sociocultural adaptation had occurred in our study area. We observed a progressive trend in the direction of an increasingly random (haphazard) distribution of pit house villages—that is, they were dispersed in a maximum way—more so than at any other period in the history of our valley. Clearly, these villages of this period had been built in removed, defensive, or generally inaccessible locations—and nearness to water was *not* a prime requisite at this time period. Hence, a more powerful determinant than nearness to water was operating and causing the people of that period to decide to construct habitation units in hard-to-reach places.

And now one asks, "What would that determinant be?"

At first we did not know, but as a result of several other tested hypotheses it seems highly probable that the reason was *fear*. At about this time, agriculture was becoming increasingly popular and many villages depended more on a farming economy than on a hunting-and-gathering one.

However, there were some people in the area who had not adapted to a farming way of life but continued to depend wholly on a subsistence procured by hunting animals and gathering wild foods.

It is probable that these latter groups looked covetously at the stored surpluses of their farmer neighbors. Hence, there would be attempts to exploit or steal these surpluses of corn, bean, and squash—and, naturally, the farmers resisted. The best protection, however, for them, their families, and their food supplies was to disperse maximally and build their houses in inaccessible, remote, defendable spots—and this is precisely what they did.

Thus, by structuring a survey in logical, deductive-inductive framework, it is possible to test an almost limitless array of hypotheses. Admittedly, some of these hypotheses might have limited value. Others, however, could deal with issues of wide scope and far-reaching significance, such as contemporary world problems—the sudden change from simple hunting-gathering cultures, or pastroal or farming cultures to industrial-manufacturing countries; or with urban problems, or with any relevant contemporary problem on which archaeologists can throw light because they deal with cultural processes that have occurred over long spans of time. Hence, we may frequently resort to predictive models that can be tested against the observed data. The goals of archaeological surveys can be anthropological and are then not different from those of social science. We can attain these goals with our own data from the past by using better and more precise techniques.

We have noted changes from 1880 to the present: from the earliest explorers who noted only the large conspicuous ruins, to a period when the area to be surveyed was well defined and when attention was focused on problems that dealt with origins, space, time, migrations, and environment, through the tremendous and exciting salvage programs some of which continue to the moment, to the present stage where one formulates a hypothesis that can be tested by data from a survey—a hypothesis that will permit us to formulate laws concerning human behavior permitting predictions with a high degree of statistical probability.

But one point should be emphasized over and over: without the work and sweat and efforts of our predecessors—no matter its shortcomings, no matter how we judge it and them—without their researches we would be unable to proceed. We build on their creations, their toil, fortitude, and their devotion to the field. Fifty years from now, archaeologists may think of our research as naïve and purblind.

Thus the tool of archaeological surveys is becoming better, sharper, more refined with time. Chances are that in ten years our survey methods will be superseded by better and more perceptive ones—or at least we hope so.

PARTIAL LISTING OF MAJOR EXPEDITIONS IN THE SOUTHWEST 1880–1970

YEAR	LEADER, PARTICIPANTS	INSTITUTION, CONTRIBUTIONS	PURPOSE	AREA	REFERENCE
1880–1885	A. Bandelier	Smithsonian Inst. Discovered Kinishba and many other sites	Survey	Between 38° and 29° Lat., 105° and 112° Long.	Bandelier, 1890

PARTIAL LISTING OF MAJOR EXPEDITIONS IN THE SOUTHWEST 1880–1970 (*Continued*)

YEAR	LEADER, PARTICIPANTS	INSTITUTION, CONTRIBUTIONS	PURPOSE	AREA	REFERENCE
1883	C. Mindeleff	Smithsonian Inst. Described Mummy Cave, White House, and other cliff ruins	Survey	Canyon de Chelly, Arizona	Mindeleff, 1895, 1897
1886–1888	F. Cushing	Hemenway Exped. Tested Casa Grande, Los Muertos, and irrigation systems	Survey and testing	Salado and Gila Valleys, Arizona	Hemenway, 1892
1890	J. W. Fewkes	Hemenway Exped. Described Ki-Akime, Pinava, and 16 other ruins	Survey	Zuni Reservation, New Mexico	Fewkes, 1891
1891	C. Mindeleff	Smithsonian Inst. Described Casa Grande and other ruins	Survey	Verde Valley, Arizona	Mindeleff, 1896
1895	J. W. Fewkes (Hodge, Judd)	Smithsonian Inst. Described Sikyatki, Awatobi, and Casa Montezuma	Survey	Red Rock Country and Verde Valley, Arizona	Fewkes, 1896
1896	G. Pepper (Nelson, Dodge)	Amer. Mus. Nat. Hist. Dug at Pueblo Bonito	Excavation	Chaco Canyon, New Mexico	Pepper, 1920
1896	J. W. Fewkes (Hough)	Smithsonian Inst. Described Homolobi, Chevlon, Chaves Pass, Cuno Pavi Pueblos	Survey	East-central Arizona near Winslow	Fewkes, 1898
1900–1903	T. Prudden (Wetherill)	Sch. Amer. Arch. Surveyed Canyon de Chelly, Mesa Verde, Chaco Canyon, McElmo Canyon	Survey	San Juan watershed, Utah, Arizona, Colorado, New Mexico	Prudden, 1903, 1914, 1918
1904–1906	E. Hewett	Smithsonian Inst. Described Rito de los Frijoles, Parjarito Park, Yapashi, Otowi, and Tshirege Puye	Survey	Jemez Plateau, New Mexico	Hewett, 1906, 1909a, 1909b

11

PARTIAL LISTING OF MAJOR EXPEDITIONS IN THE SOUTHWEST 1880–1970 (*Continued*)

YEAR	LEADER, PARTICIPANTS	INSTITUTION, CONTRIBUTIONS	PURPOSE	AREA	REFERENCE
1905	W. Hough	U. S. Natl. Mus. Excavated Tularosa Cave	Excavation and survey	Upper Gila River	Hough, 1914
1906–1908	J. W. Fewkes	Smithsonian Inst. Excavated Casa Grande	Excavation	On the Gila River near Florence, Arizona	Fewkes, 1912
1907	E. Hewett (Kidder, Morley)	Sch. Amer. Arch. Dug Pivotal group Wickyup Canyon group, Twin Towers, and others	Excavation	McElmo Canyon, Colorado	Morley and Kidder, 1917
1908–1909	J. W. Fewkes	Smithsonian Inst. Dug at Cliff Palace and Spruce Tree House	Survey and testing	Mesa Verde National Park	Fewkes, 1911b
1908–1909	E. Hewett (Chapman, Nusbaum)	Sch. Amer. Arch. Dug el Rito de los Frijoles, Sun House, Snake Village, and Talus Village	Excavation	Pajarito Plateau, New Mexico	Hewett, 1909a, 1909b
1908	S. Morley	Arch. Inst. Amer. Dug Cannonball ruins	Excavation	Four Corners Region, Colorado	Morley, 1908
1909–1910	J. W. Fewkes	Smithsonian Inst. Described Betatakin, Kitsiel, Pine Tree House, and others	Survey	Navajo National Monument, Arizona	Fewkes, 1911a
1912–1916	N. Nelson	Amer. Mus. Nat. Hist. Dug Pueblos San Cristobal, Largo Colorado, She, Blanco, San Lazaro, Galisteo, Tano	Excavation	Galisteo Basin, New Mexico	Nelson, 1914
1914–1915	A. Kidder (Guernsey, Amsden)	Peabody Mus. Harvard Dug Firestick House, Flute Player House, Olla House, Pictograph Cave, Blue Canyon Cave, Sun Flower Cave, 6 more caves, and 8 other ruins	Survey	Kayenta District	Kidder and Guernsey, 1919

PARTIAL LISTING OF MAJOR EXPEDITIONS IN THE SOUTHWEST 1880–1970 (*Continued*)

YEAR	LEADER, PARTICIPANTS	INSTITUTION, CONTRIBUTIONS	PURPOSE	AREA	REFERENCE
1914–1923	S. Guernsey (Morss, Claflin, Kidder, Amsden)	Peabody Mus., Harvard Tested Segihatsosi, Sandhill, High, Broken Roof, and Turkey Caves, Ford House, Waterfall ruin	Survey and testing	Northeastern Arizona	Guernsey, 1931
1915	N. Judd	Smithsonian BAE Described kivas and ruins in Kanab Canyon and several cave sites	Survey	Western Utah near Great Salt Lake	Judd, 1916, 1917
1915–1916	J. W. Fewkes	Smithsonian Inst. Excavated Sun Temple, Oak Tree, Willow, and Fairview Houses	Excavation	Mesa Verde National Park	Fewkes, 1916, 1917
1916–1918	E. Morris	Amer. Mus. Nat. Hist. Excavated Aztec ruin	Excavation	Animas Valley, San Juan County, New Mexico	Morris, 1928
1916–1930	H. Colton	Smithsonian Inst. Recorded 728 sites in Walnut Canyon, Doney Pk., Gourd Flat, Tolchaco Bonito Pk., Wupatki Basin	Survey	Near Flagstaff, Arizona	Colton, 1932
1916–1917	S. Guernsey (Kidder)	Peabody Mus., Harvard Explored several Basket Maker caves	Survey	Northeastern Arizona	Guernsey, 1921
1917	N. Judd	U. S. Natl. Mus. Dug Betatakin Pueblo	Excavation	Navajo National Monument, Kayenta area, Arizona	Judd, 1931b
1917	L. Spier	Amer. Mus. Nat. Hist. Described Maytsakya, Ojos Bonitos, Show Low, and Pinedale	Survey and testing	The Little Colorado south of the Mogollon rim and from Zuni to Winslow	Spier, 1919a
1917–1923	F. Hodge	Heye Foundation N. Y. Mus. Amer. Ind. Dug Hawikuh ruins	Excavation	Hawikuh, New Mexico	Smith *et al.*, 1966

PARTIAL LISTING OF MAJOR EXPEDITIONS IN THE SOUTHWEST 1880–1970 (*Continued*)

YEAR	LEADER, PARTICIPANTS	INSTITUTION, CONTRIBUTIONS	PURPOSE	AREA	REFERENCE
1918	L. Spier	Amer. Mus. Nat. Hist. Located over 20 sites and described pottery types	Survey and testing	White Mountains, Arizona, Verde Valley-Mogollon rim	Spier, 1919b
1919	J. Jeancon	Smithsonian Inst. Dug Turquoise village or Po-shu-ouinge	Excavation	Chama Valley, Jemez Plateau, New Mexico	Jeancon, 1923
1921–1922	J. Jeancon (Roberts, Allan), (Anderson, Milton, Concevitch)	Denver Univ. and Col. State Hist. and Nat. Hist. Soc. Described numerous pit houses, Pueblos, and a large kiva.	Survey and testing	Northeastern San Juan Basin, Archuleta County, Colorado	Jeancon, 1922
1921–1927	N. Judd	Smithsonian Inst. Dug Pueblo Bonito	Excavation	Chaco Canyon	Judd, 1954, 1964
1923	F. Roberts	Colo. State Hist. and Nat. Survey Hist. Soc. Described the sites of Arboles, Haystack Mt., La Boca, Mancos Canyon, and the Animas Valley	Survey	Southwestern Colorado	Roberts, 1925
1923–1928	W. Bradfield (Cosgrove, Hulbert, Goldberg)	Sch. Amer. Research and Mus. N. Mex. Dug 138 house rooms, a dump, and several burials	Excavation	Mimbres area, Grant County, New Mexico	Bradfield, 1931
1924–1927	H. S. and C. B. Cosgrove	Peabody Mus., Harvard Dug the Swarts ruin	Excavation	Mimbres Valley, New Mexico	Cosgrove and Cosgrove, 1932
1926–1930	C. Cosgrove	Peabody Mus., Harvard Tested Doolittle, Lone Mountain, Steamboat Caves, and 60 other sites	Test excavation	Upper Gila and Hueco, New Mexico	Cosgrove, 1947
1927	F. Roberts	Smithsonian Inst. Dug Shabik'eshchee village	Excavation	Chaco Canyon	Roberts, 1929

PARTIAL LISTING OF MAJOR EXPEDITIONS IN THE SOUTHWEST 1880–1970 (*Continued*)

YEAR	LEADER, PARTICIPANTS	INSTITUTION, CONTRIBUTIONS	PURPOSE	AREA	REFERENCE
1927	N. Morss (Hosmer, Boston)	Peabody Mus., Harvard Described Black Mesa and "proto-Kayenta" Pueblo I, II, III sites	Survey and testing	Kaibito and Rainbow Plateaus, Arizona	Morss, 1931a
1927	E. Hands (Fraps)	Ariz. State Mus., Univ. Arizona Dug a "pit house village"	Excavation	Tanque Verde Mountains near Tucson	Hands, 1935
1927 and 1939	E. Haury and W. Fulton (Anderson, Danson, Tuthill)	Amerind Foundation Dug Painted Cave and found early maize	Excavation	Northeastern Arizona	Haury and Fulton, 1945
1928	E. Haury (Brady, Hands, Hauck, McGregor)	Univ. Ariz. Dug at Vandal Cave	Test excavation	Lukchukai region, Four Corners County, northeastern Arizona	Haury, 1936c
1928	P. S. Martin	Colo. State Hist. Soc. Described Cutthroat Castle, Turkey House ruins, Cottonwood ruins, and Herren Farm ruins	Survey	Ackmen Area, Colorado	Martin, 1929
1928	F. Roberts	Smithsonian Inst. Dug in 80 houses, 2 kivas, 6 circular depressions, and 7 burial mounds	Test excavation	Stollsteimer Mesa, Piedra District, southwestern Colorado	Roberts, 1930
1928– 1929	N. Morss (Sanderson, Boston)	Peabody Mus., Harvard Tested 36 cave sites	Survey and testing	Fremont River, Utah	Morss, 1931b
1928– 1931	E. Campbell	Southwest Mus. Described caves, rock shelters, and campsites	Survey	29 Palms Region, San Bernardino County, California	Campbell, 1931
1929	E. Haury	Smithsonian Inst. Dug Show Low, and Pinedale ruins	Excavation	Mogollon Plateau, Arizona	Haury and Hargrave, 1931

PARTIAL LISTING OF MAJOR EXPEDITIONS IN THE SOUTHWEST 1880–1970 (*Continued*)

YEAR	LEADER, PARTICIPANTS	INSTITUTION, CONTRIBUTIONS	PURPOSE	AREA	REFERENCE
1929– 1930	N. Judd	Smithsonian Inst. Described canals	Survey and testing	Central Arizona	Judd, 1930a, 1931a
1929	F. Roberts	Smithsonian Inst. Described ruins of Kiatuthlanna—18 pit houses, 3 jacal strct., 49 rooms, and 4 kivas	Survey and testing	East Arizona, Apache County	Roberts, 1931
1929	L. Hargrave	Smithsonian Inst. Dug Kin Tiel and Kokopnyama	Excavation	Near Chambers, Arizona	Hargrave, 1931
1930– 1931	J. Steward	Univ. Utah and Smithsonian Inst. Dug Promontory Point Caves, Blackrock Cave, and others along Lake Bonneville terraces	Excavation and testing	Great Salt Lake	Steward, 1937
1930– 1931	H. Mera	Smithsonian Inst. and Lab. Anth. Tested 13 cave sites including Wildhorse, Goat, and Cremation caves, campsites, and pictographs	Test excavation	Southeastern New Mexico and southwestern Texas	Mera, 1938
1930– 1938	P. Martin (Spoehr, Rinaldo, Collier, Yule)	Field Mus. Nat. Hist. Dug Lowry ruins, 2 large kivas, 3 pit houses, and other complexes	Excavation	Ackmen-Lowry area, southwestern Colorado	Martin, 1936; Martin *et al.*, 1938; Martin and Rinaldo, 1939
1931– 1938	B. Cummings (Baldwin)	Ariz. State Mus. and Univ. Ariz. Dug Kinishba Pueblo dated at 1160–1380	Excavation	White River Apache Indian Reservation near Fort Apache, Arizona	Cummings, 1935; Baldwin, 1938
1931– 1933	F. Roberts (Miller, Kimball, Brown, King)	Smithsonian Inst. and Lab. Anth. Described and tested 20 pit houses, 3 unit ruins, and ruins of the Great Pueblo Period	Survey and testing	Whitewater District, eastern Arizona	Roberts, 1939, 1940
1931– 1933	Brew (Lancaster, Dennison)	Peabody Mus., Harvard Dug 16 pit houses	Excavation	Alkali Ridge, southeastern Utah	Brew, 1946

PARTIAL LISTING OF MAJOR EXPEDITIONS IN THE SOUTHWEST 1880–1970 (*Continued*)

YEAR	LEADER, PARTICIPANTS	INSTITUTION, CONTRIBUTIONS	PURPOSE	AREA	REFERENCE
1931–1938	R. Beals (Brainerd, Smith)	Univ. Calif. Dug Monument Valley sites from Pueblo I–III	Excavation	Kayenta-Tsegi drainage, north-eastern Arizona	Beals, Brainerd, and Smith, 1945
1932–1933	E. Hewett	Sch. Amer. Research and Univ. N. M. Dug Chetro Ketl	Excavation	Chaco Canyon, New Mexico	Hewett, 1934
1932–1933	S. Stubbs (Stallings)	Lab. Anth. Dug Pindi Pueblo, ca. A.D. 1300	Excavation	Near Santa Fe, New Mexico	Stubbs, 1953
1932	E. Haury (Hastings and Kimbal)	Gila Pueblo Described Canyon Creek ruin and other cliff dwellings	Survey	Sierra Ancha, on Fort Apache Reservation	Haury, 1934
1932	H. Mera (Stubbs)	Lab. Anth. Dug Jaritas rock-shelter and recovered textiles	Excavation	Northeastern New Mexico along the Canadian River	Mera, 1944
1932	J. Simmons	Ariz. State Mus. Dug Kings ruin, ca. A.D. 1000–1200	Excavation	Upper Verde Drain, west-central Arizona	Spicer & Caywood, 1936
1932	E. Renaud	Denver Univ. Collected Folsom points and described San Luis Valley	Survey	Platte and Arkansas Basins, eastern Colorado	Renaud, 1933
1933	L. Hargrave	Univ. Calif., at L. A. Located several sites including Pueblo ruins and cave sites	Survey	Rainbow Plateau, northern Arizona and southern Utah	Hargrave, 1935b
1933	B. Cummings and L. Caywood	Univ. Ariz. and Ariz. State Mus. Dug Fitzmaurice ruin	Excavation	Agua Fria Drain, west-central Arizona	Spicer and Caywood, 1936
1900	L. Hargrave	Mus. N. Ariz. Medicine Valley, Bonito Park, Citadel Group, Red Rock Country	Survey and testing	Wupatki National Monument, Arizona	Hargrave, 1933
1934–1938	W. Fulton	Mus. Amer. Ind., Heye Foundation	Survey and testing	Texas Canyon, Arizona	Fulton, 1934

PARTIAL LISTING OF MAJOR EXPEDITIONS IN THE SOUTHWEST 1880–1970 *(Continued)*

YEAR	LEADER, PARTICIPANTS	INSTITUTION, CONTRIBUTIONS	PURPOSE	AREA	REFERENCE
1934–1936	F. Roberts (Coffin)	Smithsonian Inst. Dug the Lindenmeier Site, Folsom complex	Excavation	Northern Colorado near Fort Collins	Roberts, 1936b
1934	L. Hargrave	Mus. N. Ariz. Described sites in Tsegi Canyon	Survey	Northeastern Arizona	Hargrave, 1935b
1935–1936	P. Nesbitt (Whiteford, Rivet, Krelschner, Bennett)	Logan Mus., Beloit Dug Starkweather Mogollon ruin	Excavation	Upper Gila area, New Mexico	Nesbitt, 1938
1936	C. Tanner	Ariz. State Mus. Described Blackstone ruins with 92 rooms	Survey	Near Tucson, Arizona	Tanner, 1936
1936	A. Krieger (Heizer, Beardsley, Lance)	Univ. Calif. Dug Humboldt Cave	Excavation	Churchill County, Nevada	Heizer and Krieger, 1956
1936	F. Hibben (Brand, Hawley)	Univ. N. Mex. Dug Tseh So House ruin dating from Basket Maker III	Excavation	Chaco Canyon	Brand *et al.*, 1937
1937	W. Duffen	William Webb Funds Dug Late Gila Polychrome site	Excavation	Graham Mountains, Bonita, Arizona	Duffen, 1937
1937–1942	H. Gladwin (Haury, Sayles, N. Gladwin)	Univ. Ariz. Dug Snaketown	Excavation	South-central Arizona	Gladwin *et al.*, 1937; Gladwin, 1937, 1942, 1948
1938	H. Colton	Mus. N. Ariz. Recorded over 100 sites in Big Sandy Valley, Aquarius Plateau, etc.	Survey	Northwestern Arizona	Colton, 1939a
1938–1942	E. Haury (Bryan, Bailey, Hayden)	Univ. Ariz. and Ariz. State Mus. Dug State Mus.	Excavation	Papago Indian Reservation Southern Arizona	Haury, 1950

PARTIAL LISTING OF MAJOR EXPEDITIONS IN THE SOUTHWEST 1880–1970 (*Continued*)

YEAR	LEADER, PARTICIPANTS	INSTITUTION, CONTRIBUTIONS	PURPOSE	AREA	REFERENCE
1939	F. Scantling	Ariz. State Mus. Dug Jackrabbit ruin	Excavation	Near Sells, Arizona	Scantling, 1939
1939	J. Brew	Peabody Mus., Harvard	Excavation	Northeastern Arizona	Brew, 1940
1939–1940	C. Tuthill	Amerind Foundation Dug site with Mogollon and Hohokam material	Excavation	Sulphur Springs Valley near Gleeson, Arizona	Fulton & Tuthill, 1940
1939	G. Vivian	U. S. Dept. Interior Dug Three-C site ca. A.D. 870–950	Excavation	Chaco Canyon	G. Vivian, 1965
1939–1946	P. Martin (Rinaldo, Wreckler, Yule, Kelly, Braidwood)	Field Mus. Nat. Hist. Dug the Su site, 26 pit houses	Excavation	Apache National Forest, Catron County, western New Mexico	Martin, 1943; Martin & Rinaldo, 1940, 1947
1939–1941	E. Sayles	Gila Pueblo Dug Cave Creek Village and San Simon Village	Excavation	San Simon Valley, southeastern Arizona	Sayles, 1945
1940–1942	E. Renaud	Denver Univ. Described numerous sites in San Luis Valley	Survey	Upper Rio Grande Valley, Colorado, and New Mexico	Renaud, 1942
1940	E. Haury	Univ. Ariz. and Amer. Philos. Soc. of Phil. Dug a large kiva and Bear ruin on Forestdale Creek	Excavation	White Mountains, east-central Arizona	Haury, 1940a, 1940b
1940	B. Cummings	Ariz. State Mus. Dug Segazlin Mesa ruins	Test excavation	Northeast of Navajo Mountain, southern border of Utah	Cummings, 1941
1941–1942	E. Renaud (Chatin)	Denver Univ. Described 20 sites, mostly stone enclosures	Survey	Cuchara Drainage, southern Colorado	Renaud & Chatin, 1943
1942	E. K. Reed	Univ. Utah	Excavation	Mancos Canyon, Colorado	Reed, 1958

PARTIAL LISTING OF MAJOR EXPEDITIONS IN THE SOUTHWEST 1880–1970 (*Continued*)

YEAR	LEADER, PARTICIPANTS	INSTITUTION, CONTRIBUTIONS	PURPOSE	AREA	REFERENCE
		Dug 3 Basket Maker III pit houses, pueblo unit, a kiva, and others			
1946	E. Danson (Dyson, Malde)	Peabody Mus., Harvard / Surveyed Mimbres, Cibola, and Pinelawn regions	Survey	West-central New Mexico and east-central Arizona	Danson, 1957
1947– 1950	H. Dick (Antevs, Mangelsdorf)	Sch. Amer. Research and Univ. N. M. / Dug Bat Cave	Excavation	Catron County, New Mexico	Dick, 1965
1948	G. Baldwin	Univ. Ariz. / Surveyed location of several structure ruins in the area	Survey	Southeastern Utah	Baldwin, 1949
1948– 1950	P. Martin (Rinaldo, Antevs)	Field Mus. Nat. Hist. / Dug Turkey Foot Ridge and other Cochise, Mogollon, and Reserve Phase sites	Excavation	Pinelawn Valley, western New Mexico	Martin *et al.*, 1949; Martin & Rinaldo, 1950a, 1950b
1950– 1953	R. Ruppé (Dittert)	Peabody Mus., Harvard / Dug Los Pilares, caves and shelters in Spider Canyon and Acoma Pueblo	Excavation	Cebolleta Mesa, west-central New Mexico	Ruppé (Dittert), 1952, 1953
1950– 1953	J. Jennings	Univ. Utah / Dug Danger Cave, Juke Box Cave, and Raven Cave	Excavation	Near Wendover, Utah	Jennings, 1957
1950	J. Lancaster (Pinkely, Van Cleave, Watson)	U. S. Dept. Interior / Dug 2 Late Basket Maker III pit houses, 3 Pueblo II Mesa Top ruins, Sun Point Pueblo	Excavation	Mesa Verde National Park	Lancaster, *et al.*, 1954
1951– 1954	E. Bluhm (Barter)	Field Mus. Nat. Hist. / Dug Sawmill or Fox Farm site	Excavation	Pinelawn Valley, western New Mexico	Bluhm, 1957b

PARTIAL LISTING OF MAJOR EXPEDITIONS IN THE SOUTHWEST 1880–1970 (*Continued*)

YEAR	LEADER, PARTICIPANTS	INSTITUTION, CONTRIBUTIONS	PURPOSE	AREA	REFERENCE
1952	E. Haury (Antevs, Lance)	Univ. Ariz. and Ariz. State Mus. Dug Naco Mammoth	Excavation	Naco, Arizona	Haury *et al.*, 1953
1952	D. Taylor (S. and J. Rudy)	Univ. Utah Dug the Garrison site of 17 mounds, 3 depressions	Excavation	Snake Valley near Garrison, Utah	D. Taylor, 1954
1952	P. Martin (Rinaldo, Bluhm, Adams, Kelly)	Field Mus. Nat. Hist. Dug Y Canyon Cave, Casper Cliff-dwelling, Hinkle Park Cliff-dwelling, O Block Cave	Excavation	Reserve area, Pinelawn Valley, New Mexico	Martin *et al.*, 1954
1953	J. Rudy (Kawakami, Brown, Taylor)	Univ. Utah Dug 9 sites, mostly multiroom structures	Excavation	Beef Basin, San Juan County, southeastern Utah	Rudy, 1955
1953	P. Martin (Rinaldo, Cutler, Bluhm)	Field Mus. Nat. Hist. Dug the Higgins Flat, Mogollon Pueblo	Excavation	Reserve Area, New Mexico	Martin *et al.*, 1956.
1954	P. Martin (Rinaldo)	Field Mus. Nat. Hist. Dug Great Kiva, pit house kiva, and sections of 3 pueblo structures	Excavation	Western New Mexico, Mogollon	Martin *et al.*, 1957
1957	P. Martin (Rinaldo)	Field Mus. Nat. Hist. Dug Little Ortega Lake Site, Laguna Salada, a pit house village, and an incipient Pueblo village	Excavation	Upper Little Colorado near Vernon, Arizona	Martin and Rinaldo, 1960a
1958	P. Martin (Rinaldo)	Field Mus. Nat. Hist. Dug Table Rock Pueblo of 50 rooms	Excavation	Little Colorado near St. Johns, Arizona	Martin and Rinaldo, 1960b
1958– 1961	W. Wasley (Schroeder, Zell, Johnson)	Ariz. State Mus. Dug Hohokam sites and several ballcourts	Excavation	Gila Bend, southern Arizona	Wasley, 1960a

PARTIAL LISTING OF MAJOR EXPEDITIONS IN THE SOUTHWEST 1880–1970 (*Continued*)

YEAR	LEADER, PARTICIPANTS	INSTITUTION, CONTRIRUTIONS	PURPOSE	AREA	REFERENCE
1959	P. Martin (Rinaldo, Longacre)	Field Mus. Nat. Hist. Dug Mineral Creek site and Hooper Ranch Pueblo	Excavation	Eastern Arizona near Vernon	Martin *et al.*, 1961
1959	F. Eddy and J. Hester (Dittert, Hammack, Pomeroy, Wendorf)	Mus. N. Mex. Dug Candelria site and Serrano site, described numerous other sites	Excavation and salvage survey	Piedra River Section, Navajo Reservoir, New Mexico	Eddy, Hester, & Dittert, 1963
1959– 1964	A. Hayes	U. S. Dept. Interior Surveyed Wetherill Mesa, kivas, towers, reservoirs; dug at Long House, Mug House	Survey and testing	Mesa Verde National Park	Hayes, 1964
1960– 1961	J. Ambler (Lindšay, Stein)	Mus. N. Ariz. Excavated 10 sites, placed between A.D. 1100–1225, some structures and several pit houses	Survey and excavation	Cummings Mesa, Arizona and Utah	Ambler *et al.*, 1964
1960– 1964	J. Ambler and M. Lambert	Sch. Amer. Research Dug several caves and surveyed Alamo Hueco Mts.	Test excavation and survey	Hidalgo County, New Mexico	Ambler & Lambert, 1965
1962	A. Johnson (Thompson)	Univ. Ariz. Dug Ringo site ca. 1250–1325 A.D.	Excavation	Sulphur Spring Valley, southeastern Arizona	Johnson & Thompson, 1963
1964– 1968	R. Lister	Univ. Colo. Dug sites 499, 875, 866, 1086, and the Far View Group.	Excavation	Mesa Verde National Park	Lister & Lister, 1964; Lister 1965, 1966, 1967, 1968

II History of Archaeological Excavations 1880–1970

Digging a site has always been considered as the "be all" and the "end all" of archaeological work. Many archaeologists have reasoned: "If one could only dig all the ruins in the Southwest, one would have in his hands the answers to all questions concerning the prehistoric peoples." Such a goal is preposterous, impossible, and unintelligent. In fact, one would end up with a mass of meaningless, incoherent data on his hands and would find himself in a sticky position, indeed, and one without any justification.

In the previous chapter we demonstrated that a well-planned survey, executed to provide data for testing various hypotheses, can and should be as rich in harvest yield as an excavation or hundreds of excavations.

It is true, of course, that a well-planned "dig" can provide answers that a survey cannot. For example, one might be interested in testing hypotheses that required answers to such specific questions as:

1. What was the date of the founding of a village or of building a house and when was it abandoned? Answers to these questions might be derived from burned wooden parts of a house, from charcoal in the fire pit, from burned or unburned corncobs, or from animal bones or teeth by means of radiocarbon dating (C_{14}); or if wooden parts of the house structure are in sound condition (burned and not burned) dates might be derived from dendrochronology (tree-ring dating); potsherds or stones lining the fire pit might be dated by means of paleomagnetic or thermoluminescence techniques; or the frequencies of the various types of fossil pollen, if recovered from the floor of a house, might be matched against a dated curve of the biotic and climatic environments for the past two millennia.

2. What plants and animals were used as a means of subsistence?

3. What tools of stone and bone were manufactured and what was the method of making them?

4. Are there definite work areas in or around houses? (That is, was butchering or tool-making, or corn-grinding confined to specific place or places?)

5. Was specialization on the increase?

6. Where were religious functions performed?

7. How complex was the social organization?

8. Was the site dedicated solely to ceremonial or religious services?

Obviously, excavation is required to answer such questions.

Excavations in the Southwest have gone on for about one hundred years. Many of the major excavations were carried on at first by eastern institutions—Peabody Museum of Harvard, the Smithsonian Institution, American Museum of New York City, Field Museum of Chicago—and it is they who own large collections.

EXCAVATION GOALS CHANGE

Interested in the change in excavation goals over the years, we decided to test the following: that archaeological excavations in Arizona during the last hundred years fall naturally into several groupings that represent the then current research goals. That is, all excavations whose purpose was goal X, we would group together. We felt very little risk in embracing this scheme because we started with two premises:

1. Human behavior is not capricious but is patterned;

2. Fashions in science, as in all phases of life, tend to run in cycles.

Thus, we felt safe in assuming that the goals of most of the major archaeologists within a limited time period would be similar if not identical. And we further assumed that no archaeologist of 1880 would suddenly introduce startling innovations such as the use of statistical manipulations, investigating ancient economic systems or varve analysis.

After accumulating the data from the last hundred years, we have tested this hypothesis and have found it to have a high degree of probability.

Accordingly, we shall discuss archaeological investigations under three principal headings or *goals*. This device, because of the premises above, causes the excavations to be ranked chronologically. What an admirable situation!

1. First Hypothesis (roughly 1880–1910). Contemporary Indian cultures are surviving examples of a single homogeneous ancient Pueblo culture.

During the time this hypothesis ruled archaeological thinking and action some of the best known American archaeologists became established—Bandelier, Cushing, the Mindeleffs, Fewkes, Hewett, and Cummings. These men viewed archaeology as living ethnology projected into the past. Culture change was explained as due to migrations of a single people—a gross oversimplification that is still heard in the halls of academe. This philosophy made life easy and simple. To explain prehistoric cultures one had only to look at analogous features in the present-day pueblos. As we shall see, this model was later cast aside and never completely revived; although as a matter of fact, archaeologists, digging in villages abandoned just prior to the advent of the Spanish (1540), often find architectural features and objects that have close parallels to similar entities in modern Pueblo villages. Hence, the idea has merit of a limited kind and may be checked by means of careful testing.

One fact that should be writ large and clear is that several students of that day did speculate about the social organization of contemporary Pueblos and that of prehistoric towns. Irregular ground plans and additions to prehistoric pueblo buildings were accounted for by assuming that matri-local residence required additions from time to time. In addition, the migration of a large social group from elsewhere would require construction of large blocks of rooms to accommodate the newcomers. Since clan was the basic unit of Pueblo social organization, Fewkes, Cushing, and Cummings assumed that clans likewise existed in prehistoric times. In short, some workers were concerned with the nature of prehistoric Pueblo societies—an interest that was considered as heresy after 1910 and quickly dropped as "speculative and not factual." Not until the 1950s did the idea of sociocultural change come again into the theoretical interest of the archaeologist.

The hypothesis then popular (1880–1910) guided research, the data that were accumulated, and the interpretations and explanations. Hence, it is not surprising to find that everything cultural in the Southwest—even including the great adobe structure at Casa Grande—was all viewed as part of a single, undifferentiated Pueblo culture, whereas now we recognize anywhere from two to five subcultures, each one of which has visible and tangible differences.

ALL SOUTHWEST PREHISTORY CONSIDERED TIMELESS

For some reason, archaeologists of this period were not concerned with temporal distinctions. They simply did not care whether village A was older or younger than village B; and no one bothered to worry about absolute time. If forced to date a village, they would give a random and often ridiculous figure (say five thousand years for the Mesa Verde ruins) and walk off in a huff because people asked such stupid questions.

The goals of the time were well described by J. W. Powell, then Director of the Bureau of American Ethnology, who wrote of the purposes of the work of the brothers Mindeleff. In his eighth annual report for 1886–87, pp. xxxiii, xxxiv, Dr. Powell said the Mindeleffs' work had consumed some five years' time and that they had studied the development of architecture and traced the origin of Pueblo architecture from a primitive conical lodge to a two- or three-storied terraced building, and that this end

product was the direct result of a defensive requirement. He further stated their researches plainly showed that the *Pueblo Indians and neighboring tribes were found to be more alike the more they were studied* (italics mine). Hence the hypothesis once popular (prior to 1880), that "all ancient buildings and ruins are the handiwork of a now extinct and vanished race," was demonstrated to be unsound and no longer needed, said Dr. Powell.

PRINCIPAL REASONS FOR DIGGING AT THAT TIME

Perhaps the biggest incentive for digging during this period of 1880 to 1910 was the need to fill museum cases and shelves. These diggers worried but little about a lofty purpose or goal; they needed pots, thousands of them, to fill spaces—and only *whole* pots were wanted. They dug mostly in graves or in large sites where loot was plentiful and rewards great. In fact, during this period, digging for "relics" was considered to be an honorable way of picking up some extra money. Many cave sites as well as open sites were thus rifled of what was then considered "treasure" and the take was sold to collectors and museums. One large museum sent a "scientist" out to the Hopi country to carry on archaeological excavations. He sat in comfort in a house near First Mesa and purchased grave goods by the barrelful—and rarely, if ever, put a spade in the ground.

Another and almost equally great demand for specimens was the market provided by the Columbian Exposition held in Chicago in 1893. Thousands of archaeological items were needed, and agents were sent out worldwide to bargain for and collect the "world's treasures" from the famous ancient cities in Mesopotamia, India, China, and Europe as well as those in North, Central, and South America.

These items now sit mutely on shelves of various museums because little or no information—no "documentation"—accompanied the specimens. The catalog entry may read "pot from Mexico, collected by World's Columbian Exposition." In fairness, the men running the show may not have realized the harm that was being done.

In sum, this period then (1880–1910) was one that produced excellent descriptions of the greater ruins then known and detailed studies of buildings and objects found therein, and saw many of the major large sites quarried in a shoddy, outrageous manner for luxury items and other prehistoric assets. No one knows how many valuable data were scrapped: roof beams, which could have been used for tree-ring work, burned by explorers in camp-cooking fires; skulls and other parts of human skeletons—all of which would have been valuable in making studies in pathology, racial affiliations—all tossed out to rot; and the layering or stratigraphic beds of burial ground turned over and destroyed. Not a period to be proud of, but no worse, no better than past events in all sciences.

Although before 1910 there may have been individuals who were interested in chronology or time measurement and the dating of sites—both relatively to one another and absolutely in terms of years—there is little mention of it in archaeological reports. Distribution of similar types of sites over a geographical area had likewise not been of interest.

Sometime before 1910 the archaeologists Fewkes, Cushing, and the Mindeleffs, who had been banking on Indian oral history and legends to provide interpretations of prehistoric ruins and a guide to their temporal sequences, had become disillusioned.

The myths contained inconsistencies and a maddening vagueness concerning points of geographic reference and cardinal directions. Every subgroup in a Hopi village had its own and differing version of its migrations. Hence, that hypothesis of extracting chronology from legends was dead—washed-out.

The casual attitude toward sequence and dating of sites referred to in the preceding section was responsible for the fact that the idea of stratigraphy (layer upon layer of cultural debris, the oldest usually at the bottom) had been previously ignored. Although this concept of layering had been known and used in archaeological circles since about 1850, the archaeologists of the pre-1910 era had held that stratigraphy did not exist in the Southwest because the remains were those of a single race—the American Indian. In all fairness, it must be mentioned that Richard Wetherill, a cattleman and of the family that "discovered" the Mesa Verde cliff houses, was the first actually to make use of natural stratigraphy. In excavating a cave in Grand Gulch, Utah, about 1890 he found an earlier culture underlying the cliff-house. Since pottery appeared not to be present in this earlier layer but since basketry was abundant, he called the culture *Basket Maker*.

Whatever the cause—and there may be many—a drastic change (about 1911) took place in the philosophy of archaeologists. Rather abruptly, *time* became very important in the thinking of the day, and with it a concern for cultural differences and their distribution in geographic space. This about-face has been termed the time-space revolution (W. Taylor, 1954*b*, p. 563).

Hence a new paradigm or model came into being. The hypothesis that best fits these interests in chronology and distribution of cultural differences may be stated as follows:

2ND HYPOTHESIS (1910–PRESENT)

"Variation in prehistoric sites is a function of their unique position in time and space."

Now in place of speculations concerning social organization and such "trivia," men settled for dating sites, for facts, then collected facts; and, in fact, these goals still dominate much archaeological research in the world.

Collecting facts is important, very much so; but collecting facts *per se* and hoping that they will speak for themselves and tell us what to *do* with our facts is poor science and a vain hope. Experience in all sciences has caused men to shun such a course of action. Instead, over the centuries it has been shown that hypotheses are not derived from empirical data but are invented to *account* for them.

At any rate, fact collecting did overturn some old notions, mainly the one that assumed that all cultures in the Southwest were merely variations of one big uniform Pueblo culture.

As early as 1911, Kidder, who was a student at Harvard University and who had heard of the value of potsherds, was collecting potsherds in the Southwest for Dr. Hewett of the School for American Research. Heretofore, sherds were tossed out, disregarded, ignored. But here was a man, who had been influenced by fresh ideas from the outside world, picking up potsherds from as many sites as he could find. He was not limited by the traditional ideas of one Big Happy Pueblo People, but on the contrary was limited only by the time and space he could devote to this work.

So far as we know, he was the first to begin what we call today a "sherd survey" —the most common attribute of all archaeological surveys today. He sorted his sherds by likeness of color and designs and thus started ceramic typology and analysis. Today, the number of ceramic types has grown uncontrollably and in the Southwest we have over six hundred types of pottery. Types are split into subtypes. Subtypes are again divided. Every time a man finds an unfamiliar type of sherd—Zow—Bang—we have a "new" ceramic type—Gallup green-on-yellow—whereas, it probably is a sherd from the Zuni pueblo area that bears a design in green lead paint that has glazed in firing. And so, sherds "breed types," and only recently has common sense prevailed and has our attention been turned to other uses of ceramic analysis.

Dr. Nels C. Nelson of the American Museum of Natural History brought about the next major archaeological event. He was interested in getting at chronologies by means of changes in pottery styles. In 1912 (Nelson, 1916) he started with the hypothesis that pottery types and decoration change through time. This was *terra incognita* and he was damned as being a radical and too far out. He tested his hypothesis in a large, beautiful, undisturbed prehistoric mound of trash or refuse at a site called San Cristobal, south of Santa Fe, where he found that the principle of layering or stratigraphy worked—that the earliest deposits were at the bottom of his garbage and the latest (broken pottery made after the Spanish entry and thus a "known" item and dated) were at the top.[1] His hypothesis checked out and he tested and retested it in other refuse. Now this hypothesis has become a law—if layers of refuse are undisturbed, those laid down first will be on the bottom—that is, stratigraphy. Thus, a chronological order could be obtained. Today, no one questions this order of things. Geologists have used the idea for two cen-

---

[1] Kidder (1962) gives Richard Wetherill credit for noting Basket Maker materials *below* that of Cliff Dwellers'.

turies; in the Southwest it is barely half a century old.

In the meantime, Leslie Spier (1919a), also of the American Museum, demonstrated in his work in western New Mexico and eastern Arizona that a random collection of potsherds from the surface of a ruin was representative of stratigraphic sequences in the ruin and of its actual time span.

The ultimate tests and intensive excavations to fill out and expand the chronological information derived from various stratigraphic tests, were carried out at Pecos, New Mexico, by Dr. A. V. Kidder over a period of about ten years (approximately 1915–24). Kidder, one of the creative geniuses of our time, analyzed, synthesized, and systematized the results of these excavations, and his work yielded:

1. (*An Introduction to the Study of Southwestern Archaeology*)[2]—the first book to pull together all the new ideas about the Southwest.

2. The Pecos Conference (Kidder, 1927; Roberts, 1936a), the first conference of Southwestern workers to discuss the new ideas that were rocking our world. It is still held annually although nowadays it is spiritless and given to mouthing old incantations; it needs a rebirth.

3. The Pecos Classification—a major ordering of cultural sequences for the northern part of the Southwest and ranked relatively in time, because no dates were then available. This ordering recognized that cultures evolved through time—an *avant-garde* idea for the Southwest in the 1920s, although not new elsewhere.

But absolute dates were still only a hope and a prayer—and then came Douglass and his tree-ring calendar. In 1929 Dr. A. E. Douglass announced the completion of the tree-ring calendar and the

[2] Published 1924, republished by Yale, 1962.

dates of several important ruins (Douglass, 1929). This method was adopted by the profession. Since that day, tree-ring research has become highly sophisticated and the dates, completely trustworthy; and the "calendar" has been extended to cover thousands of sites and encompasses some two thousand years—from the present back to about 50 B.C. Such chronological help makes it possible for archaeologists to measure culture change and improves the context of other cultural interpretations.

In 1931 Harold S. Gladwin of Gila Pueblo and several other archaeologists got together and agreed upon an ordered sequence of culture history (Hohokam) for southern Arizona (Roberts, 1936a). This was a kind of Pecos classification for the lower half of the state, while the Pecos scheme embraced only the northern parts of Arizona and New Mexico.

Thus an interest in time depth and a method for measuring it—tree rings—came into being and seemed to answer archaeologists' prayers.

PECOS CLASSIFICATION AND CULTURE HISTORY

Prior to 1910, excavations were not so numerous. A few large sites—Casa Grande by Cosmos Mindeleff, 1896—and some sites at Mesa Verde by G. Nordenskiold in 1893 were two of the important ones. Some smaller ones and many trash mounds were dug—trash mounds because therein often lay the burials and accompanying grave goods.

After 1912 the tempo picked up because archaeologists yearned for time depth. Most of the major sites that are now well known were dug between 1910 and 1940, and a few major digs continued after the war. A few of the big sites that were investigated in that period are listed below. (This is an incomplete list and names only the sites that we happen to like best. There are others, equally important—see Table at end of chapter I):

Between 1905 and 1910:
    Spruce Tree House and Cliff Palace (Fewkes).
Between 1910 and 1920:
    Aztec (Morris); Hawikuh (Hodge); Pueblo Bonito, Chaco Canyon (Judd); Tyuonyi in Frijoles Canyon (1908) (Hewett).
Between 1920 and 1930:
    Mummy Cave (Morris); Betatakin (Morris, Judd); Chetro Ketl and other Chaco Canyon sites (Hewett); Arizona Caves (Guernsey and Kidder).
Between 1930 and 1941:
    Kinishba, Arizona (Cummings); Awatobi, Arizona (Brew); Snaketown, Arizona (Gladwin and Haury); Lowry Pueblo, Colorado (Martin); Pindi Pueblo, New Mexico (Stubbs) (1922–33); and Paa-Ko (Lambert) (1935–37).

Since 1950 the National Park Service and the National Geographic Society have conducted an intensive survey on Wetherill Mesa, at Mesa Verde National Park, and have excavated several major sites.

Many reports have been published on these and other sites. They are comprehensive accounts of the digging operations as planned or envisioned by the author. They are essentially and totally descriptive but do not deal with causality. Usually the authors tried to fit the data to a growth curve or to a preconceived series of growth stages or cultural horizons so that a history of the site emerges. The Pecos Classification is the one most commonly used by archaeologists working with Pueblo cultures. The Pecos Classification, briefly, set up a series of stages that represented (at that time, 1927) what the archaeologists thought were the major factors in the development and growth of culture. For example, the earliest culture stages were called Basket Maker I, Basket Maker II, and Basket Maker III; and these were followed by five stages called Pueblo I, Pueblo II, and so on. For each stage, there was a series of diagnostic traits, usually unique for a given stage, but sometimes traits, once invested or introduced, were carried on into one or more succeeding stages. For example, the throwing stick or atlatl and coiled, rod- and bundle-type basketry were designated as two of the several diagnostic traits for the Basket Maker III period. In Pueblo I, the succeeding period, the throwing stick dropped out and in its place appeared the bow and arrow, although coiled, rod-and-bundle type basketry persisted.

Hence an archaeologist might have concluded that because 70 percent of the "culture traits" are identified as Pueblo III stage, according to the Pecos bible, then this site under discussion is a Pueblo III site and would date from A.D. 1100 to 1250. The archaeologist also usually tried to show what part his data have played in the history of the cultural development of his particular area. It sometimes took a lot of ingenious bending and twisting to make one's site fit the Procrustean bed of the adopted classification, for no site ever conformed perfectly to any preset combination of traits.

But at that time, the Pecos Classification was significant and useful because for the first time evolutionary order was brought to a chaos of conflicting ideas and evidence. It brought correlated information to a confused era. It produced a synthesis. It clearly demonstrated that in the Southwest a basic, sedentary, pottery-making culture existed and demonstrated without doubt that the culture had evolved, changed, adapted, and acquired the distinctive flavor known as Southwestern. It also made evident that there were two major provinces in the Southwest—a plateau, where the Pueblo and Mogollon subcultures resided, and a desert where the Hohokam subculture flourished. The way of life of each province developed characteristic responses to the environment and each differed markedly.

The Pecos Classification was a high-water mark in archaeological circles and was of great value to those specializing in culture history. Today, it still commands the reverence and respect of an important innovation, but it has long since ceased to be scientifically valid. Too many of the so-called diagnostic traits are useless either because they don't appear in one's dig or because in light of current knowledge they seem less important now than heretofore. But it was a great device and was one of the great contributions that Kidder made to archaeological history.

EXCAVATION METHODS
IN THE AGE OF INNOCENCE

Excavating sites has changed but little over the past sixty years and more sophisticated ideas *concerning* an excavation have only recently been devised.

In the days before tractors, back-hoes, and caterpillars, dirt in a room was loosened with picks and dug out with trowels and shovels. When a pile of dirt became a nuisance or a danger, it would again be moved by shovel or a couple of horses or mules and a scraper.

Nowadays, of course, dirt in rooms and pit houses is removed by skilled use of a back-hoe and immeasurable man-hours are saved.

Whenever possible all the rooms in a pueblo or cliff house were dug—down to the floor. If time or money ran short you did an eeny-meeny-miney-mo kind of calculation on your fingers, pointed to rooms x, y, and z and said they would be omitted from the digging schedule. If a room looked "interesting," "glamorous," "religious," or as if it were a likely place for a cache of extra-well-made pots, then, of course, those rooms were dug first.

At a large ruin in southwestern Colorado —Lowry Pueblo—we started digging at one end and continued toward the other as long as the money held out. We put aside enough money for digging a Great Kiva because at that time it was unique for the area and we dug a number of other kivas simply because kivas should be dug. We trenched a trash mound to ascertain stratigraphy and also to recover loot— whole pots, interred with the dead.

One archaeologist found two adjacent kivas jointed by a tunnel big enough for a man to crawl through. He did not like this because there was nothing in Indian legends to explain such a feature and because no one else had ever reported such an occurrence. Accordingly he walled up both tunnel entrances so tourists would not be misguided.

In the early days, all the dirt from a room was thrown out and with the dirt, all the potsherds, of course. If whole vessels stood on the floor and were not broken by the digger's shovel, they were saved and eventually ended up in a museum case or private collection. In other words, no attempt was made to look for stratified deposits. Frequently, in digging in a building that had been two to four stories high, one encountered the beams that represented a second- or third-story occupation level and the fire pit, cooking pottery and other domestic tools. Beams were torn out, whole pots and "handsome" tools were saved—but nothing so lowly as a flaked core tool or a broken mortar and pestle. Sometimes, a worker on a big dig would fail to report to his supervisor that he had reached the floor of an upper story and would continue right on down without pause.

By 1917, workers usually screened all dirt from rooms and thus recovered sherds and other artifacts. Likewise, the dirt from a room was usually separated into two levels—"fill" and "floor." "Fill" constituted everything from the surface down to within 10 cm. of the floor; "floor" meant all artifacts found on the floor proper and in the first 10 cm. above the floor.

Again by 1917 it was fashionable to save sherds from at least the two levels mentioned above. A few workers (Kidder, for one, at Pecos) put a small trench from surface to floor in the room fill and then looked for natural layers of deposition. These were taken out layer by layer and all materials segregated by levels.

The amount of material recovered from a major site was sometimes astonishingly large. When Dr. Hodge was digging the Zuni town of Hawikuh, about forty miles from the railhead at Gallup, New Mexico, he sent a train of large, horse-drawn wagons loaded with recovered materials to Gallup. It was not uncommon to ship ten freight cars of material per week from Gallup to New York City.

From Awatovi, a large Hopi city that was abandoned about A.D. 1630, Dr. Brew of Peabody Museum of Harvard University, who was in charge of this famous project, recovered well over four thousand pieces of pottery—whole or restorable; and literally millions of sherds (Brew, 1940). Awatovi, by the way, stands as one of the best digs in the Southwest. By "best" we mean careful planning, capable supervision, excellent staff, and fine laboratory analysis,

and cataloguing work. It is not the only big, well-operated dig of the last forty years, but it stands out as a model.

Another very large and famous excavation is that which took place in 1934 at the now-renowned city of Snaketown, an ancient Hohokam settlement of southern Arizona. The excavations and publications were sponsored and paid for by Gila Pueblo; Gladwin was in charge overall; Dr. Emil Haury and Mr. Ted Sayles directed the work (Gladwin et al., 1937). Here again the trenching, care taken of both potsherds and exceptional artifacts, the mapping—in short, the general solicitude for the site as a whole—were extraordinary. And when Snaketown was again (1964–65) opened up for further researches, this time by Dr. Emil W. Haury of the University of Arizona, Chief Supervisor and Director, even greater attention was paid to meticulous excavation and record-keeping (Haury, 1965, 1967).

In general, then, one can say that from 1910 to 1930 there were very few rules about what or where to dig, except those that would avoid moving a pile of dirt two or three times—and even this was not always taken into account. Too often a man has found five cubic yards of dirt deposited on top of a feature that he had only recently decided to investigate.

Mostly, excavating was a hit and miss affair, and methods did not much matter because the whole site was going to be dug anyhow.

Or if you had to skimp—and how painful that was—you tried to outguess providence and to dig where you would find the most facts or the greatest number of trait constellations. This was quite in line with the cultural-history type of inquiry whose main purpose was to place sites, events, and things in a dated horizon and in a definite place. As a result, we have excellent and complex outlines of Southwestern prehistory. It is interesting to note that although profound alterations were taking place in other fields of anthropology during the 1920–40 period, no change can be discerned in the research done by archaeologists in the Southwest.[3]

AN OVERLAP—1935 TO PRESENT

Although the second hypothesis dealt with a period labeled 1910 to Present, there is an overlap—as shown by the heading of this section. This is not difficult to understand if one remembers that after Copernicus, Kepler, and Brahe adopted a heliocentric paradigm to replace the geocentric Ptolemaic one, many astronomers still adhered to the old Ptolemaic model for several generations. In fact, astrology is still with us!

In short, while new approaches are being carried out in Southwestern archaeological circles, the older model—that is, the one that deals with a time-space-historical-cultural-trait research—still holds sway in many places and is an important adjunct

[3] I was one of those archaeologists. I was content to close "gaps" in our knowledge of certain areas, to do old things better, to keep my nose to the time-space grindstone. I know that I took new ideas about theoretical and methodological changes in my field as a personal affront, an insult to all that I had been doing and all that I stood for professionally. I did not realize that the paradigm under which I had worked for thirty years was crumbling because it no longer served and I was asking the wrong questions or at least questions in which the younger men were no longer interested.

I am glad we have the excellent and detailed outline of prehistory of the Southwest because without it we would be unable to make advances. And so before leaving the hope and accomplishments of the post-1910 era, I salute that era. It was a time of exciting new finds and new explorations and I am glad I was part of it because I can now understand the reluctance of men who worked in that era to accept something that is not tried and true. Although I can understand their reluctance, I do not share it. (P. M.)

to any archaeological work. The senior author of this volume was once a part of the time-space school and still uses those data frequently and thankfully. Now, however, there is the desire to press on beyond the restricting time-space-historical dimensions and try different approaches, some of which have deep personal conviction and meaning for the author. It is time to build on the firm foundation of the time-space model and reach new and challenging horizons.

3RD HYPOTHESIS— 1935 TO PRESENT TIME

Since 1960 a new trend has been spreading across the country—a trend that symbolizes a shift from emphasis on particularisms (that is, traits, details, minutiae) to an imaginative era in which we hold a cultural-materialist research strategy that can deal with the questions of causality, origin, and laws. The trend in anthropology toward a re-examination of goals, research methodology, and paradigms seems apparent in many fields of science and even of religion. A conceptual transformation—a revolution—has taken place and this alters the bearing, the emphasis, and the procedures of the "new" research.

Long before personal dissatisfactions became articulate and formulated, a few anthropologists from 1930 on had concluded that traditional methods were leading them astray or up against blank walls (Bennett, 1943, p. 208; Kluckhohn, 1939, p. 328; Steward and Setzler, 1938, p. 4; Strong, 1936; Taylor, 1948). They were not making contributions to our discipline, which is social science as we see it now. Our research models were not explaining why cultural systems change any more than Linnaeus explained the process of organic evolution by setting up a taxonomy and order of life forms (Binford, 1968a, p. 8). How could we reach other goals—such as explaining, predicting, or formulating laws that possess a high degree of probability?

Resolution of this impasse could only be solved—as such difficulties have always been in science—by the emergence of a new paradigm, a new model, constructed from new fundamentals, among them:

1. Cultural materialism—that is, research priority given to the study of technology as related to environment, economics, demography, ecology, etc., all of which are factors in determining other aspects of a cultural system—is accepted as a valid strategy for our research (Harris, 1968, p. 650).

2. Historical particularisms—that is, an exclusive devotion to and emphasis on historical matters—are relegated to a background position in a research schedule.

3. Acceptance of a methodological rigor and the logic of scientific methods as used by all sciences that permit the creation of hypotheses. These hypotheses will then be used to explain the processes by which cultures change and operate.

Thus the most general statement of this Third Hypothesis (1935 to present) might be stated as follows:

"Cultural differences as reflected in the archaeological record are the function of the operation of cultural processes over time." [4]

This statement of a general research goal does not exclude others. In fact, one might say that there are as many models or goals of research as there are archaeologists. But, in general the explanation of past human behavior and of changes in cultural systems —progressive and retrogressive—are among the major goals of archaeologists.

[4] Daniel Bowman, personal communication.

METHODS OF EXCAVATION, 1935–PRESENT, IN THE AGE OF SCIENCE

We must stress the close relationship that exists between survey work, excavations, and the goals of the archaeologist. In chapter I, we cited the feedback between hypotheses and survey methods. This same close relationship exists in excavations. The hypotheses that one takes to the field for testing govern what kinds of sites are to be dug. The selection of the site or sites is made on the basis of a sampling technique. Hypotheses also govern the kinds of data that one will search for. This does not mean that unused data are tossed out; on the contrary, they are tabulated, analyzed, and carefully saved so that they will be available for others who have different problems to solve.

Further, rarely are entire sites or areas excavated. A sampling technique is employed that provides reliable groups of artifacts or analysis and saves time and money as well.

Nor are sites any longer dug in order to draw praise from visiting archaeologists. We used to spend a lot of time "cleaning up" a site so that it would seem "neat" and "tidy"—but this is a sheer waste of research energy and money. Data should be secured in a precise, careful manner—all care being taken that is consonant with good scientific procedure. More than that is embellishment and unnecessary.

Hence, methods of excavation today are somewhat different from what they were in 1880. The chief differences are: the way we dig and the kinds of data we need for testing a hypothesis. These two variables are absolutely dependent, one on the other. Stratigraphy is still used and refinements such as micro-stratigraphy—that is, peeling off very thin layers that may represent a brief camping or butchering site by hunters—have come into use.

Earth-moving machinery is used more and more. After a careful survey of the area and a thoughtful assessment of the site, the number of objects that may be lost or destroyed is minimal and more than offset by the speed with which a trench or room can be dug with a skillfully operated machine.

Most research projects now need the advice, training, and help that can be given by specialists in other fields. This is not a totally new concept, as Kidder employed it in the 1930s in the research on the Maya culture. But it is more common today. Botanists, pollen experts, geologists, soil men, ecologists, zoologists, geomorphologists are called upon and used at one time or another. Sometimes they accompany the archaeologists to the field, or we call on them to aid us in analyzing data that requires special training and knowledge far beyond our own. Fossil pollen analysis is one procedure requiring such collaboration.

Up to 1950, pollen analysis was seldom used by archaeologists; today it is routine. A palynologist (pollen expert) can tell us what the flora in the vicinity of our archaeological site was; what foods were eaten; what were grown and what were wild; the kind of climate that prevailed; whether a briefly inhabited site was occupied spring, summer, or fall. In other words, a multidisciplinary approach is a common feature of modern archaeological research.

Hence, the chief differences in modern excavations stem from *what* we want to know and what data we need to test a hypothesis. Innovations are now sought that will perfect our techniques for recovering the information we want. These vary from area to area, with problems involved, with the training and experience of the archaeologist, and above all with his ability to adapt, to innovate, to invent. *But* the need for better techniques should not obscure our interest in theory and method. Techniques are tools and useful ones, but are not an end in themselves.

At the beginning of this chapter we said we would try to show why digging all the sites in the Southwest would not be fruitful or answer all questions.

Perhaps it is now clear that after an optimum number of pit houses, caves, rooms, and kivas have been excavated, the value of more excavations would diminish tremendously. The increase in knowledge gained from several excavations is not a function of the number of sites dug. The increase in knowledge gained from each new excavation (of the same time period and in the same area) becomes less and less until the amount of increase approaches zero.

We do not necessarily need more data; we need more hypotheses. Then it may be possible to test them, in part at least, by means of data in the archives of all archaeologists. If not, then you might be obliged to go to the field in order to obtain them by means of limited digging in areas chosen by sampling procedure.

But a program committed merely to digging for its own sake without establishing a working hypothesis would, frankly, in our opinion, be insane and, what's worse, would yield no intelligent or archaeologically valid results.

PART TWO

ENVIRONMENTS OF ARIZONA

III Modern Environments

The state of Arizona covers an area of about 114,000 square miles. Within its borders lies a diversity of environments that is not approached in most states. Select any variable you wish—altitude, temperature, rainfall—and its range of variation in Arizona will be immense.

However one parcels this diversity, the full range of environmental variability has been adapted to and exploited. Every region of Arizon has served as a human habitat at some time in the state's history, and the most extreme of its conditions have been overcome. In studying the prehistory of Arizona, we will learn how men met the particular problems posed by the environments in which they existed. The details of their successes and failures in coping with natural conditions will be discussed in later chapters. Our concern at the moment is to describe the state's environments as they are now.

Every culture exists in an environment. Ecology is the study of man's interaction with his natural and social environment. For the moment, the natural environment is the focus of our attention. The particular environmental variables that we will examine are those that generate the strongest selective pressures on man's culture and behavior.

1. LANDFORMS. The surface of the earth in different parts of the state makes travel easier in some areas and more difficult in others. It is easy to walk across a flat plain, but difficult to cross a mountain range. Similarly, fields can be planted on flat sur-

faces, but it is difficult to clear plots on steeply sloped land, at least without constructing terraces.

2. RAINFALL. The amount of rain that falls in an area will greatly affect the kinds of plant and animal resources that will be available there for man. Rainfall also significantly affects man's ability to practice agriculture. Some areas are too dry for agriculture, while in others there is sufficient precipitation but it comes at the wrong time of the year.

3. TEMPERATURE. The kind of shelter that man must construct and the kinds of clothing he will wear will be determined in part by the temperature in an area. Both averages and extremes of temperature are important. Temperature also affects exploitative activities. Plants and animals are sensitive to temperature variations. Agricultural products must have a certain frost-free period in order to mature.

4. PLANT-ANIMAL COMMUNITY. Throughout the prehistory of Arizona, populations relied heavily on the hunting of animals and the collecting of wild plants. Materials derived from plants and animals were also used in making shelter, clothing, and tools.

Describing environments for so diverse a situation as Arizona's necessarily involves simplification. With extreme variation in most environmental characteristics, there is no happy coincidence of topographic, floral, and faunal variables that define precisely bounded environments. Nevertheless, the variables do interact to produce discernible patterns. We will describe the patterned environmental variation in the state in terms of four environments: Plateau, Mountain, Transition, and Desert.[1]

[1] The data that will be used in describing Arizona's environments are taken from the following sources. Climate: C. Green and W. D. Sellers, *Arizona Climate* (1964); J. Hambidge, *Climate and Man* (1941); S. S. Vishner, *Climatic Atlas of the U. S.* (1966). Fauna: A. A. Nichol, *The Natural Vegetation of Arizona* (1952); V. E. Shelford, *The Ecology of North America.* Flora: A. W. Kuchler, *Potential Natural Vegetation of the U. S.* (1964); Lowe (ed.), *The Vertebrates of Arizona* (1964); A. A. Nichol, *The Natural Vegetation of Arizona.* Geography: J. L. Cross, E. H. Shaw, and K. Scheifele (eds.), *Arizona, Its People and Resources* (1960); E. H. Hammond, *Classes of Land Surface Forms in the 48 States* (1963).

FIGURE 1 Four environments of Arizona. These environments are defined by patterns in the distribution of temperature, rainfall, landforms, plants, and animals. There is less variance within each zone than between each.

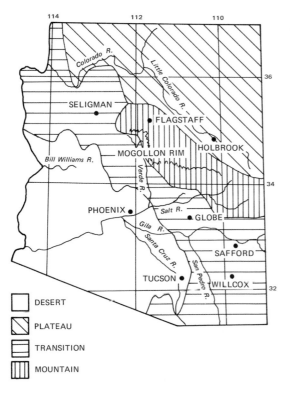

DESERT

PLATEAU

TRANSITION

MOUNTAIN

THE PLATEAU ENVIRONMENT

The Plateau environment lies north of a line running fifty to one hundred miles south of the valley of the Little Colorado and Colorado Rivers. It coincides with the territory covered by the Navajo and Hopi Reservations and the Grand Canyon National Park.

The average altitude in this environment is about 6,000 feet, ranging from 4,500 to 10,000 feet. The land is gentler in the eastern sector of the environment where the local relief averages 500 to 1,000 feet and steeper in the western sector where the averages are 1,000 to 3,000 feet. Mesas are the most common landform in this environment. Fifty to eighty percent of the land surfaces is gently sloped and this flat land occurs about equally on mesa tops and valley bottoms. There are areas of rolling hills in the environment, especially in the central sector.

Average yearly precipitation varies from about 8 inches at low altitudes to 13 inches at high ones. Precipitation is equally divided between the winter months and the summer months. The average deviation from the mean yearly precipitation is about 20 percent, so that, for example, in low-lying areas of the environment, one expects six to ten inches of rain in most years. The Colorado River is the only permanent one on the plateau, while the Little Colorado is permanent only in its upper reaches. These two rivers carry the greatest quantity of water in the month of April and are at their low points in June.

Summer temperatures average 73 degrees in high areas and 75 in lower areas. In winter, the range is from about 31 degrees at higher altitudes to 36 degrees at lower ones. There are, on the average, 140 days between the last frost of the spring and the first frost of the fall. This figure has varied from 90 to 210 days in the years for which records exist.

Four plant-animal communities predominate on the plateau. Pine forest covers about 5 percent of the land surface in the environment principally above 6,000 feet. Juniper piñon woodland and sagebrush shrubland overlap on surfaces between 5,000 and 6,500 feet. The latter lies somewhat lower and accounts for about 25 percent of the vegetation cover in the environment while the former accounts for about 30 percent. A short grass steppe covers 40 percent of the land surface, overlapping with the sagebrush shrubland between 4,-000 and 5,000 feet.[2]

Pine forest occurs on the north and south rims of the Grand Canyon, on the Defiance Plateau, and in the Chuska and Lukachukai Mountains. The dominant plant in this community is the ponderosa pine. The mule deer is the dominant animal, especially during some months. Also important are the coyote, bear, elk, mountain lion, and wolf.

Juniper piñon woodland occurs in bands surrounding the edges of the plateau environment. Its primary plant constituents are juniper and piñon. The coyote, mule deer, bobcat, and mountain lion are the most important animals.

Sagebrush shrubland extends onto the plateau in tongues at the northern perimeter of the state and grows along the Colorado and Little Colorado Rivers. Sagebrush, saltbush, and black brush are local dominants in this community. That is, they are not co-dominants over the entire area; in any given locality one is dominant. Short grass steppe is the characteristic community in the valley bottoms. Black grama, blue grama, galleta, and Indian rice grass are the most important plant constituents

of the community. The antelope was once its dominant animal but has been replaced by the jack rabbit.

These four communities account for most of the zonal variation on the plateau. In local areas where variation in altitude is extreme, the communities are interspersed on hillsides. Some other plants that are important in the plateau environment are Douglas fir, fir, aspen, Arizona fescus, buckbrush, cliff rose, elderberry, larkspur lupine, Mexican locust, mountain mahogany, mountain muhly, gambel oak, serviceberry, snowberry strawberry, algarita, blue stem, mallow, mimosa, snakeweed, spirea, rabbit bush, alkali-sacaton, cholla, fleabane, parsley, partridge pea, Mormon tea, Russian thistle, shrubby buckwheat, snakeweed, soapweed, Spanish bayonet, three awn, and yucca. Other important animals include beaver, bluebird, bobcat, chipmunk, long-tailed vole, pocket gopher, raven, robin, squirrel, tawny deer mouse, trout, chipmunk, fox, cottontail, piñon jay, piñon mouse, skunk, squirrel, wild turkey, wolf, wood rat, coyote, ground squirrel, kangaroo rat, and prairie dog.

THE MOUNTAIN ENVIRONMENT

The Mountain environment is a 200-mile-long zone along the Mogollon Rim. It is an area of high pine-covered peaks surrounded by woodland and grassland. The mountains are denser in the eastern sector of the zone and more open, with intervening plains and tableland in the western sector. The average altitude of the environment is 7,500 feet, with a range from 6,000 to 12,000 feet. Local relief varies from 3,000 to 5,000 feet in the east and from 1,000 to 3,000 feet in the west. There is little gently sloping land in this environment.

Precipitation in the mountains varies

[2] Kuchler (1964) is the principal source of data on the distribution of plant communities. He emphasizes the vegetation in the area as it probably was prior to the impact of modern American culture.

from a yearly average of 28 inches at high altitudes to 12 inches at lower ones. The precipitation pattern is a summer-winter one, with about half of the moisture falling during the growing season. Yearly departures from the mean average 30 percent. The streams that flow in the mountain environment are the headwaters of the Little Colorado, Gila Salt, and Verde Rivers. Stream flow is at a peak in April and a low point in June.

There is considerable seasonal and altitudinal variation in temperature in the mountain environment. During the summer, the higher elevations average 65 while the lower ones average about 74 degrees. In the winter, the range is from an average of 28 degrees in the heights to 34 degrees in lower areas. There are usually about 140 days between the spring and fall frosts, with extremes of 110 and 240 days.

The plant-animal communities in this environment are pine forest, juniper piñon woodland, and short grass steppe. These cover 50, 40, and 10 percent of the land surface respectively. Pine forest grows on the highest surfaces and woodland on intermediate ones. Grasslands occur as mountain meadows and at lower elevations.

THE TRANSITION ENVIRONMENT

The Transition environment lies southwest of the Mogollon Rim along a line from the southeast to the northwest corner of the state. Evaluated on any characteristic, this is the most variable of the environments. Long narrow mountain ranges are separated by equally long valleys. The average altitude in the environment is about 4,500 feet with a range from 2,000 to 8,000 feet. In the southeast sector of the environment the mountains are open and inter-

sected by broad plains; in the middle sector they are more compacted; and in the northwest corner the mountains are interspersed with mesas. Local relief varies from 1,000 to 5,000 feet in this very up and down region.

Precipitation is as high as 14 inches per year on upland surfaces and as low as 7 in the valley bottoms. The pattern is again a winter-summer one. Yearly departures from the mean average 30 percent. The Verde, Gila, and Salt are the major rivers in the environment. The San Pedro and Santa Cruz Rivers are impermanent. Runoff is concentrated in April, followed by a June low.

In the highlands, summer temperatures average about 80 degrees, while 82 is representative for the valleys. Winter temperatures range from an average of 40 degrees at high altitudes to 49 degrees at lower ones. There are usually about 220 frost-free days per year.

The plant-animal communities in this environment are quite different from those discussed so far. A few of the highest peaks in the southeastern and northwestern sectors of the environment are covered by pine forest, but this community covers only 2 to 5 percent of the land surface. In the central and northwestern sectors of the environment, juniper piñon woodland is found, and it occurs on about 10 percent of the environment's surface. Most land surfaces above 4,000 feet are covered by either chapparal or juniper oak woodland. The former accounts for about 20 percent of the vegetation cover and the latter for about 10 percent. Grama tobosa shrubsteppe covers 35 to 40 percent of the environment, primarily on surfaces between 3,000 and 4,000 feet. Below 3,000 feet, creosote bush/tarbrush/bursage shrubland predominates, covering 20 percent of the total land surface.

Juniper oak woodland grows south and east of Tucson and south of Globe. Chapparal predominates along a line running from near Clifton to near Saligman. The dominant plants in the chapparal community are scrub oak, buckbrush, and manzanita. Juniper and oak are dominant in the woodland community. The dominants of each community are subdominants in the other. No animal is clearly dominant in these communities. The major influents are an immense variety of small birds and rodents.

The grama tobosa shrubsteppe is common on midslope from Globe to the southeast corner of the state and from a point south of Prescott to the northwest corner. A variety of grama grasses as well as tobosa, filaree, mesquite, and creosote bush are the most important plants in this community. Jack rabbit, kangaroo rat, and wood rat are the animal dominants.

In the valley bottoms, creosote bush/bursage/tarbush shrubland is the principal community. These shrubs do not codominate in localities. Creosote bush is generally dominant in the northwestern corner of the environment. Creosote bush and bursage are the usual dominants along the Gila and Salt drainages.

Other plants found in the transition environment are algarita, Apache plume, buckthorn, cliff rose, cat's claw, coffeeberry, lemon bush, madrona, mountain laurel, serviceberry, shrubby buckwheat, snakeweed, twinberry, agave, bisnaga, buckwheat, curly mesquite, cholla, desert hackberry, desert willow, Joshua tree, lote bush, ocotillo, Russian thistle, ring muhly, red three-awn, sacaton, sunflower, mustard, white thorn, paloverde, palmilla, Indian wheat, squaw berry, saltbush, sophora, and yucca. The small rodents account for the greatest percentage of animal biomass in this community. Other animals include cottontail, coyote, bobcat, mule deer, skunk, squirrel, and peccary.

THE DESERT ENVIRONMENT

The Desert environment lies between the Transition environment and the southwest corner of the state. This area is one of hills interspersed with low mountains. The land is gentle and unlike the other environments the gentle land occurs on valley floors. The altitude ranges from 100 to 4,000 feet, with the average altitude 2,000 feet. Local relief ranges from 1,000 to 3,000 feet.

The lower courses of the Colorado and Gila Rivers are the environment's major drainages. An important local occurrence is the confluence of the Gila, Salt, and Verde Rivers near Phoenix. However it is measured, water in this environment is scarce. Precipitation averages 5 inches per year at all altitudes and is evenly distributed over the year. The rivers in the environment reach a maximum of flow in July and a minimum in November.

Temperature variation is slight. July temperatures average 85 degrees at all altitudes and January temperatures around 46. The number of frost-free days averages 280 with a range of 150 to 365.

Characteristic plant-animal communities in the desert environment are paloverde/cactus shrubland, creosote bush/bursage shrubland, and mesquite/saltbush bottomlands. Paloverde shrubland occurs as low as 500 feet but is most common at higher altitudes. It covers 33 percent of the land surface. The remaining two communities are complexly intertwined on surfaces between 100 and 2,000 feet. The mesquite/saltbush community grows in and along stream channels and accounts for about 5 percent of the vegetation cover in the environment. The creosote bush/bursage community predominates away from the streams and covers about 60 percent of the land surface in the environment.

The paloverde community has paloverde and saguaro co-dominants. The most important animal in the community is the rock pocket mouse. Other important plants and animals include: acacia, brittle bush, bursage, canota, cat's claw, cholla, crow's foot, six-week and needle grama, gour, Indian wheat, ironwood, lupine, morning glory, mesquite, poppy, ocotillo, prickly pear, and sangre de drago; fox, mule deer, white-tailed deer, peccary, skunk, squirrel, and many varieties of rats and mice.

The mesquite and saltbush are the dominant plants in that community. Subdominants include arrowweed, broom careless weed, cottonwood, dondia, screwbean, sacaton, salt cedar, slat grass, and willow The kangaroo rat is the dominant animal. Important subdominants are antelope, badger, carcara, coati, cottontail, coyote, burro deer, mule deer, elf owl, fox, javelina, jack rabbit, jaguar, ocelot, mountain lion, skunk, scorpion mouse, sparrow, squirrel, raccoon, and raven.

IV   Prehistoric Environmental Changes

We view culture as man's extrabiological adaptation to his natural and social environments. This chapter begins a discussion of adaptation to the natural environment. In the best of all possible worlds, we would now proceed to a discussion of the patterned distribution in prehistoric times of all those environmental variables discussed in the modern case. Unfortunately, neither our techniques nor our data permit such a discussion. It is not even possible to produce crude maps of prehistoric Arizona environments. To date, archaeologists and their colleagues in other sciences have managed to discuss changes in a relatively few environmental variables. It is to these changes that we turn our attention.

Three sets of data have been primary in these discussions: geomorphological data, palynological data, and dendrochronological data. One assumption is crucial to the use of all these data, the assumption of uniformitarianism. This proposition asserts that processes that account for environmental variability in the present also accounted for environmental variability in the past. What precisely does this assumption mean, and how is it used? Let us begin with a geographical example. We observe landforms called arroyos today. They seem to be associated with environmental conditions such as heavy summer rainfall. If we find evidence that a similar landform existed in the past, we infer that the processes that produced it were the same. We infer that heavy summer rainfall must have been common in the area at the time the arroyo was formed.

Similarly, an investigator may discover that cheno-am pollen tends to occur in localities with disturbed sediments, the disturbance frequently a result of heavy summer rainfall. If he finds a locality, a buried land surface, with evidence of a heavy cheno-am population, he infers that sediment disturbance probably caused by heavy summer rainfall existed at the time when the buried surface was the land surface. Patterns and their causes are rarely as simple as these examples. Zonal and azonal variables that affect the distribution of a particular phenomenon are always nations used above. Therefore, these exammore complex than the monocausal examples should be taken as just that, and not as rules of thumb that can be applied in the field.

In some cases where an arroyo or a heavy concentration of cheno-am pollen is found, the environmental setting and the processes that are inferred to have produced it are the same that now exist in the locality under investigation. In other instances, the modern setting and the inferred prehistoric one may differ almost totally. An archaeologist may find evidence of a marsh where a desert now exists. This contrast between the extant and prehistoric environments of a particular locality are the basic data used in inferring climatic or environmental change. In turning to the data used in environmental inferences, we will consider both the ways in which archaeologists and other students of the past have used their data and the kinds of conclusions that they have reached.

GEOGRAPHICAL APPROACHES

Interpretations of prehistoric environments based on geomorphological data are associated with the names of Kirk Bryan and Ernst Antevs. Bryan's work with this problem dates to the 1920s while Antevs' work is from the forties and fifties. These scholars relied primarily on geomorphological data, but they were not insensitive to floral, faunal, and cultural evidence of environmental change. The basic strategy employed by such investigators in their considerations of Arizona prehistory have been summarized by Paul S. Martin in his book *The Last 10,000 Years* (1963).[1] This book is the principal source of material used in this chapter and should certainly be examined by anyone with an interest in prehistoric environments.

The critical relationships that underlay the interpretations made by Antevs and other geographers are summarized in Table 1. This particular summary of the model follows that of Martin, as we feel that his account of these relationships provides a more coherent picture of the geographers' conceptual model than any they themselves offer. Seven bits of data are crucial to the interpretations the geographers make: alluviation, erosion, calichification, dune formation, faunal extinction, relict floras, and human abandonments. Each of these is associated with a minimal description of the environmental conditions that are held to have produced it. Thus, the discovery of a buried alluvial deposit would be interpreted

to mean that cool wet climate and a continuous vegetation cover existed in the locality when the terrace was formed. A similar relationship is described for each datum in the figure.

The pattern of environmental variability that emerges when this model is employed consists of three periods: the Anathermal, the Altithermal, and the Medithermal. The Anathermal lasted from about 7000 to about 5000 B.C. During these two thousand years, the climate was at first like today, but grew warmer. It was subhumid and humid. The Altithermal, lasting from 5000 to 2500 B.C.,

GEOGRAPHICAL DATUM	ENVIRONMENTAL ASSOCIATION
Alluviation	Cool wet climate and continuous vegetation cover
Erosion	Warm dry climate and reduced vegetation cover
Calichification	Warm dry climate with periods of substantial moisture
Dunes	Warm dry climate with reduced vegetation cover
Faunal extinctions (specifically the extinction of Pleistocene fauna)	Drought
Relict flora (specifically the presence of isolated stands of pine oak woodland in southern Arizona)	Humid conditions
Abandonment of an area by human populations	Drought

TABLE 1 Geomorphological data and their environmental correlates. There are many different characteristics of soils that geographers can use in making inferences about the climatic conditions that existed when the soil was formed. Different phenomena and the prehistoric conditions that they imply are shown in this table. (p. 101)

[1] This is Paul S. Martin of the University of Arizona, not the co-author of this book.

was arid and warmer than the present. From 2500 B.C. to the present the state was moderately warm, at times arid, and at times semiarid. (These definitions are based on Antevs 1948, 1952, 1955.)

PALYNOLOGICAL APPROACHES

Intensive analyses of the prehistoric pollen record in Arizona began in reaction to the paleoclimatic interpretations of the geographers. Martin's book *The Last 10,000 Years* is both a critique of the inferential model employed by the geographers and a presentation of alternative conclusions based upon pollen data. In criticizing the geographical approach, Martin notes that the environmental processes that were associated with each datum in Table 1 were not so clearly linked as the geographers implied. Alternating periods of alluviation and erosion, he argues, are more dependent upon the seasonal distribution of rainfall than on its absolute value or the temperature. A pattern of heavy rainfall during the summer months would be more likely to produce erosion than a much greater quantity of rainfall distributed evenly through the year.

Martin sees the extinction of Pleistocene megafauna as the result of cultural, not climatic, factors. That is, megafauna became extinct as a result of overkill by post-Pleistocene hunting populations, not as a result of drought. He finds that many of the species of plants and animals that are most sensitive to moisture and temperature variation did not become extinct. Extinction centered on those species that man hunted. It seems likely that both Martin and his opponents are overstating their case. An analysis that approaches the problem from an ecosystemic viewpoint and examines the interaction of environmental change, hunting patterns, animal behavior, and extinction will probably provide the most satisfactory explanation.

The process of calichification in Martin's view is the subject of far greater disagreement among geographers than the simple interpretations of the occurrence of this phenomenon in the prehistoric Southwest suggest. The cause of the phenomenon is sufficiently in doubt that it cannot be used as the indicator of any particular set of conditions. Similarly, the formation of dunes is sensitive to a series of environmenal variables such as the direction of the wind and the availability of local sands sources. Since these factors were not given sufficient consideration by the geographers, Martin finds their interpretation of dunes suspect. Finally, Martin believes that the relict stands of pine oak woodland are the result of conditions that existed in the area 20,000 years ago and inform us little of the events of the last 7,500 years.

In developing these ideas and creating alternatives to them, Martin collected pollen samples from prehistoric and modern localities in southeastern Arizona. A large number of radiocarbon dates were obtained for the profiles to provide significant temporal control.

Pollen samples were taken from desert grassland and pine parkland communities. The pollen profiles developed from these data suggested to Martin that the prehistoric communities occupying the areas from which the samples were taken were very different from the modern ones. His argument focuses on two types of pollen —cheno-ams (pollen from chenopods and amaranths) and compositae—and two broad classes of plants—hygric and arboreal.

Today, chenopods, composites, and amaranths are abundant in plant communities that occur at elevations up to 4,000 feet. These three species account for nearly 90 percent of the pollen in modern samples taken at elevations below this figure. Composite pollen tends to be dominant at the higher ranges of this altitude class. Moreover, it tends to be most important in samples taken from areas where there is a relatively high, undissected flood plain, the water table is high, and the soil nonsaline. Cheno-ams are quantitatively most important in samples taken from areas where the land surface is dissected, the water table low, and the soil saline.

Arboreal pollen is pollen produced by trees. This category of pollen is infrequent in Arizona at altitudes less than 5,000 feet. Modern samples taken from higher elevations contain much arboreal pollen. In samples taken at altitudes of 8,000 feet or higher, arboreal pollen accounts for most of the modern rain. Hygric pollens are produced by plants that grow under marshy conditions. Reeds, bulrushes, and sedges are plants that produce pollen classified as hygric. Modern samples that show a predominance of hygric pollens tend to come from damp or marshy areas.

The relationships between pollen and environmental conditions described in the preceding paragraphs are summarized in Table 2. Martin's interpretation of the prehistoric record is based upon these relationships which are in turn based upon the relationship of modern samples and profiles to modern environmental conditions from which they were taken. Martin's inferences concerning prehistoric conditions are summarized in Table 3 and Figure 2. Table 3 describes the correlation between floodplain events in the western United States, zones in the pollen profiles that Martin produced, and summer rainfall. The decreasing length of the alluvial periods and the increasing indefiniteness concerning predominant rainfall patterns as the present is approached in Table 3 reflect the more complex and comprehensive data available and the increasing difficulty in interpreting them.

The conflict between Martin's interpretations and those of the geographers are even clearer in Figure 2. The boundaries between Antevs' Anathermal, Altithermal, and Medithermal occurred at 7000 and 4000 B.P. Martin's boundaries are at 4000 and 8000 B.P. The period between the close of the Pleistocene and 8000 B.P. is as warm as, then warmer than present, and subhumid to humid in Antevs' view. In Martin's, it is warm and arid throughout with an increasingly heavy summer rainfall pattern. Antevs' Altithermal, 4500 to 7000 B.P.,

ENVIRONMENTAL CORRELATE

POLLEN	GROUND MOISTURE	SURFACE WATER	RAINFALL	TEMPERATURE	PLANT COMMUNITY
Cheno-am	low	absent	summer	warm	grassland with dissection of land surface
Compositae	high	variable	biseasonal	warm	grassland with little or no dissection
Arboreal	variable	variable	biseasonal	cool	upper parkland, forest borders
Hygric	high	present	summer	variable	standing water-marsh communities

TABLE 2 Types of pollen and the environmental conditions with which they are associated. Different plants grown in different situations. As climates change, the conditions at even a single spot change. As the conditions change, the plant cover changes, and these plants leave pollen in the soil. By carefully examining the pollen, the climate can be reconstructed. Kinds of pollen and the conditions that are inferred from them are identified.

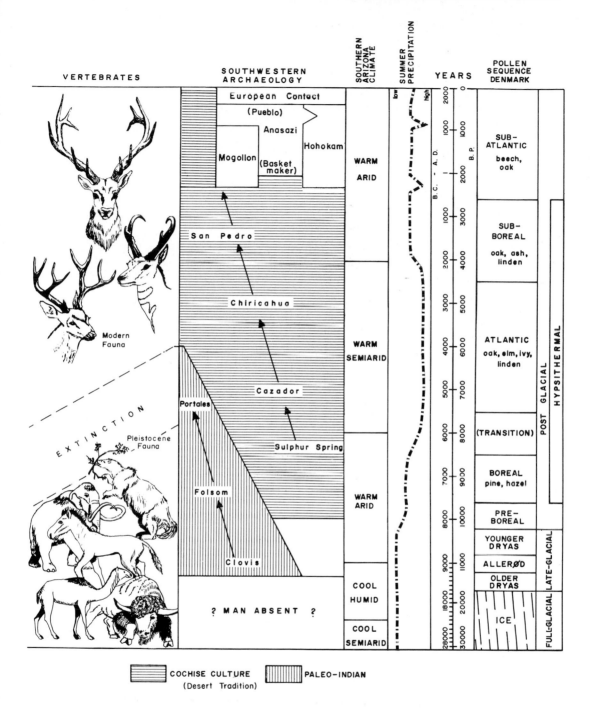

FIGURE 2 Changing patterns of southern Arizona fauna, culture history, climate, and precipitation. While there is no precise fit between culture change and environmental change, general correlations can be seen. The Desert culture, for example, begins in a period of desiccation and with the extinction of large game animals. Reproduced by permission of Paul Martin.

FLOODPLAIN EVENT	FEATURES	POLLEN ZONE	SUMMER RAINS
cutting 4	Began in late nineteenth century (Bryan 1925)	I cheno-ams	light to heavy
deposition 3	Began in most places A.D. 1200–1500[1]; continuing until 1880 or later.	I cheno-ams pine rise in northern Ariz., N. M.	" "
cutting 3	Coincided with decline of flood plain farming in many areas.	I cheno-ams	heavy
deposition 2	Twofold in several areas; upper part at most places no younger than A.D. 1100–1200[1]. Lower part dates 2200–2400 B.P.[2], occasionally to 4000 B.P. Corn pollen rare but present throughout.	II composites	light
cutting 2	The altithermal of Antevs; calichification, dune formation along certain drainages. More extensive arroyo cutting than at any time since the last pluvial. First record of corn pollen.	III cheno-ams, pine	very heavy
deposition 1	A scattering of dates suggests an age of 7000–11000 B.P.[2]. Last record of the late Pleistocene megafauna.	IV composites	light
cutting 1	The major period of erosion in valley bottoms which defined the channels filled by alluvium in postpluvial time. Probably of Wisconsin glacial age and older.	V pine, other conifers in lake sediments.	very light to absent, winter precipitation at a maximum.

[1] Pottery and dendrochronology   [2] Radiocarbon (years before present).

TABLE 3   Alluvial chronology of the western U. S. compared with pollen zones of the desert grassland. Similarities and differences in the geographic and pollen records of the past are shown in this table. Reproduced by permission of Paul Martin.

is arid and warmer than present. Martin's corresponding period is warm and less arid with a predominant summer rainfall pattern throughout. Martin sees the period between 4000 B.P. and the present as one during which the climate was warm and arid, and no pronounced summer rainfall pattern existed except for brief periods 2,500 and 1,000 years ago. Antevs' Medithermal is a moderately warm period with alternating times of aridity and semiaridity. Since Martin's interpretation better fits the data available at present, it seems the more acceptable of the two.

Martin and his students have carried out further researches that support the validity of the pollen sequence initially derived from the southeastern corner of the state. These studies have also increased the detail of the information available on the more recent portions of prehistoric time. Pollen chronologies based on work done by Martin, Schoenwetter, and Arms (1961) and Schoenwetter (1962) are illustrated in Table 4. Schoenwetter's chronology is based on pollen profiles developed from 263 samples collected in the vicinities of Vernon, Arizona, and Pine Lawn, New Mexico. One hundred of his samples are from arroyos, four from cattle tanks, 35 from archaeological sites in the Pine Lawn area, and 124 from sites in the Upper Little Colorado. While Schoenwetter's data back past A.D. 350 are sparse, the general agreement between his conclusions and those based on the southern Arizona sequence are clear.

Schoenwetter attributes the differences between the two sequences, the existence of a period of dominant cheno-am pollen with some hygric pollen between A.D. 1200 and 1350, and the subequivalence of cheno-ams and compositae in Period II to differences in both technique and data between the two studies. Schoenwetter sampled local-

| AGE | SOUTHERN ARIZONA | | EASTERN ARIZONA | WESTERN NEW MEXICO | PERIOD |
	POLLEN	RAINFALL	POLLEN	RAINFALL	
1960			cheno-am dominant with increase in arboreal	heavy summer	1-a
1350	cheno-am dominant	heavy summer			
			cheno-am dominant, some hygric	heavy summer; local standing water	1-b
1200					
			cheno-am dominant	heavy summer	1-c
1000					
	Compositae dominant	light summer	cheno-am Compositae = 1.0	light summer	II
350 A.D.					
0 B.C.					
1000					
	cheno-am dominant with less pine	heavy summer	cheno-am dominant	heavy summer	III
1420					
3000					
	cheno-am dominant with more pine	heavy summer			
5000			? ? ? ?	? ? ? ? ?	? ?
	Compositae dominant	light summer	Compositae dominant	light summer	IV

TABLE 4 Pollen chronologies in eastern Arizona and western New Mexico with associated rainfall patterns. The palynologist can infer rainfall patterns from pollen distributions and these may be similar or different in different areas. Climatic processes did not affect the entire Southwest simultaneously.

ities that are somewhat different from those sampled to the south. Moreover, he worked with a more comprehensive set of data that allowed him more detailed conclusions than were possible from the earlier study.

Schoenwetter and Dittert (1968) have summarized evidence from six studies carried out in five different areas of the Colorado Plateau in Arizona and New Mexico (Figure 3). The shaded bars define the range of variability in arboreal pollen present in modern samples taken in each area. Solid lines show changes in the abundances of arboreal pollen in prehistoric samples. Schoenwetter and Dittert argue that when the solid line is outside of and to the left of the hatched area, more trees were present in the area than exist there at present. Fewer trees were present during periods defined by the solid line moving to the right of the hatched area. The presence of more trees is associated with abundant moisture, and the presence of fewer trees is associated with drought. Conditions similar to those of the present are inferred when the solid line is within the hatched area.

Richard Hevly has studied the pattern of environmental change in the area bounded by Show Low, Snowflake, St. Johns, and Springerville, Arizona, and the Upper Little Colorado. He used pollen profiles taken from dry lake beds in the area and from archaeological sites. These data were combined with evidence of variability in tree-

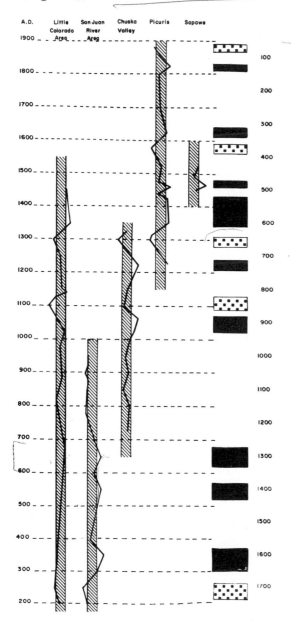

FIGURE 3 Correlation of pollen profiles in five southwestern regions and periods of moisture or drought between A.D. 200 and 1900. The curves show the frequency of arboreal pollen recovered from dated sediment samples. The hatched area superimposed on each curve represents the frequency of arboreal pollen in surface sediment samples from the Colorado Plateau at situations similar to those of the archaeological sites. When the frequency represented by a curve exceeds that included in the hatched zone, more trees are evidenced in the district than are now present. The column on the right presents an integrated interpretation of the separate curves. Stippled time horizons are those of widespread drought on the Colorado Plateau, while time periods marked as solid units are those with widespread conditions of greater moisture. Reproduced by permission of James Schoenwetter and A. E. Dittert, Jr.

ring width to produce the sequence shown in Table 5. Hevly used a very large number of samples. In addition, he was able to draw upon the earlier work done in the area by Schoenwetter (1962) and dendroclimatological studies. His work adds additional precision to our understanding of environmental variability in this area.

The data collected to date show a remarkable consistency from one locality to another. Unfortunately, all of these data are taken from the eastern margin of the state and may only poorly describe the prehistoric conditions that existed in western and central areas.

Despite the palynologists' reliance on community comparison, on statements that the profile produced by plants growing on a site at some prehistoric time is different from the profile produced by plants growing there today, maps that illustrate the distribution of plant communities in prehistoric epochs are rare. The environmental variability that palynologists have failed by and large to consider is variability in the distribution of plant-animal communities. Martin's map of the American Southwest at the height of the Wisconsin glaciation is an example of the kind of community distributional data that it would be nice to have (1965). Even more detailed, more locally precise descriptions will be required if we are to characterize accurately the interaction of prehistoric populations at their environments. Such a reconstruction for one locality and one time period will be discussed in considering the cultural ecology of Paleo-Indian populations. In general the most precise kinds of statements about community distribution available are ones that suggest that at the height of the Wisconsin glaciation community boundaries in southern Arizona were depressed 3,000 to 4,000 feet and in northern Arizona 2,000 to 3,000 feet relative to their position at

present (Martin and Mehringer, 1965). Similarly, one may read that variability in community boundaries has probably not exceeded 50 vertical meters or 50 linear miles between A.D. 1 and the present. More precise maps of community boundaries will be produced when analytic techniques such as those described earlier allow the differentiation of on site, local, and regional variability in pollen profiles.

DENDROCLIMATOLOGY

Interpretations of variability in tree-ring width have contributed importantly to our understanding of changes in prehistoric environmental conditions. Moreover, the limits of this analytic technique are quite clearly unattained. Environmental inferences from

DATE A.D.	MOISTURE CONDITIONS RELATIVE TO THE PRESENT	SEASONAL RAINFALL DISTRIBUTION
1300–1500	Increased effective moisture	Biseasonal
1100–1300	Decreased effective moisture	Summer heavy
900–1100	Increased effective moisture	Biseasonal shifting to summer heavy
600–900	Decreased effective moisture	Biseasonal
400–600	Increased effective moisture	Biseasonal
200–400	Decreased effective moisture	Biseasonal

TABLE 5 Changes in the abundance and distribution of rainfall in the Upper Little Colorado. The distribution of plants and the success of crops is affected by both the abundance and seasonality of rainfall. The table shows the record of change in both for one area of the state and indicates rather clearly that a change in one does not necessarily imply a change in the other.

tree-ring data are based on both simple observations and sophisticated regression equations that relate the width of rings in living trees to the rainfall and temperature conditions that existed during the years when the rings were formed.

While tree-ring data can be used in inferring patterns of change in any variable that affects ring width, most analyses done to date have focused on the relationship between ring width and rainfall. Mean departures from average growth curves are the basic data used in such inferences. Hevly's use of this datum in characterizing the changing prehistoric environment of the Upper Little Colorado is shown in Figure 4. When the plot of annual ring width is to the right of the long term mean, Hevly infers that the period in question was characterized by increased effective moisture. A period when the line is to the left of the mean line was probably one of decreased effective moisture. Immediately after A.D. 1100, the curve is farther to the left than at any other time. Hevly argues that during this period effective moisture was low and rainfall tended to come in the summer months. These data were used in combination with palynological evidence in Hevly's reconstruction of prehistoric Upper Little Colorado environments, and they are summarized in Table 5.

Schulman has described similar patterns of change in ring width for the Flagstaff, Tsegi, and Mesa Verde areas (1951). The tree-ring data suggest an important reason why archaeologists discuss the agricultural strategies practiced by prehistoric populations in terms of variability rather than means: the mean—whether of temperature or rainfall—almost never occurs. It is a statistical phenomenon produced by the offsetting effects of high and low periods of temperature or rainfall. It is not a phenomenon that occurs in nature.

Analyses such as these do not exhaust the potential of tree-ring data as a source of information on prehistoric environments. At the 1969 Pecos Conference in Prescott, William Robinson of the Tree-Ring Laboratory at the University of Arizona reported on new techniques that promise to produce decadic weather maps for prehistoric periods. A regression model was used in con-

FIGURE 4 Mean departures in tree-ring width for the Little Colorado area. The records in living trees were extended backwards by use of overlapping series in archaeological beams. Smoothed curves were superimposed to permit greater ease in visual comparison of the longer fluctuations. Courtesy of Richard H. Hevly.

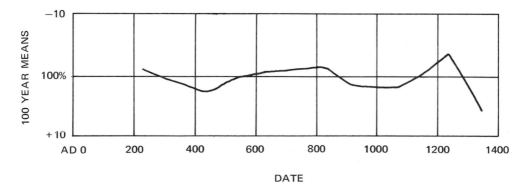

junction with a computer mapping program to produce output in the form of maps of temperature variability (measured in isotherms) and rainfall variability (measured in isohyets) for ten-year periods in sample localities in the Southwest. As these techniques are refined and data obtained from other parts of the area, archaeologists will be able to employ a far sounder and more precise set of statistics on temperature and rainfall variability.

SUMMARY

To date, the treatment of palynological, geographical, and dendroclimatic data have greatly overlapped. Archaeologists and their colleagues have used geographical data in attempting to infer patterns of climatic change. Pollen and tree-ring data have been used for similar purposes. While this complementarity of data has been important in increasing our confidence in the techniques, it will probably be much less important in the future.

While topographic variables, soil variables, plant-animal community patterns, rainfall, and temperature are dependent and interdependent variables, the correlation between each pair is not one to one. Thus, an investigator can infer temperature and rainfall patterns from geomorphological evidence, but tree-ring width is a far more sensitive indicator of these variables. Similarly, patterns of variability in temperature and precipitation can be used to infer the kinds of plant-animal communities that corresponded to the patterns, but palynological data provide the archaeologist with far more direct evidence on this score. Changes in the plant community, or rainfall, can lead to a series of conclusions about the presence or absence of erosion, but these inferences can be made far more easily from geomorphological data. With increasing specialization and sophistication, each of these analytic techniques is likely to provide the archaeologist with a firmer set of information on a more restricted set of variables. And since each variable can affect quite independently of the others the human adaptation in area, archaeologists will be able to discuss in a far more satisfactory fashion what environmental problems prehistoric populations faced and why they succeeded or failed in meeting them.

PART THREE

SPACE AND TIME DIMENSIONS

V Paleo-Indians

When did humans first occupy the state of Arizona? Whether the question of first occupation is raised in reference to Arizona or any other portion of the New World, it is a controversial one. Our most reliable evidence suggests that man entered the state twelve to thirteen thousand years ago. We can be fairly certain that it was at least this long ago, but was it longer?

Most archaeologists agree that prehistoric man entered the New World from Asia by way of the Bering land bridge, a geographical formation that connected Asia and the New World when the sea level was somewhat lower than at present. But, when did these first men cross the Bering Strait? More conservative archaeologists argue that really firm data confirm man's presence no earlier than 10,000 to 15,000 years B.P. Yet, year by year more evidence accumulates suggesting that a date of 20,000 to 30,000 years B.P. may prove more accurate. And a few archaeologists have argued that the event may have occurred 50,000 or even hundreds of thousands of years ago. To date, most such claims have been followed by argument, qualifications, and even retractions.

Why is this subject surrounded by such controversy? First, the quantity of data available from these times is minute and therefore subject to varying interpretations. Second, radiocarbon dates are few and sometimes must be based on bone, shell, and other less reliable materials. Finally, archaeologists find artifacts that look as if they may be older than some types for which firm dates are available.

Two examples should make some of these problems clearer. Several years ago, Katherine Bartlett (1943) described a series of sites that occurred on knolls overlooking the Little Colorado River in northern Arizona. The tools on these sites were different from most that Bartlett observed. She called them the Tolchaco complex. Some investigators believe that the Tolchaco complex was an example of the Pre-Projectile Point stage, a stage that preceded the Paleo-Indian stage to be discussed shortly. Others have argued that the sites were contemporaneous with Paleo-Indian sites elsewhere in the state. Some investigators have argued that the artifacts are not artifacts, that they were produced by being rolled about in stream beds.

At present, these problems cannot be resolved. The sites are gravelly knolls. They were probably used as sources of raw material for tool manufacture over thousands of years. Some of the artifacts on them are fairly recent, others may be very, very old. The sites have little or no stratigraphy, no materials suitable for radiocarbon dating have been taken from them, and none seems to exist on the sites. Without stratigraphy, without dates, with a clear case of admixtures of artifacts from different time periods, the dispute over the age of such sites will continue.

Even when dates are available, their interpretation may be disputed. Dates have been obtained on Tule Springs ("s" in Figure 5) going back to 23,800 B.P. (Harrington and Simpson, 1961). The association of the material from which the date was obtained and artifactual material is unclear, at best. Newer dates with a clearer association with cultural material suggest the occupation of the site was closer to 12,000 B.P. (Shutler, 1965). The debate over Tule Springs is not even close to an end. Nor is the debate over the existence of a Pre-Projectile Point stage.

DEFINING THE PALEO-INDIAN STAGE

The existence of the Paleo-Indian stage is not a subject of dispute. Sites of this stage are identified by the presence of bifacially worked lanceolate projectile points, extinct fauna, or both. Willey and Phillips (1958) refer to this stage as the Lithic stage. It occurs throughout the New World. In addition to the projectile points and extinct fauna, chipped but not ground stone implements, a few kinds of bone, and a few kinds of horn implements are found on sites of this stage. But, fluted and unfluted lanceolate projectile points are the principle diagnostic trait. Artifacts from this stage are so scarce that most aspects of material culture cannot even be discussed.

This situation is, however, beginning to change. Edwin N. Wilmsen (1970) has completed an analysis of Paleo-Indian data that significantly increases our understanding of the artifacts, sites, and subsistence bases of these populations. Only one of the sites Wilmsen uses in his analysis is in Arizona. Our understanding of the stage in this state will begin to increase markedly when his techniques are applied to data from the area.

Wilmsen focused on Paleo-Indian artifacts other than projectile points. He analyzed over two thousand of these artifacts in attempting to discover how they were made and how they were used. Attributes such as the shape, chipping pattern, retouch pattern, and raw material were recorded for each artifact. The artifacts were sorted into gross categories—unmodified, unutilized flakes, utilized flakes, tools (modified and utilized flakes), and fragmentary tools. Correlations of these attributes were used in defining tool types.

One attribute that is of particular interest is the edge angle of the artifacts. Wilmsen argues that this attribute can be used for making inferences about the uses to which tools were put. For example, he suggests that tools with edge angles of 46° to 55° would have been most useful for skinning and scraping hides, shredding sinew and plant fibers, and cutting bone, horn, and wood. Edge angles of 66° to 75° occur on artifacts that were probably used in woodworking, boneworking, and graving (1970, p. 70).

These tools do not occur in equal proportions on Paleo-Indian sites. Inferences concerning differences in the use of the sites are based upon the differential distribution of these types of tools as well as similarities and differences in the distribution of projectile points, chipping debris, grinding tools, and faunal and floral remains. Four of the sites that Wilmsen considered proved to be multiple activity sites, used seemingly for camping and a variety of other activities. While there were differences in the specific activities carried on at each site, they contrast sharply with five other sites that Wilmsen considers. These are limited activity sites; they were used primarily for one or a few activities involving a limited range of resources. Two of the sites were ones at which bison and mammoth were killed and butchered. A third seem to have been used primarily for processing plant material. At another, raw materials were quarried and tools made. Wilmsen's is one of the most detailed studies of variability in site use available to the archaeologist.

Only one of the sites that Wilmsen considered is in Arizona. The data published concerning Paleo-Indian sites in the state are not sufficiently detailed to permit an analysis like Wilmsen's. They were neither excavated nor analyzed for such a purpose. When such an analysis is done, our understanding of this stage in the state will be vastly increased. In our own analysis, we will use Wilmsen's typology to the extent that we can.

The locations of Paleo-Indian sites in the state and adjacent Nevada are shown in Figure 5. Although sites recorded to date tend to be concentrated in the eastern third of the state, the presence of two sites in Nevada shows that Paleo-Indian populations did occupy territory farther to the West. The majority of the sites on this map are locations where a single artifact was found and where no excavation has been carried out. Some of the sites have been excavated: Tule Springs (r), Gypsum Cave (s), Vernon (m), Ventana Cave (o), Naco (b), Lehner (c) Murray Springs (x), and Dougle Adobe (t).

GYPSUM AND VENTANA CAVES

In investigating most stages of Arizona prehistory, archaeologists have focused their research activity on sites with evidence of dwelling or habitation units. Only in studying the Paleo-Indian and Desert culture stages have archaeologists obtained substantial material from and information on nonhabitation sites. In fact, our knowledge of habitation sites of these stages is almost nonexistent. Naturally roofed space —caves—provides most of the evidence on habitation, and habitation may have been only a minor reason for the use of such caves. They may have been used more for storage.

Gypsum Cave is about ten miles north-

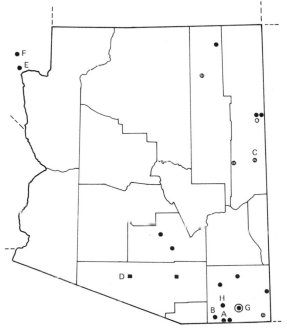

A - NACO
B - LEHNER
C - VEONON
D - VENTANA CAVE
E - GYPSUM CAVE
F - TULE SPRINGS
G - DOUBLE ADOBE
H - MURRAY SPRINGS

● CLOVIS
● FOLSOM
■ CLOVIS-FOLSOM (?)
◉ SULPHUR SPRINGS

FIGURE 5 The distribution of Indian sites in Arizona and adjacent Nevada. Some of the sites represent only a single projectile point. Others are large and have received substantial archaeological attention. Note the general absence of Paleo-Indian sites in the mountain environment. Courtesy of L. D. Agenbroad, 1967.

59

west of Hoover Dam at an elevation of around 2,000 feet. It is in a limestone ridge of the Frenchman Mountains and overlooks a lake bed that held water during some periods of the Pleistocene. This cave was known to and used by Paiute Indians prior to its excavation in 1929 and 1930 by M. R. Harrington (1933).

Extinct fauna found in the cave include sloth, horse, dire wolf, and a camelid. The cultural debris that seems to be associated with these fauna is substantial. Burned cane and sticks, fragments of a wooden atlatl, dart shafts, projectile points, an oval scraper knife, and a worked stick were recovered. In addition, two hearths were found in the same level of the cave. The cave was used by Paleo-Indian groups between 8527 ± 250 and 10,455 ± 340 B.P.

Ventana Cave (Haury 1950) is a rock shelter in the Castle Mountains, about five miles from Ventana, Arizona. Two of the lower strata in the cave contain cultural material of the Paleo-Indian stage. In the "Conglomerate," a scraper and a possible hammerstone were found in association with ground squirrel, dire wolf, coyote, kit fox, tapir, horse, antelope, and bison. Artifacts in the volcanic stratum above this one include a Clovis projectile point, one other projectile point, and a variety of knives, scrapers, gravers, choppers, and planes. A single hammerstone and one grinding stone were also found in this level. The fauna of the stratum included jack rabbit, prairie dog, badger, jaguar, sloth, tapir, horse, peccary, deer, and antelope. Undoubtedly, some of these animals lived and died in the cave. A number of the long bones, however, were charred and split as if cooked and broken to extract marrow. Shells that could have come from the Gulf of Lower California (approximately a hundred miles away) suggest that the early inhabitants of Ventana Cave were in contact with groups

from that area. The occupation level containing the Clovis point has been dated to 11,290 ± 500 B.P.

Artifacts and features in the two caves indicate that both cooking and eating occurred in them. The great variety of tools suggest that other kinds of activities may have been carried on in the cave. But, the samples are too small and the detailed evidence too slight to say much about these.

NACO AND LEHNER

Naco is an example of a kill site. It is exposed in the wall of Greenbush Creek, a tributary of the San Pedro River near the southern boundary of Arizona. The elevation of the site is around 4,500 feet.

This site was discovered by Fred and Marc Navarette and excavation was supervised by Emil Haury (Haury, Antevs, and Lance, 1953). The site is very small, covering an area of four by four meters. The culture-bearing deposit is about two meters below the land surface. Eight projectile points were recovered from the site. These were intermixed with the bones of a mammoth they were used to kill. Some bison bones were also taken from the site. No firm dates are available from the site, but on the basis of artifactual and palynological data, it seems to have been used 10,000 to 11,000 years before the present.

The Lehner Site and material recovered from it were described by Haury, Sayles, and Wasley (1959) and Lance (1959). It was discovered by and named for Edward F. Lehner. Excavation and analysis were directed by Emil Haury beginning in 1954.

The site is about two miles south of Hereford, Arizona, at an altitude of 4,200 feet. It was exposed in the bed of the San Pedro River, 2.5 meters below the modern land

PLATE 1 Bone and artifacts at the Naco Site. A meter-square block of ribs, vertebrae, and scapulae showing the location of vie spear points. Reproduced by permission of the Arizona State Museum.

surface. A bone bed and a hearth area are the two major activity loci at the site. Thirteen projectile points were recovered from the kill area. Some of these were touching the bones of nine disarticulated mammoths. Eight cutting and scraping tools, one chopper, and eight miscellaneous chips and flakes were scattered over this area. There are two hearths in the other activity area, one 40 centimeters in diameter and 35 centimeters deep, and the second 1.25 by 70 centimeters on the surface and 3 centimeters deep. Charred bison and tapir bones were taken from this area of the site. Some bones of an extinct horse were also found at the site. Radiocarbon dates on material removed from the Lehner Site range from 10,410 ± 190 to 11,600 ± 190 B.P.

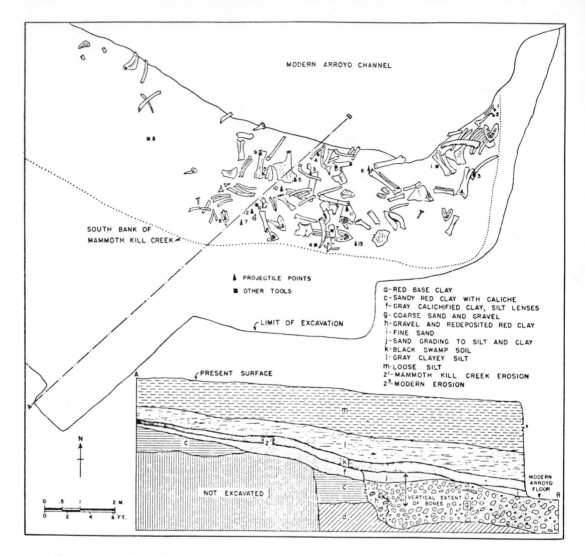

FIGURE 6   The Lehner Site. A plan view of main area of artifact and bone concentration and a geological profile of the site. Note the occurrence of projectile points and other tools in the midst of the disarticulated bones. Reproduced by permission of the Arizona State Museum.

VERNON

The Vernon Site is located to the east of the Little Colorado River Valley between Springerville and St. Johns, Arizona. Excavations at this site were directed by William A. Longacre. The artifact assemblage from the site has never been described. The site is on the modern land surface, and substantial numbers of artifacts may have been removed from it by local collectors. Excavated artifacts were used by Wilmsen in his research discussed earlier. Unfinished preforms and large quantities of chipping debris were taken from the site. A single mano was also found there. The presence of fragments of the bases of projectile points and the knowledge that Folsom points had been removed from the site by local amateurs led Wilmsen to conclude that it was probably occupied between 9000 and 11,000 years B.P.

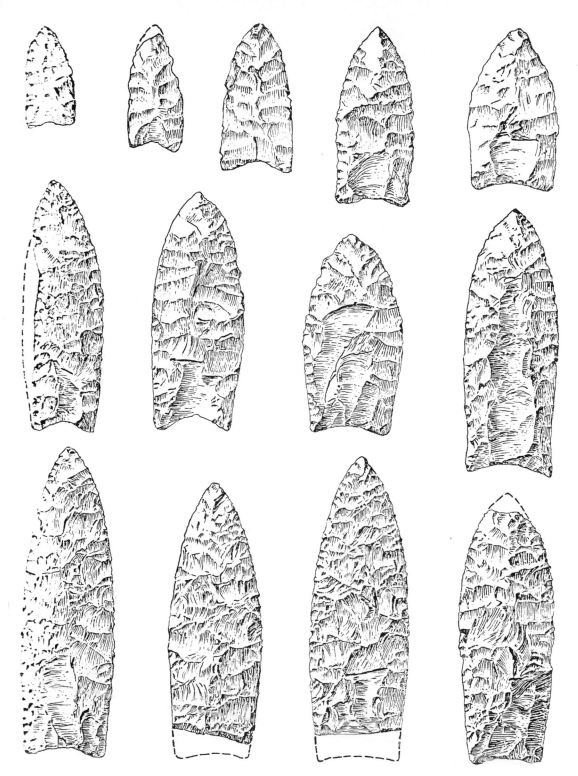

FIGURE 7 Projectile points from the Lehner Site. Notice the variation in the sizes of the point and in the fluting of the surface and shape of the base. Gorman has argued that stylistic variation on Paleo-Indian points may have served to identify the killer of the animal or the owner of portions of it. Reproduced by permission of the Arizona State Museum.

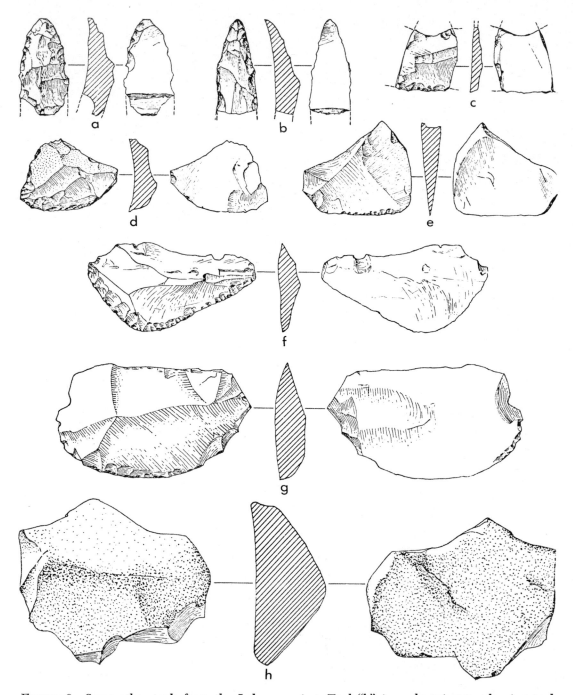

FIGURE 8   Some other tools from the Lehner Site. Tools a–g are cutting and scraping tools. Those tools with an acute edge were used for cutting and those with steeper edges for scraping. Tool "h" is a chopping or cleaving tool. The presence of such tools indicates that animals were butchered on the site. Reproduced by permission of the Arizona State Museum.

MURRAY SPRINGS

The Murray Springs Site will probably prove to be one of the most important Paleo-Indian sites excavated in the state. It is in the San Pedro Valley near Murray Springs. Excavations conducted by C. Vance Haynes and E. Thomas Hemmings (1968) recovered a partial mammoth skeleton and fragments of extinct species of bison, horse, camel, and wolf. Three thousand flint artifacts including a variety of tools and Clovis points have been recovered there. The size of this site and the amount of material being taken from it are the bases of the belief that it will prove to be important. The site dates to 11,230 ± 340 B.P.

DOUBLE ADOBE

The Double Adobe Site is in the Sulphur Springs Valley twelve miles northwest of Douglas, Arizona. This site is generally classified as an example of Sulphur Springs "stage" of the Cochise culture. We mention it here because it is a relatively early site dating to 9350 ± 160 B.P. and has associated Pleistocene fauna. Although projectile points and chipped bone implements were recovered at the site, 316 milling stones constitute the bulk of the assemblage. The predominance of food-grinding rather than hunting tools has led to the inclusion of this site in the Desert culture stage. Such a move ignores the presence of horse, bison, antelope, wolf, coyote, and mammoth at Double Adobe and sites like it (Pearce 8:10, Sonora F:10:40, Sonora F:10:17) in the Sulphur Springs Valley. These sites are only a few dozen miles from the Naco and Lehner Sites. While they may represent a culture or stage that is distinct from the Paleo-Indian one, the possibility that they

are highly specialized plant gathering stations cannot be excluded. The sites present one of the intriguing problems of Arizona prehistory.

PALEO-INDIAN SITES IN SPACE AND TIME

Some basic similarities and differences between sites discussed in this chapter are summarized in Table 6. That significant differences exist between the sites is clear. The substantial presence of preforms and chipping debris at Vernon suggest that this site was used for tool manufacture. Plant processing may be indicated by the mano found there. Naco was a kill site, and while no evidence of butchering was found there, it seems likely that some portions of the mammoth were removed from the carcass and carried away. Lehner was also a kill site, but one with clear evidence of butchering, cooking, and eating. It seems probable that the group responsible for the kills camped on the site, although no direct evidence of this activity was found.

The remainder of the sites examined were multiple activity loci. While few artifacts were taken from the cave sites, it appears that eating, processing of animal resources, and tool manufacturing occurred in them. All of these activities were carried on at the Double Adobe Site and may prove to have occurred at Murray Springs when excavation is complete.

The limited amount of data available on this stage prohibits a more intensive discussion of space-time systematics. In closing, we might explain our failure to stress the difference between what many archaeologists regard as two Paleo-Indian complexes, Clovis or Llano and Folsom. Theoretically, Clovis or Llano is the older of the complexes and is found in association with

	GYPSUM CAVE	VENTANA CAVE	NACO	LEHNER	VERNON	MURRAY SPRINGS	DOUBLE ADOBE
Hearth	+	[1]		+			+
Bone Tool	+					+	
Wooden Tool	+						
Hammerstone		+					+
Grinding Stone		+			+		+
Projectile Points	+	+	+	+	+[2]	+	+
Chipped Stone Tool	+	+		+	+[2]	+[2]	
Bison		+		+		+	+
Mammoth			+	+		+	+
Camelid	+					+	
Horse	+	+				+	+
Sloth	+	+					
Other		+		+		+	+

[1] Charcoal and charred bone at Ventana Cave suggest that cooking did occur there.
[2] Including debitage.

TABLE 6 The distribution of faunal remains and selected artifacts on five Paleo-Indian sites.

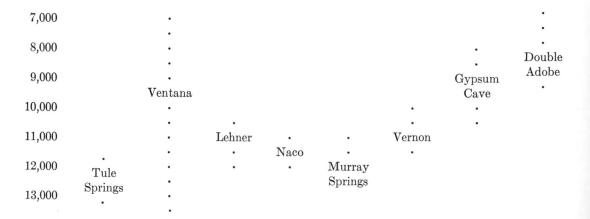

TABLE 7 Approximate dates of occupation of eight Paleo-Indian sites in Arizona and adjacent Nevada.

Pleistocene fauna, especially mammoth. Folsom is the younger complex, and Folsom points are supposed to occur in association with remains of nearly modern bison. From the limited evidence on Folsom available in Arizona, it is already clear that the two complexes overlapped temporally. Moreover, the evidence from the Sulphur Springs Valley indicates that the Clovis complex had no unique association with mammoth or other extinct Pleistocene fauna. While we don't deny that morphological differences exist between Folsom and Clovis projectile points, it seems far too early and far too convenient to explain this morphological variability by arguing for large-scale cultural differences and large-scale environmental differences in their derivations.

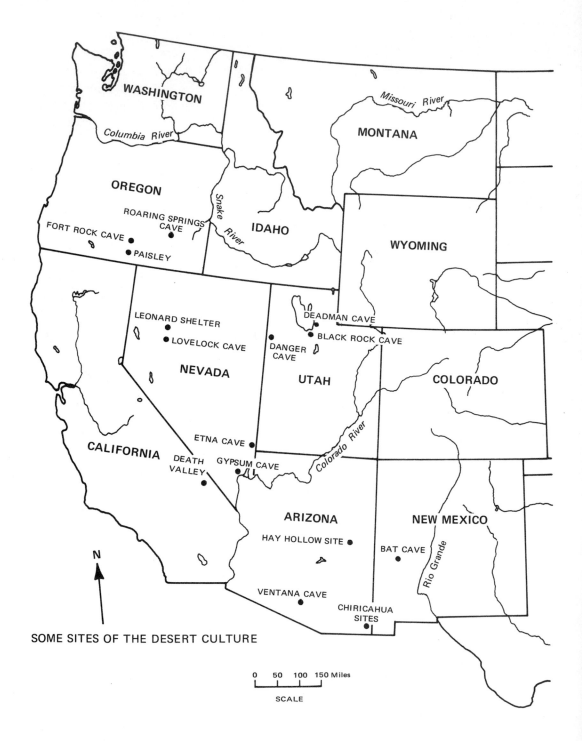

FIGURE 9   Some sites of the Desert culture.

VI   The Desert Culture: A Hunting and Gathering Adaptation

Various descriptions and analyses of the Desert culture exist, but the following is the one that is generally accepted now.

The name Desert culture is applied to the area in which numerous cultural similarities are found and which mark it as a distinctly separate assemblage and different from adjacent cultural ones. This area—the Desert West—is one of the most interesting, varied, and remarkable environments in North America. This region is known to geographers as the Intermontane or Basin-Plateau province and includes the Great Basin. It extends from southeast Oregon to the Valley of Mexico and lies between the Rocky Mountains and the Pacific Coastal ranges. Physiographically the area manifests great variety—valleys, ranges, and mountains. The structure of the Great Basin is warped, folded, uplifted, and is marked by many basins. Some of these are well-watered meadows and grasslands. Other basins are completely desiccated (Swanson, 1966, p. 140). Although the Great Basin appears to belong to a single ecological system it is characterized by a number of vegetational zones: (1) Alpine tundra zone; (2) Conifer forest zone; and (3) Grassland and desert zone (Swanson, 1966, p. 142). Although the desert occupies a lot of the area, it is actually marginal to the rest of the ecological system. Hence, the range of

these environments has affected the characted of the prehistoric cultures that are closely adapted to this setting.

Strictly speaking, then, the Desert culture cannot be taken to mean a culture of only the desert margin. The Desert culture must also be identified with ecological zones of the plains, grasslands, and forests. The culture adapted to the desert area of the Great Basin was relatively simple and was mostly confined to the central area and surrounded on the margins with specializations and elaborations of various types (Eggan and D'Azevedo, 1966, p. xvi). Swanson (1966, p. 144) suggests that both the Desert culture and the desert area are rather recent developments in this area and that the former may have developed out of the more complex cultural pattern of big game hunters. He further suggests (Swanson, 1966, p. 145) that the foundations of the Desert culture rest in an adaptation to the grassland zone or to a lacustrine zone, either of which once had a greater distribution in the Great Basin. Because of climatic change (desiccation) about 5000 B.C., the Desert culture as portrayed by Jennings (1957) may have resulted. Swanson (personal communication) dates its beginning in Nevada and Utah at about 6000 B.C. Hence, the Desert culture is a relatively recent development from a more complex Big-Game Hunting culture that adapted to a period of aridity that began about 5000 B.C.—a period that was drier than any period before or after it. The area of the desert was thus increased for a period of several thousand years because the dryness caused a shift in the Rocky Mountain ecological system that produced an increase in desert flora at lower altitudes (Swanson, 1966, pp. 144–45).

Rainfall varies tremendously, with more precipitation (about 16 inches annual fall) in the uplands and forested areas. The average annual precipitation ranges from about 4½ inches in the central desert area to 10 inches. Maximum temperatures range from about 100° to 115° F; and the minimum from about zero degrees F in the northern sector to about 20° F in the southern.

In these varied settings arose a regional adaptation, the Desert culture, that was characterized by an overall organization which grew out of and developed around specific types of food and tool production. The origins of this culture and the Indians responsible for the Desert culture are not known. All we can say from present evidence is that the Intermontane area appears to have been one of the first areas to have been settled in North America. The Desert culture, then, may have been a development out of an older Big-Game Hunting culture (Butler, 1968, p. 92). Although the Desert culture may have borne a relationship to an ancient tradition, the earliest aspects of it cannot be glimpsed until about 6000 B.C. or eight thousand years ago. Present evidence suggests that the general climate of this vast area has fluctuated considerably in the past ten thousand years, with a drier and warmer period beginning about 5000 B.C. Hence, there must have been a shift at that time in the vegetation zones with an increase in desert plants be-

low 5,000 feet elevation. Fluctuations in rainfall patterns probably occurred, but this fluctuation was seasonal and the average annual amounts were probably the same as today. Given this rigid desert environment, the floral and faunal assemblages would be limited to those adapted to this kind of setting. From present evidence it would seem that during the latter part of its existence—say 3000 to about 1000 B.C.—the Desert culture changed continuously both in actual inventory of traits and in general content and probably in social organization also (seminar research, 1968, of Southwest Archaeological Expedition of Field Museum). Hence, this characterization of the culture is a generalized and idealized one, one that might not "fit" specifically any particular time horizon. We can only present a diffuse picture of those times in a rough fashion.

One thing seems certain and that is that in the prefarming, nonherding adaptation to this arid or semiarid area, similar food could be found over the whole area: vegetable and animal, with more vegetable than animal. Hence, one may hypothesize that when man develops an adaptive response (a culture) that exploits fully the food resources offered by the environment, one may expect a broadly uniform situation—a type of culture characterized by hunting and gathering subsistence techniques. This term means that the subsistence of the population was provided *in toto* by natural resources—hunting, trapping and snaring of birds, insects, deer, antelope, mountain sheep, mice, jack rabbit, cottontail, and birds (to name only a few); and exploiting every available plant: seeds from plants and grasses, camas lily bulbs, nuts, roots, and berries.

The statement that every available plant was exploited needs to be qualified. Among contemporary Basin Indians, of the forty-four species of grasses and other seed plants present only seven were gathered by all the groups of Basin peoples. In other words, there were variations in the species of grass seeds and nuts, animals and insects collected and eaten. In the past, this may have been true also. It is probable that the quantity of a specific plant that was available at a specific time and place would determine whether or not it was collected and eaten (Downs, 1966, pp. 40–42).

Another important adaptation by the Great Basin groups was an attempt to manipuate their environment. Sowing of wild seeds may have been practiced. Burning off the plant cover may have been utilized to encourage growth of wild plants.

Downs suggests (Downs, 1966, pp. 52–55) that in societies that have successfully adapted to a relatively hostile environment one finds that they are, by virtue of their adaptation to that environment, capable of great variation from group to group, within groups and between individuals. Consequently it may be true that since hunting and gathering societies cannot depend on a single source of food, they tend to manipulate and innovate. This kind of adjustment may encourage the members of such a society to develop and to accept variations, experimentation, and fluidity in all phases of their life. The permissive and variable sociological framework of their society may have served as a favorable and nourishing medium for the growth of such ideas. Flexibility and ability to adapt are the touchstones of growth, evolution, and unfolding. To put it in the form of Service's law: "Specific evolutionary progress is inversely related to general evolutionary potential" (Service, 1960, p. 97).

In a sense, then, their adaptability and the freedom of an individual to gather foods as he chose made change easy for these societies. While these qualities might not occur in the present archaeological record, they present hypotheses for explaining the Great Basin acceptance (where climatically feasible) and development of agriculture and the development of complex forms of sociological, economic, technological, and ideological subsystems. Whether these hypotheses are valid or not, we do know that maize-growing was adapted in the southern part of the area by 3000 B.C. It is possible that the people who adopted maize may have regarded corn as merely another kind of grass seed, which it is. Furthermore, milling stones for reducing wild seeds to flour were already in use. Hence, corn probably supplemented other vegetal foods since planting and weeding required but little time. If our inferences are correct, then we visualize small groups of people whose search for food would be almost continuous. The groups moved from place to place—here in the valley in the spring, higher up on mountains in the summer, back to the ranges and valleys in the fall and winter to harvest seeds, berries, nuts, and roots as they ripened. We call such a life a "seasonal round"—moving hither and yon, searching for the areas most favorable for growth and maturing of their life-giving plants.

This, then, is the most general kind of description of the area and of the subsistence patterns in vogue during the last five thousand years.

Before dealing with specific details we wish to point out that the idea of a generalized culture characteristic of the entire region has been suggested in less or greater detail by various anthropologists since about 1930 (Kroeber, 1928; Beals, 1943; Kirchhoff, 1954; Spier, 1929; Jennings and Norbeck, 1955; Jennings, 1956, 1957).

THE DESERT CULTURE

The hunting and gathering way of life has been the most successful and enduring adaptation that man has ever achieved. Present evidence supports the idea that man *as* man has occupied the earth for about two million years; and for more than 99 percent of that time man has lived as a hunter-gatherer (Lee and DeVore, 1968, p. 3). Domestication of plants and animals by man occurred only in the last ten thousand years. Hence, in describing the Desert culture, we are presenting a generalized picture of how our ancestors and proto-ancestors lived for a very respectable length of time.

It is assumed, on the basis of many studies, that hunters-gatherers lived in small groups, consisting perhaps of twenty-five to fifty people, and probably all kin-related. The social organization may best be described as a large but elastic network of social relations with bilateral kinship ties and marriage alliances as a foundation. This network cut across ecological, linguistic, and physiographic boundaries. It has been suggested (Eggan and D'Azevedo, 1966, p. xvi) that such a network provided for the crucial transmission of information as to available food surpluses, for transportation of exotic stone, and the possibility of periodic social gatherings. About one third of the stone tools at the Blackwater Site were imported from a quarry near Amarillo, Texas, a distance of a hundred miles (Wilmsen, 1970). Certainly, the nuclear family was probably the irreducible social unit, yet other kinds of alliances may have been present: sibling ties, sororal polygamy, and marriage by exchange. Thus, extended family units and mixed groups emerged and provided a basis of bands that wintered together and cooperated in food collecting, preparation and cooking of

food, in hunting, in group security, in care of sick ones, in sharing knowledge of food surpluses and water sources, in observances of rituals, and in taking care of the children and of old people. Density of population is estimated at about one person per twenty square miles for the arid areas.

Since Desert culture people lived in small groups and were nonsedentary food collectors, we assume that they moved around a lot as food resources from a restricted area would be exhausted in a few days. It is also probable that each local group was associated with a geographical range. Wandering as they did, they must have encountered other groups; accordingly we postulate ample communication between groups. Such interaction probably brought about reciprocal visiting, food-sharing, and marriage and marriage alliances. Men hunted, while women gathered wild plants for food and healing and looked after the children.

A cave, an overhang, or any convenient rock shelter probably served as a base camp, especially in the winter time. It is also possible that temporary shelters may have been built of poles, foliage, and brush or of poles, brush, and earth, or of wattle-and-daub construction. Whether any housing was used in warm weather is not known, although it's conceivable that skin tents, windbreaks, or lodges (poles, brush, and earth) were quite likely in use. In cave shelters, bark or grass beds have been found.

EXAMPLES OF DESERT CULTURE SITES

Before Jennings excavated Danger Cave (see below) two sites in Arizona were found and excavated, the Cochise culture sites and Ventana Cave. These have become famous as they were among the first reports on manifestations of the Desert culture in southern Arizona.

The Cochise culture (Sayles and Antevs, 1941) was the first well-documented set of early sites in southern Arizona and they were soon recognized as part of the Desert culture stage. The sites are located in the southeastern corner of Arizona. The earliest stage, the Sulphur Springs stage, was exposed by recent channel erosion in White-water Creek, although the artifacts had been buried by ten feet of old river sands and gravels. The artifacts included hand-stones, milling stones, and percussion flaked tools such as knives, scrapers, axes, and hammerstones—all typical of Desert culture tools. No projectile points were found. Associated with these tools were bones of now extinct mammals: camel, horse, dire wolf, mammoth. This stage is dated by radiocarbon at about 6000 B.C.

In the same creek channel but in deposits above those containing artifacts of the Sulphur Spring stage was located another aspect of the Desert culture. This stage is called the Chiricahua and is later in time than Sulphur Springs materials. The investigators feel it is a later and continuous development of the Sulphur Springs tools. Chiricahua tools include small, one-hand handstones; milling stones that are either flat pebbles or contain an oval deep basin near the center of the stone; multi-face pestles, mortars; a crudely shaped grooved maul (?), hand axes, knives, scrapers. Most of the chipped implements were manufactured by the percussion method. Dates for this stage are given (radiocarbon dating) as about 6000–4000 B.C.

The latest Cochise stage, called San Pedro, yields stone implements, some of which are the same as those of the Chiricahua stage and some new types. In addi-

tion, tools produced by pressure flaking occur for the first time. The assemblage includes: milling stones, handstones, pestles, choppers, projectile points, scrapers, and bifaced blades. Pit houses (the earliest) occur in this stage. They are small, about 6½ feet in diameter and 20 inches deep. This stage is dated by radiocarbon at 1900 B.C.–A.D. 1.

It should be noted that pottery does not occur in any of the Cochise stages.

The significance of the Cochise culture may be summed up as follows:

1. The best and earliest documented data are described as a variation of the Desert culture for southern Arizona;

2. A typological evolution of tools plus an accretion of new types in the later stages is stated;

3. The geological antiquity is well established in addition to the carbon 14 dates;

4. It comprises three prepottery stages with houses appearing in the latest stage (San Pedro). The geological and climatic history of the deposits is fairly well worked out. The oldest stage is embedded in the final throes of the Pluvial period; the middle stage (Chiricahua) seems to have been an arid to semiarid one accompanied by erosion and cutting of arroyos during floods. The latest stage, San Pedro, enjoyed a semiarid climate with erosion cycles much like the climate of today.

Ventana Cave is on the Papago Indian reservation about a hundred miles due west of Tucson. It is not truly a cave but is more like a big rock shelter. Moisture rarely penetrated the rear, habitable area. The cave is about 190 feet long and at the deep end is about 70 feet wide. The climate of the area today is hot and dry, with a mean annual temperature of about 65° at about 2,500 feet. The average annual rainfall varies from 3 to 10 inches.

The cave was first occupied about eight

to ten thousand years ago. Above that lowest deposit four other and later prehistoric layers were identified. Throughout its history, the cave never harbored a single culture distinctive of the area. Apparently it was a kind of way station where hunter-gatherers sojourned temporarily. The earliest occupation—the Ventana complex—demonstrates culture traits that are typical of the Folsom and San Dieguito (California) complexes; the next layering produced artifacts that are typical of the Lower Colorado River Basin and of the Chiricahua stage of the Cochise culture; while just below the latest Hohokam pottery-bearing levels one finds tools typical of the San Pedro stage of the Cochise culture. Thus we have here food-collecting stages with emphasis on the grinding and milling of seeds in the earliest level, on hunting in the middle, and again on hunting and collecting of foods that were processed on milling stones in the latest prepottery horizon. In a diagram representing the changes in subsistence patterns in the cave, Haury (1950, p. 544) suggests that the people in the earliest—the Ventana complex—devoted about 60 percent of their lives to hunting and 40 percent to food gathering; but by the San Pedro level, only about 30 percent to hunting and about 70 percent to food collecting. By the beginning of the Christian era, Hohokam pottery appeared in the upper levels and agriculture not only appeared but increased in importance in the subsistence patterns. The change correlates roughly in sequence and proportions at least with other Desert culture sites.

Tools of stone, bone, shell, horn occurred at all levels. Unfortunately, perishable objects such as netting, cordage, basketry, leather and feather objects, textiles and sandals were found only in the upper pottery-bearing levels (after A.D. 1).

Human fecal material from Danger Cave (Jennings, 1957, pp. 276–77) provides an excellent notion as to what some of the Desert culture people ate. Although the fecal material was not positively identified as human, one is led to assume that some of it probably was because of the nature of the materials isolated and identified. Seeds of the pickle weed (*Allenrolfea occidentalis*) were darker than they occur in nature. Further, many were scored and abraded. Jennings suggests that the seeds of this plant had been parched and milled and utilized in some gruel-like food. Quids of vegetal fibers, often of bulrush, were found in abundance in the cave. It is assumed that these pads of matted fibers were chewed, perhaps as a means of obtaining starches or as a step in the development of raw material for making cordage.

Many, if not most, plants were used in some manner, either for food or for medicinal purposes. Wooden digging sticks were employed to dig up roots, tubers, and whole stalks of a plant. Baskets, carried by tumplines, served as containers for these plants, seeds, and nuts; and baskets lined with pitch provided excellent receptacles in which to cook vegetable foods, mush, and meat stews. The baskets were not placed on the fire but were filled with liquid and food to be cooked. Stones about as big as a man's fist were heated in a fire and when very hot were removed from the fire and dropped into the waiting basket-cum-pot. Fire was made by means of a fire drill. Other basket trays were used for winnowing or parching seeds. Seeds were reduced to flour and other plant foods were crushed and ground on flat milling stones by means of cobblestones. The presence of milling stones used in reducing seeds to flour may explain why it was easy for the Desert culture people to make a transition from grinding wild foods to grinding corn, when the latter was introduced into parts of the area at about 3000 B.C. Further, flour cooking had been practiced for several thousand years and may explain the later easy acceptance of maize and its kernels, which lend themselves to easy pulverizing and flouring. Game was procured by means of various techniques —snares, traps, and nets—and hunting was done by propelling darts, tipped with chipped stone projectile points, by means of a throwing stick (an atlatl). The bow and arrow were not introduced into the area or at least were not widely used until about the time of Christ (Tularosa Cave, Martin *et al.*, 1952). Flat, curved wooden clubs may have been used as boomerangs in hunting (?) or, more likely, for stunning or killing trapped game.

Since wild plants, seeds, nuts, and berries were not available during winter months, some method of preserving and storing food had to be developed. Seeds and other vegetable foods had to be protected from moisture and from rodents. In some instances the sides of pits may have been hardened to a bricklike consistency by building fires in them, causing the clay walls to become "tempered" or toughened to such a degree that dampness could not penetrate nor could rodents gain entrance. Food may have been placed in these pits in basket containers or without any wrapping. A covering might have been provided by stone slabs supported by horizontal poles, or by a covering of branches, twigs, and earth. When dry cave floors were available, pits were dug in them (sometimes by pecking a pit out of solid rock) and food stored therein. Or again, a pit might have been dug in the earth and lined with stone slabs. Drying or smoking meat over a fire and then hanging it out of harm's way was the preferred method of conserving it.

Clothing, although not absolutely necessary, was evidently worn, as is shown by materials recovered from dry caves, and was probably minimal. Fur cloth made of rabbit skins and bird and animal skins may have been used as robes, blankets, or capes. Sewing together pieces of buckskin was a common practice. Whether garments were produced in this manner is not known, but they may have been. Sandals made of plant fibers were woven and in use as early as 7000 B.C. Shells from the Pacific Ocean were strung together and used as necklaces.

Dogs were present as early as 8400 B.C. in eastern Idaho, but we do not know what function they served (B. Lawrence, 1968, pp. 43–49).

Games were probably played—perhaps gambling games. This inference is based on the data recovered from Danger Cave (Jennings, 1957, p. 278): flat, rectangular bars of dense animal bone as well as dozens of small wooden cylinders. These may have served as gaming counters. Such simple games appear to have been distributed widely in the world and may have an ancestry of thousands of years.

Tubular pipes of bone and stone were used for smoking and as sucking tubes for curing disease or sickness by applying suction to the affected spot. This form of "healing" was very common among many Indian tribes.

RECAPITULATION

Since Jennings produced his comprehensive and definitive contribution to the delineation of the Desert culture (1957) several publications on this or related subjects have appeared. I wish to mention one of these.

In 1966, in Chicago, an important and unusually significant symposium was held. The subject was "Man the Hunter" (Lee and DeVore, 1968). "Hunter" as used here was a shorthand term for hunters and food gatherers.

As a result of that symposium and the published papers, Lee and DeVore wrote a chapter called "Problems in the Study of Hunters and Gatherers."

Although no consensus was reached concerning all aspects of this way of life, and hence no general picture of it could be drawn, the two editors drew up a trial formulation of their views on the subject. This, it was hoped, would serve as a start for future research and discussion. We have taken the liberty of using some of their ideas to crystallize what we have been saying about the Desert culture—a way of life that was certainly based on food collection and hunting.

We use their ideas also to flesh out what is actually lacking in our knowledge concerning the Desert culture. There is a certain danger in this—the danger of mistaking theory for fact. If the reader clearly understands, however, that the various remarks about their economic, social, and ritualistic organization are to be thought of *only* as suggestions, hypotheses, theories, guesses, most of which have not been tested or demonstrated, then no harm can ensue. The trial formulation of Lee and DeVore springs from contemporary hunting and gathering societies (Africa, Asia, North and South America). If the principle of uniformitarianism holds, some of their ideas may have significance for cultures that existed thousands of years ago. On the other hand there is a chance that none of their ideas ever held true, or if they did, that we may not be able to obtain evidence for testing them.

At any rate, they carry the positive virtue of suggesting ways in which the people of the Desert culture *may* have lived, earned their living, and succeeded in conquering and adapting to and surviving in a fairly rigid desert environment.

In addition, this provides a generalized model of an adaptation that persisted in a large area for a long time. It is based on what we know about present adaptations of this sort and is consistent with known archaeological data. It is not meant as a specific reconstruction of the way of life of any particular group of prehistoric people. Rather, it provides us with a source from which hypotheses can be derived. Knowledge gained from testing such hypotheses will allow us to change the model and continually to improve its representation of the hunting and gathering adaptation.

Two basic assumptions are made: (1) the people lived in small groups; (2) they moved about, never staying long in the same spot unless it was the base camp.

The essentials of the economic system include a base camp, a division of labor—males hunting, females gathering food and tending the children—and a custom of sharing the collected food. Under this kind of arrangement, it would be well-nigh inconceivable for any member of the group to die of hunger or even to go hungry for more than a day or two.

The social system is visualized as having been egalitarian, for the reason that if people had to move around a lot to get food, the amount of personal property would have been kept to a low level—and highly portable, at that. Lack of personal property served to make accumulation of wealth impossible. Thus, differences between individuals caused by wealth differential were kept at a minimum. Basic soccial structure was a network of bands based on kinship and marriage.

The meagerness and nature of the food supply would limit the number of people who lived together. Big concentrations of people would soon reduce the food resources to nil. It is possible, however, that several bands or groups of people would have come together perhaps once a year in late summer. It was a kind of prehistoric Thanksgiving Day. On these occasions, group rituals, alliances, feasting, dancing, and exchanging information were probably important. A breeding and linguistic community probably developed from these "reunions."

The living groups or bands were composed of several nuclear families—but probably all related. The band's composition might change from year to year, but the size of the group would remain stable —twenty-five to fifty people. The force that tied these people together was based entirely on bonds between parents and children and marriage ties.

Chances are that no one group controlled the food resources of a given locality or maintained exclusive rights to them. Undoubtedly, fluctuations in rainfall brought about variations in the available food supply. This kind of situation would have been best managed by a band organization that permitted and even encouraged people to move from area to area. This fluid arrangement might have created interband arrangements so the role of host and guest alternated from season to season. Lee and DeVore suggest that "reciprocal access to food resources" might have been as important a means of communicating as was possible exchange of spouses (Lee and DeVore, 1968, p. 12). This idea in turn suggests that the social structure, kinship system, and marriage patterns were not hindered by linguistic boundaries.

Visits back and forth between various ecological and resource areas would have probably prevented any one group from claiming any "territoriality." Freedom to range over large areas was, as suggested above, encouraged by the fact that individuals and/or groups possessed little personal property, which also had to be portable. Such a flexible attitude would have permitted individuals to have changed residence location without any heartbreak. Although violence may have flared from time to time in groups and *inter* groups, arguments, disagreements, or disharmony of any kind might have been resolved by "fission" or parting company. Order was maintained, then, without elaborate social controls.

Eggan (in Lee and DeVore, 1968, p. 161) points out that in the middle of the Great Basin area one finds a culture endowed with only the bare essentials, whereas at or near the margins of the area one finds a series of specialization, including agriculture. The earliest evidence of incipient agriculture that is known to us comes from our work on the upper Little Colorado and Tularosa Cave, New Mexico (Martin *et al.*, 1952), and Bat Cave (H. W. Dick, 1965). Another early site in which maize occurred is the Hay Hollow Site.

During the summers of 1966 and 1967 with the support of the National Science Foundation, members of the Southwest Archaeological Expedition of Field Museum under the direction of the senior author carried on excavations and survey work at the Hay Hollow Site in east-central Arizona, in Hay Hollow Valley, over nine miles east of the contemporary town of Snowflake, Arizona. The valley is on the land of James Carter, rancher. John Fritz was assistant director in charge of the excavations of Hay Hollow Site. Our survey crew had analyzed the surface materials from this site and had classed it as Late Desert Culture. Excavations and analysis did not alter that classification. Analyses of all artifacts and features are still in progress by Fritz.

The reason for digging this site was to test the hypothesis: "If subsistence resources are widely dispersed in space and in time and if no single wild food stuff can provide either a large percentage of required energy or more than a specific potential of energy, then the technological, demographic, and social subsystems will take certain forms."

The site covered about two acres. About 50 percent of that was sampled and excavated. This produced five complete house floors and portions of perhaps three more. House floors were depressed slightly below the former ground surface; were modest in size (about 3 meters in diameter), round to roundish, provided with an east-facing ramp tunnel entrance, and a central fire-area. The whole was enclosed by means of insloping socketed poles set about 15 to 25 cm. apart around the circumference. These poles were covered by other poles, brush, and earth, thus forming a lodge-like structure. Presence of a central smoke hole was assumed but not known.

Two hundred eighty pits of varying diameters and depths were also excavated. Their functions are not yet determined but we suppose they were used for cooking, barbecuing, food storage, and roasting of whole animals.

Houses and pits were grouped into three principal clusters that chronologically fall into two distinct occupations. Radiocarbon dates from twenty-two discrete pieces of charcoal from house roof beams, from fire pits, and from other pits indicate the site was either intermittently occupied roughly between the dates of 300 B.C. and A.D. 300 or all occupied contemporaneously at some one period between those dates. The earliest house date is 470 B.C. $\pm$ 115; the latest, A.D. 305 $\pm$ 110. The older portion of the site (three houses and dozens of pits) yields a mean date of 30.7 B.C. $\pm$ 97.5. The younger portion (two to five houses and many associated pits) yields a mean date of A.D. 89.6 $\pm$ 94.17 years.

About 68,000 artifacts of stone and 13,000 pieces of stone used in basket cooking were recovered. Roughly 47,000 pieces of stone were utilized debris resulting from the production of stone tools; 18,000 were stone flakes modified only by use; and about 3,000 were modified over a large part of their surfaces and were used for cutting, scraping, and piercing. In addition, 170 whole or parts of milling stones were catalogued as well as 240 potsherds and 460 stones used in manufacturing stone tools. The pottery sherds are thin, brown in color, and may represent fragments of seed jars. Thermal treatment of the chert before flaking was common. Triangular blade form with corner or base notching was positively associated with 87 percent of the bifacials.

Analysis by Dr. Vorsila Bohrer, then of the University of Arizona, of fossil pollen recovered indicates that at about 200 B.C. the climate was cooler and/or wetter. The lower boundary of the juniper-piñon savanna would have been depressed by about 300 feet. Ponderosa Pine may have been within 10 miles of the site whereas today it is 30 miles away to the south. The valley floor would have had greater densities of grasses, herbs, and shrubs.

By A.D. 150, the climate had changed to a warmer, drier one—similar to that of today. A portion of the evidence for these statements was derived from the occurrence of pollen of the cattail (Typha, sp.) and of evening primrose (Onagracene) and from other significant pollen counts (Bohrer, V., 1968). Dr. Bohrer also constructed an index based on the ratio of the pore diameter of maize pollen grains to the diameter of the pollen grain. This index reflects significant differences in temperature and water regimes and is thus indispensable in determining the climatic conditions under which corn was grown in the past.

The only domesticate grown by the occupants of Hay Hollow Site was maize, the presence of which is attested to by the presence of maize pollen from several features as well as fragments of kernels and corncobs. The morphology of the cobs resembles a popcorn-like Reventador Corn or a very small form of hard flint-maize (Hugh Cutler, personal communication).

Wild plants used by the Hay Hollow people, as suggested by fossil pollen from floors of houses, from pits, and from washings of milling stones were: Alkali-sacaton grass seeds, and seeds from Amaranths and chenopodiae, which were ground on milling stones; Chola (two species), which were harvested and roasted; seeds of a long-spine compositae which were ground on milling stones; and Mormon tea.

Pollen also suggested that the houses were occupied chiefly during the winter and visited during the spring and late summer time. Pollen from maize and from the genera *Artemesia* (sage brush) tended to occur together.

As noted earlier, analyses of the mass of data are still in progress. Factor analyses on many of the data are being run on a computer. These will give us patterns of co-variation—or will indicate which artifacts and which features tend to be associated in the same or related activities.

If maize occurred on the margin of the Great Basin earlier than that from our County Road and Hay Hollow Sites, it would probably not appear much earlier than 3000 to 4000 B.C. It should also be pointed out that the appearance of the earliest maize in the area was in Bat Cave, New Mexico (Dick, Herbert, 1965). There it is dated at about 3500 B.C.

Also in Tularosa Cave, New Mexico,

(Martin *et al.*, 1952) a popcorn type of maize is dated at about 800 B.C.

Thus, the Desert culture way of life: not one of affluence perhaps, nor one of near starvation, but a transient one of constant vigilance, some satisfactions and a fatalistic attitude toward life.

Recognition of this way of life has come about because of the perceptive researches of many anthropologists (Cressman, 1942; Cressman, William, and Krieger, 1940; Kirchhoff, 1954; Kroeber, 1939; Zingg, 1933). Jennings' delineation of it (Jennings, 1956, 1957) was eagerly seized upon and used by archaeologists because it was succinct, forceful, and carefully written. It was a useful, workable conception of a hunting-gathering way of life. His principal theses were: that no significant change in Great Basin environment has occurred for some ten thousand years or more (Jennings, 1964, p. 150), that the Desert culture was a widespread uniform culture from 8000 to 3000 B.C. and that it represents the earliest culture in the arid West.

Swanson (1966, pp. 144–45) presents another model (see also Warren and Ranere, 1968; Rancre, 1970). His chief points are: that there have been major environmental shifts during the last twelve thousand years, that the foundations of the Desert culture rest in adaptation to a grassland zone and that big game hunting was *the* important facet of the culture, and that about 5000 B.C. a period of aridity set in—drier than intervals that preceded and followed that 5000 B.C. date—the net effect of which was to increase the range of xerophytic flora and the size of the desert, to make big game hunting impossible, and to bring about what we call the Desert culture adaptation.

Another model for the development of early Southwestern cultures is one created by Cynthia Irwin-Williams. In an article that Mrs. Irwin-Williams published in 1967, "Picosa: The Elementary Southwestern Culture" (Irwin-Williams, 1967), she attempts to define Picosa culture as a continuum of similar closely related preceramic cultures existing in the southwestern United States during the last three millennia before Christ. The Southwest is seen as a separate and discrete culture area and is believed to be the result of a cultural synthesis of uniform developments originating as early as 8000 B.C. Although similar to the Desert culture, the Picosa is viewed as distinct in terms of detailed inventory and historic derivation.

The idea that the Picosa culture arose as it did is a chimera that appears as the result of Mrs. Irwin-Williams' conceptual framework—the culture area (Cook, personal communication). The culture area has long been known to be useful for simple groupings of tribal entities in relationship to a geographic context. But the concept has fallen into disfavor because geographical grouping in and of itself does not contribute to an explanation of cultural differences and similarities or of human behavior. Further, lists of cultural elements are not a fruitful approach to the study of cultural processes because in an archaeological context one cannot define unit elements. As Harris puts it (Harris, 1968, p. 377) even six thousand traits might be inadequate for measuring overall similarity if the traits utilized are not systematically identified on the same level of detail. And how can one do that for traits of the Desert culture or the Picosa culture? It is impossible.

Many archaeologists fail to notice that they unconsciously change their definition of culture as they pass through time from conquest states to simple hunters and gatherers. As one goes back in time toward earlier, simple cultures, the various subsystems, such as social pattern, economy, religion, all of which are recognized by archaeologists in recent cultures, drop out, first to the inferential level, then to the "guestimate" level, and finally to zero level (Thomas Cook, personal communication).

Picosa sheds no new light on the evolutionary aspects of culture, or cultural dynamics, nor does it explain anything. It is descriptive and not very accurate at that.

The arguments continue and as new evidence is found and evaluated, models concerning the Desert culture will change.

In the meantime, Jennings and Swanson have presented cogent treatises on the subject.

VII Pit House Dwellers

At about the time of Christ, the population of Arizona began to increase rapidly. As it did, the quantity and diversity of evidence that the archaeologist would one day attempt to interpret also increased. Very real problems exist in any discussion of space-time systematics during this stage and the one following it. There are many artifacts and types of artifacts. Archaeologists frequently disagree as to whether particular artifacts are of the same type—two types share some attributes, but not others. Given a typological difficulty like this one, the probability of archaeologists agreeing on the spatial and temporal distribution of all artifact types is minute. Moreover, archaeology has no central data collection facility where information on the spatial distribution of artifacts and types is recorded. Unfortunately, reports on some excavations and their assemblages are never written. Problems in precisely locating particular types in time also exist. All dates have a ± factor. Most sites were occupied for many years and the archaeologist cannot always tell whether a particular artifact dates to the early or late occupation of the site.

These problems are more acute in the case of some artifact types and less acute in the case of others. Pottery, for example, has been intensively studied. Its morphology and spatial and temporal distribution have been investigated by numerous authors. A yearly conference is held to insure agreement in the use of terms, to update information on space-time distributions, and to discuss other problems involving pottery. Archaeologists can make few precise statements about variability in chipped stone tools. No major works, no yearly conferences focus attention on the distribution of artifacts of this category.

Even if these problems were nonexistent, our knowledge of prehistory would still be subject to reservations as a result of what we know about differential preservation. For example, archaeologists have learned a great deal more about some Pit House phases than other ones. Some villages occur on ridges and some on valley floors. In some areas the villages on valley floors have been covered by great quantities of sediments, and are difficult for the archaeologist to find. Basketmaking is a trait associated with prehistoric populations of the Colorado Plateau during this stage. More baskets and more finely made baskets are found in this area than in any other. Why? Is it because more and finer baskets were made there or because more have been preserved? This area has more dry caves where baskets are likely to be preserved than other areas in the state.

Some archaeologists prefer to circumvent these problems by concentrating on the definition of local sequences. Carried to its logical conclusion, this approach would make the writing of a book like this one next to impossible. There would be no basis for agreement on terminology from one area to the next. Other authors are lumpers as opposed to "splitters"; they see fundamental similarities in all areas of the state. Most archaeologists are uncomfortable in taking either of these positions. They recognize the great amount of work that needs to be done before space-time relationships can be accurately described. They recognize that any chronology is a set of hypotheses about spatial and temporal order in the past. Classifications are accepted as hypotheses, as efforts to order the data available at a particular time, but with an understanding of the lack of precision inherent in such cases of generalization, and the likelihood that changes in categories will be required as more data are recovered.

In pursuing this goal, Arizona archaeologists have often followed an organizational model based on an analogy with plants. They speak of roots, stems, and branches. Using this system to describe the prehistoric cultures of the Colorado Plateau, one speaks of the Anasazi root, the Eastern and Western Pueblo stems, the Kayenta, San Juan, Tusayan, and Upper Little Colorado branches. Within each root, stem, or branch, the archaeologist using this system describes phases that demarcate periods of time during which cultural traits were much the same. The root-stem-branch model is an attempt to go beyond local sequences. Branches are geographically and temporally more restricted than stems and therefore share more traits. Roots are larger geographical and temporal units than stems and the shared traits from area to area are fewer. The definition of each level is largely intuitive and archaeologists argue about them. Some see branches where others see stems. They disagree on the roots to which a particular stem should be assigned.

These same arguments over the degree of spatial and temporal similarity can be carried on with any typological model. They are more or less important in relation to one's interest in historical-diffusionary approaches. All of the models are attempts to create a viable basis for building regions from localities, and culture areas from regions. It is our belief that the data now available are neither complete nor precise enough to support accurate comparisons from one branch to another. The probability that more extensive information will show increased similarities or differences between branches or districts is high. The probability that a highly statistical, computer-based study of artifact attributes and types would produce conclusions different from those being reached at present is high. Neither the data nor the facilities for such a study exist at present. Therefore, most of our effort will be directed to roots or areal traditions. We will begin by defining and discussing the concept of a Pit House stage. Then we will consider its important traits, describe at least one site in some detail, and discuss the important spatial (regional) and temporal sub-units.

DEFINITION OF THE STAGE

Between the time of Christ and A.D. 800–1000, most of the residents of Arizona lived in villages of one to one hundred houses that were built in pits (pit houses). We have therefore focused on this trait in defining the stage as that of the Pit House dwellers. This designation roughly corresponds to the Formative in Martin and Rinaldo's discussion of Southwest co-tradition and Willey and Phillips' consideration of American prehistory, and to Daifuku's Developmental stages (Martin and Rinaldo, 1951; Willey and Phillips, 1958; Daifuku, 1952).

Martin and Rinaldo refer to the period

between A.D. 1 and 900 to 1000 as the Formative. Their list of the traits associated with this stage provides an adequate definition of it. Early in the period, most populations lived in pit houses (constructed underground), but as it came to a close they were moving into surface dwellings. Large ceremonial structures, kivas, and ball courts were built. Plainwares of brown, red, and gray were the predominant forms of ceramics. Basin-type metates were used in processing plant products in the earlier part of the stage, while trough and slab metates were more common in the later part. Basketry, netting, cotton cloth, braided sashes, twined fur, feather blankets, and sandals were made. The atlatl and dart and the bow and arrow were the major hunting tools in the early and later periods of the stage respectively. This development was paralleled by the replacement of the diagonally notched projectiles by side-notched ones. Crude chopping stones ceased to be made as finely done axes and mauls became increasingly important. Awls and spatulas were made of

PLATE 2   Pit house of Basket Maker III period (?) in southwestern Colorado, Ackmen Site, dated about A.D. 870. In left center is a circular fire-hearth filled with ash; to left of it is an upright stone deflector that prevented drafts from ventilator apparatus (left edge) from directly striking the fire. Charred remains of roof logs on floor established tree-ring dates. Roof was supported by thirty-six upright posts set in wall. Southwestern Archaeological Expedition of Field Museum, 1937. Reproduced by permission of the Field Museum of Natural History.

bone. Chipped stone tools, including projectile points, hand axes, scrapers, knives, and borers were traits of this stage. Other important artifacts common to the entire state included clay figurines, clay and stone pipes, cradles, digging sticks, stone palettes, carved shell ornaments, and hammerstones.

Much criticism of this definition has been based on misinterpretation and misuse of it. It had been argued that there are important differences from area to area within the state. No one denies this point. The definition suggests what traits are common to the entire area; it does not pretend that no differences exist. Those differences can be isolated by examining four areal traditions that existed during the stage: Anasazi,

FIGURE 10   Map of Arizona, A.D. 800–1000. The Basket Makers generally inhabited the plateau environment and the Mogollones the mountain. The Hohokam occupied the Gila, Salt, Verde, and Santa Cruz river valleys, while the Hakataya occurred throughout the remainder of the Transition and Desert environments. After Albert E. Schroeder. By permission of Albert E. Schroeder, 1962.

Mogollon, Hakataya, and Hohokam. The Anasazi inhabited most of the Colorado Plateau, the Mogollon much of the mountain environment, the Hohokam the Gila and Salt Valleys in the desert environment, and the Hakataya the remainder of the state, principally the transition environment. The distinctions between these areas have been based primarily on differences in architecture, ceramics, and burial practices. Differences in other traits are less understood. While we focus on the former, the latter will be included in the discussion. Before beginning to consider each root or tradition, we wish to make clear that the distinctions between them are not unequivocal. Over thirty years ago, Colton (1939b) showed the substantial overlap between fundamental Southwestern culture units as he saw them by plotting the percentage of the traits shared by and unique to each. His results appear in Table 8. Are culture units that share 50 percent of their traits the same unit or two different ones? Which traits should be given the greatest consideration? We raise the questions not because we have any easy solu-

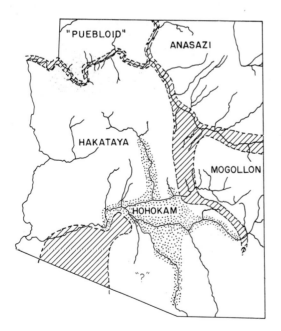

Cohonina					
Sinagua	50				
Yuman	47	25			
Hohokam	42	23	36		
Anasazi	33	47	5	8	
Mogollon	31	50	28	28	31
	C	S	Y	H	A

TABLE 8   Percentage of traits that prehistoric cultures in Arizona shared. While each culture had distinctive traits, there was considerable overlap. Within this matrix, there are two clusters, an Anasazi-Mogollon-Sinagua cluster and a Hohokam-Yuma-Cohonina cluster (Colton 1939b).

tion to them, but simply to point out the difficulties that will inevitably exist whatever units the archaeologist uses to discuss space-time relationships on a scale so large as that of a whole state. We now turn to these units.

ANASAZI

The area occupied by the Anasazi is essentially that of the Colorado Plateau. Within this area a number of regional traditions are recognized: Kayenta, Red Rock-Canyon de Chelley, Middle Little Colorado, and Upper Little Colorado. The regional traditions are characterized by regional sequences with three primary time periods: Basket Maker II from about A.D. 1 to 400, Basket Maker III or Modified Basket Maker from A.D. 400 to 700, and Pueblo I or Developmental Pueblo from A.D. 700 to 900–1000. Important sites from each region with their associated tree-ring dates when available are listed in Table 9. (These dates as well as others used in tables in this chapter are taken from the publications of the Laboratory of Tree-Ring Research: (Bannister, Dean, and Gell, 1966; Bannister, Gell, and Hannah, 1966; Bannister, Hannah, and Robinson, 1966; Bannister, Robinson, and Warren, 1967; Bannister, Dean, and Robinson, 1968.)

White Mound Village is a site in the Upper Little Colorado region that was occupied between A.D. 750 and 850. This site, which overlooks the Rio Puerco about one half mile west of White Mound, Arizona, was excavated by H. S. Gladwin in 1936. Our discussion of the site is based upon his report (Gladwin, 1945).

Six pit houses, three blocks of storage rooms, and assorted pits and other features were excavated at this site. The houses varied in size from about 10 to 15 square

KAYENTA

	A.D.
White Dog Cave (Guernsey and Kidder, 1921)	ca. 700
RB 1002 (Beals, Brainerd, and Smith, 1945)	600–700
RB 1006 (Beals, Brainerd, and Smith, 1945)	700–900
Swallow's Nest (Fewkes, 1911a, b; Hargrave, 1935a, b)	300–700
NA 2544 (Hargrave, 1935b)	ca. 1000
Church Rock (Guernsey, 1931; Taylor, 1954)	700–900

RED ROCK—CANYON DE CHELLY

Vandal Cave (Haury, 1936c)	600–700
Mummy Cave (Morris, 1938)	300–700
Obelisk Cave (E. A. Morris, 1959)	300–500
Broken Flute Cave (E. A. Morris, 1959)	450–700
Cave 1 (Ibid.)	600–700
Cave 2 (Ibid.)	600–700
Cave 3 (Ibid.)	600–700
Cave 6 (Ibid.)	500–700
Cave 7 (Ibid.)	600–700
Cave 8 (Ibid.)	600–700
Tse-Ta a (Steen, 1966)	

UPPER LITTLE COLORADO

Allantown (Roberts, 1939, 1940)	700–1000
White Mound Village (Gladwin, 1945)	750–800

MIDDLE LITTLE COLORADO

Jeddito 4a (Brew, 1941)	700–800
Jeddito 111 (Ibid.)	ca. 1000
Jeddito 169 (Ibid.)	900–1000
Jeddito 264 (Daifuku, 1961)	600–800

TABLE 9 Some important excavated Anasazi sites, by region.

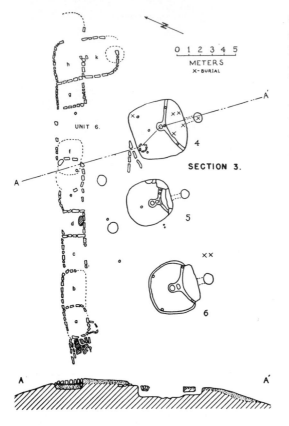

FIGURE 11 White Mound Village. This late Basket Maker site consists of several clusters of pit houses surrounded by one or more arcs of surface rooms. This is one such cluster. Reproduced by permission of the Arizona State Museum from the Gila Pueblo Collection.

meters. They were generally between .75 of a meter and 2 meters below the land surface into which they were dug. All of the houses had fire pits, ventilators, partitions separating the entrance area and the remainder of the house, and deflectors. In the majority of the houses, the roofs were supported by four posts. Storage cists or pits occurred in three of the houses. Houses 1 and 4 were abandoned and filled with rubbish while the other houses were still being used.

Storage rooms ranged in size between 2 and 6 square meters. Walls were masonry,

apparently in the Kayenta tradition. In some of the rooms, almost the entire floor had been excavated forming large storage pits.

Thirty-three burials were found on the site, most of them fragmentary. Burials were in flexed position. Grave offerings varied from nothing to pottery and ornaments.

The vast majority of the potsherds taken from the site were of a type called Lino Gray. White Mound Black-on-White and a polished red ware were the only other types present in any substantial quantity. Metates, manos, mauls, axes, hammerstones, shell and turquoise ornaments, projectile points, bone awls, bone scrapers, bone needles, bone tubes, sandals, and baskets were also found. To what extent are these traits characteristic of the Anasazi area as a whole?

Villages of this time period consisted of from one to twenty houses, three or four having been characteristic of most villages. Some villages were in caves, most in the open on ridges, and mesas. We discern no regular pattern of distribution of houses within the early villages, while houses occurred in small, perhaps kin-based clusters in later ones.

Bullard has summarized a number of important aspects of the houses built in the Southwest during the Pit House stage; our discussion throughout the chapter draws heavily on his work. Pit houses in the Anasazi area were generally circular. They varied in size from a few square meters to more than 60 square meters; the mean for Bullard's sample is 17 square meters (1962, p. 118). Considerable variability in house size existed in the region, with areas on the order of 25 to 30 square meters in the north and around 11 square meters in the south (Bullard, 1962, p. 118). The houses also varied in depth, from some that were almost on the surface to others over 2 meters deep. The roofs of the houses were dome-shaped; generally, four posts distributed in a square or rectangular pattern in the house supported the roof. In this area, the entrance to houses was either by means of a passage at the east or south of the structure or through a ventilator in the roof.

We find a variety of features on the floors of Anasazi pit houses. They frequently had a fire pit, and sometimes a small, circular ash pit in which we find no evidence of burning. Such a pit may have been used to hold overflow ashes from the fire. Between the fire pit and entrance was usually an upright slab or deflector, presumably to protect the fire from draft. Behind the fire pit and in line with it and the entrance was a sipapu or sacred hole, which in modern Pueblo ritual is the spot where the ancestors emerged from the underworld. This feature was, then, a kind of shrine in the house, perhaps used in consecrating it. Stor-

PLATE 3   Pottery from White Mound Village. It is important to keep in mind that most pottery made in the Southwest throughout its prehistory was unpainted. The extensive use of very fine lines is typical of early black-on-white pottery like this from White Mound. Reproduced by permission of the Arizona State Museum from the Gila Pueblo Collections.

PLATE 4 Projectile points from White Mound Village. Reproduced by permission of the Arizona State Museum from the Gila Pueblo Collections.

age bins were either dug into the floor or built of slabs along the walls. A slab partition frequently separated the front part of the house from the rear.

The pottery in use during the Pit House stage was characteristically either Lino Gray or Lino Black-on-Gray. (We take our descriptions of pottery types from Hawley,

1936.) Lino Gray pottery is, as the name suggests, gray in color. Coarse sand temper protrudes through the paste. Vessels made of this ware are characteristically bowls or large globular jars. This ware first appeared around A.D. 400 and was in evidence until 1300; it was most abundant between A.D. 570 and 870 (Breternitz, 1966). This same ware, manufactured with black painted designs, usually very simple and sometimes zoomorphic, is called Lino Black-on-Gray, and it dates to essentially the same period as Lino Gray.

Toward the southern edge of the plateau area a brown ware variously referred to as Adamana Brown or Woodruff Brown was made. It is morphologically identical to Lino Gray except for thte color, which probably reflects the use of an oxidizing atmosphere as opposed to the reducing atmosphere in producing the Lino wares.

Toward the end of the period a new ware, Kana-a Gray, appeared in the area. It was essentially similar to Lino Gray except for a series of incised bands around the neck. This type was most abundant on sites between A.D. 760 and 900 (Breternitz, 1966, p. 79). During this same period, other black-on-white types were produced in the region: Kana-a Black-on-White, Kiatuthlanna Black-on-White, and White Mound Black-on-White. These types were best from A.D. 725 to 816, 850 to 910, and 750 to 910, respectively. Kana-a Black-on-White tended to be most important at the northern edge of the plateau, while the other wares were more important in the south.

A number of important changes occurred in the Anasazi area during this stage. These changes are the bases of the distinction between Basket Maker, Modified Basket Maker, and Developmental Pueblo periods mentioned earlier. There is very little evidence on Basket Maker architecture in Arizona. Most of our information comes from sites near Durango, Colorado (Morris and Burgh, 1954). In these sites the pit houses are circular and relatively shallow, and have cribbed walls. In the Modified Basket Maker period, pit houses were built in villages with storage pits and cists. By the Developmental Pueblo period, these pit houses were surrounded by rows of storage rooms. Moreover, some of them began to acquire the attributes of ceremonial rooms or kivas. Surface living units appeared late in this period. There is no evidence of fired pottery in the Anasazi area that is clearly Basket Maker I. Lino Gray and Woodruff Brown were the predominant wares of the Modified Basket Maker period. During Developmental Pueblo times, Lino Gray, Lino Black-on-Gray, Kana-a Gray, Kana-a Black-on-White, White Mound Black-on-White, and Kiatuthlanna Black-on-White were most important.

Basket Maker burials were flexed, were made in pits and cists, were often found in caves and tended to be multiple interments. Bodies were frequently wrapped in cloth or fur robes. In the two later periods burials were in rubbish heaps, in pits, and under house floors. They were flexed and tended to be single interments. Anasazi Pit House dwellers made a wide variety of blankets, bags, baskets, sandals, and cord. Basketry declined in importance as pottery increased. Ornaments were made of shell, stone, bone, seed, and sometimes feathers. The atlatl and dart were important in Basket Maker and Modified Basket Maker periods but were gradually replaced by the bow and arrow. The economy of Anasazi pit house populations initially tended to hunting and gathering, with agriculture increasing in importance throughout the Pit House stage. We can say little of Anasazi lithic technology that has not been mentioned in defining the Pit House stage.

MOGOLLON

The Mogollon area during the Pit House stage was bounded by the Little Colorado River on the north, Globe on the west, and extended into Mexico and New Mexico on the south and east respectively. Six regions are recognizable within this area: Forestdale, the Upper Little Colorado, Point of Pines, and San Simon in Arizona, and Pine Lawn and Mimbres in adjacent New Mexico. The Upper Little Colorado was transitional between Mogollon and Anasazi, tending to Anasazi traits north and west of St. Johns and Mogollon traits south of that community. Similarly, San Simon was transitional between Mogollon and Hakataya. Depending on the traits one chooses to stress and the principles of classification used, the sites of this branch may be considered either.

Wheat (1955) has defined time periods that crosscut these regions. They are called simply Mogollon 1 (200 B.C.–A.D. 400), Mogollon 2 (A.D. 400–600), Mogollon 3 (A.D. 600–900), and Mogollon 4 (A.D. 900–1100). During this last period, a number of traits that are more characteristic of the Anasazi area became important in this one. Important Mogollon sites by region and time period are listed in Table 10.

The SU Site is an example of an early Mogollon village. It is in the Pine Lawn region, in Catron County, New Mexico. The site sits atop a ridge in the foothills of the San Francisco Mountains. Over the course of three seasons, archaeologists under the direction of Paul S. Martin of the Field Museum of Natural History, excavated 28 houses, over 40,000 sherds, and 1,500 other artifacts.

Houses on the site varied from around 10 to about 30 square meters in area. Some of the houses were practically on the surface while others were over a meter deep.

Numerous postholes in a majority of the houses make any interpretations of patterns of roof support difficult. The houses were constructed of logs, and chinked with mud and branches. Many storage and fire pits

FORESTDALE		A.D.
Bluff Site (Haury & Sayles, 1947)		200–300
Bear Ruin (Haury, 1940b)		550–700

UPPER LITTLE COLORADO

Site 30 (Martin & Rinaldo, 1960a)

PINE LAWN		
SU (Martin, 1943; Martin & Rinaldo, 1940, 1947)		300–500
Turkey Foot (Martin, Rinaldo & Antevs, 1949)		700–800
Twin Bridges (Martin, Rinaldo & Antevs, 1949)		650–800
Promontory (Martin, Rinaldo & Antevs, 1949)		
Starkweather Ruin (Nesbitt, 1938)		700–800
Wheatley Ridge (Rowe, 1947)		750–900
Tularosa Cave (Martin et al., 1952)		
Cordova Cave (Martin et al., 1952)		

MIMBRES		
Harris (Haury, 1936b)		600–900
Mogollon Village (Haury, 1936b)		600–900
Cameron Creek Village (Bradfield, 1931)		

POINT OF PINES

Crooked Ridge Village (Wheat, 1954)

Nantuck Village (Breternitz, 1959)

SAN SIMON

San Simon Village (Sayles, 1945)

Cave Creek Village (Sayles, 1945)

TABLE 10 Some important excavated Mogollon sites, by region.

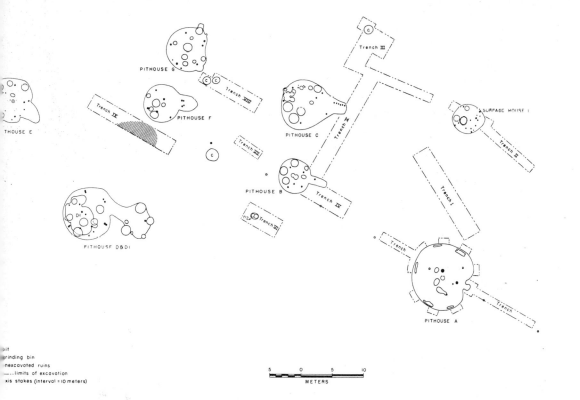

FIGURE 12 Map of the SU Site. Mogollon sites of this period varied considerably in size. The SU Site is one of the largest. Note the relatively random distribution of houses over the site and the significant variation in their size and shape. Reproduced by permission of the Field Museum of Natural History.

were found inside the houses. They were occupied principally between A.D. 300 and 500, although a few date to earlier and later periods. Large, apparently ceremonial, houses were found on the site.

Burials were found in houses, pits, and scattered underneath many areas of the site. Most were flexed. Many artifacts were buried with some individuals and none at all with others.

Fifty two percent of the sherds removed from the site were Alma Plain, 21 percent Alma Rough, 26 percent San Francisco Red, and only about 2 percent were painted (Martin and Rinaldo, 1947, p. 362). The variety of stone and bone artifacts taken from the sites is immense. Included are manos, metates, rubbing stones, mortars, pestles, polishing stones, mauls, hammerstones, pipes, projectile points, knives, scrapers, choppers, drills, hoes, bone awls, bone scrapers, bone needles, bone flakers, stone ornaments, and shell ornaments. How does the record derived from the SU Site compare to the Mogollon record in general?

Mogollon pit houses sites ranged from one to more than thirty houses, about fifteen having been typical. Houses were randomly distributed over the sites, except at Cameron Creek village where two or three houses opened on a common "plaza" (Bradfield, 1931, p. 19). Houses do not seem to have occurred in caves.

Ranging from about 5 to over 50 square

PLATE 5 Pottery from the SU Site. Reproduced by permission of the Field Museum of Natural History.

meters, Mogollon pit houses averaged 17 square meters (Bullard, 1962, p. 122). In most areas, the size of a house remained constant and close to the mean throughout the stage. In the Pine Lawn region, however, early houses averaged 25 square meters while late ones averaged about 18 (Bullard, 1962, p. 122). Mogollon houses were shallower and less variable in depth than Anasazi ones. Most were less than 1.5 meters deep. Early houses had roofs that were supported by single central posts and were more conical than dome-shaped. Later houses had a crossbeam running the length of the house, which gave the roof a kind of gabled effect. A Mogollon pit house was entered by a passageway, usually facing east.

The features that occurred inside the houses were sufficiently variable that it is next to impossible to describe a typical Mogollon pattern. Clearly, benches, partitions, fireplaces, ash pits, deflectors, heating pits, and storage pits and bins occurred in some Mogollon houses. These features, however, were never characterized by the wide distribution that was present in the Anasazi area. This pattern suggests a pronounced functional variability in the use of roofed space in the Mogollon region;

different houses had different sets of features.

The most important pottery types in the area were variants of Alma Plain and San Francisco Red. Alma Plain was made from a brown to reddish paste. Like Lino, it tends to have white angular particles that sometimes do and sometimes do not protrude through the surface. Many varieties or bowls and jars of this type were made between A.D. 300 and 950. San Francisco Red ware was made of a brown paste that was slipped with red. It appeared almost exclusively in bowls, and was abundant from A.D. 750 to 950.

PLATE 6   Projectile points from the SU Site. While there is some overlap between these points and those from White Mound Village, there are also distinctive forms found here. Reproduced by permission of the Field Museum of Natural History.

Between A.D. 775 and 950, Mogollon Red-on-Brown and Three Circle Red-on-White were common in the area. The former was made of a tan or brown paste. Bowls were slipped with light brown material and painted with red designs. Both bowls and jars were produced in the style. Three Circle Red-on-White was similar to Mogollon Red-on-Brown except for having been slipped in white. A few Black-on-White wares also appeared at this time.

Mogollon burial practices were somewhat variable. They occurred in trash mounds, in storage pits, under room floors and walls, in the open, and sometimes in caves. Usually, few offerings were placed in the graves, although at Bear Ruin, offerings were common and significant.

Wheat (1955) has described the critical changes that distinguish temporal units. Most of the important differences between Mogollon 1, 2, 3, and 4 are in pit house shape and ceramics. The earliest Mogollon houses came in a wide variety of forms: irregular, roundish, quadrangular, rounded with one flat side, ovoid, D-shaped, and bean-shaped. Roundish, ovoid, and quadrangular houses predominate in the later periods. Ceremonial houses were present throughout the sequence. Early ones (Mogollon 1) were round, D-shaped, and bean-shaped. By A.D. 600 the structures occurred in almost every shape, but by A.D. 900 roundish and quadrangular structures were the most important.

The relationship of pottery to these time periods has already been described: plainwares in Mogollon 1, plainwares and red-on-browns in Mogollon 2 and 3, and the preceding plus red-on-white and black-on-white wares in Mogollon 4. Handles and lugs did not appear on vessels made before Mogollon 3. Burial practices change very little through the sequence. Most of the other traits were present throughout the sequence. These included (again following Wheat, 1955) basin metates, unifacial and bifacial manos, hand stones, boulder and pebble mortars, pestles, digging tools, stone bowls, polishing and abrading stones, hammerstones, grooved mauls, stone hoes, pipes, and balls, diagonally notched and side-notched projectile points, flake knives, bifacial knives, drills, side-scrapers, end-scrapers, gravers, planes, choppers, bone awls, bone needles, bone tubes, and antler flakers. Ornaments were made of shell, stone, and bone. Perishable goods included wickerwork sandals, atlatls and darts, fur blankets, digging sticks, carrying bags, wooden drills, bows and arrows, coiled baskets, twilled matting, unfired pottery, wooden and bone dice, reed cigarettes, juniper berry skewers, feather-on-stick pahos, and deer-hoof charms. Many of these perishable items were evident only in Mogollon 1 and 3 as a result of the peculiarities of preservation in Tularosa and Cordova caves, but they are presumed to have been present during the other periods. Subsistence was based on agriculture— corns, beans, squash—and hunting and gathering throughout. A few important changes did occur in food-grinding tools. During Mogollon 3, trough metates with one end closed were replaced by full trough metates; rectangular manos appeared and wedge manos ceased to be made; and metate mortars and leaf-shaped projectile points also disappeared.

HOHOKAM

The vast majority of our knowledge of the Pit House stage Hohokam is based on evidence from three sites: Snaketown (Gladwin, Haury, Sayles, and Gladwin, 1937; Haury, 1967), Roosevelt: 9:6 (Haury, 1932), and the Grewe Site (Woodward,

1931). Di Peso's report on the Hohokam village at San Cayetano is the most thorough study of such a site available to date, although it is so far from the more densely settled Hohokam areas that important differences may exist between the two. The Gladwin surveys of southern Arizona (Gladwin and Gladwin, 1929a, 1929b, 1930a, 1930b), Wasley and Johnson's study of the Painted Rocks Reservoir (1965), Vivian's survey of the Gila River Valley (1965), and Morris' article on the Red Mountain Site (1969) are other important sources of Hohokam data.

Roosevelt: 9:6 was a Hohokam village occupied between A.D. 700 and 900. The site, below the high water line of Roosevelt Lake, was excavated by Emil Haury during a period of low water.

The village, which stood on the old bank of the Salt River, consisted of fourteen houses. These varied in area from around 10 to 30 meters and in depth from 30 to 60 centimeters. The pattern of roof support was different from house to house, but a pattern based on a central beam supported by two posts was the most common one. Walls were of smaller poles covered with reeds, branches, and mud. Stone supports on the ground supported a raised floor. Fire pits were found both inside and outside the house.

Pottery at the site was principally either Gila Plain, Gila Butte Red-on-Buff, or Santa Cruz Red-on-Buff. Ground stone artifacts included manos, metates, mortars, pestles, three-quarter grooved axes, paint grinders, and palettes. There were bone awls and tubes and pottery anvils made of stone and clay. Hammerstones, projectile points, and a knife formed the bulk of the chipped-stone tool kit. Yucca matting and a small fragment of basketry completed the kit. Awls and tubes were made of bones. In addition, shell ornaments and carved tur-

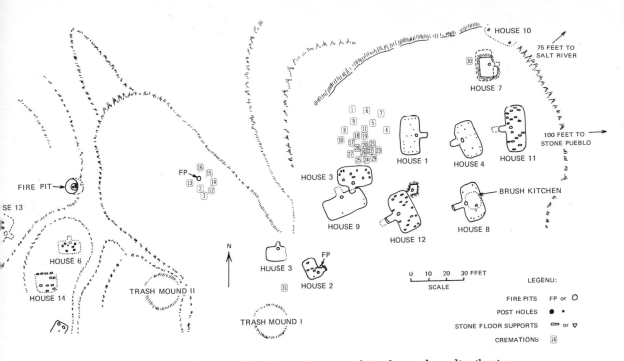

FIGURE 13 Map of Roosevelt 9:6. The houses have a relatively random distribution over the site. Their shape tends to be much less varied than that of Mogollon houses: they are rectangular with rounded corners and have a projecting entrance way. Reproduced by permission of the Arizona State Museum.

quoise were found at the site. All of the thirty-two burials excavated at the site were cremations.

Houses averaged about 23 square meters in area and were usually only about a foot deep. Pioneer period houses tended to be nearly square, while later ones were properly rectangular. The roof was typically supported by upright poles along the edges of the house, although evidence for a center support was sometimes present. Walls were usually of reeds, brush, or thatch. The floor was usually of dirt, but sometimes was of reed on a raised base of wood. A house was entered by a long passageway. Small fire pits were the only characteristic feature on the floors of Hohokam houses, suggesting that many activities performed around indoor features among the Anasazi and Mogollon were performed out of doors among

this group. Ball courts are introduced to the area at about A.D. 850.

Three pottery types are of principal importance in identifying sites of this stage. Gila Plain is a coarse brown to gray ware with sand and mica temper (Hawley, 1936, p. 107–8). It was used in manufacturing bowls, jars, and a variety of other pottery artifacts. This ware was in abundance on Hohokam sites throughout the stage. It accounted for the vast majority of sherds in sites and levels of the earlier periods, declining to 60 percent by the early Sedentary period. Other types found on sites of the Pit House stage are red-on-buff wares, principally Snaketown Red-on-Buff, Gila Butte Red-on-Buff, Santa Cruz Red-on-Buff, and Sacaton Red-on-Buff. All were made of a gray, tan, or brown paste with mica and sand temper. Designs were painted in a

PLATE 7   Red-on-buff jars from Roosevelt 9:6. The basic Hohokam painted pottery types were red-on-buff. These earlier forms had geometric designs. Reproduced by permission of the Arizona State Museum.

maroon to red paint. Jars, vessels, and a variety of other ceramic artifacts were made of these types. Distinctions among them are based primarily on variation in design elements and vessel form.

The predominant Hohokam burial practice was cremation. Individuals were burned along with clay, stone, and shell artifacts. The ashes of the individual and artifacts broken by the fire or by humans were buried, sometimes in a jar. Burial in a trench was characteristic in the early por-

tion of the stage and in plots of individual pits near trash mounds in the later portion of the stage. A strong argument has been made by Morris (1959) and others that Pioneer period burials may have been inhumations, at first flexed, then extended, rather than cremations.

Hohokam chronology is based largely on evidence from Snaketown. Three periods are defined—Pioneer, Colonial, and Sedentary—during the Pit House stage. These are divided into phases as follows:

PIONEER

Vahki, 300 B.C.–A.D. 600
Estrella, A.D. 600–700
Sweetwater, A.D. 700–833
Snaketown, A.D. 833–867

COLONIAL

Gila Butte, A.D. 867–900
Santa Cruz, A.D. 900–950

SEDENTARY

Sacaton, A.D. 950–1000

Houses were initially square but began to change toward the rectangular during the Estrella phase. By the Sedentary period, they were elliptical with bulbous entryways. Houses tended to decrease in size from early Pioneer to late Colonial periods, and to increase in the initial early Pioneer to late Colonial periods, and to increase in the initial phase of the Sedentary.

As has been indicated, plain wares were important throughout the sequence, still accounting for over half of the sherds in the Sacaton phase. Red-on-buff wares first appeared in the Estrella phase. The designs were simple and broad-lined. Chevrons, spirals, and other curvilinear designs were characteristic of the Sweetwater phase wares. Vessel forms tended to increase during this period also. During the Snaketown phase, hatched geometric designs were added to those of the preceding period. Conventionalized scrolls, geometric elements, and lifeforms were the important design elements of the Gila Butte phase. The designs became smaller and were repeated in bands or circles during the Santa Cruz phase. In the succeeding phase sectioned bands of figured patterns were important on red-on-buff vessels. Several new vessel forms—caldrons, tetrapod trays, tripods, and large mixing bowls—appeared at this time.

There were few projectile points up to the end of the Sweetwater phase. In the Snaketown phase lateral-notched points appeared, and in the Santa Cruz phase, large numbers of intricately chipped points were introduced. Reamers, whetstones, knives, hoes, and hammerstones will probably prove to have been basic components of the Hohokam tool kit.

Several types of ground stone tools were found in this area. Abrading stones were present from the Vahki through the Sweetwater phases. A few nicely rimmed palettes appeared in the Snaketown phase. These increased in number and intricacy of rim design through the Colonial period, and then began to decrease. Mortars, pestles, and stone bowls were common during the Vahki phase. Decorations were carved on the bowls beginning in the Sweetwater phase. More forms of vessels and more intricately carved vessels were introduced through the remainder of the sequence. Concave trough metates and one-handed elliptical and convex manos were important throughout the Pioneer period. During the Colonial period small, deep, angular trough metates and brick manos were introduced. The three-quarter groove axe was introduced near the end of the Pioneer period. It became smaller and more stylized during the Colonial period.

Shell work was present from the earliest phase at Snaketown. Early work included discs, bracelets, and beads. Cut shell pendants appeared at about A.D. 700 and carved bracelets by the middle of the Snaketown phase. A great variety of rings, bracelets, pendants, beads, and mosaics were made during the Santa Cruz phase. Shell etching was added to this list at the beginning of the Sedentary period. Copper bells also became important at this time.

Pinched-feature figurines were present in the Vahki phase. They became more de-

PLATE LXXXV

PLATE 8 Projectile points from Snaketown. These highly stylized projectile points are very different from those made by other cultures. There is some controversy as to whether such projectiles could have been used in hunting or whether they were too fragile. Reproduced by permission of the Arizona State Museum from the Gila Pueblo Collections.

tailed during the Snaketown phase, had modeled heads in the Gila Butte phase, and were modeled in the round and had coffee bean eyes in the succeeding phase. In the Sacaton phase, clay heads that suggest portraiture were being produced.

HAKATAYA

Whatever the approach one takes to discussing space-time systematics in the remainder of the state, the result is less satisfactory than a consideration of Mogollon,

Anasazi, and Hohokam. Whatever the shortcomings of our knowledge in these three areas, it is minor compared to the data gaps that appear elsewhere. Archaeologists have invented dozens of terms to describe the sequences of localities investigated that lie between the three major areas. In attempting to overcome this problem, we follow Schroeder (1960) in his use of the term Hakataya. Schroeder initially employed this term to refer to the cultures of Yuman origin that inhabited the transitional and desert environments of Arizona. The term embraced a number of regional traditions whose cultural affiliation has always been a matter of dispute: Cohonina, Cerbat, Prescott, Amacava, Sinagua, and Pioneer period Hohokam. We have included Di Peso's Ootam in the Hakataya root, and excluded the Pioneer period Hohokam. The latter decision does some violence to Schroeder's original concept, so we wish to make the basis of our action clear.

The debate over the cultural affiliation of Pioneer period Hohokam concerns its origin. Did it develop out of the Desert culture of the area or did it arrive in the Southwest from Mexico? Di Peso (1956, p. 19) argues that the Ootam, including Pioneer period Hohokam, was an indigenous development from the Desert culture. The Hohokam, he believes, entered southern Arizona at about A.D. 1000 and remained there until driven out at about 1300. This inference is based on the substantial number of qualitative and quantitative, technological and stylistic changes that were experienced in the Hohokam area during the Colonial period. An equally rapid and equally intense period of change occurs during the Classic period and is usually associated with the movement of Salado or Sinagua populations into the desert regions. The first period of innovation is seen to represent the arrival of the Hohokam, and the second period represents their departure. Schroeder (1960) has presented some convincing demographic evidence of a population movement into the Salt and Gila Valleys during the Classic period. However, little evidence for a movement into these valleys from Mexico has been produced, despite intensive efforts to find some.

The postulation of an invasion at about A.D. 1000 does violence to both the theory and facts of prehistory. Theoretically, there is no reason to assume or to presume that every period of rapid cultural innovation is evidence of diffusion or migration. Indigenous events do lead to change and sometimes rapid change. Seeing a migration at this point in the Hohokam prehistory ignores a number of substantial continuities in the development of artifacts and styles. From the Pioneer period on, the changes in pottery styles are understandable as an elaboration and intensification of previously existing elements. The changes in palettes, axes, figurines, manos, and metates follow a similar model. Moreover, there are basic discontinuities between the Hohokam and contemporaneous traditions in other parts of the state. Haury (1967) argues that intensive irrigation-based agriculture was present in the area from about the time of Christ. There is no evidence that this technology was used elsewhere in the state for several hundreds of years more. The Hohokam tool kit was more elaborate, more diverse, and of finer craftsmanship than that in use in other areas of the state.

Permanent villages and a high degree of sedentism are suggested in the Hohokam areas, while villages in the remainder of the regions that Schroeder called Hakataya were impermanent to such a degree that we begin to find evidence of them only during the very latest portions of the Pit House stage. We do not overlook the many similarities between Pioneer period Hohokam and Hakataya. The situation is one in which we must decide which traits to stress and which not to stress. In our estimation, Pioneer period Hohokam is best left within the Hohokam tradition. The new data from Haury's work at Snaketown and additional information that archaeologists acquire as more and more Hohokam sites are excavated will allow a far more satisfactory resolution of this problem in the future.

The primary problem encountered in attempting to discuss the Hakatayan root is the substantial lack of data. Except in the south, sites of this root tended to be impermanent and to consist of one or a few structures. Any given excavation produces relatively limited amounts of data. Moreover, few sites have been dated. These problems in the quantity and quality of data are a part of the reason why we adopt Schroeder's more general term Hakataya. The data as they stand make most arguments about regional boundaries fatuous ones. Little that is secure can be said of similarities and differences between regions. To avoid building boundaries where none exist, to avoid mistaking seasonal poses for different cultures, we believe it is more sensible to employ the more general term Hakataya.

Schroeder defines two Hakatayan stems, the Laquish and the Patayan. The Laquish were the prehistoric inhabitants of the riverine areas, while the Patayan dwelled in the upland areas. The most important Hakataya traits were impermanent, rock-encircled, round, domed jacal living units that lacked internal roof support, pottery that was fired in a variable or uncontrolled atmosphere and was gray or brown, the use of the paddle-and-anvil technique in shaping vessels, and cremation. Euler (1963) has taken issue with Schroeder on this last point arguing for inhumation. At this time

little data are available. If anything, a mixed pattern seems likely. The Laquish were distinguished by their use of Lower Colorado Buff wares. When these wares were decorated, the paints were reddish. The types include Prescott Gray, Verde Brown, Tonto Brown, Wingfield Plain, Aquarius Brown, and Tizon Brown. Breternitz argues that these are all properly varieties of Gila Plain and stresses the affinity of these regions to the Hohokam insofar as ceramics are concerned (Breternitz, 1960). San Francisco Mountain Gray Wares were important in the Patayan region. Decorations on all of these wares were typically brown or black rather than red. The clays used in upland areas were residual rather than sedimentary ones. Large cooking and roasting pits may have been more important in the Laquish than in the Patayan areas.

Since most of the Patayan and Laquish stems were current in archaeological literature before Schroeder's attempted synthesis of them, their locations are relatively precise. The Ootam region was the southeastern corner of the state, especially the San Pedro, Santa Cruz, and Sulphur Springs Valleys. The Sinagua region was around and to the south of Flagstaff, especially in the Verde Valley. The Cohonina lived in the area bounded by Kingman, Flagstaff, Highway 66, and the southern rim of the Grand Canyon. The Cerbat region was to the west of the Cohonina one, and lay between Peach Springs, Highway 66, and the Colorado River. The Prescott region was in the immediate vicinity of Prescott. The Laquish (Amacava branch, perhaps other branches) inhabited the Colorado River Valley below the present site of Hoover Dam.

A number of investigators have made important contributions to our understanding of the Hakataya. The Ootam have been discussed in detail by Di Peso (1956) and important sites excavated by Fulton and Tuthill (1940) and Tuthill (1947). Our understanding of the Sinagua region stems largely from the works of Colton (1946), Schroeder (1960), and Breternitz (1960). Intensive investigations of the Cohonina region have been carried out and discussed by Colton (1946), McGregor (1951, 1967), and Schwartz (1956). Our understanding of the prehistory of the Cerbat branch is based upon the works of Dobyns (1956) and Euler (1958). Important work in the Prescott region has been done by Spicer and Caywood (1936), Euler (1958), Dobyns (1958), and Shutler (1951). The Laquish region is known as the result of work by Baldwin (1943), Wright (1954), and Schroeder (1952, 1961a).

Because of the diversity that existed within the Hakataya root, we will describe two sites. The Gleeson Site is two and a half miles southwest of Gleeson, Arizona, at an altitude of about 5,000 feet. It sits atop a ridge in the Sulphur Springs Valley near the base of the Dragoon Mountains. The site was occupied at some time around A.D. 900.

Some thirty-five houses were excavated or explored at the site by Fulton and Tuthill (1940). The houses ranged in size from about 5 square meters to over 30. The pits in which the houses were built were universally shallow. Six-house types were identified at the site. The first two resembled Hohokam houses. They were elliptical, and there was some evidence of jacal construction techniques. The remaining four types were more similar to Mogollon architectural styles. Entrance to the houses was by way of a long narrow ramp. The walls were supported by four posts or two central posts. Each house had a small fire pit near the entrance. Small pits or "caches" were found in many houses, and storage pits in

a few. A wide variety of pits were excavated outside the houses. One hundred and eleven burials were removed from the site, only nine of them cremations. The inhumations were flexed. Some burials had no grave goods at all while others had shell, stone, turquoise, and pottery artifacts.

Stone tools used at the site included axes,

PLATE 9 Bowls from the Gleeson Site. These bowls, like those made by the Hohokam, were red-on-buff. There are some differences in design style and raw material between the types made by the two cultures. Taken from Plate XI, *An Archaeological Site Near Gleeson, Arizona*, The Amerind Foundation, Inc. Publication No. 1, 1940.

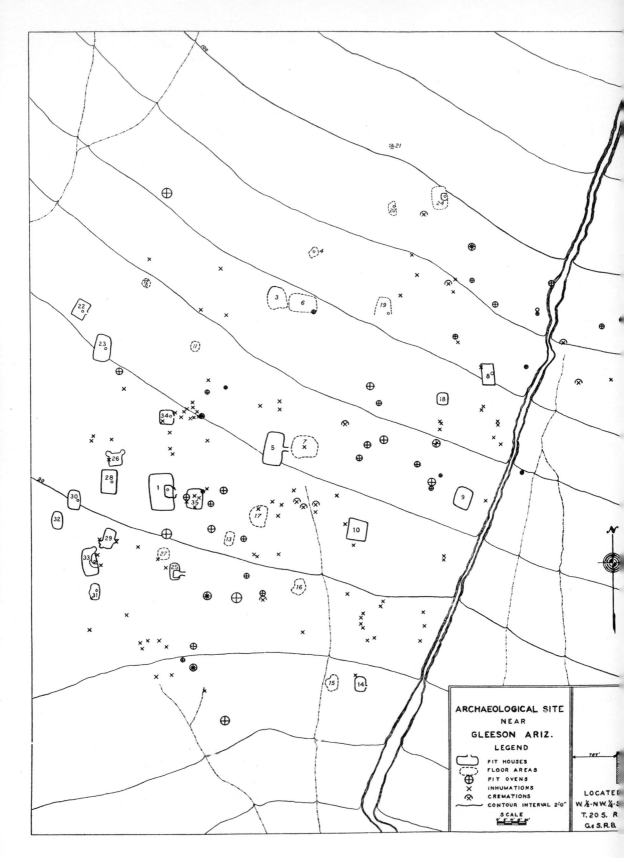

ARCHAEOLOGICAL SITE
NEAR
GLEESON ARIZ.
LEGEND

⊔	PIT HOUSES
⬚	FLOOR AREAS
⊕	PIT OVENS
×	INHUMATIONS
⊗	CREMATIONS
—	CONTOUR INTERVAL 2′0″

SCALE

LOCATED
W. ½-NW. ¼-S
T. 20 S. R
G. & S.R.B.

PLATE 10 Projectile points from the Gleeson Site. Taken from Plate XXIII, *An Archaeological Site Near Gleeson, Arizona, The* Amerind Foundation, Inc. Publication No. 1, 1940.

FIGURE 14 Map of the Gleeson Site. Some archaeologists believe that Hakataya or Ootam is a mixture of other traditions. Certainly, the variation in house size and shape on this site is extreme. However, the pattern tends toward rectangular houses with rounded corners and no entrance way. *Taken from an Archaeological Site Near Gleeson, Arizona.* The Amerind Foundation, Inc. No. 1, 1940.

palettes, combs, pipes, bowls, projectile points, carved human and animal figurines, pendants, beads, mortars, manos, and metates. Marine shells were used in making a variety of decorative items. Bone awls,

decorated tubes, bone beads, and flakers were found at the Gleeson Site.

Dragoon Red-on-Brown was the principal type found at the site. A red ware, Dragoon Red, was present, but in small quantity. It is similar to San Francisco Red. The plain ware found on the site is very similar to Gila Plain.

Breternitz excavated in the Calkin's Ranch Site (NA 2385), which is about six miles south of Camp Verde, Arizona. Five pit houses on the site were of the Pit House stage. The earliest house on the site was occupied sometime before A.D. 700. It was a small rectangular structure with a central post and peripheral roof supports. The house contained a hearth and three storage pits. It was about 12 square meters in area and less than a meter deep. Between A.D. 800 and 900, there were four more houses on the site. Houses 2, 3, 7, and 4 were approximately 24, 18, 30, and 54 square meters in area respectively. All were less than a meter deep. House 2 was a highly irregular ovoid structure that may have had a hearth. House 3 also was very irregularly shaped. House 7 was a roundish structure with a raised floor. House 4 is referred to as a communal structure because of its size and a groove on the floor. No additional evidence is offered to support this functional inference, which is frequently made in both the Sinagua and Hohokam areas. There were no sherds clearly in association with house 1C. The vast majority of the sherds in the other houses were Verde Brown. Kana-a Black-on-White and Black Mesa Black-on-White were present as trade wares. Trough metates, a variety of different kinds of manos, grinding slabs, and stones, rubbing stones, hammerstones, hoes, saws, and knives were the major artifacts in use at this time in the Verde Valley.

Village and house patterns were varied from region to region in the Hakataya area.

If one views San Simon and Cave Creek villages as Ootam, then these were the first such villages. Early villages in this region tended to be located on upper terraces, ridges, and bluffs. Houses were scattered over the sites, but occurred in groups that may have represented some sort of kin unit. Houses ranged from round to quadrangular, were generally fairly small and of jacal construction. They became somewhat larger and more rectangular during the end of the Pit House stage. In the Sinagua region, houses were generally square to rectangular and built in a shallow pit. Construction materials ranged from timber in the more northerly localities to jacal in more southerly ones. The most important characteristic of Cohonina architecture was its variability. Rarely did more than one unit occur on a site. Structures were built on or near the surface and were of varied combinations of masonry, jacal, and timber construction. Most villages were probably seasonally occupied. They occurred on both upland and lowland surfaces. Cerbat populations seem to have preferred caves to open sites, as rock shelters were the most common habitation unit in this area. The dwelling unit in the Prescott region was a rectangular pit house with rounded corners. Populations in the Laquish region used rock shelters, but the most common sites that archaeologists found were sherd areas on river terraces or the larger bars in the river. These sometimes had stone rings 2 to 3 meters in diameter that were house foundations. In Catclaw Cave, Wright found evidence of hearths, pits, and a dwelling structure of some variety.

Pottery in the Ootam area was of the Dragoon series. The brown ware similar to Gila Plain was abundant throughout the Pit House stage. It was very coarse-tempered and ranged in color from buff to light red to dark brown. Fire clouding was quite common. The techniques used in manufacturing the ware were both paddle-and-anvil and coil-and-scrape. Dragoon Red is similar to San Francisco Red, and Dragoon Red-on-Brown is similar to Mogollon Red-on-Brown. The decorations on the latter are of a Hohokam style, and were made by both paddle-and-anvil and coil-and-scrape techniques. The interior of Dragoon Red-on-Brown vessels was slipped or polished.

The pottery types common to the Patayan area were either plain brown or gray wares. The gray wares were most important in the Cohonina, Prescott, and northern Sinagua areas. Deadman's Gray was made by the paddle-and-anvil technique and fired in a reducing atmosphere. This ware had a fine sand, even micaceous temper. When it is covered with a crude red paint, that rubs off easily, it is called Deadman's Fugitive Red. When painted, it is Deadman's Black-on-Gray. Deadman's Gray was most abundant between A.D. 775 and 1200, Deadman's Fugitive Red between A.D. 775 and 1150 and Deadman's Black-on-Gray between A.D. 900 and 1100 (Breternitz, 1966). The major differences between Prescott Gray and the San Francisco wares can be explained on the basis of differences in the locally available tempering materials.

Various brown wares were also found in the Patayan area. The most important of these were Verde Brown in the Verde Valley, Tizon Brown in the Cerbat region, the Alameda Brown wares in the Flagstaff area, and Tonto Brown farther south. We have noted and agree with Breternitz's observation that these were varieties of Gila Plain, "series" rather than "wares."

Pottery in the Laquish region was of the Lower Colorado Buff ware. This ware was made by the paddle-and-anvil technique. It was fired in an uncontrolled but usually oxidizing atmosphere. Temper was of a variety of material including quartz, sherds, and sand. The Hakataya wares, then, tended to share basic aspects of manufacturing techniques. The basic differences between them seem to reflect local variability in raw materials and control of firing atmosphere.

The common burial practice is yet to be defined. Throughout most of the area, evidence either is lacking or suggests that both cremation and inhumation were practiced. Similarly, so little detailed information exists on other cultural traits that a discussion is next to impossible. Schroeder argues that the Pit House stage Sinagua used the pottery anvil, three-quarter groove axe, hammerstone, hoe, unifacial, one-hand mano, full trough metate, mortar and pestle, and chipped stone scrapers, and choppers. Projectile points were rare, especially in the north. Shell bracelets and other shell artifacts were found in sites of this stage. Bone awls were common and some other bone artifacts may have been present. McGregor feels that the principal differences between

Sinagua and Cohonina tool kits involved the presence of more artifacts and different ones on Sinagua sites (1951). Metates in the Cerbat region were distinctive. They tended to be slab metates and have heavy areas of pecking on them. They were apparently used as some sort of striking platform. Pounding stones were present in Cerbat assemblages, and projectile points may have been somewhat more abundant in this region than in those to the east. Artifacts recovered from Catclaw Cave in the Laquish area included scrapers, projectile points, knives, drills, choppers, spokeshaves, manos, metates, hammerstones, bone fleshers, awls, and spatulas, miniature pottery vessels, figurines, sandals, baskets, springs, arrow shafts, and belts. Insufficient evidence is available at present for taking any of these statements as conclusive. Moreover, we again stress the absence of dated materials for most of these areas. It is currently impossible to discuss temporal variability in them.

VIII   Pueblo and Town Dwellers

In this section devoted to culture as viewed in the related dimensions of space and time, we are interested in tracing the extent or spread of particular cultures through the variable time. In this chapter, we shall speak of various cultures as social systems that existed in relatively small and definable areas. Archaeological excavations clearly indicate that the various facets of the culture manifested trends or successive directional movements in a series of stages. One has to be able to recognize trends or directional movements in order to study culture change, because change depends on knowing what aspects of a culture are earlier and which later.

Thus in describing, for example, the Anasazi culture in space and time, I shall set forth the relative spatial boundaries of the culture and the changes that took place in the architecture and pottery through time, that is early and then later in that area.

Introduction to Town Dwellers

Although the Indians who built and occupied pit houses often lived in groupings or clusterings of from three to twenty pit houses, accommodating perhaps ten to seventy people, archaeologists tend to think of towns as consisting of surface structures. These are made up of masonry-built or wattle and daub contiguous rooms ranging in number from four to over a hundred, one or more stories high with an associated kiva or several kivas and a refuse mound nearby, all oriented usually on a north-south axis. This definition of a town is a stereotype; it does not fit all situations and is too narrow. It excludes the villages of the Hohokam Indians of southern Arizona. There—at least in the best-known site, Snaketown near Phoenix—the site was composed of houses, perhaps a hundred to a village, each of which was placed in a shallow pit the floors of which were about one foot below the desert surface (Haury, 1967, pp. 670–95).

What do I mean, then, by town dwellers? I mean an aggregation of houses—surface masonry structures or pit dwellings—that occur in fairly regular patterns of arrangements. The number of people within an aggregation is important, for the more people, the more town. Thus, an aggregation of twenty-five people or more would constitute a town; but where does one set the lower limit?

In addition to more aggregations, one must add other features, such as: increasing dependence on agriculture, well-established sedentary life with a society more complex and more tightly integrated than obtained in the culture of the Hunters and Gatherers, pottery-making, basketry, ceremonial structures, increasing population density, many villages, intervillage coordination and cooperation, and irrigation or water control devices that extended the ecological niches.

In the Anasazi area, town development

occurred at about A.D. 600; in the Hohokam, at about 300 B.C.

Thus, the term Pueblo and Town dwellers is difficult to define precisely. Involved in the definition are the number of rooms per village, population density, time of inception, control of water resources, and other intangibles such as greater intervillage and interarea coordination of production processes, social stratification, and a meshing of kinship ties. One has to "feel" what a town is and perhaps the descriptions that follow will clarify the term.

The Problem Regarding
the Appearance of Towns

One might easily ask, "Why towns?" Why did man not always live in scattered settlements? Why did he not plant, harvest, marry, raise families, worship, dance in isolation or in partnership with an uncle or a brother and their families? What forces impelled man into groups ever larger and more complex?

One reason is that the practice of agriculture made possible a higher level of productivity and a more even and stable one. Another is that an increase in population was possible because of this greater and more stable level of productivity. (This is discussed in chapter XVI, "Agriculture.") Further, more people—that is larger aggregations—lived in relatively small areas, in concentrations not heretofore found in a hunting-gathering stage.

The question "Why towns?" is not easy to answer, but an essay is devoted to them in a later section: "Great Towns." Before we can understand what is involved, we must first examine the Anasazi and Hohokam traditions because so much depends on them.

FROM ALPHA TO OMEGA,
IN THE BEGINNING

Three reliable and hearty plants—corn, beans, and squash—formed the vital economic basis of the entire sequential developments in the Southwest.

From about 1850 to 1927, archaeologists believed that this development resulted in one culture for the entire Southwest. After the Pecos Conference (Kidder, 1927) this culture was called the Pueblo culture and was subdivided into eight stages of evolution—Basket Maker I, II, and III; Pueblo I, II, III, IV, and V. Basket Maker I at that time was hypothetical; no one knew of any examples of this stage. It is now often equated with the Desert stage—Hunters and Gatherers. The Pecos classification included no absolute chronology. At present, Basket Maker stages II and III are dated roughly at A.D. 400–750; Pueblo I and II, at A.D. 750 to 1100; Pueblo III, at A.D. 1100–1350; Pueblo IV—A.D. 1350–1600; Pueblo V—contemporary pueblos. Archaeological remains that did not correspond to typical Pueblo descriptions were called "aberrant" (Kidder, 1962, p. 298).

In 1928, due to the efforts of Mr. and Mrs. Harold S. Gladwin, archaeologists were surprised to learn that the "aberrant" culture of the Lower Gila was not Puebloan but was a distinct tradition. Gladwin called it the Hohokam, from the Pima, "Those who have gone" (Gladwin, Haury, Sayles, Gladwin, 1937, p. 5). Thus by 1930 two traditions or cultures in the Southwest had been defined: the Pueblo (called Anasazi)[1] and the Hohokam.

By 1965 (McGregor, 1965, p. 73), there were seven subcultures recognized for the Southwest: (1) Anasazi, which includes

[1] Adapted from a Navajo word meaning "the old ones" or "the ones who went before."

Basket Maker and Pueblo remains, (2) Hohokam, (3) Mogollon, (4) Patayan, (5) Salado, (6) Sinagua, and (7) the Rio Grande cultures.

The earlier conception of only one culture permeating the entire Southwest was essentially correct. I think it fair to characterize the situation by stating that this culture is one of special adaptation to an arid or semiarid environment with several regional variations and adaptations. It is precisely these regional variations that give each its distinctive flavor—e.g., the Hohokam vs. the Anasazi. But all of the variants—whether Mogollon, Sinagua, Patayan, or Anasazi—despite the diversity of environments and technologies, share underlying ecological correspondences. The contents of the variants differ in detail but the structural similarities in sociotechnical organization are due to similar ecological adjustments. I think these reasons explain why one can rarely mistake an archaeological item from the Southwest for one from the Mississippi Valley.

The Anasazi and Hohokam variants will be considered here because these appear to be the two major specializations and encompass all the other variants.

THE ANASAZI

The San Juan River, a tributary of the Colorado, rises in southwestern Colorado, flows first southward, then in a generally westward direction through northern New Mexico and southern Utah. In the watershed of this river three important and now famous subspecializations of the Anasazi developed. These are (1) the Chaco Canyon, northwestern New Mexico; (2) the Mesa Verde, in and around Mesa Verde National Park area in the southwestern corner of Colorado; and (3) the Kayenta,

northeastern Arizona and southern Utah. All of these "cultures" shared many features in common, and in this sense they are similar. On the other hand, each developed a few minor variations so conspicuous that an expert can distinguish the ceramics, architecture, and village layout one from the other.

The following is a general description and does not include all exceptions and variations.

The Chaco Canyon Culture—A.D. 750–1100

The culture that developed in the Chaco Canyon and surrounding areas in west-central New Mexico has held a fascination for over a century for explorers, looters, and archaeologists.

Perhaps the environment was more attractive and verdant when the great towns were thriving centers of activity, but the area today is bleak, barren, and parched-like in appearance. It is almost a desert. There are vast wastes of undulating treeless hills, sand, rock, and when it does rain, impassable mud. It barely supports any flora and is altogether inhospitable and grim. There are few springs, no permanent streams.

Yet in this area developed a culture that was advanced in many ways, as we shall see. In spite of the great towns that developed there and the interest that the region has attracted, less is really known of the area than of almost any other southwestern district. It is amazing that so little work has been done there and so few significant reports published. There are some, of course, and reference will be made to them; but there are fewer than one would expect or hope for.

One can find here evidence for the earlier stages in the development of this culture—that is, hunting and gathering, incipient farmers who lived in pit house villages (A.D. 700), and finally surface rooms, rectangular and contiguous, with walls of excellent masonry, originally consisting of ten to thirty rooms and one story, later extending to several hundred rooms of three to four stories.

In the canyon proper an interesting dichotomy obtains.

On the south side of the arroyo are perhaps 200 to 350 small villages, each consisting of an average of twenty rooms built of slab masonry, and each possessing kivas. These villages were built and occupied from about A.D. 750 to 1100. There is no evidence for the regularity and planning apparent in the great towns (Vivian, R. Gwinn, 1970).

On the north side of the canyon are eight large towns built and occupied more or less *at the same time* as the small villages across the way. Four large towns lie outside the canyon and are also associated with small villages. All of these show evidence of careful preplanning.

Here is the puzzling situation. Why? Big towns on one side; small humble villages on the other; and both apparently occupied at the same time. We shall look into this question in a later chapter.

The arroyo that separates the two types of villages is at present some 30 feet deep and 150 to 300 feet wide. In 1849 the process of alluviation was still going on and at that time the arroyo was 1.5 feet deep and 8 feet wide (Bryan, 1954, pp. 15–16). Present evidence indicates that the present arroyo is at least the third of its kind. When the Chaco Canyon people dwelt there, alluviation was proceeding or possibly just ending. Just before the area was abandoned, arroyo cutting had started but had only cut a trench about 12 or 13 feet deep (Judd, 1954, p. 13). Apparently, then, alluviation and entrenching or arroyo cut-

ting have alternated for a long time, perhaps ever since the Canyon was first formed —perhaps during the Pleistocene period (Bryan, 1954, p. 37). The mechanism whereby this happens is not too clear, but plainly floodwaters have alternately deposited alluvium and later dissected a gully. This is believed to be due to differing patterns of rainfall. No more rain fell then, perhaps, than now, but the distribution differed. If more precipitation occurs in winter months (snow or drizzles), the moisture penetrates slowly and deeply and a cover of vegetation is emboldened to take root. The summer rains may then be quantitatively less and the moisture that occurs cannot run off quickly because the vegetation—grass, bushes, trees—restrains it. If this situation is reversed and the ground cover becomes thin, then the dashing, violent, destructive rainstorms of the summer run off quickly, cutting channels—small and large—as the water descends to the valley floor. This would encourage arroyo cutting. The present arroyo entrenchment began between 1849 and 1877 at which time it was already 16 feet deep. Alluviation began about A.D. 1250–1400. By A.D. 1500, Chaco Canyon ecological equilibrium had been re-established and would have been suitable for occupation (Judd, 1954, pp. 4–14).

The distinctive aspects of the Chaco Canyon culture pertain to masonry, shape and size of the villages, two types of kivas— small and great—and ceramics (Judd, 1954, 1959, 1964).

MASONRY

The masonry of Chaco towns is one of the most distinctive, if not unique characteristics of the area. The earlier masonry consisted of very thin sandstone slabs about 1 inch thick, large enough to span the en-

PLATE 11   Northeastern portion of Pueblo Bonito, in Chaco Canyon, New Mexico. In the foreground is a four-storied wall—the tallest wall of the town. Photo by Paul S. Martin, 1933.

tire width of the wall (that is, one end of a slab would face outward while the other end of the same slab would face inward). These were set in copious amounts of adobe mortar. Stone chips were pressed in the thick layers of mud mortar to protect the surface from the elements. Thus the wall appeared to be more mud than stone.

The later walls are of excellent workmanship and certainly mark an achievement of great technical skill. They were thicker (18″ to 23″) because they had to bear the weight of several upper stories; and were composed of a core of rubble set in mud mortar and faced on both sides by a veneer of neatly fitted, laminated, nonfriable sandstone tablets, hand-smoothed, set in even courses. These tablets were sometimes alter-

nated with bands of matched, dressed blocks of sandstone. All of the later masonry was laid with a minimum of mud. The upper story walls were thinner than those next below. Sometimes an offset or a setback provided a base for the roof floor of the superposed rooms.

All rooms in Chaco style buildings tended to be larger than those at Mesa Verde or Kayenta and with higher ceilings.

As noted above, even the surface-room towns of the early period were often built in the form of a crescent and were of one story and the masonry was exactly like the masonry of the later parts of the great towns. The latest pueblos, also crescentic in shape, were additions to the earlier rooms, were two to four stories in height and contained several hundreds of rooms. Although crescent-shaped, the open part of the crescent was eventually closed by a solid block of rooms.

KIVAS

Small kivas ranged in diameter from 13 to 26 feet; the estimated height of roof above the floor, from 7.5 to 13 feet. Kivas in the Chaco area tended to be larger than those at Mesa Verde, although many kivas at Mesa Verde had proportions that fall in the range of Chacoan measurements. But, after seeing kivas from both areas, one comes away with the feeling that Chaco "small" kivas are generally larger and deeper than those at Mesa Verde.

Generally, most small kivas were equipped with the following: a central fire pit (all kivas possess this feature); an underfloor ventilating system (this differs in form only from Mesa Verde and Kayenta kivas); a rectangular masonry-lined pit called a subfloor vault that was always located west of the fire pit; an encircling bench on which stood six to ten low pillars of masonry that served as the primary supports for the roof and from which sprang the cribwork of overlapping logs to form a domed ceiling. The bench was narrower in the southern sector, producing a recess. All Chaco kivas were round and subterranean; if not literally below ground, they were set in a square enclosure, with earth packed in around the outer perimeter of the kiva in order to simulate subterraneity. Entrance was usually via a ladder through a roof hatchway that also served as a smoke outlet. Sometimes, entrance was also by means of an underground stone-lined tunnel that led directly to a surface room. The astounding number of over 250 pine logs, small and large, were used to roof the kiva. The large logs ranged from 8 to 12 feet in length.

The subfloor vaults, like many other details, constitute a minor mystery. Their function is not known. Most of them contained clean sand and were floored with pine planks. It has been suggested that these served as foot drums.

The ventilating systems of kivas operated on the same principle no matter the type of kiva. When a fire burned in the fire pit, smoke and warmed air rose and escaped via the entry hatch. This caused fresh air to flow down the vertical ventilator shaft, through the horizontal tunnel, and thus into the kiva. All kivas were thus equipped. The unique aspect of the Chaco-type kiva ventilator system was the manner in which the new air was introduced into the kiva. Near the fire pit and between it and the southern recess was an opening in the floor that connected with the ventilator shaft. It resembled the hot-air registers set flush with the floor that were in vogue in America in the early part of the century. The fresh air entered the kiva through this floor vent. Because the fresh air escaped into the kiva in this manner, no screen was necessary to deflect the incoming air from the flames in the fire pit.

The ancestry of kiva ventilating systems has been traced to pit house entryway tunnels. In a sense, kiva ventilators are nonfunctional entrances. Take a pit house entrance, shrink it a bit, and stand it on end and you have a ventilator! Of course, in the periods when pit houses were in use, the tunnel entrance served also as an inlet for fresh air as well as enabling one to crawl into or out of the house.

GREAT KIVAS

Anything larger than a small kiva is a Great Kiva! This statement is like saying, "How long is a piece of string?" In general, anything over about 30 feet in diameter is

PLATE 12   Circular, slab-walled structure—an early Great Kiva (?). Eighty-three feet in diameter, it is one of the largest ever found. Attached to a late Basket Maker III or Pueblo I Anasazi village in southwestern Colorado. Dated about A.D. 850–875. Probably served as a sacred unroofed enclosure for ceremonial uses. Southwestern Archaeological Expedition of Field Museum, 1937.

considered a Great Kiva. Those that are called Great Kivas (Vivian and Reiter, 1960, p. 84) range from 33 feet 7 inches to 81 feet in diameter.

Approximately twenty-one circular Great Kivas have been reported for the entire Southwest, eight from Chaco Canyon alone. Twenty-three rectangular Great Kivas are known, all mostly from the Mogollon area. Great Kivas (rectangular) measure 45 to 50 feet on the longer dimension. Both types, circular and rectangular, are reported from various parts of the Anasazi and Mogollon areas. Great Kivas do not occur in the Hohokam area, so far as we know.

The circular ones date from about A.D. 650 (Broken Flute Cave, northeastern Ari-

zona) to about 1200 (Arizona P: 16:9–Forestdale area, Vivian and Reiter, 1960, p. 107). If one includes the large circular structure at Tyuonyi Site in Frijoles Canyon, near Santa Fe, New Mexico, the dates would have to be extended to about A.D. 1400.

The rectangular Great Kivas in the Mogollon area date from about A.D. 1 or earlier (SU Site, New Mexico, Martin and Rinaldo, 1940) and die out at about A.D. 1400, if one counts the plaza at Kinishba Pueblo, Arizona, as a Great Kiva (Vivian and Reiter, 1960, p. 107).

In short, Great Kivas are found in many places in the Anasazi and Mogollon areas, but are not found in western Arizona or the Hohokam area. There "ball courts" are present.

One may wonder why so much space here is devoted to this subject. This is done partly because Great Kivas are semimonumental pieces of architecture that may claim fame because they still have—even in their ruined condition—esthetic qualities that quite engross the visitor. In addition, they appear to have been most highly developed at Chaco Canyon and are relatively more abundant there (eight known) and hence are an intimate part of the Chaco tradition. Further, since Great Kivas disappeared from the scene before the Spanish invasion, there is a certain aura of mystery concerning their function. Residential rooms, on the other hand, are something that we can all comprehend because we live in such rooms, and small kivas are fairly well understood because they were in use when the Spaniards invaded the Southwest (1540) and are still in use today among contemporary Indians in the Hopi villages, Arizona, in Zuni near Gallup, New Mexico, and in Rio Grande Valley villages in the vicinity of Taos, Santa Fe, and Albuquerque, New Mexico.[2]

No one feature nor any one set of features can be set apart and called uniquely Chaco.

Most kivas are constructed with a floor of hard, smoothed dirt about 10 to 14 feet below the ground surface, although the earliest examples are less deep. Of the eleven later Great Kivas there are six in which the roof of the central chamber was lower than that of the peripheral rooms (see below). (One would think this kind of construction would have created drainage problems in times of heavy rains.) In one Great Kiva, at Aztec, New Mexico, the roof may have been carried to a minimum

height of 16 feet so that the central chamber and the peripheral rooms were all under one roof. (The Aztec Great Kiva is so reconstructed.) Very early Great Kivas were probably not roofed at all. No definite statement can be made about the others, as evidence is lacking.

The roofing of such large structures must have presented a troublesome problem to the builders. Most of the later Great Kivas (after A.D. 900) were provided with four massive stone columns or upright timbers set on bases of masonry, or with massive upright timbers that rested on great stone discs (about 3 feet in diameter), and on these upright columns—stone or wood— rested the main roof supports. Where upright timbers served as the principal roof supports, a large amount of labor was expended in constructing the seating pit for the massive timber that was to be used. Except for two early Great Kivas (Shabik'eschee and La Plata), the base of the pit was formed by one to four large thick discs of stone. The seating pit itself (3 to 5 feet deep) was rectangular and the sides of the excavation were faced with masonry. At the two early sites just mentioned, the seating pits were cut out of bed rock. The purpose of the seating pits was to provide a firm socket for the massive upright timbers so that they would not kick out at the base. (It is estimated that roof weights would have run to 70 to 100 tons and more after a rain.) After the upright timber (3 to 5 feet in diameter) had been placed in its socket, a packing of stones, cobbles, and dirt was tamped in around the upright to hold it firmly in place.

There were always four such upright supports equilaterally spaced in the kiva chamber so as to form a rectangle. The prime purpose of these four great roof supports was to carry four large horizontal wooden stringers, the ends of two resting on each

[2] Also, a personal whim impels me to dwell on Great Kivas with some loving attention. It was Great Kivas that first caught my archaeological fancy—some forty-five years ago! (P. M.)

upright, and running between them, thus forming a rectangle over the central floor area. On these in turn rested the inner ends of logs placed radially like spokes of a wheel. On them, in turn, the remainder of the roofing—smaller logs, poles, branches, and mud—was laid. If 350 logs, large and small, were required to roof a kiva only 18 feet in diameter, one can guess that to roof a Great Kiva some 40 feet in diameter would have required many more logs and many longer and thicker ones.

Placed between the upright roof supports were "vaults"—rectangular compartments —one on each side of the fire box. Built of masonry, the top surfaces were usually raised somewhat above the floor level, while their bottoms were sunk well below the kiva floor level. The function of these vaults is not known. As stated earlier in the section on small kivas, one suggestion is that planks were stretched across the long dimension and that performers danced on them using them as foot drums. Conversely, Vivian and Reiter (1960, p. 93) suggest that they might have served as small steam bath structures used for ritual cleansing. A final suggestion (*ibid.*) is that they served as places where beans and corn were ritually planted during winter months, watered, and kept warm (from the nearby big fire box) and thus forced to sprout in early spring. Thus, they may have been a sort of cold frame without the glass cover. Plants grown in the kiva would, one assumes, have ritual significance.

While every Great Kiva may lack this or that particular feature, all Great Kivas were provided with a central fire area—a shallow depression in the floor in which fires burned, or a formalized, large rectangular fire box composed of masonry. The fire box was a raised structure that rested on or extended into the floor, and was invariably located south of the center of the room. The masonry interiors are reddened from heat and all contain wood ash in quantity. Sizes varied but fire boxes were usually 1 to 3 feet deep and about 4 feet wide and 5 feet long. A draft hole was usually placed in the narrow side near the floor.

A fire screen or air deflector often occurred in Great Kivas, although their purpose is not clear inasmuch as there were no drafts that would have agitated the fire. Furthermore, the fire was well protected by the sides of the fire box. It is possible that these represented some important aspect in small kiva construction and/or ritual, and were therefore felt to be necessary appendages of some Great Kivas.

A *sipapu*—a small plastered hole—or entrance to the spirit world is a rarity in Great Kivas. Three are reported: two from Chaco Canyon and one from Fire Temple, Mesa Verde National Park.

A bench, usually of masonry but sometimes of upright slabs and earth, included the periphery of almost all Great Kivas. They were usually wider than they were high. The term bench implies that such construction was for providing seating space. In some cases, because of pole shelves or wooden cribbing over them, benches could not have so functioned.

In some Great Kivas, over the benches and in the wall of the structure, one finds crypts or niches or recesses. These apertures were usually empty, but in one Great Kiva at Chaco Canyon these niches contained artifacts that were hidden by masonry seals.

Entrance to Great Kivas was probably via an antechamber built at ground level on the north and thence down into the kiva chamber by means of a recessed stairway built of masonry. Where such conveniences were lacking, it is surmised that entrance to the kiva was by means of a ladder through a hatchway in the roof.

Peripheral rooms were small rooms, built at ground level (not subterranean), that followed the arc of the kiva proper. In the best preserved, most carefully excavated, and now restored set of peripheral rooms at Aztec National Monument, New Mexico, the rooms form a continuous ring, at ground level, around the entire arc. Each room opened into the main kiva chamber with curved walls representing segments of an arc. Peripheral rooms and Great Kiva formed one continuous unit under a single roof in this restoration.

It is probable that all Great Kivas were provided with some peripheral rooms, if not, indeed, a complete set; but hasty or careless methods of excavation may have destroyed them.

For many years, our explanation of these rooms was that they were ceremonial in nature. The latest hypothesis put forward (Plog, 1969) is that the peripheral rooms of Great Kivas served as community granaries and that the Great Kiva complex served as a center of redistribution of food for an area as well as for elaborate town or areal ceremonies.

CHACO POTTERY

Chaco Canyon pottery may be roughly divided into early (about A.D. 800–1000) and late (A.D. 1000–1150 or 1200).

Pottery in the Anasazi area was made by the coil method. A handful of properly prepared clay (paste) is pressed and patted into a saucer-shaped disc. The potter then takes more clay and rolls it out into a longish sausage of material (about one inch thick). This is a coil. One end of this is pressed onto the disc of clay and the other is guided around and spirally upward to create the walls of the vessel. Each new coil is lightly pressed onto the previous one. After several coils are in place, and have

been thinned by scraping, the incomplete vessel is set aside to let the coils dry and become strong enough to support the weight of a few more coils. If it is to be a cooking pot, the coils are lightly smoothed and only scraped somewhat. In early Chaco times, prior to A.D. 950, all the coils would be obliterated and smoothed over, thus creating a "plain ware" cooking pot. Or a few coils or wide bands might be left on the neck and upper body while those constituting the lower part of the jar would be obliterated. If the pot was to be slipped and painted, all traces of coils were removed and the entire surface smoothed over.

The earlier ware comprised an assemblage of (1) unpainted cooking pots and of (2) black-on-white painted pots. Cooking pots were either plain and smooth, or textured with wide clay bands (banded) or narrow clay strips (plain and/or indented corrugated) on the neck or upper surfaces of the pot. Bottoms were plain and smooth.

Early painted ware was slipped with a thin wash of kaolin and decorated with black paint. Hence the term *black-on-white* pottery. Designs consisted of ticked and wavy lines, interlocking whorls, squiggled or wavy hatching chiefly in curvilinear figures and thin parallel lines bordering stepped triangles. *Bowls*, the most common shape, were usually slipped on both interior and exterior surfaces. *Pitchers*, the next most common shape, were round-bottomed, full-bodied and squat, and decoration was confined to two zones—body and neck. Handles were always decorated and were mere straps of clay. Scoop *ladles* were the shape of a gourd cut in half—with no bowl-and-handle types. Designs on ladles usually ran down one side and back up the other. In descending order of numbers, were canteens, water jars or ollas, seed jars, and effigy-shaped vessels.

The paint used on early Chaco pottery designs was either organic (vegetal, derived from plant juices) or mineral (iron oxide), although mineral paint was probably used more often. It is not too difficult to distinguish between the two—especially with the aid of a hand lens. Mineral paint is usually a dense, matte black or rust color and appears to lie on the surface of the vessel. Sometimes, one can observe tiny grains of undissolved mineral in the paint.

Organic, or to use the other terms, vegetal or "carbon" paint is derived from plant juices, and is a brownish pigment before firing. When examining it with a hand lens one has the impression that it has penetrated the clay, that it had soaked in and even "run" a bit at the edges, that it looks bluish instead of matte black; and if the slip had been polished before the design was applied the black paint of the design will appear also to have been polished.

Late Chaco pottery comprised two major types: (1) cooking pots and (2) more sophisticated, generally better-executed black-on-white pots.

1. Cooking pottery consisted of all-over texturing—corrugations marked by a tool to make indentations. Hence the term *indented corrugated ware.* Usually, cooking pots are blackened and sooted on the bottoms.

2. The later black and white painted pottery came in eight shapes, listed in descending order of frequency: bowls, cylindrical jars, pitchers, ladles, canteens, water jars, and seed jars. Designs consisted of elements of straight-line hatching set within heavier framing lines, and "solids": interlocking and opposed stepped triangles of "hourglass" designs, checkerboard, scrolls pendant from the rim set in a field of diagonal hatching, panels of vertical hatching, and alternating panels of stepped triangles, and bold sawtooth triangles or a series of heavy parallel lines whose paths are interrupted by offsets.

Slip was applied thinly to interiors of bowls but usually not on exteriors. Sometimes, a band of white slip was applied to the exterior just under the rim, or a bit of slip was wiped across the exterior on the bottom. Range in size was the same for both early and late types—averaging about 9 inches in diameter and 4 inches in depth. No half-gourd scoops were made in late times; all ladles were bowl-and-handle type. Pitchers were provided with tall, cylindrical necks attached to low, square-shouldered bodies and concave bottoms. Designs occur on two encircling zones—neck and body.

A cylindrical jar shape is unique in the Southwest, and all extant examples were manufactured in the Chaco Canyon area. Two hundred of them were found at Pueblo Bonito. Their function is unknown. Some were found in rooms associated with mortuary furniture such as a cylindrical tobacco pipe, shell bracelets, turquoise beads and pendants, and "ceremonial sticks." A total of 164 cylindrical vessels were found in seven adjacent rooms.

The Mesa Verde Culture—A.D. 600–1150

The Mesa Verde area has no fixed boundaries, but it usually includes the Mesa Verde National Park, the remainder of the Mesa itself that lies in the Ute Indian Reservation and the territories drained in part by the Dolores River, McElmo Creek, the Mancos River, the La Plata and Animas Rivers, and the middle reaches of the San Juan River. Mesa Verde National Park itself is in the southwest corner of Colorado, but the *area* includes much of the famous four-corner region—that is, the area in and around the point that is common to four state boundaries—Arizona, New Mexico, Utah, and Colorado. Hence by definition the Mesa Verde culture may be found in the northeast corner of Arizona, the northwest of New Mexico, the southeast of Utah, and the southwest of Colorado.

Much, although not all, by any means, of this vast area is somewhat more attractive and less bleak and barren in appearance than that of the Chaco Canyon area. This opinion may be a personal bias, but perhaps not entirely. The less attractive portions of the area may be described as a barren, arid, plateau dissected by innumerable washes or arroyos—dry river courses—and deep, dry canyons. The only living streams in the area are the major rivers alluded to above. All other tributaries of these rivers—arroyos, canyons, and various water courses—are dry during much of the year and carry water only in early spring after snows melt or after violent thunder showers of the summer. Were it not for the thousands of springs throughout this country, at the heads of canyons or at the base of certain rock formations, much of this land would not have been habitable.

The more attractive areas—for example, a large portion of Mesa Verde Park—are higher, nearer large mountains such as the La Plata Mountains, Ute Mountain, the Blue Mountains, and receive more moisture. The average annual precipitation at Chetro Ketl in Chaco Canyon, elevation about 6,500 feet above sea level, is 9 inches (Dutton, 1938, p. 9), while at a similar elevation at Mesa Verde the average is nearly 14 inches. Where precipitation is abundant enough one finds a goodly growth of cedar (Juniper), piñon, and some oak. Of course higher up in the mountains one finds luxuriant growths of conifers as well as oak and aspen. Thus, at approximately the same elevation (6,500 feet) the Mesa Verde area is somewhat more verdant.

One must admit, however, that the present scene may differ from that of a thousand years ago. It is possible that Chaco Canyon was forested at A.D. 1000, but the roofs of the villages, towns, and kivas required so much timber that the area may have been deforested (Judd, 1954, p. 3). If that is so, then the Chaco area may also have been verdant.

Mesa Verde is famous for its cliff houses, although they do exist also in other regions—in the Kayenta area in northeastern Arizona, for example. But some of the large, striking ones were built at Mesa Verde in the shelter of caves.

However, since cliff houses, chronologically, occurred later—after A.D. 1100—our description of them will be deferred.

A.D. 600–900

The earliest pueblos, if that term be restricted to rooms built on the surface of the ground in contrast to those that are underground, developed in the area about A.D. 700.

They have been reported from southeastern Utah to the Piedra River, just west of Pagosa Springs, Colorado; and in much of the area between these sites. On one mesa top alone in Mesa Verde National Park, 147 sites like these have been documented (Hayes, 1964, p. 110). Wherever they occur there is a similarity between them as regards village plans and general arrangements. Construction of the houses varied: in the eastern area the houses were rectanguloid, with wall of wattle-and-daub construction, flat roofs upheld by four upright wooden posts set in the house floor; each room (house) was provided with an entry facing a court. Rooms were arranged in an imperfect crescent encompassing one or more subterranean chambers, all arranged on a north-south axis.

In the west, including Mesa Verde, the villages were arranged in a definite crescentic shape. The rooms were arranged in curved rows from one to three rows deep. The "front" rooms, that is, those nearest the court or plaza, were of jacal (wattle-and-daub) construction, with a doorway facing the plaza and one leading to the "rear" rooms. The walls of these rooms, in contrast, were often built of small sandstone slabs set in copious amounts of mud mortar. No doorways led from the rear rooms to the outside. Roofs were flat and were supported by upright floor posts. Each of the front rooms was furnished with a fire pit. Evidence on hand indicates that the front rooms were living quarters, whereas the rear rooms may have served as storage quarters and/or general household use. The number of rooms per village ranged from five to twenty with an average of eight per site.

As we noted in the preceding chapter the subterranean chambers—rectangular and circular—are usually called pit houses. They also possessed kiva-like features, however (bench, pit alongside the fire pit, ventilator, sometimes large enough to have served as an entrance passage, sipapu). The function of these subterranean units is not known; but they may have served as incipient religious and food-distributing foci.

The significant occurrence of this period was the development of rectangular, perpendicular-walled rooms, an evolution that permitted the building of contiguous rooms —a really great advance. Thus, we have here the beginnings of pueblo architecture, one feature of which was many contiguous rooms of one story and later of two or more stories (Hayes, 1964, pp. 89–91; Roberts, 1930, p. 166).

Rooms varied in size from 7 by 10 feet to 16 by 11 feet. Pit structures were deep— 4 to 7 feet.

The courtyard or plaza faced southward with the pit houses-kivas within or south of

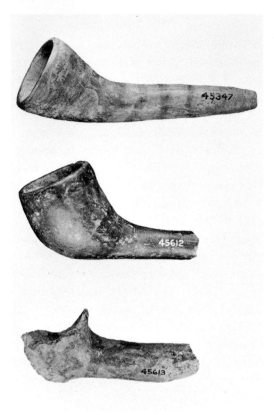

PLATE 13 Tobacco smoking pipes made from pottery. From Lowry Ruin, southwestern Colorado. Dated about 1050 (Anasazi). Smoking was not indulged in as a pleasure but was a sacred formality—e.g., as a preliminary to the invocation. The smoke was a peace offering to the Gods of rain, snow, fertility. Southwestern Archaeological Expedition of Field Museum, 1930–34.

the plaza; and sometimes, trash to the south of the pit houses. Again the several axes of the villages were north-south.

Utility vessels—jars and pitchers—were either a gray ware plain with no coil mark showing or a gray with unobliterated coil marks left on the neck or upper body.

Painted ware consisted of bowls, jars, and pitchers. Some designs appear to represent those used in basketry or textiles, "stitching designs"; some are similar to the early designs found in both the Chaco and Kayenta districts; while others bear patterns pendant from the rim with emphasis on triangles, parallel lines, concentric circles or rectangles and parallel banding lines. Paint used was mostly mineral with an occasional piece painted with vegetal paint. A small percentage of pots were slipped before the design was applied. A beautiful black on orange ware was present at this time—designs being in black on an orange or red base. On some white bowls the black paint of the design appeared as greenish glaze—apparently the result of very hot firing that caused the paint to vitrify.

While no one site evinces long occupation that would provide us with a vertical stratigraphic sequence of architecture, village plans, and pottery styles, yet we can employ what is called "horizontal stratigraphy." That is, by means of relative or absolute dating we can compose a sequence through time that will give us a working model of the development of Pueblo history. For example, if sites 1 to 7, located on a mesa, are dated as having been inhabited from about A.D. 700 to 900; and sites 8 to 20, located nearby, are dated from about A.D. 900 to 1000; and if the architecture, village plan, kiva construction, and pottery

attributes are "different" and more sophisticated, then we can begin to piece together Pueblo development.

I bring this up to make clear that the data concerning the houses, villages, pottery types that I shall now describe and refer to as "later" were derived as described above.

A.D. 900–1150

During this period, which for purposes of simplifying, represents some telescoping, villages became smaller, with contiguous, all-masonry rooms arranged in a straight line. Masonry was crude, being composed mainly of unshaped rocks with mud used only as a mortar-filler. Kivas were placed south of the room block and a trash mound to the south of the kiva. Several special developments mark this period—a "true" kiva (explained below), "true" masonry where stones were more important than the mud mortar, and the beginnings of indented corrugated pottery. The average number of rooms per village was 6; they ranged from 4 to 20 (Hayes, 1964, p. 93). Although the

PLATE 14 Anasazi unpainted pottery found with burials at Lowry Pueblo, Colorado. Dated about A.D. 800–900. Height of mug at left, 4¾ inches. Jar on right probably was used for cooking. In general, unpainted pottery is earlier than painted wares. Southwestern Archaeological Expedition of Field Museum, 1930–34.

PLATE 15   Burial 15 (extended) of a female from Lowry Ruin, southwestern Colorado. On right side of head is a mortuary offering of a pottery bowl that may have contained food for the use of the spirit in the afterworld. (Whisk broom and trowel for scale.) Southwestern Archaeological Expedition of Field Museum, 1930–34.

drop from 8 per site in the previous period to 6 may not sound dramatic, actually it is more significant than it appears. Archaeologists who have conducted extensive surveys in the area think that after A.D. 900, fission of population took place (Hayes, 1964, p. 109). This agrees very well with the results of our work in Colorado (Martin et al., 1938). Villages were mostly on tops of mesas, as in the preceding period, but distances between them were greater. It is possible that there was a reduction in population.

Gradually the fragmentation was reversed. More rooms (an average of 9) per village marked part of this change. "Unit-type" pueblos (6 to 10 rooms) were fashionable (Kidder, 1962, p. 207; Hayes, 1964, p. 100; Lister, 1964, 1965, 1966). Rooms were arranged in a single or double row, were about 6 by 8 feet in size, and were one story high. The pueblos became larger, were built with better masonry of stones that were selected for uniformity in size and were roughly shaped and laid in courses. Up to about A.D. 950 most villages were built on mesa tops, but by 1050 an equal number of villages were built in cliff shelters, and by 1150 cliff houses predominated.

"True" kivas appeared. True kivas is a term that denotes a structure that was round, subterranean, the entire interior of which was lined with masonry—from floor to roof; they were furnished with a fire pit, a deflector, sipapu, a ventilator, and southern recess, and with four to six pilasters or blocks of masonry set on the encircling bench at equal distances apart and from which the cribwork domed roof sprang. The ventilating apparatus worked like those found in Chaco kivas (see p. 111), but instead of introducing fresh air from below the floor and upward, the Mesa Verde type introduced it by means of a horizontal masonry-lined tunnel that opened into the kiva through the southern recess and above floor level. Thus, a draft from it might stir the fire too much and produce sparks. Hence a deflector—usually a stone slab— was planted in the floor between the ventilator opening and the fire pit but closer to the fire pit.

The masonry roof pillars set equidistant

produced six broad recesses, but one of them, the south one, was deeper than the others. This is called the southern recess or "altar."

The ratio of rooms to kivas was about twelve rooms to one kiva.

With the development of a "normal" or "true" kiva from a pit house structure, came another innovation—towers. Round or rectangular towers appeared in the Mesa Verde area about A.D. 950 and were usually adjacent to kivas and often connected to them by means of an underground crawltunnel. Since many of them commanded little or no view, it has been assumed that

PLATE 16 Subterranean ceremonial chamber, Kiva F, Lowry Pueblo, Colorado. Built outside the pueblo proper and at northeast side. Greatest diameter is 14 feet 8 inches; height of kiva walls five feet. Roof probably supported by upright wooden posts (note postholes). Esti-

mated height of roof above floor, seven feet. Absence of upright stone pillars for roof support and a bench makes this kiva unusual and more like those in Chaco Canyon. Southwestern Archaeological Expedition of Field Museum, 1930–34.

they were of an esoteric nature (Schulman, 1950, pp. 288–97; Hayes, 1964, p. 94). They were often two or three stories high and were constructed of brick-like stones shaped by pecking. Sometimes towers occurred alone or with a kiva isolated from any nearby dwellings. Interior features are not known because few towers have been excavated. Sometimes, the walls were pierced by openings called lookout holes or loopholes. As stated earlier they may have been associated with rituals or they might have been built for lookouts. It has been pointed out (Lancaster, Pinkley, Van Cleave, and Watson, 1954, p. 44) that towers appeared with the introduction of better, that is double-coursed, masonry and *prior* to the construction of compound pueblos. A compound pueblo (Lister, 1964) is one that was furnished with a court or plaza in which the kivas were located. Surrounding the court on all sides was a wall or rows of contiguous rooms that were blank—no openings—on the outer faces. Thus the entire town faced inward toward the court and was therefore less vulnerable to attacks from hostile people. Before the compound pueblo was conceived of, the men of the village might have been gathered in a kiva to celebrate certain rites and thus would have been hopelessly vulnerable in case of a surprise raid. Towers were built adjacent to the kivas to provide space for watchers who could give warning of impending danger. These authors also argue that our conception of what a watchtower should be may be different from that of an Anasazi Indian. They state that an uninterrupted view over great distances was not necessary; a view of the immediate area was all that was needed.

All of this suggests defense, enemies, danger, and turbulent, disturbed times. Perhaps, and even probably, so. Towers have been reported from the Ackmen-Lowry area, western Colorado (Martin and Ri-

PLATE 17   Anasazi Black-on-White pottery bowls found with burials at Lowry Pueblo, Colorado. A.D. 950–1000. Diameter of bowl at left is 5¾ inches. Southwestern Archaeological Expedition of Field Museum, 1930–34.

naldo, 1939, pp. 474–86), Hovenweep and McElmo Canyons, southwestern corner of Colorado, and from the Gallina area, northwestern New Mexico.

Great Kivas are less common in the Mesa Verde area than in the Chaco, although they exist (Martin and Rinaldo, 1939; Martin, 1936). Two have recently been excavated at Mesa Verde; one dated at about A.D. 800 to 850 is approximately 46 feet in diameter and contains earth walls devoid of masonry. The other is later and dates at about A.D. 950–1125, is about 50 feet in diameter, was provided with masonry walls, ten peripheral rooms and a north antechamber (McLellan, 1969). It resembles the one at Lowry Pueblo (Martin, 1936).

By A.D. 1150, as noted earlier, more villages were built in caves than on mesa tops. It was at this time that the large and now justly famous cliff houses came into being and large towns were in their prime. A description of them is deferred until Chapter XVII.

Pottery of this period was, as in Chaco Canyon, of two major types: culinary (unpainted) and painted.

Culinary pottery in the earliest part of the period—A.D. 900–975—consisted of jars only, with smooth bases the necks of which displayed overlapping bands 4 to 9 mm. wide that produces a clapboard effect (Hayes, 1964, p. 45) and were small, about 5 to 7 inches high, with wide mouths. Surfaces are often blackened from cooking fires.

Later, culinary pottery—975–1150—was similar all over the Southwest. It is called "corrugated" or indented corrugated. The name derives from the potters' practice of permitting the coils to remain—that is to be visible and not obliterated. As the potter pinched the coils to the preceding or lower coils an indentation was made with the thumb. This produces a rippling or a tex-

PLATE 19   Anasazi Black-on-White pottery mugs. Dated about A.D. 1050–1150. Mug at left has a double bottom with small space containing tiny pebbles that rattle when mug is used. Found at Lowry Pueblo, Colorado. Southwestern Archaeological Expedition of Field Museum, 1930–34.

tured effect that is pleasing to the eye. The entire surface of the vessel was thus treated from neck to base. There is an infinite variety of textured effects—with indentations staggered, with indentations placed to form diagonals, and alternated indented and unindented (plain) bands. These are merely the commoner variations; there are many others. Both jars and bowls occurred. Heights ranged from 8 inches to 16 inches or more. Jars were greater in height than diameter, and mouths were almost as wide as the greatest diameter. Bowls were rare, small, and were made with straight rims (Hayes, 1964, p. 49).

Painted pottery (early) was predominantly black-on-white, that is a black design applied to a white (slipped surface). Shapes included bowls, ladles, short-necked jars, canteens, pitchers, seed jars, and mugs. Designs are similar to all other Anasazi designs of this time period: solid triangles, broad-line elements, checkerboard and hatching framed between parallel lines. Paint used was of mineral origin, usually a

deep matte black. This type is called Mancos Black-on-White (Martin, 1936; Hayes, 1964, pp. 59–62).

The later black-on-white (A.D. 1050–1150) is called McElmo Black-on-White and is sometimes called proto-Mesa Verde or early Mesa Verde Black-on-White. Bowls, ladles, jars, canteens, and mugs were the common shapes. The designs are broadline triangular frets, nested chevrons, closely spaced parallel lines framing rows of dots, ticks, and checkerboards. Rims have dots on them. Organic or vegetal paint was the preferred type.

The latest pottery belongs to the "cliff house" period (A.D. 1150–1300).

The culinary or cooking pottery was much like that of the preceding period, except better and bigger. The coiling and indentations were finer, more evenly spaced and the bodies of the jars were egg-shaped, with wide mouths. Pitcherlike jugs, the surfaces of which were textured, also occur.

The black-on-white ware was of remarkable, fine quality, with a high polish and

PLATE 21 Worn-out sandals woven of yucca fiber, with designs in red and black. Basket Maker III sandals such as these were usually square-toed with fringe, whereas later, Pueblo III Anasazi, sandals had rounded or pointed toes. These sandals date from about A.D. 500 and come from a cave in southeastern Utah. Excavated in 1889 for the Chicago World's Columbian Exposition, 1893.

rather, the settlement patterns may be due to other variables, such as sociocultural behavior. Perhaps social as well as economic ties affected the settlement patterns and the random distribution of sites. In order to make fullest use of the available land, sites would have to have been equidistant in the valley bottoms, but since they were not equidistant we might assume that social ties were present.

Pit houses were the rule. They were circular, ranging in diameters from 6 to 15 feet and in depth from 6 inches to 5 feet. Fire pits were present. Either roofs were supported by upright posts, or the ends of the roof timbers rested on the banks or earthen walls of the house. Many of the houses were provided with an encircling bench. Entrance to the house was probably through the roof. Little is known of the size of villages but several villages of from one to five houses are reported (Aikens, 1966, p. 22).

Farming was becoming more important with maize and squash as the chief crops, but wild plants were extensively utilized. Wild game was obtained by means of snares, rabbit nets, atlatl or throwing stick, and darts (Aikens, 1966, p. 26). Metates, manos, hafted knives of stone, basketry containers, and twined woven bags are some of the more common artifacts. Sometime between A.D. 500 and 700, pottery made its appearance. It was a gray pottery usually not decorated and occurred in several shapes: jars, canteens, bowls, and ladles.

PLATE 22 Prehistoric "jackknives." Both are tightly held in specially prepared slats by means of some strong prehistoric "Epoxy" glue. Handles of cottonwood; blades of chert (flint). Basket Maker III, Anasazi culture, about A.D. 400–500. Object on left from Graham Canyon Cave; object on right from cave in Grand Gulch Canyon, Utah. Excavated in 1889 for Chicago World's Columbia Exposition, 1893.

Middle Period—Virgin-Kayenta Tradition
A.D. *700–1100*

More villages and an increase in population density were typical of this period, not only here but elsewhere in the Anasazi area. In addition to the valley and canyon places for village locations, the higher mesas were also now extensively occupied. Villages usually consisted of one or more pit dwellings with several associated storage units built on the surface; or they might consist of a single, small surface pueblo containing two to four dwelling rooms and several rooms used for storage. Often, a pueblo would also have several pit dwellings associated with it. The practice of building and using both surface and pit structures simultaneously was common and lasted right up to the time of abandonment of the area. This style of village layout has been mentioned before and may be much more widespread than was formerly thought. In the Kayenta area, the pueblo rooms were built along a straight axis. In the Virgin, we find the rooms were laid out in a circular or U-shaped ground plan, thus forming a courtyard. This type of village plan was also common in the Mesa Verde area, and the earlier portion of Pueblo Bonito in Chaco Canyon was laid out in the same fashion. The number of surface rooms ranged from four to sixteen; there were from two to six pit structures.

Surface rooms were usually built of masonry made up of coursed sandstone slabs, but they were sometimes, in part at least, of wattle-and-daub construction.

Pit houses were round and were of varying depths both deep and less deep. The deep ones were completely subterranean with walls of earth plastered with clay. Rarely, a pit house would be lined with stone walls. Entrance was through the roof. The less deep pit houses were those the floors of which were only 12 to 18 inches below ground. The underground portions of the house were lined with vertical stone slabs, while the upper portions were made up of slanting and upright poles the interstices of which were plugged with branches and mud. Both types were provided with fire pits.

Two types of storage units existed. One was a slab-lined pit with aboveground walls of wattle-and-daub or masonry; the other was a rectangular surface room with walls of masonry, often incorporated into a line of dwelling rooms, either in one axis or in a curve. Flagstone subfloors were sometimes placed in the latter type of storage room to make it rodentproof. Sometimes, this type also contained mealing bins and small corner hearths.

Some villages, but not all, were equipped with kivas. They tended to be simple structures, circular and subterranean or semisubterranean, containing fire pits, masonry walls, and sometimes a ventilator and deflector.

Pottery was more abundant and better made. Bowls, jars, globular cooking pots, and ladles were the common shapes. Painted pottery of excellent quality was manufactured; color and designs foreshadowed what was to be made later. The major painted wares were black-on-white and black-on-red. Plain gray and textured—neck-banded and indented corrugated—wares were used for cooking.

Designs on black-on-white vessels are similar to those from the Chaco area: two framing lines enclosing zigzags, ticked lines, scrolls, diamonds, pendant dots, and triangles. Somewhat later in the development of black-on-white pottery these designs were gradually modified in the direction of heavier, coarser treatments (Beals, Brainerd, and Smith, 1945, p. 99). These changes were associated with larger vessels.

Black-on-red vessels were made of an orange clay and slipped with a red paint. On this the designs were painted in black. The early designs were often hatched or were similar to the black-on-white designs of the period.

After A.D. 1150 the Virgin River area was abandoned and further development took place only in the Kayenta area.

The Later Kayenta Culture—A.D. 1100–1300

Aggregation on a large scale started in the Chaco at about A.D. 950, at Mesa Verde at about A.D. 1000–1050, but in the Kayenta area not until about A.D. 1150. Villages had formerly consisted of a block of front-oriented surface dwellings of two to six units, associated storage rooms, and one to several pit houses, and at least one kiva. Now they ranged from ten to forty rooms and even up to two hundred units. At that time and after, changes in the settlement pattern are noted. This may have been due to some population displacement, since the marginal areas for agriculture were less exploitable as the climate became less favorable.

At any rate, pressures of one kind or another were being exerted on the culture, and to survive, it had to adapt. Settlements were less dense and those that survived increased in size.

The new villages, ranging from ten to two hundred rooms, were built on a butte, a ridge, a mesa, always in elevated positions, or in a cliff shelter high above the valley floor. Above all, the new site was to be near arable land but not on it.

Dr. Lindsay (Lindsay, 1969) feels that the villages of this period (A.D. 1230–1300) were socioeconomic communities representing completely different patterns than had previously existed. More contiguous housing units, more people (maybe some strange and "different"), more crowding—mix these ingredients and you have troubles, new adjustments, and maybe quarrels. This situation may have been true at the other aggregations—Mesa Verde and Chaco Canyon. Perhaps they were suffering in microcosm the same sort of malaise that afflicts us. Now each village had more households living together, and each household had to have more territory.

The typical community, consisting of one or more families, was organized around a work area called a courtyard. This was a physical entity, set off from other room clusters by walls, wattle-and-daub screens, or by a room block.

Rooms were rectangular, averaging about 70 to 80 square feet of floor space, contiguous, and of one or more stories, especially in caves. The masonry typically was made up of blocks and slabs laid horizontally in copious amounts of mortar into which rock spalls and potsherds were crammed. Some rooms in the same household unit were built of jacal—wattle-and-daub—or wattle-and daub construction was employed for constructing newly added rooms or for partitions within rooms.

Pit houses occurred as individual structures separated from the main block of rooms or were constructed so as to be included in or near the room block. Sometimes a pit house was entered from a dwelling block by means of a short tunnel or ramp. The precise function of pit houses at this period is not known, but Lindsay (1969) believes they may have been used as corn-grinding rooms. It is ironic to note how old nations can be overturned at any moment. Twenty years ago we phased pit houses out of existence—in the Anasazi area—at about A.D. 500–700. Our paradigm told us that they had passed out of fashion when surface structures appeared. Here, however, in the Kayenta area, we have pit houses being built and utilized at A.D. 1250–1300. What has happened to our neat timetable? And because of the paradigm under which we operated in the 1940s and 1950s, we probably missed several pit houses that were contemporary with surface structures dating at about A.D. 1100. And when we did find and dig one (Higgins Flat Pueblo, Martin *et al.*, 1956) we were puzzled by its presence.

Living quarters were usually equipped with a fire pit and an entry unit, a kind of boxlike structure of masonry into which one stepped as he entered the room. This entry unit may be likened roughly to the foot-disinfecting bath in a swimming pool between the shower and the pool itself. The purpose of the entry-box unit was of an entirely different nature: its purpose may have been to prevent drafts from disturbing the fire. Attached to the living quarters were storage rooms for housing gear, implements, clothing, bedding, pottery and basket-containers—a kind of tack-room arrangement. It is typical of late Kayenta and is unique to the Kayenta culture.

Storage of foods was done in specially built rooms called granaries. These were

PLATE 23 Oraibi Pueblo, Arizona, as it looked between 1890 and 1900. In left foreground is a ladder leading to subterranean kiva. Though much depleted in size and population, it still exists today on the third Mesa. Photo taken by Field Museum photographer about 1890–1900.

PLATE 24 Interior of dwelling room of Hopi house, Oraibi village, Arizona, as it looked about 1900. In background are four metates or milling stones in mealing bins. Photo taken by Field Museum photographer.

built aboveground, with masonry walls of closely spaced stones set in well-spalled mud-mortar. The exterior walls were smooth and well plastered. Entry was by means of a small door or hatchway; but whatever the entry type, careful provision was made for sealing the opening from the outside to keep out pests. Floors were either bedrock, plastered earth, or paved with close-fitting stone slabs. Each extended family might have had a granary or sometimes the community shared a communal granary. Granaries might be built within a cave, in a

ledge, or under a slump of boulders usually near arable land. If they occurred within the settlement they were either separate rooms or attached to a group of rooms. Most of them appear as separate but contiguous structures in a room cluster.

Two major village patterns occurred in late Kayenta culture: the courtyard community and the plaza-oriented community.

A courtyard is an open, unroofed area of irregular or rectangular shape surrounded by two or more room clusters—that is, living rooms, storerooms and granaries, and

PLATE 26　View of a kiva interior at Mishongnovi Pueblo located on the Second or middle Mesa in the Hopi country, northeastern Arizon. Picture-taking within the village and inside of kivas is prohibited today. Photo taken by Field Museum photographer about 1900.

PLATE 25　A Hopi matron making pottery by means of the coil method. Vessels in foreground are drying slowly in the shade before being placed in a kiln. Houses in background are in the village of Oraibi, now almost defunct. Photo taken by Field Museum photographer about 1890–1900. Photograph courtesy of the Field Museum of Natural History.

sometimes a grinding room. Room clusters could stand alone but usually they adjoined other clusters and courtyards.

Doors from these rooms opened onto the courtyard. The perimeter of the court was marked by a low wall of masonry or wattle-and-daub. Entryway to the court was merely an opening in the wall. The floor of a courtyard could contain any one or all of the following features: a fire pit, mealing bins, storage pits, bedrock mortars, abrading grooves, and loom anchors. A large settlement could have many room clusters— ten or more—each with a courtyard.

A plaza-oriented community—less common than courtyard—was really a rectangular complex, part of which was composed of solid (no doorways) walls of rooms and where no rooms existed of masonry and/or wattle-and-daub walls. One ends up with a kind of hollow-square layout. A gap in the east side served as the entry to the plaza and to the room clusters, courtyards, and storage rooms. A kiva was located within the square.

Each of these village plans suggests several kinds of social grouping: extended family, lineages, lineage segments.

Kivas occurred in both courtyard and plaza groupings. Circular kivas were more common, were small—about 10 to 14 feet in diameter—and were probably older in the area. Rectangular kivas occurred only at the latest sites; they were uncommon in the Anasazi area but were very common in the area of the Mogollon variant of the Anasazi—that is, in the Mogollon mountains-Reserve area of west-central New Mexico and in the country drained by the upper reaches of the Little Colorado River. For our purposes, we shall dwell principally on the circular kiva.

A Kayenta kiva was subterranean or in a simulated pseudo-subterranean position, was somewhat simpler than the best ones in the Mesa Verde area but in general resembled the Mesa Verde type. Some were cylindrical with walls rising directly from the floor to the roof. Others had a bench encircling the perimeter and a deeper recess or "altar" on the south side. Walls were usually built of masonry, but occasionally of jacal. Roofs were flat, not cribbed as at Mesa Verde. They were supported by the outer walls of the structure and by secondary upright posts. Usually, as at Mesa Verde, the sipapu, fire pit, deflector, and ventilator were aligned more or less north-south. The ventilator apparatus was similar to those described for the Chaco and the Mesa Verde area. In the Kayenta, sometimes the fresh air was vented into the chamber from a subfloor position or at floor level.

Rectangular kivas were also small and were usually provided with a platform on the south side, a ventilator, and were often not subterranean or only semisubterannean.

The number of kivas per village varied. Sometimes a village of ten rooms had one; a village of twelve rooms had two kivas; and one of over a hundred rooms, six or seven. Great Kivas and towers, however, were unknown in the Kayenta area.

Loopholes in walls have brought forth many comments and much speculation. A loophole, here, was a small rectangular opening in the wall and resembled a slit window. Loopholes pointed straight ahead, upward, downward, or at an angle. They were most commonly found in the outer blank walls of the linear room blocks at plaza-oriented sites.

What were the loopholes for? No one knows for certain. Lindsay (1969) hypothesizes that they may have been used as a measure of defense. Late sites are located so as to have had a good view of all surrounding terrain. There are many practical reasons for locating villages on high ground, but perhaps the principal reason was so that they could watch their fields of crops. In sum, the author prefers to classify these villages as defensible. That is, they could have been defended. If defense was necessary, who was the enemy? Not the Navajo, or the Utes. Maybe the Kayenta people thought defense might be necessary against their cousins and other distant relatives who were helping to swell the size of the towns. Perhaps competition for arable, irrigable land was becoming stiffer, and one had to guard his interests.

POTTERY

Some of the superficial aspects of Kayenta culture appear (to me) to be cramped, contorted, impoverished, miserly, hostile to change. Such a judgment is subjective and

PLATE 27 "Katchina" bowl—Four Mile Polychrome. From about A.D. 1200 to 1375. Katchinas represent deified ancestral spirits who visit the pueblos to bring blessings and rain to the land. If figures do represent proto-katchinas, they are among the earliest known. Southwestern Archaeological Expedition of Field Museum, 1959.

cannot be demonstrated; it merely represents the author's feelings.

Pottery, however, was really exuberant and innovative. One has the feeling that here the people could "let go" and express themselves beyond the courtyard philosophy. Certainly, of all of the artifacts that have come down to us, ceramics were elaborate and elegant.

Again, we have two major divisions: cooking versus painted wares.

Cooking pottery was all-over corrugated. The principal shape was a large, globular-shaped jar. They were gray except when sooted from cooking. Sometimes, smaller muglike corrugated jars with handles were manufactured. Occasionally, corrugated bowls and plain gray ladles turn up.

The painted pottery consists of: (1) a black-on-white type; (2) a black-on-red type; (3) a polychrome (red designs on an orange-red background with designs edged in black), and (4) a red-on-orange. There were bowls, jars, ladles, colanders, muglike jugs. Black paint on the black-on-white type was carbon (organic origin). Designs are varied and well executed in strict geometric layout patterns. So much design was applied on the black-on-white type that it looks more black than white. They consist of interlocking frets, scrolls alternating with panels of plain or ticked lines; or interlocking flags; crosshatched lines or checkerboard motifs that are called "mosquito bar" design because of its resemblance to netting.

Lindsay (1969) considers that the black-on-reds, polychromes, and black-on-orange types stem from an early (Pueblo I) black-on-orange ware found in the Mesa Verde-Ackmen-Lowry areas in Colorado and at Alkali Ridge, Utah.

Designs on the orange ware and polychromes are not the same as those used on black-on-white types and almost belie description. Simple- and crosshatching, terraces, encircling stripes, an S center arrangement, quartered layouts, a meander in the form of a swastika, and interlocking scrolls are merely a few of the design elements. It is felt here that these black-on-white and orange types are the most beautiful of prehistoric ceramics.

What became of the Kayenta people? Why was the area abandoned at about A.D. 1300? Where did they go?

Upper Little Colorado River Valley

We have excavated several pueblos in the vicinity of Springerville, Show Low, and St. Johns, Arizona (Martin and Rinaldo, 1960a, 1960b; Martin *et al.*, 1962; Martin, Longacre, and Hill, 1967).

The *Thode Site* on the banks of Mineral Creek near Highway 60 and about twenty miles west of Springerville may represent a transition between pit houses and a pueblo. The eleven irregularly shaped rooms resemble shallow pit houses built fairly close to one another; they might be called semicontiguous. All were small, were of one story and were built of crude masonry. No kiva was found. The estimated

date of the pueblo is about A.D. 1100; population, 20 to 25 persons.

Rim Valley Pueblo, on the ranch of Rob Hooper, stands near the edge of a mesa overlooking the Little Colorado River. The building consists of nineteen contiguous rooms built of masonry, disposed in a straight row running north and south, two rooms wide. Eleven rooms were dug.

A similar row of double rooms may lie to the west across a plaza. Masonry was inferior and was made up of upright slabs and cobbles.

The pueblo may have consisted of about twenty-five rooms of one story. One room, larger than the others, possessed a few features that suggested it may have served as a ceremonial place. An estimated date of about A.D. 1225 was made for this town; population about 50 to 60 persons.

Hooper Ranch Pueblo, on the ranch of Rob Hooper, is situated east of Rim Valley Pueblo and is right on the east bank of the Little Colorado River. Indeed, it is possible that floods have carried away parts of this town.

The size of the pueblo has been estimated at sixty rooms and probably contained two stories.

The major distinction of this pueblo is that it was provided with three kivas: one small, one intermediate, and one Great Kiva, all rectangular. The small one was floored with slabs and furnished with a platform or bench on the west side, and a ventilator. Adjoining it, to the south, was the intermediate-sized kiva provided with a packed dirt floor, a central fire pit, a vault, a ventilator, and a platform or bench on the south side.

Adjoining that kiva to the south was the Great Kiva, constructed apparently after the others. It was of noble proportions and measured 50 by 47 feet. The major features were: a ramp entry over 7 feet wide and about 7 feet long leading eastward; between the inner part of the ramp and the fire pit was a mammoth slab—about 7 feet long and 3 feet high—that served as a deflector; a bench abutted all four walls; crude vaults were located in the north and south halves of the floor area; in the south half of the floor was a crypt 15 by 14 inches and 11 inches deep roofed with a ring slab and sealed with a sandstone slab. In the crypt were a female effigy painted in stripes of yellow, blue, red, and black, and a painted miniature jar that contained black and white stone beads. The figure is a rare if not unique type and is considered to be a cult deity rather than a proto-katchina Martin *et al.*, 1962, pp. 64–74).

A pollen study indicated that heavy summer rainfalls were frequent. Nevertheless, our impression was that irrigation or water control of some kind was also practiced (Martin *et al.*, 1962, pp. 168–206).

The probable date of the kiva was A.D. 1230 (a carbon 14 date); population of pueblo, about 250 persons.

Some aspects of this site showed relationships with Zuni pueblos—about 60 miles to the north and east.

Table Rock Pueblo, which we excavated in 1958 (Martin and Rinaldo, 1960b), is located just two miles east of St. Johns on the east bank of the Little Colorado River and is on the ranch of Mark Davis. The pueblo, situated on a very low rock outcropping, probably consisted, at one time, of sixty to a hundred rooms. We excavated fifty rooms and two kivas. Rooms were only one story high. The plan of the village followed the contour of the hillock, the rooms were strung out in two ranks, each three rooms wide. Almost all the southernmost rooms had fire pits; these may have been the living quarters. Rooms averaged 9 by 7½ feet.

One rectangular kiva (about 13 by 12 feet), incorporated into a house row, was floored with fitted slabs (a most unusual and a Hopi- and Zuni-like feature), had an altar on the south, and was provided with a rectangular fire pit and adjoining ash pit. Loom holes were located east of the fire pit. The other kiva—15 by 13 feet—was below the mesa, and was less well built.

The relationship between this site and those of the Zuni and/or Hopi Indians is pronounced, especially in the architecture and pottery (Zuni glazes).

The construction date of the pueblo is presumed to have been about A.D. 1350. Estimate of population: 100 to 125 people.

Carter Ranch Site, property of James Carter, lies nine miles east of Snowflake, Arizona, and overlooks Hay Hollow Wash, a tributary of the Little Colorado River. It was a two-story pueblo of about forty rooms, two kivas, and a Great Kiva. Twenty-three rooms were excavated, which were built in the form of a hollow square and the enclosed plaza contained the medium-sized kiva and a small rectangular kiva with platform on the east, various fire and roasting or barbecue pits, and an extraordinarily large jug-shaped storage pit, about 6 feet deep and about 6 feet in diameter at floor level. It had been covered by a stone cap. On the bottom of the pit was a quantity of shelled, charred corn.

The burial ground lay to the east of the eastern boundary wall and yielded some thirty burials. The analysis of the burials, associated pottery and pottery designs made by Longacre resulted in the first research on the sociological implications of ceramic analysis in the Southwest (Longacre, W. A., *in* Martin *et al.*, 1964, pp. 155–70). Briefly, Longacre found that two lineages had inhabited the town and that males of status were buried in the central part of the cemetery.

The Great Kiva located about 40 feet

PLATE 28 Looking into crypt in which stone effigy figure was found. Slab that covered "ringslab," at left. Pottery jar and right side of effigy (lying upside down) may be seen as first discovered on slab floor of crypt. Arrow (30 cm. long) points north. Southwestern Archaeological Expedition of Field Museum, 1959.

PLATE 29 Female image, carved from sandstone. Probably of great sanctity. Height, 8¼ inches. Dated about A.D. 1230. Southwestern Archaeological Expedition of Field Museum, 1960.

northwest of the village, was round (about 55 feet in diameter), and contained five masonry pillars to support the roof, a fire hearth, and a ramp entry leading out to the east.

The report on Carter Ranch (Martin, *et al.*, 1964) contained several other "firsts." Freeman and Brown ran a statistical analysis on the pottery on a Univac computer, the first time such an analysis was ever done on ceramics from the Southwest. They demonstrated that four groups of pottery may have been used for functionally diverse purposes. One type was probably used for mortuary or ceremonial purposes. The grouping also indicated that there were four room types each devoted to different cultural activities; and one pottery type seemed to have been used both within the rooms and on the rooftops.

The environment of the area for the past seven thousand years was derived by the study—paleoecology—of fossil pollen obtained from cores from Laguna Salada, a now dry lake bed. The work was done by Dr. Richard Hevly and extended our knowledge about climate and climatic changes for the Southwest by several millennia.

The report also contains a synthesis of Upper Little Colorado prehistory covering three thousand years (Longacre, *in* Martin *et al.,* 1964, pp. 201–15).

Carbon 14 dates for the pueblo indicate that it flourished from about A.D. 950 to 1200; population, about 200 persons.

Broken K Pueblo, in Hay Hollow Valley, also on the ranch of James Carter, is located about nine miles east of Snowflake, Arizona, and about five miles north of Carter Ranch Site. It was a pueblo of about ninety rooms, one story high, built in the form of a hollow square. The plaza contained one kiva and several fire and roasting pits. Within the house block itself were two small kivas floored with slabs. The forty-eight rooms excavated were chosen by a random sampling technique—the first site in the Southwest to be so treated. Hill (*in* Martin, Longacre, and Hill, 1967) directed the operations and wrote a doctoral dissertation on the results (Hill, 1970). By means of analysis based on ceramic and ceramic designs, fossil pollen, sizes and uses of rooms, and stone artifacts, Hill concluded that the pueblo was inhabited by five uxorilocal residence subgroups that fell into two larger units (clans?). This was the second time that a sociocultural analysis was done for a Southwestern prehistoric site.

The pueblo was dated by carbon 14 and tree-ring methods at about A.D. 1150–1280. The population estimate is about 150–200 persons.

PLATE 30 Four bins in which food were milled or ground, Broken K pueblo, Carter Ranch, Arizona. The grinders, female, perhaps two or three at a time, knelt in the space between mealing bins and wall of room 92 (top of photo). In each compartment was a milling stone (metate) and at lower end (nearer the reader) were hollowed stones that acted as receptacles for collecting ground foods. In the middle of the room was a rectangular fire pit and adjacent to it was the ash pit. Charcoal from fire pit dated at about A.D. 1250. Southwestern Archaeological Expedition of Field Museum, 1963.

Patayan Culture
(Lower Colorado River Culture)

Up to this point, we have dealt with the Anasazi culture at some length—Chaco Canyon, Mesa Verde, Kayenta, and the Upper Little Colorado areas. We have alluded to the Hohokam and Mogollon cultures. Both will be discussed later; the latter to be treated in chapter X, "Adaptation of Man to the Mountains." We will now describe a Patayan site.

Patayan is the term given to a peripheral prehistoric culture that has only recently been recognized as such. It differed some-

what from the Anasazi, Hohokam, or Mogollon cultures and yet was influenced by
both Hohokam and Anasazi. As we now
know it, the Patayan culture apparently
was not as distinctive and able to stand on
its own feet as were the Hohokam and
Anasazi. It is a kind of useful classification
for taking care of all those traits that are
not clearly and unmistakably Anasazi or
Hohokam. Its locus is mainly the Lower
Colorado River Basin.

This anomalous culture has had ardent
defenders beginning with Rogers (1945),
Colton (1945), and ending up with Schroeder (1957, pp. 176–78). Originally the
culture was called "Yuman" by Rogers because the Colorado Valley was occupied
by Yuman Indians. But Colton and others
objected to this ethnic, linguistic term for
the archaeological cultures of the area because the term assumed without proof that
all the archaeological complexes of the
Colorado Valley were of Yuman Indian
derivation. This may be so or partially so,
but it has not yet been demonstrated.

At any rate, Colton suggested that the
Yuman word for "old people"—*Patayan*—
be employed to designate all prehistoric
Lower Colorado River Valley archaeological manifestations. The term Patayan includes several major subdivisions, namely
the Cohonina who occupied the country
south from the Grand Canyon to the San
Francisco Mountain volcanic field, the Prescott, the area in and around the city of
Prescott, Arizona, and the Cerbat, who occupied the area in the big bend of the
Colorado River, near Needles, California.
Schroeder in 1957 suggested that the term
Hakataya—which means Colorado River
in the Walapai and Havasupai Indian languages—be employed to cover Patayan and
all the archaeological remains of the southern California area. The argument is complicated and rests in part on taxonomic se-

mantics and a willingness to see differences,
disregarded by some workers, of importance. For the time being, until more hypotheses are stated and tested, we shall
continue to use the term Patayan for the
western Arizona-Lower Colorado River
Valley basin areas.

Briefly, the Patayan (Hakataya) culture
is not well known, sites are not numerous
(perhaps due to recent alluviation and silt-
ing that may have covered ancient sites),
and the poverty of material remains make
it difficult to set forth a bold, distinctive
picture of what the culture was really like.
Nevertheless, there appears to be an archaeological record in the area significantly different from the Anasazi, Mogollon, and Hohokam traditions and worthy
of more research. It is not unlikely that the
Patayan-Hakataya arguments may end up
like those concerning the separateness of
the Mogollon culture. During the 1940s,
several of us were hell-bent on demonstrating that the Mogollon culture was not only
a separate taxonomic and important subdivision of Southwestern cultures, but one
of equal rank with Hohokam and Anasazi.
We seized on any difference—shape of
pots, of houses—to stress our point. True,
ceramics and agriculture may have been
older in the mountainous Mogollon area,
but today the feeling is that we were arguing about unimportant entities and missing
the fact that the Mogollon culture was a
special adaptation of some Cochise-Hoho-
kam-Anasazi characteristics. The main
point was that it was both Anasazi and
Hohokam with special adaptations to a
rugged environment. Hence, the argument
was really much ado about nothing, especially when the meaning of the various
traits is not known and yet overemphasized.

The antecedent culture of Patayan is a
branch of the Desert culture. Rogers
(1945) calls this antecedent the Amargosa

(about 1000 B.C.). The earliest houses were fragile pole and brush structures, circular and built on the surface of the ground. Mortars and pestles were employed to reduce foods to a cookable state, and meat and vegetal products were roasted outside the houses in pits. Maize was eventually added—about A.D. 400—to the previous subsistence of hunting and gathering. Irrigation was not practiced as such, but inundation from spring freshets was used to supply the plants with water. Pottery, introduced about A.D. 400–600, was plain ware, brown or gray in color after firing, and was made by a paddle and anvil technique. After A.D. 1050 ceramics reflected influence from the Hohokam with some red-on-buff decoration. Cremation was the usual method of disposing of the dead, although this may not hold true for the whole area. Trade with both Anasazi and Hohokam peoples has been noted.

Very few Patayan sites have been dug; however in 1949, McGregor excavated some twenty-one sites (McGregor, 1951). They are located near U.S. Highway 64 between Williams and Grand Canyon.

The houses were surface structures and were round, rectangular, and irregular in shape. Walls were of wood or brush or very low, crude masonry, never over five feet high. Of the twenty-one wood and stone units dug, only two were shallow pit houses. Most houses were provided with a roofed porchlike affair—called a patio, or a shade, or a ramada. Here cooking and other activities were carried on, as fire pits were never found within the sleeping rooms. The patios must have been pleasant, cool places for doing kitchen work as the sides were open to the breezes.

The principal pottery types were Deadman's Gray, mostly plain-ware jars; Deadman's Gray Tooled—with wide-neck coils present, but otherwise like Deadman's Gray; and Deadman's Black-on-Gray—in bowl forms with designs resembling those from the Kayenta area on the interior.

Subsistence data are rare, but corn was probably grown as well as squash. Antelope, mule deer, jack rabbits, and cottontails were probably eaten, as bones from these fauna were found in the refuse.

Percussion-flaked choppers were used instead of the ground stone-axes elsewhere. Sea shells were imported from the Gulf of California and were traded to other Southwestern groups.

Part of a human skeleton was found in a cave, but the manner of disposing of the dead at these particular sites is not known.

The houses yield a spread of dates from about A.D. 748 to 1070.

The Cohaninan subculture is the best known of the various subgroups and Schwartz (1966, pp. 469–84) has also added to our knowledge concerning this branch of the Patayan culture. Among other researches, he has shown that the Cohonina people entered the plateau country around the Grand Canyon at about A.D. 600. By A.D. 900, they had reached a population climax and maintained that climax for about two hundred years and even expanded into and near the bottom of the Canyon. By A.D. 1100 or 1200 they had completely abandoned the plateau and even their houses in the Canyon bottom and took refuge in cliffs and easily defended canyons. There is some evidence for assuming that the contemporary Havasupai Indians are the cultural descendants of the Cohonina.

The Sinagua Tradition

The Sinagua as well as the Patayan are subcultures about which there are interminable arguments concerned with their origin and their place in the cultural galaxy.

These are based mostly on taxonomic or classificatory quibbles. Since the various scholars who have worked with cultures of the Arizona area in the regions of Flagstaff, the Verde River, Prescott, and the northwestern quarter of the state do not agree among themselves on the disposition of the several dozen cultural manifestations, it is obviously impossible to set forth a clear schematic representation. Again, the trouble lies in the traditional definition of what culture is. The concept used is outmoded and relies on the *forms* of tools, house styles, pottery colors and shapes—in short, a trait list. This definition does not lend itself to the kinds of questions that archaeologists now think are relevant. The traditional concept of culture does not recognize that culture is a system whose parts are in mutual interaction. It is adaptive; it is a response to a total ecological situation—social and environmental. The arguments about whether the Sinagua tradition had slab houses and black-on-white pottery or the Patayan brush shelters and a gray pottery are irrelevant. In doing research, one often finds pages devoted to minutiae of pottery types and perhaps a paragraph devoted to subsistence, ecology, demography, social groups, and settlement patterns. Our preoccupation with tabulations of data and charts showing presence and absence of arrow smoothers, hoes, and nose plugs forces the conclusion that we are unwilling to wrestle with the problems and objectives of our discipline. Mere dating and classifying are no longer considered important in conceiving theories for framing strategic researches.

For our purposes, we accept Colton's feeling that the Sinagua is a cultural entity and that it is more closely related to the Mogollon than to any other culture. The Verde Valley, the areas around Winslow, Arizona, Flagstaff, and the central part of the state are the chief areas where the Sinagua sub-branches are found.

There are many Sinagua sites—beginning about A.D. 500 and reaching a climax about 1300. House types included pit houses, surface rooms with kivas, and pueblo-like architecture with a cellular arrangement of rooms. Since most of the features of these sites resemble those of the Kayenta culture, a breakdown of traits is omitted because it would be a duplication of others already given.

One remarkable natural event that occurred between A.D. 1046 and 1070 was the volcanic eruption of Sunset Crater. About 800 square miles of the area between Flagstaff and the Little Colorado River at Winslow were covered with a layer of black volcanic ash.

People who were living in the area in pit houses fled and left behind their homes and belongings, which were totally buried under volcanic ash. The original populations plus newcomers returned sometime between A.D. 1100 and 1200 and resettled the area, which now had greater agricultural potential. The cinders when cooled and settled acted as a mulch to conserve moisture and this made growing crops a much simpler matter. Stick a seed in the earth below the cinder mulch and you were able to produce a plant. Present feelings are that the news of this new, rich territory spread far and wide and attracted the unsuccessful, the dreamers. The population of the area expanded enormously after the eruption. After a time, perhaps two hundred years, the cinders were blown about and gradually formed dunes so that the heavy clay soil was no longer covered and the people began to move away. By A.D. 1300 the area around the Flagstaff area was abandoned.

The Sinagua site described below is the Ridge Ruin, a small masonry ruin about twenty miles east of Flagstaff, Arizona. It was chosen because it dates from the post-eruption era, because it is fairly typical of the area, and because it yielded a burial, the like of which in the Southwest has never been equaled.

The pueblo sat astride a small cone overlooking a valley. It consisted of about twenty-five rooms, many of which were two stories in height. Masonry belonging to the earlier section was of good true courses, resembling that of Chaco Canyon; the later walls were of basalt boulders. Rooms averaged 36 square feet. Near the main pueblo were several masonry-lined pit houses, a feature common to many Kayenta pueblos. About 400 feet away lay a ball court of the Casa Grande type. It was probably in use during the lifetime of the pueblo, which dates at about A.D. 1080–1175.

In the middle of the floor on one of these pit houses a pit had been dug and carefully roofed with poles. In this pit was found a most remarkable burial. (For an exacting account of this see McGregor, 1943, pp. 270–98.) The body of a man had been placed in the three-feet-deep pit. After offerings had been placed with the body, the pit was roofed with poles and they in turn with dirt. The room was never again used for any purpose since it was quickly filled up and obliterated with refuse. The burial is dated at about A.D. 1125.

With the deceased were over six hundred articles, many of which were of such excellent workmanship and unique execution that the burial represents one of the richest ever found. If it had been in a dry cave, even more objects—cloth, leather, basketry, wood—would have been preserved.

One should consult the original report, which contains reproductions in color of some of the strange, barbaric ritualistic objects. The following is a partial list of the objects:

25 whole pots, most of which were bowls.

8 fragments of baskets, some plain, some coated and then painted, and one covered with a mosaic made up of turquoise, red argillite rectangles, and orange-colored rodent teeth ground down to match the other tesserae.

420 arrow points (3 of bone).

Stone ornaments such as turquoise ear pendants, turquoise pendants and 107 turquoise beads, 3,600 stone beads, a button made of jet (lignite), a bracelet containing 73 turquoise beads, a nose plug made of argillite with turquoise ends; a cap, like a skullcap, made of beads; two ear pendants carved from Californian shell, fishhook blanks; ceremonial sticks carved and painted to represent hands, and antelope feet all of which lay across the pelvis.

Crystals, minerals for paint (?)—hematite, ocher, copper ore.

Bags filled with cinnabar.

Mountain lion claws, painted and drilled canine teeth, parrot skeletons.

The age of the individual at death is estimated to have been thirty-five or forty years. He had been about 5 feet, 8 inches tall. Some of the pottery bowls contained remnants of food, lac (a natural resinous substance), corn meal, bear (?) hair, squash rinds, and seeds (not identified).

Obviously this man was a person of importance, even of superior importance. It does not seem too far-fetched to regard him as a man of high status. Apparently individual wealth and social stratification may have existed eight hundred years ago among these Sinagua people.

THE HOHOKAM CULTURE
C. 300 B.C.–C. A.D. 1200–1300

Earlier, we mentioned that there were two principal cultural variations in the Southwest: the Anasazi and the Hohokam.

Up to about 1928 the Hohokam culture was considered as an aberrant or peripheral form of the Basket Maker-Pueblo (Anasazi) culture. As stated before, Mr. and Mrs. Harold S. Gladwin, who founded the research institution called Gila Pueblo, Globe, Arizona, demonstrated that the culture of the Gila-Salt River Valleys was a configuration distinct from the Puebloan. This tradition we shall now examine. Haury (1967), who is one of the authorities on this tradition, refers to the Hohokam as the first masters of the American Desert.

Another specialist on the cultures of Gila-Salt River Valleys of southern Arizona is Dr. Charles Di Peso. His researches have led him to a different interpretation of the history of the area. The matter is complex and rests on differing constructions, explications, and readings of the evidence. Both Haury and Di Peso are scholars, careful workers, and well-informed men. Here, we will attempt to present both sides but briefly.

Haury postulates that the Hohokam tradition is an outgrowth of the Cochise stage of the Desert culture. This development has been well documented in Ventana Cave. Added to the Hohokam culture at various times were borrowed increments from Mexico.

Haury divides the Hohokam culture, after A.D. 1000, into two branches: the Desert branch and the River branch. The River branch was represented by the classic Hohokam whose villages centered on the Gila and Salt Rivers. The Desert branch people inhabited southwestern Arizona, known as the Papagueria, lying west of Tucson and now set aside as the Papago Indian Reservation.

The best way to illustrate the differences of these two branches of the Hohokam culture is to list them as Haury did (Haury, 1950, p. 547):

RIVER BRANCH	DESERT BRANCH
Cremation	Earth burial
Red-on-buff pottery, not polished	Red-on-brown pottery, polished
Red ware, black interiors	Red ware, red interiors
Full-troughed metate, well shaped	Block metate, some shaping, not troughed, as a rule
Great array of projectile points, delicate workmanship	Limited projectile point types, few in number, workmanship poor
Well-developed carved stone	Carved stone weakly represented
Few chopping, scraping, and cutting tools	Abundance of roughly chipped chopping, scraping, and cutting tools
Slate palette	Slate palette, little used
Stone and shell jewelry, abundant and elaborate	Stone and shell jewelry, rare and simple
Figurine complex strong	Figurines, rare
Large-scale irrigation systems drawing water from streams	Limited irrigation canals, designed to catch surface runoff
Subsistence primarily agriculture	Subsistence primarily collecting
Heavy Salado intrusion after 1300	Little affected by Salado

Summing up these classificatory differences, it seems apparent that the Desert branch division is merely an indifferent copy of the classic or River Hohokam.

Di Peso's interpretation of the various historical sequences of the area is that the earliest phases at Snaketown and elsewhere in the Gila-Salt drainage should be attributed to the Ootam (a word taken from the Pima Indian language and the term by which the Pima, who still inhabit southern Arizona, refer to themselves). Ootam is classed by him also as an offshoot of the Cochise (Desert) culture. The early "formative" of the Ootam people is dated by Di Peso as existing between A.D. 1 and about 400 or 500, and late formative Ootam from A.D. 500 to about 1000. These time spans would embrace the Snaketown periods of Pioneer, Colonial, and about half of the Sedentary period. Then at about A.D. 1000 the Ootam (Gila-Salt drainages) were taken over by a band of intruders, the Hohokam, from Mexico. Some of the Ootam were absorbed by the Hohokam; and others were pushed back into the fringes of the area where they survived as a group known as the Desert branch of the Hohokam.

The Hohokam intruders are credited with having introduced a number of new culture traits: large, intricate irrigation systems, new races of maize, large village concentrations, new technical skills in working stone, bone, wood, and shell, as well as new pottery designs and shapes, mosaic plaques (mirrors), copper bells, etched shell, nose buttons, ear plugs, ball courts, and perhaps a new social system that included caste or class divisions (Di Peso, 1956, pp. 253–64).

Still another conjecture concerning Hohokam origins was advanced by Schroeder (1960). His proposition is that the earliest period of Hohokam (the Pioneer period, about 300 B.C.–A.D. 500) was brought about as a fusion of Patayan and Sinagua traditions and he would lump them all into a Hakataya base culture equal taxonomically with Anasazi and Hohokam. He would also (like Di Peso) class the later periods of Snaketown—post A.D. 500—as the result of a Hohokam intrusion from Mexico.

It is apparent that there are a few similarities and many differences in these points of view. One factor that is common to the theories of the three scholars is that much of Hohokam culture was derived from Mexico—by borrowing, diffusion, or invasion.

After one handles and studies the artifacts from the Gila-Salt drainages, it is easy to see why the simplistic explanations of either diffusion or invasion sprang into existence. Nothing could be more natural.

From our point of view the explanations offered are superficial and do not take into account the fact that all of them are suppositions that have not been scientifically tested and demonstrated. It is a complex problem, and postulation of diffusion, borrowing, or invasion explains nothing.

In 1934–35, the staff of Gila Pueblo excavated portions of a large ancient site, called Snaketown, about thirty miles south and east of Phoenix, Arizona (Gladwin, Haury, Sayles, and Gladwin, 1937).

Snaketown is one of the largest known Hohokam sites and covers an area three quarters of a mile north and south and about half a mile east and west. In 1964–65, Haury spent another seven months there doing an intensive study of other portions of the city. Another report on that work is in progress.

Investigations in other Hohokam sites have been undertaken (for example, Di Peso, 1956) but some are not reported in publications, while others represent unpublished theses. Recently, Wasley and Johnson (1965) presented an excellent report on their salvage operations in the region of Gila Bend, Arizona, southwest of Phoenix.

Snaketown lies in the southern Arizona desert—a level sandy area dotted thickly with salt bush and mesquite. Nearby are the twin peaks of Gila Butte and farther away are some low-lying mountains—the Santon to the east, the Estrella to the west, and the Salt River mountains to the northwest. The elevation of the desert there is about 1,000 feet above sea level. Temperatures range from summertime highs of well over 100 degrees, and in wintertime, down to about 30 degrees. Rains occur mostly in the winter and average 8 inches annually. It is an arid area—but here people lived, raised crops, and flourished for over fourteen centuries, or from about 300 B.C. to A.D. 1100.

Houses were individually built and were not contiguous as in the Anasazi area. The floors of the houses were dug down below the desert floor about one foot. Vertical posts set in the bottom of the pit supported the roofs and sides, which were constructed of a matting of twigs, reeds, and grass, all of which was covered with earth. The side walls were not perpendicular but slanted inwards. The walls and roof were erected in a pit and independent of it. A house was entered through a vestibule usually parallel-sided, near the middle of one side. Entrances did not always face east or southeast as was usually the case among the Anasazi, but often opened toward any one of the cardinal directions. A basin-shaped fire pit was placed in the floor near the entrance.

The earliest houses were usually larger (about 26 feet by 28 feet, or over 700 square feet of floor space) than the later ones (10 feet by 20 feet, or about 200 square feet of floor space). Shapes also changed: early houses were more or less square; later, rectangular; and latest, elliptical in shape.

Haury (1967, p. 690) estimates that a village may have been made up of a hundred houses at any one period of time. Not too much is known, however, about the settlement patterns and village plans for the Hohokam. Haury (1956, p. 7) states that the dispersal of Hohokam houses was determined largely by access to water and to arable land. Thus, Hohokam villages were mainly confined to river valleys. But even these two basic requirements did not result in compact, concentrated house clusters. The Snaketown people settled in random clusters of houses dispersed over a large area.

From Di Peso's excavations at San Cayetano (Di Peso, 1956, pp. 118–22; and pp. 219–29), we gain a better idea of what an early Hohokam village (A.D. 900–1200) plan was like. The houses, fifty-eight of them, were clustered in five irregular rows that ran north and south. The houses were not contiguous but were separated one from the other by a meter or so. Vestibules or entryways of houses usually faced east. A hard-packed clay area between each row of houses may have served as a street. Cooking pits were scattered about the house units apparently at random. Cremations were placed in a single burial area centrally located. One house, larger than the others and better constructed, is believed to have been devoted to ceremonies. Because compound walls were lacking and since the arrangement of the houses seemed less rigidly fixed, Di Peso felt that the occupants of this village placed more emphasis on village unit than upon a kin unit.

Later, that is after the Hohokam control of the area was broken (about A.D. 1250–1650) by a "reassertion of the Ootam people" (Di Peso, 1956, p. 264), the typical Ootam village plan was reintroduced. This village plan was characteristic of earlier Ootam villages and had lingered on in out-of-the-way valleys during the intrusion of the Hohokam people. Now it reappeared in a more developed form.

The contrast between the earlier village plan and this one is striking. During this period of "reassertion of Ootam people," the entire village of San Cayetano was enclosed by a nondefensive village wall of stone; and within its confines were twenty distinct compound units. Each compound was separated from the others by enclosure walls of adobe, posts, hill terrace levels, or cobblestones. The number of houses in one compound was usually six; and each house faced inward toward the plaza. Burials—inhumations—were placed in a restricted area in the plaza. Certainly, this kind of village plan suggests a clan or an extended family. Houses were built in pits with superstructures of wattle-and-daub.

In this description of village plans, one may have a clue as to what villages in the Hohokam area looked like. But, one must remember that these descriptions come from only one village, and may not fit all time periods in the entire area. But it is the best that can be presented at this time. Some credence is lent the situation, however, by the work of Wasley and Johnson for the Citrus Site near Gila Bend, Arizona.

Recently, Wasley and Johnson (1965, p. 38) partially excavated the Citrus Site There they found evidence for one type of Hohokam settlement pattern: namely, an irregular grouping of the Hohokam *wattle-and-daub in a pit* type of house arranged around a plaza.

Ceremonial Structures

Kivas were unknown in the Hohokam area. Another but very different kind of structure is associated with the Hohokam area. It is often referred to as a "ball court."

Ball Courts

The first of these structures ever to have been thoroughly investigated was at Snaketown (Gladwin, Haury, Sayles, and Gladwin, 1937, pp. 36–49). The structure was a large elongated depression flanked on the longer sides by earthen walls. Its length was estimated to have been about 182 feet; its width, about 55 feet; side walls rose some 13 to 18 feet. Its general shape was an elongated oval.

In the center of the floor and at each end of the court were small stone "markers." It was estimated that this court was built between A.D. 500 and 900.

A second court was excavated at Snaketown. Its general shape is oval and is smaller than the first one (about 72 feet long, 33 feet wide, and with low side walls). End markers were located. The date of construction was placed at about A.D. 900 or later.

Other "ball courts" have been reported from various sites distributed across southern Arizona, from the Gila Bend area to the extreme southwest corner of New Mexico; and up the Verde and Oak Creek Valleys northward to the Little Colorado drainage east of Flagstaff (Ferdon, 1967, p. 4).

What were these courts used for?

They were recognized as some sort of special feature by early explorers (Bandelier, 1892; Cushing, 1890; Fewkes, 1912) and speculation regarding their function ranged from water-storage reservoirs to threshing pits, clay quarries, and sun temples. Pinkley, a former superintendent of Southwestern Monuments, was the first person to trench one of these mysterious depressions and as a result he hypothesized that they were places used for ceremonies, games, or festivals (Pinkley, 1935, p. 388, cited in Gladwin, Haury, Sayles, and Gladwin, 1937, p. 37). In seeking an explanation for their use, Haury was moved to consider them as inspired by the numerous and famous ball courts of Meso-America. According to ethnohistoric documentation the ball game was played by knocking a rubber ball through stone rings set high up in the walls. Players were permitted to use their hips, knees, or elbows for impelling the ball through the ring but were not permitted to use their hands or feet.

Were the courts in Arizona used for a similar game? Haury thought this was a possibility (Gladwin, Haury, Sayles, and Gladwin, 1937, pp. 47–49).

Recently another explanation has been proposed (Ferdon, 1967). The evidence is carefully examined by Ferdon, who concludes that the ball court hypothesis was not demonstrated.

Ferdon (1967) found that contemporary Piman-speaking Indians of southern Arizona, who are regarded as the cultural descendants of the Hohokam Indians, performed a ceremony—the Vikita ceremony—whose function was to prevent floods.

To buttress his argument, he cites the fact that the Pima-Papago Indians possess traits that reflect prehistoric Hohokam traditions—such as house types, red-on-buff pottery, and cremation. He asks, is it not logical to assume that the principal ceremonies, although attenuated, also reflect ceremonies that were handed down from the Hohokam culture?

His answer is in the affirmative, although he admits that ball-court structures of the ancient types do not now exist. But a crude and simple ceremonial complex does exist, the most permanent feature of which is a dance ground or court. It is an elongated area in the desert, 50 to 100 feet long. Temporary enclosures are erected at each end. Ferdon argues that both the ancient ball court and the modern Pima-Papago dance ground may have served as integrating ceremonial devices that were useful in welding together the people in a socio-religious system.

Platform Mounds

In the most recent excavations at Snaketown, Haury (1967, p. 685) located two structures that appear to have had special significance. One of these was a low flat mound, 3 feet high and 50 feet across. The mound was composed of dirt and trash and the top was capped with a coating of adobe. The other was a truncated cone, made up of clean desert soil. In Mexico, such dirt structures evolved into great pyramidal stone-faced structures (Haury, 1967, p. 685). Were ceremonies performed on these specially prepared platforms of the Hohokam? Were structures erected atop these platforms? Platforms also existed at Los Muertos.

In the Gila Bend country, Wasley found another platform mound (Wasley and Johnson, 1965, p. 18). Excavations in it demonstrated that the final stage in the aboriginal construction of it was the sixth in a series of repairs, modifications, and enlargements of it. In all of the preceding stages as well as in the final one, the mound was flat on top, with battered or sloping sides and rounded corners, and was composed of an earth core. In plan view, it was more or less square or rectanguloid in outline. The flat tops as well as the sides of all versions of the mound were covered respectively with a plaster made of caliche a calcium carbonate—or with caliche and adobe mixed together. A house-like structure of wattle-and-daub had been erected on the fourth stage. In its final stage the mound measured—at the base—70 by 95 feet and rose about 12 feet above the plaza floor (Wasley, 1960a).

Pottery, Stone, and Shell Artifacts

While the architecture of the Hohokam villages may not win any prizes, this cannot be said of their pots and tools.

Hohokam pottery was of several types— plain red, plain brown-gray, and decorated, all of which are decorated with red paint on a gray background (early) (red-on-gray), or on a buff background (red-on-buff). No indented corrugated and no black-on-white wares were manufactured. Incising or grooving—emphasizing the troughs between the coils—did occur.

The red-on-buff types are a delight to behold and occurred in bowl forms of many varieties, in jar forms with and without a "shoulder" (the abrupt inward turn of the outer walls of the vessel) low down on the vessel, legged vessels, effigy forms, scoops, and plates. The forms were distinctive and did not resemble, for the most part, any Anasazi form.

The designs were mostly geometric, but the manner in which they were used demonstrated a consummate ingenuity, artistry, skill, and a drollness that are indescribable. Of course, there were scrolls, hatchings, terraced figures, bull's eyes—but these are merely conventional terms and do not convey the unconventional uses of them nor the whimsical ways in which they were combined. The life-forms were entertaining and zestful. Birds, animals, lizards, people, and masked dancers were portrayed with abandon. The facial expression of some of the birds was life-like, solemn, and waggish.

Many of the stone artifacts exhibit a beauty and symmetry often lacking in Anasazi counterparts. Metates and manos, for example, were symmetrical and well shaped. Some of the stone vessels were striking in proportions; they were often polished, incised, and carved in relief to show snakes, frogs, lizards, mountain sheep, and people. Other stone vessels were effigy forms representing tools, birds, bears, mountain sheep, ducks, and coiled snakes.

Stone palettes were one of the distinctive Hohokam traits. They consisted of a flat oblong slab of smoothed stone, usually slate, with a raised border often sculptured and a depressed mixing surface. They were not large—perhaps 2 to 7 inches wide and 4 to 10 inches long. But the sheer delicacy of manufacture is impressive. Their use is not known.

Ornaments of shell were worn—carved bracelets, carved rings, beads, and pendants. Most of these objects exhibit skillful artistry. Some shell ornaments bore designs in relief produced by means of acid etching. Bells of cast copper, turquoise pendants, nose buttons of soapstone, and ear plugs were some of the items of fashion; bells may have been worn on ankles or wrists in ceremonial dances.

One extraordinary type of ornament was a mosaic plaque or "mirror," one surface of which was encrusted with angular pieces of iron pyrites. Seventy-five such specimens were recovered. These are thought to resemble closely the mirrors from Meso-America. Local manufacture of these was suggested by Haury (Gladwin, Haury, Sayles, and Gladwin, 1937, pp. 130–34), although the possibility exists that they are instances of trade between Meso-America and Snaketown.

Disposal of the Dead

GENERAL REMARKS

Pottery, tools of bone and stone, ornaments have been discussed in the preceding sections and in this one. Perhaps it is not clear that the archaeologists find these artifacts in several places: in dwelling or storage rooms, in kivas, in trash mounds, and principally as grave goods accompanying burials.

Burials were often interred in trash mounds, which explains why pot hunters, looters, and archaeologists as well avidly look for cemeteries. They are not really cemeteries as we use the term with nothing but graves and tombstones. But trash mounds or middens are sometimes called cemeteries because they often contain burials. Burials are also found in odd places: beneath the floors of houses, beneath kiva floors, in kiva ventilators, on house and kiva floors after the structure was no longer used for its original purpose, in caves and in cave floors, and sometimes in clefts in cliff walls.

No major burying ground has been found for the big, late structures in the Chaco, Mesa Verde, or Kayenta areas, although burials have been found in abandoned rooms in these areas.

HOHOKAM DISPOSAL OF DEAD

In the Hohokam area, the dead were usually cremated, as opposed to noncremation or inhumation in the Anasazi area. Cremation, however, was sometimes practiced among the Anasazi and noncremation among the Hohokam.

Cremations or the remains after cremation as well as noncremation burials were usually grouped in areas that were apparently used only for disposal of the dead.

The method varied through time somewhat; but in general the body and various mortuary offerings were burned, after which the unconsumed bones, ash, pottery, stone objects such as palettes, stone bowls, and other offerings were gathered up and placed in a small pit or in a pottery jar.

Sometimes the pits showed evidence of fire and contained large quantities of wood ash, all of which suggests that the cremation took place in the pit. Usually along with the wood ashes and calcined human bones in these pits, one finds pottery vessels, ornaments, stone objects, and even perishable materials. These had been burned with the body and then the whole pit was filled with earth. Naturally all of the objects that went through the crematory fire were cracked, broken, injured, or partially destroyed or were intentionally smashed by human beings. Hence, many of the pottery vessels, stone bowls, effigy bowls, shell ornaments, slate palettes, clay figurines, and the like that one sees in Hohokam reports and in museum exhibitions are pieces that were removed from cremations and restored by patient technicians.

Sometimes, after cremation the remains were placed in a pit in a bowl and covered by another inverted bowl or a large sherd.

At Snaketown (Gladwin, Haury, Sayles, and Gladwin, 1937, p. 91) a total of 530 cremations were found and 10 instances of noncremations.

Subsistence

Hunters and gatherers flourished in the Hohokam area. Evidence for this came from the Cochise culture (Sayles and Antevs, 1941) which is considered as part of the Desert culture (see chapter VI), from Ventana Cave (Haury, 1950), and from the Lehner and Naco Sites where mammoth remains and projectile points were found in association (Haury et al., 1953; Haury, Sayles, and Warloy, 1959).

The next stage for which we have good evidence is that of the Hohokam culture with its irrigation canals, the dates for which hover around 300 B.C. or earlier (Haury, 1967, p. 691). Here is a going culture—full blown. How did they manage to grow crops and produce irrigation canals

—for without irrigation, crops would not have been possible. Or did the climate change?

The dates for the earliest aspects of Ventana Cave are given as about 8000–7000 B.C., and those for the Cochise (Sulphur Spring stage) as about 7000 B.C. The later aspects of the Cochise date from about 3000 to 2000 B.C. Hence, there is a hiatus of some fifteen hundred years or more between these last-mentioned dates and the earliest for Snaketown (300 B.C.), for which we have data. The evolution of Hohokam irrigation and their transition from hunting to horticulture are steps for which data are now lacking. Explanations for the origins of the Hohokam culture and many of its traits (irrigation, ball courts, copper bells, mirrors) are: diffusion or migration from Mexico, and a development in place.

At any rate, irrigation was present at 300 B.C. or earlier, and from this we assume that they grew crops, or perhaps irrigation was for some other purpose—perhaps merely to bring domestic water within a convenient distance or to be used for fish traps.

Although corn was present, evidence for it at Snaketown does not appear until A.D. 500 (Gladwin, Haury, Sayles, and Gladwin, 1937, p. 158; Wasley and Johnson, 1965, p. 108); however archaeologists assume that it was present before that date, but perhaps gathering wild foods was more important than one thinks. As yet, evidence for beans and squash has not been found.

Snaketown was apparently abandoned by A.D. 1100 or 1200. What happened to the Hohokam culture after that will be dealt with in chapter XVII.

DEVELOPMENT STAGES*	SOUTHWESTERN CO-TRADITION**	PECOS***
Elementary Southwest Culture About 3000 B.C.–A.D. 1 (Desert Culture) hunting, gathering, some horticulture	Pre-Ceramic 2000 B.C.–1000 Early Agricultural	— Basket Maker I
very early Hohokam	1000 B.C.–A.D. 1	Pre-Christian era
Formative Southwest Culture A.D. 1–A.D. 700	Formative	Basket Maker II & III
Basket Maker-early Hohokam	A.D. 1–1000	A.D. 1–700
Florescent Southwest Cultures A.D. 700–1300 Pueblo I–Pueblo III-Later Hohokam	Classic A.D. 1000–1350	Pueblo I–Pueblo III A.D. 700–1300
Fusion Period A.D. 1300–1600	Renaissance A.D. 1350–1700	Pueblo IV A.D. 1350–1700

* Daifuku, 1952   ** Martin and Rinaldo, 1951   ***Members of the Pecos Conference

PART FOUR

THE EVOLUTION OF SUBSISTENCE—SETTLEMENT SYSTEMS

IX   Adaptation of Man
to the Desert

The succession of human ecosystems in the Desert and Transition environments will be discussed together. In part because of the data available in these environments and in part because of the ways in which archaeologists have approached or failed to approach them, we know somewhat less of the prehistoric ecology of these environments than of the Plateau or Mountains. At the same time, it is clear that there was substantial interaction between populations that inhabited these environments. Finally, treating two environments at once will provide us opportunity to deal with ecological relationships in a comparative framework.

Our discussion of each of these environments during each stage of prehistory will focus on four questions: What did the environment look like during this stage? Which of the environmental resources were used? How was the society organized for the exploitation of these resources? How was the organization of the society affected by the resources? The principal data used in the discussion fall under the heading of subsistence and settlement. What kinds of sites were there? Where were these sites located? What resources were used on these sites? Unfortunately, the available data will not permit as precise or as quantified a discussion of between-site or within-site variability as would be desirable. But we can describe more general relationships between the distribution of sites and the distribution of resources and the interaction between these two patterns.

Our understanding of prehistoric cultural ecology in these environments will be somewhat enhanced by examining some critical aspects of modern adaptations to them. Data on the Maricopa, Cocopa, Mohave, Yuma, Pima, and Papago in the Desert environment and on the Walapai, Havasupai, Yavapai, Western Yavapai, Southeastern Yavapai, Western Apache, and Chiricahua Apache in the Transition area will be examined both to show the kinds of organizational and exploitative variability that are possible within these environments and to construct a series of models and derive a series of propositions that will be useful in working with the prehistoric data. This information is taken largely from Murdock's *Ethnographic Atlas* (1967). Where possible, additional information has been included so as to create a description of these societies as they were prior to the immense changes caused by the arrival of the white man.

Information concerning each of these populations is summarized in Table 11. The subsistence base is described in terms of the relative percentages of hunting-gathering, agriculture, and fishing resources. The type of agriculture practiced is identified as either intensive irrigation, floodwater farming, ahkchin irrigation, shifting fields, or casual. This typology reflects both the

155

amount of human effort put into crop producing and the means by which water was brought to the plants. Intensive irrigation involved the construction of irrigation channels. Floodwater farming, practiced in the valley of the Colorado, relied on seasonal floods to carry water and mineral nutrients to the fields. Ahkchin irrigation involved planting fields on alluvial fans and constructing ditches or terraces to carry water to the plants. Shifting fields had no built-in processes for restoring soil nutrients that were lost in growing crops. Groups practicing this form of agriculture periodically moved their fields. Casual agriculture involved putting seeds in the ground and leaving

	% HUNTING-GATHER-ING	% AGRI-CULTURE	% FISH-ING	TYPE AGRI-CULTURE	AGRIC. LOCUS	PRI-MARY HG LOCUS	SECOND-ARY HG LOCUS	SEDEN-TISM	SIZE MAX LOCAL AGGRE-GATE	SEASONALITY
Maricopa	50	30	20	II	V	V	U	S	50–99	All seasons in river valleys; gathering mainly in summer
Cocopa	40	40	20	FW	V	V	U	S	Hmstd.	All seasons in river valleys; gathering mainly in summer
Mohave	50	40	10	FW	V	V	U	S	Hmstd.	All seasons in river valleys; gathering mainly in summer
Yuma	30	50	20	FW	V	V	U	S	500+	All seasons in river valleys; gathering mainly in summer
Pima	41	50	9	II	V	V	U	S	100+	All seasons in river valleys; gathering mainly in summer
Papago	50	50		AI	V	U	V	SS	1–2 Fam.	Growing season: shifting camp; remainder of year: upland well villages
Walapai	100	P		C	V	U	V	SN	>50	Gathering-agriculture camps in valley bottoms in summer; permanent upland villages in fall, winter
Havasupai	40	60		II	V	U	V	SS	100–200	Spring-summer: agriculture-gathering in valleys; fall-winter: gathering in uplands
Yavapai	100	P		C	V	U	V	SN		Probably similar to Walapai
W. Yavapai	90	10		SF	V	U	V	SN	50–99	Probably similar to Walapai
S. E. Yavapai	90	10		C	V	U	V	SS		Probably similar to Havasupai
W. Apache	70	30		SF	V	U=V		SS	>50	Spring-fall: agriculture fields with permanent camps; fall-winter: shifting low-altitude camps
Chiricahua Apache	100	P		C		—U=V—		N		Shifting camps

KEY: AGRIC. TYPE—II = Intensive Irrigation, FW = Floodwater, SF = Shifting Fields, C = Casual
LOCI: U = Upland, V = Valley
SEDENTISM: S = Sedentary, SS = Semisedentary, SN = Seminomadic, N = Nomadic

TABLE II Economic and organizational characteristics of modern populations inhabiting the Desert and Transition environments.

them largely or wholly untended through the growing cycle while all of the other forms required at least some tending of crops through the growing cycle. The loci of both agricultural and hunting-gathering activities are identified next. Sedentism refers to the annual pattern of movement of the populations. Groups who remain in one camp through the entire year are referred to as sedentary. Those who remained in a single camp through most of the year but moved into secondary camps for some portion of it are labeled semisedentary. Those who moved or were in secondary camps for the greater portion of the year are called seminomadic, and those who were continually on the move are nomadic. The size of the maximum local aggregate refers to the largest group that lived together for some substantial portion of time during the year. Finally, the seasonal pattern of population movement is described.

The extant variability in these environments should be clear. Within the Transition environment, reliance on agriculture varies from about 60 percent to nearly zero. In the Desert, the variation is somewhat less substantial, from 30 percent to 50 percent. It is important to note that no modern population even approaches a 100 percent reliance on agriculture. It would seem unlikely that any prehistoric populations in these environments did so either. Agriculture is generally practiced in the valley bottoms. The only apparent exception to this is the Western Apache who summered in the mountainous areas of the Transition environment that today constitute their reservations and wintered in the lowland Salt River Valley. No similar pattern of migration is recorded for any of the other agricultural groups, and this is therefore atypical. Moreover, within the upland area, the Western Apache did not plant crops in the valleys. Those populations that were sub-

stantially dependent on agriculture tended to hunt and gather in the valley bottoms primarily and in the upland areas secondarily. Those less reliant on agriculture tended to hunt and gather principally in the uplands and secondarily in lowland areas. The size of the maximum local aggregate varies substantially in both areas, from family-size homesteads to villages of five hundred or more in the Desert environment and from units of a few families to villages of about 200 in the Transition area.

Despite this variability, a number of generalizations can be made concerning these data: (1) Within any region, agricultural populations tend to have more nucleated and permanent settlements; (2) larger settlements, if the settlement system is seasonally differentiated, tend to occur in the primary resource area—the one in which most of the population's resources are attained; (3) concomitantly, smaller settlements or impermanent camps are found in secondary resource areas.

Using these principles and the data summarized in Table 11, a series of settlement models can be formulated that illustrate the differences among these populations. These models are shown in Figure 15 and labeled with the names of the modern populations whose settlement patterns they approximate. The settlement system models are composed of five types of settlements: nucleated villages, small permanent villages, permanent homesteads, semipermanent villages, and temporary camps. These settlements are distributed among valley, upland, and mountainous areas. (Again, the Apache models are somewhat out of scale with the other models since these groups cover a more substantial amount of territory.) The archaeologist may find settlement data that closely reflect one of these distributions. When he does—say he finds a model that resembles that of the Havasupai—he does

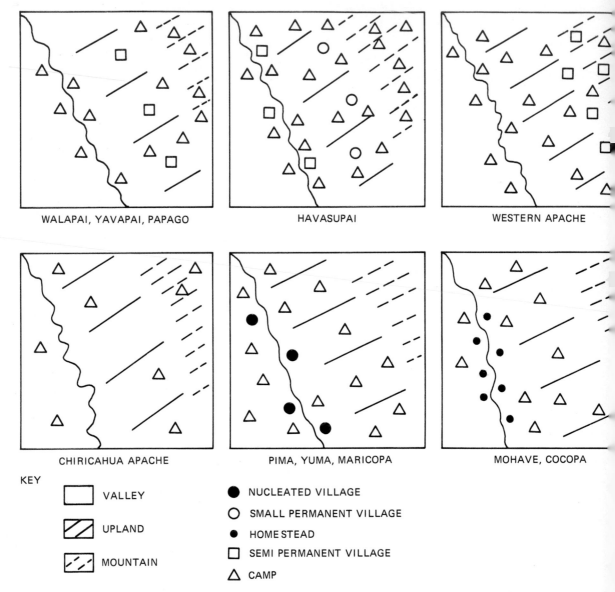

FIGURE 15 Models of settlement pattern. These are models of the settlement pattern of modern populations inhabiting the desert and transition environments. Settlements are spread over mountain, valley, and upland or piedmont areas. Five types of settlements are present, though no one population has all five. The kinds and locations of settlements reflect the relative importance of the different natural communities.

not conclude that he is dealing with the prehistoric ancestors of the Havasupai. However, he may conclude that he is dealing with a population that exploited resources in much the same way that the Havasupai do. Having done so, he makes a series of predictions concerning the kinds of resources that he would expect to find in the upland and lowland sites: the valley sites would be expected to contain more agricultural materials and to be associated with evidence of irrigation or fields, while the upland sites would be expected to contain more hunted and gathered materials. Moreover, the hunted-gathered resources within the sites should reflect animals available in the valley and upland communities. (If we had postulated hunting and gathering in both communities from a single permanent settlement, we would have expected to find resources of both communities equally represented in each site.) In this way the settlement models can be used to direct us to data that will increase our understanding of prehistoric subsistence practices in a given area. Unfortunately, detailed settlement surveys that would allow this mode of inference are rare in the two environments. Let us now turn to the data at hand.

SUBSISTENCE AND SETTLEMENT IN THE PALEO-INDIAN STAGE

It is important to recall that most of the Paleo-Indian sites recorded in Arizona (chapter V; Figure 5) are surface finds of a single point or a few artifacts. Moreover, most of the excavated sites are kill sites. These biases substantially reduce the number and the quality of the inferences we can make about subsistence and settlement in Paleo-Indian times. Nevertheless, some patterns are clear.

The vast majority of the sites occur in the Transition rather than the Desert environment. Those that occur in what is now Desert are so close to the Transition boundary that it seems very probable that at their time of occupation they were in plant communities that we would now identify as Transition ones. The only possible exception to this is Ventana Cave.

What did the environment of the area look like at the time these sites were occupied? Mehringer (1967) has discussed the probable differences between early post-Pleistocene environments in southern Arizona and modern ones. He argues that vegetation zones were depressed by around 1,000 meters between 18,000 and 9200 B.C. Just before 5500 B.C. he infers a depression on the order of 300 to 600 meters. Thus we might imagine a far more restricted distribution of the creosote/bursage/tarbush shrubland and significant increases in both juniper and oak woodland, grama tobosa shrubsteppe, and pine forest. The shrubland communities may have been completely pushed from the Transition habitat and existed primarily or solely in the Desert region. Pollen taken from Paleo-Indian sites suggest that valley bottoms in the Transition environment were grasslands with substantial numbers of scattered oak trees. Streams probably ran during the entire year and standing ponds of water were present in these valleys.

It is becoming increasingly clear that many of our ideas of how Paleo-Indian groups adapted to their environments are grossly oversimplified. It is no longer reasonable to believe that earlier Paleo-Indian or Clovis groups hunted only mammoths and that later ones hunted only bison. In the first place, bison and mammoth are both found on sites such as Lehner, Murray Springs, and Double Adobe. Moreover, many other animals were hunted by these groups. The list included horse, tapir, camelid, antelope, peccary, sloth, deer, prairie dog, squirrel, jaguar, rabbit, badger, coyote, fox, wolf, fish, and shellfish.

Even to think of Paleo-Indian populations as full-time hunters is a mistake. Modern big game hunters in subarctic areas rarely rely on large and small game animals for more than 50 percent of their diets (DeGarmo, 1970). Wilmsen's evidence of the importance of plant processing artifacts on Paleo-Indian sites suggests that we will ultimately have to allow flora an important role in subsistence and maintenance activities during this stage. The evidence is already beginning to appear. For example, hackberry seeds were found in abundance at the Levi Site (Wilmsen, 1970).

The only way that archaeologists have been able to maintain so single-minded a focus on Paleo-Indians as hunters is by systematically ignoring contrary evidence. The Sulphur Springs stage sites of the Cochise culture in the Sulphur Springs Valley are quite clearly as old as Folsom sites found in the Southwest. These sites contain substantial numbers of grinding stones that archaeologists agree were used in processing plants. Pleistocene fauna are found on these sites and they are above the grinding tools. One Clovis point was found associated with these grinding tools (Sayles and Antevs, 1941). Yet most archaeologists would still argue that these are Desert culture and not Paleo-Indian sites.

This position seems to us an unreasonable one. Archaeologists have evidence that Paleo-Indian populations did not subsist on meat alone. They know that functionally specific hunting sites existed during this stage. Why then, when we find sites specialized in meat processing, sometimes with evidence of associated plant materials, and sites specialized in plant processing, with some evidence of meat processing, and these sites are within a few dozen miles of each other, must we attempt to force the data to support the idea of two different traditions or cultures? It is clear that the behavior that occurred at the two sites was different, but this behavioral difference by no means implies a cultural one. Until evidence can be developed showing why and how an only meat-eating and an exclusively plant-eating culture should have developed side by side in a single valley, the presumption based on ethnographic and archaeological evidence must be that these are functionally specific sites of a single tradition. That such evidence could be obtained seems most unlikely.

It is nevertheless the case that in the Paleo-Indian stage, populations were far more substantially organized in a fashion oriented to hunting, and in the succeeding Desert culture stage to plant gathering. In what ways did a heavy reliance on hunted resources affect the social organization of groups that existed at this time? Wilmsen has argued that Paleo-Indian groups assumed a number of structural poses during an annual cycle. There is evidence of multiband, band, and family-size settlements in the archaeological record. Small sites occupied seasonally and for highly specific purposes were probably settlements of family units. Large sites such as Lindenmeier were gathering spots for many families or bands. The raw materials used in making artifacts at Lindenmeier were brought from source areas as far away as Wyoming and the Texas panhandle. Apparently, groups who occupied this site wandered and traded over vast territories in band or multifamily units.

How might these poses have been helpful in resource exploitation? Let us first consider bison and then mammoth hunting. DeGarmo (1970) has noted that large game animals tend to summer in plains or open valley environments and to winter in smaller, more closed valleys in foothill or piedmont regions. It is common in near-mountain environments to find that small piedmont valleys are somewhat warmer and less snowbound than nearby open areas. These foothill areas would have served as a winter haven for bison, a variety of other game animals, and man.

Gorman has observed that during winter

months bison tend to travel in groups of five to twenty individuals while in the summer they move in herds of several dozen to many hundreds of animals (Gorman, 1968). He argues that the bison kill sites the archaeologist finds should reflect this pattern. During the summer months bison were slaughtered by large groups of individuals who drove them to and over precipices at the edge of or on the plain. A number of families or even bands might have cooperated in this activity. During the winter months, a few individuals could have hunted successfully. Animals were surrounded in depressions in the foothills and killed. The number of animals slaughtered was much less at any kill site during winter than during summer months. Population aggregates were probably also smaller during these months with families or small bands constituting the dwelling unit. Gorman has discussed significant amounts of data that support these arguments. While he is principally concerned with bison, the organizational and hunting techniques he describes might have been used in taking other herd animals.

Gorman (1969) has also discussed techniques of mammoth hunting practiced by Paleo-Indian populations. Hunting these large animals was a very different proposition from taking bison. Modern elephants, and probably prehistoric mammoths, wander in herds of a few individuals to a few dozen individuals. They generally cover a territory of fifteen to twenty-five miles each day. While they travel along relatively predictable routes, their pace is so rapid that a man on foot would have difficulty keeping up with them. A running elephant can easily outdistance a running man. Gorman argues that Paleo-Indian hunters would certainly have been familiar with the paths that mammoths followed through rich browsing and grazing areas, from water hole to water hole. They would also have known that wounded animals tend to run to the nearest water hole. The hunters might then have distributed themselves along one of the mammoth trails. The animals were wounded with a spear or atlatl dart. Most of the initial thrusts were to the ribs, vertebra, and legs of the animals (that is where the archaeologist finds imbedded projectile points when he excavates mammoth kills), and seem to have been intended to retard the movement of the animal rather than to kill it outright. As the animal ran toward water, other hunters waited along its route to further wound it. By the time it reached water, it was near death or so incapacitated that it could no longer escape its predators. Some animals, mostly young ones, did escape—we find points in these animals but not evidence that they were butchered.

A large mammoth would have provided enough food for about twenty individuals to live for a month if they ate around ten pounds per day. Of course, the meat could not have been refrigerated, but not all human populations share our scruples about the freshness of meat. With this much food available from a single kill, mammoth hunting populations could have remained in a single locale for substantial periods of time.

Gorman argues that color and stylistic variability in projectile points served to indicate what animals had been killed by a particular individual or what portion of an animal belonged to an individual. We will consider this argument in more detail later.

Following the ideas of Wilmsen, De-Garmo, and Gorman, we might expect that as archaeologists find more Paleo-Indian sites, the subsistence-settlement system that emerges will look something like the following. Sites found in lowland areas will be large. Some of these will be kill sites where large numbers of animals were slaughtered.

Others will represent base camps where the women and children remained while the men hunted. (The Sulphur Springs sites seem likely candidates for this role in the settlement system: they are relatively large and contain evidence of both plant and animal processing.) Some evidence of uxorilocality might be found in these sites since the women were making the majority of day-to-day decisions for the band as a whole. At higher altitudes, sites will be much smaller. The sites were both kill sites and dwelling units of relatively small population aggregates. At middle altitudes, a third type of site represents spots where large populations aggregated before moving up to the highland areas in the winter and down to the plains in the summer.

Paleo-Indians were not passive inhabitants of their environment. One of the most heated debates in American paleoanthropology concerns the role that man played in the extinction of Pleistocene megafauna. Some investigators argue that mammoth, camel, horse, tapir, and early bison became extinct as a result of the climatic changes that marked the end of the Pleistocene. Others believe that man was the primary agent in the demise of these life forms. Those who argue for the agency of man point out that there is no clear coincidence between climatic change and the extinction of these animals. They did not become extinct at a single point in time, and other animals that were equally sensitive to climate did not become extinct at all. Those who argue for climate maintain that there is no evidence that human populations in the late Pleistocene and early post-Pleistocene periods were so large that they might have had this drastic an effect on their prey.

It seems strange that a group of individuals, most of whom call themselves ecologists, should engage in such a debate.

Man, climate, and animals were participants in a single ecosystem. It seems most unlikely that the extinction of Pleistocene megafauna reflects the unique effects of man or climate. Nevertheless, we have no good model that shows how the interaction might have resulted in the extinction of megafauna. Instead, the debate is a fruitless one that is most frequently argued in nonecological, nonsystemic, either-man-or-climate terms. There are any number of ways in which man and climate could have had a compounding effect that resulted in the extinction of the megafauna. Until this kind of argument is made, and the appropriate evidence sought, the debate will remain unresolved in the minds of most archaeologists.

SUBSISTENCE AND SETTLEMENT IN THE DESERT CULTURE STAGE

Desert culture populations were probably equally distributed between the Desert and Transition environments. Most of the sites described in the literature are in the Transition environment. However, a few sites found in the desert plus the knowledge that these populations were abundant in similar areas of California and Nevada and the likelihood that these sites in the Arizona desert might lie under deep layers of alluvium, suggest that archaeologists have not found as much evidence of these hunter-gatherers as probably exists in the Desert environment.

Irwin-Williams and Haynes (1970) have recently summarized the available evidence concerning climatic and environmental change during the Desert culture stage.[1]

[1] This article was not yet published when the chapter on prehistoric environments was written. It seems to us that it retains the best of both geological and palynological arguments and summarizes the available data in simpler but more precise terms than the syntheses discussed earlier.

Their inferences concerning changes in effective moisture are based on both palynological and geological evidence. Late Paleo-Indian and early Desert culture populations that existed between 8500 and 5500 B.C. lived in an environment that was cooler and wetter than at present. The period between 8500 and 8000 B.C. and that between 6500 and 6000 B.C. were especially wet. Around 6000 B.C. effective moisture began to decrease and the period between 5000 and 3000 B.C. was perhaps even drier than at present. Effective moisture began to increase at about 3000 B.C., reaching a maximum between 2000 and 2500 B.C. and then declining to about the time of Christ. Most of the differences between this interpretation and Paul Martin's can be attributed to the somewhat more detailed reconstruction now available.

Plant communities during this period of time were probably distributed much as they are at present, although during periods of increased effective moisture highland communities may have occurred 100 or more meters lower and lowland water-dependent communities may have spread outward from stream banks. Whatever, differences exist between Desert culture and modern environments, they were not nearly so pronounced as the differences between modern and Paleo-Indian stage environments.

Both cave and open-air sites are recorded for this period. Sites found in the transition zone are predominantly open-air sites immediately alongside stream channels. This distribution may reflect a heavy reliance by Desert culture populations on near-stream environments or it may reflect the increased probability that the archaeologist will find deeply buried sites where alluvium has been cut by a stream channel. Some of these open-air sites had houses, although there is certainly no evidence that populations were sedentary. The Cienega Creek Site (Haury, 1957) is a relatively large open-air site where food-processing activities were carried on. A large number of cremations were found at this site suggesting that it may have been the seasonally occupied base camp of a relatively large band.

Resources found on Desert culture sites show some significant spatial patterning. Chiricahua period sites in the southern transition zone contain remains of antelope, jack rabbit, bison, deer, mollusc, and turtle. Somewhat later San Pedro period sites contain remains of coyote, turtle, and mollusc. The molluscs may have been brought to the site by agencies other than man. However, there is no reason why Desert culture populations might not have used them as a food resource. The land mammals were all ones that ranged through the transition environment and would have been equally available in all of the plant communities, although principally in those occupying valley bottoms and midland slopes. These sites vary considerably in size: some contain a few dozen artifacts while others have several hundred of them. However, sufficiently detailed analyses to permit sound inferences about differences in site specialization have not been made.

The faunal record from Ventana Cave in the Desert environment is substantial, complex, and our principal source of information concerning Desert culture adaptations to this environment. Between 75 and 90 percent of the faunal remains from Desert culture levels of this cave are remains of mule deer, jack rabbit, coyote, badger, cottontail, pronghorn antelope, and bighorn sheep. Deer and rabbit were the most important subsistence resources within this group. Tortoise was the most important of the reptiles that were used for food, and red-tailed hawk the most important bird. Dog, possibly domesticated and possibly used for food, was represented in some Desert culture levels. Other animals eaten by the inhabitants of the cave included squirrel, wildcat, fox, porcupine, prairie dog, wood rat, mountain lion, wolf, skunk, bear, cacomistle, chipmunk, road runner, white-winged dove, pocket gopher, kangaroo rat, horned toad, snakes, lizards, raven, owl, turkey vulture, and brown pelican.

This diverse list of animals lived in most of the communities that exist in the vicinity of Ventana Cave. However, most of them came from a single community—the mesquite-saltbush bosque—or reached their greatest density there. This community has a very restricted distribution in the modern desert environment. It might, however, have been far more widely distributed under somewhat wetter conditions. The community does have the highest carrying capacity of any in the desert region, so while the inhabitants of Ventana Cave seem to have used it as a base camp for exploiting a variety of plant-animal communities, they seem to have been specializing from the earliest times in exploiting the relatively rich mesquite-saltbush community. Unfortunately, there are no plant remains from Desert culture levels in Ventana Cave that would permit confirmation of this argument. Nevertheless, it does seem that the pattern of exploitation of animals was far more specialized than that in the Transition environment.

Some of the contrast between the evidence from the Transition and Desert environments may of course be due to the fact that sites in the Transition environment are open-air ones and Ventana Cave is a cave. This issue may be clarified somewhat by comparing the evidence from Ventana Cave with that from Bat Cave in New Mexico (Dick: 1965).

Bat Cave is in a kind of transitional en-vironment on the east side of the continental divide. The cave is just below high mountains and overlooks a broad plain that is the remnant of glacial Lake San Augustin. This lake may have held water at some points during the Desert culture stage occupation. Faunal remains from the cave include bison, mountain sheep, deer, antelope, elk, wolf, badger, porcupine, jack rabbit, cottontail, pocket gopher, and wood rat. These animals, excepting bison, all live within a thirty-mile radius of the cave today. Most of the bison remains are from relatively late prehistoric times and seem to represent a movement of bison back onto the plains during late prehistoric times. Bison bones are present, however, in levels that date back to 2000 B.C. or earlier. In part, then, Bat Cave seems to have been a site that was occupied during some part of an annual cycle specifically for the purpose of hunting bison. More basically, it seems to have been used as a base camp for gathering a variety of plant products that lived within a relatively substantial portion of the surrounding area.

This conclusion is substantiated by the floral remains in the cave. The author of the report assumes that the floral record at Bat Cave primarily reflects climatic change. This assumption is not a reasonable one. Did the prehistoric inhabitants of Bat Cave collect their plant products from a 100 square meter area in front of the cave so that all of the changes in the cave deposits simply represent changes in the plants that grew in this small area? Such an assumption does a great deal of violence to our knowledge of the behavior of hunting-gathering groups. Yet, this is the assumption that we are being asked to make when we are told that plant remains in the cave vary because climate changes. It is typical for such populations to range over relatively substantial territories, and the distribution of floral remains in the cave are certainly consistent with this pattern of behavior.

Each of the varieties of plants found in the cave is recorded as either present or absent in each of the levels in which the cave was excavated. These data are somewhat difficult to work with since presence/absence data are not necessarily good indicators of covariation. However, it is possible to evaluate some inferences using these kinds of data.

For example, the author of the report concludes that levels II and III in the cave were formed when the climate was wet because rushes, aspen, and reeds were found in these levels. It is assumed that these plants were growing on the playa floor when strata in question were deposited. This argument fails to consider the possibilities that other plants found in levels II and III and other plants that covary with aspen, rushes, and reeds may not support the inference of wetter conditions on the playa floor. If we examine these plants and other plants found in the cave that grow in moist environments, we find that they occur just as frequently in other levels as they do in levels II and III. There is some tendency to a concentration in levels II and III but not a pronounced one. If, on the other hand, one examines the plants that would not be expected to have grown on the plain if it had been wet and supporting populations of aspen, reeds, and rushes, it is apparent that such plants are present in levels II and III in the same quantities that they occur in other levels. It does not seem, then, that the patterned distributions of remains between the levels imply climatic change.

These remains can be re-evaluated on the assumption that their patterned distributions reflect patterns of human behavior. One may hypothesize, for example, that

the variation in plant remains should reflect variation in the purposes for which the plants were collected, variation in the season during which they were collected, and variation in the community from which they were collected. In terms of use, we can use ethnobotanical data to identify plants that were used for food, for medicine, for maintenance, and for ritual purposes, at least insofar as the prehistoric functions of these plants were similar to modern ones. Studies of plant community constituents can be used to identify the kinds of communities from which particular plants might have been collected. Similarly, plant remains can be described in terms of the season of the year during which they would have been available.

If plants are divided into groups based upon their patterns of covariation through the levels, these groups prove to have functional, ecological, and seasonal patterns. Group I consists of plants that occur in all levels of the cave: corn, squash, sunflower, piñon, yucca, and walnut. These are all plants that were general purpose ones in that they were used for a variety of purposes—food, medicine, maintenance, and ritual. They were harvested in the late summer–early autumn. Another group of plants occurs only in levels I and II: eupatorium, juniper, saltbush, and muhly. These are principally scrubland-woodland plants that were used for medicinal purposes. The group of plants that occur exclusively in level III of the cave are plants that would have grown at the edge of a stream or marsh and have been collectable in late summer or early autumn. Not all of the covarying groups within the cave can be associated with precise functional or ecological patterns. But, significant patterns are present. Variability in floral remains in the cave is not a product of climate but of the time of the year that prehistoric populations visited the cave, the kinds of plants they sought, and the plant communities to which they traveled in attempting to acquire them. In any given level, the pattern of covariation is complex and suggests that the cave was occupied at several points during the year by a group or groups with very different wandering territories. Moreover, unlike the situation in Ventana Cave, the floral remains in Bat Cave suggest that this unit was used by populations exploiting a variety of communities and using the cave as a base camp. There is little or no suggestion that one community was primary.

There is very little evidence concerning the size of local aggregates of the Desert culture stage. Based upon anthropologists' knowledge of the relationship between floor space and population, Bat Cave might have been inhabited by up to forty individuals and Ventana Cave by around thirty. Both of these sites seem more likely to have been the abode of a band than of a single family unit. No reasonable estimate can be made of the size of the groups that occupied open-air sites in the Transition environment. The large numbers of cremations at the Cienega Creek Site, however, suggest that it might also have been occupied by a band-size unit.

Archaeologists—and most Americans, for that matter—believe in progress and tend to see human societies over time increasing in size, in quality of life, and so on. While this characterization may be accurate in the long run, it is not necessarily the case that any two points in time will stand in the relationship more sedentary to less sedentary, for example, just because they also stand in the relationship younger to older. This point should be clear from an examination of modern data—immense variation in sedentism exists within both the Transition and Desert environments. Just as sed-

entism varies in space it varies in time. There is no a priori reason to assume that Desert culture populations were more sedentary than Paleo-Indian ones. If anything, the opposite might have been true. Hunting large herds of macro-fauna may have necessitated cooperation among large numbers of individuals. Females and children were left in base camps while males hunted. No similar necessities existed for Desert culture populations. The resources used by groups during this stage could have been more efficiently exploited by large population aggregates but in no sense would have required them. Moreover, meat resources acquired by Paleo-Indian hunters might have necessitated dwelling in the vicinity of the kill while those acquired by Desert culture hunters could have been moved. Deer and antelope are far more portable than bison or elephant. The heavier reliance on plant products by Desert culture populations might have required moving over substantial areas to acquire the needed quantities of sparsely distributed plant resources. Animals, on the other hand, have home territories and remain in them. Just because the Desert culture stage was later than the Paleo-Indian one, was it characterized by more sedentism? Such a conclusion would be reached by many archaeologists. Yet, there are many reasons to believe that this might not have been the case, and conclusive evidence for one argument or the other is still wanting.

The same argument must be made with respect to population. We cannot assume that there were more people in Arizona during the Desert culture stage than during the Paleo-Indian stage. It is true that archaeologists have found more Desert culture than Paleo-Indian sites. But, the Paleo-Indian stage lasted for about four thousand years and the Desert culture stage for about seven thousand. Furthermore, Paleo-Indian sites are more deeply buried and more difficult to find. It is not clear that there are a sufficiently larger number of Desert culture sites to firmly conclude that population was greater during this stage. Moreover, there are some blocks of time during the stage (e.g., 5000–3000 B.C.) when there is little or no evidence of human occupation of the state.

Given the environmental conditions in the state, the heavier reliance on hunting by Paleo-Indian populations may have provided for a more secure subsistence than a principal reliance on gathered plants. Drought at a critical point in the year may have sometimes killed all or most of the plants eaten by humans. While this drought would also have reduced the animal population, some individuals would have remained for humans to exploit. Moreover, animals were a readily available winter resource and plants were not. It is certainly the case that the later agricultural populations in these environments were larger and more sedentary. But, the Desert culture stage prior to the advent of agriculture may have been characterized by sparse populations and tenuous subsistence and existence. In any case, we cannot assume that Desert culture groups were larger and more sedentary simply because they lived later in time than Paleo-Indian ones.

CULTURAL ECOLOGY OF THE HOHOKAM

To this point our discussion has focused on the cultural ecology of the populations that existed in the Transition and Desert environments during specific stages. In discussing them, our hypotheses and inferences were based upon excavated materials from a substantial number of the known sites of the stages. This approach is no longer an acceptable one in dealing with the Pit House and Town Dweller stages. So little ecological data are available from the two environments under discussion that the focus will be primarily on those sites and site reports for which good information is available. For example, most of our knowledge concerning the Hohokam is based upon material from one site—Snaketown. Yet there are hundreds, perhaps thousands, of Hohokam sites in the southern desert. Archaeologists have very limited evidence concerning the similarity between sequences at Snaketown and those at other Hohokam sites. This problem would be further compounded if we attempted to discuss the general subject of adaptations to the desert based upon evidence from Snaketown. Fortunately, we have two excellent ethnobotanical analyses of prehistoric floral remains, both written by Versila Bohrer, one for the Transition environment and one for the Desert environment, that provide us with substantial information concerning the adaptation to specific segments of this environment.

Hohokam sites are generally distributed through the valleys of the Gila, Salt, and Verde Rivers during the Pit House and Town Dweller stages, but they tend to a maximum of density near the confluences of these rivers. With the possible exception of the prehistoric populations that inhabited the lower Colorado River Valley, no other prehistoric group was so dependent on large rivers and their flow. Most of our evidence concerning the subsistence resources employed by the Hohokam are from the two expeditions to Snaketown. The first expedition produced primarily faunal evidence and the most recent one principally floral evidence. Bohrer (1970) has described the floral remains and the role that plants made in the Hohokam subsistence system. While her analysis is based primarily on evidence from the late Pit House stage, it probably is an accurate description of the practices that existed during most of the occupation of this site.

Floral remains from Snaketown include seeds of cholla or prickly pear, hedgehog or strawberry cactus, saguaro, cocklebur, coyote melon, goosefoot, little barley grass, mesquite, screwbean, sedge, spiderling, trianthema-chenopodium, and walnut. The cactus seeds would have by and large been collected in the saguaro-palo verde community that covers hillsides in the area, while the remaining seeds would have been taken in the mesquite-saltbush community. Faunal remains from the earlier expedition (those of the more recent one are as yet unreported) include domestic dog, coyote, gray fox, ground squirrel, pocket gopher, kangaroo rat, pack rat, muskrat, jack rabbit, cottontail, mule deer, pronghorn antelope, mountain sheep, bison, raven, golden eagle, turkey, sage hen, blue goose, owl, tortoise, and Colorado salmon. Jack rabbit and cottontail were the most important animal products used at Snaketown, followed by antelope and deer. Although rabbit bones were more numerous, it is likely that antelope and deer were a more important resource because they carry more meat. The most striking aspect of these resources is their great similarity to those found in Desert culture levels of Ventana Cave. Like the remains from Ventana Cave, most of the hunted animals were inhabitants of the mesquite-saltbush community or at least attained their greatest density there. Like the Desert culture populations who inhabited the region thousands of years earlier, the Hohokam seem to have concentrated their exploitative efforts on this community.

Unlike their predecessors, however, the Hohokam were significantly reliant upon agricultural products. The first canals were built at Snaketown when the site was founded at about 300 B.C. Maize was grown in the fields that these canals watered. Beans were first grown during the Estrella phase, cucurbits during the Snaketown phase, and cotton during the Sweetwater phase. (While cotton fibers for making cloth were the principal product of this plant, seeds may also have been cooked and eaten.) Tansy mustard, little barley grass, horse purslane, and various amaranths and chenopods undoubtedly grew as "weeds" in the Hohokam fields. While these plants were neither planted nor cultivated, they were allowed to grow, and were undoubtedly used as a food source.

Bohrer also analyzed the materials that the Hohokam used in constructing their houses. These included cypress, cottonwood, mesquite, Douglas fir, ash, juniper, and reed grass. House remains from both

FIGURE 16   The Pima ecosystem. The Pima ecosystem was probably very similar to that of the Hohokam. Crops were planted not on the basis of local rainfall, but when rivers filled with summer and winter runoff. Saguaro and mesquite provided resources that backed up the domesticated crops. Taken from "Ethnobotanical Aspects of Snaketown, a Hohokam Village in Southern Arizona." *American Antiquity* 35: 413–30. Courtesy of Versila L. Bohrer.

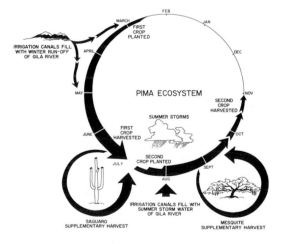

the Sacaton and Sweetwater phases show that a variety of materials were used in constructing individual houses. Apparently, the accessibility of raw materials was primary in determining which were used in particular construction tasks. Bohrer argues that some of the conifers may have been carried to Snaketown when the river was in flood.

All of these various data are tied together when Bohrer paints a composite picture of the Hohokam ecosystem. She argues that these people planted two crops each year, one in February and one in July. The crops planted in February were watered by win-

ter runoff that filled the Gila and Salt Rivers. The second crop was watered by summer storms in the mountain areas that filled these same streams. Saguaro was harvested in July and mesquite in September. The extent of the harvest of these two resources, which seem to have been the most important ones to the Hohokam, was largely a function of the agricultural product. When crops were good, little saguaro and mesquite were collected, but in bad years the collection of these wild resources was extensive and necessary to the survival of the Hohokam.

To understand changes in the subsistence

FIGURE 17 Stress at Snaketown. The increasing reliance on leguminous seeds suggests that crop failure was becoming more and more characteristic as the Hohokam evolved. Taken from "Ethnobotanical Aspects of Snaketown, a Hohokam Village in Southern Arizona." *American Antiquity* 35: 413–30. Courtesy of Versila L. Bohrer.

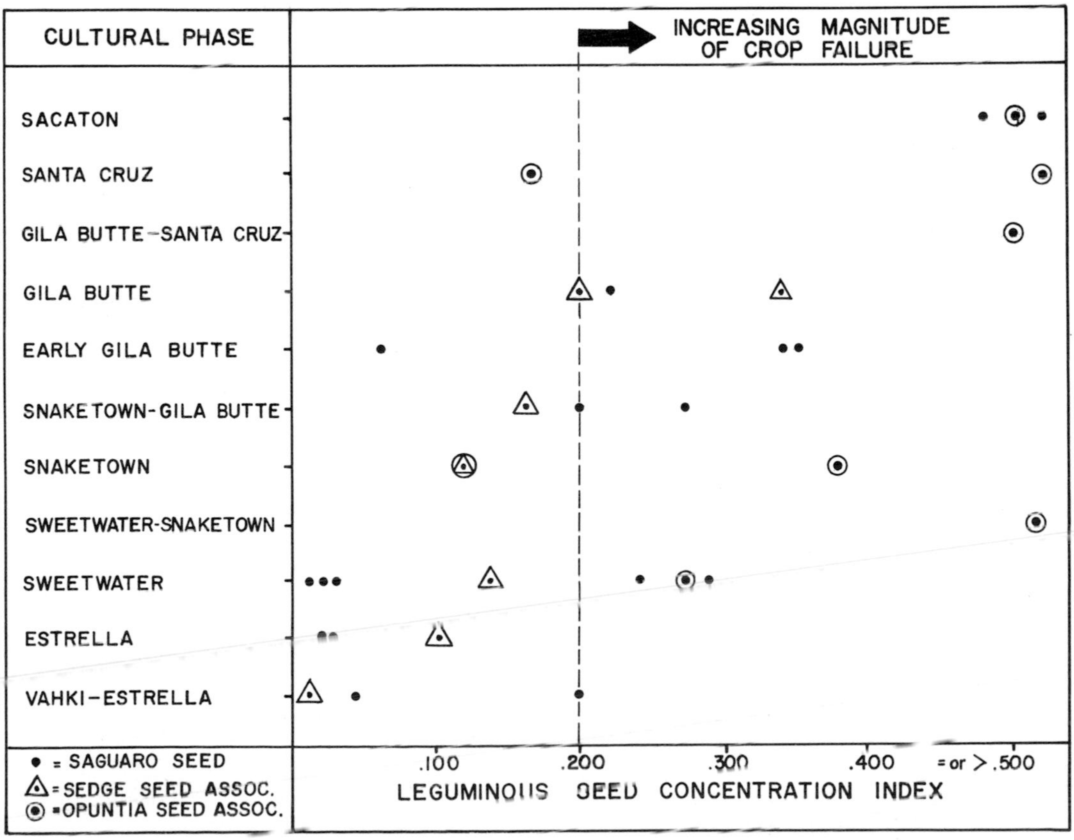

record over time, Bohrer plotted the relationship between the number of leguminous seeds and the total volume of plant material in the samples she analyzed. She argues that this "seed concentration index" is a good measure of changes in the use of saguaro, mesquite, and cholla or prickly pear. The patterns of these changes is shown in Figure 17. In this figure, the greater the index, the greater the inferred probability that crop failure was characteristic. The chart shows that a period of agricultural stress began in the late Sweetwater and early Snaketown phases. A second period of stress began in the early Gila Butte phase, when reliance on wild legumes and seeds began to increase. Unfortunately the record lasts no longer than the late Sacaton phase with reliance on gathered seeds still increasing.

The only evidence that modifies this picture comes from two Hohokam sites south of Tucson, BB 13:41 and BB 13:50 (Bohrer et al., 1969). A number of pottery vessels filled with seeds were recovered from this site. Maize and about 400 milliliters of tansy mustard seed were found at BB 13:41, which dates to around A.D. 900 to 1200. One olla at BB 13:50 contained 890 ml. of tansy mustard. Maize was predominant in a house at the site that was occupied between A.D. 700 and 900. House 12, dated to A.D. 900–1200, contained pottery vessels with 572 ml. of maize, 30 tepary beans, 50 jack beans, 2,040 ml. of amaranth (goosefoot), a pod segment of mesquite, 5 ml. of stickleaf, and 360 ml. of cholla buds. Tansy mustard and goosefoot seem to have been more important at these sites. It is not currently possible to say whether this difference was produced by differences in the behavior of the populations that inhabited the sites or differences in the preservation of the materials.[2] It is

reasonable to believe that the Hohokam used the wild plants that grew in their fields in much the same way that they used cholla, mesquite, and screwbeans. When irrigation water was insufficient to produce an abundant agricultural harvest, it may still have been sufficient to cause "weeds" such as tansy mustard and amaranth to grow in abundance. These resources may have been used as a dietary supplement in drought periods throughout the sequence or only during later phases as the evidence from BB 13:40 and 13:51 suggests.

Bohrer was able to obtain a limited amount of pollen data from Snaketown. She believes that the pollen record primarily reflects increases in the importance of agriculture in the area. Low-spine composites increase from the beginning of the record up to Sacaton times. Composites are usually associated with abundant moisture and disturbed soil. Bohrer observes that from Sweetwater to Gila Butte phases, when the seed concentration index indicates that agricultural products were in abundance, low-spine composite pollen is also in abundance. New irrigation ditches and new fields would have produced the disturbed sediments and moist sediments in which composites would have grown.

The evidence of increasing agriculture based on the patterned variation of low-spine composite pollen is consistent with other data from Snaketown. For example, the first Snaketown expedition recovered burials from the successive periods at the site in the following numbers: Pioneer, 25; Colonial, 175; Sedentary, 123; and Classic, 75. If we divide these figures by the lengths of the respective periods, the following record of burials per hundred-year period is obtained: Pioneer, 3; Colonial, 44; Sedentary, 62; Classic, 25. It may be necessary to increase the estimate for the Classic period since Snaketown is not a Classic period site

---

[2] Substantial quantities of pigweed and goosefoot were recovered by the first expedition to Snaketown (Castetter and Bell 1942:33).

in the same sense as Casa Grande or Los Muertos. On the other hand, there is little evidence at this point that the population of such sites was any greater than the Classic period Snaketown. These data suggest, then, that the population in the Snaketown area may have reached its peak during the early Sedentary period when agriculture seems to have been most important. The increase in reliance on wild plant products in the following phases may be paralleled by a decline in population.

The organization of Hohokam communities for the performance of subsistence tasks is still somewhat of a mystery. It appears that villages contained a few houses to a few dozen houses. Later settlements were somewhat larger than earlier ones. Houses do not seem to have varied greatly in size or function. Evidence of ceremonialism in the Hohokam villages includes ball courts, platform mounds, and a few houses that are far larger than the average and therefore inferred to have been ceremonial. Each of these features could, however, have served a variety of functions other than ceremonial ones. Evidence for pan-village ceremonialism among the Hohokam is not nearly so certain as for the Mogollon or Anasazi until the appearance of the great houses of the Classic period.

Scheduling decisions were certainly made by Hohokam groups. Someone had to decide that the agricultural crops would be insufficient during a given growing season and that the population should turn its efforts to gathering. The construction and maintenance of canals, the coordination of work in the fields while men were away hunting, and the organization of the harvest would have necessitated similar decisions. However, there is no reason to assume that pan-village functionaries or institutions would have been required for these decisions and activities. They may have been handled by families or by casual cooperation between family groups.

The principal organizational change in the Hohokam record is that between the Sedentary and Classic periods when brush villages were replaced by large adobe compound sites with great houses. Archaeologists have tended to account for this change in terms of invasion by Salado or Sinagua populations. We shall speak of this idea in a moment. However, the appearance of site and settlement patterns in the Hohokam region that are related to ones found in areas to the north and northeast should not blind us to important changes that were occurring in the Hohokam area anyhow.

In the first place, the advent of the Classic period is associated with the construction of many new sites. Less than 10 percent of Sacaton phase sites survive to the Soho phase. These new sites tended to be built somewhat closer to the river than those of the preceding period. Prior to A.D. 600, sites were built relatively close to the river, but between A.D. 600 and 1150 they were built somewhat farther away. The transition to the Classic period represents a return to near river situations. Bohrer's evidence suggests that the transition may have been associated with deteriorating agricultural conditions. This in turn could have had a variety of causes. The major rivers might have been carrying insufficient water to irrigate fields that were far away from the river. Alternatively, lands away from the river might have been overused. We shall mention in a later chapter the problems created by alkali or salt deposits in heavily irrigated areas of the southern desert. As agricultural problems and stresses increased, the utilization of resources from the mesquite-saltbush community increased and may ultimately have created a stress situation in this niche. While the carrying capacity of the community is high, it has a finite distribution. The switch from wood and brush structures to adobe might indicate a shortage of these resources. A more formal organization with strong pan-village institutions might have been required to schedule labor so as to increase the quantity of now scarce resources that the population could acquire. This situation might easily have resulted in the adoption of new organizational patterns.

It does seem reasonably clear that the changes that occurred at this time involved more than the adoption of new organizations. New populations seem to have been moving into the valley. The most insightful analysis of this event has been made by Schroeder (1960). He notes that during the Classic period there seem to have been about 140,000 acres of land under irrigation in the vicinity of Phoenix. This land was associated with about 27 cities, yielding an average of about 5,200 acres per city. Assuming that 13 or so acres of land were required to feed one person, some 400 people would have lived in these cities during the Classic period and the population of the valley would have been about 10,800. Schroeder estimates that the population in the area reached a maximum of around 12,000 people at about A.D. 1300. He contrasts this with an estimate of around 9,000 people for the preceding Sedentary period.

This analysis would seem to indicate that population was increasing from the Sedentary to the Classic periods. However, Schroeder presents a strong argument that a substantial portion of this increase was due to the migration of populations from the Sinagua area to the Salt River Valley. Based upon the abandonment of sites in that region, he argues that around 8,000 individuals left the Flagstaff area at about A.D. 1200. Approximately 3,000 of these individuals went to the Salt River Valley. This migration is reflected, Schroeder argues, in the approximately one third to one fourth

of Classic period burials (at Los Muertos) that are extended, not cremated in the Hohokam style. Analyses of these skeletons also suggests that the individuals were not of Hohokam stock. In other words, the indigenous population seems to have remained stable or even declined between Sedentary and Classic times. The addition of so substantial a population to a system in equilibrium or perhaps already threatened by a deteriorating natural environment could easily have resulted in significant organizational changes. Alternatively, Salado populations and Salado organization might have been brought to the valley to solve problems that already existed there. In any case, the transition from the Sedentary to the Classic periods deserves a far greater explanatory effort with equal emphasis on the dynamics of the Hohokam subsistence settlement system prior to the change and the possible role of immigrating groups.

One final aspect of the relationship between Hohokam populations and their environment deserves comment. By 300 B.C., when populations in other parts of the Southwest were still principally nomadic or seminomadic, the inhabitants of the Hohokam region were already sedentary. They lived in permanent villages, manned a complex irrigation system, and were agriculturalists. This discontinuity has led many archaeologists to assume that the Hohokam moved into the area from Mexico as an already "developed" culture. Many archaeologists still hold to this belief despite the fact that several decades of searching have still failed to produce the postulated source area in Mexico. There is no reason to doubt that early Hohokam populations were in contact with Mexican ones. Nevertheless, it is equally clear that many important components of the Hohokam subsistence system were present among Desert culture populations in the same area.

The most important of these is the heavy focus on exploitation of the substantial biomass of the mesquite-saltbush community. The high carrying capacity of this community might have permitted or selected a drastically reduced pattern of seasonal movement at a very early date. Given that a resource such as corn was known to a population whose exploitative system was attuned to this community, the pressures for its adoption would have been great. Corn is harvestable at points in the year when naturally available resources would have been low, and would have been a natural complement to these resources.

Bohrer (1970) points out that the double cropping which was practiced by the Hohokam would have led to a much more rapid rate of change in the genetic characteristics of corn and other cultigens, and a much more rapid selection for varieties particularly suited to the southern desert. A more rapid rate of growth and development among the Hohokam would have been expected as a result of these relationships. The rate of departure from other Desert culture behavioral patterns would have been rapid as would the continued rate of evolution. Thus, the rapid adoption of innovations in this area may be explained by internal processes rather than by postulating diffusion from Mexico. Taking this approach, we would not need to overlook other traits such as the domestication of the dog and cremation that were present during the Desert culture stage. There is of course no guarantee that this approach would work. But we must try in the coming decade to understand the changes that occurred in prehistoric Arizona in terms of the internal dynamics of the changing systems rather than by invoking the deus ex machina of diffusion or migration. Archaeologists cannot reject the occurrence of migrations when evidence of their occurrence is substantial—as in the case of Schroeder's argument concerning migration to the Salt River Valley. But neither can they afford to invoke them every time they see a change, even if it is an unusually rapid one.

CULTURAL ECOLOGY OF THE HAKATAYA

The Transition environment covers approximately the same percentage of Arizona's land surface as the Desert and Plateau ones. Yet, the variety of adaptations to this environment during the Pit House and Town Dweller stages greatly exceeded that of any other environment in the state. This variability is probably a reflection of both the great variation in natural environmental variables and of continual contact with adjacent Hohokam, Mogollon, and Anasazi populations.

Most of our evidence concerning subsistence-settlement systems in this area comes from the Town Dweller stage. While there is little good evidence, it appears that environmental variables were within their modern limits and plant communities were distributed over the environment much as today.

Bohrer (in Steen et al., 1962) has described the use of natural materials by the inhabitants of two late Town Dweller cliff houses in the Tonto National Monument. Her study provides a base line for interpreting somewhat more limited data from elsewhere in the Hakataya region. Rock and adobe were used in constructing these cliff dwellings. A variety of plant and wood products were used in building the roofs. Piñon, juniper, and sycamore were used for beams. Juniper shakes, saguaro ribs, willow withes, agave and sotol stalks, and reeds were interwoven to form the roof cover. Bohrer notes that the residents of these sites consistently selected building materials that grew in areas some distance upland from the site and did not use more locally abundant materials.

A variety of household items were found in these ruins. Agave and saguaro were used to make drill and hearth sticks for fire-making. Brushes were made of yucca and grass. Pine pitch and lac were used as glues and as coating materials for baskets. Hard-woods were used to make spindle whorls and battens for use in weaving. Weapons were also found at the sites: bows of hackberry branches, reed arrowshafts, and mesquite and screwbean clubs.

Cotton, agave, and yucca fibers were used in making cord and were woven into textiles. Cloth made of bighorn sheep and goat hair was also found at the site. Sandals were made of woven yucca, agave, and sotol strips and from juniper bark. Bear grass and sotol were the primary plants used in basketmaking.

Maize, beans (including common beans, tepary beans, lima beans, and jack beans), and squash (Cucurbita pepo, mixta, and moschata) were grown and eaten by the inhabitants of the Tonto Ruins. Food amaranths were present and may also have been cultivated. Gourds that were used for making containers may have been collected, tended, or cultivated. Cotton was grown in the vicinity of the sites. "Weeds" that grew in the agricultural fields were also used for subsistence. Little barley grass, canary grass, cocklebur, and amaranths were the most important of these plants.

Wild foods gathered by the inhabitants of the Tonto sites came from every plant community in the vicinity, and no one community seems to have been primary. The most important resources were as follows:

NUTS: acorns, piñon, walnut, jojoba
FRUIT: cholla, hedgehog cactus, hackberry, juniper berry, wild grape, yucca
GRAIN: bristle grass, cocklebur, paloverde, thistle
LEGUMES: catclaw acacia, mesquite
GREENS: cholla, agave, buffalo gourd

Bohrer believes that Saguaro fruit was probably eaten, although no seeds were found in the ruins.

The most important wild food resource at this site seems to have been agave, and indeed this cactus was a critical resource throughout the Transition environment. The cacti were collected by men in the early spring, carried back to the village, and roasted. The leaves were eaten, or allowed to dry and then beaten into a cake. The juice was used in making an alcoholic beverage. These plants are large, and the collecting expeditions may have required some organization. They were abundant in the environment, growing on many of the sloping surfaces. Di Peso (1956) has observed that the use of and probable reliance on agave by the Ootam was one characteristic in which they were distinct from the Hohokam, who do not seem to have used this plant resource. The residents of the Transition environment were probably not able to grow more than one crop each year. These resources were largely used up by spring, just when the agave was ready for harvesting. For this reason, it was probably a very critical resource throughout the Hakataya area.

Deer was the most important animal resource used by the inhabitants of the ruin. Antelope, jack rabbit, cottontail, bobcat, badger, fox, quail, mountain lion, mountain sheep, prairie dog, pocket gopher, kangaroo rat, pocket mouse, porcupine, wood rat, white-footed mouse, snake, turtle, and fish were also exploited.

It is impossible to describe in any detail the organization of these people on either an inter- or intra-site basis. Many of the sites in the area are compound sites. Houses were built inside a compound wall, and there is some suggestion that the entire community cooperated in building the compound.

Somewhat more information on organizational patterns is available in areas to the north and south of Tonto. The inhabitants of sites such as Hidden House, Tuzigoot, and Montezuma's Castle in the Verde Valley area grew corn, beans, squash, and cotton. Yucca, acacia, and agave were the most important gathered plant products. They hunted elk, mule deer, antelope, beaver, rabbit, turtle, and fish.

Mindeleff (1891) did a relatively thorough survey of this area, and his data shed considerable light on settlement patterns in the area. He found that a great variety of different sites were built in the Verde and adjacent valleys. There were large villages of twenty to several hundred rooms, cliff dwellings of a dozen or more rooms, cavate lodges—small limestone caves in which one or a few rooms had been built—and small boulder rings.

The distribution of these different types of sites is significantly patterned. (However, the lack of detail in Mindeleff's maps creates some problems in this regard.) Sixty percent of the large villages occurred in the main valleys, 24 percent in tributary valleys, and 17 percent on upland surfaces. The cliff dwellings were about equally distributed between the tributary valleys and the uplands, but only around 20 percent of them occurred in the Verde. Cavate lodges show a similar pattern of distribution. About 42 percent of them occurred in tributary valleys, 30 percent in the uplands, and 28 percent in the main valleys.

If this same pattern is observed taking drainages as the base, a distinctive pattern is still evident. In the large lowland valleys, 57 percent of the sites were villages, 40 percent cavate lodges, and 3 percent cliff dwellings. Sites in the tributary valleys were about 20 percent villages, 10 percent cliff dwellings, and 70 percent cavate lodges. Twenty-five percent of the upland sites were villages, 10 percent were cliff dwellings, and 65 percent were cavate lodges. The large villages had more rooms than cliff dwellings or cavate lodges, and therefore held more of the population than these percentages indicate. The distribution of the boulder rings is not clear. They seem to have occurred throughout the area on ridges overlooking field areas.

The pattern is a suggestive one. Large population aggregates were concentrated in the main valley and a few villages elsewhere. Cavate lodges were probably the homes of families. Cliff dwellings were inhabited by a group of intermediate size. This pattern could indicate that the adaptations to the different drainages were different. Upland valleys by and large supported less population than lowland ones. But the pattern could also have resulted from seasonal behavior. Populations might have come together in the lowland villages during one part of the annual cycle and dispersed to family or lineage units during the remainder of it. In any case, it does not seem that the resources available in the lowland valleys were sufficient to support the entire population of the region during the entire year. Population was either breaking up on some seasonal basis or was permanently dispersed with some families living away from the main centers. Nevertheless, the resource focus does seem to be on the lowland areas.

What resources in these lower-lying areas would have made them more important? Irrigation ditches at Montezuma's Well and Tuzigoot as well as others reported by Mindeleff indicate that at least by the Town Dweller stage irrigation was practiced in the valley bottoms. Minckley and Alger

175

(1968) report that 194 fishbones were recovered from one site (ASU N-4-2) that dated to A.D. 1300 to 1400. One hundred and twenty-four of these were identifiable and these were predominantly Gila sucker and Sonora sucker. Humpbacked sucker, roundtail chub, and squawfish were also eaten at this site. While fishing is not of critical importance to the modern populations living in this environment, it may have been so in prehistoric times. Agave pits were found near some of the sites in this area (Schroeder, 1960). It is not clear whether this resource was basically a lowland or upland one, although heavy reliance on it might have made it scarce in the densely populated valleys. Until archaeologists undertake excavations that provide detailed faunal and floral evidence from upland and lowland sites, this issue will remain unresolved. However, it seems likely that some element of economic difference between the upland and lowland site was critical to the success of subsistence efforts in this area.

Most of our information concerning subsistence in the Transition environment to the south of Tonto is the result of the work of the Amerind Foundation (Tuthill, 1947; Di Peso, 1951, 1953, 1956, 1958; Burt, 1961). Most of the sites in the region occurred on low ridges overlooking valleys. Irrigation canals found below some sites indicate that the valleys were used for farming. Remains of Colorado salmon, humpbacked sucker, and a large (6-foot) minnow were found at Quibori, indicating that rivers in the region carried more water than at present and were fished.

Plant resources found on the sites in this region do not differ significantly from those of Tonto. At the Upper Pima village of San Cayetano, corn, agave, and beans were the most abundant plant resources, in that order. Bear grass seed, pigweed, and walnut were also used there. Remains of corn, beans, squash, agave, cotton, walnut, and yucca were also found at Babocomari village. Very few plant remains were found in the Hohokam village at San Cayetano. The absence of agave at this and other Hohokam sites led Di Peso to his conclusion that agave exploitation was a major difference between the Hohokam and Ootam.

Rabbits accounted for about 40 to 50 percent of the animal bones found on sites in this area. Ungulates (white-tailed deer, mule deer, antelope, bison) account for around 30 to 60 percent of the bone debris. Fox, badger, squirrel, prairie dog, pocket gopher, kangaroo rat, wood rat, beaver, and some other smaller animals were eaten. Indian dog was also present at the villages and may have been used as a food resource. Hawks, owls, doves, quail, ducks, geese, turkeys, ravens, and robins were also eaten. Wild animal bones occur in substantially the same proportion at the Hohokam and Upper Pima villages of San Cayetano.

Reeve Ruin and the Davis Ranch Site were in Di Peso's view sites occupied by Salado migrants to the region. These sites are just across a river valley from each other. He argues that the Salado hunted somewhat different animals from the Ootam. The inhabitants of Reeve Ruin seem to have hunted white-tailed deer rather than mule deer or antelope, cottontail rather than jack rabbits, and to have taken many more birds than the inhabitants of the Ootam villages of San Cayetano and Babocomari. The deer remains from the Davis Ranch Site support this inference, but jack rabbit was far more important than cottontail. There are other significant differences between these two sites. They represent the ends of the range of the proportion of ungulate bones to all bones in the region; 31 percent of the bones at Davis were ungulates and 60 percent at Reeve. The inhabitants of

Davis were either not hunting deer so heavily or were leaving the carcasses on the trail. About half of this difference is made up by an increase in the percentage of rabbit bones at Davis and the remainder by a greater abundance of small game animals and dog. Differences in preservation may be at work here, but the patterned distribution of animal waste bones between the sites could indicate some degree of cooperation between the communities or slightly different cultural affiliation.

The pattern of organization of these sites is an interesting one. The earliest sites in the area such as Gleeson were a relatively random scattering of dwelling units. All of the later sites, however, were at least in part organized into compounds bounded by walls, terraces, or lines of rocks. The earlier compounds at Tres Alamos contained five to seven jacal houses. The later ones had about twice as many houses of adobe. Some houses at the site lay outside the compounds. There were about forty houses at Babocomari village organized around five plazas with some suggestion that these may have been compounds. The Ootam village at San Cayetano had about seventy houses and ten or eleven compounds. Bidegain ruin consisted of a single compound enclosing three houses. (By way of contrast, the Hohokam village at San Cayetano was not organized into compounds.) Late Salado sites in areas to the north were also compound sites. What does this unit of organization represent? There is some suggestion that the compounds at San Cayetano may have been economically differentiated, but it is not conclusive. Until detailed analyses of differences in economic specialization and style between the compounds are undertaken their meaning will be unclear. But their existence alone is an indication that some organizational unit smaller than the site was important in the Transition environment. Given the diversity in this environment it seems likely that these units may have played specialized economic roles.

Outside of the Verde, Tonto, and Ootam regions, our information concerning subsistence and settlement systems is much spottier. Most information concerning the Cohonina culture is the product of research carried out by John C. McGregor (1951, 1967) in the Mount Floyd area and northwest of Flagstaff. McGregor's efforts have produced a picture of immense variability in house forms in the area. This variability includes both the construction material and the arrangement of rooms on sites. Single pit houses, single surface rooms, alcove houses, patio houses, and forts all occur with some frequency in this region. Many investigators have argued that this variable pattern was produced by groups from different cultures who wandered through or lived in the area. Again, this argument is a tenuous one in that behavioral differences represented in the construction of different kinds of dwelling units do not necessarily imply cultural differences. Given what we know of the great natural variation in the Transition environment, it seems equally probable that these different sites may have been used by groups of different sizes engaged in different activities at different times of the year.

Unfortunately, the research plan that McGregor has pursued in the area, at least in its published form, is not of much help in resolving the problem. Site maps are not precise and it is difficult or impossible to determine the patterns of variability in the location of sites with respect to plant, animal, land, and water resources. McGregor's emphasis seems to have been on testing a variety of sites and not on intensively investigating a few. Of course, these techniques were appropriate to the spatial-temporal problems that he had in mind, but not to ecological explanations. Nevertheless, we can say something about subsistence and settlement in the region.

About 65 percent of the faunal remains recovered from McGregor's sites were rabbit. Rats, squirrels, prairie dogs, and other small animals accounted for another 15 percent of the animal resource base. Antelope and deer bones made up most of the remainder, but birds and carnivores were present. This seems a substantially heavier reliance on small animals than that which was characteristic in most areas of the Transition zone. While antelope and deer were undoubtedly still important given their greater biomass, the smaller animals seem to have been a much more important subsistence resource here than elsewhere. Animal remains tend to be most abundant in upland or upstream cave sites or impermanent irregular pit house sites. The more permanent sites seem to have been built in the larger lowland river valleys. Squash seeds have been recovered from some sites, but agricultural products have not proven abundant in the area. Nevertheless, the overall pattern is one of at least semipermanent villages in the lowland with upland hunting camps and temporary open-air dwellings. Variation in site size is still so great that it would be more than speculation to discuss demographic or organizational patterns.

Euler (1958) has described important subsistence resources that were used at sites where substantial quantities of Tizon Brown Ware (which he associates with the Cerbat Branch) were present. Unfortunately, these sites are spread out over an area enclosed by the Grand Canyon, Colorado River, Bill Williams River, and Agua Fria River. Thus, reliable ecological inferences are not possible. Nevertheless, we can obtain some idea of the subsistence resources used by these groups. Most of the sites that contain substantial subsistence evidence are cave sites. Only a few pit houses, usually located in valley bottoms, are known from this area.

Jack rabbit, cottontail, deer, antelope, and mountain sheep were the most important hunted resources in this region. The ungulates seem to be the most important single resource, even without taking their greater weight into consideration. Walnuts, mesquite beans, hackberry seeds, and gourds were the most important wild plant resources that these groups used. Sunflower, squash, corn, beans, agave, cotton, juniper berry, cholla, piñon nuts, paloverde, and yucca were also important. All of these resources suggest a fairly heavy reliance on the chapparal community. Some of the caves contain no plant materials at all and may have been used exclusively as hunting camps. Others are close to arable land and contain dwelling-like structures, so that they may have been used as collecting and agricultural stations.

Wright (1954), Baldwin (1943), and Schroeder (1952, 1961b) have described settlement patterns in the Colorado River Valley. Dwelling units occurred in rock shelters and on the first terrace above the flood plain of the river. Occupational levels were evident on sand bars and in dune fields near the river. These may represent loci where agriculture was practiced. Stone workshops and small storage pockets in cliffs are the remaining site types in the area.

Inhabitants of these sites ate bison, bighorn sheep, cottontail, jack rabbit, ground squirrel, kangaroo rat, wood rat, bobcat, coyote, quail, owl, hawk, and chuckawalla. A variety of fish, especially suckers and large minnows, were also eaten. It appears that populations living in this valley relied heavily on the valley bottoms for agriculture and wild resources. Nevertheless, they also hunted in highland areas where animals such as mountain sheep could be procured.

Most sites seem to have been the domicile of a single family or at most a few families. The major departures from this pattern are in the area now occupied by the Yuma. The more extensive and richer agricultural land, as well as being an ideal habitat for dense populations of water fowl, supported a much denser population in this area.

SUMMARY

Most of the conclusions reached in this chapter are hypotheses. Data required to test them adequately are not available and will not be available until more thorough jobs of collection and rigorous analyses such as those at Snaketown are undertaken. We could have continued, as many of our colleagues have done, to have extensively used ethnograpic data on the assumption that the prehistoric inhabitants of these environments exploited them in the same way that the modern ones do. We think that there is already substantial evidence indicating that prehistoric adaptations were very different from modern ones. If this is the case, then subsistence remains from archaeological contexts must be analyzed in their own right and not simply interpreted in relation to ethnographic data. Until this is done, we will not adequately understand the relationship between environment and organization in these areas.

X   Adaptation of Man
to the Mountains

In this chapter we deal specifically with the resources exploited by the Mogollon Indians and how the resources changed through time. We also deal with the patterns of organization that evolved as a result of the exploitative configurations. Adaptation is the key word, for to understand how these people lived we must understand how they adjusted to their environment.

Before settling down to subsistence and settlement patterns, we wish to speak briefly of the Mogollon culture and point out why it is merely a subsystem of Southwestern culture and not a distinct and independent cultural entity within the Southwestern system.

THE MOGOLLON CULTURE

In the mountainous area that bestraddles the Arizona–New Mexico border, a special cultural adaptation arose that in its earlier stages was functionally and even structurally different from Anasazi and Hohokam cultures. We refer to what is called the Mogollon (Moh-guh-yown) subculture. By "functionally different" we mean differences in the way activities of a culture are carried on as means of adaptation to the overall environment. We do not mean any differences in the systemic organization of societies or in the ways they are linked to the ecological communities in which they are situated. For example, visualize two cultural

systems both of which base their subsistence on gathering. One system occupies a desert and the other a mountainous, well-watered, cool environment. Naturally, we know that there would be many different ways in which things were done in the two cultural systems—due to the gross environment. There would be the differences in wild foods available and eaten, the tools used for carrying on daily activities, differences in seasonal activities and even perhaps in social organization. Hence, we would say that the differences in the foods collected and eaten, tools made, etc., were merely functional. In effect, the peoples of the two systems may be said to occupy similar ecological niches or places where they naturally live—their habitats. Since they are all hunters-gatherers they are structurally similar but the differences in the foods harvested are the result (the function) of their habitat and not due to a structural difference (Binford, 1968b, p. 324).

There is also the possibility that there were structural differences between the Mogollon, in their high mountains, the Hohokam in their low-altitude desert, and the Anasazi who inhabited the generally elevated Colorado Plateau.

What are structural differences in ecological niches? As the word implies, it means different kinds of "building," "organizations," or arrangement of parts. In short, it means different cultural systems reacting in different ways to a particular niche. If two cultural systems live in the same gross environment but occupy different ecological niches in that environment, we would expect to note differences in the ways in which the two cultures adapt and unite all parts of their systems to their particular niches.

An excellent example comes to mind in the case of the Hopi and the Navajo Indians of Arizona. They live side by side, so to speak. The Hopis are farmers; the Navajos are pastoralists. Each system has become linked ("articulated") to its own ecological niche in very different ways. In other words, structural differences imply different relationships, different adaptations between the cultural systems and the various elements in the ecological communities in which the cultures exist even though the gross environment is the same.

It follows, then, such cultural systems enjoying different ecological niches would be exploiting different elements and attributes of their niches and hence would be subject to different and differing types of selective pressures.

If a situation such as I have described for the Hopi and Navajo Indians had existed in prehistoric times (and, of course, it did) pressures in the form of *demographic* variables on either group would have caused a disruption of some kind.

Now in speaking of the Mogollon subculture, we are suggesting that it differed from Anasazi and Hohokam both functionally and also structurally. In the earlier stages of development they were all food collectors, then food collectors and farmers, and finally, all farmers. But they operated in different environments—and some of the differences in adaptation between these three best known Southwestern subcultures were functional only. But there were also, at least before A.D. 1000, some structural differences between the three cultural subsys-

tems. As time went on, each became more and more subject to qualitatively different types of selective pressures—population, climate, food, and so on.

We stress these points somewhat because much has been made in the past of the "trait" differences between these three cultural subsystems.[1]

ADAPTATION TO THE MOUNTAINS—THE MOGOLLON

In dealing with adaptation to the mountainous area, we should like to speak briefly of the variability of kinds of sites, the natural resources that were available for subsistence, the balance between gathering and agriculture, and what the settlement patterns were, and what the organization was that made the adaptation successful. In essence, we shall sketch briefly the evolution of the subsistence settlement system and how it exploited, processed, and stored foods.

The country occupied by the Mogollon people lies in two environmental zones: the mountain and the transition environments. It lies roughly in a rectangle about 300 miles east-west and about 270 miles north-south—a rectangle that is about equally divided east and west by 108° longitude. Within this rectangle are such places as St. Johns, Springerville, Albuquerque, El Paso, Reserve, Forestdale Valley, Cibecue, Grasshopper, Point of Pines, Show Low, Pinedale, Snowflake, and Silver City. The area is rugged, beautiful; that which is north of

[1] I think, however, that I have paid too much allegiance to differences in house types, tool types, and pottery types and not enough to the variables that direct change in the internal structuring of ecological systems. I often forgot that cultural differences and similarities are adaptive adjustments in the varieties of *ecosystems* within which the prehistoric Indians operated and within which they were participants. (P. M.)

the Mogollon Rim is 6,500 feet or over in elevation. Some of it is verdant and well watered, dotted with volcanic cones, and mountains, including the Mogollon Mountains. The Little Colorado, the Gila, and the Rio Grande Rivers lie within this area. Some of the area formerly occupied by the Mogollon people is south of the Mogollon Rim (see section B, chapter I).

The first inhabitants may have expanded from an on-going system to the south into this (Mogollon) uninhabited region. We have only a few data on early sites, the earliest perhaps being the Cochise tool kits that we found in western New Mexico (Martin, Rinaldo, and Antevs, 1949). This manifestation dates from about 2500 B.C.

Since so few sites of 2000 B.C.–A.D. 1 have been reported, it is not possible to say anything about settlement systems of earliest Mogollon times. Most of our evidence comes from sites that date roughly about 300 B.C. to about A.D. 1200, at which time the "inner," higher, the most rugged parts of the area that sits astride the Arizona and New Mexico borders were abandoned.

In order not to load the reader down with too many indigestible details, we shall consider the evolution of subsistence settlement systems in two sections: "early," about A.D. 300 to about 700, and "late," about A.D. 700 to about 1200.

SITE LOCATIONS

The early and earliest habitation sites of the Mogollon area tend to be located some 300 to 600 feet above valley floors on and at the extremities or tip ends of mesa tops —Forestdale Valley and Reserve areas (Haury and Sayles, 1947; and personal researches). The steep sides of the cliffs on three sides would have discouraged unwelcome visitors from attempting to enter the

village, while the open avenue of approach was protected by a wall or walls that sealed off the village by extending across the mesa top from one cliff edge to the other. All the villages on the high precipitous mesas were fortified in this manner.

Other villages were on lower terraces overlooking arroyos where concern for defense seemed to have been of less importance, but no village of this earlier period was ever built in valley bottoms.

Whether the higher, fortified villages are older than the ones on lower terraces, no one knows. But one wonders why the high defensible locations. One reason may have been that these villagers were on a tension zone created by the advent of these Mogollon sedentary farmers (corn, beans, and squash were present in the area by at least 3000 B.C.) who disrupted the population equilibrium balances of a nonsedentary group. Their supplies of wild food resources and hunting enclaves would have been diminished by the takeover of the farmers. Hence, one can suppose feuding ensued and something and someone had to yield. It is probable that strong selective pressure would have favored the people who were the more efficient in developing food production—in a word, the farmers. This kind of struggle reminds one of the hostilities between the cattle and sheep ranchers in the 1870s in Arizona.

Perhaps the villages on lower terraces were not on the edges of tension zones or they were built and occupied after the disappearance of the hunter-gatherers (Binford, 1968b, p. 332).

After A.D. 900, villages were rarely built on high mesas but were placed, rather, along or near streams in valleys. Defense, if once required, was no longer essential and one finds greater and greater numbers of villages taking advantage of verdant valleys where good arable land abounded and

PLATE 31 Artist's reconstruction of SU Site (Mogollon) pit house village, New Mexico. SU Site consisted of twenty-six pit houses, ranging in diameter from 15 to 20 feet; tunnel entrance to east, about 2 to 3 feet deep. From about A.D. 350 to 500. Southwestern Archaeological Expedition of Field Museum, 1939.

where water was flowing in streamlets. Irrigation may have been practiced in a limited way, especially after A.D. 1000 in Hay Hollow Valley (Plog, 1965) and at Grasshopper Pueblo (Longacre, personal communication).

DISTRIBUTION

Mogollon villages are extensively known in western and central New Mexico (Apache Creek, Datil, Reserve, Pine Lawn, Alma, Glenwood, Cliff, Mimbres Valley, El Paso) and in east-central and southeastern Arizona (Hay Hollow Valley, Snowflake, Show Low, Forestdale, Pinetop, Pinedale, the Ringo Site, and Grasshopper).

SIZE AND FORMS OF SITES

Early Mogollon villages were composed entirely of round pit houses. Indications of the sites consist of shallow depressions, sometimes so shallow that they can only be discovered by looking for them shortly after sunrise, when shadows are longest. Sometimes there is no evidence of pit house depressions, but there are other telltale signs that are useful in locating such villages. These are scatters of potsherd and debris from stone-tool manufacture with definable limits that range from one quarter of an acre to four or more acres. Sherds are not much larger than big crumbs and, since they and the natural gravels are brownish in color, it takes sharp observing to note them. The number of houses per village ranged from four or five to fifty or more. The total number of such sites is unknown, but survey data from our own work alone in New Mexico and Arizona suggest that there are hundreds of them.

Later Mogollon villages—after A.D. 900–1000—were composed of contiguous surface rooms with walls built of stone masonry, albeit of inferior quality. The rooms were strung out in a straight north-south axis or in the shape of an ell. Still later, rooms were built in a large block of contiguous rooms, massed so as to form a plaza, and often two stories high.

EXPLOITATIVE AND MAINTENANCE ACTIVITIES

Not many early sites have been excavated (Hough, 1920; Haury, and Sayles, 1947; Martin, 1943; Martin and Rinaldo, 1940, 1947). Furthermore, data concerning such items as activity areas, areas of social distinction, tool kit assemblies, sociotechnic items, food remains, raw materials, and earth ovens are sometimes lacking. But some statements can be made with a fair degree of accuracy.

Tools that were used for hunting and butchering, and for reducing seeds to flour (metates and manos) and for breaking up

PLATE 32 Pottery jar with polished red surface and narrow mouth, from about A.D. 500 to 700, found in the entryway of a Mogollon pit house (c), Pine Lawn Village, western New Mexico. (The white areas are restored portions.) Used for storage of dry foods and/or water, but not for cooking. Southwestern Archaeological Expedition of Field Museum, 1939.

PLATE 33 Excavating Tularosa Cave, Apache National Forest, Catron County, New Mexico. Photo taken from inner deep trench looking outwards. Materials in cave dated from about 2500 B.C. to A.D. 1000. Southwestern Archaeological Expedition of Field Museum, 1950.

nuts or woody and tough edibles (stone mortars and pestles) occur in high frequencies. Large choppers, hammerstones, and hand axes—all used for manufacturing tools that would have been used in food procurement or preparation—turned up more often than any other tool types. Tools of bone occurred rarely. Miniature animal effigies and fetishes of stone were recovered in sufficient numbers to permit one to infer that they represented ritualistic items. Sometimes, they were found with the very rare burials.

In the floors of houses, we found numerous deep, cylindrical storage pits. In one house we found six such pits. These had probably been floored over with planks. Many pits were also found outside of houses. Some had been used for barbecuing as the walls of the pits were reddened and baked hard from heat. The uses of many of the pits is conjectured as data concerning their contents are lacking. If we had employed flotation processes and/or analysis of the dirt for fossil pollen, we might have learned much about pit uses.

In later times and with the advent of masonry, storage facilities were provided in masonry-walled rooms, often with floors lined with stone slabs.

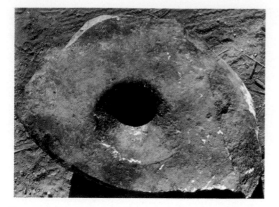

PLATE 34 Mortar for crushing seeds, nuts, and herbs, pecked out of a natural large boulder. Such mortars have a long history that extends back into the Hunting and Gathering stage. Overall length, 18 inches; weight, 30 pounds; date, about A.D. 500. Southwestern Archaeological Expedition of Field Museum, 1950.

PLATE 35 "Ceremonial" items from Tularosa Cave, Apache National Forest, Catron County, New Mexico. Field Museum Southwestern Archaeological Expedition, 1950. Top: atlatl or throwing stick, weights or "charm" stones; middle: crude pendant with sinew string still attached; bottom: "cloud-blower" type of tobacco pipe with bone mouthpiece and remnants of dottel of wild tobacco and effigy "feet," possibly bear paws. Dates: atlatl weights, 150 B.C.–A.D. 700; tobacco pipe, A.D. 700–900; pendant, A.D. 500–700; and foot effigies, A.D. 700–900.

SUBSISTENCE

Fortunately, we do know a lot about foods gathered or grown and about other plants collected for medicinal, and ceremonial and magical importance. This happy circumstance came about through the excavation of a relatively small cave (Tularosa Cave, Martin *et al.*, 1952) in which the deposits had been perfectly preserved. It probably yielded more knowledge concerning subsistence than any other cave in the Southwest up to that time. The deposits were bone dry, undisturbed, and laid down in a fairly orderly fashion so that the stratigraphy was clear. The chronological sequence was established by means of typolo-

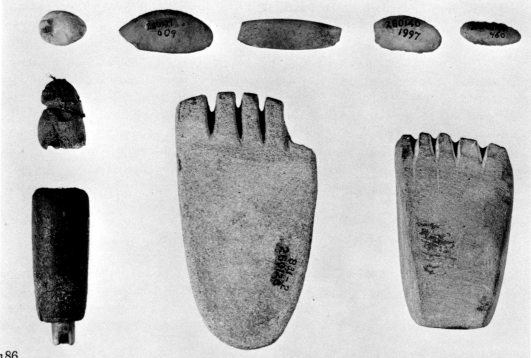

gies (not too exact) and by means of radiocarbon dating (much more satisfying).

Since the number of food plants—both wild and domesticated—is large, we merely list them and briefly indicate the uses to which they were put. The list includes plants utilized by the Mogollon and Anasazi (to be discussed in the following chapter) because the list of wild and domesticated foods is approximately the same. The Anasazi area produced a few wild plants not common to the Mogollon-mountainous area, and these are added at the end of the list of plants that grew in both areas and were exploited by both groups.

PLATE 36   Mortar and pestle of very tough igneous rock, found in a SU Site pit house, New Mexico, in a Mogollon village dating at about A.D. 200. Such tools were commonly used by hunters and gatherers and less frequently by agriculturists. Southwestern Archaeological Expedition of Field Museum, 1941.

PLATE 37   Storage basket with hinged lid, woven by tie-twine process, from about 300 to 150 B.C. The foundation is a bundle of grass; twining elements are narrow strips of yucca. Diameter 58 cm., height 37 cm. Southwestern Archaeological Expedition of Field Museum, 1950.

The accompanying list is an abbreviated one and shows astonishingly well what a variety of resources were exploited for a wide spectra of needs.

In addition to these plants we found bones of deer, bison, turkey, and muskrat—with deer being the most bountiful.

LIST OF PLANTS EXPLOITED BY MOGOLLON AND ANASAZI[2]

FAMILY OR GENUS	USE (as determined by ethnographic studies)
Pine Family— Juniper	Firewood; decoction from leaves drunk for medicinal purposes
Piñon	Nuts for food
Grass Family— Lovegrass, grama, Indian rice, reeds, dropseed, and corn	At least five genera were used for food; others were used in basketmaking; reeds, for roofing, pipe stems, cigarettes
Lily Family— Mariposa lily, bear grass, yucca	Food Weaving, sandals, baskets, soap
Agave Family	Food—drink
Willow Family (Cottonwood and willow)	Firemaking apparatus, effigies, medicinal (aspirin)
Walnut Family	Nuts used for food
Beech Family—oak	Acorns for food; wood for atlatls
Goosefoot Family (Chenopodeaceae)	Food
Amaranth Family	Food
Four O'clock Family	Medicinal
Barberry Family (Holly grape)	Arrow shafts, spindle shafts, medicinal
Mustard Family Tansy mustard	Eaten as greens
Caper Family— Rocky Mountain beeweed	Food; paint for pottery
Rose Family— Mountain mahogany	Dying skins and basket strands

LIST OF PLANTS (Continued)

FAMILY OR GENUS	USE (as determined by ethnographic studies)
Cliff rose	Medicinal
Pea Family— Kidney bean	Food
Mallow Family— Cotton Globe mallow	Weaving Medicinal
Cactus Family— Prickly pear Cholla cactus	Food Food
Evening Primrose Family	Ritual, medicinal
Potato Family Jimson weed Tomato (wolf berry) Wild tobacco	Medicinal Food Ritual smoking
Pumpkin Family— Gourds, squash, etc.	Food, utensils (?)
Sunflower Family— (includes sunflowers, sagebrush, thistle)	Food, medicinal
Horsetail Family	Scouring purposes

ADDITIONAL PLANTS EXPLOITED ONLY BY THE ANASAZI (COLORADO PLATEAU)

FAMILY OR GENUS	USE (as determined by ethnographic studies)
Mormon Tea Family	Medicinal
Grass Family— Corn	More rows and varieties than early Mogollon
Sedge Family— Rushes	Ceremonial

[2] The list of Mogollon plants is from Cutler (Martin et al., 1952, pp. 478–79). Additional plants for the Anasazi are after Whiting (1939).

Although this cave was used more or less continuously for about three thousand years, it would never really be called a house or a village. It may have served as a camping or storage place, but the smallness of the floor area would have restricted its use to a mere handful of people; and as the debris, ash, and discarded items increased, the amount of headroom declined proportionately. When we first entered it, one could crawl in, but certainly not stand up. Nevertheless, the contents provided us with a real gold-mine of information.

Several "mummies"—desiccated bodies— were discovered wrapped for burial. A "darning" basket filled with about a dozen balls of cotton yarn, a ball of human hair, and mummies of two wild turkeys were found with one individual.

VARIABILITY IN SUBSISTENCE-SETTLEMENT SYSTEM

As we have indicated from the above list of foods, maize was one of many. The earliest corn, found in the lowest levels of the cave, dates from about 2000 B.C. The cobs were small and of a "primitive" or early type of corn.

A study of plant remains from about 2000 B.C. to A.D. 500 in the cave by level showed that maize was slowly becoming more frequent in proportion to wild foods. But at

PLATE 38   A desiccated body of a male Indian of the Mogollon culture, wrapped in a rush mat tanned deerskin hide. Dated at about A.D. 100–300. Arrow (30 cm. long) points north. Field Museum Southwestern Archaeological Expedition to Tularosa Cave, Apache National Forest, Catron County, New Mexico, 1950.

about A.D. 500 there was a marked decrease in the amounts of cultivated foods and a proportionate increase in the amounts of wild foods utilized by the occupants. Whether this shift was due to the whims of the cave inhabitants or whether it was a widespread phenomenon, we do not know. Assuming that this change reflected a shift in subsistence activities of the general area, we are confronted with an interesting question. Why give up maize cultivation in favor of a regression to a subsistence economy based more on gathering wild foods? I estimate that the amount of corn found in the cave layers dating from about A.D. 400 to 700 fell by more than 80 percent. In other words, corn production fell almost to zero.

One explanation is that corn growing was difficult or impossible because of a decline in rainfall from about A.D. 500 to 700. This drought or really a series of short periods of below normal rainfall may, indeed, have been a factor in the shift in subsistence pattern at that time (Bluhm, 1960, p. 543; Martin *et al.*, 1952). We are somewhat wary of this explanation but have none other to offer as a substitute.

Be that as it may, the cave evidence suggests that the Mogollon people had achieved a nice balance between hunting-gathering and horticulture and when local selective pressures began to operate—for whatever reasons—they were able to step back in time—as it were—and adapt to the pressures that forced them to eat more wild foods for a few decades and more or less abandon corn-growing.

How long this turnabout lasted is conjecture, but our guess is about two hundred or possibly three hundred years. We should also like to add that according to our surveys the number of sites, the number of pit houses, and the area of space in square feet per house was the lowest during this period (about A.D. 400–700) for any of the

time spans in the fourteen centuries of the culture-history that we established for the Mogollon area.

It seems probable that some pressure or pressures were operating during the period from about A.D. 500 to 700. At any rate, the Mogollones did not become extinct but some of them hung on by the skin of their teeth and eventually made a comeback.

After this "depression," we found that pit houses were no longer round or oval but were square or rectangular, and the red-on-brown decorated pottery and plain brown ware utility vessels were gradually superseded by a pottery bearing designs in black paint on a white background and the utility pots also showed changes in color (gray instead of brown) and in the amounts and types of texturing (indented-corrugated). Interesting covariances, but we don't believe they were due to migration, although interaction and trade with other peoples undoubtedly contributed to the rapid transmission and integrative innovations from the Anasazi cultural system.

GENERAL TRENDS IN SUBSISTENCE-SETTLEMENT

The following remarks are based on complete data from Pine Lawn Valley, west-central New Mexico, where the senior author carried on research for fifteen years, but they will probably hold true for all Mogollon sites of the early period. The average size of dwelling rooms decreased through time. Before A.D. 500, the average floor space of pit houses was about 30 square meters (about 333 square feet); after that date the average fell to 18 square meters per house, and after A.D. 1000 the average size slipped again to 12 square meters per dwelling room. Thus in about one half of a millennium, the floor areas fell about 60 percent.

A reciprocal change took place synchronously in the average number of rooms or houses per village. As floor area of the houses decreased, the number of rooms increased. Thus, at or before A.D. 500 the average number of units per village was 17 pit houses; by A.D. 700–1000 the number of units increased to 50 per village (two pueblo rooms were counted as the equivalent of one pit house dwelling unit); by A.D. 1000 the average almost tripled to 136

units per village (again two pueblo rooms were classed as one pit house); and finally, at about A.D. 1100–1250, the number dramatically dropped to 6 units (double rooms) per village.

Thus, while floor areas decreased in size through time, the number of dwelling units increased in number. The explanation for this covariance has not been satisfactorily demonstrated. Several obvious inferences come to mind: a change in social organization from extended families living together in a few large houses to nuclear families,

PLATE 39   Room A, a dwelling room, Higgins Flat Pueblo, Mogollon-Anasazi, western New Mexico; about 12 feet by 18. Floor shown belongs to earlier occupation; slab-lined, ash-filled fire pit (center) and mealing bins (upper left) rest on unexcavated pillars of dirt belonging to later floor. Tree-ring dates establish occupancy at 1239–49. Southwestern Archaeological Expdition of Field Museum, 1953.

PLATE 40 "Ceremonial" objects (restored) of stone painted in reds, blacks, greens, and yellows; found as a group in a room next to a kiva. Top left to right: mortar, and two "bears"; bottom left to right: mortar, "sun" disc, and tobacco pipe. Colors may represent cardinal directions. Mogollon-Anasazi. Dated about A.D. 1200, Higgins Flat Pueblo, New Mexico; Southwestern Archaeological Expedition of Field Museum, 1953.

occupying less space, but, accordingly, needing more houses. That is, the population may not have increased very much; but theoretically a village consisting of say 17 large units each capable of holding 10 people or a total of 170 people is one thing, but if each nuclear family of 2 to 4 (average 3) people needed a separate dwelling, then 170 people would constitute a village of about 56 houses! Population may also have been increasing, but it is not the only reason for more house units.

But why change from houses holding extended families to those accommodating only nuclear ones?

We don't know the answer, but we think it has to do with subsistence activities. We suggest that if larger, corporate groups (extended families) could better cope with the procurement of food then that desider-atum would reinforce the size of the group in relationship to work activities. Since hunting-gathering may have been more important than agriculture in pre-A.D. 500 times, a big household would be an advantage.

Then later, when agriculture tended to be more important (post-A.D. 700), perhaps a nuclear family might have been the maximum optimum economic unit for handling food procurement.

Amid these changes other noteworthy changes were taking place: (1) the number of metates and manos per house decreased in frequency from early to late; (2) metate types shifted from basin-type metates (early) (more seeds and nuts to process) to trough types in late times as corn production increased; and (3) all other artifacts (stone tools) including knives, scrapers, choppers, drills, saws, projectile points decreased in frequency per room from early to late; (4) shapes of pit houses changed from round (pre-A.D. 700) to rectangular; and by A.D. 1000, surface, rectangular, contiguous masonry-wall rooms appeared although pit structures accompanying the surface pueblos continued to be built and used right up to the time of abandonment of the area (about A.D. 1250). Their function is unknown.

The shapes of kivas followed the pattern of the dwelling units. Early (pre-A.D. 700) they were round but larger than dwellings; when rectangular pit houses appeared, the kiva shape was rectangular; and after surface pueblos appeared (A.D. 1000) Great Kivas developed and they too were rectangular.

SUMMARY

Settlement systems are concerned with the manner in which man disposes himself and his buildings over the country in which he resides. It includes dwellings, ceremonial structures, and other buildings

PLATE 41   Great Kiva, Higgins Flat, New Mexico. Note axis of earlier kiva (lower floor where men are standing) is different from that of later (upper) kiva. Ramp of later kiva may have been used for entrance of priests in sacred procession. Deep holes were for gigantic (about 39 inches in diameter) upright wooden posts supporting the roof; deep grooves (man at left standing in one) may represent remains of "foot drums" (an oblong trench over which long planks were laid and on which ritual performers danced. Dated about A.D. 1200–1350. Southwestern Archaeological Expedition of Field Museum, 1954.

and their arrangements and relationships, one to the other. An analysis of a settlement system plus the configuration of exploitative and maintenance activities reflect many things: ecology, adaptation to the total environment (social and natural), the level of technology reached by the occupants of the settlement and, of course, the social institutions: social control and social organization.

In this section, we have dealt with the variability of site locations, site-size, changes in architecture, the natural resources that were exploited, what the settlement patterns were and what the changing patterns of adaptations were.

The big events were: (1) change from round to rectangular pit houses and eventually the latter plus surface pueblos of contiguous rooms predominated; (2) a slow steady adoption of maize, beans, and squash from about 200 B.C. to A.D. 500; (3) a regression to hunting and gathering for about 200 years (A.D. 500–700); (4) development of kivas from small ones to Great Kivas; (5) an increase through time in number of houses per village and an increase in number of villages, except for the "depressed" period of A.D. 500–700; and (6) a trend of Mogollon culture toward being functionally and structurally similar to the Anasazi culture to the north. This began soon after the "depression" referred to above.

This Anasazi "takeover" may best be explained by the proposition: "if two or more different kinds of sociocultural systems occupy adjacent environmental zones, the one that can be altered or adapted to fit the adjacent environmental zone will expand at the expense of the resident system" (the Mogollon, in this case) (Binford, and Binford, 1968b, p. 331). This is an application of the Law of Cultural Dominance (see Sahlins and Service, 1960, pp. 69–92). The Mogollones may have been reeling from their setback of A.D. 500–700 and ripe for being dominated, and we would expect the Anasazi system that was growing anyhow and becoming dominant in its own territory to expand into the juicy, verdant Mogollon zone and adapt to it. They needed an area to spread into. Certainly, all of our evidence indicates Anasazi influence and perhaps daughter communities that grew stronger with time. The surface pueblos, the Great Kivas, the Chaco-like black-on-white pottery, especially, suggest that a new cultural system had been able to alter their adaptation and expand. We also know that after about A.D. 900 the number of Anasazi villages grew in numbers and that Anasazi expansion of daughter communities was surging and spreading in several directions but especially toward the Mogollon area. For all intents and purposes the Mogollon area after A.D. 1000 became an Anasazi one. Eventually, diminishing food resources would result from a population density that would be greater than the area could carry and then a regression and finally abandonment would occur. This is exactly what happened, and after A.D. 1250 the region was permanently abandoned and the resident population shrank and withdrew northward toward the villages of the Zuni area.

We have not spoken too much of the balance between hunting and gathering and agriculture except to suggest in gross terms that gathering gradually diminished in importance as agriculture took over—except for the sad regression from A.D. 500 to 700.

XI Adaptation of Man to the Colorado Plateau— the Anasazi

The Anasazi culture in Arizona covered roughly the northeastern part of the state (about one third to one half). Some of this area was covered by the subculture known as Kayenta.

Data for this area on the subject of subsistence and settlement systems are sparse and uneven in character, especially for some periods. Consequently, occasionally we will draw on information from adjacent regions (Colorado, Utah, New Mexico) to round out the picture.

For the sake of convenience we will treat our data, when available, as: *early* or pre-A.D. 500 (Basket Maker II); *middle* —A.D. 500–900 (Basket Maker III and Pueblo I); and *late*—A.D. 900–1300 (Pueblo II and III). We will not describe the various environments for the Arizona Anasazi since it is more varied than the Mogollon. Suffice it to say that most of it lies in the Plateau environment (see chapter III for full description).

SITE LOCATIONS

Early and Middle

The most favored locations for early sites were a low mesa, a low terrace or bench overlooking a stream, a low ridge, and the base of a mesa. Prior to A.D. 900 the locations of villages were distributed in roughly equal proportions on mesa tops and valley ridges with a slightly higher number found on the former. No attempt was made to provide for any defense. This is in contrast to some Mogollon sites. Some canyon sites utilized cliff shelters, ledges, and crevices, some of which were high up in the canyon walls.

Late

After A.D. 900 villages were situated in fairly even numbers on the tops and sides of mesas, valley ridges, and on valley floors. After A.D. 900, villages were located in uplands areas (4,500 feet or higher), in or near river valleys, in the lower portions of tributary canyons and close to arable land and overlooking it, in cliff shelters, and in the open on sand dunes or upper ends of sandy ridges (Lindsay, 1969, p. 215).

After A.D. 1150 the inhabitants abandoned Grand Canyon and the upper Glen Canyon. It is assumed that a portion of the population increase that took place in the Kayenta area was made up of people from Glen Canyon. The shift in village locations after A.D. 1150 was toward increasingly frequent inhabitation of mesas and valley ridges and a corresponding decline in the density of settlement distributions on valley floors.

After A.D. 1230 this trend became more sharply characterized, principally through

PLATE 42 A rock shelter (behind trees) and a cave site, both of which were occupied by Indians of the Basket Maker III period—about A.D. 500–700 in Allan Canyon, southeastern Utah. Perishable articles such as yucca-fiber sandals, stockings knitted from human hair, and wooden spoons were found in the upper cave. These were preserved because no moisture ever penetrated the cave. Photo taken by diggers about 1889 searching for specimens for the Chicago World's Columbian Exposition.

the rapid disappearance of village sites located on valley floors. After A.D. 1230, in the Kayenta region, villages were built on terraces, low ridges, and higher mesas; but more frequently and increasingly, they were built in cliff shelters (Lindsay, 1969, p. 220). Distances between settlements became greater and settlements were often somewhat remote from arable lands. Hence, farmers had to travel greater distances to

their fields. Accordingly, "field" houses or seasonally occupied structures built at or near the cornfields came into being (Lindsay, 1969, p. 224).

After A.D. 1300 the Kayenta area was virtually abandoned and large villages developed in what is now called the Hopi Country and in the area around Flagstaff, Winslow, and in the rugged country just south of the Mogollon Rim. Some were located in pine forest, on ridges overlooking a stream, and on hills overlooking the Little Colorado River.

A recent survey in eastern Arizona (the Chinle Ganado, Fort Defiance areas) (Lee, 1966) indicated that the preferred location for sites in that area changed little from A.D. 500 to 1300. The exceptions were the pueblos built after A.D. 900 in narrow canyons where the bottom lands were too valuable to be wasted on domiciles. In these cases, the villages were erected in alcoves or in almost inaccessible caves.

VARIABILITY AMONG OCCUPATIONAL UNITS

Size of Villages and Village Plans

EARLY, PRE-A.D. 500

In Hay Hollow Valley, east of Snowflake, Arizona, the Field Museum excavated five houses at Hay Hollow Site that date from about 300 B.C. to A.D. 300. The village layout is not clear because five houses are too few to show clearly what the village plan was —if indeed there was one. On the basis of present evidence, it appears that there were two clusters with accompanying storage and cooking pits. The floor levels of the houses were four to ten inches below the present ground surface. The houses were provided with a short tunnel entrance that faced eastward or southeastward. A reddened basin-shaped area, centrally located, indicated a fire pit.

In another season, the Field Museum excavated three houses that were part of an extensive village that was situated in the alluvial flat bordering Hay Hollow Wash. The size of the village is not known but we estimate that it may have contained upward of ten to twenty houses or even more. It is likely that the entire alluvial flat was occupied more or less simultaneously and

may have accommodated several villages. The portion that we sampled dated from about A.D. 500 to 700. The village plan is not known, but we think that the houses may have been placed in random fashion.

In the Pine River Valley, northern New Mexico, two early villages called Valentine and Power Pole sites were excavated by Eddy for the Museum of New Mexico (Eddy, 1961). The portions excavated revealed fifteen structures (dating from A.D. 100 to 400), most of which were round surface houses. They were situated on a bench or terrace overlooking the river. The arrangement of houses appears to have been random. The house shapes were round to oval; several are referred to as being dumbbell-shaped because of the antechambers that were appended to the east or southeast side of the structure. Fire pits and storage pits occurred within the structures. The archaeologist who dug the site refers to two types of house structure: ring house type and nonring type. The ring type is distinguished by a ring of cobbles laid as a paving around the interior, shallow, basinshaped floor area. No explanation is given for the function of these cobble pavings.

Jennings (1966, p. 53) suggests that these cobble pavements or aprons may represent early experimentation with mud-stone masonry. In other words, they may be toppled walls. I agree with this suggestion.

One or two of the structures were large— one especially contained almost 70 square feet for the main part of the house, and 29 square feet in the antechamber, making a total of almost 100 square feet under a roof.

MIDDLE

Anasazi villages (about A.D. 500–900) consisted of (1) round, oval, or rectangular pit houses with accompanying storage pits, all grouped in a semicircle (Shabik'eshchee Village, New Mexico, Roberts, 1929); (2) pit houses arranged in clusters of three to six houses with accompanying surface storage structures (Kiatuthlanna Village, Roberts, 1931; Flat Top Village, Wendorf, 1953); or (3) a series of units of surface rooms, each unit comprising a double row of contiguous rooms, the rear rooms being built of crude masonry and the front rooms of wattle-and-daub. These units were laid out in the form of a crescent or an arc. The rear rooms were used for storage of foods; the front rooms were dwellings. The arc usually faced south or southeast and within the area embraced by the arc were pit houses or kivas (Martin and Rinaldo, 1939; Gladwin, 1945; Brew, 1946; Wendorf, 1953).

The number of pit houses per early village ranged from 3 (Roberts, 1931) to 50 (Bullard, 1962); and the accompanying surface rooms from 4 (Gladwin, 1945) to over 100 (Roberts, 1939; Martin and Rinaldo, 1939; Brew, 1946).

LATE

Anasazi villages became increasingly large (after A.D. 900), ranged in size from 20 to 200 rooms and were often multistoried. Before A.D. 1200, walls of pueblos were not straight, and corners were curved. Pit houses occurred individually and separated from the room block and also within the house block (Lindsay, 1969, p. 121). After A.D. 1200 the rooms and walls were more precisely built; and when rooms were added, the builders were careful to align the walls with the older walls and to make the corners square (Lindsay, 1969, pp. 122–23). Rooms were arranged in a straight line or in the shape of an ell or a semicircle. Sometimes extensions of walls were built to form a court area; or rooms were added to

form a plaza. It is interesting to note that the numbers of activity areas found in domestic and ritual structures were roughly equal prior to A.D. 900. This balance appears to have continued until approximately A.D. 1050, and thereafter the number of activity areas in living units declined while those found in ritual buildings increased to a point where there were nearly three times as many activity areas in kivas relative to the number which characterized houses in any one village.

EXPLOITATIVE AND MAINTENANCE ACTIVITIES

Early, Pre-A.D. 500

At Hay Hollow Site, Arizona (300 B.C.–A.D. 300), numerous metates were recovered—troughed (scoop-shaped with the trough closed at one end), grinding slabs or "basin metates," and manos of the one-hand type. These plus the presence of corncobs and corn pollen demonstrate that corn was crushed on them as well as wild plants, listed below.

In addition, we have an excellent and unique report on the paleoecology for the area (Bohrer, 1968). Bohrer's essay illuminates many facets of the subsistence patterns and climate. We shall briefly highlight a few aspects of her report:

1. Hay Hollow Valley received higher effective soil moisture at the beginning of the Christian era.

2. A piñon-juniper woodland belt surrounded the valley similar to what is found today fifteen miles to the southwest.

3. Wild plants probably used at Hay Hollow Site: alkali-sacatan grass, chenopodia and amaranths, cholla, one of the long-spine sunflower family, and Mormon tea.

The presence of over 250 pits at this site testifies to the fact that storage of surplus food and the roasting of cholla, maize, other food plants, and meat were important parts of the subsistence pattern, and indicated a fairly permanent village.

Tool kits consisted of choppers, bifacial blades, stone pounders and hammerstones, metates, manos, and some pottery. Much of the work of preparing food and manufacturing of tools was done out-of-doors, although some grinding of seeds may have been carried on in the houses. No bone tools were recovered, although we do not know why.

The slightly younger "Basket Maker" village (A.D. 500–900) that was situated on the Hay Hollow alluvium yielded bits and pieces of corncobs, Mormon tea, beeweed, mustard, beans, and Amaranth. These domesticates (corn and beans) and the wild plants were the mainstays of the vegetal diet. In addition, meat was provided by rabbits, deer, gophers, and prairie dogs as indicated by the faunal remains found in the houses.

In the Los Pinos phase sites in northern New Mexico (dated at about A.D. 100–400), a number of tools were found on floors of houses. These included choppers, projectile points, bifacial blades, scrapers, drills, stone mortars, hammerstones, punches, awls, manos, and metates. Some of the same tools were found outside of houses in work areas. About thirty fired brown ware sherds, similar to the few found at Hay Hollow Site, were recovered. They probably represent jars and bowls. In addition, unfired gray sherds turned up. It was felt that their preservation was due to the fact that they were unintentionally baked when the houses burned down.

Corn is the only food mentioned in the published report (Eddy, 1961, p. 94); but one supposes that wild foods were also collected and eaten. If not, the occupants of these sites were unique.

Middle Period, A.D. 500–900

Metates and manos found on the floors of pit houses and in storage rooms suggest that corn and perhaps seeds and nuts were crushed where most convenient. Metates were not enclosed in bins but were propped up on a stone of proper size so that the closed end of the metate was closer to the grinder and the meal would tend to slide down into a container—a basket or a bowl. Other evidences of activity were: mauls, for battering and pounding; hammerstones for pecking grooves into metates and for manufacturing blanks from which projectile points, knives, and scrapers were made by flaking; stone axes for cutting and chopping wood and roof timbers; stone bowls that may have served as mortars; utility pottery for cooking, and decorated pots for storage and for serving food; stone palettes for grinding paint pigments; knives, choppers, projectile points for butchering and hunting; drills for piercing wood, bone, shell, and turquoise. Tubular pipes, found on pit house floors, may have been smoked in ceremonies. (Since smoking was only performed for ritualistic purposes by Indians of the recent past [A.D. 1600] it is assumed that that custom obtained in the far past [A.D. 500]. Further, ancient pipes were made of stone, measured three or four inches in length, weighed many ounces, and were not ideally shaped to hold in the mouth except when supported by at least one hand. True, many pipes in ancient times were supplied with a bone stem; but this merely facilitated drawing on it.)

Tools made from deer bones occurred. Awls and bodkins were used for basketmaking, piercing, stitching leather, and making sandals from apocynum and yucca fibers.

Storage pits were dug into the ground near the houses. Diameters varied from

PLATE 43 Objects from a cache found with a burial in a cave in Grand Gulch, Utah. Most of the objects date from A.D. 700 to 900. From left to right: a potsherd, bone weaving tool, piece of rush matting, squash stem, pendant, miniature pitcher of pottery with projectile point leaning against it, a basket woven from vegetable fibers; a "whiskbroom" or floor brush inside basket; two projectile points in front of basket; two stone fetishes; two leather pouches; a wooden notched object; two projectile points, and a small wooden mortar (?). Excavated in 1889 for Chicago World's Columbian Exposition of 1893.

three to six feet and depths ranged from eighteen inches to six feet. Often a conical superstructure of poles, brush, and mud plaster was erected over these pits to shed moisture and to keep the contents of the pit dry. Sometimes the floors were paved with stone slabs and the walls lined with slabs (Roberts, 1939).

Cave storage pits were dug into the floor and lined with stone slabs. The cover consisted of funnel or dome-like structures made of poles and brush which were covered by mud plaster (Roberts, 1939, p. 8).

These storage pits served primarily as granaries for storage of corn since many of them, when dug, have contained sizable amounts of burned corn—both shelled and on the cob. Burned seeds from wild plants have also been recovered from storage pits.

In sum, the evidence indicates that from pre-A.D. 500 to 900 the villages were active settlements—small to large—that demonstrated a degree of homogeneity as reflected

in the generally constant orientation of surface rooms, to pit houses, to trash. Granaries, and clusters of tools in houses, in storage rooms, and in "work" areas indicate activity areas. Food was gathered, planted, and hunted; surplus was stored in specially built, vermin- and rain-proof storage pits or in surface storage rooms. Pottery vessels, fragments of pottery, and charred remains of baskets attest to the inference that cooking and processing of food (winnowing wild seeds from stems) took place at the village. Manufacture of tools of bone and stone, of baskets, of rabbit nets, of textiles, of pottery, butchering, unworked fragments of deer bones in the refuse suggest that we are dealing with some of the minutiae of daily living of people who lived much or all of the year in permanent villages. The magnitude of their round of activities—hunting, planting, harvesting, butchering, reducing corn or seeds to flour, cooking, manufacturing of tools, baskets and pottery, playing games, and performing rituals—suggest that all communities functioned as social and physical entities. In short, a successful and adaptive way of life and a selective exploitation of plants, animals, and natural resources reflect a social system that was well articulated with the environment.

PLATE 44   Human hair yarn ready for coiled netting and a pair of bone needles (top); leggings fashioned by means of coiled netting method from human hair yarn (middle); and hank of human hair ready to be spun into yarn. Found in a permanently dry cave in Butler Canyon, Utah. Excavated in late 1880s for Chicago World's Columbia Exposition, 1893.

PLATE 45   Apron of yucca strings from grave of Basket Maker III, Anasazi Indian, about A.D. 500–700. From Battle Canyon, Utah. Excavated in 1889 for Chicago World's Columbian Exposition of 1893.

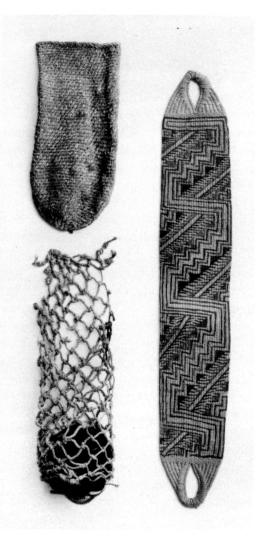

PLATE 46   Grave offerings from Basket Maker III, Anasazi, burial, A.D. 500–700. Top left: pouch of woven buckskin strips; bottom left: crocheted pouch or sock containing ball of human hair ready for spinning; right: tump line (forehead band) woven from yucca fibers and bearing a design painted on surface with mineral paints. Tump line was placed around forehead and a load of firewood or a basket of seeds carried on the back was fastened to the tump line loops by means of yucca rope. From Battle Canyon, southeastern Utah; excavated in 1889 for Chicago World's Columbian Exposition of 1893.

Late

Many statements concerning the exploitative and maintenance activities that are given above will also hold for the later time periods. But, there are also *some* differences, some of which are due to more data and better preservation, especially villages in dry caves.

Metates and manos occurred. They have been found in all types of rooms; and examples of metates in various stages of manufacture have been discovered in courtyards (Lindsay, 1969, p. 152). Flat, slab-type metates were more commonly used and usually were found set in a mealing bin. A mealing bin is a stone-lined box, without cover, large enough to hold at least one metate in a fixed slanting position with the grinder's end elevated several inches. Two, three, and four metates have been found adjacent to each other with vertical slabs between them. When such a multiple assemblage is found, metates range in texture from coarse to fine. Occasionally, bins have been found containing several metates made from different kinds of stone (sandstone to volcanic) but with similar grades of texture. Such metates have been washed with distilled water that was then examined for fossil pollen. This ingenious type of investigation has indicated that metates were sometimes used for grinding different *kinds* of foods. In one case (Hevly, 1964, and personal communication) Dr. Hevly found that one metate had been used for crushing corn, another, for cactus, and the third for piñon nuts.

Sometimes several sets of bins were arranged in pairs, side by side or facing one another. We know from experience that grinding enough corn for daily needs required a lot of time and hard work. It is probable that several women carried on this activity simultaneously, thus providing an outlet for gossip, exchanging news, and socializing.

Metates and/or metate bins occurred in rooms of all types and in courtyards where women of the same residential unit may have done their daily grinding chores.

Another distinction between early and late is that the Indians of the later period often constructed grinding rooms, that is, rooms which provided a suitable spot in a cluster of rooms (living and storage) where food preparation could be carried on. Nearby was a fire pit to provide heat in the winter, or heat for some step in food preparation, or for cooking. The last seems unlikely because the grinding rooms were often small. The pit houses, not connected with the block of living rooms, may also have been used as grinding rooms (Lindsay, 1969, p. 122).

Tools used for the following activities were found in abundance: for food preparation, cooking and serving—pottery vessels, jar covers of sandstone discs, mortars for crushing nuts, metates, manos, fire hearths, and fire dogs; for hunting and butchering—arrow points, utilized flakes, choppers, knives, and scrapers; for manufacture of tools—hammerstones, cobbles, anvils; drills for drilling holes in a cracked pot, one hole on either side of the fracture after which the two parts were bound together with string, and for drilling holes in wooden slabs, the use of which is unknown; axes for maintenance and building and chopping trees down; and mauls and hammerstones for pecking metates.

Workshop activities were often carried on at the quarries, as is demonstrated by the fact that finished and unfinished tools as well as tool blanks have been found there (Lindsay, 1969, p. 280).

In addition to these tools found mostly in open sites, a study has been made of artifacts made from perishable materials and found in dry cave villages, especially in the Kayenta area (Anderson, 1969).

For food preparation and serving, there were scoops, ladles, and bowls that were made of wood and squash or gourd rinds; for food tongs, tied sticks and bent branches; for stirring, paddles of wood.

For containers: baskets in bowl and try shapes; well-decorated pottery; cloth and animal hides were fashioned into sheaths, bags, and pouches.

For carrying or suspension of pots: nets of yucca leaves or of string; for carrying loads of wood, etc., tump straps and lines made from human hair or plant fibers.

Covers and stoppers were made from wood, mud, corncobs, and gourd rinds; piñon pitch was used for coating baskets to make them water-tight, for repairing broken pots, and for fastening handles to tools such as chipped stone knives.

Torches were fashioned from strips of juniper bark and bound with yucca twine.

Bone tools such as gouges, fleshers, awls, and the draw scrapers were used for working hides. For doorway covering there were plaited mats of cattail reeds and sewn mats of bulrush; or stone slabs.

Cradle frames were made of wooden rods tied to a U-shaped branch.

For manufacture of cloth, there were weaving tools from which it is inferred that the true loom was present; loom holes in kiva floors for tying down the bottom of the loom; raw cotton, spindle whorls, and cotton plants, from which cotton was carded by wooden combs. Loom parts, such as bent-stick loom floor anchors, roller bars, warp rods, battens, shuttles, shed and heddle rods, a device (a temple) for keeping cloth stretched to the proper width during the weaving, have been recovered.

Clothing forms are not well known, but archaeologists have found sandals woven from yucca leaves and bast cordage with ties of bast, leggings of hide and human hair, and breechclouts of yucca, doeskin, or cotton cloth. Robes and blankets of rabbit fur or feather-wrapped cordage were used perhaps as blankets and certainly as robes. Mantles of deerskin were also worn.

Planting of seeds was done with digging sticks of oak by punching a hole in the ground, dropping the seeds therein, and neatly closing with the stick or the big toe (personal observation of Maya Indians).

Wooden sticks may have been employed as hafts for hoes.

Artifacts of bone and wood, called "dice," may indicate gaming activities. Each die was incised on one surface.

Ceremonial items were: bull-roarers, a box for storage of feathers, fetishes, and altar (?) pieces. Cigarettes made from cane and stuffed with true tobacco were smoked. Painted objects of wood which represent sunflowers and a bird were cached in Sunflower Cave (Kidder and Guernsey, 1919).

PLATE 47   Darning basket with five balls of cotton yarn—black, yellow, red. Found with a late burial in a cave in Battle Canyon, south-eastern Utah. Pueblo III—or about 1150–1300. Excavated in 1889 for Chicago World's Columbian Exposition, 1893.

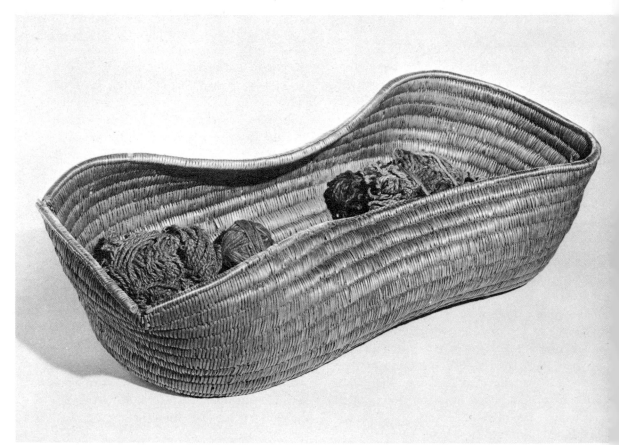

SUBSISTENCE

In some ways, the exploitative economy of the Anasazi was similar to that of the Mogollon. In other ways, it was somewhat different in that more microadaptations had to be made and that the technique of exploitation was perhaps more complex.

From the earliest settlements comes evidence of agriculture. Certainly the pit house villages of Flat Top (Wendorf, 1953), White Mound (Gladwin, 1945), Kiatuthlanna (Roberts, 1931), and Allantown (Roberts, 1939), all of which date from about A.D. 700 to 1000 were dependent on corn agriculture to a certain degree. Charred corn was found in granaries and rooms. It seems fairly safe to assume that corn was known in the area as early as A.D. 500 and perhaps earlier. In addition, beans, Indian rice grass (Oryzopsis hymenoides), and piñon nuts (Roberts, 1939, p. 264) were found in the cultural deposits of one village. It is supposed that they supplemented the maize diet. Bones of antelope, deer, and rabbits were also found in the refuse, and their presence may indicate that they provided meat.

It seems highly probable—a statement based partly on our work in Hay Hollow Valley, Arizona, and by observations on contemporary Hopi Indians (Whiting, 1939, pp. 19–20; Beaglehole, 1937, p. 50)—that wild plants were gathered and used to enrich and supplement the agricultural products, especially when crops failed.

No one knows precisely how much of prehistoric diet was made up of agricultural resources versus those that were gathered (wild plants) and hunted. Recently, Schiffer (1970) has attempted to measure the extent to which Basket Maker III populations (about A.D. 500–800) depended on domesticates. His tentative conclusion is that about one half of the diet consisted of domesticated plants.

For the later periods (A.D. 900–1540 we have more data, especially for the Kayenta area.

Corn continued to dominate the scene as the most important agricultural product, with beans and squashes following in that order. Again, wild foods were important—especially prickly pear cactus and beeweed. Thus a blend of domesticates, wild gathered foods, and deer, mountain sheep, antelope, and rabbits permitted the people to exist. Sometimes, depending on crop success, subsistence was ample; other times, it was not. It all depended on a combination of resource staples and how they were integrated and on rainfall or irrigation. The Indian always had two aspects of his environment to consider—wet and dry years. Experience may have taught them how to forecast these cycles in a rough sort of way and how to brace themselves against total failure. They undoubtedly tried to choose arable land where experience showed them that rain was more likely to fall or where irrigation or floodwater farming could be used to expand an ecological niche. But it was all very chancy, and there was no way to hedge their bets.

We do not know anything about the number of cultivated acres that were necessary for a settlement to survive. A glance at Hopi Indian agricultural practices may be suggestive. For about forty years (1890 to 1930), they have farmed three to four acres per person (not counting infants) with about 55 percent in corn, 30 percent in beans, melons, and vegetables, and about 15 percent in fruit trees. (Fruit trees were introduced by the Spaniards and were totally unknown before A.D. 1540.) In prehistoric times, this 15 percent of land presently devoted to fruit trees may have been divided between maize, beans, and squash. One acre of corn produced (in 1892) about 12 bushels or 672 pounds, which barely supported the needs of one person, since the annual consumption of corn per person was estimated to have been 692 pounds (Woodbury, 1961, p. 38). Thus, theoretically, a settlement of a hundred persons would have required cultivation of 300 to 400 acres. It is possible that as a guarantee against crop failures in certain fields, more than four acres per person might have been planted in scattered plots.

Some sorts of water control devices came into being about A.D. 1000. Three systems seemed to have been in use: (1) the diversion of excess water; (2) improvement of water distribution and retention methods; and (3) transport of water to land usable only if irrigated (Woodbury, 1961, p. 87). These systems were made to function by means of: (1) terraces or low walls built across the bottom of a small rocky dry stream bed. The purposes of the terrace were to hold soil so that a series of small farming plots was created and to slow runoff rainwater so that it would soak into the ground; (2) linear borders consisting of rows of boulders piled two or three high that ran across the slope to prevent erosion and to slow down runoff from heavy rains; (3) grid borders which were lines of stones or low walls arranged in two directions, usually more or less perpendicular to each other. Their purpose, also, was to control soil erosion and to slow ruinously fast runoff (Woodbury, 1961, pp. 11-13). Lindsay suggests that grid borders, in addition to controlling erosion, acted as borders for individual fields (Lindsay, 1961, p. 183); (4) ditches consisting of two parallel lines of stone slabs about 8 to 15 inches apart. At intervals, notched stones, set at right angles to the ditch walls, were fixed to serve as turn-out gates. The function of the ditches, which were relatively short (30 to 100 feet long) was to carry water to areas not usually watered by other sources. The water sources for the ditches is unknown but may have been from springs or rain runoff (Lindsay, 1961, pp. 183-84; and 1969, p. 209).

One of the more remarkable water control devices was found in Utah (Sharrock, Dibble, and Anderson, 1961). It is rare because of its distance from a community and because of its complexity. The device consisted of a large masonry spring-fed reservoir (27 feet long by 11 feet wide by about 4 to 6 feet high) capable of storing about 10,000 gallons. This may seem pint-size to modern ranchers, but it probably helped the ancient farmer more than we can imagine. The drainage complex was ingenious. At one end, there was a drain in which was set a perforated slab. The flow of water may have been controlled or turned off by the use of a stone slab placed partially or entirely over the drain hole. The water ran from the reservoir into a stone-lined ditch, a short section of which was located and cleaned out. The date on this reservoir was placed tentatively at A.D. 1100-1200.

Some of the plants gathered or grown by the Anasazi Plateau people are listed near the end of the previous chapter. As we mentioned earlier, plants utilized by both Mogollon and Anasazi were identical although the Anasazi exploited a few peculiar to their area and cultivated more varieties of maize.

GENERAL TRENDS IN SUBSISTENCE AND SETTLEMENT SYSTEMS

Anasazi sites on the Colorado Plateau have two characteristic locations—no matter whether early or late: (1) ridges, low terraces, and higher mesa; (2) in cliff shelters or caves or at the base of caves.

The shapes of pit houses varied from round, through oval to rectangular. Some houses were supplied with a rather long entrance tunnel through which the occupant crawled to gain entrance to the house proper. It has been suggested that this lateral entryway was a result of trade or intercourse with the Mogollon culture (Wasley, 1960b, pp. 34–35). After A.D. 800 or thereabouts the lateral entry-antechamber complex was converted to a ventilating system. The distribution of round or rectangular houses with or without lateral entry-antechamber-ventilator units was probably due to functional and adaptive differences rather than to caprice.

Later and late sites consisted of aboveground pueblos with contiguous rooms, storage rooms, as well as subterranean grinding rooms or pit houses and kivas. Almost all pueblos were "front oriented"— that is, they all faced out onto a common passageway or street. Later, the courtyard developed out of these front-oriented room blocks. Courtyards consisted of an open, unroofed area lying in front of several domestic rooms. They occurred at both open and cliff sites. Sometimes a village contained several courtyards. Plazas, also unroofed, were a somewhat more formal organization of houses, walls of masonry or wattle-and-daub, completely enclosing an area that usually included a kiva, centrally located. Plazas occurred only at open sites. Secular activities were carried on within this enclosure and perhaps ritual dances also. Plazas and courtyards were mutually exclusive; sites with plazas had no courtyards (Lindsay, 1969, pp. 160–69). Toward the end of the fourteenth century, rooms were built en masse all facing inward toward a square. Villages built in caves were obliged per force to fit their buildings to the shape of the cave but were usually arranged so that rooms of a residential unit opened into a courtyard and it, in turn, toward the canyon, many of which are spectacular.

High frequency of storage pits and excellence and durability of the heavy framework of the pit houses (about A.D. 500–900) suggest permanent villages. In addition, permanent and integrated social systems are indicated by: (1) workshops for manufacturing stone tools; (2) clusters of tool kits used in food procurement and preparation found on floors and in butchering areas outside of houses; (3) evidence of recreational and ceremonial activities.

Certainly, later sites were permanent towns without question. The sturdy masonry walls of surface rooms, the elaborate provisions for storage and preparation of food, the evidence of nearby irrigation devices for extending the ecological niche, the evidence of developed crafts (spinning, weaving) for rituals, for games, for manufacture and construction, all suggest sustained occupation and a culture well adapted to its environment.

SUMMARY

After reading these descriptions, one may say: "Well, so what?" To counteract this, let us see if we can draw a few conclusions from these data and suggest a few hypotheses as to the meaning of these changing patterns of adaptation.

In earliest times (see A.D. 300) the Anasazi exploited at least six principal kinds of wild plants and some maize. The tool kit assemblage was fairly simple and consisted of approximately nine different classes of stone tools (metates, manos, bifacial items that would include knives, scrapers, and gravers; stone bowls, grooved tools, and odds and ends of stone flakes that were discarded when stone tools are manufactured. Some of these flakes were collected and used in various ways; hence, the term utilized flakes.)

After A.D. 1000 the Anasazi consumed corn, beans, squash, and at least ten wild foods. The classes of stone artifacts in the tool kit numbered about thirty to forty, most of which were manufactured for particular tasks.

Thus, it is evident that the ratio of food types to tool types increased in direct proportion from early times to late. The tools of the late periods used in exploitation and preparation of food stuffs and for general maintenance were more specialized for efficient processing of foods and were adapted to more specific tasks.

Elsewhere, we have noted that the Anasazi began to aggregate from about A.D. 1000 onward. There were fewer towns per square mile, but the towns that did exist became larger. Archaeologists are not sure what caused this tendency to crowd together in increasingly larger towns. Steward (1955, p. 167) suggested that the concentration was caused by a nonecological factor—in this case, the need for defense. However, as Harris (1968, p. 670) points out, increased strife leading to the need for defense would have been a probable effect of ecological factors such as population increase. At any rate, such population movements did occur. They might also have been caused by cultural, as well as environmental, stress that was linked to a generally constant decrease in the varieties of environments which the people had formerly been accustomed to exploit. Eventually, some of the population would have been obliged to relocate in defensible positions (cliff shelters) or ecologically marginal areas where more stress may have resulted (Gorman, personal communication).

Finally, arable lands were probably limited in extent and at a premium. Thus, with the total pueblo area shrinking in size, it is not difficult to hypothesize that a situation existed in which changes in the entire cultural system occurred and made interaction between the cultural system and the environment difficult or impossible. If my assessment of the situation is roughly correct, then it might be interesting to advance a hypothesis by Miller relating to changes in systems. Miller (1965, p. 401) says, "As stress increases it first improves system output performances above ordinary levels and then worsens it. What is extreme stress for one subsystem may be only moderate stress for the total system."

It seems likely that by A.D. 1000 or even 1100, stress was widespread in the Anasazi area. The florescence and exuberance in the proliferation of pottery forms, colors, and designs (black-on-white, black-on-red, black, red, and white and other polychromes), in the burgeoning of classes of specialized tools, in the perfecting of the "classical" and beautiful small kivas and the overpowering Great Kivas, in the excellence of masonry and multistoried pueblos, and in the irrigation and the hydraulic devices for extending the ecological niches appear to be examples of cultural activities above earlier levels. These experiments with the technoeconomic systems and the merging of formerly localized lineages into clans probably offset the stress for a time, but after A.D. 1200 or 1225 (Lindsay, 1969) environmental conditions appear to have worsened and the whole cycle of stress and adjustments to it resumed. The population was obliged to depend on increasingly large amounts of wild foods since maize plants often starved for rain. The layout of villages and the groupings of rooms and storage areas suggest increasing coordination and cooperation among the various kin groups. Experimentation was resorted to in the way the fields were scattered in order to take advantage of areas where local rains most frequently fell and in the frenzied building of more reservoirs, garden terraces and irrigation ditches; in the probable increase in rituals that would induce the rain gods to look with favor on the plight of the people, nevertheless a viable equilibrium was never again attained, and by A.D. 1300, or shortly after, the Kayenta and the entire northern section of the Anasazi system collapsed. It is at about this time that the Hopi towns (Oraibi, Awatobi, Shungopovi, Walpi, etc.) began to increase in size swelled by the refugees from the stricken areas. By A.D. 1400 all the towns in northern Arizona, in the Mesa Verde area, and in the Chaco Canyon were abandoned. Many of the great towns farther south (Kinishba, Grasshopper, and others) began to grow with the arrival of displaced persons.

Among other matters discussed in the earlier parts of this chapter, we touched on the location of sites, sizes of villages, and exploitation activities. One of the crucial questions that archaeologists may ask is how did changes in the economic subsystem affect the social subsystem. Below are two models designed to explain different aspects of these relationships.

Zubrow (personal communication) has suggested an evolutionary model of the relationships between land, labor, kin groups, and band or village communities. He defines two analytical units, the village (an aggregate unit) and the producer (the smallest social unit or kin group involved in production). In this model the differential marginal productivity[1] of land and labor is used to explain changes in the relationships of the variables mentioned above.

In early times (300 B.C.–A.D. 300) when gathering of wild foods was more important than agriculture, it is possible that extensive enclaves of land would have been of paramount importance for maintenance of band-group-villages, while manpower would have been of greater importance to kin groups since each had to fend for itself. The marginal productivity of land is suggested to be greater than the marginal productivity of labor for hunting and gathering economies at the village level. On the other hand, the marginal productivity of labor would have been greater than of land for the producing unit.

In late times (post-A.D. 1100) when agriculture had become more important than hunting and gathering, the situation appears to have become reversed. In this case it is possible that land (in the form of farm plots) would have been more important to the kin groups while communal labor organized on a nonkin basis was of greater significance to a village (for ceremonies, defense, and construction and maintenance of buildings, water control systems, and other "public works" projects). In other words, as Mellor (1969, p. 210) notes, the level of production and output of the individual producer in subsistence agricultural economies is a function of their land, while the production of the aggregate unit is a function of labor.

This model has not been tested but might be productive if tested. The second model has been tested and is concerned with economic and social autonomy.

One hypothesis that has been tested is one that is concerned with economic and social autonomy (Leone, 1968). The hypothesis reads as follows: "With increasing dependence on agriculture, the social distance between minimal economic units will

[1] Marginal productivity is an economic term which means the additional amount of production which results from an additional unit of input—such as adding one more person to the labor force.

become increasingly great." We cannot summarize Leone's whole array of arguments; we can only cite a little of the evidence.

1. Variability in types of tools indicated increasing reliance on agriculture rather than food collecting.

2. Pottery styles were shown to be related to social groups and kinship.

3. Increased reliance on agriculture and increased matrilocality suggest a trend toward endogamy. That is, males from another kin group within the village provided marriageable partners for the women.

4. Hence, cooperation within the village would have counteracted tendencies toward fission. (In other words, villages were independent units with little dependence on nearby villages.)

In later times (after A.D. 1000) the reverse became true. Due to a possible shift in rainfall patterns, corn-growing became more and more difficult. Dependence on collected wild foods became a necessity. With this breakdown in corn-growing and a *decreasing* dependence on agriculture, social distance became less. Thus one would expect a shift in social relations and greater extension of ties and cooperative efforts between kin groups. This is exactly what we see reflected in the architecture of late large villages. Social distance was no longer possible.

Another hypothesized relationship between architectural and environmental aspects of Anasazi settlement was tested (Gorman, personal communication). The hypothesis proposes that the amount of diversity in archaeologically defined components of Anasazi villages is proportional to the diversity of village settlement over a spectrum of prehistoric environments. Simply stated, correlations exist between the frequency of site location in each of three broad, yet distinct, types of environment and the frequency of architectural features characterizing some or all prehistoric villages inhabited during each of four arbitrarily defined periods of time.

By necessity, analysis of this sort is structural for it involves evaluating the association of two different kinds of phenomena through application of an abstract measure —that of diversity, or specifically, levels of diversity. The aim of this approach is not one of defining the role of prehistoric cognition involved in the adaptation of the Anasazi to their environment. Rather, the study focuses upon changing relationships between empirically defined aspects of the total environment which may have affected the adaptive propensity of the Anasazi world view at four points in a sequence of time ranging from A.D. 650 to approximately 1250. The assumption is made that a population's capacity for viable adaptive response to environmental change is roughly proportional to the amount of cultural diversity (however this is defined) which exists in that population.

Indices of diversity were derived for four successive eras, three of which are approximately two hundred years in length. Forty-four villages were analyzed in the study. All traits used in the analysis were drawn directly from archaeological monographs and site reports. Bluhm's monographs (1957a, 1960) were used as an aid in the classification of data for comparison. The analytical procedure is described in the following paragraphs.

Architectural and environmental features that characterized the total range of the Anasazi settlement system were ordered to form a matrix in which the frequency of the items diagnostic of village settlement in each era were plotted. The matrix also contained the maximum number of non-repetitive trait combinations within each category of phenomena association that was analyzed. Eleven categories of associated features were held constant throughout the analysis as was the maximum number (66) of nonrepetitive associations. This was theoretically feasible because the inventory of Anasazi settlement features did not increase in geometric proportions through time. Settlement attributes characteristic of early periods were not always found in succeeding ones.

The second step in the analysis involved evaluating the degree to which attribute associations characterizing the population of villages in each era were diverse. Ratios were derived for the actual number of diverse associations in each category by comparing them to the corresponding maximum number of nonrepetitive associations theoretically possible in each category. The sum of these ratios for all categories within a period were then averaged to render an approximate index of diversity. A compensation factor was introduced to prevent statistical skewing which would arise from ignoring unequal sizes of populations of villages within the different periods. The number of villages from each period was subtracted from the total population of villages used in the study. The resulting number from each of the four periods was multiplied by the index determined for each period. Eleven villages comprised the sample dated between A.D. 650 and 850, fourteen within the period A.D. 850–1050, thirteen villages formed the population dated from A.D. 1050 to 1200, and six were placed within a period dated A.D. 1200–1250.

Maximal diversity for each and all cases is theoretically represented by the unit value 1, when the actual number of diverse associations matches the number of possible associations. In order to make this value relevant and consistent in relation to the compensation factor, the number was multiplied by the total population (44) of villages. The index of theoretical maximal diversity then became forty-four.

Analysis of architectural aspects of Anasazi settlement correlated prehistoric use of (1) angles and curves in floor shapes to (2) their positions above, on, or below the contemporary surface of the ground; floor shapes to (3) the shapes of interior features; floor shapes to (4) spatial configurations of the village; (5) numbers of building materials to (6) numbers of functional types of architecture. Numbers of building materials were also compared to (7) the number of floor shapes in each village. Activity areas in (8) storage, (9) living, and (10) ritual units were also compared. These factors were in turn related to the frequency of village locations on (11) the surfaces of mesas, valley ridges or terraces, and valley floors. Analysis revealed that the quantitative measures of relationships between architectural components of Anasazi settlement varied with the degree to which the population of villages in each of the four periods approached numerically even distributions of settlement in all three types of environment. This does not reflect a simple univariate correlation between architectural and environmental types.

The following indices were derived for each of the four periods in the development of Anasazi culture: A.D. 650–850, index 14.5; A.D. 850–1050, index 22.3; A.D. 1050–1200, index 17.6; A.D. 1200–1250, index 18.6.

The last index may not be truly representative for it reflects the smallest population of villages in the study, one which is approximately half the size of the three populations of earlier villages. A definite decline is seen to exist, which indicates that optimal cultural diversity in the Anasazi settlement system occurred between A.D. 850 and 1050. This period appears to have been one of intense experimentation for it

211

is statistically probable on the basis of this study that only one of every two architectural definitions and uses of environment was repetitious. Equally significant is the trend of gradual decline among these indices of architectural and environmental diversity during the two centuries following A.D. 1050. Architectural and environmental facets of Anasazi culture appear to have become disturbingly homogeneous by A.D. 1250 for slightly more than half of the manifest possibilities for previously efficient domestic uses of space were ignored for some reason. The earliest index is particularly significant for it permits the estimate that about two of every three relationships were repetitious, and shows a very high degree of patterned behavior in settlement. The index pattern also shows the assumption of proportional relationship between adaptive capacity and cultural diversity to be relative. Continuity in the archaeological record between A.D. 650 and 1050 indicates that viable adaptive responses were made by the Anasazi from a period marked by the lowest diversity in settlement systems to a point in time marked by the highest degree.

The results of the study demand a redefinition of the problem. Either Anasazi settlement itself was of little adaptive significance or the kind of environmental change that occurred shortly before A.D. 1000 was not the same as the second which appeared around A.D. 1250. It is equally possible that the two shifts in environment were of the same type but that different rates of change in each required different levels of cultural diversity for adaptive response. In this case, rapid change around A.D. 1250 may have necessitated more experimentation with settlement system than that which characterized this period. The problem of predicting a corresponding lack of diversity in all components of a cultural system from the homogeneity characterizing one category of behavior cannot be dealt with here, so the relative importance of dysfunctional settlement systems as a major cause of cultural disintegration among the Anasazi remains unknown. If criticism of this approach provokes better insight into the quantification of culture as adaptive behavior then the study will have served its purpose.

Subsistence patterns and settlement systems are thus seen to be important facets in the evolution of Southwestern adaptive responses to particular and changing ecological situations. These in turn are related to social organization and all are articulated in such a delicate fashion that when one subsystem changes (economy or subsistence) we can predict that changes will occur in other parts of the cultural system, such as social organization or rituals.

PART FIVE

THE EVOLUTION OF TECHNOLOGY

XII Tools, Changes in Artifact Morphology and Distribution

In previous chapters, we have suggested that varying patterns of behavior and of social organization manifested in the cultures of the Southwest evolved—sometimes, slowly, sometimes, swiftly—toward greater complexity. These developments, according to our philosophy, are seen as responses to changes in the patterns of subsistence, settlements, technology, social organization, and systems of communication that may have reduced conflict that was likely to have broken out between members of a family, between related families, and between larger groups (lineages and clans) of people related by blood and by marriage. In general, the same kinds of evolution of artifacts may be noted in manos, metates, projectile points, and all other tools as one examines them from early to late. In fact, we can say that most artifacts probably changed through time in response to technoenvironmental variations in subsistence and settlement patterns; but data concerning many tool types (particularly those of wood and bone) are scarce and even wanting. These deficiencies are in part due to differential rates of preservation since stone tools and ceramics are long-lasting whereas wooden and bone objects tend to molder in a relatively short time. Gaps in our knowledge concerning the more perishable types of artifacts are also due to unevenness in reporting, since one archaeologist may be more interested in ceramics, for instance, and without meaning to might slight the descriptions of artifacts in which he has less interest.

We shall not go through the whole inventory of tool types (there are at least seventy types and subtypes) because mere descriptions are boring and explain nothing. We prefer to dwell on a few types for which there is excellent documentation and exploit them as examples of evolution in tool types. We would then venture to suggest, that scantiness of data notwithstanding, our remarks might stand as generalized nomological explications that would hold true for all types of tools.

An empirically substantiated generalization concerning artifact morphology and distribution might read as follows:

Changes in the technology of tools will arise in response to a technological need and will be directly related to changes in subsistence, settlement patterns, and patterns in communication. For example: hand choppers (roughly flaked massive tools) may have served as axes in pre-A.D. 500 times, but as the need arose for more precise and greater amounts of wood-cutting, grooved stone axes appeared while choppers went out of existence. If a tool type is good and sufficient for its purpose and if the purpose does not change over time, it may be altered little, if at all; for example, a stone drill or a scraper.

In the following examination of tool evolution we will discuss first metates and manos; then projectile points and finally baskets.

For many decades manos and metates have served as relative time indicators. It is now apparent that the variations in these food-processing tools may also reflect changes in the subsistence economy and the efficiency of grinding.

To understand the meanings of variations in metates and manos, we must first explain that our researches in Hay Hollow, east-central Arizona (Burkenroad, 1968, and Schiffer, 1968) indicate that two surges of population occurred there—one at about A.D. 500 and another one at about A.D. 800. It has been suggested by Boserup (1965), Birdsell (1966), and Clark (1967) that population increases may take place before a change in subsistence economy. A population might have expanded by having encouraged budding groups to move into unoccupied niches. When no more niches were available, the population still continued to increase, the effect of which might have been to force the population to find a new niche or to develop a new food resource— corn agriculture, for example.

These models may not completely explain all the facts in Hay Hollow Valley, but the fact remains that population did increase by severalfold, especially around A.D. 800. The response to this dramatic increase was an intensification of agriculture and a reduction in the amounts of gathered wild plants. As a measure of increasing dependence on agriculture, Burkenroad (1968) and Plog (1969) have shown that manos and metates change accordingly.

Our researches at early sites, 300 B.C.–A.D. 300, indicated that subsistence consisted mainly (more than 90 percent) of wild foods, with corn agriculture making up a mere fraction of the total. At these sites (Hay Hollow and County Road Sites)

manos were round or oval cobbles that fitted into the depression of a "basin metate," that is, in a slab containing a basin-shaped depression. These types (cobbles and metates with basins) are known to be early and associated with a subsistence pattern that was almost wholly a gathering one and are assumed to be associated with grinding gathered wild seeds. Hence, "early" manos and metates are well fixed chronologically and by documentation. Also noteworthy is the fact that there was great variety in the kinds of stone chosen for grinding kits, in the colors of the stone, in the sizes and shapes. Some metates and manos were made of vesicular basalt which is very rough, while others were of another or "prettier, more attractive" stone. Undoubtedly, some of the variety was for functional purposes to accommodate the specific wild foods. But such varieties in shapes, colors, and sizes may have also been due to other causes, that is, used to assert or demonstrate ownership, pride of ownership, or to discourage indiscriminate borrowing.

Conversely, in sites that date at about A.D. 1000 (Longacre, *in* Martin *et al.*, 1964; and Hill *in* Martin, Longacre, and Hill, 1967), at which corn, beans, and squash made up the bulk of the subsistence, we found different and more standardized types of food processing tools, that is, metates and manos. At this time, manos were thin, rectangular, shaped slabs of stone; and metates were flatter, longer, and troughed with both ends open. Still later, the troughs disappeared and the grinding surface became the entire flat surface of the mill.

In the space of about one thousand years, then, we have evidence of an evolution in food processing tools, the trend being toward more efficiency since pulverizing of greater quantities of food had to be done. In other words, technological innovations occurred during the transformation from gathering of wild food to farming (Plog, 1969). The innovations consisted of increasing the effective grinding surface of the milling stone. At first, it consisted merely of the depression in the center of the metate. In trough metates, the grinding surface covers most of the top side of the mill, the ridges being the limiting factor. In late metates (post-A.D. 1100), the entire top surface of the metate was available for grinding. The same trends may be seen in manos. Round cobbles used in one hand are typical of early times when metates accommodated a small depression or basin. In the latest periods, manos had flat or beveled grinding surfaces. This variation increased the percentage of grinding surfaces that were in contact with the metate; and the eventual development of two-handed manos completed the evolution by increasing the grinding surface by about 50 percent and permitting more force to be employed to the food-grinding process (Burkenroad, 1968; Plog, 1969).

Another explanation for changes in types of milling stones is offered by Gorman (personal communication, 1970).

An earlier article by him, however, makes clear his point of view and the principle that is involved (Gorman, 1969, pp. 91–102). He became interested in the mammoths found in southern Arizona and excavated by the University of Arizona. In ruminating about the hunters who killed these elephants and why they would have left about thirty of their projectile points (called "Clovis" type)—all in perfect condition—in the carcasses of these creatures, Gorman made an interesting discovery. Analysis of the points indicated that they were deliberately left in the carcass. But, more important, it showed that there was a correlation between types of colors, kinds of lithic materials used, and proportional

differences in size. For example, a pair of intact projectile points both being made of a reddish-brown material called chert were found close together in the carcass; another pair made of clear quartz were associated. These correlations are based on data from five different mammoths, found at three different sites, and on a total of twenty-four projectile points. This pattern of abandonment of projectile points—all in good condition—singly or in pairs cried out for an explanation. Gorman (1969) offered several suggestions for this phenomenon. One was that a hunter probably made his own projectile points and hence would have recognized his own handiwork, his favorite color of stone, and the size of his own points. The presence of his own points in the elephant may have given that hunter an unquestionable claim to certain portions of the carcass or to a certain measure of the meat. Thus conflict over distribution of the meat might have been avoided and this would have been no mean attainment since each man hunted for his immediate family.

This theory, when applied to metates and manos, means, in essence, that in the era of hunting and gathering each family may have possessed ways of identifying its own metates, manos, projectile points, baskets, and general tool kits. Ownership may have been set apart by some distinguishing hallmarks, such as color, kind of stone, shape, method of manufacture, design, or some natural flaw or oddity in the raw material (e.g., the inclusion of a fossil). This emphasis on ownership may have lessened tensions and reduced causes for squabbles and misunderstanding. It is a form of communication that would have wordlessly signaled that this is *my* tool kit, not *yours*.

Now, back to manos and metates and a supplementary explanation for their evolution from basin-like affairs to flat ones with large grinding surfaces.

By the time that these peoples had developed a more sophisticated technology, social organization, and ritualistic life (after A.D. 1000–1200), other forms of silent communication may have developed (Gorman, personal communication). If this be so, perhaps it was no longer necessary to have distinctive manos and metates because men may have organized their lives in such a way as to relate one subsystem with another in a different manner. Thus integration may have been achieved at other levels so that individual ownership or distinctive hallmarks of tool kits were no longer essential. Metates, as noted earlier, were transformed from "basins" to trough types, and eventually became more or less flat, with the entire top surface given over to a grinding area. Almost all of them (over 85 percent) were made from sandstone (Woodbury, 1954, p. 55); manos, made predominantly of sandstone, became somewhat longer and more uniform in form. In other words, the attributes of dissimilarities declined in importance at lower levels of contrast. Metates and manos "grew up," became more efficient grinding tools, and emphasis on one's hallmark as a trait of ownership may have well nigh disappeared because people had now (by A.D. 1000–1200) organized a different system for perceiving material phenomena, events, behavior. They related to one another in more complex ways and did not need to distinguish one tool kit from all others. In a large extended family group, made up of fathers, mothers, children, as well as many kin on the maternal side, all corn grinding was done as a cooperative, group activity of women of the clan. No one cared whether he was using his own tool kit or that of his sister's uncle!

Now, let us turn to projectile points. The term implies that this type of tool was used for hunting or for warfare, but it should be pointed out that this name "projectile"

point is misleading. A point might have served as a projectile tip, a knife, a scraper, or in other ways; just as our screw driver is often used or misused to tighten or loosen screws, to pry open lids, to knock a hole in a can, or to serve as a chisel.

For our purposes, however, we assume that most points were used for hunting unless careful examination of the edges of the implement indicated that the tool was used for scraping or cutting.

Projectile points, as in the case of manos and metates, have been used by archaeologists to assign approximate dates to sites. It is possible that changes in shape, size, and especially in manufacturing processes may also reflect a shift from hunting and gathering to farming.

Analysis of 120 points from four sites in Hay Hollow Valley—sites ranging in time from about 200 B.C. to A.D. 1000—demonstrated that the one variable that many archaeologists have overlooked is that of manufacturing (Traugott, 1968). His researches further indicated that the manufacture of projectile points up to about A.D. 750 involved four cumbersome steps: (1) subjecting the core to a long, sustained heating process that facilitated the flaking operation by altering the crystalline structure of the siliceous materials (heat treatment observed in 60 percent of specimens); (2) removal of a projectile point "blank" from a core; (3) thinning the "blank" by flaking; (4) secondary flaking to shape the blank to the desired form.

Statistical tests supported Traugott's hypothesis that heating the chert was related to the flaking process. Here we have evidence of a fairly complex manufacturing process that was in use until about A.D. 750 and that produced projectile points of varying styles, shapes, and lengths.

Since these weapons were used by a people who depended more on hunting than on agriculture, we may have here another instance where emphasis on individuality of type, shape, and length of the point as well as on the color of the stone was important so that ownership of game could be established by the hunter.

After A.D. 750—at which time population had surged upward—the subsistence pattern was reversed with more emphasis on agriculture and with less dependence on hunting. At about that time, the manufacturing process of projectile points was simplified, using only two steps instead of four. In the opinion of lithic experts (Traugott, 1968; Plog, 1969; and Crabtree and Butler, 1964, and personal communication), this simplified process was a more efficient way of manufacturing with the result that the points became more standardized in length and shape.

It seems fair to assume then that since hunting had declined in importance, less time, energy, and raw stone materials were needed for turning out a projectile point and that novel shapes, colors, or sizes were no longer of importance. Food procurement was not now the business of the individual family but may now have been shared by means of other mechanisms (the kin group, the clan); and communication may have developed into a system whereby people treated goods and services as community effort that functioned in such a smooth way as to reduce conflicts and tensions.

When we turn to baskets, we are dealing with a perishable product, which unless protected from the elements, will not long survive. In their study of Anasazi basketry from Basket Maker II through Pueblo III, Morris and Burgh (1941) reported on approximately two hundred specimens. Undoubtedly, there are more in private and public collections to which they did not have access. But, even if one doubles or

triples that figure, the total is still small compared to extant stone tools and pottery.

Two basket forms persisted almost unchanged from earliest times (pre-A.D. 500) down to the end of the archaeological aspects of Anasazi culture—perhaps—A.D. 1540. These are plaited-twill-ring baskets, still made today by the Hopi Indians, and trays and bowls. The latter probably constituted the work-horse class of basketry of the day because they are most abundant and many of them are worn, scarred, torn, and mended. The plaited twill baskets lacked freedom of form because this type of basket weaving combined with the materials used restricted the weaver's efforts. A plaited container is merely a mat woven flat and then warped into the form of a tray or a shallow bowl (Morris and Burgh, 1941, pp. 28–29).

The forms that appeared to have had the greatest significance in an evolutionary development from about A.D. 400 to 1300 were: the carrying basket and a bowl-like shape (Morris and Burgh, 1941, pp. 27–28). Since the carrying basket more completely illustrates the development about which we are talking, we shall confine our remarks to that shape.

In the third and fourth centuries after Christ, and perhaps even earlier, this form evolved. Such baskets were more or less conical in shape, with holes midway between rim and base for attachment of a burden strap. They were fairly large (about 15 inches high and 31 inches in diameter) and may have had a carrying capacity of one and a half to two bushels of wild gathered foods. (Author's estimate based on measurements in Guernsey, 1931, p. 95, and Morris and Burgh, 1941.) By A.D. 500–600, these baskets became more graceful in shape, were more elliptical in cross section and were provided with a flattish bottom instead of a pointed one as in the preceding or earlier type. They were beautifully decorated with red and black designs of "unusual intricacy" (Morris and Burgh, p. 33) and of great variety, thus, perhaps, indicating ownership.

Women, who were probably the chief gatherers of wild foods, carried these large baskets on their backs, support being given by means of the burden strap that passed across the forehead. Edible tubers (collected in early summer) were rooted out by means of a sharpened digging stick and tossed into the basket. In late summer, when wild seeds were ripening, the women also carried a basket tray. Holding their trays perhaps in the left hand and their sticks in the right hand, they proceeded from one clump of grass to another knocking off the seeds into the trays. When the trays were full, the seeds were emptied into the burden or carrying basket (Amsden, 1949, p. 76).

Simultaneously, miniature carrying baskets were manufactured, six of them having been buried with one infant (Morris and Burgh, 1941, figure 28). Not only were they small (7 inches in diameter at the rim and 6 inches high) but were wedge-shaped instead of conical. Such tiny baskets probably served no utilitarian purpose, especially when one is told that tiny clay replicas of carrying baskets appeared at the same time and in great numbers. From the available data, it appears that these clay replicas (at first of unfired clay but within a few years of fired clay) are not necessarily associated with burials but were found scattered throughout the cave dust. And along with them, crude effigies of human females.

Morris and Burgh (1941, p. 54) suggested that the miniature carrying baskets, the replicas of them in clay, and the associated female clay effigies may have been emblems of a fertility cult. The miniature form of the carrying basket persisted until about A.D. 1300.

But we are straying from the main thread of our discourse. Shortly after A.D. 900, at the time when the practice of gathering wild foods was being replaced by sedentism and farming, the carrying basket as such disappeared since it was no longer essential. Only the memory of it and its function persisted in the miniatures of basketry.

Harvesting corn, beans, and squashes did not require this kind of a facility since the yield could be transported more easily by other means (in trays and in cloth bags) especially since one had only a short distance to walk from the field to the pueblo.

Carrying baskets, then, illustrate the evolution of a useful seed and wild plant container at a time when the gatherers had great distances to traverse in order to procure food. But, like buggy whips, they vanished when no longer useful or necessary.

XIII   Facilities

In this chapter we shall discuss spatial and temporal variability in facilities, roofed structures and pits in particular, and some ways in which this variability can be explained. It should be clear from the preceding discussion of variability in space and time that whatever the time level one chooses, immense variability in facilities can be observed. The prehistoric residents of Arizona lived on and used sites with many different kinds and many different combinations of facilities evidenced as features. We briefly recapitulate these data.

Archaeologists know little of the facilities that were characteristic of the Paleo-Indian stage. These populations used caves for shelter. Hearths were found both in the cave sites and in some open-air sites. We can say little more. However, it seems likely that there will be a good deal more to say in the future. Populations at this stage of development in other areas of the world lived in tents or tent-like structures, and archaeologists have recovered evidence of them. While the existence of similar structures in Arizona is unproven, evidence of them may come to light as we find and excavate non-kill sites of the Paleo-Indian stage and as our sensitivity to the very minor modifications of the land surface that mark the former existence of a tent increases.

Caves were still in use during the Desert culture stage. Ventana Cave, Bat Cave, Tularosa Cave, and Cordova Cave are examples of cave sites that were used by these populations. Such cave sites almost always contained hearths, or other evidence of the use of fire. They sometimes contained pits full of cultural debris that were probably used for storage. Martin *et al.* (1952) reported a row of post holes in Tularosa Cave that may indicate a barrier of some sort was erected across the mouth of the cave. Some later Desert culture populations lived in pit houses on open-air sites.

Caves were a less important dwelling unit in the Pit House stage. Pit house villages were sometimes constructed in caves, but open-air sites were far more common. These sites had from one or two houses to several dozen of them. Houses varied in size and shape both within sites and from region to region. Pits were sometimes dug inside these houses and sometimes outside of them. In some areas near the end of the Pit house stage, masonry structures occurred on predominantly pit house sites. The first evidence of ceremonial structures appeared during this stage in the form of exceedingly large houses with distinctive features.

This trend to diversity continued into the stage of Town Dwellers. While aboveground masonry structures were predominant on sites of this stage, the variety of features from site to site and area to area was immense. Kivas carried forward the tradition of pit houses. Jacal ramadas occurred side by side with sophisticated masonry dwelling units. Size, shape, and morphology of facilities all varied immensely.

How does the archaeologist make sense of these patterns of variability? How does he try to explain the fantastic variety of features that existed and were used prehistorically? In the past, he has frequently attempted to isolate and define "templates" or ideal plans for the construction of such features that prehistoric individuals carried around in their heads. The fashion in which a particular feature was constructed was a result of the template or templates that the individuals doing the construction carried in their heads. Each culture had its characteristic templates, and archaeologists attempted to discover what they were.

As we have indicated several times, this normative sort of approach is not an appealing one. It has little to do with what social scientists have learned concerning the causes of behavior in the modern world. We prefer to view these features as results of particular decisions and particular patterns of behavior that prehistoric Arizonans made and engaged in. These decisions and patterns of behavior were shaped by the knowledge of the individuals in question, but also by the social and environmental situations in which individuals and groups found themselves. Ideas were important, but so were available resources, available tools, and existing patterns of organization of labor.

We will try to follow this approach in answering two questions: How and why do facilities vary in construction material and technique? How and why do they vary in size, shape, and arrangement on a site?

CONSTRUCTION MATERIALS AND TECHNIQUES

Prehistoric residents of Arizona and the adjacent Southwest used a variety of materials and techniques in constructing features. Our emphasis will be on dwelling structures, with some attention to pits. In

Digging the house pit   Framing the house walls

Framing the house roof   Thatching and plastering

The doorway   Hearth and baseboard

Backfilling the pit   Building the raised floor

FIGURE 18 Building a house (Upper Pima). While the materials being used and the design of the house cannot be generalized, the steps being used to build this house are those that would have been undertaken in constructing any subterranean or semisubterranean dwelling. Taken from Figure 14, *The Upper Pima of San Cayetano del Tumacacori*, The Amerind Foundation, Inc. Publication No. 7, 1965.

looking at these features, we need to understand the different combinations of materials and techniques that can be used in any particular construction task. Both wall and roof construction are important in this regard.

Wall Construction

The most important techniques of wall construction were as follows:

1. Walls were made of brush, thatch, or mats either laid against timber supports or,

in the case of brush, self-supporting. Walls of this variety usually required a ring of boulders or stones to anchor the material. This ring of stone is the primary evidence of the existence of such structures.

2. Deep pits were dug into the ground providing a natural earthen wall. These walls were lined with timber, stone, or plaster, or were left unlined.

3. Shallower pits frequently served as foundations for walls. The walls were constructed of timber set into the ground in upright rows around the circumference of the pit or leaned against some central support. Holes between logs were chinked with branches and mud.

4. In similar shallow pits, small poles were set at close intervals from each other in upright fashion. These poles were interwoven with reed mats or plastered with adobe. The architectural form that employs a plaster coating over the preceding is called *jacal*.

5. Walls were built of unhewn natural boulders with a matrix of adobe or smaller stones.

6. Walls were built of stone that was coursed, laid on relatively even rows. When well-hewn blocks were employed with very little mortar matrix between them, the style of architecture is called Mesa Verde.

7. Fine coursings of thin stone slabs were set on both sides of a core of adobe, or adobe and rubble. This fashion of wall construction is associated with Chaco Canyon and the Chacoan tradition.

8. Rough-hewn blocks, irregular slabs, and a great deal of adobe were mixed together in a somewhat unsystematic manner to form a wall. This style of masonry, Kayenta, is common in much of northern Arizona.

9. Adobe by itself or over a core of poles was used to form walls. The walls were built using wooden forms. These forms were placed on top of and next to already hardened sections of wall.

10. Adobe bricks were formed away from the site and used in construction.

Once again, it is important to remember that more than one of these techniques was frequently used on a single site. Thus, while we may identify trends and tradi-

FIGURE 19 Styles of masonry. Three styles of masonry were predominant in Arizona: Chacoan (A), Mesa Verde (B), and Kayenta (C). These styles have no exclusive identification with the areas for which they are named. Chacoan walls have an exterior of thin stones, Mesa Verde of well-shaped blocks, and Kayenta of irregular blocks. Reproduced by permission of the Field Museum of Natural History.

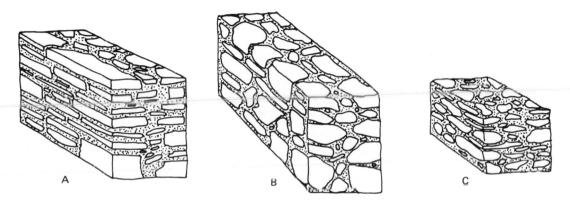

tions, we must not forget the more minute levels at which this variability exists. When more than one architectural tradition occurs on a single site, archaeologists often infer that individuals or groups from two different cultures lived on the site. We believe that such fanciful explanations must be forgone and ones more firmly rooted in available resources, tools, organizations, and ideas sought.

Roof Construction

It is not always possible to distinguish between walls and roofs. In a dome structure, for example, such a distinction would be meaningless. In structures where a roof can be distinguished, the basic construction technique is similar throughout Arizona. Logs or poles were laid in some regular geometric pattern. Interstices were filled with twigs, branches, mud, and adobe. Occasionally, reed matting was used just above the timbers. Variability from region to region is primarily in the size of timber used and in the particular geometric pattern followed.

A good deal more variability existed in the manners in which roofs were supported. Bullard (1962) has summarized the important techniques used in constructing pit house roofs. These same methods were appropriate for building a pueblo roof.

1. Some houses had no interior support for the roof. That is, the roof was supported by the walls of the house. In larger structures, such as great kivas, cribbing, constructing offset, and overlapping polygons were used to increase the strength of wall-supported roofs.

2. Roofs were supported by four timber posts in a square or rectangular pattern. The supports were generally at the corners of the house. Bullard feels that this tech-

nique was the most widespread one in pit house construction.

3. A conical roof was built employing a single central support with timbers laid against it.

4. When a crossbeam was set on a series of post running along the axis of the house and timbers leaned against it, a gabled roof resulted.

5. Pilasters, square masonary posts, were used for roof support. This practice was especially common in late kivas.

6. The pattern of roof support was sometimes complex, involving the use of more than one technique described above, or involving the use of a great number of regularly spaced posts.

7. In some cases, the postholes found in a house are so numerous and the pattern so irregular, that no clear judgment can be made as to what technique of support was used.

Explaining Variability in Construction Materials and Techniques

The first section of this chapter as well as more detailed descriptions of the distribution of architectural traits in the chapters on space and time indicate that these different construction techniques did have some spatial and temporal integrity, they tended to be more important at some times and places than at others. Yet, intraregional and even intrasite variability are important. Dealing with this complex a pattern would require a very long and very statistical anlaysis. A computer would be necessary to accumulate the data, define spatial and temporal variability at all necessary levels of detail, and test the hypotheses that might explain this pattern. While such an analysis would be interesting and is necessary, it is not possible in the time and with the data available to us now. Therefore, we offer some suggestions concerning the kinds of factors that might be important in formulating such an explanation. Five such factors are important: natural resources, tools, function, labor, and know-how.

Variability in available natural resources, raw materials to be used in construction, explains some of the similarities and differences in the construction of features. It was impossible to build a timber structure in an area where timber was unavailable locally. Thus, archaeologists tend to find jacal structures in the Gila and Salt River Valleys and evidence of brush structures in the lower Colorado River Valley. Adobe is a common construction material in the southern part of Arizona. The use of stone might have necessitated hauling that material over great distances. But, calcareous muds were abundant in the broad alluvial valleys. Similarly, in the rocky and heavily timbered mountains, these two materials were more frequently used. In the Transition environment, where many different sources of construction material existed, houses were correspondingly varied in construction material and technique. At whatever time period one chooses, there is probably more variability in facilities in this environment than any other.

Similar patterns shaped intraregional variability. The kind of stone used in building masonry walls varied. If sandstone outcrops with even and narrow cleavage planes occurred, a Chacoan style was more probable than if cleavage patterns were grosser. If no stone that could be easily shaped was available locally, some technique employing unshaped blocks was likely. From region to region in the state and from locality to locality within any region, the availability of raw materials caused some construction techniques to be practiced while others were not.

Even where a particular raw material was abundant, it may have gone unused if its use would have served no particular purpose. A deep, heavily timbered pit house would have provided substantial protection against snow and cold weather in environments with those attributes. A house built in this style was of much less utility in the hot arid regions of the lower Colorado River Valley. This does not mean that only one raw material is appropriate for a given environment. Where reeds occur in mountainous areas, they may be used for ramadas or summer shelters, even though they are inappropriate for winter houses. Similarly, we would not expect that the same time and effort spent in constructing a unit to be used for three days would be spent in constructing one to be used for thirty years. Different structures had different functions related to the environments in which they occurred and the kinds of activities that were practiced in them. Lighter, less durable structures are found in less severe environments and associated with shorter-term activities.

We must also consider function in the relation of parts of a structure to each other. Thus, a gabled roof may be more appropriate for a narrow rectangular structure than any other roof form. Jacal or brush can be used in constructing small units. But, a great kiva of brush would collapse under its own weight. A reed wall probably won't support a timber roof. One particular architectural trait may be necessary as a result of the function a given structure is to serve. It may then necessitate the use of materials or techniques not related to the primary function of the structure, but to this functionally important trait.

When a particular kind of structure was needed and the materials for erecting it were available, construction might not have

Type 2 Cooking Pit

Type 1 Shallow Cooking Pit
This shallow, circular
cooking pit was the most
popular form.

The figure 8 form of
cooking pit was the
second most popular
form.

Type 3 This Adobe Lined
Pit is an Ootam trait
with a wide distribution
in Pimeria Alta.

Type 4 The Stone Lined
Cyst may have been used
for storage. 2 types were
noted, a single slab wall
and a double slab wall.

Type 6 Deep Pits were
found scattered through
out the ruin. No evidence
was found as to the use
of these pits.

Barro Pits consisted
of those areas from
which clay was removed
for construction.

FIGURE 20   Types of
pits. Pits were used for
a variety of different
purposes. Their shapes
and sizes reflect the
tasks for which they
were used. These are
Upper Pima pits, but
they are typical of those
found in most societies.
Taken from Figure 16,
*The Upper Pima of
San Cayetano del
Tumacacori*, The
Amerind Foundation,
Inc. Publication No. 7,
1965.

been undertaken if the proper tools were unavailable. Archaeologists have acquired very little detailed knowledge of interregional variability in tool kits. While tools seem to be very similar from one part of Arizona to another, more diversity will become apparent as our typologies improve in detail and coherence. A group that lacked tools for felling large trees and found itself, perhaps by force of population pressure, in an area where the use of this resource was desirable or necessary might have been unable to exploit it. Similarly, one group that observed a near neighbor employing coursed masonry in construction could not have employed this construction technique unless it had the tools for quarrying the raw materials and for shaping the blocks.

Even with the proper raw materials, purpose, and tools, a technique of construction might have gone unused if a population lacked the labor or organization needed to employ it. The Salt and Gila drainages provide an example. During most of the Pit House and Town Dweller stages, jacal and reed architecture were the predominant technique used. Later, adobe pueblos appeared. They did so at about the same time that large ceremonial structures, great houses like Casa Grande, appeared. It may have been that the impetus to go from single jacal units to adobe ones was present for some time but the organization of labor required for the use of the latter technique was absent. A particular population fifty miles from a source of timber may have foregone the use of this resource if they lacked the quantity of labor or the organizational devices necessary to arrange for transporting the resource over this distance. Thus, even the availability of resources is relative to the quantity and organization of labor available for acquiring them.

Finally, the ideas and know-how associ-

226

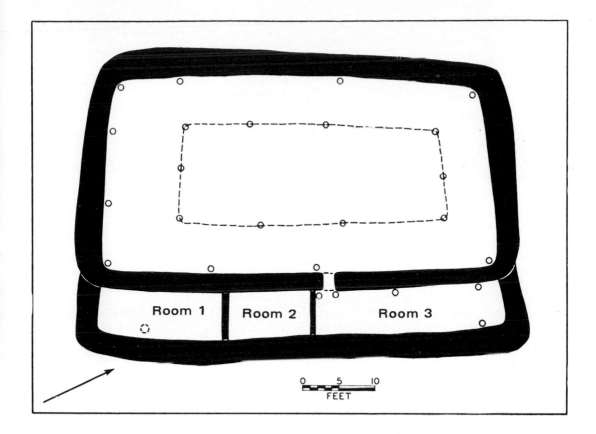

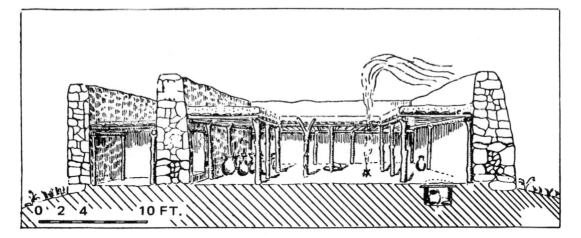

FIGURE 21 A Cohonina fort. The top portion of the figure shows the archaeological evidence of the fort, the walls and postholes. Below is the reconstruction. Courtesy of the Museum of Northern Arizona.

ated with different construction techniques were not present at all times and places. We tend to feel that ideas spread relatively rapidly in prehistoric Arizona, and that

some of our colleagues overemphasize the role of the slow diffusion of ideas in their explanations of architectural variability. They rely too heavily on ideas and forget

227

FIGURE 22 Reconstruction of a SU site house. A typical house on the SU site in the process of construction. Reproduced by permission of the Field Museum of Natural History.

FIGURE 23 Reconstruction of a house at Roosevelt 9:6. The lumber shell was covered with twigs, reeds, and adobe. Reproduced by permission of the Arizona State Museum.

the functional, ecological, and organizational factors that may have determined whether those ideas were acquired and whether they were used by a particular population.

Nevertheless, it would be foolhardy to argue that Desert culture populations knew about Chacoan architecture but chose not to construct dwellings in this style. Knowhow is not evenly distributed in time and space. Inventions occur and ideas are dif-

fused or borrowed. The rate of invention and borrowing varies throughout Arizona prehistory. But, the archaeologist cannot assume a one to one correlation between the geographical distribution of an idea and the geographical distribution of a construction technique. We must learn what kinds of social or natural environmental problems led populations to invent or to borrow particular patterns of behavior.

In any case, it is clear that whatever the

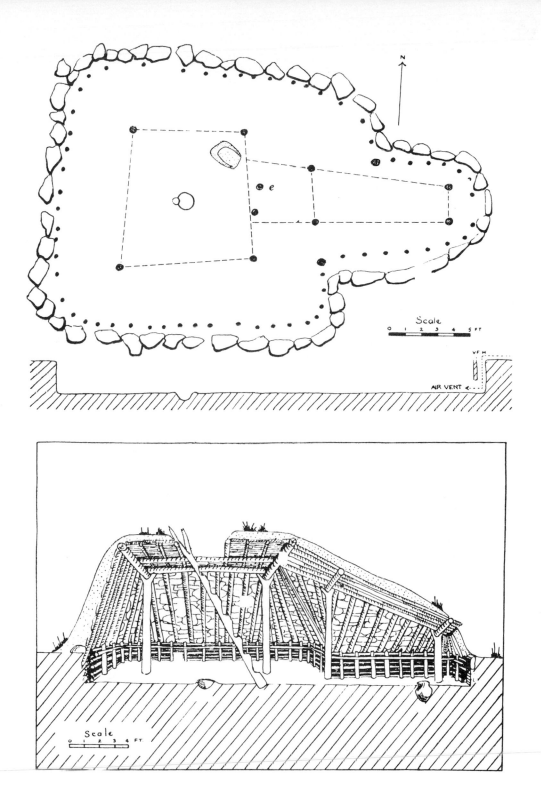

FIGURE 24 An alcove house. This house takes its name from the projection or alcove on the eastern end. The timber structure was covered with slabs and dirt. Entrance was through the hole in the roof. Courtesy of the Museum of Northern Arizona.

predominant architectural practice in any area at any point in time, other techniques were available or known to the group in question. People observe their neighbors' activities. While they may not imitate everything observed, the observations are remembered, and, if imitation becomes appropriate, it occurs. Moreover, populations don't use the same ideas in every set of activities they undertake. When prehistoric Arizonans were still living in brush or hide structures, they began to hew wood for fuel and tools. The lessons learned in these activities were soon applied to others, and trees were hewn for house supports.

This pattern of change, applying a lesson learned in one activity set to a different set, or applying lessons learned in small-scale activities to large-scale ones, is particularly clear in the relationship between pits, work rooms, and dwelling rooms. In Arizona, many architectural innovations seem to have been used in constructing pits and limited activity structures before they were used in constructing dwelling units. Storage pits were dug before pit houses were dug. The first pit house (Desert culture) has a very large storage pit in it. Slab-lined and plastered pits appeared before slab-lined and plastered pit houses. On the Colorado Plateau, surface rooms were used for storage and work before surface houses were built for dwelling. Pits may have been dug initially to protect subsistence resources from the natural environment or to hide them from competing groups. This style of environmental protection was then used in protecting the human builders or the pits. Pits may have been slab-lined to reduce seepage and spoilage in wet caves. If this problem was encountered in a pit house, a similar solution may have been applied. Adobe was used to prevent or reduce water loss in canals in southern Arizona and to fill niches in jacal structures before massive adobe structures were built. When confronted with a problem that cannot be solved using customary practices, a population will borrow ideas from its neighbors, combine ideas of its own with those of neighboring populations, and transfer or combine ideas from among its own different activity systems. Problem solution is the principal stimulus to invention and diffusion.

All of these factors—natural resources, function, tools, organization, and ideas—can be used by archaeologists in explaining variability in the construction of features. Their relative importance will vary from case to case. But, in every situation every factor will be important. "Available natural resources" cannot be defined without establishing whether the tools and organization necessary to acquire the resources were present. They may not have been used if they were unneeded or if their utility was not recognized. For example, we have mentioned the great variety in construction materials and techniques in the transition environment. This variety may reflect the great diversity of natural resources available there. It could reflect seasonal and altitudinal variability in the environmental problems that populations had to solve. These same factors might have acted to prevent a rapid flow of ideas from one population to another. The variety could have resulted from variability in any one of the factors, and it probably resulted from interaction between all of them. Until archaeologists working in the area collect the relevant technological, ecological, and organizational data, we will remain unsatisfied as to the real explanation for diversity of architectural style in this area. Until archaeologists in all areas of the state collect these kinds of data, we will be able

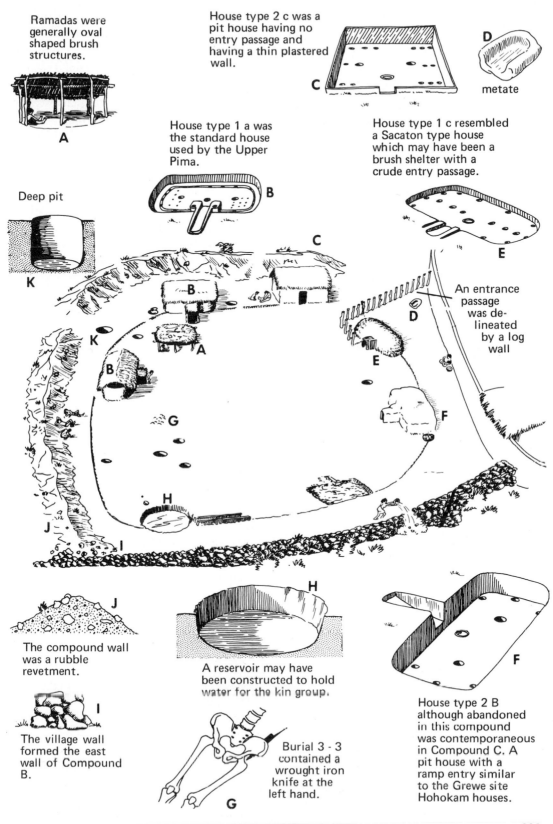

Ramadas were generally oval shaped brush structures.

A

House type 2 c was a pit house having no entry passage and having a thin plastered wall.

C

D

metate

House type 1 a was the standard house used by the Upper Pima.

B

House type 1 c resembled a Sacaton type house which may have been a brush shelter with a crude entry passage.

E

Deep pit

K

C

B

A

K

B

An entrance passage was de- lineated by a log wall

D

E

F

G

H

J

I

The compound wall was a rubble revetment.

J

The village wall formed the east wall of Compound B.

I

H

A reservoir may have been constructed to hold water for the kin group.

Burial 3 - 3 contained a wrought iron knife at the left hand.

G

House type 2 B although abandoned in this compound was contemporaneous in Compound C. A pit house with a ramp entry similar to the Grewe site Hohokam houses.

F

233

investigators (summarized in Hill, 1970) have constructed equations that link the size of a dwelling unit and the number of individuals occupying it. Similarly, we estimate the population of sites by counting the number of habitation rooms, thereby acknowledging the fact that the number of people on a site affected the number of rooms. A given population may have had no residential-organizational unit larger than the family. If it adopted such a unit, the change would have been reflected in the size and number of features on a site. Thus, in the Upper Little Colorado, most sites occupied at about A.D. 800 consisted of one or two dwelling units and a storage pit or two. Both a few hundred years earlier when the population of the region was lower, and a few hundred years later when it was higher, the population lived on sites consisting of ten to forty dwellings. This pattern suggests changing organization quite independent of population size per se. And that changing organization is reflected in the number of dwelling units on a site.

Spatial and temporal variability in the shape of features can be explained using similar factors. For example, a storage facility, be it a room or a pit, can be shaped in any variety of ways. In caves, irregularly shaped niches were walled and used for storage. Since subsistence resources were small, they could be fit into a variety of different configurations. Human beings are bulkier than their subsistence resources. They will fit into a far less varied set of shapes. We expect, and find, that dwelling facilities are considerably less varied in shape than storage ones.

Archaeologists interested in architecture are very concerned with the question of shape. In most areas of the state, round belowground dwelling structures were replaced by rectangular aboveground ones between A.D. 700 and 1000. Why did this change in shape occur? At least three different but related causes were probably involved. Increases in population and changes in the organization of that population resulted in more families living on sites. At the same time, many functionally specific tools and features were appearing, many of them in aboveground rather than belowground loci. Since it is easier to combine timber, reeds, stone, and other construction material in freestanding forms with square rather than round corners, most of the roofed limited activity loci were rectangular or square. It is easier to use these materials in enclosing a cube than a cylinder or hemisphere. Moreover, more square structures can be fit into a given area than round ones of equal area. Finally, in a village of pit houses being built closer and closer to each other as a result of the population changes, the danger of collapsing dirt walls would have been high. Thus, initial changes in population and kinds of work space probably created a situation in which square structures were more efficient with the use of available resources, the use of available on-site space, and the durability of the product. A more comprehensive explanation can undoubtedly be developed. It seems wiser to us to move toward explanations that stress the interaction of technological, environmental, and demographic changes than toward ones that focus on templates or ideology and see the change as a result of round-orientation being replaced by square-orientation.

Finally, archaeologists try to explain similarities and differences in the relation of features to each other. We believe that our basic set of factors are adequate to this task. Environmental interaction is an important cause of variability in feature associations from site to site. In the transition environment where there is firm evidence of seasonal variability in the subsistence settlement system, we find upland sites with different features from those on lowland sites. Why did some pit houses in the state have storage pits dug into the floor while others had slab bins constructed along the walls? It would be no surprise if differences in soil moisture and local populations of burrowing animals accounted for this variability.

The particular kinds of activities carried on at a site affected the distribution of features there. One of us (Plog, 1969) has discussed variability in the features and artifacts found on nonhabitation sites in Hay Hollow Valley near Snowflake, Arizona. The definition of nonhabitation or limited activity sites is based upon the observation that not all sites have dwelling structures on them. Some sites have only a single fire pit. In virtually every part of the transition, mountain, and plateau environments, small caves were walled and used for storage. These were storage sites. Similarly, archaeologists sometimes find a site that consists of a fire pit and a row of boulders that might have anchored a wind break. Distributions of these different kinds of nonhabitation sites usually correspond very closely with the distribution of different resource zones. Different activities are carried on in different resource zones and these require different combinations of features.

Some of the most productive work done in recent years has focused on the relationship between social organization and features on a site. The impact of this knowledge with regard to social organization is discussed in another chapter. Here we simply wish to examine the interaction of organization and site plans. The spatial relationships of different kinds of rooms and features and the order in which these units were constructed are the most critical activities in this undertaking. Some sites show a high degree of planning while others seem

essentially unplanned. Why? We suggest an answer by examining three sites scattered over this continuum.

Dean (1970) has analyzed the growth of a number of Tsegi phase sites. By defining different kinds of rooms and building a construction sequence based upon detailed tree-ring data, Dean was able to arrive at some firm conclusions on the construction and organization of the sites. The basic unit of construction at the site was the room cluster. A room cluster consisted of "one living room, one to six storage chambers (granaries and storerooms), occasionally a grinding room, and in all but a few cases a courtyard" (1970, p. 155). When building

FIGURE 27 Tsegi phase room cluster. The rooms are very similar in construction, although different kinds of activities were carried on in each of them. Each cluster was used by a nuclear or extended family. Courtesy of the Laboratory of Tree-Ring Research, the University of Arizona.

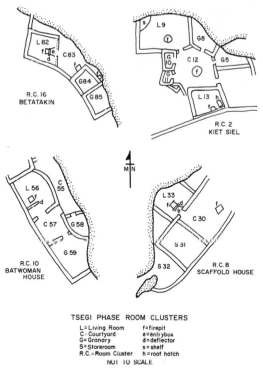

TSEGI PHASE ROOM CLUSTERS

L = Living Room   f = firepit
C = Courtyard   e = entrybox
G = Granary   d = deflector
S = Storeroom   s = shelf
R.C. = Room Cluster   h = roof hatch
NOT TO SCALE

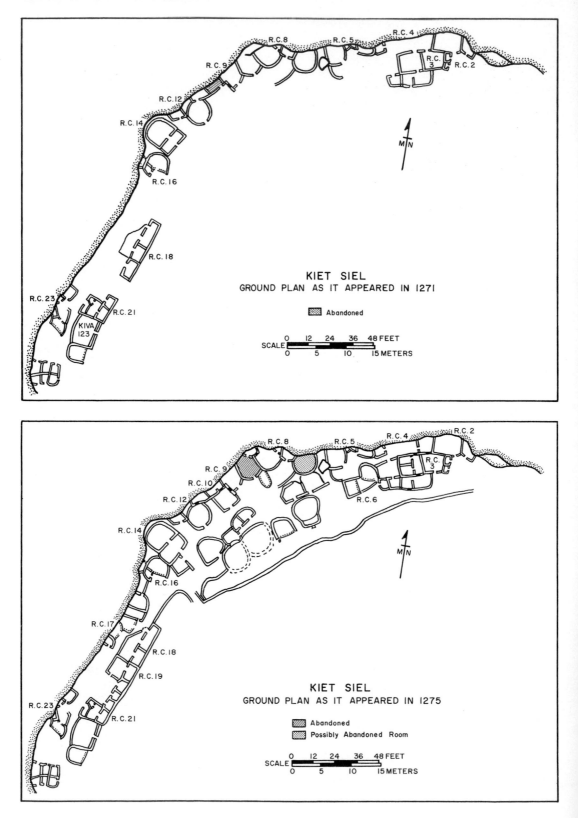

KIET SIEL
GROUND PLAN AS IT APPEARED IN 1271

Abandoned

SCALE
0   12   24   36   48 FEET
0   5   10   15 METERS

KIET SIEL
GROUND PLAN AS IT APPEARED IN 1275

Abandoned
Possibly Abandoned Room

SCALE
0   12   24   36   48 FEET
0   5   10   15 METERS

FIGURE 28 Growth of Kiet Siel. Kiet Siel is an unplanned village. New rooms and family units were built as they were needed. There is no overall plan to the growth of the village. Courtesy of the Laboratory of Tree-Ring Research, the University of Arizona.

activity occurred, it usually involved the construction of a room cluster, not just a room, and not a series of clusters. Dean does define a subsite unit larger than the room cluster, the courtyard complex consisting of two or more room clusters with a shared courtyard. The clusters in such complexes were built at different times, and when rooms were added they were added to a cluster, not a complex. Dean believes that the room clusters were occupied by extended families and the courtyard complexes by related families. The kivas on Tsegi phase sites are not associated with courtyard complexes and show little spatial

patterning. There is no evidence of a local group larger than that occupying the courtyard complex and smaller than the site. The only evidence for cooperation in construction activities is evidence that beam cutting may have been a community activity. Planning and construction were household activities.

The situation at Kiatuthlanna (Roberts, 1931) was a quite different one. The unit of construction was a room block. At the center of the room block was a kiva, and the kiva was surrounded by six or more dwellings and four or more storage rooms. Thus, the social units that planned and constructed the site were multifamily units tied to a single kiva. A strong social unit that was intermediate between the household and the community is suggested.

In Chaco Canyon, New Mexico, the pattern was even more complex. Vivian (1970) has discussed evidence suggesting that large

FIGURE 29 Growth of Kiatuthlanna. The growth of Kiatuthlanna illustrates the construction sequence at a "planned" village. In speaking of planning, the archaeologist is observing that each new unit of construction involves more than the number of rooms that would be

associated with a single family. In this site, a kiva and six to twenty associated rooms were erected in each stage of the building process. Sites like Chaco Canyon evidence even more extensive planning. Courtesy of the Smithsonian Institution.

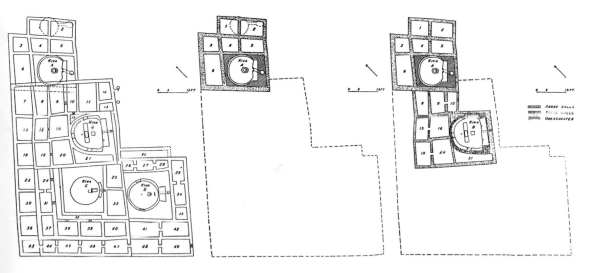

towns were built, razed, and remodeled within relatively short periods of time. Entire villages with hundreds of rooms in each village suggest an overall planning of the community as a whole. Some additional aspects of the organizational complexity at Chaco Canyon have been discussed elsewhere.

Organizational inferences can be drawn and architectural variability explained by examining the co-distribution of storage rooms, habitation rooms, and kivas on a site and between sites in a region (see Plog, 1969, for example). Storage rooms were sometimes randomly distributed in a village. This was particularly true in early Town Dweller sites. On other sites the storage rooms were attached to habitation rooms or occurred in clusters with them. This was the case with Dean's Tsegi phase sites. In still other cases, storage rooms were attached to kivas and great kivas. This last pattern existed just prior to the abandonment of many areas of the state. All of these patterns apparently reflected differences in the regulation or control of subsistence resources. When resources were controlled and storage done by families, the storage facilities were associated with other family facilities. When some or all of the resources were controlled and stored by larger social units, the rooms in which the resources were kept are in evidence and they were attached to facilities such as kivas that are associated with larger social units.

The distribution of storage facilities over a series of contemporaneous sites was not always egalitarian. Some sites may have had an inordinate number of storage rooms while others had fewer than the average. This situation existed in the Mesa Verde area. Cliff Palace had a greater number of storage rooms than was average, compared to other excavated sites such as Spruce Tree House or Balcony House. It also had proportionally more kivas than these sites, and the number of habitation rooms was much lower than what would be expected on the basis of the number of storage rooms and kivas. Too few people and too many storage and ceremonial facilities were found at Cliff Palace. Apparently, this site played some special role in organizing and controlling the resources of the area.

SUMMARY

It is easy to observe spatial and temporal variability in the size, shape, arrangement, and techniques of construction of features. It is difficult to explain this variability. We have attempted to show how explanations might be constructed by referring to aspects of the social environment, natural environment, and cultural system of a particular population that shaped its decisions and behavior in architectural matters. Natural resources, tools, organization, activity-structure, and ideas are all important in this regard. If and when such explanations are constructed for particular sites and particular regions, it may be possible to construct explanations for the state as a whole.

XIV Portable Containers

The prehistoric inhabitants of Arizona made and used a wide variety of portable containers including bags, pouches, baskets, and pots. These were made of skin, cloth, bark, twigs, reeds, clay, and a variety of other plant products. Archaeologists have learned more about ceramic containers than about any other kind, and our discussion will be focused on them. First, let us look at baskets, probably the most important container prior to the invention of pottery.

BASKETRY

Archaeologists do not know when prehistoric populations first began to make baskets. A fragment of a basket found in Gypsum Cave may date to Paleo-Indian times. It is clear that baskets were used by Desert culture groups and all of the later populations that inhabited the state. Despite the long record of this artifact, few systematic statements can be made about it. The material of which baskets were made does not preserve well, and archaeologists find few of them relative to other kinds of artifacts. Because preservation is poor, it is difficult to know whether observed patterns of spatial and temporal variability represent real differences in the manufacture and use of baskets or simply differences in preservation from area to area and time period to time period. Furthermore, baskets and basket fragments are usually fragile and difficult for the archaeologist to work with.

Nevertheless, archaeologists have obtained some systematic knowledge about baskets. While precise patterns of variability cannot be described, it is clear that baskets made in prehistoric Arizona were different in the raw materials of which they were made, the technique of manufacture used, their shape, design, and use. The most important raw materials used in making baskets were pliable twigs such as those from willow trees, the leaves of cacti like yucca and sotol, and a number of hardier grasses. Grasses and twigs were often used in the same basket, the twigs to give it a firm shape and the grasses to provide a tight surface.

Baskets were made in three different ways: by coiling, by twining, and by twilling. The maker of a coiled basket first made ropes of grass and of spliced twigs. The basket was built up from the base in spiral fashion. Each new layer of material was sewn to the layer below it. In making a twined basket, the craftsman began with a series of radiating spokes. Twigs of fibrous strips were then intertwined with the spokes. Twilling is a kind of weaving technique in which strands of the raw material were continuously overlapped. The baskets were sometimes coated with pine resin or lined with sun-dried clay.

Baskets were made in a variety of different shapes, probably more than archaeologists now know about. Large and small jars, bowls, platters, and bags were all made. Modern Southwestern Indians make baskets in virtually all of the shapes of pottery vessels, and there is no reason to assume that their ancestors were less talented.

Designs on the baskets were usually of black, brown, and/or red. In some instances the design was painted on the surface of the basket after it was made. In others, the materials of which the basket was to be made were colored and the design woven into the basket.

Baskets were used for a variety of different purposes. Some were made to hold liquids; they were woven tightly or were lined with resin or clay. Baskets were certainly used to hold and store seeds and grains. They were even used for cooking. Of course, the basket could not be placed over an open fire. But, if it could hold water, then rocks hot enough to bring the water to a boil could be dropped into it, and plant or meat products cooked in it.

At about the time of Christ, pots began to replace baskets as the most important type of container. Why? Two factors probably contributed to this change. First, prehistoric populations had been experimenting with clay as a material for lining baskets. As they used this material they undoubtedly learned that for some uses it was superior to woven plants. Moreover, they learned that clay placed in a fire forms an even harder more durable surface than that dried in the sun, and that this material is self-supporting, it does not require an outer framework of basketry to give it shape or support. Thus, clay was present as a kind of variety in the containers these groups used.

Pottery could never become important in a nonsedentary population that made baskets. Baskets were far less susceptible to breakage than pots and, therefore, more useful to wandering groups. Pots, however, are more useful than baskets in around-camp activities like cooking and storing. It

is not surprising that pots became more important as prehistoric populations became more sedentary.

The earliest Southwestern pottery was found by Paul S. Martin in caves of the Pine Lawn area of New Mexico. The sherds he found dated to about 600 B.C. Pottery was important by the Pioneer period in the Hohokam area and by Mogollon 1 in the mountains. It did not become important until somewhat later in the Colorado Plateau or in the northwestern portion of the state. Pottery is the most important single artifact that archaeologists have found on sites dating to A.D. 900 or later in most parts of Arizona.

HOW THE ARCHAEOLOGIST LOOKS AT POTTERY

Spatial and temporal variability in ceramic artifacts has been the most important single datum used by archaeologists in building chronologies and defining culture areas. The association between culture and pottery is so strong in the minds of some archaeologists that they speak of the "brownware people" or the "buffware people." For reasons that will be discussed later, so close an identification of the two phenomena is unreasonable.

Nevertheless, pottery is an important tool. McGregor (1965) has summarized a number of reasons why this is the case. Pottery is practically indestructible and is readily preserved. As a result, it is abundant in late prehistoric sites. It was a widespread phenomenon; prehistoric pottery is found throughout the state. It is "plastic," reflects minute spatial and temporal changes. Finally, it is relatively easy to collect, handle, and study.

All of these arguments are valid. Nevertheless, they ignore one important reason why ceramics have become so important an archaeological tool. In many parts of Arizona, prehistoric peoples made very beautiful pottery. Pottery vessels were highly prized and much sought after in the early days of Southwestern archaeology. Museums wishing to classify these vessels began to develop relatively sophisticated typologies well before other artifact classes were subject to much analysis at all. The precise nature of the spatial and temporal variability in this artifcat became clear, and archaeologists began to use it in mapping old and defining new cultural units. This utilization led to further improvements of typologies which made pottery more useful a tool which led to further improvements in the typologies and so on.

It may be that pottery is more "plastic" than other artifacts, but in large part this plasticity is a product of the archaeologist, not the artifact. By learning to differentiate minute details of pots and potsherds, we have created a good deal of the plasticity. For example, archaeologists know much more about decorated types of pottery than about undecorated types. Some archaeologists prefer to spend their time analyzing decorated vessels and sherds and practically throw away plain ones. Yet, the great majority of sherds on sites in Arizona (often 75 percent or more), even late ones, are undecorated. By focusing on designs, and studying spatial and temporal variability in designs in great detail, archaeologists have created plasticity. It remains to be shown that chipped or ground stone tools would not appear equally plastic if subjected to the same minute attribute analyses that have been made of pottery. The usefulness of any artifact to the archaeologist is to a very substantial extent a function of what he trains himself to see in the artifact and how he uses the observed variability.

Another attribute of pottery that makes it useful to the archaeologist is the fact that sherds (small broken pieces of vessels) are useful in a way that bits of projectile points or chipped stone tools are not. Archaeologists do not have to find whole vessels in order to make use of this artifact.

There are hundreds, even thousands, of attributes of pots and potsherds that archaeologists might choose to look at and record. Only a limited number of these attributes have proven useful in working with ceramic variability. Attributes of sherds can be used to obtain information about the raw materials used in making pots, the techniques of constructions used, the way the product was used by its maker, and the way the vessel looked. Only a limited number of these attributes have proven important in working with ceramic variability, and it is to these that we turn our attention.

A page from *Pottery Types of the Southwest* by Harold S. Colton (1955b) is reproduced here. This page illustrates the format that archaeologists use in defining pottery types. By working through this definition, we can see what the archaeologist regards as relevant to pottery classification.

The name of the type that is being defined consists of a geographic term, followed by a descriptive term. Simply by reading this term, we learn that this type is found generally in the Kayenta region and is white with black paint.

Before archaeologists reached agreement on the designation and definition of this type of pottery it was referred to by other names. These names, the names of the archaeologists who used them, and the works in which they were used are listed under SYNONYMS. Under the heading DESCRIBED BY, the names of the individuals who have published the most extensive descriptions of this type and the publications in which the descriptions appear are listed. The individual who first employed the name now being used to denote the type is identified in NAMED BY. Publications in which ILLUSTRATIONS of the type and museums where examples of the type can be examined are listed next. The STAGE and TIME PERIOD to which the type belongs are based in some instances on relatively firm radiocarbon or tree-ring dating while in others they are relatively crude guesses. A map in the

KAYENTA BLACK-ON-WHITE

SYNONYMS   (a) Black-on-White Ware, Kidder & Guernsey, 1919, pp. 130–134; (b) Kayenta Black-on-White Ware, Kidder, 1924, Pl. 30, 31; (c) Tokonabi (Kayenta) Ware, Fewkes, 1926; p. 9; (d) Sagi Black-on-White, Gladwin, W. & H. S., 1934, Fig. 7.

DESCRIBED BY   Kidder & Guernsey, loc. cit. Revised by Colton and Hargrave, 1937, p. 217.

NAMED BY   Kidder, 1924, p. 71.

EXAMPLES   Sherds Nos. AT 128, 1043, 3076–3093 at the Museum of Northern Arizona.

TYPE SITE   Long House Pueblo (NA 897), = Ruin A (Kidder & Guernsey, 1919), Marsh Pass, Navajo County, Arizona.

STAGE   Late Pueblo 111.   TIME   ca A.D. 1250–1300.

DESCRIPTION   *Constructed:* by coiling. *Fired:* in reducing atmosphere. *Core:* usually light gray. *Carbon streak:* rare. *Temper:* small amounts very fine quartz sand, usually almost invisible; occasional small opaque angular fragment, red or black. *Vessel Walls:* very strong. *Texture core:* very fine. *Fracture:* shattering. *Surface finish:* bowl interiors, jar exteriors, compacted; well-polished. *Surface color:* dead white to light pearl gray. *Forms:* jars, (predominate) bowls, colanders. *Recorded range thickness jar walls:* 2.2 to 8.6 mm.; average (98 sherds), 4.3 mm. *Decoration:* painted. *Paint:* black, occasionally brownish, almost always rich and dense; never gritty. *Pigment:* carbon, sometimes indicates of iron (test by Colton). *Design:* execution, excellent; characterized by negative or "mosquito-bar" effect; wide stripes frame rectangular or triangular panels in which occur narrow-line cross-hatching, usually diagonal, with solid elements as triangles, bars, stepped elements; occasionally opposed stepped elements in panels without hatchure; rarely interlocking scrolls; rarely finely barbed wide lines or stripes.

COMPARISONS   *Hoyapi Black-on-White,* surface color never dead white, often fairly dark pearl gray; decorated surfaces less well-polished, scraping marks often conspicuous on unpainted surfaces; execution of design considerably less excellent; hatchure lines not always exactly parallel or evenly spaced; paint generally gritty and frequently purplish in spots. *Betatakin Black-on-White,* surface color never dead white, often dark pearl gray; painted surfaces only moderately polished, scraping marks often conspicuous on unpainted surfaces; execution of design considerably less excellent; open-work rather than negative design.

RANGE   Tsegi Canyons south to Hopi Mesas, northern Arizona.

REMARKS   The Kayenta Style of decoration is more widespread than the type and has thus given rise to erroneous impressions of the distribution of Kayenta Black-on-White. It may be a style variation of Tusayan Black-on-White.

FIGURE 30   Sample description of Black Mesa Black-on-White. This description shows both the form and content (attributes) of an archaeologist's definition of a pottery type. Courtesy of the Museum of Northern Arizona.

upper right-hand corner of the page (not shown) shows where this type of pottery is found.

The most important part of the definition is the DESCRIPTION.

Attributes that the archaeologists will use in identifying specimens of this type are recorded. Some archaeologists have argued that the type is the most basic unit of ceramic analysis. It should be clear that no one can recognize a type without knowing the attributes associated with the type. The attribute, not the type, is the most basic element in our analyses. Each of the attributes in the definition is important. Our discussion of the meaning of the attributes is based upon Anna O. Shepard's *Ceramics for the Archaeologist* (1956).

CONSTRUCTION

The vessel walls can be constructed or built up in many different ways. Clay can be modeled, turned on a wheel, or put into a mold.

The archaeologist is able to infer how a particular vessel was made because these techniques leave distinctive marks on the vessel walls. Vessels made in a basket carry impressions of the basket. Vessels made by coil-and-scrape have striations or scrape marks on some surfaces. The coils are sometimes still visible on the surface of these vessels. Modeled vessels still retain finger and hand marks. The round head of the anvil left characteristic markings on the interior walls of vessels made by the paddle-and-anvil technique. Kayenta Black-on-White vessels were made by the coil-and-scrape technique.

FIRING

Once a vessel has been formed, its walls are made fast by exposing it to heat. Some early vessels were hardened simply by setting them in the sun. During most of the prehistory of ceramics in Arizona, vessel walls were hardened by exposing the vessel to a burning or smoldering fire.

CORE COLOR

The color of the paste of which vessels were made depended both on the raw materials used and on the firing technique.

CARBON STREAK

Some clays are rich in carbonaceous material. When such clays were used, they left an attribute referred to as a carbon streak.

TEMPER

When vessels begin to dry, they shrink somewhat. In order to keep the vessels from cracking or breaking as they dried, prehistoric potters added nonplastic materials called temper to their clay. Some of the earliest pottery made in the Southwest had organic temper. Typically, however, potters used sand, crushed rock, and crushed sherds for temper. Mica, tuffs, black sand, water-worn sand, and other very distinctive materials were used in some localities.

VESSEL WALL STRENGTH

This attribute is an estimation of the force required to snap a sherd.

FRACTURE

When a sherd is snapped, the break may be a clean or a crumbly one.

SURFACE FINISH

The surfaces of vessels were finished in a variety of different ways. Sometimes coils or parts of the coils were still visible on the surface of the vessel. This surface finish is called corrugation. Vessels whose surfaces were scraped to evenness but were still bumpy, gritty, or dull are called rough-finished. A smooth stone or gourd shell was sometimes repeatedly rubbed over the surface of a vessel to polish it to a very high luster. Some potters coated their vessels with a layer of extra high quality clay referred to as a slip.

SURFACE COLOR

The color of the surface as opposed to that of the paste is characterized in much the same way as that of the core.

VESSEL FORMS

Most of the vessels that prehistoric potters made were either bowls or jars. Some other forms into which prehistoric potters shaped their vessels are shown in Figure 31.

RIM TYPE

The rims of vessels were formed in a variety of different styles. Archaeologists classify rims on the basis of the shape of the side wall, the direction of the lip, and the form of the rim.

RECORDED RANGE OF THICKNESS OF BOWL AND/OR JAR WALLS

The archaeologist notes a mean thickness and a range of variation in his type definitions.

DECORATION

Decorations were painted on the surface of vessels and/or cut into them.

PAINT AND PIGMENT

Archaeologists are interested in several attributes of the paints and pigments used by prehistoric potters. White, red, black, green, and brown paints were all used. The combination of paint and surface color that the potter created provides the name that the archaeologist uses in referring to the types: Black-on-White, Red-on-Buff, Black-on-Red, Red-on-Orange, and Polychrome (red, white, and black on the same vessel).

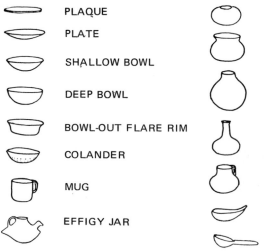

PLAQUE
PLATE
SHALLOW BOWL
DEEP BOWL
BOWL-OUT FLARE RIM
COLANDER
MUG
EFFIGY JAR
SEED BOWL
WIDE MOUTH JAR
NARROW MOUTH JAR
VASE
PITCHER
SCOOP
LADLE

FIGURE 31 Vessel forms. These are some of the shapes of vessels that were made by prehistoric inhabitants of the Southwest. Vessels of different shapes were used for different purposes, although not exclusively so. In many cases, different raw materials and techniques of construction were used in making different forms of vessels. Courtesy of the Museum of Northern Arizona.

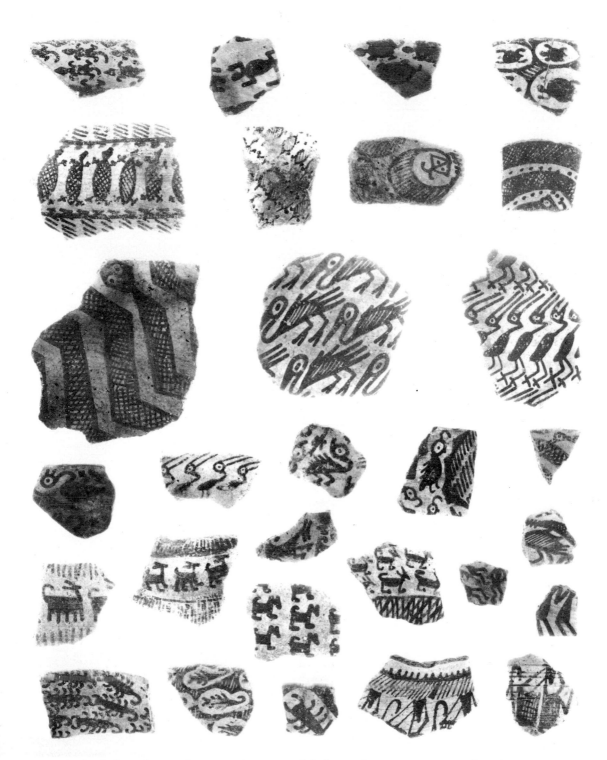

PLATE 48   Hohokam design elements. A variety of different designs were painted on pots by prehistoric potters. In some areas, these were primarily geometric forms. The Hohokam are noted for the use of finely executed animal forms on some pottery types. Reproduced by permission of the Arizona State Museum.

DESIGN

Describing the designs that were painted on vessel surfaces is by far the most complex task facing the archaeologist. As one can see from the description of designs common to Kayenta Black-on-White, these descriptions usually take the form of a mixture of statements about the sizes of lines, the direction of lines, commonly occurring geometric, zoomorphic, or anthropomorphic figures, and the relationship between all of these.

A design element is the basic unit of design. It is an attempt on the part of the archaeologist to infer the most basic symbols from which designs were created. The design element concept is useful in working with sherds as well as whole vessel, because a sherd is typically covered by one or a few design elements.

Whole vessels were painted with many different design elements. Recurring groups of elements are called *motifs*. The motifs were enclosed by *framing lines*. Motifs were alternated, repeated, interlocked, and opposed. The portion(s) of the vessel that the painter covered with designs are usually described in terms of *layouts*.

Design is the last attribute considered under DESCRIPTION. The next category is COMPARISONS. Archaeologists use this section to describe the differences between the type being defined and similar but not identical types. The RANGE of the type is described next. Finally, the archaeologist adds any additional remarks or warning that he feels will assist his colleagues in working with the type.

ORGANIZING THE ATTRIBUTES

All of these diverse attributes can be organized in terms of two different schemes. First, we can view the attributes as they might have been viewed by the prehistoric potter. Second, we can view them as they are viewed by the archaeologist defining his types. Some archaeologists believe that artifact typologies are "arbitrary," that they are ultimately the creature of the archaeologist. Others believe that they are or should be real; that they should closely approximate the way in which prehistoric populations viewed the phenomenon under study. We subscribe to the latter viewpoint and believe that the more closely our typologies reflect the cultural reality of the potter the more useful they will be to us.

In this regard, we can think of all these attributes in terms of the decisions made by the potter. From the beginning he had some concept of the form and style of the vessel he would construct. This idea was not carried as a "template" but as a series of decisions he knew he would have to make in effecting his product. The first decisions concerned the choice of raw materials. He selected clays, tempering material, pigments, and fuel. In part his selection was shaped by the availability of different materials in his environment. In part it was shaped by what he had learned of the qualities of these raw materials. He chose between a variety of different techniques and combinations of techniques for building the walls of his vessels. He may not have known of all the techniques that were used in prehistoric Arizona, but he certainly knew of some of them. He built a jar, bowl, colander or ladle depending on the purpose for which he needed the

FIGURE 32 Ceramic techniques of the Upper Pima. This illustration shows the different steps involved in making a pot. Taken from Figure 44, *The Upper Pima of San Cayetano del Tumacacori*, The Amerind Foundation, Inc. Publication No. 7, 1956.

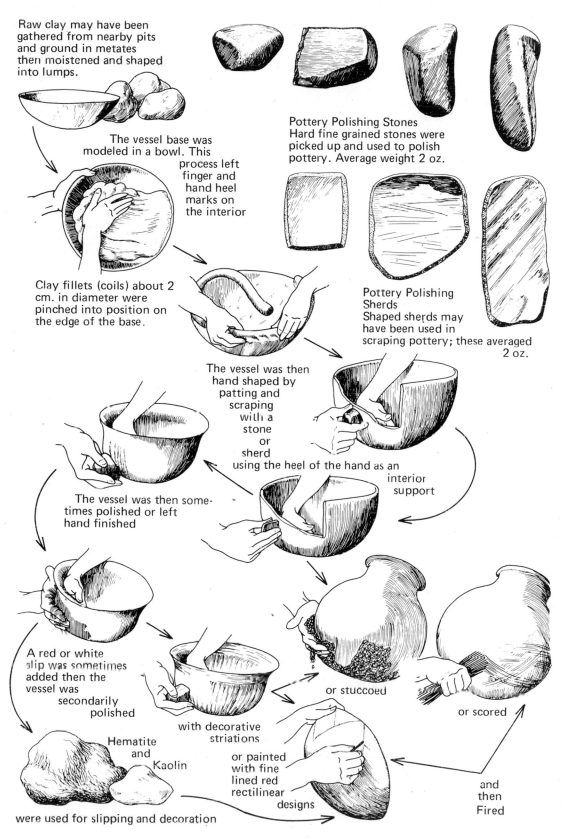

Raw clay may have been gathered from nearby pits and ground in metates then moistened and shaped into lumps.

The vessel base was modeled in a bowl. This process left finger and hand heel marks on the interior

Pottery Polishing Stones
Hard fine grained stones were picked up and used to polish pottery. Average weight 2 oz.

Clay fillets (coils) about 2 cm. in diameter were pinched into position on the edge of the base.

Pottery Polishing Sherds
Shaped sherds may have been used in scraping pottery; these averaged 2 oz.

The vessel was then hand shaped by patting and scraping with a stone or sherd using the heel of the hand as an interior support

The vessel was then some-times polished or left hand finished

A red or white slip was sometimes added then the vessel was secondarily polished

with decorative striations

or stuccoed

or scored

Hematite and Kaolin

or painted with fine lined red rectilinear designs

and then Fired

were used for slipping and decoration

TECHNIQUE OF
CONSTRUCTION   FIRING ATMOSPHERE   TEMPE

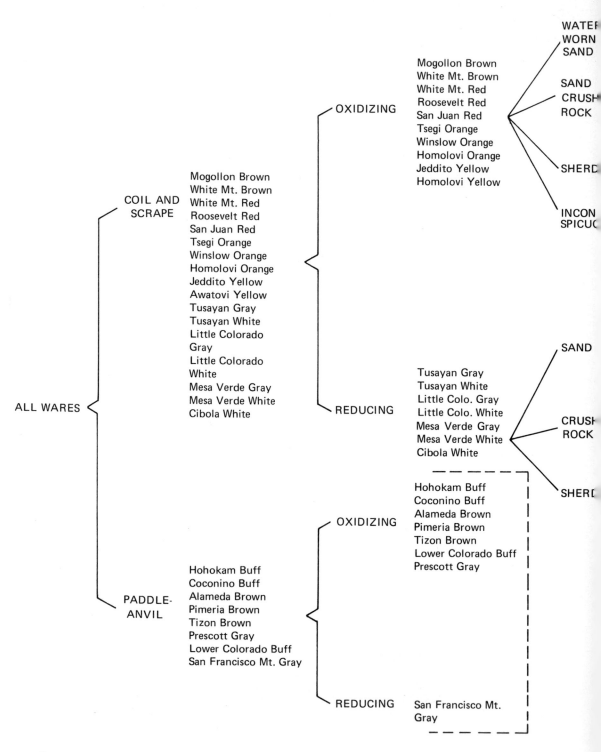

WATER
WORN
SAND

SAND
CRUSH
ROCK

SHERD

INCON
SPICUC

OXIDIZING

Mogollon Brown
White Mt. Brown
White Mt. Red
Roosevelt Red
San Juan Red
Tsegi Orange
Winslow Orange
Homolovi Orange
Jeddito Yellow
Homolovi Yellow

COIL AND
SCRAPE

Mogollon Brown
White Mt. Brown
White Mt. Red
Roosevelt Red
San Juan Red
Tsegi Orange
Winslow Orange
Homolovi Orange
Jeddito Yellow
Awatovi Yellow
Tusayan Gray
Tusayan White
Little Colorado
Gray
Little Colorado
White
Mesa Verde Gray
Mesa Verde White
Cibola White

ALL WARES

REDUCING

Tusayan Gray
Tusayan White
Little Colo. Gray
Little Colo. White
Mesa Verde Gray
Mesa Verde White
Cibola White

SAND

CRUSH
ROCK

SHERD

OXIDIZING

Hohokam Buff
Coconino Buff
Alameda Brown
Pimeria Brown
Tizon Brown
Lower Colorado Buff
Prescott Gray

PADDLE-
ANVIL

Hohokam Buff
Coconino Buff
Alameda Brown
Pimeria Brown
Tizon Brown
Prescott Gray
Lower Colorado Buff
San Francisco Mt. Gray

REDUCING

San Francisco Mt.
Gray

SURFACE TREATMENT   CORE   PAINT
(polished or slipped vs. rough)

```
Roosevelt Red ───────── P, S ───────── DARK ───────────── ORGANIC
                                        DARK    San Juan Red ──── MINERAL

⎧ White Mt. Brown ────── P, S San Juan Red
⎪ Winslow Orange              Winslow Orange   LIGHT   Winslow Orange ── MINERAL
⎨ Homolovi Orange
⎩ Awatovi Yellow ────── R Homolovi O.          PINK    Homolovi O.
                           Awatovi Y.
                                              YELLOW   Awatovi Y.
⎧ White Mt. Red ─────── P, S White Mt. Red     DARK    Tsegi O. ──────── MINERAL
⎨ Tsegi Orange               Tsegi Orange
⎩                                             LIGHT   White Mt. Red ── MIXED

Jeddito Yellow ─────── P, S ───────────── YELLOW ──────────── MINERAL


                                                      ORGANIC Tusayan W.

                                                      MINERAL Cibola W.

⎧ Tusayan G.            P, S Tusayan W. ── LIGHT    Tusayan W.
⎪ Tusayan W.                 Cibola W.             Cibola W.
⎨ L.C. Gray
⎩ Cibola W.             R Tusayan G. ──── DARK     Little Colo. G.
                           L.C. Gray
                                         LIGHT     Tusayan G. ── ORGANIC Mesa Verde W.

⎧ Mesa Verde G.         P, S Cibola W. ── LIGHT    Cibola W.        MINERAL Cibola W.
⎨ Mesa Verde W.              Mesa Verde W.         Mesa Verde W.
⎩ Cibola W.
                       R Mesa Verde G. ── VARIABLE ───────── ORGANIC

Little Colo. W. ────── P, S ─────── DARK
```

FIGURE 33 A tree diagram of major pottery wares. When the wares are divided into groups on the basis of the presence or absence of particular attributes, a unique definition of each ware is generated. Some meaningful groups are generated early in the diagram also. For example, paddle and anvil pottery was made principally below the Mogollon Rim and coil and scrape pottery above it.

vessel. He chose between finishing the surface by corrugation, polishing, scraping, slipping, or painting. In part this choice was shaped by the intended function of the vessel and in part by his future intentions for decorating it. The potter knew of many different designs and combinations of designs that he might use on the vessel. If he was painting it he chose some of these. This choice was not capricious and some reasons why particular choices were made will be discussed later. The vessel was fired, perhaps refired, and the potter exercised a good deal of control over the changing color patterns on the vessel. This complex process of decision-making produced the vessel that was used, then eventually broken, and from which an archaeologist finds two sherds a thousand years later.

The archaeologist's typology may reflect all or some of this decision-making process. The typology in terms of which most of the ceramic variability in Arizona has been ordered is that created by Harold S. Colton and first described by Colton and Hargrave (1937). Three concepts are basic to this typology: the type, the series, and the ware. These are defined as follows:

A pottery type is a group of pottery vessels that are alike in every important characteristic except vessel form, including surface color, technique of manufacture, texture of the core, chemical composition of the temper, chemical composition of the paint, and style of design.
A Ware is a group of pottery types that has a majority of the above characteristics in common but that differ in others.
A Series is a group of pottery types within a single ware in which each type bears a genetic relation to each other. The geographic occurrence of a series is usually limited to a definable subdivision of the ware area. (After Colton and Hargrave, 1937, pp. 2–3.)

Using these concepts, Colton divided Southwestern pottery into some fifty wares, over sixty series, and over six hundred types.

Not all of these wares were important in Arizona prehistory. In Colton's thinking, vessels assigned to a single type should resemble each other in very great detail. Those assigned to the same series should be somewhat more dissimilar and those within a single ware even more so. At the same time, types falling in a given series should be more similar to each other than to types falling in different series, and series and types falling within a single ware should be more similar to each other than to series or types falling in different wares.

Some of the strengths and weaknesses of this approach are apparent when one asks exactly how wares differ from each other. We can distinguish between wares by looking at a few attributes or, alternatively, the answers to a few questions:

1 Was the vessel constructed by the paddle-and-anvil or coil-and-scrape technique?

2 Was the vessel fired in an oxidizing or reducing atmosphere?

3 Was the tempering material water-worn sand, sand, crushed rock, sherd, or inconspicuous?

4 Was the surface of the vessel painted/slipped or left relatively rough?

5 What is the color of the paste?

6 Was the paint used on the vessel mineral or organic?

Fig. 33 is a tree diagram in which wares have been systematically divided into sets and subsets based on the answers to these questions.

Colton's typology is the most important one that has been created. Nevertheless, there are problems with it that archaeologists continually work to improve. The first problem is that the number of types is proliferating rapidly; so many types have now been defined that it is very difficult for an archaeologist to keep track of them. This problem was discussed in 1958 by

Wheat, Wasley, and Gifford. They suggested that this proliferation could be stopped by using the term variety to describe some of the minute differences between kinds of pottery that archaeologists were citing in defining types.

It should be obvious that this suggestion stops the proliferation of types but does not stop the proliferation of names of different kinds of pottery. Given Wheat, Wasley, and Gifford's suggestion, varieties rather than types will proliferate—the archaeologist will have just as many names to keep track of.

Typologies don't become overly complex because of the names that archaeologists give to types. Complexity is a product of the number of attributes used in construct-

ATTRIBUTE	POSSIBLE CONDITIONS	COMBINATIONS OF CONDITIONS	POSSIBLE TYPES THIS ATTRIBUTE	AGGREGATE NUMBER OF POSSIBLE TYPES
Technique of Construction	paddle-anvil/coil-scrape	either/or	2	2
Firing Atmosphere	oxidizing, reducing	either/or	2	(2 × 2 =) 4
Temper Type	sand, sherd, mica, crushed rock	any three, any two, any one, none	14	(14 × 4 =) 56
Temper Size	v. coarse, coarse, medium, fine, v. fine	any two, any one	15	840
Carbon Streak	present/absent	either/or	2	1680
Core Color	white, gray, yellow, orange, red, brown, black	any one	7	11760
Core Texture	same as temper	any two, any one	15	176400
Surface Finish	corrugated, rough, polished	one exterior/one interior	9	1587600
Surface Color	same as core color	one ext./one int.	49	77892400
Paint	red, white, black	any two, any one, none	7	545246800
Design Elements	25 (assuming archaeologists could agree on only 25 elements in terms of which types would be defined)	any combination of five or fewer including none (assuming that types could be defined in terms of 5 or fewer design elements)	*	

* The expression for computing this combination is as follows:

$$\text{Combinations} = \frac{25!}{5!(20!)} \times \frac{25!}{4!(21!)} \times \frac{25!}{3!(22!)} \times \frac{25!}{2!(23!)} \times 25 + 1$$

TABLE 12 Computing the number of logically possible types in a typology. Each attribute is listed followed by a description of the values or conditions the attribute can take. The manner in which the values can be combined (either or, three at a time, two at a time) are basic to the calculation of the possible types based on this attribute alone. These are then multiplied in calculating the aggregate of possible types.

ing the typology and the number of distinctions that archaeologists must make in identifying an attribute. A typology has a number of logically possible types based upon the combination of attributes in it—in just the way that we defined wares based on attribute combinations. Not all of these logically possible types will be found to exist, but there will be a tendency to fill all of the slots that exist. And the number of slots, the number of possible types, in a typology like Colton's is enormous, as Table 12 shows.

A second problem with Colton's and many other typologies is that they confuse the morphological attributes of a vessel with its space-time coordinates. It is true that every type is found within spatially and temporally bounded areas. But, this does not mean that an archaeologist can classify on the basis of space and time. If he wants to learn about the space-time distribution of particular types or even pottery-making traditions, the typology itself must be based on morphology alone. If space and time are used in defining the typological units, the archaeologist is assuming his conclusions. Unfortunately, we are afraid that the Colton typology has become so ingrained in the Southwest that many archaeologists are classifying sherds on the basis of when and where they are found rather than by paying careful attention to the attributes of each sherd or vessel.

A third problem is the archaeologist's inability to say just how different two types are from each other. Taking all of the different types of Black-on-White that Colton defines, we find that about 75 percent of the distinctions between types (within wares) are based on differences in design elements or design layouts, 10 percent are based on differences in temper, 5 percent on attributes of the paint, and the remaining 10 percent on attributes of the

clay. Of those types that are distinguished on the basis of design elements, some are differentiated by one or two elements and others by many. In short, we can say that types are different. But in the existing typologies they are different from each other in different ways (different attributes) and to different degrees (different numbers of attributes). There is no formal basis for precisely stating the degree of difference between types in existing typologies and it would be useful to be able to make such statements.

Archaeologists are rapidly learning that no single typology will serve for all of the problems that they try to solve. Nevertheless, it is necessary to have a typology that will facilitate precise communication. A typology such as this would: (1) be based on formal attributes of the artifacts, not their spatial or temporal locus; (2) be based on attributes that closely reflect distinctions that might have been made by prehistoric peoples; (3) define a limited number of types; (4) permit statistical confirmation of the existence of types; and (5) allow precise statements of the degree of difference between types. Archaeologists are working toward such a typology. Colton made an excellent beginning, but his work can and will be improved.

SPACE AND TIME DISTRIBUTIONS

Our criticism of the Colton typology was made in an attempt to suggest improvements in it. No disrespect for Colton and his major contribution to archaeology is implied. He has created the most orderly approach now available to Southwestern pottery and one that we will use in discussing space-time relationships.

In Table 13 and Figure 34 the wares that were important in prehistoric Arizona are located in space and time. The maps of the spatial distributions of the wares are taken from Colton's studies of Southwestern pottery types. When such maps were not available, we drew our own.

Some patterns of spatial and temporal variability are clear. Mogollon Brown, Pimeria Brown, and Tusayan Gray are the earliest wares in the Mogollon, Hohokam and Hakataya, and Anasazi areas, respectively. These wares continue to be important into late prehistoric times, accounting for the majority of sherds on even late prehistoric sites. Hohokam Red-on-Buff, Mogollon Red-on-Brown and Red-on-White (Glenwood Series, Mogollon Brown Ware), Red-on-Brown types of Pimeria Brown Ware, Cibola White Ware, and San Juan Red Ware were most important in their respective areas in the last centuries before A.D. 1000. Tusayan White Ware, Little Colorado Gray and Little Colorado White Wares, Mesa Verde Gray and Mesa Verde White Wares were important on the Colorado Plateau during the centuries on either side of A.D. 1000. At this same time, pottery was becoming important in the northwestern Transition environment as recorded by the appearance of Tizon and Alameda Brown Wares, Lower Colorado Buff Ware, and San Francisco Mountain Gray Ware. In the Hohokam and southern Transition areas, types of Hohokam Buff and Pimeria

TABLE 13 The time spans during which major Arizona pottery wares were made. These values represent the maximum span and not periods of peak abundance. The number of series and types in each ware are also given.

WARE NAMES (NUMBER OF SERIES, TYPES)	BEST DATES
Mogollon Brown Ware (13 series, 120 types)	600 B.C.–A.D. 1300
White Mountain Brown Ware (6 types)	A.D. 1000–1300
White Mountain Red Ware (3 series, 25 types)	A.D. 950–1400
Roosevelt Red Ware (12 types)	A.D. 900–1400
San Juan Red Ware (6 types)	A.D. 600–1300
Tsegi Orange Ware (4 series, 28 types)	A.D. 1000–1400
Homolovi Orange Ware (2 types)	A.D. 1300–1400
Winslow Orange Ware (2 series, 9 types)	A.D. 1300–1400
Awatobi Yellow Ware (7 types)	A.D. 1300–recent
Jeddito Yellow Ware (24 types)	A.D. 1250–recent
Tusayan Gray Ware (3 series, 23 types)	A.D. 350–1400
Tusayan White Ware (2 series, 20 types)	A.D. 650–1400
Little Colorado Gray Ware (1 type)	A.D. 700–1300
Little Colorado White Ware (6 types)	A.D. 700–1400
Mesa Verde Gray Ware (2 series, 8 types)	A.D. 350–1300
Mesa Verde White Ware (4 types)	A.D. 950–1400
Cibola White Ware (5 series, 35 types)	A.D. 650–1300
Hohokam Buff Ware (10 types)	A.D./B.C.–A.D. 1100
Coconino Buff Ware (3 types)	A.D. 800–1100
Alameda Brown Ware (6 series, 41 types)	pre-A.D. 700–1400
Pimeria Brown Ware (6 series, 42 types)	300 B.C.–recent
Tizon Brown Ware (7 types)	A.D. 700–1400
Lower Colorado Buff Ware (7 series, 31 types)	A.D. 800–recent
Prescott Gray Ware (5 types)	A.D. 1000–1400
San Francisco Mountain Gray Ware (6 types)	A.D. 700–1200

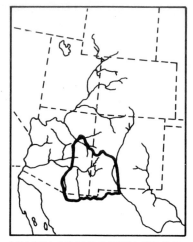

MOGOLLON BROWN WARE

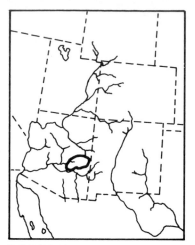

ROOSEVELT RED WARE
(SALADO)

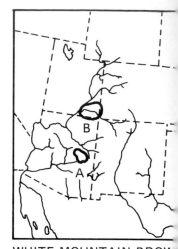

WHITE MOUNTAIN BROW
WARE (A)

SAN JUAN ORANGE WAR
(B)

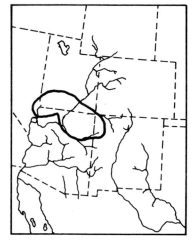

TUSAYAN GRAY AND
WHITE WARE

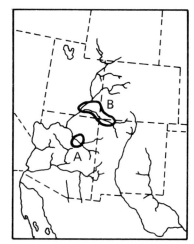

LITTLE COLORADO GRAY
AND WHITE WARES (A)

MESA VERDE GRAY AND
WHITE WARES (B)

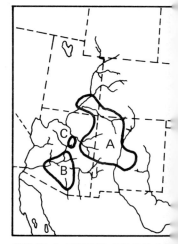

CIBOLA WHITE WARE (A

HOHOKAM (B)

COCONINO BUFF WARES

Brown Wares continued to be important. A number of red-on-black and polychrome types were abundant in the plateau and mountain environments after A.D. 1000, especially White Mountain Red and Brown Wares and Tsegi Orange Ware. Roosevelt Red Ware had a very substantial distribution over the Transition, Mountain, and Desert environments during this period. It is also called Salado Red Ware and its distribution is used by some archaeologists in arguing for Salado migrations or invasions. A buff ware, Coconino Buff, was produced at the edge of the mountain and plateau environments after A.D. 1000 and Prescott Gray Ware was made in the vicin-

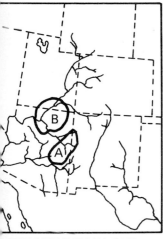

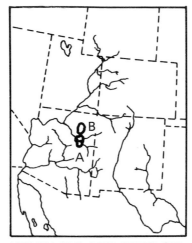

HITE MOUNTAIN RED
WARE (A)

EGI ORANGE WARE (B)

HOMOLOVI AND WINSLOW
ORANGE WARES (A)

AWATOVI, JEDDITO YELLOW
WARES (B)

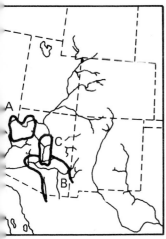

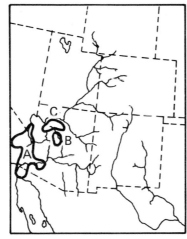

ZON BROWN WARE (A)

AMEDA, PIMERIA (B)

OWN WARES (C)

LOWER COLORADO BUFF
WARE (A)

PRESCOTT GRAY WARE (B)

SAN FRANCISCO MOUNTAIN
WARE (C)

FIGURE 34 Spatial distribution of major wares. The maps show the areas where each of the major pottery wares of Arizona are indigenous. These wares may have been traded more widely, but archaeologists believe that they were made principally within these home areas. Courtesy of the Museum of Northern Arizona.

ity of Prescott. After A.D. 1300 the centers of pottery innovation were in the Hopi region where Homolovi Orange, Winslow Orange, Awatovi Yellow, and Jeddito Yellow Wares were introduced and in the Ootam region of southern Arizona where various new types of Pimeria Brown were made.

To continue this chapter to a description of the spatial and temporal distributions of series and types would press this chapter into hundreds of pages and the book into volumes. Therefore, we leave the discussion of space-time variability and begin to seek explanations of why these patterns of variability developed.

EXPLAINING PATTERNS
OF CERAMIC VARIABILITY

Most of Arizona archaeologists' efforts to explain ceramic variability have employed the concept of spread by diffusion. This has been true whether the investigator was dealing with wares, types, or particular attributes of pottery. Diffusionist studies involve assumptions about changes in the abundance of pottery in space and in time that we find unacceptable. These assumptions are modeled in Figures 35 and 36. We wish to make our reasons for rejecting these models clear.

Diffusionist models assume that pottery types were invented at particular points in time, increased in popularity, and then decreased. This, the path of the variable "abundance of type X" measured over time would approximate the curve in Figure 36:A, with even rates of increase and decrease and the peak period of abundance in the middle of the temporal distribution. Some types do indeed vary over time in a way that approximates a normal curve. But, for other types the increase is very rapid and the decline very slow (Figure 36:B). For still others, the increase is slow and the decrease rapid (Figure 36:C), and for still others the rate of change in the abundance of the type may fluctuate substantially (Figure 36:D). This variation in the pattern of abundance graphed over time is caused by the fact that different pottery types are adopted at different rates by different populations who are adapting to different environmental conditions.

Some feeling for such patterns of variability can be derived from a close examination of Breternitz's study of tree-ring-dated pottery. Breternitz gives a broad range of dates for each pottery type and a range of best dates. We can use the clus-

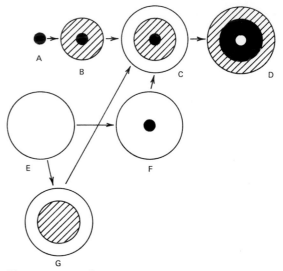

FIGURE 35   Alternative patterns of change in the abundance of pottery in space. Any given spatial pattern in the distribution of a single pottery type may be produced by a number of different spatial processes. The basic pattern that diffusionists assume as well as possible alternatives are illustrated.

FIGURE 36   Alternative patterns of change in the abundance of pottery in time. Archaeologists have unwisely assumed that the appearance and disappearance of a pottery style follows a temporal trajectory that approximates a normal curve. Charts of the adoption of new pottery styles and other innovations are considerably varied in time.

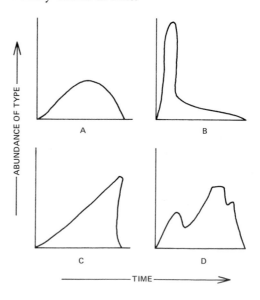

tering of dates as a crude indicator of periods of abundance in the type. In some instances, the best dates and the range of dates correspond rather closely. Alma Plain for example has a range of dates from A.D. 265 to 950 and is best from A.D. 300 to 950. Relative to its total range of dates, Alma Plain increased and decreased in abundance relatively rapidly and remained at a high level of abundance for most of its history. Pinto Polychrome has a range of dates from A.D. 1110 to 1385 and was best from A.D. 1345 to 1385. It increased in abundance at a relatively slow rate and decreased rather quickly. Kana'a Black-on-White increased rapidly and decreased slowly. Its best dates are from A.D. 725 to 815 and its range from A.D. 635 to 1325. There are, of course, other types in which the best dates occur in the middle of the range and the patterns of increase and decrease in abundance are similar. The point is that changes in the "popularity" or abundance of pottery types are variable and cannot be assumed to occur at any particular rate or in any particular pattern.

A similar problem exists with respect to the spatial distribution of types. Diffusionary models assume that pottery types were invented or introduced at specific spatial loci and spread at even rates from these loci. A model of spatial variability at any point in time is assumed to show a central zone in which the type is most abundant and concentric zones in which it is decreasingly abundant (D in Figure 35). The pattern of change in spatial variability over time would look like the sequence from A to B to C in Figure 35. A type was introduced at A, spread to B in a succeeding time period and to C in a still later one. Since the rates of adoption are assumed to have been constant, A must show the greatest abundance, B somewhat less, and C still less. Once again, we know that different

patterns of spatial variability are possible and did occur. For example, a given type sometimes became important over a region, then important at some particular locus, and then important in the territory surrounding the locus in the fashion suggested by the arrows from E to F to C in Figure 35. Other patterns, like E to G to C can result in a distribution that looks like C. Moreover, C is not necessarily the final pattern. If the importance of the pottery type at its initial locus of manufacture began to decrease, a pattern like D might result.

Some sense of this variability can again be obtained by looking at Breternitz's data, this time comparing the best dates that he gives for each type with its trade dates. For some types, the period of abundance as a trade ware falls at about the middle of the period of abundance in the indigenous area. Kana'a Gray, for example, has a range of dates from A.D. 675 to 1190 and was most important as a trade type from A.D. 800 to 965. Black Mesa Black-on-White is recorded as a trade ware (A.D. 875–1130) before it was indigenous in any one area as defined by either the earliest range (A.D. 975) or best (A.D. 1060) date. Excluding the concept of trade, the dates suggest that the type achieved a relatively widespread distribution before it became important in any restricted area. Little Colorado Corrugated does not appear as a trade type (A.D. 1265–75) until its period of peak abundance in its indigenous area is passed. We might expect that a pattern similar to that in Figure D would have existed under these circumstances. There are many possible patterns for the spatial distribution of a type and many different processes by which this pattern can be achieved.

The rate of adoption of artifacts including pottery does not vary uniformly in time and space. Therefore, diffusion or the rate of diffusion is not an explanation of anything; it is a phenomenon which itself warrants explanation. Trade did indeed occur among prehistoric populations. Not only things but ideas spread in this fashion. But their spread is not an explanation of anything; it is an event wanting an explanation. Let us look at a number of examples of the way in which archaeologists have explained or might explain variability.

The material used in tempering pottery shows considerable spatial and temporal patterning. The earliest pottery made in Arizona was tempered with organic material. Sand, crushed rock, and sherds were probably the most important materials through the bulk of the ceramic sequence. Sherd temper was very important late in the ceramic sequence. In northern Arizona gray and white wares, sand seems to have been the primary tempering material used in types made in the center of the plateau while crushed rock was more important in wares and types made nearer the plateau's mountainous peripheries. In some areas crushed rock was used in making red wares and sand in making white wares. How might the archaeologist begin to account for these differences?

Some of them can undoubtedly be explained by differences in the local availability of raw materials. One would guess that sand suitable for temper is more abundant in the broad alluvial and colluvial valleys of the plateau than in the narrow mountain canyons. Of course, sand or crushed rock may be the most readily available resource within regions where another raw material is more abundant. In any case, we might guess that variability in the use of tempering materials will closely reflect variability in available raw materials.

The availability of raw materials did, of course, change over time. Particular sources were used up or forgotten. After pottery had been made for a number of centuries, prehistoric potters had a ready source of tempering materials in their own garbage heaps. At this point, it may have become more efficient to recycle the sherds than to walk several miles in search of a natural material.

The type of clay used in building the vessel walls may have been responsible for some differences in the selection of temper. It seems curious that red and white wares made in the same areas had very different tempers. The clay or firing techniques associated with the color differences may have required the use of tempering materials with different plastic characteristics. Southwestern potters undoubtedly learned from each other the location of raw materials and the relative merits of these materials in producing particular colors or types of vessels. By experimentation with the results of combining different raw materials and by mapping the locations of natural sources of raw materials in the field, the archaeologist can begin to build explanations of ceramic variability that are linked to raw materials.

Vessel shape has less to do with either the raw materials that were available to potters or the informational networks in which they participated than with the purpose for which the vessel was to be used. Archaeologists' notions of vessel function are so well formed that they are virtually built into descriptions of vessel shapes. Prehistoric Arizonans made some vessels that were short cylinders with a capacity of a pint or so and had handles. We call these cups or mugs because they resemble our own drinking utensils. In the same sense, flat circular vessels are called plates. Large round vessels with necks and handles are called pitchers, again because they resemble our own utensils. Very large jars without handles were used for storing water or grains, and somewhat smaller ones were used for cooking. Archaeologists differentiate between the two on the basis of whether vessel exteriors show evidence of continuous and repeated burning. Bowl-shaped vessels were used for storing, cook-ing, eating, and decoration. It is often dif-ficult for the archaeologist to determine which of these functions they served. How-ever, bowls may be found with other eating or storage or cooking utensils that provide the archaeologist with some contextual ev-idence as to how the bowl was used. In any case, most of our attempts to explain var-iability in vessel form will be made in terms of function and not raw material.

Explaining variability in design elements is a particularly difficult but nevertheless interesting problem. Longacre in his study of Carter Ranch pueblo and Hill in his study of Broken K pueblo defined micro-style zones within prehistoric communities. There are localized areas within these pueblos where distinctive design elements and combinations of elements occur. In both Longacre's and Hill's studies the ma-jority of design elements were associated with the pueblo as a whole. Those that were not defined the micro-style zones. Cook (1970) was able to show that this same pattern existed in the valley in which the communities were located. He noted that sites were not evenly distributed over the valley but occurred in clusters. He found that there was significantly less variability within these clusters than between them.

What do these patterns of variability re-flect? Why are some elements associated with regions, some with groups of settle-ments, some with particular settlements, and some with groups of rooms within the settlements? Most archaeologists seem to agree that these style zones reflect learning: potters watched and copied the styles of nearby potters. There is more shared in-formation within settlements than between settlements, within settlement clusters than

between settlement clusters, and so on. Longacre and Hill argued that the informa-tion exchange system was an even more organized one. Mothers taught their daugh-ters to pot. In a matrilocal society where a daughter brought her husband to live in her mother's dwelling, the designs passed from mother to daughter would have remained localized within a given part of the settle-ment. Leone (1968) analyzed variability in marriage patterns in the Upper Little Colo-rado and found that this variability could be explained in terms of changes in the eco-nomic base that would have favored or militated against matrilocality. Plog (1969) observed that the micro-style zones in both Longacre's and Hill's analyses consisted of about eight habitation rooms. He went on to show that sites in the Upper Little Colo-rado tended to have multiples of eight habitation rooms (8, 16, 24, etc.). It seems more reasonable to believe that these eight-room style zones represented some basic organizational unit than to believe potters just happened to imitate each other in groups of eights. So, we can view this as-pect of ceramic variability in terms of pat-terned exchanges of information about pottery-making and refer these exchanges to the organization of the society in which the exchange occurred and the social and natural environmental factors that affected the organization.

Explaining similarities and differences in an attribute like the color and color com-binations on vessel surfaces necessitates drawing on all of the different factors dis-cussed so far. The clays, tempering mate-rials, and pigments that were available in a particular area determined what kinds of colors could be produced. Prehistoric pot-ters learned about the color characteristics of some of these materials later than others. They also had differential knowledge about firing atmospheres and differential abilities to manipulate them to vary the color by this method. Polychrome vessels were generally later than bichrome ones, which in turn were later than plain wares. Why did decades or centuries pass before a society that made both red-on-black and red-on-white vessels begin to make polychrome ones? Was the change the result of the accidental creation of a blend that became popular? Or did the need for more complex symbol systems to carry information of vessel surfaces act as a selective pressure favoring the adoption of polychromes? Answers to questions such as these will come as archaeologists abandon their diffusionary models and seek explanations of ceramic variability in terms of cultural and behavioral factors.

PART SIX

CHANGING PATTERNS
OF SOCIAL ORGANIZATION

XV   The Growth of Complex Systems

INTRODUCTION: CULTURE AND CULTURAL SYSTEMS

Culture is regarded as a thermodynamic system. It is made up of attributes or units or traits (e.g., things, attitudes, events). Thus, culture is a complex adaptive system —a whole that functions as a whole by virtue of the interdependence of its parts (Rapaport, 1968, p. xvii). Or, expressed differently, culture is an organization of cultural elements without regard to chronological sequences. A cultural system is an organization of things, ideas, attitudes, and events so interrelated that the relationship of part to part is determined by the relationship of part to whole (White, 1959a, p. 17). The major subsystems of culture are: technological, sociological (having to do with the nature of society), economical, and ideological.

The function of culture is to make life secure, tolerable, and lasting. Man employs his extrasomatic, nonbiological culture to keep himself going and to perpetuate the race. Culture makes it possible for man to relate to his total environment, for man to relate to other men, and to his habitat. It enables him to live, to propagate, to fight off enemies, to be confident and happy.

Social Organization Defined

Social organization and social structure are principal elements of a major subsystem of culture necessary for the effective conduct of life and the survival of man. They are just as necessary and important to the total environment as are technological adjustments.

Social organization is concerned with the arrangements and relationships of human beings one to the other. These arrangements and relationships are determined by three elements: subsistence, offense-defense, and total environment.

Social organization is never static. It changes, develops, and evolves. As a society grows from simple to more complex, so does social organization. Greater complexity means more parts; more parts require more effective integration of the whole which accommodates the parts (Service, 1962, p. 180). It is a kind of feedback loop that carries a continual flow of information between the social system, the other subsystems, and their environment. The combination of technology and ecological adjustment may bring about a particular type of social organization. When technology and other ecological commonalties change, the other subsystems change. This hypothesis has been criticized (Service, 1962, pp. 72–76), but this strategy still merits support (Harris, 1968, p. 667).

Before going further with comments on social organization, it might be well to define a few terms that will be used in this section.

Social structure refers to the component groups of a society and to the configuration of their arrangement. For example, domestic families, lineage villages, and territorial bands are sometimes called residential groups. The important point here is that they live together or close to one another (Service, 1962, pp. 18–22).

Social organization, as used here, is a broader term that refers to both *structure and status,* the latter being defined as a social position that is named, e.g., "brother," "father," "cousins," "uncles," etc. *Status* applies to people who have assigned appropriate attributes for the regulation of their interpersonal conduct (Services, 1962, p. 54). Other terms will be explained as they occur.

The main purposes of this chapter are: (1) to call attention to the probabilistic kinds of social organization that may have been associated with the various stages and subculutres in the Southwest; (2) to show how changing patterns of social organization are adaptations to changing technologies, resources, physical conditions, or environment, and how we can hypothesize that with these changes, social organization, as part of a system, could not remain static; and (3) to suggest that the social organization is a response to a certain ecological and technological situation and that the resultant organization makes good sense in exploiting certain resources, in the division of labor, in extracting a living, and in redistributing the harvest.

As White puts it: "The degree of organization of a system is proportional to the concentration of energy within the system" (White, 1959a, p. 145). Thus, a large concentration of energy within a system means a complex social organization. Hence, social organization is directly related in a systematic way with subsistence and technology, or tools, to cover all material means for doing work (energy). Tools are a means for harnassing and transforming work (energy) into products (goods and services) for the everyday needs of man. Technology and ecological adjustment go hand in hand; they cannot be separated.

Sociocultural Levels

In earlier chapters of this book, we outlined several kinds of "cultures" or adaptations: hunters and gatherers, pit house dwellers, pueblo and town dwellers.

We now propose to look at these stages of development from another perspective and to suggest the kinds of social organization that may have characterized their levels of sociocultural development.

In 1962, Service named three stages as being important in the evolution of primitive social organization: (1) band level of integration; (2) tribal level of integration; and (3) chiefdom level of integration. The names are not important, but the changing patterns of complexity are.

The point of view we are advancing does not imply that all societies must, or do, go through these stages. Some societies might remain at band level and never become more complex. We are merely calling attention to a taxonomic description of the social organization of many societies.

Hunters and Gatherers

From earliest times to the introduction of agriculture in Arizona and the Southwest, the land was exploited by peoples who subsisted on wild plant food and game.

What kind of network of relationships held these gathering societies together? Given the technoenvironmental conditions under which they lived, how were they able to establish an adaptation that assured them foods, protection against hostile people, and survival and reproduction of their species?

The answer is the sociocultural type of integration called the *band level.* It is the simplest form of social structure and was a practical form for people who hunt and gather and whose population density was too sparse to make possible the formation of villages.

It is believed that all societies at the band level of integration, or unity, are foragers, but not all foragers are at the band level. Where natural abundance of wild foods (or sea food) exists (e.g., northwest coast of North America), one finds the people living in complex communities (Service, 1962, p. 60). The bases for hypothesizing that the band level is the earliest and simplest type of social organization are founded on primate social life, on the archaeological record concerning early man, and on studies of this form of society still retained by some living groups (the Arunta of Australia, for example).

What is a *band?* A band is a local group made up of several families who habitually camp together, who hunt and gather together, and who migrate together seasonally. Bands are politically autonomous and are composed of a small population that is subdivided into several nuclear families. These families are permitted to hunt or gather on lands controlled and owned by the band. Briefly, the band adjustment to the environment, or habitat, may be described as follows: low productivity of the hunting and gathering techniques in semi-arid areas with a consequent limitation of population density (about one person per square mile). The social aggregates are restricted and small with perhaps ten to fifty persons to a band. The band is larger than the nuclear family because a band is more efficient in providing security against hostile persons and in assuring food for the whole band (Steward, 1936).

This type of adaptation to the techno-environment probably implies: (1) sharing and making friends by sharing, both of which lead to reciprocity (sharing food,

giving help in various situations); (2) marriage to stabilize mating when sexual division of labor was established; (3) marrying outside the group (exogamy) to reduce jealous male conflict within the group and to form alliances between bands to increase the lands available for food collecting and to swell the number of relatives who may be called on for cooperation and assistance.

While marrying outside the group may have been the ideal, perhaps one was encouraged to marry not *too far* outside the group, for in doing so, group solidarity was weakened. Marriage then took place between groups and was reciprocal; women were the "gifts" and the male group that accepted the woman was the recipient. Reciprocity was established by means of a countergift of goods or of a female.

There are two types of bands: *patrilocal* and *composite*. A patrilocal band, as the name implies, is a band in which the bride moves to or near the parental home of the groom. The term implies exogamy and virilocal residence. A composite band, although not referred to again, is defined as one that lacks the rules of exogamy and virilocal residence.

The patrilocal type probably came about because a group organized around a nucleus of males has great advantages in obtaining food, in hunting, and in defending the group.

Thus, we have strong reasons for advancing the hypothesis that the desert hunters and gatherers lived in bands that practiced virilocality, exogamy, and reciprocity. Their economy was a family matter; group control was in the hands of the heads of families; religion was a family-band matter and was probably concerned mostly with curing ceremonies. The nuclear family and the band ran the whole show—economies, politics, ideologies.

Farmers of the Southwest:
300 B.C.–A.D. 1100, Hohokam;
and About A.D. 200–
A.D. 900, Anasazi

Included in the term "farmers" are all people who built and occupied pit houses, villages, surface villages, big houses, and cliff houses. This means people who relied on a crop subsistence rather than *only* on hunting and gathering. By definition this would, of course, include the Anasazi, Hohokam, Mogollon, and others with emphasis mainly on the Anasazi.

Obviously, the band level of integration would be too simple to handle the activities and social relationships of groups whose lives were drastically altered by agriculture and made more complex. Again, ecology and integration would have been the key causative factors in bringing about an adaptation to changed conditions.

The situation was not simply a matter of population increase, for a more complex social structure does not arise solely as a response to more people (Carneiro, 1967, p. 239). In fact, a dense population and a concentration of it in small areas may cause a breakdown in the social structure. One may find instead a reversion to a simpler organization or even almost chaos (as found in ghettos, for example). If a critical point in size is reached without the development of new organizational features, a society might break up into smaller, semiautonomous units. But changes in subsistence or defense requirements may bring about new structural features in the sociocultural system without more population (Carneiro, 1967, p. 239).

If, however, we wish to assume that the society in question, e.g., that which flourished in Chaco Canyon for about two hundred years (roughly A.D. 900–1100), was becoming larger and that it was already unified and integrated, then we have to assume

that the social organization became more elaborate.

Earlier, we pointed out that culture was a system with its parts so interrelated that a change in one part would bring about changes in another. It is therefore not out of line to suggest that when the number of social units increases, the social system will respond by elaboration of the social structure because more coordination is required to keep the individuals and the social units operating as a going mechanism. At this point, social organization of larger aggregations of people in towns moves on to what Service calls tribal organization (Service, 1962, pp. 110–42).

What are some of the features of *tribal level* of sociocultural integration? It is more complex than a band; it is usually composed of economically self-sufficient residential groups or families; the nature of the society continues (from band level) to be egalitarian and hence there is a lack of political leadership; the familistic groups, therefore, appropriate the private right to protect themselves and to punish wrongdoing. Since feuds are disruptive and tend to perpetuate themselves, it seems probable that the factors that brought about internal unity were external strife and competition among tribes (Service, 1962, p. 114). Integration was achieved in part by residential-kinship ties (lineages) and an increase in clans (sodalities).

A *lineage* is a consanguinal residential group, whose numbers can trace their common relationship genealogically and feel that kinship ties are stronger in either the male or the female line. Marriage is exogamous (Steward, 1955, pp. 152–54). Even if a lineage becomes large, members of the lineage still feel and preserve a sense of kinship even when they cannot actually trace genealogical ties. Belief in descent from a common ancestor (e.g., a bear or a frog), ceremonies held by lineages, common residence, or perhaps some emotional bonds contribute to their sense of relationship.

When a lineage becomes large, it breaks up into several lineages and is called a *clan,* whose members believe the myth of a common ancestor, practice exogamy because of a common name, and share common rituals. Some authors (Service, 1962, p. 116) call a clan a *kinship sodality.*

A clan, or a sodality, may be represented in one or several villages. For example, among the Hopi Indian villages, the Bear clan was present in four villages on several different mesas.

A clan is a culturally created factor in social structure and implies a relationship that may be actual or fictional. This relationship is nonresidential, nonlocal, and has integrating powers because it crosscuts residential ties and unifies all of the members. Thus, clans (lineal sodalities) emerged in the Southwest as the new level of integrating tribal elements. The natural tendency of the residential groups to disintegrate is like a centrifugal force. But since culture is not capricious, to prevent chaos sodalities emerged as an integrating force that is centripetal.

The preceding is a long way of saying that the greater aggregations in towns and the accompanying changes in social structure toward greater complexity (tribal integration by means of clans) were the result of a change in exploiting the environment, in technology, and in production (agriculture).

Tribal organization of early town dwellers seems predictable given a certain set of environmental and technological conditions (rainfall agriculture, not irrigation). Thus, towns and population concentrations were a result of the feedback in the system between the social, technical, and economic subsystems.

Whether the rules of residence of the early farmers in the Southwest were uxorilocal or virilocal, with descent reckoned through the mother-line or the father-line, is not known. It is more difficult to retrodict about these matters because we lack adequate data from archaeological sites. It is only recently that interest in prehistoric social organization has awakened. Further, hypotheses and their implications must be conceptualized with great sensitivity to arrive at acceptable demonstrations concerning social organization.

Evidence from contemporary societies indicates that uxorilocal-matrilineal organization is typical of rainfall agriculture where the planting is done by the women; a number of families form a close-knit residential group (as is a pueblo with contiguous rooms); and harvesting and food-processing cooperation are carried out by women. It is possible that the virilocal-patrilineal type of organization (sometimes ascribed to the Hohokam people) was present in agricultural societies where warfare was more important (Service, 1962, p. 121).

Steward, in an essay on ecological aspects of Southwestern society (Steward, 1955, pp. 161–72), set forth his views on the transition from a lineage to a clan. He bases his history of western Pueblos on archaeological data. Briefly, it is as follows:

In Basket Maker III times, the arrangements of the pithouses and the number per village suggested lineage with farm plots becoming more important which, in turn, brought about new factors of property ownership that affected social structure.

Pueblo I clusters of rooms around a kiva probably housed a lineage. As villages got bigger, the blocks of rooms housing lineages were no longer separated geographically from one another. In Pueblo II and III, formerly localized and independent units merged. People tended to concentrate in large villages, with houses of more than one story located in the open or in caves. The reason for merging was ecological, that is, population pressures and the need for defense. Increase in the number of people, agriculture, value of farm plots, and other technological and environmental changes were sufficient to bring about pressure of some kind, possible strife. Strife, if present, probably would not have consisted of conquests but more likely would have been niggling little hit-and-run affairs with a threat of more such tactics ever present.

We see then that given a certain set of technological and environmental conditions, a change will occur in all the cultural subsystems resulting in a multiclan town. Contemporary Hopi towns exemplify this kind of unilateral (matrilineal, in this case) concentration left over as a kind of anachronism. The original motives for these town concentrations have vanished; at present, there is a tendency toward decentralization.

Besides Steward's work, we should mention three other archaeological studies that examined the nature of social organization in prehistoric sites as reflected in the patterned nonrandom spatial distribution of cultural materials.

In 1950 we[1] wrote an essay that was concerned with social organization of the Mogollon Indians (Martin and Rinaldo, 1950b, pp. 556–69). Our hope was to proceed beyond traditional, descriptive archaeological presentations. After summarizing the sequence in the area designated Pine Lawn Valley, we suggested that there was a direct correlation of change in metate types with the introduction of corn; and that size of houses was gradually reduced and probably restricted to nuclear family residence. We hypothesized that matrilineal residence, matrilineal descent, and inheritance gradually

increased with extended families building their residences near pit dwellings of relatives. With the development of surface houses having perpendicular masonry walls, extended families added on increments to the rooms of the mother house. A village may have been made up of only one lineage.

This outline of development of social organization was not sophisticated because it lacked testable hypotheses that could have governed our research and collecting of data. But it was an attempt to break away from the traditional time-space limitations.

In 1964, Longacre (*in* Martin *et al.*, 1964, pp. 155–70; and 1970) described his research on the sociological implications of ceramic analysis of the Carter Ranch Site (circa A.D. 900–1150). His hypothesis was that social demography and social organization are reflected in the material cultural system.

Analysis of pottery designs on potsherds and whole vessels found at the site showed that there was a definite nonrandom distribution of pottery design elements and element groups. Longacre also demonstrated that a twofold pattern of design elements emerged for the village. The evidence suggested that the pueblo had been occupied by two localized lineages or lineage segments. This suggested that Carter Ranch Site had been occupied by two matrilineal descent groups practicing matrilocal residence. Social stratification was likewise suggested because of the central location of some burials and because of the more than usual amount of grave goods that accompanied these individuals.

Hill (*in* Martin *et al.*, 1967, pp. 158–67; and 1970) excavated Broken K, another site in the same valley. His purpose was to study the nature of the social structure and changes in that site. The evidence that he recovered seemed tentatively to establish

---

[1] Reference here is to Martin and Rinaldo, rather than to Martin and Plog.

the existence of five uxorilocal residential units. Although these essays have been criticized, they are persuasive and, if the evidence is accepted, tend to strengthen Steward's (supra) position. Even if further work discounts in part the work of Hill and Longacre, their efforts represent an innovating step in the direction of conceiving of Archaeology as Anthropology and therefore a social science.

We have stressed social organization as it may have been structured among the Anasazi. The other subcultures, the Hohokam in particular, have not been omitted through oversight. Less attention by archaeologists has been paid to social organization of the Hohokam. This is due, in part, to the fact that their literary "existence" spans only forty years; and, in part, to the fact that Hohokam village plans and settlement patterns of the early periods were only hazily perceived. We believe, certainly, that they had progressed from the band level to the tribal by 200 or 300 B.C.

For the latest periods in the Hohokam area, we have some information concerning the village plans at Los Muertos ruin, near Phoenix, Arizona, (Haury, 1945) and for San Cayetano ruin on the Santa Cruz River, about fifty miles south of Tucson (Di Peso, 1956, p. 262). The houses were clustered in groups or in irregular rows. At Los Muertos and Cayetano (both post-A.D. 1300), they were usually within compound walls.

It is difficult to make any generalizations about social organization in the Lower Gila Valley because such statements would be based on the village plans of only six to ten sites. In the Anasazi area, we have many more village plans for study and to use in a comparative way.

In general, however, we feel that the present evidence indicates multilineage and clan concentrations of people in the Hohokam area after A.D. 500. Before that time,

the available evidence also indicates that small groupings of houses sheltered lineages. They were probably unilateral, but whether they were uxorilocal or virilocal is not known.

Farmers of the Southwest: Latest Periods

When we come to the period of Great Towns, or incipient urbanization, as exemplified by large pueblos in Chaco, Mesa Verde, Kayenta, Hopi (Jeddito) areas and the Great Houses in the Gila and Salt River Valleys, we may have had a level of social integration approaching *chiefdoms* (Service, 1962, pp. 143–77). Irrigation and water control devices were common. The great concentrations of people probably brought about a different level of social organization; but what can one deduce from water control devices? Population of prehistoric settlements can be very roughly estimated as of the order of one-tenth the floor area in square meters (Naroll, 1962, pp. 587–89). The only practical difficulty is that most site reports do not present sufficient data with which to apply this formula.

It has often been assumed that water control devices brought about large-scale cooperation, centers of authority, communal discipline, and a mechanism for recruiting labor for canal construction and maintenance (Haury, 1956, p. 8; and Eggan, 1950, pp. 318–19). Cooperation, yes, by all means.

Certainly, if a group of people successfully handled an irrigation system, especially where water supplies were limited, some devices must have been created to integrate the various relationships between individuals and towns and to minimize potential conflicts that were bound to arise. Conflicts arise today in the Southwest, and many a feud has started over water rights. But the particular ways in which these situations are juggled will differ from place to place. Recent studies have suggested that a centralization of authority is an *exceptional* response to problems concerning distribution of irrigation waters (Millon, 1962).

In a recent review of the ecological and other factors that led to the growth of cities, Adams (1960) discusses the role of irrigation in intensive agriculture. He distinguishes between small-scale irrigation, including floodwater techniques and short canals, and large-scale irrigation. The former may make available for agricultural purposes only a small portion of the possible total water supply. Construction and maintenance of this small-scale irrigation works would not have needed any elaborate reorganization of social structure beyond that of cooperation. It would not have required big labor gangs for work that could have been done easily by a family or a lineage. *Perhaps,* this kind of low-key irrigation would have brought about some social stratification for those who were owners of better and more easily watered land.

Large-scale irrigation is a horse of a different color: it requires technical and social demands beyond the small-scale type. Not only more workmen would be needed, but someone also would have to coordinate their efforts; and, perhaps, such supervision would become permanent. Giving each farmer his fair share of the water would require a Solomon, especially when one considers that the downstream farmers are bound to feel cheated by the upstream guys who would tend to hog it all. One can see where the birth of a politically integrated "state" would almost necessitate a strong man at the top of the heap to keep things running smoothly, especially the water. Adams advances the hypothesis that great networks of irrigation canals were a *consequence* of the appearance of dynastic state organizations rather than the *cause* of them.

In our present study, however, we do not have to worry about large-scale irrigation works since the Hohokam ditches probably never exceeded a total of 200 miles of main canals and were not all contemporaneous. Because their construction was carried out over five or six centuries, no great amount of labor would have been required for their initial excavations (Woodbury and Ressler, 1962, p. 49 *in* Woodbury, 1962).

There seems to be no need for postulating big work crews to do the work. Instead, cooperation between kin groups and villages might have taken care of the matter without a centralized authority in charge of the whole network. Small groups of independent, but cooperating, lineages might have kept the system functioning.

Because irrigation may not have been a factor in bringing about powerful central authority, a despot, or the need for gangs of slave-diggers, we may discount those possibilities in considering the chiefdom level of integration.

The important aspects of a *chiefdom* are: a denser society in response to better agriculture—both ecological in nature; centers that might coordinate economic, social, and religious activities; and an incipient specialization in production and redistribution of produce from the controlling center. The whole system now functions in a more complex adaptive way because all of the interdependent parts—demography, agriculture, clans, irrigation, religion, ecology—are producing feedbacks that interact and carry a continual flow of information between the subsystems.

The evidence for all this in the Southwest is meager and, at the moment, merely indicates a trend. We do not have much evidence on specialization but we infer that it existed. The technology of where to put irrigation ditches and how to control water and make it flow where it was needed must have produced incipient engineers. Building a large multistoried building, such as Pueblo Bonito in Chaco Canyon, must have required some minor specialists in stress and strain. The making of certain luxury goods may have produced some artisans; and even the making of arrow shafts and projectile points may have been more efficiently done by "specialists" (Longacre *in* Martin, Longacre, and Hill 1967, p. 125).

The notion that produce was redistributed is a fairly new and significant interpretation. It was first suggested by Longacre (Longacre *in* Martin *et al.*, 1964, p. 209).

The matter of redistribution is reported with great clarity and thoroughness by Plog (Plog, 1969, pp. 149–65). On the basis of all available evidence, he suggests that kivas may have taken on redistributive functions even in Pueblo II times since they were pan-village institutions and not a family one; and that Great Kivas, some of which were surrounded by an arc of peripheral rooms, may have served as distributing centers, the peripheral rooms functioning as centralized storage granaries.

Distribution of a common supply of food would probably require people of status to handle the situation (Plog 1969, pp. 158–65). Plog cites several examples of the existence of such people: high status burials going back to Pueblo I times (circa A.D. 600–800); at Grasshopper Pueblo (A.D. 1275–1400), status roles had developed to the point of becoming hereditary (Griffin, 1967).

Thus, it is probable that a chiefdom level of integration had developed in the South-west. The evidence is not yet conclusive because our ideas and theories have advanced faster than archaeological techniques. But it is suggestive.

SUMMARY

If one accepts changes in a system through time as the result of a progressive matter-energy process that occurs at all levels of the system—increase in population, rise in the number of components in the system (agriculture, irrigation, clans, etc.), and increasing complexity in all parts of the system—then there seems to be no doubt that changes and developments in the social system took place also.

We can certainly show that the following variables increased through time: (1) population; (2) differentiation (activities areas within and between sites, room to room variability, specialization, and redistribution); (3) integration (kivas serving an economic activity and role differentiation of certain individuals); and (4) technology (technological innovations, central storage to guard against fluctuating harvests) (Plog, 1969).

At the beginning of this chapter, we stated that culture is regarded as a cultural system; if one subsystem changes, the others also will. It is evident that as the cultural subsystems in the Southwest changed from the hunter-gatherer stage to that of the late farmers (A.D. 1300 or 1400), so did the social system change from band, to tribe, to chiefdom levels.

PART SEVEN

THE GREAT EVENTS
IN PREHISTORIC ARIZONA

XVI Agriculture

During the last two decades, archaeologists and their colleagues in botany have focused increasingly great attention on the study of prehistoric agriculture. Our discussion of prehistoric agriculture in Arizona will focus on four topics: (1) the kinds of plants that were cultivated; (2) the agricultural techniques that were used in growing them (some of the most important work on agricultural techniques, especially insofar as they involved irrigation, has been done in Arizona); (3) the distribution of these plants and techniques in space and time; and (4) some possible explanations of the spatial and temporal variability.

The record of domestication and cultivation is at best an unclear one. Of all the evidence that prehistoric man left concerning his economy and subsistence, the record of plant exploitation is the spottiest. Plant material is less likely to be preserved than bone or stone tools. Until the last few years when archaeologists began to sift sediments that might contain seeds or other plant remains through fine screens, many of these remains were not recovered, even when present. Preservation varies from plant to plant—corn is more durable and more frequently preserved than beans—and from area to area—less plant material is preserved in the desert than the other environments. The care taken in collecting these material varies considerably from investigator to investigator. Some investigators look for evidence of prehistoric agricultural practices, and others ignore them. As a result of all these problems, some of the

spatial and temporal variability that we observe may have more to do with preservation and archaeological technique than with the behavior of prehistoric populations.

(The importance of animal domesticates in the state is quite unclear at the moment, and we have chosen to ignore this topic. The dog, parrot, and, perhaps turkey were domesticated. The turkey was clearly used for food, but we have not yet determined whether the birds so used were domesticated or wild. Parrots are found in high status burials in some parts of the state, and parrot cages have been found in sites in northern Mexico. Dogs may have been kept as pets, used in hunting, or used for food. There is very little more to be said of animal domesticates.)

PLANT DOMESTICATES AND THEIR DISTRIBUTION

Corn, beans, and squash were the primary plants cultivated in prehistoric Arizona. The archaeologists and the botanists who study prehistoric agriculture distinguish a number of different types of each of these plants. In defining them, these investigators rely upon attributes of the plants in much the same way that the archaeologist relies on artifact attributes. When different genuses, species, and varieties have been defined, archaeologists can begin to discuss their spatial and temporal distribution and the factors that affect that distribution. While our knowledge of these topics is somewhat scanty at present, a number of important facts are known.

Corn

Corn was the most important agricultural subsistence resource in prehistoric Arizona. Evidence of the presence of corn appears earlier than that for any of the other domesticates, and we tend to find more of this plant in excavations than either beans or squash. Corn is a grass, and the early ancestors of corn resemble grass to a far greater extent than does the corn with which we are

PLATE 49 Corn from Tularosa Cave. This plate illustrates the great variety in the sizes and shapes of corn that were grown by the same population in prehistoric Arizona. Early corn was smaller than our own. But, most varieties of corn were more suited to the climate conditions of the Southwest than our modern hybrids. Reproduced by permission of the Field Museum of Natural History.

familiar. The corn plants were smaller and less stocky. Kernels were smaller, and, in the earliest corns, the corn and cob were not larger than the little finger. In these early forms, a husk sheathed each kernel on the corn fruit rather than enclosing the entire fruit as it now does. Beginning many thousands of years ago, modifications of this primitive corn by accidental and purposeful crossbreeding of corn with a number of related grasses began the process of change that eventually resulted in the corn familiar to us today.

Different varieties of corn are defined on the basis of a number of attributes of the kernels and the cobs. Corn kernels vary in color, from white or yellow to blue, red, purple, orange, and even black. The shape of the kernel may be ovoid or round. Sometimes the top surface is convex and sometimes it has a dent. The number of rows of grain on the corncob varies also. This attribute is recorded either by counting the number of rows on the cob when it is found, or measuring the angle formed by the edges of the kernel and dividing 360° by this figure. The width of the cupule, the pocket in which a kernel sits on the cob, is sometimes used in defining races of corn. The length and width of the cob are other important attributes. The hardness of the corn kernel, however, has probably been the most basic attribute employed by botanists in discussing corn. The kernels of some varieties of corn, those with a high starch content, are hard throughout. Popcorn is an example of this type. Those kinds of corn that have soft kernels throughout are called flour corn. A third type, flint corn, is soft in the center but has a hard starchy layer near the surface of the kernel.

Cutler (Martin et al., 1964) defined a number of races of corn using these attributes. Two races, Chapalote and Reventador, had small cobs, a cupule width of 6 millimeters or less, and a flinty kernel. These corns had from eight to sixteen rows of kernels, with ten or twelve rows the most frequent number. Harinoso de Ocho was an eight-rowed flint corn. Pima-Papago is a flour corn that usually has about ten rows and a cupule width of 8 millimeters or more. Onaveño was medium-sized corn with a cupule width of 6 to 9 millimeters and eight to twelve rows. Apparently it was produced by hybridization of flour and flint corns.

There is at present no evidence that wild maize is native to Arizona. It is, however, native to Mexico. Pollen of wild maize has been found in cores drilled deep into now-dry lake beds around Mexico City. These pollen grains are up to 80,000 years old (Manglesdorf, MacNeish, and Galinat, 1964, p. 543). The earliest evidence of domesticated maize is from the Tehuacán Valley, Mexico, at about 5000 B.C. (MacNeish, 1962, pp. 9–10). By 3400 to 2300 B.C., there was a significant amount of corn under cultivation (Manglesdorf, MacNeish, and Galinat, 1967, p. 189).

The first evidence of corn in and around Arizona occurs during the Desert culture stage. Corn pollen was recovered from sediments at the Cienega Creek Site in southeastern Arizona (Martin and Schoenwetter, 1960, pp. 33–34). This pollen was deposited at 2000 B.C. or earlier. Corn dating to 2000 or 3000 B.C. was found at Bat Cave in west-central New Mexico. Over 30,000 corncobs were recovered from Tularosa Cave in the Pine Lawn Valley in New Mexico. Some of this early corn is morphologically a Chapalote. From 300 B.C. on, the evidence of corn is more and more abundant from all over the state. It seems increasingly likely that where archaeologists have not found evidence of corn by the time of Christ or a few centuries thereafter, it is because the corn has not been preserved or not been found, not because it was not grown. Evidence from Tularosa Cave and the Navajo Mountain area (Lindsay et al., 1968, p. 364) suggests widespread distribution of the plant in the early centuries of the Christian era or before. Corn was present at Snaketown in the Hokokam area by 300 B.C. (Bohrer, 1970). Corn may have been relatively important in some areas at this time, and not all groups in every area used it. But the plant itself had spread relatively widely.

The earliest corns were of a Chapalote type. Between the time of Christ and about A.D. 700 the size of the cobs and the number of rows on them increased. In addition flour as opposed to flint characteristics became more important. At sometime around A.D. 700, the Harinoso de Ocho appeared, and, when crossbred with the existing races, produced a variety with a smaller number of rows and a flintier texture. This product seems to have been a somewhat heartier plant, more adaptable to some of the marginal areas of the state. Carter (1945) has noted the tendency to find flour corns in the southern half of the state and flintier corns in the northern half. While this tendency is apparent, it is important to note that many different varieties of corn, including older ones like Chapalote, were present on late sites. Neither the races of corn nor their attributes follow an absolutely discrete pattern of distribution.

Beans

Four kinds of beans were grown in prehistoric Arizona: Phaseolus vulgaris, the common or kidney bean; P. lunatus, the lima bean; P. acutifolius, the tepary bean; and Canavalia ensiformis, the jack bean. Phaseolus coccineus, the scarlet runner bean, may also have been grown, but the evidence is less certain. Of all the prehistoric Arizona cultigens, archaeologists have found the least evidence of beans. Beans lack the husk cob of corn, and the peduncles and hard-covered seeds of the pumpkin and squash. Therefore it is probable that the dearth of material stems from the plant's poor quality of preservation. There is no reason to infer that beans were a less important subsistence resource than squash on the basis of the evidence available now, although this may yet prove to be the case. The most important work on the prehistory of the bean in Arizona and the Southwest was done by Lawrence Kaplan (1956) and our discussion will rely heavily on his.

The different varieties of beans are distinguished on the basis of seed coat, shape, size, color, and the texture of the seed coating. The shapes and sizes of different parts of the seed are also used in this activity. Parts of the bean plant other than the seed are rarely found by the archaeologist. Kaplan has summarized the basic differences between the species of beans described above, and has defined a wide range of different types of beans within the species.

Kaplan has also discussed the origin and distribution of these beans. The common bean was domesticated in Mexico some five to seven thousand years ago. It was used in both the Tehuacán Valley and the Tamaulipas area at about this time. Common beans spread to the Southwest at some time between 1000 B.C. and 500 B.C. They were found in levels at Bat Cave (Dick, 1965, p. 100) and Tularosa Cave (Martin et al., 1952, p. 499) that date to this period. The common bean was the most important one in the mountain and plateau environments of Arizona throughout the state's prehistory. It was found in sites of the Transition environment, and seems to have been less important in sites of the Desert environment. A bean dated to 100 B.C.–A.D. 100 was found at Snaketown (Bohrer, 1970).

In the southern part of the state, the tepary and jack beans were more important. The tepary was domesticated either in southern Arizona or along the western coast of Mexico. Carter (1945) notes that wild ancestors of the tepary are found in this area. Moreover, he indicates that the variety of teparies is greater here than anywhere else in the region where it is found. Some botanists accept the argument that the point of origin of a particular species or plant corresponds to the area where the greatest formal variety in that plant occurs. Those who reject this argument have been very critical of Carter's argument and believe that the first evidence of domestication for the tepary bean will be found farther south.

Teparies were important in the Hohokam and Hakataya areas. No precise evidence is available on the dates of their first use, but they were present at least by the Sacaton phase at Snaketown (Castetter and Bell, 1942, p. 32). They were found in other parts of the Southwest, even at relatively earlier dates, but never attained the importance there that they did in the southern part of the state.

Canavalia occurs primarily in the Hohokam and Hakataya areas (Kaplan, 1956; Bohrer in Steen et al., 1962). The date of its appearance and information on its importance are not available. The lima bean seems to have been brought into the state during the thirteenth and fourteenth centuries; however, good data on the distribution of lima beans are again unavailable. It is not clear that the runner bean was of any importance in prehistoric Arizona, although it is used by some modern Indian groups.

Squash

When archaeologists use the term squash, they are frequently referring to what most people would call squash, pumpkins, and gourds. All of these plants, except some gourds, are cucurbits, species of the genus cucurbita. The common gourd is of the genus Lagenaria. Squashes, pumpkins, and gourds were used for food and for making containers by prehistoric Arizonans. The seeds, flesh, roots, and leaves of the plants were all used.

Cutler and Whitaker (1961) have described in great detail the morphology and distribution of the cucurbits. They distinguish five that were important in Arizona prehistory: C. pepo, C. moschata, C. mixta, C. foetidissima, and Lagenaria siceraria.

PLATE 50 Cucurbits from Tularosa Cave. Most preserved plant remains such as these squashes and pumpkins come from dry caves like Tularosa, although some subsistence remains are found in open-air sites. Reproduced by permission of the Field Museum of Natural History.

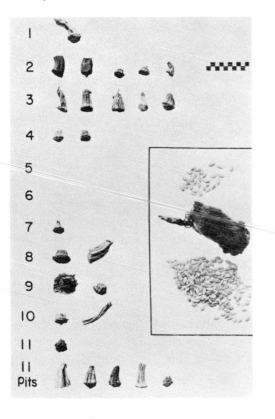

The New England pumpkin, Zucchini, Summer Crookneck, and Acorn squashes are examples of C. pepo. (It should be clear that the distinction between pumpkin and squash that modern Americans make crosscuts the botanical definitions.) The Kentucky Field pumpkin and the Butternut squash are varieties of C. moschata. The cushaws are the main type of C. mixta. C. foetidissima is the Buffalo gourd and L. siceraria the common gourd. Characteristics of the peduncle (stem), seeds, and fruit are used in classifying these species. The stem and seeds, because they are more frequently preserved, are most important to the archaeologist, and the botanist who works with him.

As was the case with beans and corn, the first evidence of domesticated cucurbits is from Mexico at about seven thousand years before the present. The earliest evidence for the Southwest is from Bat Cave where C. pepo was found and dated to 2000 B.C. or earlier (Dick, 1965). At Tularosa Cave, C. pepo dated to 300 B.C. It was in use in the Anasazi area by the second century A.D., and seems to have become abundant at about A.D. 900–1000. Cucurbits at Snaketown appeared as early as the Snaketown phase but they may have been wild species (Bohrer, 1970).

C. moschata did not appear in the Southwest until about A.D. 1000. Its importance is still unclear, but it seems to have been present in the plateau, mountain, and transitional environments. C. mixta was found at Ventana Cave in a level that dates to A.D. 900. It began to appear at sites in the mountain, plateau, and transition areas a century or so later. Lagenaria occurred in the lowest levels of Tularosa and Cordova Caves, but evidence of its widespread use was not found until about A.D. 400–600. Wild cucurbits were also in use throughout this sequence, C. foetidissima the most important of these. Whether the slim evidence for the use of squash in the desert area during prehistoric time is real or an accident of preservation remains to be seen. Most of the modern and historic tribes of the area grew squash. It seems that it should have been an important Hohokam crop, but we find little evidence that it was.

Cotton

We know less of the prehistory of this plant than any other major cultigen, although cotton was present in Arizona at least by A.D. 100–300 (Bohrer, 1970) and may have been there earlier. It has been found in Hohokam, Hakataya, Mogollon, and Anasazi sites. Our knowledge of cotton is based upon discoveries of seeds, fiber, and cotton cloth.

Prehistoric inhabitants of the state may have grown or experimented with a variety of other plants. Chili, wild potato, wild dock, beeweed, and lamb's-quarter are but a few examples. Our evidence concerning these plants and many others is simply too spotty to permit any conclusive statements.

EXPLAINING SPATIAL AND TEMPORAL VARIABILITY IN THE DISTRIBUTION OF DOMESTICATES

As should now be clear, the evidence concerning domestication currently available is incomplete. For this reason, it would not be particularly profitable to attempt an explanation of the distribution. However, a discussion of some explanations that have been offered for domestication is warranted. If we do not develop potential explanations, it is unlikely that appropriate data will ever be collected. Our discussion of some potential explanations for domestication will be followed by a loose consideration of the data now available in Arizona.

By far the greatest portion of archaeologists' efforts to explain the spatial and temporal variability in the occurrence of domestication has focused on the temporal dimension of this variability. Especially during the last two decades, the question of how and why man began to domesticate plants and animals has been primary in the archaeological literature. Two specific items of man's behavior have received particular attention: the behavior that resulted in genetic and morphological changes in the plants and animals that were domesticated, and the behavior associated with greater and greater utilization of these products.

The vast majority of attempts to explain domestication have employed a model that focused on the origin and dispersal of domestication. Archaeologists sought to identify the geographical location of the first domestication and the spread of the practice from that spot. Domestication was assumed to have been invented only once or a few times and to have diffused from the loci of invention. Areas where wild relatives of domesticated plants grew were considered the most likely spots of origin. Natural corridors following a river system or a series of linked intermontane valleys along which domestication might have spread were identified. Most of the investigators employing this model were unconcerned with the behavioral changes associated with domestication. They assumed that if men began to live in a location where potential domesticates grew they would learn to domesticate as a result of learning to live in the habitat.

This approach has fallen into disfavor for a variety of reasons. The data that archaeologists collected in evaluating the model did not suggest a few "hearths" of domestication. Europe, the Near East, Southeast Asia,

North America, and South America all seem to have been the location of domestication of one or more of the many plant and animal resources that were so modified. Within some of these areas, it is no longer unusual to discover that the inhabitants of a particular site were in the process of domesticating one local resource while borrowing domesticated resources of other varieties from nearby regions. Many scholars were unhappy with the vitalism inherent in the notion that domestication would be learned because of some innate human impulse to learn. The analysis of the origin of food production took on an air of the quest for a holy grail as archaeologists sought to find the very earliest evidence of this practice. The probability that archaeologists can be sure that a particular site was in fact the locus of the first domestication of some particular resource is slight. Our time is better spent in attempting to explain the presence or absence of food production at a particular site or in a particular region whether the occurrence is early or late.

Most importantly, a number of archaeologists began to argue that from an explanatory viewpoint the distinction between invention and diffusion implicit in the model was not a useful one. Historically speaking, it may be interesting to know whether the domesticates used at a particular site were domesticated there or borrowed. However, the laws useful in explaining these two events are likely to be the same. Whether a particular trait, artifact, or bit of behavior first appears locally or first appears in some distant region, the most important question that the social scientist must answer is why is this trait adopted, why does it become important in a particular society?

Human groups are aware of many more items and patterns of behavior than they practice. Today, we know of many items that we could eat that we do not eat. We know that these items could be eaten because they are consumed in some other society or because a few individuals within our own society have discovered that they are edible and have begun to do so. We can make similar statements about tools, about organizations, about all sorts of behavioral patterns.

When biologists deal with evolution, they speak of variety and selection. A variety of genetic traits are present in any breeding population. Some of these traits are more common than others. Variety is caused by mutation (accidental changes in genes), and by combining different genetic traditions, by breeding outside the population. In the absence of some selective pressure favoring them, these deviant genetic characteristics disappear. But, if the individuals possessing them are able to compete more successfully, the deviant characteristics become common ones. Changes in an organism's environment may render characteristics that have conferred no competitive advantage at one point in time advantageous at a later point.

These same principles operate in the case of behavior. As a result of accidents, socialization processes gone astray, and the observation of different modes of behavior in nearby societies, there is behavioral variety in any society. This variety may be present in the form of facts kept in the heads of individuals in the society or in the form of the deviant behavior of a few individuals. If this information or behavior confers no competitive advantage on the individuals holding or practicing it, it soon disappears from the society's pool of variety. But, if it does confer such an advantage, it will become common or normal behavior for the group in question.

In the case of food production, we know that this practice was present in most societies for hundreds, sometimes thousands, of years before it became important. It was a part of systemic variety before it became the common way of acquiring subsistence resources. Every human group has some idea of the relationship between seeds and the growth of plants. Almost every group manipulates plant growth in some minor fashion. Why did this idea and this bit of behavior which were relatively unimportant in the populations that we call hunter-gatherers become critically important in those that we call agriculturalists?

In attempting to answer this question, let us return to the two more specific questions with which we began this discussion. Under what conditions would man's behavior have begun to produce the morphological and genetic changes in plants that he exploited? Under what conditions would he have begun heavier and heavier exploitation of these resources? The most interesting answers to these questions developed to date are ones that postulate causal connections between the increasing utilization of particular plant resources, the increasing modifications of the plants' genetic and morphological traits, and increasing modification of plant productivity. In discussing it we draw heavily upon the works of Kent V. Flannery (1965, 1968) and Lewis R. Binford (1968b) who formulated the most important ideas in it.

Let us consider the relationships in the model one at a time. The increasing utilization of a wild plant resource tends to increase the rate of modification of the plant's genetic and morphological traits. We know that simply by using a particular plant resource humans become one of the selective forces operating on it; they are potential sources of modification of the plant's genetic and morphological traits. In some cases humans modify the evolution of plants by design, as when agronomists in the modern

world produce hybrids by cross-pollination. But, some changes in the plants are unintended consequences of utilization. For example, many hunting-gathering groups cover a great deal of territory and travel through a large number of habitats in the course of a year. In the course of this travel, they may carry food resources collected in an area with one set of environmental conditions into an area with very different ones. Plant seeds or roots may be dropped and/or abandoned in this area. If the seeds sprout, the plants will grow under a new set of environmental conditions. The selective pressures effecting the evolution of the plant will be different, and the plant may undergo drastic modifications. Such changes do not always occur. Nevertheless, assuming no more than the random dispersal of seeds over a particular region, we can argue that the greater the utilization, the greater the modification. The more a particular resource is utilized, the more different environmental situations into which seeds will be carried, the more varied the set of selective pressures to which the plant is responding, and the greater the probability of modifications.

On much the same ground, we can argue that increasing modification leads to increasing productivity. Not all of the modifications of a plant resulting from moving seeds to new environments will be ones that increase the productivity of the plant. But, if we assume that productive change, unproductive change, and no change are equiprobable outcomes of the seeds sprouting in a new environment, the greater the modification, the greater the number of productive or more productive varieties of the plant in question.

Moreover, we can once again identify unintended consequences of human behavior that make productive modifications of the plant a somewhat more likely outcome. In nature, plants must have seed dispersal mechanisms. If all the seeds on a particular plant fell at its base, they would force each other out of existence. Therefore, in nature, there is selection for mechanisms that disperse the seeds. In some species, a strong gust of wind is enough to shatter a seed pod and scatter the seeds. While desirable in nature, this attribute is not desirable for man. If every plant that he touched possessed a shattering seed pod, an individual subsisting on wild resources would soon starve. Plant gatherers tend to utilize those species that don't shatter. Moreover, within any species particular plants that through mutation or whatever have developed non-shatter characteristics are the ones most likely to have their seeds collected and transported to new environments. Therefore, the plants that are undergoing selection in new environments are likely to be ones that already possess some productive advantages for human exploitation. It is important to note that this same process of change increases the extent to which plants are dependent on man. Nondispersal is being selected for because man is becoming the primary agent of dispersal.

Again, we can argue that increasing productivity will lead to increasing utilization. If a particular plant becomes more productive, more food or energy is acquired for a constant expenditure of human effort. Operating on simple Malthusian terms, these additional resources will result in an increase in population. The additional population will commonly fluctuate as an equilibrium situation is sought. When the population is above the equilibrium point, increased utilization of resources is likely to occur. In addition, the users of this more productive resource will hold a competitive advantage and are likely to spread in the habitat in question at the expense of non-users.

Thus, we have a cycle in which increased productivity leads to increased utilization leads to increased modification leads to increased productivity leads to increased utilization and so on. This process operates given only unintended consequences of human behavior. It ignores intentional behavior and learning. Humans do learn and they do behave intentionally. In attempting to explain the accelerated operation of this cycle that we associate with the adoption of food production techniques, we may turn our attention to these topics. We may ask under what conditions humans might become especially concerned with the productivity of plant resources.

Two of the most promising answers suggested to date concern population increases and the seasonal availability of resources. Binford (1968b) has focused on the competition that would occur in a situation where a sedentary society maintained a population equilibrium by exporting population into an adjacent area that was already occupied by a less sedentary group. He argues that an intense concern with and competition over productive resources would result in such a situation. We might also note that a great deal of social psychological evidence suggests that it is when individuals and groups are in unfamiliar environments or situations that the successful behavior of one individual or group is likely to be rapidly imitated by the others. Flannery (1968) has investigated the role that the seasonal availability of resources might have played in the adoption of food production. He notes that hunter-gatherers in some parts of the world face situations in which two or more important food resources in widely separated areas become harvestable at the same time. Such groups must make scheduling decisions—decisions as to how they should allocate their productive effort to obtain the greatest quantity of resources. If resources in a particular location become more productive, it might become less worth while to travel to a distant area and collect alternative resources. Such a decision would contribute to the more rapid operation of the model just discussed.

Most prehistoric hunting-gathering societies possessed information and behavior that are basic to food production. Unintentional behavior by these populations could have resulted in modifications of both subsistence practices and the morphology of plants being exploited. Under conditions of subsistence stress occasioned by population pressure or conflict in the scheduling of exploitative activities, decisions that would have increased the rate of these modifications would have been made. This process is what we call domestication or the development of food production.

The argument or explanation for the development of domestication is a complex one. The reasons why such a practice once developed might not be adopted in all areas having knowledge of it are not so complex. The practice may simply have proven inappropriate, for a variety of reasons, in some of the subsistence systems into which it was introduced. Those reasons would include the precise genetic composition of the domesticate in question, the nutrition it provides, the natural environment of the population adopting it, and that population's organization and technology.

In studying domestication, botanists strive to define characteristics of plants that permit them to distinguish between domesticated and nondomesticated forms. As was indicated earlier, however, they also seek to define various races of domesticated and nondomesticated species. These differences may have important consequences in determining what success a particular population will have in using a particular domesticate.

Minute differences may be responsible for the success of one race in a particular region and the failure of another. The Harinoso de Ocho race of corn, for example, appeared in Arizona at a time when the use of this subsistence resource was rapidly increasing. It seems probable that Harinoso de Ocho possessed some genetic trait that made it particularly adaptive to areas that had previously been marginal ones.

The dietary needs of human organisms also have an important effect on patterns of adoption of domesticates. Corn, for example, cannot be used as a major source of protein because it lacks lysine, a major amino acid. Beans, however, are rich in lysine (Flannery, 1968). Corn and beans together can form the basis of a particular population's diet in a way that neither could alone. It is not surprising that prehistoric populations in Arizona did not seem to have begun to rely heavily upon corn until after beans were also present in the region.

A number of natural environmental variables may be important in explaining why a particular domesticate was or was not adopted. For any given domesticate or race of domesticate we can specify a set of environmental conditions in which the plant can be grown and ones under which it cannot. Corn, for example, usually requires a growing season of about 120 consecutive frost-free days and 4 to 6 inches of rainfall during the warm season (Carter, 1945). Many plants will not grow where the alkali content of the soil is high. The natural plants that were present in a particular area had an important effect on the resident populations adoption of domesticates. If more productive plants occurred naturally, domesticates were not adopted.

Finally, characteristics of the population that acquired the domesticate had an important effect on adoption. If a particular domesticate required soaking in order to break down its husk or some complex proteins and a particular population lacked vessels in which the soaking could have been done, the domesticate would not have proven useful. Large-scale technologies such as irrigation rendered usable areas in which the practice of cultivation had previously proved impossible. New and more complex modes of social organization were required before agriculture could be practiced in other areas. While a nomadic band would have lacked both the spatial stability and the coordination of manpower required to man a complex field system, a sedentary tribal group would have been capable of such an accomplishment.

The archaeologist has no reason to assume that one of the factors or kinds of factors discussed above will prove to have been critical in a particular instance. Complex patterns of interaction may have existed between them. In a single area, naturally available resources may have been more productive with one form of organization, domesticates with another. Two populations with a similar organization and very different technologies may have followed quite different courses in adopting domesticates.

Nor can the archaeologist forget that the presence of domesticates or potential domesticates may have acted as a selective pressure with respect to changes in technology or organization. If the domesticate did represent a more productive food source than any available naturally, this would have been especially so. The presence of a domesticate in an area can lead to changes in natural conditions by replacing particular plant communities or removing man as an agent of selection on formerly important wild species.

All of these ideas discussed in the last few pages are used by archaeologists when they attempt to explain domestication. However, we still have a long way to go. No research effort to date has combined the theory, analytical tools, and data now in existence to produce a sound explanation of the adoption of domesticates. It is certain that we will not find the world's first corncob in Arizona. No archaeologist anywhere will ever know for certain that he has the first; that is why the quest for origins is more often a game than a legitimate scientific effort. But there is no reason why the record of adoption of domesticates in Arizona cannot be used in constructing the first complete explanation of this phenomenon.

AGRICULTURAL PRACTICES

One cannot understand prehistoric agriculture without understanding the techniques used in practicing it. In discussing practices, we will be concerned not with the tools—hoes and digging sticks—that prehistoric Arizonans used, but with the ways in which they modified the surface of the earth in order to make plants grow. We now know that there was immense variability in these practices, even in historic times. In some areas of the southwestern United States, wandering bands simply planted crops in the spring and left them, not to return until harvest time in the fall. No time or effort was spent in cultivating or watering the plants. In other areas, groups built ditches to carry water to areas where wild plant resources grew in order to increase their abundance. These plants were not domesticates; there is no evidence that their genetic composition had been modified, but some agricultural techniques had been applied to growing them. At the opposite end of the continuum, we can describe groups that would not exist were it not for their sophisticated irrigation systems. Hack (1942) and Castetter and Bell (1942; 1951) have described the techniques employed by the Hopi, Pima, Papago, Mojave, Yuma, and Cocopa. The practices of these groups probably define rather completely the range of agricultural techniques employed by prehistoric groups in Arizona.

Hack has listed the principal types of fields that are used by the Hopi today (1942, p. 26). With a few modifications, this list can be made to include the field types of southern Arizona populations. Therefore, we follow his outline and ideas. Hack defines four primary types of fields: fields watered by surface runoff, fields watered by rainfall, fields watered by subsurface seepage, and fields watered by irrigation.

Floodwater farming involves planting crops in fields watered by surface runoff. Fields watered in this fashion usually occur in one of four locations: on alluvial fans at arroyo mouths, along the course of shallow arroyos or rivers, in the lower terraces of arroyos, and in the bottom of arroyos. The success or failure of these fields depends on the rain that falls in the watershed of the channel in question, and thereby on the stream flow or flooding in the watercourse. In some areas, like the Colorado River Valley before the river was dammed, the flood was a yearly event. In the Hopi and Papago areas, where semipermanent or impermanent streams are more common, the flood in any particular drainage is and was a far less predictable event. By planting crops at varying distances from the stream channel, in the channel, on the terraces, near the channel, the probability of success is increased. In both northern and southern Arizona, modern Indians use a number of techniques to increase the amount of water that the plants receive. In the Colorado River Valley, dams were built to direct the annual floodwater into low-lying areas

in which crops were to be planted. Small dams to spread the water away from the stream channel over a fan or a terrace, or to slow the water in the case of fields planted in arroyos, are used by the Hopi.

Other fields are watered by rainfall. In a few areas of the state, this can be done on ordinary colluvial soils. The crops may be planted and tended by a sedentary group or planted and left by a wandering one. In the Hopi area, most of the rainfall farming is done in dune fields. In contrast to colluvial soils, dune sand is very porous and holds rainwater for long periods of time. Deep-rooted plants, such as beans, can tap this valuable source of water. The chief danger to plants being grown in this situation is damage from sandstorms. Therefore, windbreaks are built along the field borders or even around individual plants.

Seepage fields occur primarily at the mesa edges in the Hopi area. Underground seepage from aquifers waters both colluvial soils and sand dunes. The latter association makes for superior fields.

Finally, fields are watered by irrigation. The irrigation water may be taken from rivers, springs, or slope wash, and it may be carried for long or short distances. Ditches may bring water into the field on a regular basis, or only when the river is in flood. The ditches may range from very small channels scratched in the earth to canals that are several feet wide and several feet deep.

A variety of different construction or excavation tasks are associated with the practice of each of these techniques. It is these activities as they were employed in the past that provide the principal evidence of prehistoric agriculture. The most important evidence is provided by canals, terraces, linear grids, and linear borders.

Canals were dug to transport water. Their channels can sometimes be identified in aerial photographs or by the archaeologist doing ground survey research. Some channels have been excavated, a few of which can be seen by the public at Montezuma's Well National Monument and at the Park of Four Waters in Phoenix. Prehistoric ditches have been found at San Cayetano (Di Peso, 1956), Snaketown (Haury, 1967), the Casa Grande and Los Muertos vicinities (Midvale, 1965), the Verde Valley (Mindeleff, 1896; Breternitz, 1960), the Upper Little Colorado (Bandelier, 1892),

the Flagstaff area (Breternitz, 1957a, b), southern Utah (Sharrock, Dibble, and Anderson, 1961; Lindsay, 1961), Mesa Verde (Rohn, 1963a), and Chaco Canyon (Vivian, 1970).

Terraces were constructed to hold water or soil or both. Sometimes they were built in stream channels (these are called check dams) and sometimes on hillsides. Terraces are known from the Point of Pines area (Woodbury, 1961), from the vicinity of Young, Arizona (Rodgers, 1970), Mesa

FIGURE 37   Point of Pines terraces. These terraces or check dams impeded the flow of soil and water in the natural drainage channels. This prevented erosion downstream. Crops may

also have been planted on the terraces. Reproduced with the permission of the Arizona State Museum from "Prehistoric Agriculture at Point of Pines, Arizona" by Richard B. Woodbury.

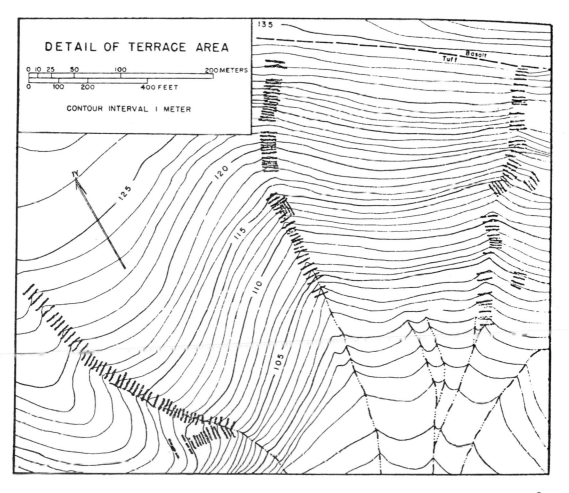

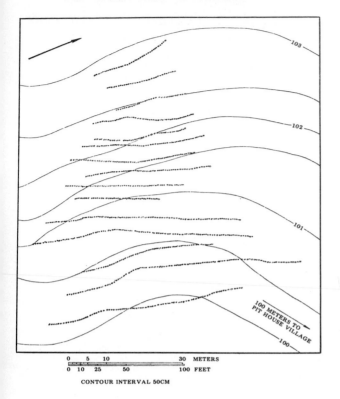

0 5 10   30 METERS
0 10 25   50   100 FEET

CONTOUR INTERVAL 50CM

effect on slope wash but more probably
served to demarcate plots or to anchor
windbreaks. Linear grids and borders are
known from the Young area (Rodgers,
1970), Cave Creek (Ayers, 1967), the
Upper Little Colorado, Point of Pines
(Woodbury, 1961), Mesa Verde (Rohn,
1963a), Valhalla Glades (Hall, 1942), and
southern Utah (Lindsay, 1961). (The preceding distributional descriptions are taken
from Vivian, 1970, in large part.)

When none of these techniques was used
in practicing agriculture, it is difficult for
the archaeologist to find any evidence of
that practice. However, minute soil differences can sometimes tell us where a prehistoric field was located, even if water,
soil, or wind control devices are absent.
Schraber and Gumerman (1969) have suc-

FIGURE 38   Point of Pines borders. These borders or grids served much the same purpose as
terraces. They were located on hill slopes rather
than in drainage channels, and caused moisture
to soak into the ground rather than flowing
over it. Reproduced with the permission of the
Arizona State Museum from "Prehistoric Agriculture at Point of Pines, Arizona" by Richard
B. Woodbury.

Verde (Rohn, 1963a), the Upper Little
Colorado, Shihump Canyon (Schwartz,
1960), Valhalla Glades (Hall, 1942), and
southern Utah.

Linear grids and linear borders are rock
structures one or a few rocks in height.
They are generally lower than terraces.
When constructed perpendicular to the
slope, the feature (linear grid) had much
the same effect as contour plowing in slowing slope and soil wash. When constructed
parallel to the slope or in polygonal patterns
(linear borders), they may have had some

0   10m
scale

FIGURE 39   Cave Creek borders. This complex
system of borders is composed of lines of rock
that in some cases intersect at right angles. The
system serves the same purpose as less complex
ones. It is not clear whether the rectangles
formed by the intersecting rows were plots of
individuals or families. Reproduced with permission from The Kiva.

288

cessfully used infrared photography in locating buried prehistoric fields.

We would undoubtedly have more evidence of the use of water and soil control techniques from other parts of the state if archaeologists had been more interested in them. By and large, they have not been. It is clear that where techniques like these are not found it is in part because of the archaeologists' failure to look for them. It is equally clear that not all of the techniques were used in all areas at all times. Canals were in use at Snaketown by the time of Christ (Haury, 1967). In no other areas of the Southwest has substantial evidence been found indicating that water control systems were in use before about A.D. 1000. During the succeeding century, water control systems were constructed all over the Southwest. Information concerning water control systems had been present in the Southwest for many centuries. Why had this information gone unused for so long? When the construction of water and soil control devices began, the same techniques were not used everywhere; in some areas, canals were predominant, in others terraces, and in still others grids. How can we account for this spatial and temporal variability?

FIGURE 40 The Beaver Creek system. The Beaver Creek system illustrates the complex set of grids, terraces, and ditches that may be necessary to successfully practicing agriculture in an arid environment. Courtesy of the Museum of Northern Arizona.

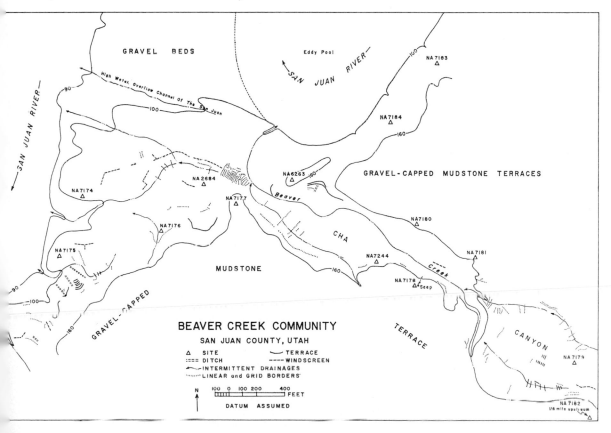

PLATE 51 Beaver Creek Ditch. Ditches, especially when they carried water over sandy soils, had to be lined. The Hohokam lined their ditches with adobe. On the Colorado Plateau, some ditches were lined by ponding water and allowing the silt to settle out, forming a compact bottom. This ditch was stone-lined. Museum of Northern Arizona photo.

EXPLAINING SPATIAL AND TEMPORAL VARIABILITY IN THE DISTRIBUTION OF AGRICULTURAL PRACTICES

Arizona archaeologists have generally explained variability in agricultural practices by reference to differential patterns of diffusion from Mexico. For reasons already discussed, we do not find this approach a legitimately explanatory one. There is little in the archaeological literature outside of the American Southwest that guides the archaeologist in developing explanations of varying agricultural practice. There are typologies that, for example, distinguish between horticulture and agriculture on the basis of the complexity of the techniques employed. And there are theories that attempt to link the appearance of irrigation with states and despotisms. However, few works provide working models for dealing with inter- or intra-cultural variability in agricultural practices.

The theories and models that seem to us most viable are ones that operate in terms of the relative costs and benefits of particular subsistence strategies in their respective habitats. The use of any set of agricultural techniques can be associated with a set of approximate or relative costs and similar sets of benefits. The relationship between the costs and benefits that alternative subsistence strategies carry is the most crucial determinant of the distribution of these strategies.

In what sense do the costs associated with particular agricultural practices vary? First, there is variability in preparation costs. A population that simply sowed seeds over an unprepared ground surface or punched holes in the ground with a digging stick spent little time in preparation and incurred minimal preparation costs. When ground surfaces were prepared more thoroughly, say by hoeing, the preparation cost to the population was higher. Constructing canals or terraces increased these costs even more. Maintenance costs are the second important item. Groups that planted seeds and then left the area, allowing the crops to grow unattended, incurred no maintenance cost at all. Hoeing fields to remove weeds involved some costs. The costs of repairing terraces and cleaning and repairing canals were even higher. Finally, there were opportunity costs. Planting a field and then leaving it to follow some seasonal wandering pattern involved little in the way of opportunity costs. A population's time was still basically free for other pursuits. Weeding committed populations to remain at or return to the fields for longer periods of time, thereby reducing the population's ability to exploit alternative resource sets. Irrigation may have required groups practicing it to remain at the fields for the entire growing season, considerably reducing the time available for other subsistence pursuits. Finally, there were costs associated with the negative effects of some practices on their natural environment. It seems likely that prehistoric populations in the area overirrigated the land, raised the soil alkalinity, and were forced to abandon the fields for some period of time, perhaps even permanently.

Different agricultural practices can also be associated with different benefits. Some of them result in increases in the production of a crop per unit of labor input. Others act to increase gross product without necessarily increasing productivity. Still others act to increase security by, for example, making a resource available at some point in an annual cycle when resources in general are critically short. There need not have been any precise relationship between these three benefits. Prehistoric populations may have found that the subsistence strat-

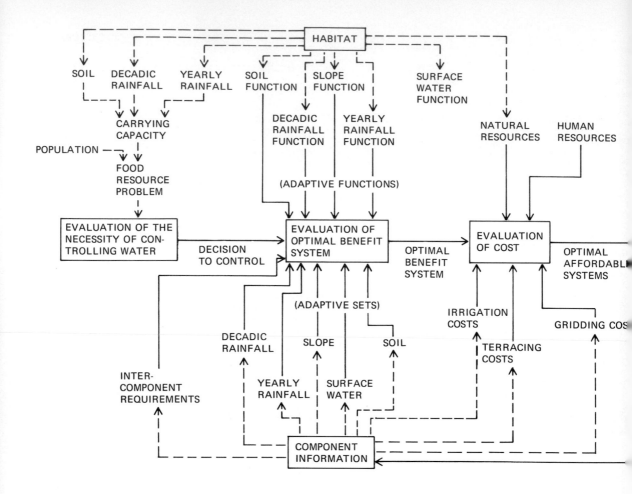

egy that resulted in the greatest product did not provide them resources at the time of years those resources were needed. Similarly, there were undoubtedly situations when the most efficient agricultural practice did not result in sufficient product because the area in which it could be used was too limited. Thus, the problem of evaluating benefits is and was a complex one.

Moreover, the costs and benefits that can be derived from a particular agricultural technique varied with the habitat in which populations resided. In areas where plant communities were very broad, the opportunity cost associated with using field systems was high; a population that was tied to its fields could not wander freely into other resource zones. In a more fine-grained environment, where many different com-

munities occurred in a given locality, gathering was carried on in the vicinity of the fields and the opportunity cost was lower. This same kind of qualification must be made for each cost and benefit. The archaeologist may develop formal models that operate in terms of costs and benefits, but he must remember that the costs and benefits associated with even a single practice will vary from habitat to habitat as the environmental conditions that affect these values vary.

In using these ideas to explain spatial and temporal variability in the adoption of different agricultural practices, the archaeologist must choose between two assumptions. He can assume that populations are constantly striving to improve their cost/benefit situation or he can assume that they

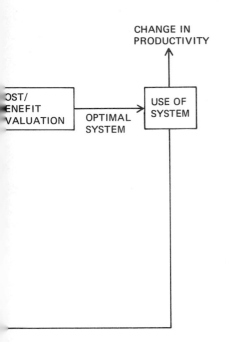

CHANGE IN
PRODUCTIVITY

OST/
ENEFIT
VALUATION

OPTIMAL
SYSTEM

USE OF
SYSTEM

FIGURE 41   A model of
the relationship between habitat and water control strategies.

change practices only in response to unfavorable cost/benefit situations, costs exceed benefits, and situations in which benefits are insufficient to support the population. Both of these assumptions seem
reasonable to us. The first assumption was
probably most important in day-to-day and
year-to-year decisions concerning the practices that were appropriate in a given situation. The second provides the better clues
to explaining periods of rapid change in
agriculture practice. Humans do learn. On
a day-to-day basis they increase their understanding of behavior that is in their
best interest. But, this day-to-day learning
rarely results in major behavioral modifications. The latter are more likely to result
from stress situations.

Plog and Garrett (1970) have constructed

a model based upon cost/benefit evaluations for explaining some aspects of variability in prehistoric Southwestern water
control systems. Water control systems in
this model have three components: canals,
terraces, and linear grids. The primary question upon which the analysis focuses is,
"Why do the relative proportions of these
three components in spatially discrete loci
vary?"

It is already clear that one cannot speak
of Mogollon, Anasazi, Hohokam, or Hakataya water control systems. A great deal
of valley-to-valley and region-to-region variability within each of these areas has already been reported. Therefore, the valley
or locality seems the proper unit of analysis.

The model used to explain valley-to-valley variability is represented in Figure 41. It is first and foremost a model of how an archaeologist might go about explaining variability in water control systems. However, if it accurately predicts differences in the component ratios from valley to valley, it must also closely reflect the decision-making process characteristic of the prehistoric population in question.

Two data sets are primary to the model: information on the habitat in which the system is being constructed and information on the tolerance of system components for relevant habitat variables. The initial decision to control water is viewed in terms of a food resource problem. It seems unlikely that so expensive a system as water control would be undertaken in the absence of such a problem. The food resource problem is defined in terms of the balance between population and carrying capacity. When the population of a valley approached the aggregate population that the valley could carry, a stress situation resulted. Such stress situations led to the decision to control water.

The most important habitat variables for determining what system will provide optimum benefit in a particular locality are soil, slope type of surface water available, yearly rainfall distribution, and decadic rainfall distribution. For each of these variables, we can specify a value at which each system component will provide optimum benefit and a range in which it will provide some benefit. For example, we can examine the relationship between gridding, terracing, and irrigation, and the variable slope. Modern water and soil conservation data can be used to determine the slope on which each technique is maximally productive and the range of slopes on which it can be practiced. (Contour plowing is used as an analog for gridding.) The results of such an analysis are in Table 14.

The relationship of each system component to each variable may be evaluated in a similar fashion. Moreover, the selection of one component sometimes necessitated the selection of one other. For example, it was sometimes necessary to build a canal in a position where it was threatened by a small arroyo cutting across it. In such cases, small terraces or check dams were built in the arroyo above the canal. These dams slowed the processes of erosion and protected the canal.

With all of the components and habitat variables that are relevant to the design of the water control system, it is likely that more than one system would have been adaptable to a particular habitat. When this was the case, the cost of alternative systems would have been the principal factor that determined which system was in fact put to use. The relative cost of each of the components per unit of land can be estimated. Today, terracing is about twice as costly as gridding, and irrigation is twice as costly as terracing. The relative costs were probably much the same prehistorically. Both the resource and maintenance costs associated with gridding were low. The use of this technique required a few rocks and the time needed to arrange them in rows. Terraces were probably much more costly. More rocks are needed and

COMPONENT	BEST GRADE	TOLERANCE RANGE
Irrigation	1%	.1–10%
Terracing	12%	5–35%
Gridding	5%	1–20%

TABLE 14 The relationship between system components and the variable slope. The distribution of these three techniques should reflect the distribution of land surfaces of varying grades within the area under study. Southwestern data on the slope locations of the components suggesting that this is probably the case are shown in Figure 41.

more time to build walls. In some cases, time was spent in filling the area behind the terraces with soil. Finally, terraces required more repair work than grids. Canals were the most expensive proposition. They required the movement of soil, careful design to assure an acceptable grade, the construction of a silt or adobe bottom when the course flowed over sand or some permeable sediment, the removal of vegetation that obstructed the flow of water, the construction, maintenance, and use of gates to let water into the field, and some mechanism for allotting the water in the ditch between the cultivators sharing it. If we conceive of these costs in terms of human and natural resources, the use of these techniques probably could not be afforded by some prehistoric populations.

Even after the costs of alternative systems were evaluated, it is likely that more than one system proved optimal and affordable for a given habitat. The one that was put into use within this set was probably relatively accidental. This type of accident served as one source of variety in the systems that existed in different regions. Once a given system was put into use, it had some effect on the resource base and may have partially or completely alleviated the food resource problem with which the chain of events began. The use of different systems and system components modified the population's understanding of the costs and benefits of the components so that similar decisions at later points in time were based on different and more complete sets of information.

This model attempts to deal with only one of a number of aspects of variability in water control systems. Archaeologists are interested in others. It does not deal with the problem of whether water control or some other strategy will prove the best response to a particular stress situation. The Hopi plant crops in many locations within a single drainage. At any given locations seeds may be planted in the stream channel and at different elevations above the bed. This diversified system acts to insure that some crops will grow whether a particular year is cold and wet or warm and dry. If the year is cold and wet, crops at lower, warmer elevations receive enough water to grow. If it is warm and dry those at higher elevations and those growing in stream channels at lower elevations receive enough water to grow. This strategy may be more effective in marginal areas of the Southwest than more technologically complex ones. A more complete model of agricultural practices must include options such as this one.

While this model shows some promise in that currently available facts of the type that it was created to explain tend to fit predictions, it has been revised a number of times and will require further revision. Archaeologists need much more information about water control systems in order to test any explanatory ideas or models.

SUMMARY

In attempting to show how far short of explanation many of our efforts have fallen, we may have conveyed the impression that archaeologists have learned little concerning agriculture in prehistoric Arizona. Focusing on theories in terms of which facts may be explained has a similar effect. Therefore, let us end the chapter by returning to some of these facts.

We may break the development of agriculture in prehistoric Arizona into three periods lasting from about 2000 B.C. to about 700 B.C., from about 700 B.C. to about A.D. 700, and from about A.D. 700 to historic times. Evidence for the first cultigen, corn, in Arizona dates to about 2000 B.C. There is no evidence that this resource was important for another 1,000 to 1,500 years. Prehistoric groups lived at sites like Bat Cave and Tularosa Cave for only limited portions of the year. Sites of this period contain little evidence of occupation for more than restricted portions of a given year, and show relatively few signs of permanence. A few plants may have been sown in front of caves or other sites in the spring and harvested in the fall. But there is nothing to suggest that the plants were tended through their growth or that their product was of dietary importance. Tools or facilities especially appropriate to processing agricultural products were not present.

By about 700 B.C., a number of important changes had occurred. Beans and squash have been found at sites dating to this period. A few villages with indications of permanence or at least semipermanence date to the early to middle portion of this period. Pottery that might have been used in processing agricultural products appeared just before the time of Christ. Storage facilities began to increase in both quantity and variety. In the southern desert, populations began to practice irrigation and to rely heavily on agricultural products by 300 B.C. Agricultural resources were certainly important during this period, but there is still little evidence suggesting that they were primary.

An important period of change began at around A.D. 700 in most parts of the state. New races of corn, beans, and squash, some of which are more adaptable to marginal areas of the state, appeared. Cotton becomes an important resource. Populations in most parts of Arizona lived next to their fields for most of the year. Pottery was abundant and manos and metates changed in ways that may have made them more efficient for grinding cultigens. Ceremonial structures often have associated storage facilities and may have served as inter- or intra-site redistributional centers. Irrigation, terracing, and gridding were all practiced. Archaeologists still lack a precise indication of the importance of agricultural products in the diet. However, populations during this period of time were organized in a manner that seems particularly appropriate to the practice of agriculture.

The transitions between these periods share some patterns. There were increases in the quantity of cultigens, the number of different cultigens, and the extent of the technology appropriate to exploiting them. At each transition, settlement pattern and community organization changed in ways that would have made the use of cultigens easier and more profitable. Each is associated with an increase in the abundance of archaeological evidence relative to the preceding period. No clear pattern of environmental change is associated with the transition. Thus, an explanation for the changes seems most likely to involve population, organization, and technology rather than the environment. We will take up this topic in a later chapter.

XVII   Great Towns

Earlier in the book we asked the question, "Why towns?" Here we will try to give an answer.

THE FORMATION OF GREAT TOWNS —AN EXPLANATION BASED ON TECHNOENVIRONMENTAL AND TECHNOECONOMIC DETERMINISM

One of the goals of anthropologists has been to explore the processes leading to the evolution of a large aggregation of people —an urban society, such as flourished in Mesopotamia, Meso-America, Peru, China, Egypt (Steward, J., 1949, pp. 1–27; and Adams, 1966). Is there a single processual pattern, with regional variations, that explains the evolution of all urban societies? Are there regularities in 'human behavior that recur over and over due to similar technoenvironmental situations? As we shall see, the answer to both questions is "Yes."

While our examination of the prehistory of Arizona will not lead us to actual urban societies such as those mentioned above, we do have cultural manifestations in Arizona and the Southwest that may properly be considered as pre-urban. These manifestations represent examples of the earlier portions of developmental sequences that appear to have been levels of sociocultural development in the evolution of urban societies in arid and semiarid areas. That is, the general sequence of social, religious, and technical patterns ran roughly a parallel course in all urban societies. Steward

(1949) created several models in his developmental sequence of urbanism. Some of these are, from early to late: Hunting and Gathering; Incipient Agriculture; Formative; Regional Florescence; and Conquests.

These models share the same general features for Mesopotamia and Meso-America regardless of time of occurrence. The time of actual occurrence of Incipient Agriculture, for example, is several thousands of years earlier in Mesopotamia than in Mexico. I am proposing that the first three of these—Hunting and Gathering, Incipient Agriculture, and Formative—also occurred in the American Southwest and later than in Meso-America.

The rationale for equating these levels of development, wherever they occur in arid or semiarid countries, is this: similar causes under similar conditions lead to similar results, and human cultures tend to evolve along essentially similar paths when they are confronted with similar technoenvironmental situations (Harris, 1968, p. 686).

In this chapter I am interested in the covariance of technological controls, for example between technological efficiency and ecology, or food controls, or a social organization and institutions that integrated increasingly larger concentrations of formerly localized and independent units.

In thinking about the reasons or causes for greater concentrations of people in larger Southwestern villages, I cannot use prediction, but I can and will use retrodiction. What I am saying is that if urban societies evolved independently, both in the Old World as well as the New, from a mass of similarities in form and process, and if one of the parallel "stages" in this development was the regularly occurring feature of hunters and gatherers slowly advancing through various degrees of complexity to a phase in which population density and proliferation of villages resulted, then I think it is appropriate to regard the period of Town Dwellers in Arizona as a phase akin to Steward's Formative in his global-scale cultural evolution.

Some of the parallels (or similarities) between the arid or semiarid places (Mesopotamia, China, India, Peru, Meso-America) where urbanism developed and our Southwest are:

1. A food-producing revolution (Adams, 1966, p. 40). By this I mean a process by which food was produced not by gathering it, as in the Desert culture, but by planting and harvesting it. Increase in population seems to have been the cause of greater food production. As gathering of wild foods was gradually replaced by planting and harvesting maize, and later beans and squash (about 1500 B.C.–A.D. 700), many adaptive changes occurred in the subsystems of the cultures under study. The technological subsystem is the most obvious and easiest to document and directly influences the sociological and ideological systems. In the Southwest, certainly, food production was one of the technological changes and only a minor one at first. Along with this transformation, I assume that there were increased yields and an extension of the ecological niche that was available for crops by means of clearing, seeding, weeding, and some simple form of water control.

2. A new tool technology developed during this phase that showed increasing complexity. The grinding tool complex indicates a remarkable trend toward more efficiency.

The earliest metates (lower part of a corn mill) were large heavy boulder-stones in the upper face of which a basin had been pecked. A round cobble was used as a mano (upper part of the mill). This type of metate was inefficient as it provided a very small grinding area. By contrast, the late metates were slab-shaped, flat on top, and the entire surface was available for grinding. A similar change in manos occurred with a two-handed flat stone being used, thus increasing the percentage of grinding surface that was in contact, at any one time, with the flat face of the metate.

Since emphasis on hunting was slowly declining as agriculture increased in importance, one would expect a more standardized kind of projectile point that could be manufactured quickly and without fuss. And this is exactly what happened (Traugott, 1968). Early, four major steps were required in making a projectile point: (1) removal of the projectile point *blank* from a core; (2) primary flaking to thin the *blank;* (3) secondary flaking to shape the *blank;* (4) thermal treatment of core or blank before flaking (in 60 percent of all specimens prior to A.D. 750).

Later, only two steps were needed to produce a point, since primary flaking and thermal treatment were eliminated. And these late points were standardized to the extent that variability was decreased by 50 percent.

3. Another technological change involved the amount of food storage space, which is regarded as a variable that measures both changes in the availability of food resources and changes in the efficiency of a productive system (Plog, 1969). In early times, storage space was most frequently found outside of the houses; in late times, all storage was within the pueblo or in specially constructed, vermin-proof granaries. The

storage space relative to the dwelling unit increased from early to late by about forty times (in one area).

4. Another technological shift concerns habitations. Pit houses were gradually abandoned as domiciles, as places for various household activities and for family ceremonies. In some areas, notably the Kayenta, pit structures continued in use and are associated with surface rooms in late pueblos (A.D. 1100–1300). Their use is unknown. Eventually, they were used only for group ceremonies and as clubhouses for men in nonceremonial parts of the year. Replacing them as domiciles were surface structures (pueblos) of contiguous rooms built of masonry. At first only four to six rooms in size, these pueblos became multiroomed and multistoried. This expansion in numbers of rooms per pueblo was accompanied by greater residential stability, density of population, and numbers of villages per square mile.

5. And then we come to the notion that urbanism was accompanied by social stratification—class, chiefs, and so on. How did that come about?

The assumption has always been that a "surplus" of food supplies was likely to bring about an increase in population and, therefore, an increase in leisure time. During this unused time, instead of sitting around and doing nothing, these lucky folk —the well-fed men of leisure—sat down and thought: "Now, what can we do with this leisure? We have a surplus of food, we have a good thing going, how can we improve our society?" And the answer they presumably came up with was that they could invent, they could become specialists, and they could create luxury goods. And so, the fairy tale ran, they invented writing, and calendars, and mathematics; they made jewelry and other valuable trinkets; they built towns and irrigation works and they all lived happily ever after. In other words, "surplus" would automatically create social stratification and chiefdoms.

But, of course, some anthropologists came along, vigorously attacked these ideas and rejected them as naïve, untenable, and out of tune with the facts (Harris, 1959, pp. 185–99). If sitting around on your hands and having leisure time to spare are responsible for cultural development and advances, then one rightly wonders why hunters and gatherers did not produce cities, and writing, and the concept of place enumeration, and complex, stratified societies. They certainly had leisure and then some.

No, the fact is that increase in *population* brings about an increase in food production; not the other way around (Boserup, 1965). But increase in and variations of food production and supply are in turn related to technological development, to population density and to ratio of food-producers to non-food-producers, and hence to specialists, priests, chiefs.

If by "surplus" one means *necessary* food supplies rather than superfluous amounts of them, then we can hypothesize as follows: "If significant quantitative and qualitative changes occur in the nature of a surplus, significant changes will take place in the social organization, especially those related to an increase in economic, religious, and political specialization. Social stratification will be based upon the *unequal* rights of access to strategic supplies" (Harris, 1959, p. 195).

What force would make the food producers willingly surrender a portion of their necessary food supplies in order to support a class of nonfood producers, specialists, priests, artists, craftsmen, merchants, chieftains, and tax collectors? The answer is that probably an elite class was able to control food supplies, and this meant control over the source of energy that motivates culture to move (Harris, 1959, p. 195).

Flannery, in his researches in Iran, adds substance to Harris' argument concerning the relationships of population, social stratification, and subsistence. In order to understand his reasoning, we shall briefly recapitulate one or two relevant points. He adopts the view of Binford (1968b, p. 326) that prehistoric gathering populations tended to remain stable at a density below the point of maximum resource exploitation and that this equilibrium between population and environment would not be changed unless some event disturbed that equilibrium (Flannery, 1969, pp. 76–96). If some of the population exploited a habitat where a high level of edible resources existed, that population would take advantage of the optimal carrying capacity of their territory. This might result in a higher population. Then, instead of arguing that a climatic change caused people to adopt a different pattern of subsistence (that is, agriculture), both Flannery and Binford reason that a change in demography would raise the population too close to the limits of the carrying capacity of their territory. Accordingly, one reason for this culture change might have been the pressure of the expanding population who inhabited the "optimal," that is, the most favorable, area on their less fortunate neighbors who inhabited the marginal, less favorable areas. From the more favorable areas a swelling of greater population density, emigrations, or budding groups might have occurred (to lighten the load on the carrying capacity of the motherland). Such emigrations would have moved into the marginal areas, caused disturbances in the equilibrium there, and might have tended to deplete the energy or carrying capacity of the area.

This kind of a situation—that is, pressures for finding new and exploitable sources of food—might have resulted in seeking other food sources not yet tapped —water fowl, fish, acorns, molluscs, wild grains—and thus set the stage for the later domestication of plants. It should be noted that exploitation of new food sources would probably occur, not in the centers of population growth, but around the margins of growth (see also Service, 1960, pp. 93–124).

After domestication of plants occurred, a period of dry farming followed, the net effect of which was to have altered the native plant cover and this in turn may have prevented the people from returning to the previous food-gathering pattern of subsistence procurement. Eventually, irrigation may have developed as a new technological innovation in a response similar to that described above—that is, it took place in a less favorable habitat that was adjacent to an area of population growth. Peoples living in marginal areas were being crowded by budding daughter groups who were moving in on them. More food was needed than the dry-farming method could produce; hence, the response was to introduce water to nonproductive areas to increase the carrying capacity of available land. Population density would have again increased.

It is this situation that set the stage for social stratification. Flannery points out that as population increased with changes in subsistence from gathering to dry farming to irrigation agriculture, the amount of land that was "highly productive" under the successive modes of subsistence *decreased*. (In Iran today the irrigated 1 percent of the total land area produces 30 percent of the yearly crop.) Under these conditions of a widening gap between population size and the size of the arable land on which the population was most dependent for food resources it is suggested that an inequitable system of land ownership and tenure would have developed. Thus, a small, elite class (as suggested by Harris) would have controlled the differential access to water and food resources, and it is this kind of a situation which is the basis of ranked or stratified societies.

This kind of a relationship between population, arable land, and subsistence technology appears to have given rise to highly stratified societies in the Near East, and may have been part of the evolutionary development in the Southwest where irrigation was important (Chaco Canyon, Mesa Verde, the Upper Little Colorado area, the Kayenta area, and certainly the Hohokam area of southern Arizona; see also Aschmann, 1962, pp. 1–14).

Accompanying these shifts in technology were changes in the social organization, because that is determined largely by technology. A change in food production or type of house will produce new patterns of behavior and these patterns will interlock and bring about an integrated social system. Again, because of the changes in the techno-environmental aspects mentioned above, there will also be a correlated change in ideology. When technological controls are slight, supernaturalism flourishes; and as these controls increased in scope, supernaturalism decreased. So, as technological structuring of experience changes, so do the philosophy and ideology (White, 1959a, pp. 16–23).

Hence, we can retrodict that religious ideas had altered and the importance of priests had been enhanced along with the innovative technologies. Kinship ties gradually weakened as more aggregation took place and special mechanisms of social integration and control came into play, and, therefore, social stratification occurred.

In brief, we appear to have a Formative period in the Southwest—that is, manifestations of similarities or parallels that oc-

curred independently in several arid or semiarid areas in the world and at different times. This is what one means by cultural regularities for which anthropologists have been seeking. It is a sample of recurring phenomena that have come to pass.

In northern Arizona, aggregation began roughly about A.D. 700 and reached a climax about A.D. 1500.[1] In southern Arizona (the Hohokam) aggregation started much earlier—perhaps about 400 B.C. and came to an end about A.D. 1300–1400. We call this the Formative Era. Unfortunately, further development, if possible, was thwarted by the arrival of the Spanish military in A.D. 1539.

In summary, the concept of the Formative Era in the Southwest and elsewhere is one of the major, successive organizational levels that is an indispensable model in comparing the apparently parallel, independent, and discontinuous processes of sociocultural development. As stated earlier, this occurred in several different world areas at different periods of time.

And, at least so far as Mesopotamia and Meso-America are concerned, these came about independently. The vital steps in each sequence were achieved without dependence on the other. Emphasis is not on a constellation of features or traits but upon technological innovations and ever more varied social organization.

The steps from hunting and gathering, to incipient agriculture, to formative eras represent one of several transformations. In both the Old World and the New the first

[1] Actually, aggregations continued after A.D. 1500 —the Pecos Indians moving to Jemez, the Tewa-speaking people from Santa Clara pueblo to the first mesa in the Hopi country. The contemporary aggregations in the Hopi, Zuni, and Rio Grande pueblos fall into a special class. The need that gave rise to these towns has now disappeared. We now are witnessing a reverse tendency among these towns—the pueblos shrinking as the population spreads out to build individual houses on the outskirts (Zubrow, 1969b).

of these transformations is economic, that is, from food-gathering to food production. Agriculture, however, appeared only in a relatively few areas in the world and in arid or semiarid ones at that. But the dates of the appearance of the food-producing revolution varied greatly from area to area. In Mexico, settled village communities were formed by 2000 B.C., although maize was probably known by 5000 B.C. and beans and squash by 7000 B.C.

In Arizona and the Southwest, settled village communities of pit houses that relied on fully developed agriculture probably did not come into existence much before 400 B.C. (the Hohokam).[2]

We have traced sociocultural evolution in the Southwest from the Desert culture of hunting and gathering, through the stage of the pit house dwellers or incipient agriculturists to the stage of aggregations or pueblo and town dwellers—all moving in a direction fundamentally similar to that taken earlier by the Indians of Meso-America and Peru and even earlier by the peoples of Mesopotamia.

Diffusion of traits from Meso-America are accordingly ruled out as far as general structural and functional categories are concerned. It should be remembered that, as Harris says (1968, p. 378), "A diffused innovation, no less than an independently invented one, must withstand the selective pressures of the social system, if it is to become part of the cultural repertory. In this larger sense, the adoption of diffused and independently invented innovations must be viewed as part of a single process." Since many of the features of Southwestern

sociocultural traits are to be found in many scattered parts of the world, it seems rather sterile to explain cultural similarities between Meso-America and the Southwest by "appealing to the nonprinciple of diffusion." Diffusion really explains nothing.

This is not to say that diffusion never occurred. That is an absolutistic statement. We know for instance that soon after the discovery of the New World many cultural elements rapidly spread from there achieving a pan-world distribution. Tobacco and the smoking of it is one excellent example of this mechanism. Others are maize, the potato, beans, tomatoes.

Briefly, then, we do not wish to state categorically that diffusionary processes have never operated. The principal point we wish to stress is that if an innovation is diffused it must withstand the selective pressures of the social system. Perhaps, too, we might add that an innovation will not be adopted unless a society has a need for it and unless it resembles and is consistent with pre-existing usages.

In the case of the spread of maize, beans, and squash, one can demonstrate that the pre-agricultural Southwestern people were accustomed to selecting certain foods and reducing them to a flour by means of a milling process. Perhaps that usage helped the newly adopted foods withstand the pressures of the social systems of their new home.

GREAT TOWNS IN THE SOUTHWEST

The term "Great Towns" is, of course, a relative one. We are accustomed today to regard great towns as cities of many millions of peoples. Cities of that magnitude are relatively modern. Ancient cities were much smaller. For example, cities of the

---

[2] I make these comparisons because traditionally I used to suggest—directly or indirectly—that cultural developments in the Southwest were the result of "influences" or borrowing of ideas from the urban state societies in Mexico. I no longer hold with this idea. I now believe that an independent evolution, not a mere borrowing process, took place. (P.M.)

'Ubaid period (about 3800 B.C.) in Mesopotamia such as Ur, Eridu, and Ugar are estimated to have averaged about two thousand people each (Adams, Robert, McC., personal communication). Ancient Tikal in the jungles of Meso-America is believed to have been populated with about ten thousand people. Teotihuacán at about 100 B.C. is thought to have held about ten thousand people in the urban center.

The towns of the ancient Southwest were minuscule by comparison. Considering their limited technology, some of the towns were large enough to command our respect.

Not all of the towns to be mentioned were in Arizona, but since we cannot slice up the prehistoric Southwest to conform to our requirements, we shall take the liberty of selecting large towns from the various subareas—Chaco, Mesa Verde, Kayenta, the Hopi area, and the Hohokam. Further, for Pueblo Bonito, a building of some eight hundred apartment rooms, we shall include details concerning the ancient mode of living. This will serve as a template for the remainder of the towns. Although each differed from the others, the general details of sleeping, eating, furniture, amount of space allotted, location of storage space, means of entrance, and so on were more or less alike for the entire area.

The Chaco Area—A.D. 830–1130

In the Chaco area there are remains of twelve large towns scattered along a twenty-mile stretch. Pueblo Bonito, one of the best known, was built according to a preconceived plan. The ground plan is D-shaped or semicircular with an open plaza. The open part of the crescent was eventually closed by a block of rooms. Large units of this extraordinary town were constructed at one time. Eventually, it consisted of about eight hundred rooms and covered three acres. Of all these large late towns, Pueblo Bonito is the only one to have been totally excavated (Judd, 1954, 1964). We shall therefore describe it and let it stand as a type of the other eleven towns.

One tangential issue should be mentioned at this point. Dr. Judd was the archaeologist from the United States National Museum who directed the seven-year operations at Pueblo Bonito, the expenses for which were borne by the National Geographic Society (1921–27). In his final reports, Judd speaks of the "Old Bonitians" and the "Late Bonitians." He hypothesizes that in the eighth century a group—the "Old Bonitians"—built the first row of rooms and expanded crescentically to the right and left as the lineage expanded. Then in the 1000s—perhaps about 1025—the original local population was swelled by the arrival of a second group—the "Late Bonitians." The newcomers took over in a big way because they were numerically and culturally superior. They built onto what was there, tore that down, and then built it up again (urban renewal) and twice enlarged it. Judd thought that he could perceive differences in the masonry, pottery, and general architectural style of the newly arrived immigrants. He also thought that they seemed aware of the possibility of strife because they made the pueblo more impregnable.

At the present time, this idea is not generally held. It seems more likely that the whole town as well as the others was the result of an *in situ* development. There was no "Old" or "Late" Bonitians in the sense that the latter were immigrants. All the evidence points to a gradual development by the local people from small simple villages to large, multistoried complex ones (Vivian and Matthews, 1966, p. 108).

All of these late, large towns were built

according to a preconceived plan, were multistoried (four stories high) and conformed to a ground plan that was D-(Crescentic) or E-shaped with a court enclosed by rooms.

The masonry of the older portions of Pueblo Bonito is distinctive. It consists of sandstone slabs as wide as the wall was thick. Ample mud mortar and spalls were used to bed and level the slabs. This is a simple type of wall with surfaces that were relatively smooth but not covered by a veneer. This type of masonry was in vogue from about A.D. 830 to about 940.

About A.D. 1000 (Vivian, R. G., 1970) there was a marked expansion of building activities at many of the towns—remodeling, razing of the unfaced slab walls, and additions—lateral and vertical. With this upswing in the building trade came the introduction of a better kind of masonry, called *cored, faced masonry*. This type of wall construction called for a core or an inner hearting of rubble laid in adobe mortar and a facing on both sides of neatly laid stonework. Often, the veneer was banded and thin tabular pieces of sandstone were laid so as to form a decorative pattern. A study of dated wall constructions is helpful in placing undated sites in a relative time scale.

The ground floor rooms may have been used mostly as storerooms. The living quarters were in the upper stories.

Entry to the living quarters was by means of doorways in the walls facing the plaza. There were usually no door openings on the rear wall facing away from the plaza. Some had been included in the original building plan but they were later blocked up with masonry and sealed. Eventually after the open side of the court was closed by means of a block of doorless rooms, the Bonitians themselves had to enter or leave the town by means of ladders that led up to and across the rooftops. Thus the town was as impregnable as the occupants could make it. Such provisions against unwanted visitors leads one to suppose that either the Bonitians were paranoiac and imagined that they were going to be attacked or that danger was real and menacing. By pulling up their ladders, they could prevent attackers from gaining a foothold, or at least discourage them.

Living quarters were not sumptuous but fairly adequate. Each family with extensions of aunts, uncles, and grandparents occupied a suite of three or four rooms, size of the suite depending on their needs. One of the main residence rooms probably was provided with a small fire pit that furnished heat for cooking and for comfort and to give light. There were no windows; light filtered into the room through the doorway. Doorways, after A.D. 1000, were large, rectangular, with sills raised about eight inches above the floor; they were either rectangular or T-shaped. A few diagonal doorways existed—that is, a doorway that went diagonally through the corner of a room. In bad weather, this opening was closed by means of a skin or matting. Smoke found its way out via the doorway or through a small ventilator, with which some rooms were provided. Smoke probably did not annoy the families in the upper stories because they were set back in terraces. People slept in the rooms of their suite on the floor on mats wrapped up in a rabbit-fur blanket, a skin, or a woven blanket of cotton. Storage rooms were at the rear of the terrace and were dark; living quarters faced the plaza. Living quarters measured about 12 by 18 feet, giving a floor space of about 216 square feet; ceilings were about eight feet high. A total of over 1,700 cubic feet was the average for the late type rooms.

When weather permitted, cooking was done out of doors on the ground or on the

rooftops belonging to the story below.
Food was placed in bowls on the floor and
the family dipped into the stew or gruel
with a tortilla-like bread. No eating utensils
such as forks existed. If the family was
matrilineal and matrilocal, then it would
be composed of father, mother, married
daughters and their husbands, children, and
perhaps grandparents.

The furnishings of a room were meager:
clothes racks consisting of poles set in the
masonry and running across the narrow
dimension of the room; shelves made up of
poles; cupboards created by sealing a doorway or ventilator; and wall pegs.

As noted above, rear rooms were dark
and served admirably for storing dried
beans, shelled corn and sunflower seeds in
jars; husked corn stacked like firewood,
dried pumpkins, gourd water jugs, baskets,
stone mortars, gourd rattles, ceremonial
masks, tortoise shells, pots, and odd implements ranging from the profane to the
sacred. Floor sweepings and refuse were
carried to the nearest community dump.
Sometimes a room was set aside as a privy.
Otherwise, the whole out-of-doors was
available for toilet facilities.

The population of the canyon is estimated to have been about 4,400 persons
for the period A.D. 950–1075 (Vivian and
Matthews, 1966, p. 108) and to have decreased to about 3,300 for the period A.D.
1075–1130.

Thus in a period of about three hundred
years (A.D. 830–1130) this area witnessed
the development of towns of remarkable
architectural sophistication. Along with
these large clusters of cell-like rooms and
the 200 to 400 smaller villages on the south
side of the canyon, there were the significant water control systems that were associated with the large towns on the north
side of the canyon. These command our
respect.

Although abandonment of the towns is
believed to have begun shortly after A.D.
1130, some groups remained there until
about A.D. 1300.

One hypothesis for explaining the great
towns on one side of the wash and the
small contemporaneous villages on the
other, is that the elite lived in the great
towns (where the luxury goods were
found), and the less important people occupied the smaller, one-story villages. A
chiefdom type of social organization may
have been present with the elite controlling
and distributing the food supplies.

The Mesa Verde Area—A.D. 1150–1300

In the recent survey of great towns on
just one mesa—Wetherill Mesa—100 were
found in caves and 53 on mesa tops. It is
estimated that there are perhaps 500 to
1,000 cliff houses in the Mesa Verde proper.
Besides this, there are some other cliff
houses (usually small) outside of the National Park itself plus hundreds of medium-
size towns on mesa tops. This preference
for placing a town in a cave was on the
upswing during this period, rising from
about 20 percent of all sites dated at
roughly A.D. 950 to 66 percent of all sites
in A.D. 1150. This movement to caves may
signify that the people felt a need for protection against potential troublemakers
(Hayes, 1964). The greatest amount of
building activity was done between A.D.
1230 and 1260.

In general, the villages in caves show no
definite plan because the rooms, towers, and
kivas had to fit the available space. Storage
rooms were placed at the rear of the caves;
dwelling rooms were in front of them, with
kivas the farthest forward. Most of the
caves selected opened toward the south,
the east, or the southeast. Since most of the
towns in caves were "new" buildings and

PLATE 52 Artist's reconstruction of Lowry Pueblo (Anasazi), Colorado. Dated at about A.D. 1050–1150. In foreground is circular Great Kiva. Pueblo proper was two and three stories high. Ladders projecting from smaller circular features indicate small clan kivas. Excavated by Southwestern Archaeological Expedition of Field Museum, 1930–34. Anne Harding Spoehr, artist.

did not spring from older building (as at Pueblo Bonito in Chaco Canyon) it is difficult to see any preconceived building plan. Kivas were placed near or in a block of dwelling rooms. Since the shape of the buildings had to conform to the configurations of the caves, some small changes in architecture may be noted. If the cover overhang was sufficient, the uppermost floors were sometimes not roofed with timbers, since the walls were built right up to the cave roof. This provided the ceiling for the upper rooms. Where space permitted, the linear type of pueblo found in earlier periods continued to be erected with a grouping of living quarters suggesting that lineage social organization was important. A "unit" of six to ten rooms arranged around a tower and kiva or just around one or more kivas is not uncommon. The location of the kiva in reference to the lineage house-unit in open, mesa-top situations was fairly standard with the kiva to

the south or southeast of the house row. In a cave, however, it was easier to build the kiva at the front regardless of what direction the cave mouth faced. Hence, the former orientation of kiva vis-à-vis houses was no longer regarded as important. In many caves, the kivas were to the *north* of the houses. (The rule for open sites was to have the kiva to the south.)

The number of stories in height varied from one to three. Cliff Palace, the largest town of the area, contained 200 rooms and 23 kivas; Spruce Tree House, about 120 rooms and 8 kivas; and Long House, 150 rooms.

The best of the masonry in the towns compares favorably with some of that at Chaco Canyon. Walls were sometimes composed of a core and a facing, the latter being made up of rectangular sandstone blocks, the faces of which had been carefully dressed by grinding and pecking. Repeated blows of a pecking stone produced a dimpled effect which was most characteristic of the best and latest masonry. The usual wall was of a single course, that is, one stone would extend from inside to outside. This, of course, made for thinner walls but structural sturdiness was lacking. Where upper stories were lacking, the masonry was not of high quality. On the whole, Mesa Verde masonry of this big town period lacks the aesthetic appeal, the substantial quality, and the rugged characteristics of Chaco Canyon masonry. Mesa Verde walls, especially when made up of dimpled stones, are useful in establishing relative chronology but lack the sensitive chronological traits that characterize Chaco masonry.

Room usages were the same as those given for Pueblo Bonito. Rooms were small; they contained perhaps 140 to 160 square feet and ceilings were a mere 5 to 6 feet high.

The estimates of population for Wetherill Mesa as given by Hayes (1964, p. 110) are as follows: 100 cliff houses with about 730 living rooms would yield a population of about 730 to 1460. Since he surveyed only about 10 percent of the Mesa Verde, a projected figure of about 7,000 persons (total) for all the big towns is given, but with misgivings. In the period just before A.D. 1100, dense populations were found at elevations ranging from 6,700 feet to 7,200 feet. After A.D. 1100, sites tended to be above the 7,000-foot contour level. More precipitation falls in the country above 7,000 feet and this may have been a factor in causing the people to move.

PLATE 53   Cliff Palace, Mesa Verde National Park, southern end, dated from about 1100 to 1275. There were over a hundred ground floor rooms, many of which contained a second and/or third story, and twenty-three kivas. Photo by Paul Martin, 1948.

GREAT TOWNS IN NORTHERN ARIZONA—A.D. 1300–1540

Now let us move into Arizona proper and take a glance at some of the larger sites that flourished in the centuries just prior to the Spanish Invasion. The sites are listed in alphabetical order.[3]

Name: CHEVLON RUIN (CAKWABAIYAKI)

Primary drainage: Little Colorado River

Secondary drainage: Chevlon Creek

Ecological zone: Upper Sonoran (desert grassland and tamarisk)

Elevation: 4,950 feet

Location of site: About 15 miles east of Winslow, Navajo County, Arizona

Position of site: Top and sides of prominent gravel ridge. Three room blocks—east, west, and south. The unit to the east is the largest.

Fields: Probably on the valley floor of Chevlon Creek and the Little Colorado River

Size: 60 × 100 meters (total)

Number of stories: Probably 2

Masonry: Sandstone slab

Number of rooms: ca. 300±

Population estimate: 200–400

Kivas: Probably

Plazas: Possibly

Burials: Just outside the outer wall of the pueblo at varying depths, in extended position; no evidence of cremations

Relative date: Pueblo IV (A.D. 1400)

Excavator: Fewkes

---

[3] The information that follows was compiled under the direction of Dr. Alexander J. Lindsay by students Donald C. Fiero and Daniel Schecter. I turned for help to Dr. Lindsay of the Museum of Northern Arizona, Flagstaff, because much of the data I needed was not available in complete form. The Museum at Flagstaff, of course, is without peer in research in northern Arizona; and I knew the information that would be sent me would be complete and up-to-date. I thank Dr. Lindsay and Messrs. Fiero and Schecter for their assistance and gratefully acknowledge their contributions. (P.M.)

Date: 1896

Institution: Smithsonian Institution

References: 22d BAE, Annual Report 1904, pp. 89–90

Name: GRAPEVINE PUEBLO

Primary drainage: Canyon Diablo

Secondary drainage: Grapevine Canyon

Ecological zone: Upper Sonoran

Elevation: 6,900 feet

Location of site: 32 miles southeast of Flagstaff, 10 miles southeast of Mormon Lake, Coconino County, Arizona

Position of site: On north edge of Grapevine Canyon, immediately south of ephemeral lake on mesa top

Fields: Possible terracing on natural benches

Source of water: Grapevine Spring below pueblo

Size: 20 × 70 meters

Number of stories: One

Masonry: Crude basalt and sandstone cobbles and slabs, walls about 1.5 meters high

Number of rooms: 45±

Population estimate: 30–60

Kivas: Possibly

Plazas: Possible plaza areas

Relative date: Pueblo III–Pueblo IV (A.D. 1400)

References: Colton, 1946, p. 213

Name: GRASSHOPPER PUEBLO

Primary drainage: Salt River

Ecological zone: Mountain—open low mountains

Elevation: 6,000 feet

Location of site: About 15 miles west of Cibecue, Fort Apache Indian Reservation

Position of site: Two large units of rooms, plazas, and great kivas separated from one another by the Salt River Draw. It rests on lava and is in a yellow pine forest.

PLATE 54 "Montezuma's Castle" (a misnomer), cliff pueblo, about forty miles south of Flagstaff, Arizona, overlooking Beaver Creek, a tributary of the Rio Verde. Four to five stories high and accessible only by means of ladders, it was occupied sometime between A.D. 1300 and 1500. Photo taken by Field Museum photographer about 1900.

Source of water: Salt River Draw, a permanent stream at time of occupation

Masonry: Blocks of sandstone

Number of rooms: 500 rooms or more; some parts, two stories high. One of the largest, if not the largest in Arizona.

Kivas: Small rectangular kivas and at least one great kiva

Burials: Several cemetery areas in trash on the east side, and in clusters to north and south of the main ruin. Burials of persons of high status occur mostly under the floor of the great kiva that was at one time a plaza. The mortuary offerings of these burials were particularly rich in grave goods.

Cultural affinity: Late Mogollon or Western Pueblo

Relative dates: A.D. 1275–1400

Institution: University of Arizona Archaeological Field School under direction of Chairman Raymond H. Thompson (1964–65) and Professor William A. Longacre—1966 to present

References: Thompson and Longacre, 1966; Griffin, 1967; Clark, 1969

Name: HOMOLOVI I

Primary drainage: Little Colorado River

Ecological zone: Upper Sonoran (willow and cottonwood in the floodplain)

Elevation: 4,880 feet

Location of site: Apache County, Arizona

Position of site: Rolling grass-covered hills formed by alluvium of the Little Colorado River

Source of water: Little Colorado River

Size: 1.5–2.0 acres

Number of stories: 2, possibly 3

Masonry: Sandstone slabs (wet and dry)

Number of rooms: ca. 230 rooms

Population estimate: 150–300 persons

Plazas: One

Relative date: Pueblo IV (A.D. 1400)

References: Museum of Northern Arizona site files

Name: KINNIKINNICK PUEBLO

Primary drainage: Canyon Diablo

Secondary drainage: Grapevine Canyon

Ecological zone: Upper Sonoran (piñon-juniper forest, ponderosa in the canyon below)

Elevation: 6,900 ± feet

Location of site: 30 miles southeast of Flagstaff on Anderson Mesa on the south rim of Kinnikinnick Canyon, about 1 mile above the confluence of Grapevine Canyon; Coconino County, Arizona

Position of site: The large easterly and smaller westerly room blocks rest upon a lava flow on the south edge of Kinnikinnick Canyon.

Fields: Basalt walls north of ruin are possible agricultural terraces.

Source of water: Some seepage in the canyon directly below pueblo; good supply at Kinnikinnick spring 1¼ miles up the canyon

Size: Both pueblos ca. 40 × 50 meters

Number of stories: 2 to 3

Masonry: Crude basalt and sandstone slabs

Number of rooms: West unit 13, east unit 60 ground floor rooms

Population estimate: 100–150

Burials: Multiple reinterment of 5+ individuals from the western side of Kinnikinnick Canyon, 100 yards below the rim of Anderson Mesa and 150 yards from the west unit

Relative date: Pueblo IV; ceramic dates—A.D. 1200–1325

Tree-ring date: Dates from the one room excavated cluster at A.D. 1308

Excavator: Milton Wetherill, Sidney Conner, and Theodore Stern

Date: 1940

Institution: Museum of Northern Arizona

References: Conner, 1943; Colton, 1946; Wilson, Winston, and Berger, 1961; Bannister, Gell, and Hannah, 1966

Name: KINTIEL (WIDE RUIN, PUEBLO GRANDE, BUTTERFLY RUIN)

Primary drainage: LeRoux Wash

Secondary drainage: Wide Ruin Wash

Ecological zone: Upper Sonoran

Location of site: At Wide Ruins Trading Post, 18 miles north of Chambers, Apache County, Arizona

Position of site: A very large pueblo built in a hollow oval or "butterfly" (crescentic) shape on either side of a small wash which is an eastern tributary of Wide Ruin Wash

Fields: Possibly to the north and to the west

Source of water: Masonry-walled spring, west end of pueblo

Size: 550 × 300 feet (our estimate)

Number of stories: Two

Masonry: Excellent, rather uniform construction

Number of rooms: 150–200

Population estimate: 300–500 (Fewkes)

Kivas: 2 excavated

Plazas: One

Burials: On the eastern side of the northern section, burials made close to the outer walls of the buildings. No orientation noted.

Cultural affinity: Hopi

Tree-ring date: From two excavated kivas; Kiva KT-2's dates cluster at A.D. 1275, while the dates from KT-1 range from A.D. 1226 to 1276

Excavator: Fewkes; Hargrave

Date: 1900; 1929

Institution: Smithsonian Institution; Smithsonian Institution and National Geographic Society

References: V. Mindeleff, 1891, pp. 91–94; Fewkes, 1904, pp. 124–28, 100, 181; Haury and Hargrave, 1931, pp. 80–95; Bannister, Hannah, and Robinson, 1966, p. 25

Name: KOKOPNYAMA (HORN HOUSE, COTTONWOOD RUIN)

Primary drainage: Little Colorado River

Secondary drainage: Jeddito Valley

Ecological zone: Upper Sonoran (juniper, pine, and fir)

Location of site: 1 mile northeast of the Jeddito Trading Post on the north side of Jeddito Valley, and a "few miles" south of the Keams Canyon Agency

Position of site: On the edge of Antelope Mesa

Source of water: Possible spring just below the mesa, nearly opposite the center of the village

Size: 10–12 acres

Number of stories: 2 or more

Masonry: Poor quality of stone used, no attempt at coursing apparent

Number of rooms: Several hundred

Kivas: 5 excavated or tested

Great kivas: 7

Plazas: 2–4

Cultural affinity: Hopi

Relative date: Pueblo III and Pueblo IV

Tree-ring date: Two clusters, one in the late 1200s and the other in the late 1300s. The latest date is 1400.

Excavator: Hargrave

Date: 1929

Institution: Smithsonian Institution and National Geographic Society

References: V. Mindeleff, 1891, pp. 50–51; Hough, 1903, pp. 288, 337–39; Haury and Hargrave, 1931, pp. 95–120; Hargrave, 1935a, v. 8, no. 4, pp. 18–19; Bannister, Robinson, and Warren, 1967, p. 18

Name: PAYUPKI

Primary drainage: Little Colorado River

Secondary drainage: Corn Creek, Polacca Wash, Wepo Wash

Ecological zone: Upper Sonoran (margin of piñon-juniper)

Location of site: Summit of a bold promontory south of the trail from Walpi to Oraibi; about 6 miles northwest from Mashongnavi

Position of site: Hollow square pueblo located on spur of mesa isolated by a saddle

Source of water: Unknown; possibly from head of valley to the northwest or from wells

Size: 300 × 250 feet

Masonry: Poorly dressed due to use of soft sandstone, use of stone of varying sizes

Number of rooms: ca. 200

Population estimate: 150–250

Kivas: Two

Plazas: One

Relative date: Pueblo III, Pueblo IV, Pueblo V (A.D. 1200–1700)

References: V. Mindeleff, 1891, pp. 59–60; Fewkes, 1904, pp. 583–84

Name: PINEDALE RUIN

Primary drainage: Little Colorado River

Secondary drainage: Silver Creek

Ecological zone: Upper Sonoran (yellow pine, juniper, and oak)

Elevation: Approximately 6,400 feet

Location of site: 0.5 mile southeast of Pinedale, Arizona, 16 miles west of the Showlow Ruin.

Position of site: Hollow rectangle pueblo in flat, open pine forest

Size: 250 × 250 feet (estimated)

Number of stories: 1 and 2

Masonry: Dressed stone, chinked; well-made

Number of rooms: 200±, 21 excavated

Population estimate: 200–400

Kivas: 1 (excavated)

Plazas: 1, central, rectangular

Burials: Fewkes removed some burials from the east midden

Tree-ring date: A.D. 1275–1325

Excavator: Haury, E. W.

Date: 1929

Institution: Smithsonian Institution and National Geographic Society

References: Fewkes, 1904; Spier, 1919a; Haury and Hargrave, 1931; Bannister, Gell, and Hannah, 1966

Name: STONE AXE (BLACK AXE) RUIN

Primary drainage: Little Colorado River

Secondary drainage: Rio Puerco

Ecological zone: Upper Sonoran

Elevation: 5,400 feet

Location of site: 2.8 miles southeast of Agate Bridge in Petrified Forest National Park, 15 miles southeast of Carrizo, Apache County, Arizona

Position of site: Series of mounds on point of ridge between two small washes

Source of water: Only permanent water below bed of wash near Agate Bridge in Petrified Forest

Size: 150 × 100 meters

Number of stories: One

Masonry: Sandstone slabs

Number of rooms: 200+

Population estimate: 150–300

Plazas: Yes

Burials: 3 "cemeteries" at north end of site. Hough (1903, p. 321) estimated from 150 to 200 burials

Relative date: Late Pueblo III–Pueblo IV (about A.D. 1300–1400)

Excavator: Walter Hough

Date: 1901

Institution: Museum-Gates Expedition, U. S. National Museum

References: Hough, 1903, pp. 320–25

SOUTHERN ARIZONA—HOHOKAM AREA ABOUT A.D. 1300 TO 1450

The towns in the Gila-Salt River drainages were larger and more numerous than in northern Arizona. Unfortunately, not very much is known about them since many of the adobe buildings have melted away or were reduced to mounds of rubble that have since been plowed over and destroyed. Pueblo Grande, in the city of Phoenix, has been partly saved and restored. But within a circumference of about twenty miles of Phoenix there were six to ten other large towns. No one knows how many other big towns flourished in the whole Hohokam area from A.D. 1300 on to about 1500. A rough guess of the number of such towns for the whole area ranges from fifteen to thirty.

Some of the more interesting aspects of these towns are the "great houses," the compounds, and the village plans and house architecture.

The only Great House still standing is at a site called Casa Grande about sixty miles southeast of Phoenix, and it is fragmentary, having been ravished by weather and vandals. It was supposed to have been three to four stories high. It measures about 40 by 60 feet, contained five rooms on the ground floor and perhaps a total of fifteen rooms. The walls were four feet thick at the base and were made of puddled adobe. This is a type of construction that calls for building of walls of mud by means of movable forms. The mold, three to five feet long and four feet thick, was constructed of canes, poles, and woven reed mats forming two parallel planes, about four apart. Into this was dumped wet mud (adobe) mixed with small stones and tamped and rammed and then permitted to dry. After the adobe was firm and dry, the mold or form was moved and the process repeated.

At Casa Grande there were at least two of these "great houses."

The present standing one stood within a compound wall that is estimated to have been seven feet high. It enclosed a space of about 65 acres. Against the walls of the compound and within it were the Hohokam houses. No one knows what the "great houses" were used for, but later on we suggest that at this stage of development of the Hohokam, chiefdoms had emerged and that the elite lived in the big houses.

Our greatest source of information on Hohokam great towns comes from the ancient city of Los Muertos excavated by the Hemenway Southwestern Archaeological Expedition, 1887–88, under the direction of Dr. Frank H. Cushing. The collection of some five hundred specimens, notes, and sketches were loaned to the Peabody Museum of Salem (1888) and later bequeathed by the trustees of the estate of Mrs. Hemenway to Peabody Museum of Harvard University in 1894. Forty years later Emil W. Haury conducted research on the collection for his doctoral dissertation and in 1941 the manuscript was revised for publication (Haury, 1945). Cushing himself never finished his account of the work of the Expedition. Haury's task, therefore, was a pleasant but most difficult one—namely, the revival of work that had been done some forty years earlier and without the aid of adequate detailed notes and photographs. Fortunately, a topographer accompanied the expedition and drew plans of the excavations, but no sections. Without this great contribution of Haury's, we would have a most limited idea of what Hohokam classic culture was in the fourteenth century of this era.

The enormous ancient town called Los Muertos (so named because of the numerous cremations and inhumations) was about 6.5 miles from Tempe, Arizona, a satellite of Phoenix. The elevation of the large plain on which it lay (scarcely a vestige of any kind of this great town now remains) is about 1,100 feet above sea level. Annual average rainfall is about 8 inches and the summer temperatures may rise to 130° F. Since this rainfall is not enough to permit dry farming, irrigation was extensively employed (see below). The size of this great town may be partially comprehended when one is told that the city covered an area 5 to 6 miles in length and .5 to 1 mile in width. In this vast area were some twenty-five to thirty mounds. Dr. Matthews, who was a member of the expedition, estimated that the population was about 13,000 inhabitants, although it is unclear how he reached that figure. We do know that of the twenty-five mounds that Haury mentions (1945) most of them were partially or wholly explored. Judging from the plans that Haury published, we estimated that about 400 rooms were dug. It is impossible to know whether the excavations covered 10 or 90 percent of the area. Our guess is that Los Muertos probably contained over 500 rooms of various kinds and sizes and perhaps even 1,000. At any rate, by Southwestern standards this was a big site.

Great Houses

As we mentioned earlier, only one of these multistoried houses still exists (at Casa Grande site); but it was stated by Matthews (Matthews *et al.*, 1893) that each site formerly had one of these great multi-storied houses usually centrally located in the town, and that one city had seven such buildings. There is no way of verifying these statements, nor can one tell from the published plans in Haury whether each of the excavated units at Los Muertos possessed one or not. The exception, of course, is Ruin I, the plan of which indicates a "big house." It measured 80 feet (east–west) by 120 feet (north–south). Cushing stated that it had been four to seven stories high, but Haury thinks it was more likely only four stories (Haury, 1945, p. 17). The walls at the base were 7 feet in thickness. If each compound at Los Muertos possessed one of these puddle-adobe four-story pueblos, then there may have been twenty-five of them. This is conjecture.

The multistoried building that we are sure of at Los Muertos (in Ruin I) stood within a compound formed by a massive adobe wall, some 7 feet thick and perhaps 7 feet high. The dimensions of the compound area were 200 by 320 feet. The area, bounded on all four sides by this wall had contained plazas, and clusters of rooms some of which abutted the compound wall. No more can be stated about the "great houses"; hence they provide a mystery of sorts.

Compounds

Almost every unit of the various subdivisions of the city was enclosed on all four sides by a compound wall, and within the compound were several disparate house clusters and plazas. Sometimes the rooms were incorporated into the wall; sometimes, a compound wall served as the outer or fourth side of a house unit; sometimes a room stood alone and, more often, the houses abutted on one another. Ruin XIV contained one of the most extensive house clusters (perhaps thirty rooms) but courtyards between the several clusters may have lent a spacious air to the unit. When more rooms were needed, they built outside the compound wall.

Houses

The data on these structures are maddeningly scanty. Judging from the ground plans in Haury (1945) many of the rooms were contiguous and this implies vertical walls. Apparently, they were of puddled adobe similar to those excavated by Tuthill at Tres Alamos and Di Peso at San Cayetano. Whether they were one story high or not, we do not know, although Cushing's note suggests that several floors were encountered and that they may have been two stories high. If one looks at the ground plans only and is willing to forget for a moment that this was a Hohokam town built entirely of puddled adobe, the resemblance to ground plans of houses of towns at Mesa Verde, the Kayenta and Flagstaff areas, Lowry pueblo, and late sites on the upper Little Colorado River (Hooper Ranch Site) is remarkably similar. We do not mean the "great houses" or the compound walls; we refer specifically to the contiguous, cellular characteristics of many of the room clusters. The sizes of the rooms varied greatly—from 10 by 10 feet to 12 by 20 feet.

Whether each family occupied a room or a suite of rooms is unknown. But certainly the grouping of dwellings within a walled compound reminds one of San Cayetano (Di Peso, 1956) and suggests an extended clan relationship.

Platform Mounds

It is likely that some of the mounds that Cushing observed were what are now called platform mounds, the purposes of which are not understood (see description of one at Gila Bend, p. 149). This type of mound was created by first building retaining walls, and then filling the area then enclosed with soil and refuse. There is some evidence for believing that brush or wattle-and-daub structures were placed on top of these mounds. The height of these is not known, but at Snaketown they were only several feet high. It also appears that the great multiple-storied adobe houses were erected on top of these walled mounds.

Ball Courts

No ball courts were reported for Los Muertos; but were reported from nearby great towns. (In a previous chapter, it was pointed out that these might not have been ball courts but large ceremonial dance plazas roughly akin to great kivas [?].)

Disposal of the Dead

For some time, Gladwin, Haury, Di Peso, and others have hypothesized that the even flow of Hohokam life was interrupted by the peaceful arrival at about A.D. 1300 of an immigrant group called the Salado. Their homeland was supposed to have been in the northern part of Arizona (the Little Colorado), and they are credited with introducing several new cultural items to the Hohokam: inhumation; Gila, Pinto, and Tonto polychromes; multistoried pueblos of adobe, since building stone did not exist in Hohokam land, the custom of deforming their roundheaded skulls; dogs, turkeys, and so on.

The chief evidence for this invasion consists of four items: multistoried houses, skull deformation, a different pottery style, and inhumation versus the Hohokam cremation.

This idea has governed most of the work and ideas of archaeologists of the Gila-Salt-lower Arizona area for over thirty years.

It is our belief that the so-called Salado developments were all developments that took place in the Gila-Salt area as the result of a natural evolution (see forepart of this chapter)—an *in situ* development.

The Anasazi once built and occupied pit houses (A.D. 500 or so) but by A.D. 800–1100 were building contiguous stone-walled pueblos of several (2 to 4) stories. Their pottery and many other items changed dramatically during the same time.

Why, then, if the Anasazi could have evolved from pit houses to 800-room, terraced, stone-walled pueblos—all of which demonstrate astounding virtuosity—could not the Hohokam Indians have evolved an architecture that flowed from flimsy, brush, noncontiguous huts to the kinds of great houses, ordinary houses, and impressive compounds that have just been described?

It seems reasonable that they might have done so. We do not have the data with which to demonstrate this proposition, but it is put forth as an alternate explanation that is more in line with contemporary research trends. After all, no one seriously suggests that the Great Towns in Chaco Canyon were the result of an invasion. Of course, for the Anasazi we have more data that suggest in-place development. Such masses of data are lacking for the Hohokam area, but the evidence suggests that our proposition for *in situ* growth merits consideration, meager though the evidence is.

Really, what the Hohokam experts have implied is that the Hohokam were not bright enough to have developed great houses of several stories, compound walls, and the like.

Now, let us examine the burial customs on which so much emphasis has been placed.

Haury states (1945, p. 43) that not a single burial (inhumation) was found in the trash mounds outside the compounds. All such burials were found within the compound under the plazas or under floors of rooms. All the cremations were located in trash mounds outside the compounds.

The data concerning the head forms of unburned versus burned skeletons is inconclusive and according to contemporary research may not have much meaning. Haury (1945, pp. 47–49) suggests that skull deformation was not practiced by the cremating Hohokam and that they were long-headed, whereas the unburned skulls appear to have been round-headed. The number of unburned skeletons recovered from below plaza and house floor was 122, while the number of cremated individuals may have been between 300 and 400. This represents a ratio of cremations to burials of about 3:1. Haury suggests that the burials represented a Puebloan racial stock—the

Saladoans—from the north; and the cremated individuals, the original Hohokam population. Recent excavations at Casa Grande suggested to the investigator that there was no invading group (Steen, 1965, p. 80).

One highly suggestive point is that Cushing stated that the more luxurious articles were found within the compounds and the "priests' temples," that is, the "great multi-storied houses" (Haury, p. 37).

Now Cushing is described as a visionary person with uncanny insight (Haury, 1945, p. viii). He may have dreamed up these differences—luxury items interred with burials with the compounds and the "great houses" as opposed to art remains of a less fine order interred with cremations. But if he did not, this strengthens our suggestion that an elite—even "chiefs" and families—occupied the "great houses" and the houses within the compounds. It also agrees with the evidence from Chaco Canyon where the "luxury" items were found mostly in the great multistoried pueblos and not in the more humble villages across the canyon ("on the wrong side of the railroad tracks"!).

Cushing became so ill in 1887 that Dr. Washington Matthews, U.S.A. surgeon, was sent to the camp at Los Muertos to give medical care to him. While there, Matthews developed an interest in the burials that were being excavated. In his account (Matthews, Wortman, and Billings, 1893), Matthews said that with inhumations from below plaza floors and from

. . . wall sepulchers were found various household utensils and articles of personal adornment and others of a sacerdotal character. In the mural burials of the temples [he means the "great houses"] the articles of a sacerdotal character were particularly numerous and elaborate. This is one of the many reasons we have for believing that those buried without cremation were of a sacerdotal and higher class in the community, while those who were cremated were of a lower class, and laymen. The pottery buried with adults in the graves (not cremated) was left whole and not broken or "killed" in the manner to be described of burials after cremation; . . . (quoted from Turney, 1929, pp. 16–17).

Perhaps Cushing imagined that the burials in compounds and "great houses" were better endowed with luxury mortuary items; and perhaps Matthews got this all secondhand from Cushing and did not really witness the resurrection of articles of a sacerdotal character.

But somehow this all rings true, especially when Fewkes found a similar situation at Casa Grande (Fewkes, 1912, pp. 108–10).

It might be worth while if we take a second look at this evidence since it suggests social stratification, an elite, a "chiefdom" stage of social evolution. Thus the differences in burial customs, burial locations, and more luxurious grave goods suggest that the inhabitants of the compound and of the "great houses" were *different*—not necessarily a different physical type but of a higher rank. This idea seems consonant with what we know of social evolution and with the ideas set forth at the beginning of this chapter. This elite—these non-food-producers, perhaps, were of a higher rank because they controlled the food supplies and had the rights of access to strategic sup-

plies—energy. And hence, they built bigger and better houses for themselves and kept the food producers from associating with them by building compound walls to keep out the lower classes.

Now we come to the much-talked-about Salado Polychromes (Pinto, Gila, and Tonto) that were found exclusively with the inhumations. As a matter of fact, Haury notes that five polychrome pots were found with cremations, and five Hohokam red-on-buff pots with burials.

It has been held (Haury, 1945, p. 63) that the Salado polychromes originated to the northeast, in the region between the Mogollon Rim and the Little Colorado River, and that they were introduced to the Hohokam area by the Saladoan invaders.

As a matter of fact, no one knows where this polychrome pottery originated or if it had an area of dispersal. We do know that like St. Johns Polychrome, it was popular all over the Southwest, was traded even down to northern Mexico, and may have been made in hundreds of kilns in many sites and the general design style copied by many potters. It seems fantastically strange to imagine that it was made in one place only. It probably represents a type that for the elite of Los Muertos was functionally different and that the "upper class" reserved to themselves the privilege of using for some particular purpose.

XVIII   Abandonment

From the time of Christ to about A.D. 1100 populations were growing and expanding all over Arizona. Previously unoccupied areas of the state were colonized; within both old and new regions settlements became more dense, and these settlements grew larger. By about A.D. 1000 it was probably possible to cross the state in just about any direction without being more than a few miles or a few dozen miles from a settlement. In the Upper Little Colorado area for example, major clusters of sites occurred every five to fifteen miles. Within these regional clusters, local clusters occurred every few miles, and within the local clusters sites were a few hundred yards to a mile or so apart. Undoubtedly, some areas of the state (e.g., the south-central and southwestern portions) were still thinly populated. But this was not true over most of the state; settlement was more continuous than it is at present.

In most areas of the state, or at least most areas of the Colorado Plateau where the best demographic data have been collected, there was a decline in population at about A.D. 700. This apparent decline may prove to represent a period of increasingly great seasonal movement. In any case, population began to increase between A.D. 850 and 1050 and grew by factors of four to forty during the succeeding one hundred to two hundred years. During the next one to two hundred years vast areas of the state were abandoned and people and settlements were more sparsely distributed everywhere.

This is the phenomenon that archaeologists call the abandonment. It seems to have occurred all over the Southwest in much the same pattern as in Arizona. Most of the information that archaeologists have collected concerning abandonments comes from the Colorado Plateau. It is clear that population movements and rapid increases and decreases in growth occurred elsewhere in the state. But many of the inferences about such phenomena in other portions of Arizona are based upon very shaky evidence. Moreover, the extent of abandonment may have been somewhat greater in this area. Therefore, our discussion will focus principally on the plateau and the Anasazi groups that lived there.

There are at least three kinds of evidence of abandonment that archaeologists work with. The first consists of changing distributions of cultural units.

Figures 42 and 42a are maps of the distribution of cultures in Arizona at about A.D. 1125 and 1500. The area inhabited by the Anasazi shrank from the whole northern quarter of the state to a small territory in the vicinity of the modern Hopi villages. Hohokam groups that had been widely distributed in the Gila, Salt, Verde, and Santa Cruz drainages became restricted within the Gila and Salt River Valleys between the mouth of the Verde, the Gila-Salt confluence, and the Gila-San Pedro confluence. There were still settlements in the Hakataya and Mogollon regions at A.D. 1500, but these were few in number and discontinuously distributed. The hatched area in Figure 42

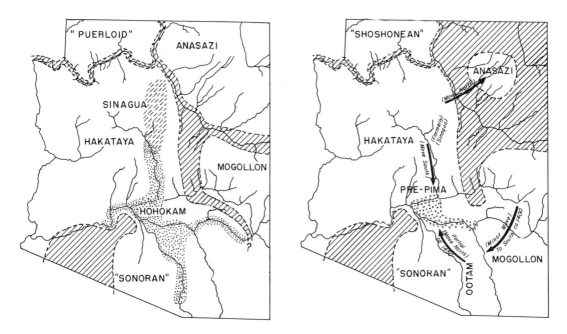

FIGURE 42 The distribution of cultures in Arizona in A.D. 1500. The two maps show the pattern of abandonment that occurred over this 400-year period. Undoubtedly, there were scattered populations all over the state, but the major centers were now restricted to the Hopi mesas and the Gila and Salt river Valleys. After Albert E. Schroeder, 1962. By permission of Albert E. Schroeder.

surrounding the Hopi mesas is an area that was more or less completely abandoned by sedentary populations. If there were humans in this area in any substantial number, they were nomadic groups that left little or no record of their presence.

John C. McGregor has plotted the terminal dates for dated sites that were occupied between A.D. 400 and 1500 (1965). He argues that the terminal date is an indication of when the site was abandoned. Between A.D. 600 and 1500 the number of sites abandoned during fifty-year time blocs was relatively constant except between A.D. 1000 and 1150 and between A.D. 1250 and 1350. One could argue that this pattern simply reflects the greater number of sites that existed in late prehistoric times. Such an argument would not explain why sites weren't abandoned between A.D. 1150 and 1250. And,

since population was generally greater in later settlements than in earlier ones, these periods represent very substantial population shifts.

Stephen Plog (1969) employed variation in the number of dwelling units on dated sites to construct population growth curves for selected regions in the Anasazi region. The evidence in these regions is summarized below. It shows that populations began to increase over the Plateau between A.D. 850 and 1050. Population peaks were reached a few hundred years later, and all regions but the Hopi were abandoned in another few hundred years.

These, then, are the basic data on the basis of which abandonments are inferred. Most of the concepts that we will use in interpreting these data are taken from the works of Hill (1970), Jett (1964), and

REGION	BEGINS	PEAKS	DE-CLINES	ABAN-DONED
Chaco	900	1000	1000	1150
Mesa Verde	900	1250	1250	1325
Flagstaff	1050	1100	1100	1325
Houck	1000	1050	1050	1150
Jeddito (Hopi)	1250	1400	1500	1700
Tsegi	950	1250	1250	1325
Canyon de Chelly	1000	1200	1200	1325
Upper Little Colorado	850	1200	1200	1500
White Mountain	1050	1200	1300	1450

TABLE 15 Summary of demographic events in different areas of northern Arizona and the adjacent southwest. For each area, the table shows when rapid population growth began, when it reached a peak, when it began to decline, and when abandonment occurred. It is clear that only the Hopi area which was not finally abandoned reached any kind of population equilibrium. (After S. Plog, 1969)

S. Plog (1969). Before we begin to consider some of the hypotheses that have been offered to account for abandonment, we must point out one very grave weakness in the data and inferences that archaeologists have been using and that we will have to use: we de not know precisely what kind of population change the abandonments reflect. Jett, for example, assumes that the basic behavior represented in the abandonments was migration—the population decline in a particular area is interpreted as a migration of families from the area. But there are other possibilities. Populations might have remained in the areas but decreased in number as a result of rapidly increasing death rates or rapidly decreasing birth rates. Or, the great towns that began to appear just prior to or during the period of abandonment may have been large enough to have absorbed the population of the many smaller settlements that previously existed in the area that was being "abandoned."

Unfortunately, we cannot now say which of these demographic processes or which combination of processes was in fact operative. Archaeologists became interested in "explaining" abandonments and did not stop long enough to characterize accurately the nature of the variability that they were trying to explain. Are we observing variability in birth rates? in death rates? in aggregation? in mobility? While evidence that would permit us to distinguish between these different demographic processes does exist in the archaeological record, it has been either not collected or not analyzed.

For example, careful analyses of patterns of longevity in burial populations would throw considerable light on the problem. Similarly, archaeologists and physical anthropologists specializing in paleopathology can determine what kinds of diseases or nutritional stresses prehistoric populations were subject to. We could determine whether the young or old were dying in equal or different proportions and what they were dying from.

One of the most difficult problems is determining whether the group in question remained in an area or moved from it. This issue has generally been resolved by referring to the spread or movement of pottery types or other cultural traits. It was simply assumed that if the traits moved, people must have been moving too. Unfortunately, we now know that this assumption is not a viable one; objects are traded and copied as well as carried to new areas.

S. Plog has begun to analyze migrations using demographic rather than stylistic data. After plotting the curves of population growth discussed earlier (and demonstrating that these correlated significantly with curves constructed on somewhat more subjective bases by archaeologists working in the areas), Plog used correlation coefficients to estimate the probability that population was actually moving between two regions. He reasoned that population flow from A to B would be indicated if population was rapidly declining in A and rapidly increasing in B. This pattern would be shown by a negative correlation between population growth curves in the same area. Of course, if the flow were equal in both directions, the population of the two areas would vary together. And the increases and decreases in the areas could be independent of each other. But if the substantial migrations that archaeologists have inferred in fact occurred, and since the inferred migrations have always been unidirectional, some evidence should be reflected in the demographic data.

Plog found that only four movements were indicated for the entire period between A.D. 300 and 1700. These movements were from the Tsegi, Canyon de Chelly, Mesa Verde, and Upper Little Colorado regions to the Hopi mesas between A.D. 1250 and 1350. (It is of course possible that movements to the Zuni and Rio Grande pueblos would be indicated if population curves had been available for these regions.) Of all of the various movements that archaeologists have inferred, only these find even minimal support in the demographic data.

Plog next used a gravity model to estimate the magnitude of the movements that might have occurred. Such models are based upon the observation that the movement of people or things between two regions is directly proportional to the pop-

ulation of the regions and inversely proportional to the distance between them. The best estimate that can be derived from this model is that between twenty and fifty families moved from each of these regions into the Hopi region. About half of the population of the Tsegi, Mesa Verde, and Canyon de Chelly regions and about a third of the population of the Upper Little Colorado may have moved to the Hopi mesas.

Plog's inferences are consistent with some of the more intuitive arguments that archaeologists have made in the past. The inhabitants of the Flagstaff region are supposed to have moved to the south. Plog's data indicate no correlation between population curves in the Hopi and Flagstaff regions. Similarly, populations in the Houck and Chaco regions are supposed to have moved to Zuni or the Rio Grande pueblos. Archaeologists have argued that the populations of the Upper Little Colorado and White Mountains moved to Zuni, to the Hopi region, and southward into the Salt River Valley. Plog's analysis suggests that only some of the population of these regions went to the Hopi mesas. Nevertheless, the analysis indicates that substantial portions of the population in these areas prior to the beginning of abandonment remained in them and died or moved to regions other than the Hopi mesas. Plog's inferences are remarkably consistent with the evidence of migration inferred from stylistic data. But, they show that there were probably far fewer migrations than have been postulated. The techniques that Plog used and the data that were available to him were not ideal. But his analysis represents a direction in which archaeologists must go if they are to understand the nature of the demographic variability that they have lumped under the all-inclusive concept of abandonment.

SOME HYPOTHESES

Remembering that archaeologists cannot precisely characterize the variability that they are trying to explain, let us examine some of the hypotheses that have been offered to account for the occurrence of abandonment. Climate and Athapaskan raiders are probably the most common causes of abandonment discussed.

Abandonments have been associated with three different climatic changes: drought, erosion, and shifts in the seasonal rainfall pattern. The evidence for drought is largely dendroclimatological. Between A.D. 1215 and 1299 in general, and especially between A.D. 1276 and 1299, pine trees in some areas of the plateau were forming very narrow rings. A number of archaeologists have argued that these rings are associated with drought conditions. They argue that the Anasazi were driven from the plateau by drought conditions that made the continued practice of agriculture impossible.

This argument has been challenged on a number of grounds. First, tree rings are better indicators of winter moisture than summer moisture. Even if drought was occurring during the winter months, there would be no necessary indication of summer drought. Moreover, many of the areas that were abandoned have in historic times been somewhat less drought-prone than areas that weren't. For example, the Navajo Monument area was abandoned by populations that moved to the Hopi mesas. Yet, parts of this area are less likely to have droughts than the Hopi area. In addition, the dates of the abandonment and the dates of occurrences of the postulated drought do not correspond closely. Abandonments in some areas came two hundred years before the drought.

A similar argument focuses on the possible role of erosion in the abandonments. Proponents of this approach argue that populations inhabiting the plateau area at the time of the abandonments relied heavily on floodwater farming. Arroyo cutting would have had a disastrous effect on this kind of farming: the spring floods that watered the valley would have been contained within deeper watercourses, topsoil would have been lost, and the water table would have been lowered. Even irrigation farming would have become more difficult as watercourses became deeper and more steepsided. The erosion might have resulted from a climatic shift, from the overuse of valley bottomlands by farmers, or from cutting trees on the slopes above the valleys. Indeed, there is evidence of arroyo cutting in Chaco Canyon at about the time it was abandoned, and pollen data indicate that once substantial pine forests had been all but eliminated from the mesa tops above the canyon. Erosion channels have also been observed in the Hopi region dating to Pueblo II and IV times, in Tsegi Canyon at Pueblo II, and in the Navajo Mountain region at A.D. 1150 or 1225–1300. Evidence of an erosional cycle on the plateau is present by A.D. 1100, and the erosion seems to have been worst during the 1200s.

This argument has been criticized for a number of reasons. Erosion, some investigators have argued, was not a phenomenon that affected whole valleys at a single point in time. It proceeded upstream, and soil was cut from an upstream source and deposited at some point lower in the valley. (This must have been small comfort to those populations living in areas that were being cut!) Areas where erosion occurred do not always contain evidence of heavy population. There is no evidence that the areas that were eroded are ones that supported a large population and extensive farming. Moreover, erosion occurred in some areas that weren't abandoned (e.g., the Hopi mesas) and didn't occur in other areas that were (e.g., Canyon de Chelly). Finally, this argument fails to take into account the fact that populations just prior to the period of abandonment were employing a wide range of soil and water conservation devices.

Many of the most recent arguments for a primary role for climatic causality are based upon pollen data. The period when tree rings became narrow corresponds to one when cheno-am pollen was being deposited with increasing intensity and arboreal pollens were in a corresponding decline. These changes in the pollen record suggest a period of substantial sediment disturbance. A variety of investigators have argued that decreasing effective moisture and an increasingly strong tendency for precipitation in the form of summer thunderstorms would have produced soil disturbances in general and erosion in particular. The rainfall during the period of the year just prior to and during the planting of crops would have been minimal. Such a shift of rainfall to the summer months might easily have produced the pattern of winter drought that is recorded in the tree rings. And it would also have produced the widespread erosion that the geologist observes. Thus this argument is the most economical of the climatic ones. Pollen records seem to show two periods of disturbance at about A.D. 1100 and 1300 that correspond rather closely to the periods of abandonment. Although these data are not available from many areas of the plateau, they seem to suggest that the phenomenon is widespread. There is no basis for concluding, at least at the moment, that areas that weren't abandoned were less affected by this climatic shift.

The majority of archaeologists who reject climatic causality focus on the movement of new populations into Arizona at approximately the time that abandonments were occurring. The Apache and Navajo were relative newcomers to Arizona; they were the last new populations to enter the state before white men came. They are different from other Indian groups with respect to a variety of characteristics, the most important of which is language. The languages spoken by these two populations are most common in areas far to the north of Arizona. The Navajo and Apache evidently migrated from these areas. Languages change at definable rates, and the differences that do exist between the languages of the Apache and Navajo and those spoken in the source areas indicate that the groups began to move southward toward Arizona at about A.D. 825 and 1100 respectively.

A number of the changes associated with abandonments of particular areas suggest that the movement of these new populations into the state may have involved fighting and raiding. It is then argued that the fighting and raiding led to abandonments. What is this evidence?

In the first place, most of the population movements or migrations that archaeologsts have inferred are to the south, west, or east, but rarely to the north. On the Colorado Plateau the trend of the inferred population movements is generally to the south, and pueblo populations are believed to have moved into southern Arizona, extreme southern New Mexico, western Texas, and northern Chihuahua at about this time. Sinagua populations moved into the Salt River Valley.

A good deal of the arguments concerning invasions and reactions to them have revolved around the concept of defensive sites. No one can climb down a ladder into Balcony House at Mesa Verde National Park and then squeeze out through the narrow exit without feeling that the inhabitants of this site didn't want to be noticed and wanted to be able to exclude unwelcome visitors. Casa Malapais near Springerville, Arizona, is a similar case. With miles and miles of rich valley bottomland and gentle hills and terraces to choose from, the prehistoric inhabitants of this area chose to build their site on the side of a mesa. And, of all of the miles and miles of mesa side that they had to choose from, they chose a spot where a village could be built and crops planted that would be invisible from the valley below and visible from only a few spots on the mesa above. There are other such sites in the Upper Little Colorado, and all over the plateau.

Were they defensive sites? Intuitively, they certainly convey the impression of having been such. But intuition has no boundaries. Cliff dwellings, large aggregated villages, sites on mesa tops, sites that cannot be seen from above or below, and sites with a substantial view of the surrounding area all had advantages for defense. But these locations and village patterns could be associated with entirely different causes. What most archaeologists seem to have in mind when they speak of defensive sites are sites that were difficult to see and difficult to gain access to but which commanded a substantial view of the surrounding area. It has not yet been demonstrated that sites with these attributes were built exclusively or primarily during the abandonment period. A systematic analysis of the relevant data might, however, prove this to be the case.

A number of other site attributes are associated with defense. At about this time period on the northern edge of the plateau, sites that were essentially towers were constructed. Again, a tower is a kind of site with restricted access and a substantial view of the surrounding territory. Sites of this time period are said to have had narrow entranceways or entrances from the roof that would have required ladders. Some archaeologists argue that many doors and windows were filled in. A systematic analysis of the data might show that tower sites, roof entrances, walled-in doors and windows, and narrow entrances have a strong nonrandom association with the period of abandonment, but such an analysis has yet to be done.

Similarly, some archaeologists argue that burned buildings, burned bodies, unburied bodies, and skeletons that show signs of violent death are associated with the abandonment period. Such arguments frequently cite evidence from the Rosa and Largo-Gallina phases in northwestern New Mexico. Rosa phase pit houses are said to closely resemble Navajo hogans. Largo-Gallina houses contained pottery that is very similar to that made by the Navajo (some archaeologists agree and some strongly disagree with this interpretation). Most Largo-Gallina sites were burned and skeletons with crushed skulls were recovered from them. Again, these data are impressive. But a clear and nonrandom association between burned sites and violent deaths and the period of abandonment has not been demonstrated. All of these different indicators of defensiveness and warfare are appealing. But the proponents of this argument must precisely define the attributes of defensiveness and clearly demonstrate that they are associated with the period of abandonments. To date they have not done so.

There is another major difficulty, however, with the invasion hypothesis. Whatever the linguistic evidence indicates, archaeologists find no direct evidence of the presence of Athabaskan populations in Arizona or the Southwest until A.D. 1390–

1500. Evidence that such groups were present is not substantial until the 1600s. Moreover, there is both prehistoric and ethnohistoric evidence suggesting that the Pueblo and Navajo were, at least some of the time, on friendly terms. Navajo hogans occurred in association with Pueblo tower sites. The Pueblo and Navajo traded with each other and in some times of trouble took refuge with each other.

Furthermore, even if all of the evidence of defensiveness were acceptable, it would remain to be proven that the defenses were built against Athapaskans. The Pueblo did fight among themselves. Turner and Morris have recently described a skeletal population from Polacca Wash ten miles south of the Hopi villages. "Thirty Hopi Indians of both sexes and all ages were killed, crudely dismembered, violently mutilated, and probably cannibalized about 370 years ago" (Turner and Morris, 1970). The date of this massacre and other of its details correspond closely with legendary accounts of the destruction of the prehistoric village of Awatovi by Hopi from other villages. And there are many other accounts of intra-Pueblo warfare.

A variety of other explanations have been offered for abandonment. There was a period during which temperatures were lower than normal and the growing season too short for crop-raising. Disease and epidemics were widespread. (This argument is appealing in that populations experiencing a dietary change and aggregation might well have experienced nutritional and other health stresses. Paleopathological data are not so good as to allow a careful evaluation of this argument.) Wild game animals were overhunted. Soil was depleted or became too alkaline. None of these arguments has received the support of the others just discussed.

ETHNOHISTORIC DATA

Archaeologists sometimes express the opinion that they would be far more capable of interpreting and explaining prehistoric events if they had written records. In the case of abandonments what records do exist do not make the picture any clearer. J. Charles Kelley has described the abandonment of Pueblo settlements in the lower Rio Grande and Rio Conchos River Valleys (1952). His reconstruction of the abandonments is in part based on archaeological evidence and in part on historic Spanish documents. That reconstruction is as follows.

At about A.D. 1000 Pueblo populations began to expand southward in the Rio Grande Valley toward the Rio Conchos area. They occupied lands that were marginal for agriculture but were usable as a result of increased rainfall. A symbiotic relationship developed between the Pueblo groups and adjacent nomadic groups in which the agricultural products of the former were exchanged for hunted products of the latter. Shortly thereafter, precipitation began to decrease, threatening both the viability of farming and the symbiotic relationship with the nomads. The situation was further complicated by the movement of new nomadic populations, the Jumano and Cibola, into the area from the plains to the east. By about A.D. 1400 the few communities that remained were in areas where soil was richer and water more plentiful. Symbiotic relationships continued between these communities and the Jumano and Cibola. When rainfall conditions improved, some of the marginal areas were reclaimed; new communities were founded in them.

In the late eighteenth century, the Jumano and Cibola were conquered and became a part of the Apache. Populations identified as Apache moved into the Rio Conchos area at about the same time that another cycle of adverse climatic conditions began. Again, both agricultural and symbiotic relations were upset, leading to the abandonment of communities in more marginal locations.

It seems likely that the movement of nomadic populations into the area was itself a product of deteriorating climatic conditions on the plains. Both marginal nomadic and marginal sedentary populations faced subsistence threats that led to a deterioration of the relations between them and to conflict. The records that Kelley examined indicated that the inhabitants of abandoned settlement always cited the threat of the Apache as the reason for abandonment. But their ability to cite specific incidents was poor. It was also clear that the villages that were abandoned were in marginal areas relative to those that were not.

Kelley's work indicates the difficulty of interpreting the data even when they are more complete. Nomadic and sedentary populations do not necessarily fight with each other, but under certain conditions they do. Informants may identify the Apache as the reason for abandonment when other causes can be inferred from the pattern of abandonment itself. Kelley's analysis does not resolve the problem; it suggests that we are dealing with a multicausal relationship. And it seems likely that the same would be true in other instances (Galisteo, Pecos, Gran Quivira) where the influence of the Apache on abandonment is a matter of record.

SOME ALTERNATIVE HYPOTHESES

While all of the arguments discussed in the preceding pages add rich detail to our understanding of the context in which abandonments occurred, they are not and do not point in the direction of explanations. They embody no stated regularities that render this event or any class of events predictable. There are many instances of drought that are not accompanied by abandonment, and many instances of abandonment that aren't associated with drought. There are many instances in which abandonments occurred with invasions and many instances in which invasions occurred without abandonments. Over the course of human prehistory and history, there is no necessary connection between these events.

Perhaps we can begin to formulate an explanation by returning to some of the basic facts that archaeologists have learned about this period of abandonment. First, the situation is one in which a rapid period of population increase was followed by a rapid period of decline. In most areas population reached a peak that lasted for a very short period of time. The absence of a plateau at the population maximum in these curves is important: it implies that an equilibrium of population was not reached in these areas prior to abandonment. Population was in the process of reaching an equilibrium point or had exceeded it, and when the correction began, the reaction was too extreme. Those areas that did achieve a stable equilibrium or at least fluctuation around the population maximum are the ones that were inhabited until A.D. 1500 or later. Returning to Table 16, the regions that show essentially no equilibria were on the average abandoned within 125 years of the beginning of the decline. In areas where an equilibrium was maintained for a hundred years or more, populations survived for an average of three hundred years. Abandonment did not occur in the context of a stable situation in which something went wrong. Populations on the plateau were in the midst of a major change. And those areas that came closest to achieving a new equilibrium were the ones where population survived, at least for a few hundred more years.

A second important aspect of abandonment is the fact that small sites were abandoned first. Larger sites were founded and received population from smaller ones, and sites in certain locations grew into large ones during a short period of time. Aggregation was occurring concurrently with abandonment.

Aggregation may have involved a good deal more than people coming together. The larger sites into which populations moved may have had very different kinds of organization from those that were abandoned. Recall (from chapter XV) that the localization principle operative at Carter Ranch and Broken K was far weaker at the latter site than the former. Grasshopper pueblo, a few dozen miles to the southwest of Carter Ranch and Broken K, was occupied later than these sites. Clark's (1969) analysis of the burial population there indicated that a high status group was associated with the kiva. And while Clark found no evidence of redistribution at Grasshopper, many of the late great kivas in the Upper Little Colorado are surrounded by rows of rooms that, typologically, are storage rooms. These kivas may have been redistributive centers. In any case, there are indications of organizational change as well as demographic change at the time of the abandonments.

Finally, there is evidence of significant disruptions in the natural and social environments of the populations living at this time. Tree-ring, geomorphic, and pollen data all indicate that climatic conditions were not ideal for the practice of agriculture in many areas and during many years between A.D. 1100 and 1300. Further difficulties resulted from the movement of new populations into the area and possible conflict between established ones. While we doubt that any one of these disturbances can be uniquely associated with abandonment, there seems to us little reason to doubt that the abandonments occurred in the context of substantial environmental disturbance.

It is possible to formulate an explanation that involves law-like statements and accounts for these basic facts. It is not possible to offer an adequate test of the hypotheses and will not be for a substantial number of years—until many new and different kinds of data are collected from Arizona and other parts of the Southwest. We are stretching data and speculating. But we regard our formulations as hypotheses and will present test implications for evaluating these hypotheses.

1. If a population is expanding in a fine-grained environment, then increasingly marginal areas will be occupied. By A.D. 1100 the practice of agriculture was well established on the Colorado Plateau. Those areas that were ideal for the practice of this subsistence technique were filled with people. Undoubtedly, agriculture had been tried in other situations, but the normal operation of selective pressures resulted in the concentration of population in those areas that were best suited to agriculture.

The entire Southwest is a region that is relatively marginal for the practice of agriculture. And ideal areas are a very scarce resource. When populations began to grow, and groups budded off from parent pueblos, the new communities were founded in localities that were less practical for farming than the ones in which the parent pueblos were located. The newly populated areas were marginal with respect to some combination of soil quality, rainfall, the abundance of surface water, and temperature. In Hay Hollow Valley, Zubrow (1969, 1970, 1971), has shown that population growth involved the founding of new communities and that these new communities were in increasingly marginal locations. The greater the population expansion, the greater the marginality of the areas that were being colonized. Less marginal areas were filled with populations before more marginal areas were.

If this argument is accurate, then population growth up to A.D. 1100 should have involved (1) the founding of new communities at a rate equal to or greater than the growth of population in existing ones; and (2) the use of increasingly more marginal areas as population growth continued.

2. Marginal populations adopt innovations at a more rapid rate than nonmarginal ones. This idea is not a new one. A host of social scientists over the last several decades have argued that innovation and evolutionary progress tend to occur among marginal populations. In nonmarginal areas where there is a successful and ongoing subsistence and organizational strategy, selective pressures tend to favor the further development of the existing system. If a population has survived by planting corn in a certain way in a certain kind of location at a certain time of the year, that practice will spread and be reinforced. Those individuals and communities that follow the practice will be more successful and have a higher rate of survival than those that don't. These processes operate today and they operated in prehistory.

When populations moved into marginal areas the situation changed. In the first place, a new set of selective pressures in the form of new natural and social environmental conditions were introduced. Furthermore, behavioral variety in the populations increased as the pre-existing reinforcement devices were removed and as the new communities attempted to meet the changed conditions in different ways. With greater variety and new selective pressures, the adoption of innovations was likely. Thus, in the Upper Little Colorado water and soil control devices—ditches, terraces, and grids—were adopted in marginal areas such as Hay Hollow Valley two to three hundred years before they were adopted in nonmarginal ones such as the valley of the Little Colorado proper. Water and soil control devices would provide an excellent test of this idea. If the argument is valid, then in other parts of Arizona water and soil control devices would have been adopted in marginal areas before nonmarginal ones.

3. Under stress, differences in available resources (standard of living) between marginal and nonmarginal areas will increase. Innovations such as ditches, terraces, and grids were productive in both marginal and nonmarginal environments. They were not initially adopted in nonmarginal environments because there was no need for them. But given that they had been adopted by nearby populations and adapted for use in the region in question, they were adopted by nonmarginal groups. When they were combined with the more productive natural resources in these areas, more products resulted and the gap between the marginal and nonmarginal areas increased. If this argument is valid, population should have continued to grow in parent communities and areas at a rate faster than that in daughter communities and areas.

4. If it is to survive, a population must be characterized by at least as much variety as that in the environment to which it was adapting. The statement is called the Law of Requisites Variety. It suggests that populations living in situations where critical environmental variables are either spatially or temporally varied must be capable of adjusting their organization and/or their subsistence practices to meet these exigencies. Populations in less variable environ-

ments are organizationally and nutritionally less diverse.

Perhaps the import of this law can be made clear by contrasting two different techniques of doing agriculture that were employed in the prehistoric Southwest. Some prehistoric populations employed canals, terraces, and grid systems in practicing agriculture. There is no doubt that the use of these techniques improved the productivity of the land.

The Hopi were probably never significantly reliant upon large-scale agricultural technologies. Modern Hopi live between an area that is in some years too cold for crops to grow but is quite wet and another that frequently too dry for crops to grow but is always warm enough. Hopi fields for any given village are spread out over an area of twenty-five or more miles north and south of the villages. Fields to the north are in the colder and wetter zone and those to the south in the warmer and drier one. Most growing seasons in the Hopi region are either warm and dry or cold and wet. It is difficult to predict what a given growing season will look like and within any ten-year period both kinds of seasons will occur. But whether the season is warm and dry or cold and wet, some crops will grow. If the year is a warm dry one, crops in downstream areas may receive insufficient rainfall to grow, but with higher temperatures in upland areas and some rainfall there, these crops will mature. In a cool wet year, the growing season will not be long enough for crops planted in the upland areas to mature. But the increased moisture reaches the lowland areas and these crops grow. Similarly, along the drainages, the Hopi plant some crops in the stream channels and some on terraces. If only a little water flows in these streams, the crops in the channel itself are watered. If a lot flows, plants in the channel may be washed away, but those on the terraces will be well watered.

This system which is suggested by modern Hopi practices is far more sensitive to environmental conditions like those that exist on the plateau than one based on irrigation. You can't move a canal to catch the rainwater. And hundreds of acres of irrigated land or terraces built either in the upland or lowland areas would fail to produce successful crops in some years. Thus, a system like that suggested by the Hopi would have been far more adaptive given the environmental variability that existed at the time of abandonments than one based on irrigation or terrace agriculture. It is more varied and would have more successfully met the demands of a variable environment.

Requisite variety can be discussed in terms of organization as well as subsistence strategy. For example, the residents of some Rio Grande pueblos are divided into two groups or moieties—the Summer moiety and the Winter moiety. Today, the members of the Summer moiety are principally interested in or concerned with agriculture and the members of the Winter moiety with hunting and gathering (Dozier, personal communication). There is some suggestion in the traditions of these people that at some point in the past there was a real division of economic activities between the moieties following the same lines as the modern "interests." This kind of organization that brings together two cooperating groups, one specializing in hunting-gathering and one specializing in agriculture, would be very advantageous in a situation where agriculture is somewhat tenuous.

A redistributional system uniting upland and lowland communities would have a similar effect. In years when the crops in one area failed, some claim could be made on the produce of the other areas. This is

329

why the evidence that great kivas may have served as storage centers is important.

Given that northern Arizona is a marginal area for agriculture and critical variables do vary substantially in both time and space, selective pressures should favor subsistence and organizational strategies that are sensitive to variety. If this argument is correct, archaeologists should find evidence that those areas that were not abandoned had such strategies as opposed to those areas that were abandoned.

5. Population tends to flow from marginal to nonmarginal areas. This hypothesis was developed and used in explaining the behavior of populations in the modern world by Gunnar Myrdal. He was able to show that in the case of economic development in the modern world population tends to flow from less developed to more developed regions. The "tends" is important. Population flows may not actually occur if the nonmarginal areas create institutions for staving off the flow. Our immigration barriers are a device that limit the flow of population from developing nations to the United States. Aid to depressed areas within the United States has the effect of raising the standard of living in these areas and slowing the flow of population to urban areas.

It seems more than mildly contradictory to have argued a few pages ago that population was expanding into marginal areas and now to say that it tends to flow to nonmarginal ones. There is no contradiction, however. It was observed earlier that the movement to marginal areas occurred only when nonmarginal areas were filled up and even then it was to the least marginal areas. The hypothesis that we have now offered simply suggests that this was not necessarily a happy state of affairs, that those groups living in marginal areas would have "preferred" to be in nonmarginal areas where subsistence was easier and more secure and

the standard of living was probably higher. When for one reason or another space became available in a nonmarginal area, population tended to flow back into it. This might have happened, for example, when the application of irrigation increased carrying capacity.

There may have been institutions in prehistoric Arizona that did act to retard the flow of population to nonmarginal areas. Redistribution or some other exchange arrangement between mother and daughter communities might have allowed the daughter community to claim some portion of the produce of the parent community in years when conditions for agriculture were adverse in marginal areas. It may have required the sacrifice of some subsistence resources on the part of the parent community to make the population budding system work, to keep daughter communities in the marginal areas. If this were so, we should find that the great kivas served as redistributive centers and we should find other evidence of exchange networks that linked parent and daughter communities.

There were instances in which population does seem to have moved during the period of abandonment, and in these instances archaeologists should find evidence that the flow was from marginal to nonmarginal areas. For example, a good deal of evidence suggests that migrations did occur into the Hopi region. Can we argue that this was a nonmarginal area? S. Plog (1969) has summarized a number of ways in which the natural environment of this region is more suitable to the practice of agriculture than any other part of the Colorado Plateau. Floods that cover valley floors are frequent in this region. The prevailing winds pile sand carried by the streams against the mesa sides. Sand is very water-retentive and the dune fields along the mesas have been an important farming locus. Sand also allows for better soil drainage and retards arroyo cutting. It also serves as an intake for water that later flows out in springs. Because of this and other geological peculiarities, the region has many springs. We have already argued that the subsistence strategy employed in this region was a superior one. Thus, it may have been nonmarginal in more than one way. Similarly, the advantage of the Rio Grande region may have been both the natural potential and the particular form of organization that evolved there. Evaluated over any consistent set of productive criteria, archaeologists should find that the communities and regions into which population flowed were nonmarginal ones.

Now, let us switch tracks for a moment. An important assumption has underlain all of our arguments—the assumption that environmental stresses were present at the time of abandonments. We discussed earlier some of the major changes in environmental variables that archaeologists have inferred and then argued were causes of abandonments. Now we want to suggest that it is probably unnecessary to search for major environmental disruptions.

6. Any given environmental variation will have a greater effect on marginal than on nonmarginal areas. Factors that are no more than normal variance in a secure environment may constitute major stresses in a marginal one. If rainfall was barely sufficient to grow crops in the average year, an only slightly less-than-average precipitation record may have caused crops to fail. Where soil was not good to begin with and surface waters carried few mineral nutrients, soil depletion may have occurred rapidly even though farming was neither more intensive or extensive than in nonmarginal areas. When little topsoil was present to begin with, very slight erosion may have removed it. Even if environmental conditions

had not changed one whit from A.D. 1100 to 1300, crises could have resulted from the use of areas that were not really appropriate to agriculture.

7. When organizational or subsistence ties are maintained between communities in marginal and nonmarginal areas, a stress situation in one area will create stresses in the other. Human cultural systems are not closed; substantial quantities of matter, energy, and information cross their boundaries. To the extent that these flows are significant between two systems, events in one will affect events in the other. To the extent that organizational or subsistence ties were important between prehistoric communities or populations, the events that affected one affected the other.

Populations that underwent subsistence stresses did not simply sit around and die, they sought to make up the deficiencies in the availability of resources that they suffered. In some instances, this meant a return to heavy reliance on hunting and gathering. But it also meant pressures on whatever exchange channels existed between marginal and source populations. If redistributive systems existed, the marginal populations would have called for a redistribution of food resources to make up their deficit. If trade occurred between populations, they would have brought increasingly great quantities of hunted and gathered products to the agricultural communities to trade. If these demands exceeded the productive capacity of the agricultural communities, they too would have been placed in a stress situation

If demands by marginal populations could not be met by peaceful interaction, they probably turned to more violent forms. F. W. Hodge (cited in Jett, 1964) has argued that at about A.D. 1550 there were nineteen "Navajo" clans. Only four of these were clearly Athabaskan groups. Two were

Yuman, five Puebloan, one Shoshonean, one Ute, and six unknown. This is not to deny that Athabaskan populations moved into the Southwest. It simply suggests that the nomadic populations lumped under the term Navajo may have included both originally nomadic groups and ones that turned to wandering because sedentary agriculture was no longer possible.

A parallel situation existed on the northern frontier of Meso-America. The Chichimecs, responsible for the establishment of the Aztec empire, were originally thought to be wandering "barbarians." But recent investigations have shown that the term included a great variety of groups that lived on the Meso-American frontier: wandering nomads, indigenous agriculturalists, indigenous part-time agriculturalists, colonial groups who moved from the valley of Mexico to the frontier area to practice agriculture, and colonial populations that became semisedentary under stress conditions. Armillas has argued (1969) that between A.D. 1300 and 1500 the frontier zone north of the valley of Mexico was subject to environmental stresses similar to those experienced in Arizona. This led to a contraction of the frontier of "civilized agriculturalists" and the movement of all of the groups called Chichimecs southward toward the valley of Mexico.

Raiding and strife do seem to have occurred concurrently with the abandonments. It seems pointless to argue as to whether the strife represents an invasion or internal warfare. All of the ethnohistorical evidence available to us indicates that the Athabaskan populations moving into the Southwest did not come spear in hand and already at war. These populations were probably joined by sedentary agriculturalists who found the practice of agriculture impossible, and the pattern of raiding was a response to subsistence stress.

A final stress would have resulted from the increasing failure of population-budding to maintain an equilibruim situation. If marginal agriculturalists were not surviving, populations would have been increasingly unwilling to move into marginal areas. Population would have grown in the source areas, possibly to a point where carrying capacity was taxed.

If these arguments are valid, then periods of stress in marginal areas should be followed by increases in evidence of nomadism, raiding, and subsistence stress in source areas. Additional evidence will be found suggesting that "Athabaskan raiders" were an amalgam of legitimate nomads and marginal agriculturalists.

The series of events that led to the abandonment of vast areas of the Colorado Plateau may be summarized as follows. At about A.D. 900 population began to grow rapidly all over the plateau. (Although we have not attempted it, this event in itself clearly demands an explanation.) The population increase was handled by budding— as existing communities became larger, groups moved from them and established new communities in nearby areas. These areas, however, were marginal ones; agriculture had proven less successful there than in the areas that were now densely populated.

Agriculture in fact proved more difficult in these daughter communities. In attempting to establish and equilibrium, the populations adopted technologically complex forms of agriculture. In order to maintain the population budding system, to insure the survival of daughter communities, redistributive links were created with communities in parent areas.

However, marginal areas *were* marginal areas. And, as population continued to grow in the parent areas if not in the less marginal ones, increasingly marginal areas were brought under cultivation. Environmental variability that had insignificant effects on agriculture in parent areas was stressful in marginal ones. Practices that were well within tolerance limits in parent areas were harmful to the environment in marginal ones.

Stress in daughter communities led to stress in parent ones. This stress led to the adoption of technological innovations in parent areas. By increasing productivity, the use of canals and terraces may have temporarily alleviated the problem. But, in the long run differences in the subsistence resources available to marginal and non-marginal populations increased.

These problems were all compounded by the movement of new populations onto the plateau. Moreover, there was a period when rainfall patterns shifted making agriculture more difficult everywhere. Greater stress and ultimately death, population movement, and strife resulted. Population tended to move from marginal to nonmarginal localities within regions and from marginal to less marginal regions. It ended in areas with subsistence or organizational strategies that met the spatial and temporal variability in environmental variables critical to the practice of agriculture more effectively than floodwater farming or even irrigation agriculture. In some instances, the success of the adaptation was primarily a result of a sensitive subsistence strategy—such as that employed by the Hopi. In other cases, organization was more important as in the Rio Grande pueblos where cooperation between agricultural and hunting-gathering specialists was maintained by the moiety system, or at Grasshopper pueblo where ranking systems seemed to be developing.

Again, we recognize that this argument has been a highly speculative one. It seems to cover neatly the events in the Upper Little Colorado, the part of the plateau that we are most familiar with, and fits what we know of events in other areas. We have tried to point to data that fits our explanation. Moreover, we have stated some test implications of our hypotheses so that, if wrong, they may be disproven. In order to prove these arguments wrong, it will be necessary for archaeologists to look at a good deal of data in their respective areas that they have commonly ignored, and to be far more careful in defining terms like "defensive sites." In the process, we should all learn a good deal more about abandonments.

Finally, we apologize for ignoring events below the plateau. Some archaeologists have argued that substantial population shifts and stresses were also characteristic there. But good data concerning these events are very limited and to have treated them in the same fashion that we have dealt with the Anasazi data would have been worse than speculation.

PART EIGHT

SOUTHWESTERN PREHISTORY—
AN EXPLANATION

XIX   A Diffusionist or Migration Model

Notions of diffusion and/or migration of peoples to explain cultural changes by the spread of languages, customs, ideas, cultural elements, inventions, styles, decorative motifs in pottery and basketry, or the radiation or dispersion of peoples who carried their ideas and culture elements with them, is an old, stale, overworked concept. It has fallen into disfavor precisely because it has been employed without discernment or due caution. Indeed, as Harris puts it (Harris, 1968, pp. 373–92) diffusion is a nonprinciple and is incapable of accounting for the origin of a given trait except by "passing the buck" back through an infinite regression.

An early attempt to explain similarities between culture areas resulted in the formation of the German school of anthropologists who called their approach the *Kulturkreise* or Culture Circles. This notion implied that large complexes of traits had spread from six world "centers" and had become global in distribution. Thus, remnants of similar activities such as pyramid-building, mummification, systems of writing, and other configurations of culture traits located in Egypt, Mesopotamia, Meso-America, Oceania, and Europe were "explained" as having diffused from one or more of the culture centers.

The Pan-Egyptian School (about 1910), represented mainly by G. Elliot Smith and W. J. Perry, developed the idea that the whole inventory of world culture had evolved in Egypt and spread from there.

These two examples illustrate the extreme form that diffusion has taken.

A classic example of the judicious use of the concept is Spier's perception of the relationships that existed in the eighteenth and nineteenth centuries between several manifestations of the Sun Dance on the American Plains (Spier, 1921, pp. 451–527). His analysis indicated that the Sun Dance originated among the Arapaho and Cheyenne and was disseminated by them to neighboring tribes, primarily the Crow, the Kiowa, the Sioux, the Blackfoot. His study was wisely limited to diffusion within a natural geographical region—the Great Plains area. He took into account the dynamics of diffusion among the Indians of the area and he used ethnohistory for checking his ideas by comparing the mechanics of diffusion between the Indians inhabiting the Plains. He found that the Sun Dance form spread by means of warfare, trade, and ideas (stimulus diffusion), the latter being the more important. He concluded that symbols were readily diffused between neighboring tribes but were given entirely different meanings. That is, a neighboring tribe would copy a painting or would accept a medicine bundle from the Arapaho, but the functional context and the meanings of these symbols would be utterly different from those of the donor Arapahos. A crude analogy might clarify this kind of shift in meaning. In homes where electricity is available, electric refrigerators are commonly used, but in rural areas where no

337

power is available, an electric refrigerator becomes a status symbol in which to store heirlooms and stands in a conspicuous position in the parlor.

Within the last few years, Deetz (Deetz and Dethlefsen, 1965) introduced the archaeological implication of the Doppler effect in relation to the seriation method of chronological ordering. (Seriation is a method of ordering or ". . . the placing of items in a series so that the position of each best reflects the degree of similarity between that item and all other items in the data set." [Johnson, 1968: pp. 1–2].) Seriation is linked to the concept of diffusion by a mutual concern with tracing trends (for example, the rise and fall of pottery types) through time and geographical space and the spread of traits. Deetz and Dethlefsen show that the trends in frequency in the seriation will be altered if one has by chance chosen to seriate traits from successive sites that are "traveling" counter to the original direction of the diffusion or sites that are "flowing" toward the "original" center of diffusion. These men demonstrated the validity of the hypothesis by analyzing the origin and spread of tombstones carved by well-known masons in Massachusetts in the 1700–1800s. Their model illustrating the Doppler effect on diffusion added a methodological refinement to seriation by suggesting rates of changes and the reasons for this phenomenon (Clarke, 1968, pp. 426–62).

Recently the possibility of trans-Pacific diffusion has again become popular. The most recent example postulates that pottery was introduced to the coast of Ecuador by a canoe-load of fisher folk from Kyushu, Japan, some five thousand years ago. This hypothesis is based on parallels in decorative techniques, motifs, and rim and base forms of ancient pottery found in Japan and equally ancient ceramics found in Ecuador by Meggers, Evans, and Estrada (1965). Ferdon (1966), who is an expert on the subject of trans-Pacific migrations and contacts, Polynesian origins, and cultural diffusions regrets that a single hypothesis was employed by Meggers, Evans, and Estrada to explain these cultural similarities (although the latter died before the monograph was written). Although Ferdon thinks such diffusion was possible, brought about by accidental or purposeful seafaring voyagers from the New World to Polynesia or from there or Japan to the New World, he seems to think that the Meggers, Evans, Estrada hypothesis was premature and not adequately tested.

Archaeologists previously invoked the principle of diffusion more frequently than at present to explain similarities between cultures and changes in culture, and we could cite many other instances. But nothing is gained by flogging a dead horse.

The factor that really throttled the concept of diffusion, or at least made people sit up and think about it, was the fact that independent invention was shown to have occurred on a massive scale in the New World. The independence of the cultures of the New World has been demonstrated many times over. Few, if any, anthropologists still hold that New World cultures are the result of diffusion from the Old World. Since this is the generally held belief, diffusion is no longer a tenable explanatory device, but is the "very incarnation of antiscience" (Harris, 1968, p. 378). Since independent invention has been demonstrated for the New World, we need no longer worry about the assertion that man was by nature uninventive (Harris, 1968, p. 382). In fact, it can be shown that given similar causes under similar conditions, similar results may be expected (Harris, 1968, p. 683). For example, when men in the Old and the New World were confronted with similar technoenvironmental situations they invented agriculture, systems of irrigation, aggregation of people (towns and cities), writing, pottery, weaving, metallurgy, boats, temples, basketry, class systems, and theocracies—to name only a few of the independent inventions of both the New and Old Worlds.

In short, it is more in keeping with the method of science to *explain* causes and similarities by discovering laws, regularities, or uniformities and linking particular events to these laws to render them predictable (Hempel, 1966, p. 50). Additionally, diffusion is a single causal explanation. Clarke (1968, p. 79) cautions that all necessary causes should be used in accounting for a phenomenon. Applying the converse of Occam's axim, he suggests that "large numbers of complex factors may well be involved in changes in cultural systems and that to invoke barely sufficient or single causes may be mistaken" (Clarke, 1968, p. 79).

Diffusion *has* occurred—and perhaps more often than we realize. Examples of undoubted diffusion are: the spread of systems of writing all through the Near East—Egypt, Mesopotamia, Phoenicia, Greece; the dissemination of tobacco, potatoes, maize, peanuts, from the New World to many parts of the globe; the spread of European languages to India; the plow; copper-smelting; the Athapascan languages (in North America); the spread of pottery-making, the wheel; fire; algebra; the automobile; the steam locomotive; the telephone; wheat, barley, and domesticated animals. But these many documented instances of diffusion add nothing to the explanatory powers of the concept.

Actually, the concept of diffusion has been more of a deterrent than a help to the discovery of lawful principles that govern sociocultural phenomena. Steward, in speaking of the consequences of relying on culture area typologies (a kind of ethnographic map of a continent on which tribal entities or archaeological traits are grouped in relation to some geographical aspect of the environment) points out: "that culture centers or climaxes and the boundaries of the area may shift from period to period; the nature of the culture may change so profoundly in successive periods that the culture in a given period may have greater resemblances to cultures in other areas than it did to its predecessor or successor in the same area; and, portions or subdivisions of the area although representing a basic tradition in terms of diffused culture elements, may have very unlike structural patterns" (Steward, 1955, pp. 82–83).

The above criticisms apply very well to the Kroebers' Greater Southwest Area (Kroeber, 1939). Archaeological research does not confirm or even hint at a single stable center, nor several small climaxes. We do know that there were two principal developmental sequences: (1) the Desert culture—(Cochise) hunting and gathering subsistence system evolving into the Hohokam (Desert and River branches) and other subcultures; (2) the Desert culture (pre-Basket Maker-Anasazi) hunting and gathering economy developing into the Anasazi. And, finally, despite similarities in culture content, the area has been partly taken over again by hunting and gathering peoples (Navajo-Apache) who have adapted to their new homeland and to the sedentary people living there.

Certainly we may be able to learn a bit about historical development in Arizona by studying diffusion, but as a concept or a model for studying sociocultural changes or for searching for regularities, for questions concerning causality and origins, or for applying the principle of technoenvironmental determinism, it is inadequate precisely because one cannot test its implications for explanation and prediction.

MIGRATIONS

We shall have little to say about the use of the model of migrations of people to explain adaptations or culture changes.

We do not deny that there have been migrations—many of them. The American Indians moved from Asia into America, and that could be termed a movement of peoples or a migration. But we do not use this fact to explain why native American cultures were able independently to achieve every technological innovation that had been known in the Old World.

There have been documented movements of peoples in the Southwest. In 1838 the few survivors at Pecos pueblo moved to join their linguistic relatives at Jemez pueblo. After the abortive Indian uprising against the Spaniards in 1696, a Tewa-speaking group of Indians fled from the Santa Fe area to the Hopi country to escape the wrath of the Spaniards. The newcomers settled on the First Mesa near the Hopi town of Walpi, and their town is called Hano. The Hano people still speak their language (Tewa), which is distinct from Hopi, but make pottery just like that of the Hopi and have tied their social and ceremonial systems to those of the Hopi Indians. Certainly, in this case one could not possibly use the fact of their migration to explain any part of their culture (except their language) because their culture is completely Hopi and swings with the tides of Hopi cultural changes (Eggan, 1950, p. 139).

A recent study concerned with the carrying capacity and consequent depletion of an area in the Santa Fe-Albuquerque regions (Zubrow, 1969b, pp. 89–103) hypothesized that as population contact increased, the importance of climate in determining the perimeters of Pueblo population decreased. As a subsidiary part of this hypothesis, Zubrow was concerned with the migratory response to population contacts and pressure from non-Indian groups. He was able to demonstrate that with the encroachment of Americans, the Pueblo population tended to move south and westward and that the Pueblo Indians regrouped themselves in such a way that distance between themselves and Americans was increased so that contacts would be minimized.

Zubrow shows that Spanish and American immigration into the area of the New Mexican Pueblos produced a strain on the limited resources of the Rio Grande area and forced the Pueblo Indian population to migrate south and westward and to aggregate to a certain extent. But nowhere does the author explain culture change by these migrations. Instead, he views pressures on resources caused by contact and climatic deterioration as causal.

Archaeologists have been prone to choose an easy way out by invoking migrations in the Southwest to explain similarities between pottery types, architecture, and stone tools found in widely separated places. For example, a migration of people from Mesa Verde to Aztec pueblo and Chaco Canyon sites has been used to explain: (1) small rooms or large rooms made smaller by poorly constructed partition walls; (2) the presence of certain kiva features; and (3) the presence of pottery types allegedly manufactured only in the Mesa Verde area. Further, this postulated migration supposedly explains Mesa Verde-like masonry and Mesa Verde pottery in the area around Santa Fe. Another example of the use of migration as an explanatory tool is the presence in southeastern Arizona of Kayenta-like masonry and pottery as evidence for a migration from the Kayenta area. Maybe these dispersions were brought about by diffusion and/or migrations. But these ideas have never been set up as hypotheses and tested by scientific methods. The use of diffusion or migration obscures the problems of cause and effect and engenders explanations of cultural origins that explain nothing (Steward, 1955, p. 183). Certainly, such an explanation fails to explain process. Regularities can be found if we look for them, but they will be valid only if a rigorous method is devised for testing the propositions (Steward, 1955, p. 183).

A measurement and explanation of prehistoric population movements was demonstrated by Plog (see preceding chapter) (S. Plog, 1969). He developed techniques for rigorously measuring population movement by testing the validity of such movements into and out of the Hopi country. He predicted that all areas into which people were moving should show indications of a growing or leading economy. His analysis showed that there were four population movements into the Hopi area during the period of A.D. 1250–1350. He was able also to demonstrate that the Hopi country could justifiably be labeled a leading area ecologically speaking; he also showed that it was a leading economic area in terms

of population, differentiation (development of more autonomous and specialized structural units), sociocultural integration and technology. Consequently, the Hopi country (A.D. 1250–1350) was in the process of economic growth. The presence of water control devices and varieties of corn especially adapted to the extraordinary climate of the area also contributed greatly to Hopi economic growth. These data are the more interesting because prior to A.D. 1200 the Hopi area was marginal. The upshot of all this is that the Hopi area fortified and sustained its growth at the expense of stagnant areas.

Finally, Plog demonstrated that there were population movements from lagging areas (Mesa Verde, northeastern Arizona, east-central Arizona in the thirteenth century) to leading economic areas. Since the Hopi area was a leading area, ecologically and economically, people poured into that country between A.D. 1250 and 1350.

Here is an example of population movement or migration that has been tested and reasons given for the movements. It illustrates the fact that diffusion and migration are cultural processes that need to be and can be explained. Using these concepts alone as explanations of archaeological phenomena adds nothing to our understanding of those phenomena.

XX   An Evolutionary Model

In presenting a diffusionary summary of Arizona prehistory, we have attempted to be fair—to describe the archaeological record in the state from a viewpoint we have neither espoused nor followed. We have, however, tried to take a consistent ecological and evolutionary approach to the state's prehistory. In that sense, this entire book is an evolutionary summary. It is also a series of suggestions as to how a more thorough understanding of cultural and behavioral evolution of prehistoric populations in Arizona might be achieved. Most of the work done in Arizona has not been ecological; even when social and natural environmental events have been considered, they have been used to define natural areas in much the same way that cultural variability has been used primarily to define cultural areas. Systemic analyses have been rare. If archaeologists are to answer some of the interesting questions that the use of evolutionary paradigms guide them to, they must begin to collect kinds of data and to undertake kinds of analyses that they have not traditionally undertaken.

In this chapter, our concern will be threefold: (1) to formulate a concise statement of the evolutionary paradigm as we have used it; (2) to tie together some loose ends, to answer some questions not fully answered in the body of the text and to raise some new ones; and (3) to describe in detail the research that we have carried out in northeastern Arizona so as to make clear what kinds of data and what kinds of analytic tools are required if we are to gain a fuller understanding of Arizona's prehistory. Some of these ideas will be ones we had clearly in mind when we began the book. Others we have learned in writing it, for the act of writing this book has taught the authors a great deal about the theory of evolutionism and about Arizona's prehistory.

ECOLOGY AND PROCESS

No magic phrase can neatly describe cultural ecology. As we have used the term, it implies a commitment to three analytic concepts; systemic analyses, technoenvironmental determinism, and processual explanations. Systemic analyses and technoenvironmental determinism have been thoroughly discussed in the archaeological literature. "Process" and "processual explanations" have not. What, then, is process or processual explanation?

Let us begin to answer this question by going back to a more basic one: What is an archaeologist? An archaeologist is a social scientist who seeks to explain spatial and temporal variability in the distribution of artifacts or cultural forms. When archaeology is done carefully, formal variability, space, and time are not confused. We have emphasized the need at the more detailed levels of archaeological research to construct typologies for describing artifacts that are based upon variability in the formal attributes of those artifacts alone. Once formal variability has been characterized accurately, the artifact can be located in the space and time dimensions, but spatial and temporal considerations should not be built into artifact typologies.

This is the case for two reasons. First, if archaeologists are going to explain spatial and temporal variability in artifact distributions then space, time, and form must be measured independently. It is misleading and wrong to date sites in a region on the basis of some formal trait and then turn around and argue that the trait has a discrete temporal distribution. We cannot argue that a series of sites are Pueblo III sites because they are large rectangular villages and then argue that during Pueblo III most villages were large and rectangular. We cannot infer that Arizona Black-on-White was made between A.D. 700 and 800 and then contend that pottery made at about this time has the attributes of Arizona Black-on-White. If the spatial and temporal variability we seek to explain is to have any meaning at all, then it must be based upon independent measurements of spatial, temporal, and formal variability. Second, a focus on formal attributes provides us with a far clearer idea of how and why the prehistoric inhabitants of Arizona made and used the artifacts that archaeologists study. In discussing ceramics, we pointed out that Colton's classification of pottery wares and types was based upon a series of attributes that very closely approximate the steps a potter goes through in constructing a vessel. While Colton did not do it, such a typology could be used to discuss very precisely the differences in the ways pottery was made in different areas. Moreover, because the typologies reflect the steps in the pottery manufacturing process, it helps us to understand some of the anomalies that the archaeologist confronts. For example, archaeologists have begun to learn that design elements on painted pots do not vary with the classical types. This fact makes a good deal of sense if one notes that painting is one of the last steps in the pottery-making process and is not nearly so interdependent as some other attributes, such as the kind of raw material used and the color of the paste.

All this is not to say that techniques like seriation that use artifactual variability for dating are invalid. Formal variability can be used to make inferences about the spatial and temporal affiliation of a site or an artifact. But if the formal variation is not understood in its own right initially, the archaeologist misses a good deal of information that he might obtain concerning manufacture and use in prehistory. Moreover, we suspect that seriations are far more precise and effective when formal variability is well understood and controlled than when it isn't.

Independent measures of space, time, and formal variability are a first step to the understanding of process, but they do not get us all the way. A second important step is realizing that spatial variability in artifact distributions can be understood only as a result of processes that have a temporal distribution. It is possible to correlate the distribution of artifacts at a single point in time with the distribution of social and natural environmental variables; we have done this sometimes, but only when available data and theory allowed us little more. Basically, when the archaeologist observes such a correlation he is simply describing events as they were and not as they came to be. He is describing associations between cultural and natural forms, but *he is not describing causal relationships.*

Causal statements must always be formulated in temporal terms. A given spatial pattern can be produced in a variety of different ways; review, for example, the model discussed earlier of the ways in which patterns of pottery distributions could have been produced. The same pattern could have resulted from different sequences and the same sequence could have produced different patterns. This problem is not one that is unique to archaeology; social anthropologists have it too. Most of evolutionary theory was invented to account for spatial variability in cultural forms and this paradigm still suffers from a dearth of properly temporal data. Some evolutionists have tried to correct this flaw by inferring temporal processes from spatial distributions. Graves, Graves, and Kobrin (1969) have demonstrated that this approach is highly misleading.

Social anthropologists rarely have good temporal data to work with. But change over time is the archaeologist's stock in trade. The important contribution that we can make to social science is to study change in time per se rather than having to infer processes of change from spatial variability.

In general when the term "process" is used it simply refers to a series of linked events. Rather than talking about process in general, however, we wish to focus on particular processes of change and their effects on spatial and temporal distributions. Both processes that are operative when the environment to which a population is adapting is stable and those that occur when it is changing will be discussed. In that regard, a precise definition of both environment and change is necessary. In discussing processes of change, environment refers to those variables that have a specific effect on the cultural form being studied, or those aspects of the natural and social environment with which the population in question is interacting. Change does not refer to any change. For any environmental variable that is specified, a given population will have some acceptable range of tolerance. This is the justification for the earlier statement that populations adapt to variability and not to norms. For any environmental variable, there will not be simply a unique value at which the system can effectively function but a range of variability. The variable will fluctuate within these limits and can do so without affecting the system. But when variation in the environmental variable exceeds these limits, it has an effect on the system in question and this kind of variation above or below a tolerance limit is what social scientists mean by change.

PROCESSES OF SYSTEMIC CHANGE IN STABLE ENVIRONMENTS

In the context of a stable environment, three processes of change are constantly occurring: negative feedback, the generation of variety, and selection on that variety. Negative feedback is a process by which systems counteract the regular variation in environmental variables. We spoke of a number of examples of this process. Bohrer's discussion of the Hohokam comes to mind first. The Hohokam were basically agriculturalists, but in those years when the harvest was not abundant, they turned to mesquite, screwbean, and suguaro for subsistence. In years when the harvest was good, these crops were used, but not in great quantity. Crop failure in the prehistoric Southwest was probably a relatively regular event. Agriculturalists knew that in one or two years out of ten, either the rainfall or temperature conditions would be such that the harvest would be meager. Falling back upon some alternative set of subsistence resources in these years was a regular part of the subsistence system.

A second example of this process was mentioned in discussing Bat Cave. Toward the end of the sequence at this cave, buffalo seem to have been killed and slaughtered in substantial numbers. But the tool kit at the cave does not reflect this change in subsistence to any marked degree. Apparently the tool kit made and used by the population that lived in Bat Cave was so general that a variety of different emphases in the exploitation of subsistence resources were possible with a little or no change in technology. This raises another crucial point: some systems are more varied than others. It seems unlikely, for example, that the Hohokam could have responded to the presence of bison without significant changes in technology, but the Mogollon could.

A final example of deviation countering changes that occur on a regular basis is the variability in house types in many, but especially the northern, parts of the Transition environment. The house types in this area were highly variable and we hypothesized that with further and more detailed work, this variation would prove to have environmental and seasonal concomitants. In the Transition environment, subsistence resources seem to have been distributed so unevenly that it was most efficient for populations to be in different parts of the environment at different points in the year. Thus we find radically different types of sites in radically different spatial loci that are a result of resource seasonality and the scheduling of population and domiciles to meet it. It will undoubtedly prove to be the case that in some instances where archaeologists have defined different cultures or two different time periods on the basis of formal variability in the attributes of sites, seasonality during the annual cycle will have been the cause. These seasonal poses countered expectable variation in the environment.

A second process that occurs in human populations even when the environment is stable is that of variety generation. The factors that produce variety were discussed earlier and include accident, mislearning, inability to execute learned behavior, and borrowing of ideas or things from other cultures. Each of these factors is operative whether the environment is changing or not. We tried to point out that most if not all of the technological and subsistence resources that were ultimately used by populations in prehistoric Arizona were present in the state for a very long time before they were adopted. Undoubtedly, many more such items and resources were present for decades and centuries as variety but were never adopted by the populations in question.

Of crucial importance in this regard is the eternal concern of Southwestern archaeologists for the topic of diffusion from Mexico. We have no doubt that many of the practices that were ultimately adopted by Southwestern populations were introduced into Southwestern systems by the specific mechanism of contact with Mexico. Mexico was the source of a great deal of variety. If anything about this relationship is surprising, it is the fact that Mexico did not have an even stronger influence on the developmental sequence in the Southwest than we now know about. Perhaps evidence of a greater influence will be obtained in the future. We have not been so concerned with Mexico as this statement implies because it is of historical more than explanatory interest.

Even though new variety was introduced into prehistoric cultural systems by the process just discussed, significant changes in these systems did not occur when the environment was not changing. This failure to change was a result of the constant action of selective pressures and processes of selection on these populations. As long as the environment was not changing, the character of the maximally efficient adaptation to these conditions did not change. The force of selective pressures acted so as to reduce the variety present in the system. Maximally efficient patterns of behavior grew at the expense of less efficient ones. This resulted from both conscious and unconscious processes. Inefficient behavioral systems either failed to survive or were outcompeted by more efficient ones. Moreover, prehistoric peoples learned as we do, and when it became apparent that a particular pattern of behavior was advantageous, they adopted it. This notion has been summarized by Sahlins and Service (1960) as the Law of Cultural Dominance: that adaptation or behavioral system that more effectively harnesses the energy resources of a given environment will spread in that environment at the expense of less effective systems. This law is undoubtedly what in implicit fashion led archaeologists to assume that the pattern of adoption of artifacts and behavior by humans approximated a normal curve or grew with some rapidity. While the law is a valid one, the deduction made from it is not, for the reasons discussed earlier.

PROCESSES OF CHANGE
IN CHANGING ENVIRONMENTS

Environments do change. Critical variables do exceed the acceptable tolerance limits. And when such events occur, the effect on populations in question is generally a drastic one. We can speak of four processes that operate under such conditions: variety generation, selection, positive feedback, and growth.

There is little evidence at the moment to inform us as to what happens to variety generation under changing environmental conditions. While systemic change is a more ubiquitous event under conditions of environmental change, it seems to have more to do with processes of change other than variety generation. Since some sources of variety are random events, they would not increase or decrease with any environmental or systemic variable. On the other hand, under changing environmental conditions it might prove impossible for individuals or groups to behave as they had been taught to behave, or at least more difficult than under stable environmental conditions. This would, of course, add to variety. Moreover, we might suspect that during such periods a population might consciously and explicitly consider the behavior of nearby populations in a search for alternatives to that which is beginning to fail them. Again, increased variety might be characteristic during periods of change.

The situation with respect to selective pressures is far clearer. Environmental changes represent a shift in the selective pressures affecting a population. The ability of a population to survive such a shift will depend on whether appropriate variety is represented in the population. Of relevance to this situation is what Sahlins and Service call the Law of Evolutionary Potential: the more specialized a culture the less its potential for going on to the next evolutionary stage. We might make this somewhat more general by saying that the more generalized a culture the greater its potential for surviving an environmental change; the more specialized, the less its potential.

We have discussed a number of instances when this seems to have been the case. The most dramatic example was in the case of those populations that survived the period of abandonment between A.D. 1100 and 1300. The populations inhabiting the Hopi mesas seem to have been practicing an aberrant form of agriculture relative to other areas in the Southwest. Regions like Grasshopper were characterized by a social organization that was somewhat different from the normal. But given the changes that occurred in the environment, these regions found themselves at an advantage. Moreover, populations of other areas, realizing this, began to move into these regions. Both conscious and unconscious processes of selection were operative.

A similar case was presented in the evolution from pit houses to pueblos. Pit houses were serviceable dwelling units until a critical variable in their environment—population density—changed. When pit houses were built close enough together on sites to meet the change in this variable, the walls collapsed. On sites where the distribution of rooms was dense, aboveground masonry walls proved far more stable. Prior to the increase in density, aboveground masonry structures had been used for storage and some work, but not basically for living. But after the increase in density began, there was a rapid selection for this architectural form because it far more adequately met the requirements of the changed environment.

In some instances, the action of selective processes acted to produce two populations where one had previously existed. The Pima and Papago are populations that are very similar to each other with regard to a variety of biological and behavioral traits. The principal distinction is subsistence base; the Pima use agricultural products for about 60 percent of their diet, while among the Papago the figure is only about 25 percent. The Pima practice agriculture in irrigated fields of the broad Gila Valley while the Papago tend to use family plots on alluvial fans in smaller mountainous valleys.

But it is clear that these differences are far more extreme than they were at some point in the past. There were "Pima" who practiced floodwater farming and "Papago" who irrigated in larger valleys. Hackenberg (1962) has observed that there was a continuum of agricultural behavior with villages ranging from entirely hunting-gathering Papago to the most agricultural of the Pima villages. (Archaeological evidence in the area certainly does not contradict this argument.) Whether we are dealing with a situation in which the distribution of communities over a continuum of agricultural to hunting-gathering practice had a single mode with those to the agricultural side called Pima and those to the hunting-gathering side called Papago, or whether the typical Pima and Papago had different modes that were much closer than at present is unclear. However, it is clear that the two populations at some point in the past were far more similar than at present.

What, then, caused the divergence of these two populations? Unfortunately, the record of climatic change in the part of the state inhabited by these groups is so poor that the role of climatic shifts in causing the differentiation cannot be evaluated. It is clear, however, that the entry of two new populations, the Spanish and the Apache, at about the same time had an important effect. The Spanish brought wheat, a winter crop that fit nicely into the subsistence cycle of the most agricultural of the Pima but was of little utility to less agricultural groups. The entrance of the Apache also favored the organization of the Pima in that large villages had stronger chiefs and the importance of these chiefs grew to meet the Apache threat. Very small and mobile Papago groups may have been able to avoid the Apache. Medium-size villages that were neither mobile nor organized so that they could become adapted to warfare tended to disappear. The middle of the continuum disappeared and two populations with fundamentally different subsistence strategies remained. Thus selective pressures can operate on both ends of a curve simultaneously, thereby producing two different populations where there had been one. In any case, under conditions of environmental change, it is the tails of the curve rather than the norm that are important to the survival of the population in question. (Parenthetically, that is why freedom is important. Cultural systems that permit substantial behavioral variability have a much higher survival potential than those that do not.)

A third process of change under conditions of changing environment is positive feedback, or deviation amplification. This is the pattern of change in which tolerable changes in the environment lead to behavioral responses that push the environmental variable close to or past the tolerance limits of the cultural system. Rather than leading to an equilibrium, as was the case with negative feedback, positive feedback leads to further changes. Obviously, the preceding causal chain isn't a clear-cut instance of environmental change; human behavior is ultimately responsible for the macro-environmental change that produces the systemic change. We choose to consider it under environmental change because of the drastic effects that this process characteristically has on the cultural systems in which it occurs. It is an important process because it gets us out of that fatalistic attitude toward the world in which humans simply sit and wait for their environment to change and into one in which environmental changes and thence changes in cultural systems are themselves a product of human behavior.

Probably the most significant case of this kind of change that we discussed earlier was the beginning of the process of agriculture. By accidentally carrying seeds to new environments, human behavior produced changes in the genetic characteristics of plants and thus changes in their productive capabilities, further and more rapid transport to new environments, further genetic changes, and so on. This process ultimately led to a situation in which the use of previously marginal plant resources was selected for.

A similar situation probably existed at about the time of abandonment. Zubrow's work has strongly indicated that population surplus, at least in the Upper Little Colorado, was handled by budding—exporting population to new sites in adjacent areas. Unfortunately these areas were more marginal for the practice of agriculture than that in which doner populations had subsisted. In order to practice agriculture in these marginal areas, populations adopted intensive agricultural techniques, which led to a more rapid depletion of soil and water resources, making the area more marginal, and so on. Additionally, budding continued pressing population into more and more marginal areas, with greater and greater difficulty. Deviation amplification continued to a point at which cultural systems in the area suddenly and drastically changed.

A final instance of deviation amplification occurred in the Salt River valleys and other areas of Arizona where soil alkalinity was a problem. Increasing alkalinity led to decreasing crop yield. If this had led to more intensive agriculture and more frequent irrigation, the rate of alkalinization would have increased, further decreasing crop yield, and so on. Unless some technique for stopping the increase in alkalinity had been found, such as letting fields lie fallow or flushing them, the process would have continued to a point at which the fields were essentially unusable.

GROWTH

The final process of systemic change under conditions of environmental change is growth. Our reason for separating this process from the others is not theoretical. We separate it because this process has been a major target of study by Plog (1969) and to some extent by the Southwest Archaeological Expedition of the Field Museum of Natural History of which Martin is the director and Plog formerly an assistant. We will use our discussion of growth both to provide a detailed record of evolutionary processes in a limited portion of Arizona and to suggest the kinds of evidence that archaeologists must begin to collect if they are to use ecological theory in studying growth.

Our concept of growth follows but is somewhat simpler than that of James G. Miller (1965): Growth is a matter-energy process that is characteristic of all living systems and involves increases in the size of systems, increases in the number of kinds of parts, increases in the strength and changes in the kinds of interaction between the parts, and increases in the quantities of matter, energy, and information that the system is processing. Each of these components of growth is viewed as a dimension of variability in much the same way that time and space are. Any cultural form varies in size, in the number of parts it has, in the integration of those parts, and in the matter, energy, and information they are processing.

Far too frequently, in attempting to deal with changes in cultural and behavioral systems, archaeologists have focused on origins. It is certainly interesting and important to know about origins, to know, for example, when agriculture began to be practiced. But it is fruitless to carry this concern to the point of looking for the very first corncob or the very first garden plot. Having gained some general ideas as to when a particular behavioral system appeared, we should then look for answers to two questions: Why was it adopted? And why and how did it affect the system that adopted it? The variety-selection model allows us to answer questions concerning adoption. The growth model is one designed to allow us to describe and explain the effect of the new system on the society that adopts it. Any invention that is adopted by a society has a direct effect on at least one of the dimensions that we discussed. In this sense, the dimensions that we are discussing are those over which we might construct scales in dealing with variability in behavioral systems in our variety-selection models.

In attempting to apply this model to the prehistory of the Upper Little Colorado in general and Hay Hollow in particular, we realized that one very basic archaeological tool would prove useless. It is very difficult to study processes of change when the usual chronological units—stages, phases, etc.—are employed. These units are useful to space-time summaries, and that is the fashion in which we have used them in this book. But they are not useful for explaining change. Such units are created so as to minimize variability within units and maximize variability between units. That is to say that the investigator tries to draw the boundaries between units so as to define time periods when cultures did not change much and to place into different units time periods in which culture was very different. Our Pit House stage was a period when cultural systems all over the state were very much the same and very different from the preceding Desert culture stage and the succeeding Pueblo stage.

For the study and explanation of change, this procedure has two important negative consequences. First, it compresses periods of change onto the lines that form the boundaries between units or it places these periods of change half in one unit and half in another. It obscures precisely the phenomenon that the investigator who wants to study change is most interested in. Second, it is a crude summary of variability in behavioral systems and artifacts. All archaeologists know that cultural variables do not vary on a one-to-one basis. Chronological units are convenient summaries, but if one is interested in the interaction among different behavioral systems, he must examine each of them independently. The investigator cannot afford to use a typology constructed to describe ceramic variability as if it were also an adequate summary of variability in population. He must specifically look at population to see if it varies. For both of these reasons, in approaching the problem of growth, we decided to look at each variable as it varied over time on a continuous basis rather than a categorical one. Rather than defining stages we sought to record some idea of variation in each dimension for every fifty- or one-hundred-year interval. In the long run, archaeologists will need even more precise measures.

Before testing the ideas about growth with archaeological data, a wide variety of modern data bearing on growth were examined. These led to the conclusion that we were basically correct in our perception that growth and the specific dimensions defined were important. Moreover, they were useful in formulating a set of ideas concerning the interaction and causal relationships between these dimensions. Not all of the data appropriate to studying growth could be obtained from the archaeological record, but we found that we could focus on four sets of data: population, differentiation, integra-

tion, and the adoption of technological innovations, the latter of which would have made energy-processing more efficient.

Data Collection

Evaluating the utility of the concept of growth and the approach to change that we wished to take required a very detailed set of data. We were fortunate in that the long experience of the Southwest Archaeological Expedition in the area had provided a great deal of detailed information on many aspects of cultural and natural variability that we required. Nevertheless, new material to be used in the analysis was collected during the summers of 1967 and 1968. (These data were in some cases used by other investigators working on different problems. With careful planning it was possible to make sure that the data collected would be appropriate for all of the research at hand.)

Hay Hollow Valley covers an area of about seventy-five square miles. During the summer of 1967, a block of approximately five square miles at the north end of the valley was surveyed. Five square miles is an area some surveyors claim to be able to cover in a day. The expedition's decision to devote an entire summer to an area of this size was based upon the belief that many sites are missed when a region is surveyed so quickly. Surveying was done by approximately eight people who worked in the field five days a week for ten weeks. A small area was isolated for reconnaissance and worked by a team of three or four individuals during the course of a day. They crossed and recrossed the area, noting *all* cultural occurrences, sherd scatters as well as habitation sites.

During the second season of the survey (1968), its scope was enlarged. The previous season's work at the north end of the valley provided a picture of variability on the floor of the valley and on the top and sides of Point of the Mountain, the basalt flow that forms the eastern boundary. It seemed desirable to examine the margins of the valley as well as its center and to consider additional variability. An area of about twenty square miles was surveyed to the east and west of the block surveyed in 1967. To survey these twenty miles in the same detail that we surveyed the original five-mile block would have required four years of work. Making such a large commitment of time and personnel was unwarranted. Therefore, a 25 percent sample of the area was taken. We had good reasons to believe that a sample of this size would produce about the same information that surveying all of the area would have produced.

Data were recorded on a total of 325 sites. This means that in the entire 25 square miles investigated by the block survey and sample survey, there are probably about a thousand sites. In many site surveys done in Arizona about fifty sites are recorded in a 25-square-mile area. This figure should give an idea both of the detail of our survey and of the number of sites that most archaeologists fail to observe.

Most of the intrasite data to be used in the study were to be taken from sites that had already been excavated. However, the expedition had no data from the time period between about A.D. 500 and 700. Survey research in the area suggested that sites of this time range were predominantly small villages or even homesteads of two to ten houses. These were distributed along the western side of Hay Hollow Wash along the valley floor. An area of about 75,000 square meters alongside the wash was studied in great detail. While we believed that there would be only scattered sites in the area, we began by assuming that the area contained one village. By applying a regres-

sion equation to be discussed later, it was determined that if this area were a single village it should contain about three hundred pit houses.

The entire area was then investigated. Each of the concentrations of cultural debris was tested to a depth at which either the presence or absence of pit houses was indicated. The area between concentrations was sampled using heavy machinery. Five pit houses and a similar number of intensive activity loci were located within the area. We were satisfied that this was not a single large village but isolated clusters of a few pit houses and activity loci. This same pattern seemed to be continuous all along the valley floor. Four of the five pit houses were excavated in their entirety. The work space immediately adjacent to the pit houses and the limited activity loci were also sampled. These data were then used in constructing some of the variables that we used in our analysis.

Population

The first variable considered was population. Archaeologists have used a variety of different techniques in estimating the prehistoric populations of both sites and regions. The quantity of refuse left at a site, the number of rooms on it, the number of burials in the burial ground, the quantity of storage space, the number of sites in a region, and the number of rooms in a region have all been used by one investigator or another. This analysis of population was based principally on the number of habitation rooms on sites and the number of habitation rooms in the region. A great deal of evidence has been collected to show that there is a linear relationship between the size of a site or room and the number of people that lived on or in it. In the Upper Little Colorado, pit houses and storage rooms are about the same size and prob- ably held about the same number of people. Modern Pueblo and Navajo dwelling units tend to hold about the same number of people. The procedure by which we es- timated the total number of rooms per unit of time was as follows:

1. Location of sites: Sites were located by the site survey.

2. Estimation of the number of rooms on the site: In order to estimate the number of rooms on sites that were surveyed but not excavated, we examined the relationship between the size of the rubble mound prior to excavation and the number of rooms that were ultimately uncovered on sites that had been excavated in the Upper Little Colo- rado. It was necessary to use sites from diverse areas of New Mexico and Arizona in order to compare site size and number of rooms for pit house sites. Using regres- sion techniques, we were able to construct the following equations:

Number of pit houses on a site = .0047 × site area in square meters + 1.2

Number of rooms on pueblo sites = .10 × area of rubble mound in square meters + 4.0

(These equations will undoubtedly vary from region to region and should not be mechanically applied elsewhere.)

3. Estimation of number of habitation rooms on a site: Not all rooms on a site were habitation rooms, some were used for storage and some for the performance of ceremonies. Pit house sites were composed almost entirely of habitation units. Once the number of rooms on a pueblo site was es- timated, a certain percentage of rooms was subtracted from the total to remove cer- emonial and storage rooms from the figure. The number subtracted was again deter- mined by studying the number of ceremo- nial and storage rooms on excavated sites.

4. Dating: Sites were dated using Breter- nitz's study (1966) of tree-ring-dated pot- tery types.

5. Correction for the developmental his- tory of the site: Sites were not built in a day. Therefore, it was necessary to make assumptions about the history of the growth of the site. Works such as Dean's (1970) analysis of the growth of Betatakin and Kiet Siel will ultimately allow us to do this with great precision. In the meantime, we knew that from modern pueblos only about 78 percent of the total number of rooms on a site were occupied at any one time. We assumed that the point of maximum occupa- tion occurred somewhere near the midpoint of the time span during which the site was occupied. Therefore, the maximum occu- pancy was plotted at the midpoint of the occupational span, it was calculated at 78 percent of the total habitation rooms on the site, and for each fifty-year period moving away from the midpoint in either direction, the occupation was assumed to have been about half that reached at the occupational maximum.

6. Summation: Population curves for each individual site were summed to create a curve for the valley as a whole.

This technique was then used in meas- uring variability in the aggregate popula- tion of the valley, the mean distance between sites, and the density of sites. Demographic trends in the valley can be summarized as follows:

1. Population increased from A.D. 200 to 400. This increase was associated with a relatively constant number of sites per square mile and a regular distance between sites. The increase was the result of the internal growth of four large sites located on mesa tops or high terraces overlooking the valley.

2. From A.D. 500 to 800 population de- creased. Sites were far more dense and

were randomly spaced. Sites were by and large very small.

3. Population increased rapidly from A.D. 800 to 1050. The number of sites per square mile also increased rapidly and they were closer to each other. Sites were still small with only a few rooms per site.

4. From A.D. 1050 to 1200 population was at a maximum. The density of sites began to decrease and sites were almost randomly distributed. The average number of rooms on the sites began to increase near the end of the period.

5. From A.D. 1200 to the abandonment of the region, population and density in the valley decreased. The aggregation of sites decreased and the number of rooms per site first increased and then declined.

This interpretation of demographic trends is quite different from the traditional one. It indicates that Basket Maker II sites were much larger than Basket Maker III sites. During Basket Maker II times, population reached a relatively stable equilibrium and was concentrated in a few villages. Both Basket Maker III and Pueblo I were periods of relatively low population. The former was a period of population decrease and the latter one of increase. In both periods sites were small and were very closely packed on the valley floor. This suggests that some new resource associated with the valley floor that supported a very dense population was adopted at about this time. All of the demographic indices changed most rapidly during the period that is associated with the Pit House–Town Dweller transition. We simply note that these patterns would have been obscured had we chosen to look at prehistory in Hay Hollow Valley using a stage or phase approach.

Differentiation

A second dimension of growth that was investigated was differentiation or special-ization. Social scientists use these and a variety of other terms to describe the fashion in which human populations organize their activities into sets. Populations vary in both the number of such sets they have and their discreteness or boundaries. The number and discreteness of activity sets both between and within sites were examined for the case of Hay Hollow Valley.

Approximately 250 of the sites catalogued in Hay Hollow Valley were limited activity sites. These sites did not have habitation units built on them. Sites with habitation units tended to be the locus of both habitation and a variety of other activities. Limited activity sites, on the other hand, were the locus of one or a few activities. We were able to differentiate thirteen different types of limited activity sites, ten of which were used in the analysis. The differences were defined on the basis of four attributes: presence/absence of pottery, presence/absence of lithics, presence/absence of features, and site size. Thus, one type is a site of 15 to 75 square meters that has both lithics and pottery but no features. Another type also has lithic and ceramic debris and no features but is from 100 to 1,000 square meters in area. A third type has pottery and features but not lithics and ranges from 2 to 180 square meters in size. These different combinations of artifacts and features suggest that different activities were carried out on the sites. Moreover, it was possible to demonstrate that the types tended to be associated with landforms and biotic communities, to the extent that the latter vary with landform. Since the tools and features found on the sites and the resource zones on which they were located both varied, we concluded that these were specialized sites used for the exploitation of particular resources.

When changes in the distribution of limited activity sites over time are plotted, a number of interesting patterns appear. From about A.D. 400 to 700 there was one meter of space on limited activity sites for every ten meters of space on habitation sites. In other words, when the areas of habitation and limited activity sites were measured, the ratio of the two was 10 : 1. Then the ratio began to decrease and did so until A.D. 800–900 when it was 1 : 1; that is, there were equal amounts of space on habitation and limited activity sites. After A.D. 900 the ratio began to increase again and indicated that by A.D. 1200 there was eight times as much habitation as limited activity site space.

A similar pattern existed when variation in these sites was examined. Between A.D. 900 and 1200 many different kinds of limited activity sites were present. Prior to and after this time, only a few of the total range of site types were represented. Similarly between A.D. 900 and 1200 sites tended to occur in far more varied topographical and biotic situations than prior to or after this period.

Thus, specialization as recorded by the quantity of limited activity site space present and variation in the kind and location of this space is very generally associated with the Pit House–Town Dweller transition in the area. An interesting pattern was evident when these data were combined with the demographic data just discussed. Basketmaker, or the Pit House stage, in the valley is associated with habitation sites on mesas and high terraces overlooking the river valley. Pueblo, or the Town Dweller stage, is associated with sites in the river valleys. In the former stage limited activity sites tended to occur on the valley floors and during the latter stage they tended to occur on mesas and high terraces. Limited activity sites intrinsically represented a kind of variety in the subsistence settlement system; they were located in those areas that

were not primary but nevertheless were an important source of subsistence items. Some selective pressure that reversed this pattern occurred. The valley bottoms became primary and the mesas secondary. The distribution of limited activity and habitation sites simply flip-flopped. Moreover, the period of time during which the flip-flop occurred was one marked by a great diversity in the kinds and locations of limited activity sites. In response to a question raised earlier, it now seems that experimentation did increase during periods of substantial change. Similarly, as we noted in discussing demographic trends that the change that occurred was one that resulted in greater densities of human population, we can now note that the focus of exploitation after the change was on the valley floor.

The analysis of activity areas within sites, while informative, deserves somewhat less emphasis in that it is based on data from only three sites: the County Road Site occupied sometime between 1000 and 300 B.C., the Gurley Sites occupied between A.D. 500 and 700, and Broken K occupied between about A.D. 1000 and 1200. In general it was shown that the association of tools with rooms became stronger over time. Tools tended to be more strongly associated with particular kinds of rooms and different kinds of rooms tended to have more discrete tool kits.

One surprising result of this analysis was the discovery that three of the four pit houses excavated on the Gurley Sites were significantly different from each other. One had a predominance of manos, metates, and vessels suggesting that grinding and storing was the primary activity carried on in it. Another had substantial quantities of cores, lithic debris, hammerstones, and anvils suggesting that it was a specialized tool making locus. Still another was largely deficient in artifacts; it may have been a sleeping area.

If pit houses prove to be so functionally diverse, then the population maximum associated with Basket Maker II will be much lower than is recorded in our chart. We leave it as is because the predominance of available evidence from other areas suggests that pit houses by and large were not functionally differentiated.

Integration

A substantial portion of the information that archaeologists have obtained about the social organization of prehistoric societies has come from Hay Hollow Valley. However, since archaeologists have only recently brought sophisticated analytical techniques to bear on this problem, less information is available concerning it than most other topics. In considering growth, we were concerned with three specific integrative variables. We first examined the number of habitation rooms that were found on the largest site at each time period as the percentage of the total of rooms that occurred on large sites. An increase in population does not automatically imply an increase in the size of sites. There were periods of time in the history of the valley when population increases were not associated with larger sites. Moreover, large aggregated sites were strongly associated with the population decline near the end of the sequence in the valley.

The size of the maximal local aggregate is an indication of integrative principles in a region more than of population per se. Moreover, there is a surprising consistency between site size and what we do know of organizational patterns in pueblos. The residence units defined by Longacre at Carter Ranch and Hill at Broken K each consisted of about eight habitation rooms. At Carter Ranch the pueblo was divided between two such residence groups. At Broken K there

were five groups and these were further divided into one group of three residence units and one of two. Thus, it appears that when there were three or more residence groups on a site, an additional level of organization developed.

We examined settlement pattern data looking principally at the percentage of habitation rooms that fell on sites with more than twenty-one habitation units. Between A.D. 350 and 550, a high proportion of the rooms fell on such sites. There is no evidence, however, to indicate that a complex organizational pattern characterized relatively randomly arranged pit house sites. The percentage of rooms on such sites was zero between A.D. 550 and 850 and then began to increase again. After a slow beginning, the increase was rapid until some 76 percent of the rooms in the valley were on large sites by A.D. 1250. This evidence suggests that there was a substantial organizational change associated with the transition period that was evident in examining both the demographic and specialization data.

A number of architectural indicators of integration were also used. It is clear that three kinds of rooms existed in pueblos in the Southwest: habitation rooms, storage rooms, and ceremonial rooms. The pattern of association of these different kinds of units provides important clues to changing patterns of organization. For example, archaeologists have known for some time that the ratio of habitation to ceremonial rooms changes rather drastically over time. In late prehistoric and early historic times, there were many more habitation rooms per ceremonial unit than in earlier times (Steward, 1955). This changing rate suggests that over time the "scope" of integration increased. More and more families came to share a single ceremonial unit.

This pattern of change is associated with another one in which storage units became associated with ceremonial units. Early in the Town Dweller stage, habitation units and storage units were generally attached to each other, with storage units separate. In later times there were room blocks that seemed to be centered on a kiva surrounded by a row of storage rooms and then an outer row of habitation rooms (re-examine the earlier figure of Kiatuthlanna for example). Later on we found in the Upper Little Colorado and other parts of the Southwest Great Kivas that had an outer row of rooms that were typologically storage rooms. Moreover, archaeologists have found that in some areas, if not most, both storage and ceremonial rooms were nonrandomly distributed over sites within the same region. For example, at Cliff Palace, Spruce Tree House, and Balcony House in Mesa Verde, the ratios of kivas to secular rooms were 1 : 7, 1 : 12.5, and 1 : 20, respectively. At the same time, Cliff Palace had 1.25 storage rooms per habitation unit and Spruce Tree House only 0.33. There is a strong suggestion, then, that Cliff Palace had a dearth of habitation units and an excess of storage and ceremonial rooms and may have played a ceremonial and storage (perhaps redistributive) role in the Mesa Verde settlement pattern.

There is not enough detailed information available yet in either the Upper Little Colorado or the remainder of Arizona to perform a strong quantitative analysis of this relationship. But the suggestion is a provocative one. The changes in site size and organization seem to be associated with a pattern of change in which storing and ceremoniality were increasingly strongly associated.

The final line of evidence followed in discussing changes in organization was burial data. Unfortunately, large burial populations are not so abundant in the Upper Little Colorado that our data could be taken from this area alone. Two hundred thirty-one burials from fourteen sites were examined. The number of burials that showed some indication of high status and the structure of burial populations were noted. Of the eighty-two burials associated with pit house villages, 3 or 4 percent were high-status burials. The number was so small that it was more probably associated with random variability than with any kind of significant patterning. Of the 148 burials associated with pueblo sites, 37 (that is, 25 percent) had burial offerings that indicated a substantial degree of deferential treatment when compared to the burial population as a whole. The details of this variability have already been considered. At sites like Carter Ranch there were burial grounds associated with residence units in the pueblo and some indication that a percentage of the burials might have played some pan-village role. At Grasshopper, a site occupied a few hundred years later, one group buried in the plaza and kiva area were quite clearly accorded deferential treatment. Not only adults but infants were buried with distinctive offerings suggesting that whatever status was marked by the burial treatment it was one into which an individual was born rather than one which he achieved.

Archaeologists have now uncovered a large number of provocative suggestions concerning organizational change. Nowhere is the record so complete as to permit a detailed description. It is clear, however, that this organizational change is generally associated with the Pit House–Town Dweller transition.

Energy Flows

At the time that this analysis was performed, the record of subsistence change in the valley was perhaps the weakest aspect of available data. During the past few years a number of investigators have concentrated their attention on this phenomenon. In another few years, it is likely that we will be able to consider the problem of growth using a detailed record of variation in subsistence resources.

At this time, however, most of our evidence concerns variability in tools and processes of tool manufacture. Two important points can be made with available subsistence data. First, there is only one significant indication of change in the subsistence base; at about A.D. 950 a new variety of corn that was far more suited to the climatic conditions of the area came into use. Time may prove that this resource innovation was important enough to have had a substantial effect on cultural systems in the area, but there is no good reason to believe that such was the case at the moment. Second, the transition from the Pit House to the Town Dweller stage was not the result of a beneficent climate. Palynological data from Hay Hollow Valley indicated that conditions were most ideal for the practice of agriculture between A.D. 400 and 600 and between A.D. 1300 and 1500, not during the period when the transition occurred. However, the initial movement of population from the mesa tops to the valley floor did occur during a period that was wet and was characterized by an even distribution of rainfall during the entire year. Again, further research may show that the combination of a new, more adaptive variety of corn and favorable environmental conditions resulted in the shift to the valley floor and were the stimuli to the period of growth that followed, and that problems resulting from a deteriorating environment also had important effects. But it is impossible to reach such conclusions at present.

Most of the evidence of change in energy processing available now concerns the tools that were used. It is clear that the transition from Pit House to Town Dweller stage was associated with significant changes in the efficiency of tool manufacture and tool use. This pattern of change is most evident when projectile points and manos and metates are examined.

There were two different processes of projectile point manufacture in the valley. The first involved four steps:

1. The projectile point blank was removed from the core.
2. The blank was flaked so as to thin it.
3. The blank was flaked so as to shape it.
4. In some instances, the core was heat treated before the blank was removed so as to increase the quality of flaking.

In the second process there were only two steps: a flake was removed from a core and then it was shaped. The difference between these techniques is traceable to the work habits and motor control of the individuals who made the points. In the first process, the "blank" removed from the core was large and required a great deal more thinning and shaping to form the actual point. In the second, the blanks removed from the core were very thin and their shape closely approximated a point. The work remaining to be done after the flake was removed from the core was minimal. The second process was far simpler and more efficient than the first. Furthermore, it resulted in a far more standardized product. The length, for example, of points made by the first process is about twice as variable as that of points made by the second. The second process of projectile point manufacture began to replace the first at about A.D. 600. The increase in the adoption of the second process was most rapid at about A.D. 850. Most projectile points made by Town Dwellers in the valley were made by the second process.

New kinds of tools used in grinding plant

resources were also being adopted at about this time. In the case of metates, the change was from basin metates with very limited grinding surfaces to slab metates with very substantial surfaces. A concomitant change in manos occurred, so that together they permitted the processing of a far greater quantity of plant product for about the same effort as had previously been used. The adoption of these new devices began at about A.D. 700 and the greatest increase in the rate of adoption is again associated with the Pit House to Town Dweller transition.

SUMMARY

This study led us to a number of conclusions about the study of change and about ecology.

1. The more minute the record of variability in cultural and natural variables the archaeologist can record, the stronger the explanation he can formulate. We have tried to avoid summarizing variability in our natural environmental variables by creating "natural areas" and in our cultural variables by creating cultural ones. We cannot assume all variability is at the level of cultures; we must look at interpopulation and intersettlement variation.

2. If archaeologists are going to study change, they must adopt conceptual tools appropriate to this effort. We learned a great deal about the transition from the Pit House to the Town Dweller stage that we might not have learned if the change had been studied in terms of concepts such as stage. Continuous records of variability are always more appropriate to the study of change than categorical ones.

3. Transition periods, or at least this one, can be conceptualized in terms of the proc-

ess of growth. Again there is no doubt that it is important to identify the key event that triggers a period of growth. But archaeologists have always been interested in this search for origins. We must learn to explain what effect a change will have on existing organization given that we know it has occurred.

4. Growth is a systemic rather than a unilateral process. We could approach the question of causality in dealing with the interaction of population, differentiation, integration, and energy by simply asking what changes first and assuming that the variable that changes first is the one that "caused" the others to change. If we did so, we would conclude that changes in tool technology and differentiation changed first and at about the same pace followed by changes in population and finally integration. Our data indicated that in fact there was substantial variation of a cyclical type in these dimensions before a rapid increase began. Were our data more detailed, this initial variability would probably be even more profound and make it more difficult to clearly identify the variable that changed first.

In any case, we are less interested in answering the questions about first causes than in exploring the systemic connections among the variables. To this end we did a statistical analysis of the relationships among the variables and found that the dimensions were excellent predictors of each other. This analysis also suggested that the major difference in the transition period was a strong positive feedback between tool innovations and the rearrangement of work space. This linkage seems to have been the most important one. We are in the process of extending this statistical analysis to the point of constructing models that simulate the changes that occurred in the Upper Little Colorado. We already know that variability in any one of these dimensions can be successfully explained by reference to systemic connections among the other variables.

5. Archaeologists must learn a good deal more concerning organization and organizational variability than they now know. It is clear, for example, that two societies organized in different ways may have totally different potentials for exploiting a particular environment. Moreover, the first change that initiated a period of growth may frequently have initially affected organization. In the Transition environment, for example, it appears that compound organizations had a long history. The spread of compound sites has frequently been associated with Salado or Sinagua invasions; we suspect it may simply have been an organizational change. We will not know for sure until we understand what the compounds in a site like San Cayetano represented. It is clearly improbable that the walls built between compounds on a site were for defensive purposes. But they did draw an important organizational boundary. What was the nature of the interaction between the units that occupied the separate compounds? Did they specialize in the exploitation of different resource zones? There were early sites with compounds in the Transition environment, Bidegain and Tres Alamos, for example. The "Salado invasion" may represent no more than the spread of a form of organization that was highly effective in the Transition environment, but we shall not know until the nature of the organization itself is understood.

We suspect that the reluctance of archaeologists to study organization and ceremonialism is in part due to the fact that archaeologists have tended to assign provocative but elusive patterns to ceremonialism. For example, we have frequently heard archaeologists note that pit houses tend to face east and to suggest that this is an indication of sun worship. Now, such an argument is a very tenuous one, indeed. But it could easily be made more secure. Pit houses and all underground structures in temperate climates are coldest in the early morning hours. It would be advantageous to locate these houses on slopes facing eastward to catch the morning sun. Given that a house or a village had been built on an east-facing slope, the entrance would have to be built facing east, or downhill also. If it had been built in an uphill direction, the pit house would have become a swimming pool every time it rained. We suspect that a study of pit house locations would verify this argument. Even if, however, this proved to be true, it might have been the case that sun worship or ceremonial was the code in which the information that pit houses should face east was carried. And a change in this code could ultimately have led to change in the society that possessed it. This has been known to happen. But we shall never know if it has happened in prehistory until archaeologists begin carefully to study organization, ritual, and symbolism in their own rights rather than attributing every unusual artifact or pattern to them.

6. Finally, we have shown that societies do not continually go onward and upward. Population varied in Hay Hollow Valley; it did not continually increase. Archaeologists have probably missed the dispersed homestead-based population that was characteristic in the late Pit House stage because they assumed that population continually increased. Similarly, we argued earlier that Arizona may have been less populous during the Desert culture stage than the Paleo-Indian stage. Despite the more secure position of Desert culture populations on the food chain, we feel they may have been relying on a specific set of resources that

were more variable than those used by Paleo-Indian groups. In any case, archaeologists cannot simply assume that population increases during a given period of time; they must demonstrate it.

Similarly, the efforts of archaeologists to study organization have been impeded by the assumption that the existing Pueblo societies must be the most complex that have existed in the indigenous Southwest, that they represent the highest point on the evolutionary chain. It seems clear now that Chaco Canyon had a far more complex organization than any that exists today, and we guess that the same was true in other areas.

Archaeologists must cast off their assumptions about how things grow, how they change, and how variability is organized in time and space. They must record space and time variability in detail and then seek to explain it. As long as we assume more than we observe, we will not learn more of Arizona's prehistory.

XXI Prehistoric and Contemporary Problems[1]

In this final chapter we should like to suggest that the results of archaeological research can be used in dealing with contemporary problems. Recent changes have occurred in the theoretical orientation of archaeology, and it is these changes that make it possible for archaeology to be relevant in a modern context. Archaeology has always had the potential for relevance and has produced broadly relevant general knowledge, but we wish to suggest that a more immediate and substantial contribution is possible. In *no* way does this mean that archaeology has to justify its existence by being relevant. The following is simply a statement relating the recent directions in archaeological research to possibilities for the uses of archaeology.

GOALS AND METHODS IN ARCHAEOLOGY— NEW DIRECTIONS

Archaeology has undergone a revolution in the past decade. Formerly, the archaeologist was thought of as an adventurer who found lost cities, dug for exotic objects, and spent time counting potsherds; he was seen as concerning himself with unwritten history. Archaeology itself was essentially an enterprise rather than a science.

It is true that archaeology has con-

tributed significantly to general knowledge. It has established the probable antiquity and origins of man, contributed substantially to the delineation of Biblical and Classical history, and made contributions toward defining the origin and antiquity of American Indians. Further, archaeology has demonstrated the separate development of cultures in the Old and New Worlds; outlined the evolution of cultures, the origins of agriculture, and the development of systems of writing; and has aided in the destruction of myths and folklore concerning giants, superior races, and human origins. These achievements do not, however, explain or predict cultural phenomena and remain on the descriptive level.

This stereotype of activity remains true for many archaeologists, but new directions are being sought and followed. No longer is the archaeologist concerned with simply digging up artifacts and classifying them, or in creating culture sequences by noting the presence or absence of material traits in time and space. Today, archaeology is viewed as anthropology and as a social science. It is a social science because its goal is to explain human behavior. Archaeology is anthropology because it uses the concept of culture. Because its goals are accomplished by using data from the past, the science is archaeology.

The methodology employed by archaeology for arriving at laws of human behavior is broadly described as the scientific

[1] Co-authored by Paul S. Martin and David A. Gregory.

361

method (see Hempel, 1966, Braithwaite, 1960, and Hanson, 1965). Tentative hypotheses are formulated to give direction to scientific investigation. Such hypotheses determine what data should be collected at a given point in an investigation by means of stated test implications. Test implications state what would be expected in a certain class of data if the hypothesis is correct. Positively tested hypotheses become tentative probabilistic statements or laws of human behavior.

Laws that have a high degree of probability are as important to archaeology, anthropology, and social science as they are to any "hard science." Without the laws of organic chemistry there would be no synthetic drugs; without the laws of celestial mechanics there would have been no space shots. With rigorously tested laws in our "tool kit" we could proceed toward explaining human behavior.

The value of this "new" approach lies in the fact that it revolutionizes our methods of thinking and permits us to view our inquiries in a different way and with greater scope. It is a new way of regarding the archaeological record. Additionally, it produces results that have the logical power of deduction behind them.

THE CONCEPT OF RELEVANCE

Caution must be exercised in dealing with the proposed relevance of archaeology to contemporary problems. It would be easy to state that man in the twentieth century faces problems similar to those that have existed throughout the human career. Pollution, racial tension, wars, and food shortages could be immediately suggested as phenomena with which man has always had to deal. Consequently, it could be argued that the archaeological record is important in understanding such phenomena and

should therefore be studied. This argument is plausible and superficially logical, yet is simplistic and misleading. Like the concept of diffusion, relevance has such broad implications that we must take care in our uses of it. We must not allow it to become simply a litany recited by archaeologists to glamorize and justify their work. Nor should the concept be used in a nonrigorous manner so that, like diffusion, it will quickly fall into misuse and disfavor. Rather, we must carefully define relevance and state its relationship to the broader goals of archaeology.

The concept of relevance may be stated in the following relationships. Archaeology is a social science and seeks to uncover and explain patterns of human behavior. Explanations take the form of laws that are by definition valid regardless of their temporal or spatial contexts. These laws may be invoked to explain past and present behavior and to predict future behavioral conditions. Therefore, we can use the results of archaeological research to define, explain, and construct solutions to problems experienced by human populations today. When we say that archaeology is relevant, we mean that it produces cultural laws and that this knowledge may be used operationally in dealing with problems extant in today's world.

The relevance of archaeology, then, depends ultimately upon the theory from which archaeology operates. Given the recent shift in the goals and methods of archaeology, the concept of relevance is an obvious by-product of these changes. Relevance itself, however, is not a goal or driving force for archaeological inquiry. The encompassing goal is to produce laws of human behavior. The possibilities for the relevance of archaeology result from striving for this goal and from the nature of the results of this endeavor.

THE ADVANTAGES
OF ARCHAEOLOGY

In relation to other social sciences, archaeology has some unique perspectives and advantages to offer in the study of human behavior. We do *not* agree with the viewpoint that:

The archaeologist primarily interested in formulating laws about sociocultural processes might better become a social anthropologist or ethnologist and work with existing or historically well documented peoples rather than with the more refractory material of archaeology (Trigger, 1970, p. 35).

Because he can contribute perspectives unavailable to the social anthropologist or ethnologist, the archaeologist could only limit knowledge of sociocultural processes by turning to these disciplines. To say that archaeology itself cannot contribute to social science would be to eliminate many possibilities for the understanding of human behavior. Specifically, this denial of the social scientific value of archaeology would limit our understanding of contemporary problems.

We do not wish to suggest that archaeology has the only perspective from which modern problems should be approached. It should be obvious that the greater the understanding of any problem, the greater are the chances for constructing a workable, meaningful solution. The perspectives and advantages of archaeology, when added to the knowledge of the contemporary behavioral scientist, can contribute a new dimension to the understanding of modern social problems.

Processual Completeness

Perhaps the most powerful advantage of archaeology is that it can view patterns of human behavior and cultural change over long periods of time. The archaeological record provides a laboratory with a time span unavailable to other social sciences. Only archaeology commands the temporal ranges necessary for a study of long-term cultural change. This great temporal perspective allows us to relate the structure and patterning of behavior at a given point in time to gradual and encompassing change. As a result, patterns of behavior that may defy explanation by the social anthropologist or ethnologist are often apparent in the archaeological record as manifestations of change over long periods of time.

The study of completed processes of cultural systems would be extremely important if applied to the construction of solutions for modern problems. Programs designed to alleviate social problems are often initiated with an eye toward immediate resolution. This approach too often proves inadequate and superficial in the long run. An applied knowledge of long-term change would enhance greatly the possibilities for success in social engineering.

Experimental Morality

Archaeological research is carried on using the remains of extinct populations. The archaeologist is therefore able to actually perform experiments and test hypotheses using human populations; yet, he remains humanistic in orientation because he does not disturb living populations in any way.

This ability to use human populations extensively in discovering laws of human behavior eliminates some of the guesswork in operationalizing programs to solve social problems. Plans designed to alleviate contemporary problems can be constructed around archaeologically derived laws of human behavior and cultural process. This approach is more likely to produce successful solutions than those based on political motivations, ethnocentric biases, and untested assumptions about cultural process.

Economy

Archaeology is unparalleled in its potential for maximum return with minimum input of time and money. Any archaeological site contains the products of myriad behavioral events compressed into an effectively manageable unit for study. One excavation provides data that can be used in testing numerous differing hypotheses about human behavior. Additionally, there is an abundance of archaeological data in museums that has never been subjected to analysis. This could be cheaply and effectively used.

As suggested above, using tested hypotheses about human behavior in constructing solutions to contemporary problems is likely to produce positive results. This is certainly more economical than waiting for abortive programs to use up time and money in a trial-and-error approach. If we can predict behavior, we can predict the areas that are likely to respond to structured change and use our resources in these areas.

Analytic Objectivity

The use of archaeological data has the advantage of immediately eliminating the guesswork inherent in studying living peoples. Never does the archaeologist have to be concerned that his presence will alter significantly the patterns of behavior of the population he is studying; nor are his results and interpretations directly subject to his own prejudices about living peoples.

This objectivity could also be advantageous in social programs and public education. Prejudice, both recognized and unwitting, is a major barrier to effective solutions to problems faced by society. If such problems can be understood by the public (and, indeed, by the administrators of social programs) in terms of laws of human behavior rather than in the shadow of their ethnocentric beliefs, prejudices will be softened and solutions can be effective. Consequently, dealing with contemporary problems in the light of archaeologically tested hypotheses has educational value.

To illustrate some of these advantages and the possible applications of archaeologically derived statements about human behavior, it is necessary to give a concrete example. We will use as an example certain characteristics of the phenomena that has been called the urban ghetto. These characteristics will be explained briefly in terms of hypotheses tested on archaeological data. This example is hypothetical and suggestive in nature: No attempt has ever been made to apply archaeological research to contemporary problems in a rigorous way, and this example does not serve to perform such an application. *The possibilities*, however, for the valuable use of the concept of relevance should be apparent.

A brief statement describing the general characteristics of the ghetto is necessary at this point. This summary will sufficiently support the assumptions that the ghetto represents a highly aggregated population attempting to exploit an area that is depleted with respect to energy (economic, social, and political).

The economic structure of the ghetto is perhaps its most obvious characteristic. Thomas Gladwin in *Poverty U.S.A.* states:

Being poor . . . consists in a lack of sufficient money to function effectively in the economic system through which everyone is forced to seek the necessities of life. (1967, p. 48)

He goes on to elucidate very effectively the economic patterns of the poor and demonstrates how our capitalistic system tends to maintain poverty:

. . . if only *equal* opportunities are extended to the minority poor and they are therefore subject to the same rules of business which govern middle-class people their limited cash resources will prevent them from deriving any lasting advantages from this "equality." (1967, pp. 58–59)

Gladwin shows how the lack of simple facilities like cars and telephones can severely inhibit the ghetto dweller trying to find and keep a good job, can keep housewives from doing effective shopping, and prevents the urban poor from obtaining professional services readily. In short, these simple things prevent the poor from exploiting the economic resources outside of a very limited area (pp. 55–56). Without effective means of utilizing the resources of the total urban setting, the population must remain in the aggregated area and attempt to use the limited resources present there or do without. Within this area of low economic base, jobs are limited in number and kind, and wage scales are low. The capitalistic system by its very nature cannot function in this economically poor area effectively without either putting the businessman out of business or charging the poor the same or higher prices in relation to the rest of the urban area. Often this is extended to blatant exploitation of the poor because there is simply no other place for them to do business. (See Gladwin, 1967, pp. 48–59.) A low level of economic energy is thus maintained in the ghetto.

The opportunity structure for the poor is an important factor in maintenance of the ghetto·

The undereducated, the underskilled, the Negro and the aged worker are at a competitive disadvantage in the labor market. They must accept the job opportunities that have been rejected by others—unstable, low-paying work which is generally unprotected by the institutional safeguards of better paying jobs. Many of these jobs are economically exploitive; some of them easily lend themselves to mechanization or automation with the result that even this meager opportunity structure for the marginal worker in low-paid employment is shrinking, making predictability in economic and social life difficult, if not impossible. (Ferman, Kornbluh, and Haber, 1965, pp. 316–17)

Again, effective exploitation of the economic energy resource outside the ghetto is blocked.

Many of the ways in which economic energy is maintained at a minimal level in the ghetto are related to social energy acting within, or more importantly, directed against the ghetto population. Prejudice and discrimination act as two of the most effective mechanisms for maintaining the social and physical boundary between the ghetto and the surrounding urban area: "Discrimination rests upon negative expectations, upon unfavorable stereotypes, or in a word, prejudice" (Gladwin, 1967, p. 76). The aggregation of the poor population in ghettos magnifies and reinforces the social differences and stereotypes that cause prejudice. Further, prejudice encourages the ghetto population to remain within the relative friendliness and security of the ghetto itself.

The assumption that the poor are different from the other members of our society affects not only the economic and social interaction between ghetto and the larger urban community, but influences the programs supposedly designed to alleviate poverty in various ways. Attempts at population control are illustrative of this:

The argument for family planning, which is addressed to middle-class people states that through this means they will be enabled to love all their children because they will have only as many as they want. Should it be otherwise for poor people? Do only their numbers matter? The final turn of the screw is the widespread denial of family planning services to unmarried lower-class women. Thousands of illegitimate children are born to lonely and bewildered young women because of a prudish policy based on a single totally unfounded assumption. Ignoring mounting evidence to the contrary, this assumption posits that the sexual morality of poor people depends significantly upon reasoned decisions regarding the likelihood that conception will result from any given act of sexual intercourse. (Gladwin, 1967, p. 94)

This is an example of how social energy maintains poverty through the effects of prejudice and discrimination on the economic resources of the ghetto and on those "objective" programs to alleviate poverty:

The fact that the larger society, impinging upon each of its disadvantaged ethnic minorities, tends to treat them all in similar ways underscores, but also generalizes, Liebow's observation that what we are really seeing is the way our national culture molds the lives of the poor people within it. (Gladwin, 1967, p. 84)

Welfare programs often reflect the prejudices of the larger society, prejudices often unwittingly directed against the poor. Welfare represents an attempt to channel economic energy into the poverty area that has failed. This failure is due largely to the effects of the social energy represented by attitudes of the larger society and injected into welfare programs:

. . . existing welfare policies and the philosophy underlying them would have to be drastically overhauled before welfare agencies could effectively serve these new goals. Ever since the Poor Law of 1834 in England public welfare has operated on the premise that all able-bodied and morally upright people should be gainfully employed; any able-bodied person who requires welfare support must therefore have a defect in his character, a defect which should not be encouraged by any reward of money. Welfare laws have therefore been designed on the basis of an essentially negative philosophy, that of discouraging idleness. If welfare is to be productive it must instead encourage productive lives by providing the security and facilities essential to that end. Instead of supporting disablement, welfare should strive for enablement. (Gladwin, 1967, p. 69)

Current welfare programs insist that once a participant obtains a job, the amount of his salary is deducted from his welfare check, or that the check stops all together. This completely ignores the need for establishing a stable economic base for the poor in order to wipe out poverty. Even if a person gets a job, it is essentially replacement of a welfare check with a paycheck. In a situation where job stability is low, motivation is lacking because of low pay, previous failures, and the apparent futility of the work, a ghetto worker may go back and forth between welfare and brief employment until frustration or other combinations of factors cause him to give up and remain on the welfare rolls. This circumstance reinforces the stereotype of the lazy poor. This is certainly no effective channeling of increased economic energy. Instead, poverty is maintained:

Public assistance payments are so low and uneven that the government is, by its own definition, a major source of the poverty on which it has declared unconditional war. (Gladwin, 1967, p. 70)

The relationship of welfare to politics makes obvious another area of social interaction in which the urban poor are lacking in energy and power, the realm of politics itself.

The growth of the bureaucracies of the welfare state has meant the diminished influence of low-income people in public spheres. This has come about in two ways: first, the bureaucracies have intruded upon and altered processes of public decision so that low-income groups have fewer occasions for exercising influence and fewer effective means of doing so; and second, the bureaucracies have come to exert powerful and inhibiting controls on the low-income people who are their clients. (Cloward and Piven, 1965, p. 223)

Bureaucracies also reduce the amounts of money actually being spent on poverty programs: "It has been estimated that one out of every five welfare dollars is spent simply in policing eligibility . . ." (Gladwin, 1967, p. 70). The combination of a high degree of aggregation and low degree of organization (in terms of the sociopolitical system operating in the larger society) in the ghetto, and the economic and educational factors that keep good leadership from developing, prevents effective and equal political representation. Political energy of an organized and unified sort does not exist in the ghetto (Gregory, 1969).

The above is only a brief description of selected characteristics of the urban ghetto but will serve as a basis for demonstrating how archaeologically derived statements about human behavior can provide a valuable perspective. Further, we can make constructive criticisms about the programs that have been designed to alleviate the problems of the ghetto and suggest alternatives to these already tried approaches. Again, the important fact to recognize is that archaeological research can produce laws of human behavior that have explanatory and predictive validity.

In archaeological investigations carried on in east-central Arizona, Zubrow has done work concerning the relationship between a population and its area of resource exploitation (Zubrow, 1969a). Zubrow has demonstrated a definite and predictable relationship between the amount of available energy and the population of a given area: The number of people an area will support is determined by the resources available for exploitation by the population. When the level of population a given area will support is reached, or when the energy level for some reason decreases, two alternatives are available if the population is to survive. First, the population may move into and begin to exploit more favorable resource areas; second, the population may change its organization to more effectively exploit the original area of its occupation. A third alternative, of course, is the extinction of the population.

It should be obvious that the ghetto population is largely unable to move into a more favorable resource area, due to economic and social factors suggested above. From our knowledge of the archaeological record, we would predict that one way to lessen the pressure of the ghetto would be to effectively disperse people into the larger urban area so that a greater resource base would be available (jobs, recreational facilities, etc.). This is easier said than done, but had this knowledge of human behavior been applied to social problems we could have avoided the mistake of viewing urban renewal as a step toward eliminating urban poverty. The crucial factor is not the newness of the buildings, but the concentration of people in the area. Urban renewal may be viewed as simply a rearrangement of slum space, often a rearrangement that is detrimental rather than helpful:

Slum clearance programs have replaced the slum dwellings of the poor with higher cost housing which low income families can't afford. The poor are concentrated in ever shrinking land areas of slum housing. (Ferman, Kornbluh, and Haber, 1965, p. 316)

We could have predicted that dispersion was necessary, instead of the construction of new and "better" housing. The money spent on urban renewal could have been

367

used to develop programs that would find ways to disperse the ghetto population. We might have eliminated the misery of people now living in high rise slums by not subjecting them to our hit-or-miss program.

The organization of the population living in an urban ghetto is complex and difficult to understand. Broadly, we may suggest that the alternative forms of organization practiced by people in the ghetto represent attempts at dealing with the low energy level present in the ghetto. If an individual needs money and cannot get a job because he is unqualified or because an employer is prejudiced, the next most effective way of getting money may be by stealing it. Thus the ghetto has a high crime rate. If a father in a family must exploit the kinds of jobs available to him in the ghetto (transient labor, odd jobs, etc.), he must necessarily be away from home a great deal both performing this type of labor and looking for it. His energies cannot be spent with his family. Additionally, if a father fails his family by being unable to get or hold a job, his home and family represent something he does not want to be reminded of. Consequently, he stays away as much as possible. It appears to the larger society that the father is an irresponsible and unloving villain. These are examples of the kind of behavior that is often the source of misunderstandings, false beliefs, and resulting prejudices on the part of the larger society; yet it is behavior that represents an attempt to cope with the situation in which ghetto inhabitants must exist. From the archaeological record, we know that populations experiencing energy depletion use organizational change as an adaptation to this condition. If the public were to understand the ghetto in these terms, prejudices could be combated and social programs designed without bias.

The possibilities for change and for more effective ways of exploiting energy resources have been severely limited for people that live in ghettos. We know that when these possibilities are blocked, the population becomes extinct. The widespread riots in our cities may represent populations in their death throes. Riots are destructive and ineffective uses of energy that the people of the ghetto cannot afford, given their already minimal energy resources. Yet all other avenues for change have been largely blocked, so that the ghetto dweller turns to violence in a maladaptive expression of the panic and despair he faces. Assistance in constructing avenues for change can come from archaeological perspectives.

Ghettos exist in Arizona today, as do many other problems that must be dealt with. Three minority groups, Indians, Mexican-Americans, and Blacks, inhabit the state along with the Anglo population. These four groups have unique problems and lifeways that must be mutually understood if they are to successfully coexist. In addition to urban ills, the problems of extensive agricultural exploitation and the constant need for water face the people of Arizona. Arizona also encompasses one of the most extensive areas of archaeological remains in the world. These prehistoric populations may be studied in order to give insight into the problems of today, not only in Arizona, but wherever explanations of human behavior are important.

By using the concept of relevance, we have shown how archaeology can be useful in the modern world. Archaeology produces laws of human behavior and contributes unique perspectives and advantages in the study of human behavior. In this way, archaeology can be a significant (though as yet untapped) resource in understanding and solving contemporary problems.

APPENDIX

TREE-RING DATES

Prehistoric populations in the Southwest often located their villages on the borders of forest vegetation belts where this type of environment provided timber for architecture, agricultural land in areas from which forest was cleared, and a relative abundance of edible faunas.

Dating seasonal growth increments of certain species of tree beams excavated from these sites enables Southwestern archaeologists to estimate according to our calendrical system the years in which these materials were cut and used by prehistoric populations for architectural proposes.

This is achieved by measuring specimens against relative or floating tree-ring chronologies derived from archaeological sites in the Southwest which have been cross-dated with modern tree-ring chronologies. In theory, then, the archaeologist can derive absolute dates for many Southwestern sites (Osborne and Nichols, 1967). The archaeologist must deal with two criteria which structure the meaning of tree-ring dates obtained from archaeological sites. The first concerns the representativeness of the cross-dating of modern ring chronologies. Some prehistoric chronologies used to date tree-ring specimens are based on modern chronologies that are not indigenous to the region from which the archaeological specimen was obtained. The most trustworthy archaeological chronologies are cross-dated with modern chronologies obtained from trees that inhabit the same environment, such as the Wetherill Mesa tree-ring series (Smith and Nichols, 1967), for example. The second criterion concerns the representativeness of dates obtained from each archaeological tree-ring specimen. Individ-

ual dates obtained from specimens excavated at archaeological sites do not date the site. At best, each dates only the archaeological context from which the specimen was obtained. In certain situations outlined below, even dates of restricted utility should be considered suspect.

The significance of tree-ring dates in their archaeological contexts can perhaps best be understood by outlining some of the prehistoric environmental and cultural factors that complicate the definition of a sample population of tree-ring dates obtained from any archaeological site:

1. Dendrochronologists must evaluate ancient regional ring chronologies of different quality, consistency, and areal extent that were as varied in prehistory as are modern chronologies made from the study of living trees today. Variations in the seasonal ring widths of trees used by past and present people in these locations probably resulted from regional differences in temperature precipitation and river runoff.

2. Archaeological tree-ring specimens often occur in the form of charcoal fragments which are the result of decay or burning at a site. Estimation of the cutting dates requires that these specimens contain bark cells. In situations where clusters of fragments are retrieved from one locus, archaeologists often accept the most recent dates obtained from very few fragments having rings that contain bark cells.

3. A single archaeological tree-ring specimen may have lost a considerable portion of the outside; consequently the final dated ring may in actuality be far from the cutting date of that specimen.

4. Prehistoric specimens may have been

cut or died during a critical period of climatic change. Consequently some rings on the exteriors may be absent. On specimens having rings that do not extend far enough beyond such a period to permit a check on these critical years, there is no way to determine whether there was in fact any measurable growth during the period in which the tree was cut. In this situation a plus sign which is affixed to some dates indicates that the specimen dates at least to the assigned year and possibly beyond (Smiley, 1951, p. 8).

5. Coniferous species of prehistoric tree beams are usually considered to be datable, but archaeologists often recover and submit for analysis other species of undatable quality that were used in prehistoric construction.

6. Dated specimens are often excavated from dubious archaeological contexts reflecting the prehistoric practice of reusing tree beams taken from abandoned architecture to build other dwellings. The archaeologist must integrate the derived dates with archaeological data to determine which dates are incongruous as a result of prehistoric cultural activity involving the reuse or repair or replacement of original beams at a site.

Dendrochronologists deal with problems in measuring tree-ring specimens that also complicate archaeological interpretation.

1. In most cases multiple measurements taken from an ancient or modern tree-ring specimen have a high degree of correlation. While this is desirable there have been cases where two or more dendrochronology laboratories have made collections from the same ruin, leading to a duplication among the specimens dated. Where this is the case all specimens must be considered as individuals even though the possibility remains that they are duplicated (Smiley, 1951, p. 9). It is still possible however for variation to occur when more than one measurement is made on different portions of one sample. Dendrochronologists (Fritts, 1963; Smith and Nichols, 1967; Nichols and Harlan, 1967; Ferguson, 1969) are currently investigating this problem through the use of statistical tests of correlation and covariance among multiple measurements made of geographical populations of living trees.

2. Adequate evaluation remains to be made of the degree to which ranges of dated archaeological features are statistically representative of the site as a whole. The suggestion has been made (Smiley, 1951:9) that a normal ratio should exist between the number of tree-ring samples obtained from an architectural feature and its type or size as well as the number of such features at a site.

The assumptions and methods used by dendrochronologists to measure tree rings are changing. One new dating technique derived from the study of living trees is densitometric analysis (Polge, 1970). Wood density variations in tree rings obtained by evaluation of X-ray negatives are thought to be more characteristic of rings formed in a given year than are the ring widths themselves.

In the near future this technique may well be applied to archaeological specimens that occur in the form of charcoal (Polge, 1970, p. 2). Therefore, the dates in the following list are to be taken as approximations of the time of occupation of the sites. With the exception of the sites marked with an asterisk these dates are taken from Bannister *et al.* (1966, 1967, 1968, 1969, 1970). The dates for the sites marked are from Breternitz (1966).

FREDERICK GORMAN
*Doctoral Candidate,
University of Arizona,
and tree-ring specialist*

ALLANTOWN

DATES
Pit houses A.D. 844–53
Pueblo A.D. 1002–16

LOCATION
About 3.5 miles south of Allantown on U. S. Route 66 in Apache County, Arizona. South of the Puerco River and west of Whitewater Creek in Section 34, Township 22 North, Range 30 East.

DESCRIPTION
A large multicomponent site covering a large area. The main excavated portion consisted of two groups of pit houses with some surface architecture, trash mounds, detached granaries, ovens, shelters, and a dance court. A small masonry pueblo with a circular kiva was excavated at the foot of the talus below the main site as well as another similar pueblo about 1 mile upstream.

AWATOVI

DATES
A.D. 1200–1700

LOCATION
About 10 miles southwest of the Jeddito Trading Post on the southern tip of Antelope Mesa, between Tallahogan Wash and Jeddito Wash in Navajo County, Arizona.

DESCRIPTION
A large sandstone ruin that covers about 20 acres and was occupied from about A.D. 1200 to 1700. The earliest occupation was in the Western Mound, which represents the prehistoric period of occupation. The site is also the location of a Spanish Mission established in 1629 and occupied until about 1700.

*AZTEC RUIN

DATES
A.D. 1110–25

LOCATION
New Mexico

BATWOMAN HOUSE

DATES
About A.D. 1250–80

LOCATION
In a shallow overhang near the head of a large cove 3.5 miles upstream in Dogoszhi Biko from its confluence with Kiet Siel Canyon. The two canyons flow together for only a short distance before joining the main Tsegi Canyon approximately 6 miles upstream from Marsh Pass, Navajo County, Arizona.

DESCRIPTION
Sixty rooms and courtyards situated on a series of ledges in a shallow arc.

BEAR RUIN

DATES
A.D. 641–713+

LOCATION
In the Forestdale Valley approximately 8 miles south of Show Low, Arizona, and 1 mile southeast of Forestdale trading post, on the Fort Apache Indian Reservation. It is on the highest of five terraces on the east (left) bank of Forestdale Creek about 4 miles above its confluence with Corduroy Creek, a tributary of Carrizo Creek.

DESCRIPTION
About half of the village, consisting of 13 round and square pit houses, two storage rooms, and one circular great kiva, was excavated.

BETATAKIN

DATES
A.D. 1267–86

LOCATION
Betatakin is a unit of Navajo National Monument and is near the head of a small side canyon entering the main Tsegi Canyon from the southwest about 6 miles upstream from Marsh Pass in Navajo County, Arizona.

DESCRIPTION   Since its discovery in 1909 by Byron Cummings, Betatakin has been one of the best-known cliff dwellings in northern Arizona. It lies in an arc-shaped cave and has about 135 rooms, some two-story, and a single rectangular kiva.

BLUFF SITE

DATES   A.D. 238+–322+

LOCATION   Site is on a bluff just east of and above the Forestdale Valley, about 8 miles south of Show Low, and 1 mile southeast of Forestdale trading post on the Fort Apache Indian Reservation. It is about 1.5 miles downstream from the Bear Ruin, and is about 3 miles above the confluence of Forestdale Creek and Corduroy Creek, a tributary of Carrizo Creek.

DESCRIPTION   An early pit house village of approximately thirty houses and a great kiva dug into bedrock. House shapes included both circular and subrectangular types with some slab-lined.

BROKEN FLUTE CAVE

DATES   A.D. 470–652

LOCATION   In the extreme northeastern corner of Arizona in Apache County. Cave is in the head of the easternmost tributary on the north side of Atahonez Wash which is a western tributary of Prayer Rock Wash which drains into the Red Wash that runs from near Red Rock Trading Post north to the San Juan River.

DESCRIPTION   A very large cave at the top of the talus slope. It contains at least seventeen Basket Maker pit houses, more than fifty storage cists, and a possible great kiva.

BROKEN K PUEBLO

DATES   A.D. 1150–1280

LOCATION   In the drainage of Hay Hollow Wash, 11 miles east of Snowflake, Arizona.

DESCRIPTION   A rectangular, single story masonry pueblo with about ninety-five rooms.

*CANYON CREEK RUIN

DATES   A.D. 1323+–48

LOCATION   Arizona

CANYON DE CHELLY, MISC. 1 (HOGAN 1, GROUP 1; HOGAN 6, GROUP 3)

DATES   A.D. 1800–70

LOCATION   In Canyon de Chelly National Monument, Apache County, Arizona, along Spider Rock Road.

DESCRIPTION   These are Navajo Hogans.

CARTER RANCH SITE

DATES   A.D. 1116–56+

LOCATION   Nine miles east of Snowflake, and less than 1 mile southwest of Point of the Mountain Mesa. The site is near Hay Hollow Wash.

DESCRIPTION   A Pueblo III masonry pueblo with thirty-nine rooms built in a rectangular block which includes a small plaza. Within the plaza are a large D-shaped kiva, a large storage pit and a small rectangular kiva with a platform. A detached circular great kiva lies 10 meters to the northwest of the north wing.

CHAVEZ PASS

DATES   About A.D. 1375

LOCATION   About 30 miles southwest of Winslow and about 20 miles southeast of Mormon Lake. It is on a high mesa north of the road which runs south from U. S. 66 past Meteor Crater to state route 65.

DESCRIPTION   The site consists of a large mesa-top pueblo built of lava rock. It has one hundred to two hundred rooms on the ground floor built in two house groups around two courts.

*CHETRO KETL

DATES   A.D. 911+–1116

LOCATION   New Mexico

DESCRIPTION   More tree-ring dates from Chetro Ketl than any other Southwestern ruin.

*CLIFF PALACE

DATES   A.D. 1210–73

LOCATION   Colorado

CROSS CANYON GROUP

DATES   Pit houses A.D. 875–910
Pueblo and Kiva A.D. 1002–24

LOCATION   On the south bank of Ganado Wash about 7 or 8 miles east (upstream) of Ganado, Apache County, Arizona.

DESCRIPTION   A complex series of sites consisting of a fifteen-room, L-shaped masonry pueblo with a circular, full-bench kiva in the plaza to the south. An earlier pueblo underlay this as well as another circular kiva under the west wing and perhaps four pit houses. In addition, two Great Kivas were nearby: one to the south and earlier than the pueblo and one to the north and somewhat later than the pueblo. At least five other pit houses were excavated nearby.

FORESTDALE RUIN

DATES   A.D. 1080–1115

LOCATION   In the Forestdale Valley approximately 8 miles south of Show Low, and 1 mile southeast of Forestdale trading post, on the Fort Apache Indian Reservation. The ruin is on the left bank of Forestdale Creek, a few hundred yards downstream from the Bear Ruin. Both sites are about 4 miles above the confluence of Forestdale Creek with Corduroy Creek, a tributary of Carrizo Creek.

DESCRIPTION   A twenty-one room masonry pueblo, with a small kiva and a circular stone-walled great kiva located about 25 meters southwest of the room block. The great kiva had a stair entry to the southeast and several rooms attached to its outside wall. About ten rooms and the great kiva were excavated.

FOURMILE RUIN

DATES   A.D. 1380+

LOCATION   On a bluff on the west bank of Cottonwood Creek, also called Pinedale Creek. It is about 4 miles south of Snowflake and 2 miles west of Taylor, Arizona.

DESCRIPTION   A large, three-story, roughly rectangular pueblo with walls of stone and adobe. There are burial areas on the flats away from the pueblo.

*GILA PUEBLO

DATES A.D. 1345–85

LOCATION Arizona

DESCRIPTION Regarded as a typical late Salado site.

GRASSHOPPER RUIN

DATES A.D. 1275–1400

LOCATION Ten miles west of Cibecue on the Fort Apache Indian Reservation. It is on both sides of the Salt River Draw, a northern tributary of the Salt River.

DESCRIPTION Pueblo contains more than five hundred masonry rooms, some of which were two stories high. Rooms are grouped in two major blocks, one on either side of the creek. These are surrounded by a number of smaller room blocks with twenty to thirty rooms. There is a great kiva within the western room block, and a number of smaller kivas.

HAWK'S NEST CLIFF DWELLING

DATES A.D. 1273

LOCATION In a cove on the east side of Sage (Sand) Valley in northern Navajo County, Arizona. The valley, although draining into Nakai Canyon, lies only a few miles north of the divide between that drainage and Cow Springs Wash which flows south to the Klethla Valley.

DESCRIPTION Perhaps poorly named. It has about twenty single-story storerooms set among large boulders in a long arc.

HAY HOLLOW SITE

DATES 300 B.C.–A.D. 300

LOCATION On a terrace overlooking Hay Hollow Wash, about 9 miles east of Snowflake, Arizona.

DESCRIPTION Desert culture

INSCRIPTION HOUSE

DATES A.D. 1220–71

LOCATION In a cave south of Navajo Mountain and about 25 miles NNE of Tonalea, northeastern Coconino County, Arizona, on an eastern tributary of and near the head of Navajo Canyon.

DESCRIPTION Well-known cliff ruin is part of Navajo National Monument. It has approximately fifty rooms of masonry, adobe, and jacal construction with extensive use of T-shaped doorways.

JEDDITO, SITE 4

DATES Latest horizon A.D. 1235–75

LOCATION On the southern rim of Antelope Mesa 1 mile west of the Jeddito Trading Post in Navajo County, Arizona.

DESCRIPTION Site has two Basket Maker III slab-walled pit houses (one actually called a room), a Pueblo I–II house unit of three rooms and an associated kiva which is superimposed on top of one of the earlier pit houses, and an early Pueblo III D-shaped kiva associated with a three-room pueblo. A seven-room structure was built as an extension of the Pueblo III room block. The D-shaped kiva is connected to the room block by a passageway.

JEDDITO, SITE 4A

DATES   Pit houses A.D. 800–5+

LOCATION   Two hundred yards west of Site 4, about 1 mile west of the Jeddito Trading Post on the rim of Antelope Mesa in Navajo County, Arizona.

DESCRIPTION   Pueblo II site has ten rooms and a D-shaped kiva. The pueblo and kiva overlie several pit houses.

JEDDITO, SITE 104

DATES   About A.D. 1280–83

LOCATION   Site is located in a side canyon of the Jeddito Valley and in the rocky breaks below Pink Arrow about 1 mile west of the Jeddito Trading Post, Navajo County, Arizona.

DESCRIPTION   A Pueblo II–III pueblo community consisting of a series of separate house units, of which nineteen rooms and one kiva were excavated.

JEDDITO, SITE 264

DATES   Pit houses A.D. 670–730

LOCATION   On a spur of Antelope Mesa which juts into the Jeddito Valley between Kawaikuh and Chakpahu. It is about 5 miles southwest of the Jeddito Trading Post, Navajo County, Arizona.

DESCRIPTION   A small Basket Maker III–Pueblo I village of six pit houses and 43 other units including slab-lined pits and other pit structures. A Pueblo II surface room overlies one of the pit houses.

JUNIPER COVE

DATES   About A.D. 650–75

LOCATION   At the base of the South Comb about 9 miles southwest of Kayenta, Navajo County, Arizona. It is approximately 1 mile north of highway U. S. 164 between Tuba City and Kayenta.

DESCRIPTION   A large Basket Maker III pit house village located on a stabilized sand dune directly adjacent to the sandstone outcrop of the South Comb. It contains more than a hundred units—pit houses and slab cists—and a circular Great Kiva.

KAWAIKUH

DATES   A.D. 1350–1469

LOCATION   On the southeastern edge of Antelope Mesa between two gorges and about 3 miles east of Awatovi in Navajo County, Arizona.

DESCRIPTION   The largest Pueblo III–IV ruin in the Jeddito area. The pueblo is of irregular arrangement with a large number of courts enclosed by large and small room clusters.

KIET SIEL

DATES   A.D. 945–1286

LOCATION   Kiet Siel is another unit of Navajo National Monument. It is in a cave 5.5 miles upstream from the confluence of the main Tsegi Canyon with its major left-bank tributary, Kiet Siel Canyon. The confluence is approximately 6 miles up the Tsegi from Marsh Pass, Navajo County, Arizona.

DESCRIPTION   Ruin has been described as the largest cliff dwelling in Arizona and it may well be. The long arc-shaped cave contains about a hundred and fifty rooms, courts, and plazas and five kivas.

KING'S RANCH RUIN

DATES About A.D. 1204

LOCATION About 35 miles north of Prescott on a gravel terrace overlooking the east bank of Chino Creek. It is about a half mile below the mouth of Walnut Creek and about 10 miles northwest of the confluence of Chino Creek with the Verde River.

DESCRIPTION A pueblo with mud and boulder walls. There are twelve ground-floor rooms and a second story existed over at least part of the masonry rooms and a second one was located in the burial area to the east of the pueblo. Room 6, which provided all of the tree-ring dates, was centrally located and was one of the best-preserved and most typical of the pueblo rooms.

*KINISHBA

DATES A.D. 1233+−1307

LOCATION Arizona

KINNIKINNICK PUEBLO

DATES About A.D. 1308

LOCATION About 30 miles southeast of Flagstaff, on Anderson Mesa, on the rim of a canyon tributary to Grapevine Canyon.

DESCRIPTION A masonry ruin with a large easterly and a smaller westerly room block of some sixty ground-floor rooms, some of which were at least two stories high.

KIN TIEL (WIDE RUIN)

DATES A.D. 1226–75

LOCATION At the Wide Ruins Trading Post, about 18 miles north of Chambers, Apache County, Arizona in Section 5, Township 23 North, Range 27 East.

DESCRIPTION A very large masonry pueblo built in an oval or "butterfly" shape on both sides of a small wash which is an eastern tributary of Wide Ruin Wash.

KOKOPNYAMA

DATES A.D. 1275–1380

LOCATION On the edge of Antelope Mesa approximately 1 mile northeast of the Jeddito Trading Post in Navajo County, Arizona.

DESCRIPTION A large pre-Spanish Pueblo III–IV masonry pueblo which encloses a large quadrangular plaza. In addition to the plaza and its surrounding room blocks, the pueblo stretches north for about 600 feet along the mesa edge. The Pueblo III dwellings and the Pueblo IV kivas are located on the slope below the mesa edge.

LENAKI

DATES About A.D. 1106+−1127+

LOCATION In a cave near the head of Dogoszhi Biko about 9 miles upstream from its junction with the main Tsegi Canyon. This confluence, in turn, is approximately 6 miles upstream from Marsh Pass, Navajo County, Arizona.

DESCRIPTION A small masonry cliff dwelling of about eight rooms and a circular kiva that was evidently never completed.

LUKACHUKAI, MISC. NO. 1

DATES	About A.D. 500
LOCATION	One and a half miles southeast of Lukachukai Trading Post.
DESCRIPTION	Basket Maker III?

MUMMY CAVE

DATES   Basket Maker A.D. 300–700
      Pueblo A.D. 1280

LOCATION In Canyon de Chelly National Monument, Apache County, Arizona. Cave is in east wall of Canyon del Muerto about 10 miles upstream from the confluence of Canyons de Chelly and del Muerto.

DESCRIPTION The cave consists of two large alcoves connected by a ledge about 110 feet long. They are about 80 feet above the natural talus slope and some 300 feet above the stream bed. Culture-bearing debris falls continuously from the cave over the top of the natural talus to the canyon floor. The western alcove is about 100 feet across and 75 feet deep. The eastern portion is over 200 feet across and 100 feet deep.

Both alcoves and the bench hold Pueblo III masonry structures with Mesa Verde affiliations. There are seven Pueblo III rooms on the bench. Most of these were more than one story in height and the easternmost is a three-story tower. These rooms are about 20 feet wide from front to back and 10–15 feet wide. They are solidly constructed with walls nearly 2 feet thick. Groups of wooden prayer sticks were set in the wall joints of the tower and others were laid beside each of the main roof timbers. The roof of the tower has a parapet.

No pit houses were found under the Pueblo III rooms in the alcoves but there were slab-lined Basket Maker houses on the bench. These were buried by a rockfall whose upper surface was made level with stones, timbers, and earth to provide a smooth floor for the overlying Pueblo III rooms and tower. To further increase the floor space of the bench, a retaining wall was built as far out on the cliff as possible and the space behind it was filled.

As houses became buried under trash, others were built at a higher level. Each of these houses was surrounded by a number of storage bins. These were of irregular shape and depth, and were 2 to 6 feet in diameter. They were lined with large thin slabs set on edge, the cracks and joints being sealed with mud reinforced with shredded bark, reed leaves, or corn husks. Two had roofs in place consisting of jug-like necks of adobe reinforced with sticks and covered with circular slabs. Some of the cists held corn, gourds, and seeds. In every respect these dwellings and cists fit the description for a Basket Maker III occupation. The precise association of the numerous tree-ring dates is occasionally to a house or cist structure, some of which may date to Basket Maker II times.

MUMMY CAVE NO. 2

DATES   Pueblo I about A.D. 700–800

LOCATION In Canyon de Chelly National Monument, Apache County, Arizona. Located 300 yards south of Mummy Cave in Canyon del Muerto.

DESCRIPTION A cave with at least two pit houses. Perishable materials were present. Ceramics include Lino Black-on-Gray and Kana-a Black-on-White.

NEW ORAIBI

DATES A.D. 1910–71

LOCATION Pueblo is situated at the base of the southern face of Third Mesa just west of Oraibi Wash in Navajo County, Arizona.

DESCRIPTION Founded in 1910–11 by people who remained in Old Oraibi after the 1906 split but who were too progressive to remain. The pueblo is constructed of well-dressed standstone with the majority of the houses being larger and more isolated than those in the other Hopi villages.

OBELISK CAVE (CANYON DE CHELLY)

DATES A.D. 325–480 (thirteen dates)

LOCATION In the extreme northeastern corner of Arizona in Apache County. Cave is in next drainage south of the canyon which contains Broken Flute Cave. This is a tributary of Prayer Rock Wash which drains into the Red Wash that runs from near Red Rock Trading Post north to the San Juan River.

DESCRIPTION Cave contains at least one pit house and some surface storage rooms. Ceramics include Lino Gray, Obelisk Gray, and unfired fiber-tempered pottery.

ORAIBI

DATES A.D. 1150–1971

LOCATION On the southeastern tip of Third Mesa, a southern projection of Black Mesa, 55 miles north of Winslow in Navajo County, Arizona.

DESCRIPTION Once the largest of the Hopi pueblos. It is composed of several linear room units forming parallel streets, rather than plazas. The pueblo is constructed of sandstone and rises to four stories in a few places. It has been continuously occupied since about A.D. 1150, but in 1906 a split occurred which depopulated the pueblo. Since then, Oraibi has been one of the smaller Hopi villages.

PINEDALE RUIN

DATES A.D.1305–80+

LOCATION About 16 miles west of Show Low and a half mile southeast of Pinedale, Arizona. It is 1 mile west of Mortenson Wash, a tributary of Silver Creek which runs north to the Little Colorado River.

DESCRIPTION A large Pueblo IV ruin of the Pinedale and Canyon Creek phases, consisting of two masonry units in an open pine forest. One is a large rectangular area surrounded by a row of single-story rooms. The other is a more compact pueblo of multiple story rooms around a rectangular plaza. It included a small rectangular kiva. An additional wing, several rooms in breadth, extended about 100 feet east of the northeast corner of the Pueblo. All of the testing and tree-ring specimens represent the compact room block.

*POINT OF PINES RUIN

DATES A.D. 1201–90

LOCATION Arizona

DESCRIPTION Room 11, with a single date of 1294+, is a Canyon Creek phase room. All other dated rooms are Maverick Mountain phase, representing occupation of the Point of Pines ruin by a group of migrants from the Kayenta-Anasazi (Haury, 1958). The six tree-ring specimens having neither the Point of Pines chronology nor the ring structure are thought to be from trees grown in the Kayenta area. All the dated tree-ring specimens from northern Arizona are small and probably represent artifacts carried to the Point of Pines region; they are not part of construction beams.

POLLOCK SITE

DATES
: Earlier part A.D. 1250
Pueblo about A.D. 1275

LOCATION
: About 40 miles east of Flagstaff, at the mouth of Kinnikinnick Canyon on the east slope of Anderson Mesa.

DESCRIPTION
: The ruin has two distinct parts. One (NA 4317) is a masonry pueblo of at least thirty rooms with small courts or large rooms forming part of the main mass. The second portion (NA 5817), located 300 yards away, is a group of rectangular room outlines. The only excavated outline contained a pit house.

PRAYER ROCK CAVE (PRAYER ROCK COVE, PRAYER ROCK CLIFF DWELLING)

DATES
: A.D. 1238–77

LOCATION
: In the extreme northeastern corner of Arizona in Apache County. Cave is near the mouth of Atahonez Canyon which is a western tributary of Prayer Rock Wash which drains into the Red Wash that runs from near Red Rock Trading Post north to the San Juan River.

DESCRIPTION
: Small Pueblo III cliff dwelling. Most remaining rooms are storerooms. Probable affiliations with the Mesa Verde area.

°PUEBLO BONITO

DATES
: A.D. 828–1126

LOCATION
: New Mexico

DESCRIPTION
: Two main building periods stand out—the first in the early part of the tenth century and the second in the latter part of the eleventh century. Minor construction seems to have gone on continuously, and repair work was carried out until 1130 at the least.

RED HOUSE

DATES
: About A.D. 1250

LOCATION
: At the southern base of Navajo Mountain, about 2 miles east of Rainbow Lodge, in northeastern Coconino County, Arizona.

DESCRIPTION
: A large, masonry, surface pueblo of a basic rectangular pattern enclosing a central plaza.

CAVE 2 (RED ROCK)

DATES
: A.D. 626–70

LOCATION
: In the extreme northeastern corner of Arizona in Apache County. Cave is in the same northern tributary of Atahonez Wash as is Cave 1. Atahonez drains into Prayer Rock Wash which drains into the Red Wash which runs from near the Red Rock Trading Post north to the San Juan River.

DESCRIPTION
: A small cave containing four Basket Maker III pit houses and at least three cists.

CAVE 6 (RED ROCK)

DATES	A.D. 660–74
LOCATION	In the extreme northeastern corner of Arizona in Apache County. Cave is in north wall of Atahonez Canyon a short distance upstream from Pocket Cave. This is a western tributary of Prayer Rock Wash which drains into Red Wash which runs from near Red Rock Trading Post north to the San Juan River.
DESCRIPTION	Cave is badly eroded with vestiges of three Basket Maker III pit houses, two or three cists, and thick trash deposits. Ceramics include Lino Gray, Kana-a Gray, fiber-tempered unfired pottery, and some later Pueblo Black-on-White sherds.

*RIDGE RUIN

DATES	A.D. 1085–1207
LOCATION	Arizona
DESCRIPTION	Assigned to the Elden phase.

SCAFFOLD HOUSE

DATES	A.D. 1274–85
LOCATION	In a large alcove on the left bank of the main Tsegi Canyon just below the mouth of the tributary Bubbling Springs Canyon and about 8 miles upstream from Marsh Pass, Navajo County, Arizona.
DESCRIPTION	Ruin has about thirty-five rooms and two kivas scattered along rock ledges and talus in a long arc. The feature which imparts the name to the ruin is a platform in a crevice high above the ruin at the east end.

SHIPAULOVI

DATES	A.D. 1700–present
LOCATION	On the summit of a low rocky knoll on Second Mesa on the Hopi Indian Reservation, 17 miles west of the Keams Canyon Trading Post, Navajo, Arizona.
DESCRIPTION	The smallest of the Hopi Villages. It is a good example of the enclosed court-type village. There is only one break in the wall in addition to three roofed entries. There are two rectangular kivas, one on the rocky summit near the houses and the second on the lower ground beside the trail that leads to the village.

SHOW LOW RUIN (WHIPPLE RUIN)

DATES	First occupation A.D. 1200–1300 Second occupation A.D. 1335–84
LOCATION	Fifty-five miles south of Holbrook, in the town of Show Low, on the west side of Show Low Creek, a tributary of Silver Creek and the Little Colorado River.
DESCRIPTION	An E-shaped masonry pueblo, mostly of one story, with possibly two hundred rooms. The northeast corner rooms were apparently abandoned and stripped, and most of the remainder of the Pueblo burned. Twenty-nine rooms were tested, many of which provided tree-ring specimens. A two-phase occupation.

SHUMWAY SITE

DATES   A.D. 938

LOCATION   In the Silver Creek drainage, 12.3 miles north of Show Low.

DESCRIPTION A round pit house was sectioned by a road cut. It was excavated into native soil, no rocks were seen, and the walls were plastered. Burned logs were found on the floor.

SHUNGOPAVI

DATES   A.D. 1680–1971

LOCATION   Pueblo is located on the southern edge of Second Mesa on the Hopi Indian Reservation in Navajo County, Arizona.

DESCRIPTION Pueblo was founded about 1680 after the destruction of its Spanish mission and abandonment of its previous site. It is a plaza-type pueblo constructed of stone and rises to three stories in some places. There are five rectangular kivas.

SICHOMOVI

DATES   A.D. 1750–present

LOCATION   Pueblo is located on top of First Mesa between the adjoining pueblos of Walpi to the south and Hano to the north on the Hopi Indian Reservation, Navajo County, Arizona.

DESCRIPTION Sichomovi has two long linear room blocks which enclose a narrow plaza. Two contiguous kivas are located in the plaza. The pueblo was founded about 1750 by some people from Walpi and the Rio Grande pueblos.

SITE 30 (FIELD MUSEUM)

DATES   A.D. 820–50

LOCATION   Three miles south of Vernon, Arizona, and several hundred yards west of Vernon Creek.

DESCRIPTION Site consists of eight irregularly shaped pit houses with the diameter varying between 2.65 and 5.3 meters and the depth varying between .45 and 1.95 meters. The dwellings were apparently stripped and burned.

SLIDING RUIN

DATES   A.D. 829–986

LOCATION   In Canyon de Chelly National Monument, Apache County, Arizona. Cave is on the north wall of Canyon de Chelly about 3+ miles upstream from the confluence of Canyons de Chelly and del Muerto.

DESCRIPTION A masonry pueblo with thirty to fifty rooms, some with two or three stories. There are three circular kivas. There is some Basket Maker III and Pueblo I material present.

*SPRUCE TREE HOUSE

DATES   A.D. 1020–1274

LOCATION   Colorado

DESCRIPTION The site was occupied in late Pueblo III.

SWALLOW'S NEST

DATES	Basket Maker A.D. 667–78 Pueblo A.D. 1252–70
LOCATION	In a cave on the left bank of the main Tsegi Canyon about 3 miles upstream from Marsh Pass, Navajo County, Arizona.
DESCRIPTION	Swallow's Nest is a two-component site. Pueblo III remains consist of a masonry cliff dwelling of eighteen rooms and a circular kiva. These are arranged in stepped tiers without the usual courtyards. A Basket Maker III occupation was also present in the cave as witnessed by a single excavated pit house.

TABLE ROCK PUEBLO

DATES	About A.D. 1370+
LOCATION	About 1 mile east of St. Johns. It is on top and between two low natural hills of sandstone about 500 feet east of the Little Colorado River.
DESCRIPTION	A Pueblo IV masonry one-story pueblo consisting of sixty to a hundred rooms and at least two kivas. Fifty rooms and the kivas were excavated. The latter were rectangular, with benches across one end.

NA 8300 (THREE MILE DRAW)

DATES	A.D. 730–860
LOCATION	On the left bank of Laguna Creek about 3 miles west of Kayenta, Navajo County, Arizona.
DESCRIPTION	NA 8300 is a pit house village with at least twenty pit houses, some with contiguous surface storage rooms to the northwest, outside fire pits, and other associated features.

TURKEY CAVE

DATES	About A.D. 550+–1025+
LOCATION	A few hundred yards upstream from Kiet Siel on the same side of Kiet Siel Canyon. It is also approximately 12 miles upstream from Marsh Pass, Navajo County, Arizona.
DESCRIPTION	Turkey Cave has a deep trash deposit, two circular kivas, and a number of associated masonry structures which may be turkey pens. Material in the trash ranges in time from pre-ceramic to late Pueblo III. Excavations in the trash have disclosed at least two pit houses in the cave.

TUSAYAN RUIN

DATES	A.D. 1180–90
LOCATION	South rim of the Grand Canyon in Coconino County, Arizona. It is nearly due south of the bend where the Colorado River resumes its westerly course.
DESCRIPTION	A small, masonry, U-shaped pueblo with eight living rooms, associated storerooms, and two circular kivas. One kiva was incorporated in the room block; the other isolated a short distance away.

TUZIGOOT

DATES
1st period—no dates
2nd period—about A.D. 1200
3rd period—about A.D. 1386

LOCATION
About 2 miles east of Clarkdale and 2 miles north of Cottonwood. It is about 400 yards from the Verde River on the top and slopes of a sharp ridge near Peck's Lake.

DESCRIPTION
An extensively excavated masonry pueblo with an overall length of about 500 feet and a maximum width of about 100 feet. The initial rooms were on top of the ridge. These were razed and replaced by others. Growth by accretion of room blocks proceeded down the slopes and finally ended in three outlying room blocks of less than ten rooms each. The area between the main room block and the outlying unit to the north served as a plaza area. Eighty-six rooms were excavated and 411 burials recovered from thick trash deposits on the slopes.

TWIN CAVES

DATES
About A.D. 667

LOCATION
On the western side of the Lukachukai Mountains, Apache County, Arizona. Cave is at the head of the central fork of Hospitibito Canyon, a tributary of Chinle Wash.

DESCRIPTION
Both east and west caves contain perishable materials. The east cave contains at least one Basket Maker III house.

TWIN CAVES PUEBLO

DATES
A.D. 1272–80

LOCATION
This cliff dwelling is . . . located on the right bank of Dogoszhi Biko, about 5 miles upstream from its confluence with the main Tsegi Canyon. Dogoszhi Biko enters the Tsegi approximately 6 miles upstream from Marsh Pass, Navajo County, Arizona.

DESCRIPTION
Twin Caves Pueblo lies on a series of ledges at the head of a rincon. It is divided into three distinct parts; a low middle section, and higher sections on each side. It has an aggregate of over sixty rooms and three circular kivas, the latter all located in the high western section.

VANDAL CAVE

DATES
About A.D. 650–80

LOCATION
Due east of Los Gigantes Buttes on the western side of the Lukachukai Mountains, Apache County, Arizona. Cave faces southwest from north wall of a SE–NW-running tributary of the central branch of Hospitibito Canyon, a tributary of the Chinle Wash.

DESCRIPTION
A Basket Maker III occupation, including three circular pit houses associated with early ceramics, corn, the bow and arrow, perishable remains, and seven dolichocephalic mummies and skeletons, is overlain by traces of later slab-house construction. Superimposed is a late six-room masonry pueblo with four associated burials, characterized by pottery and material culture analogous to those in the Mesa Verde and Tsegi Canyon areas.

WALPI

DATES A.D. 1680–1971

LOCATION Pueblo of Walpi is located on the southern tip of First Mesa, about 70 miles north of Winslow, Navajo County, Arizona.

DESCRIPTION A compact, linear unit due in part to topographic limitations. It is constructed of sandstone masonry and rises to four stories. There are five kivas in the village. Walpi was constructed at this location shortly after A.D. 1680 when its previous locations below the mesa were abandoned.

WHITE HOUSE

DATES From lower ruin A.D. 1050–1275

LOCATION In Canyon de Chelly National Monument, Apache County, Arizona. Site is located on north side of Canyon de Chelly about 1 mile upstream from the confluence of Canyon de Chelly and Canyon del Muerto.

DESCRIPTION A large masonry pueblo with about forty-five to fifty rooms on bottom land next to the cliffs and about twenty rooms in a cave some 35 feet up in the canyon wall. The postulated height of the lower group is four stories, which would bring the roofs to the height of the cliff dwelling rooms. There is one circular kiva in the lower cluster.

WHITE MOUND VILLAGE

DATES A.D. 783–803

LOCATION About 400 yards north of the Puerco River and 2 miles east of Houck, Apache County, Arizona.

DESCRIPTION A village of six excavated circular pit houses with rows of rectangular surface masonry storerooms and associated hearths and cists.

*WINGATE

DATES A.D. 863+–80+

LOCATION New Mexico

*WINONA VILLAGE

DATES A.D. 1089–1131

LOCATION Arizona

*WUPATKI

DATES A.D. 1028+–1205?

LOCATION Arizona

BIBLIOGRAPHY

ABERLE, S. D.

1948   The Pueblo Indians of New Mexico, their land, economy and civil organization. American Anthropological Association, Memoir No. 70. American Anthropologist, Vol. 50, No. 4, Part 2. Menasha.

ADAMS, ROBERT MCC.

1960   Early civilizations, subsistence, and environment. In, City invincible, edited by Carl H. Kraeling and Robert McC. Adams, pp. 269–95. University of Chicago Press. Chicago.

———

1966   The evolution of urban society. Aldine. Chicago.

ADAMS, WILLIAM Y.

1960   Ninety years of Glen Canyon archaeology, 1869–1959. Museum of Northern Arizona, Bulletin 33 (Glen Canyon Series No. 2). Flagstaff.

———, LINDSAY, ALEXANDER J., JR., and TURNER, CHRISTY G., II

1961   Survey and excavations in Lower Glen Canyon, 1952–1958. Museum of Northern Arizona, Bulletin 36 (Glen Canyon Series No. 3). Flagstaff.

AGENBROAD, L. D.

1967   The distribution of fluted points in Arizona. Kiva, Vol. 32, pp. 113–20. Tucson.

AIKENS, C. MELVIN

1965   Excavations in southwest Utah. University of Utah Anthropological Papers, No. 76 (Glen Canyon Series No. 27). Salt Lake City.

———

1966   Virgin-Kayenta cultural relationships. University of Utah Anthropological Papers, No. 79 (Glen Canyon Series No. 29). Salt Lake City.

AMBLER, J. RICHARD, and LAMBERT, MARJORIE F.

1965   A survey and excavations of caves in Hidalgo County, New Mexico. Monographs of the School of American Research, No. 25. Santa Fe.

———, LINDSAY, ALEXANDER J., JR., and STEIN, MARY ANNE

1964   Survey and excavations on Cummings Mesa, Arizona and Utah, 1960–1961. Museum of Northern Arizona, Bulletin 39 (Glen Canyon Series No. 5). Flagstaff.

AMSDEN, CHARLES AVERY

1949   Prehistoric southwesterners from Basket Maker to Pueblo. Southwest Museum, George Rice & Sons. Los Angeles.

ANDERSON, KEITH M.

1969   Tsegi Phase technology. Doctoral dissertation, University of Washington, Seattle. University Microfilms. Ann Arbor.

ANTEVS, ERNST

1935   Clovis Lake. Philadelphia Academy of Natural Science Proceedings, Vol. 87, pp. 304–11. Philadelphia.

———

1948   Climatic changes and pre-white man. University of Utah Bulletin, No. 38, pp. 168–91. Salt Lake City.

———

1952   Arroyo cutting and filling. Journal of Geology, Vol. 60, pp. 375–85. Chicago.

———

1955   Geologic-climatic dating in the West.

American Antiquity, Vol. 20, pp. 317–35. Salt Lake City.

ARMILLAS, PEDRO
1961 Land use in pre-Columbian America. *In,* A history of land use in arid regions, edited by D. Stamp. UNESCO. Paris.

———
1969 The arid frontier of Mexican civilization. Transactions of the New York Academy of Sciences, Vol. 31, pp. 697–704. New York.

ASCHMANN, HOMER
1962 Evaluations of dry land environments by societies at various levels of technical competence. *In,* Civilizations in desert lands, edited by Richard B. Woodbury, pp. 1–14. Anthropological papers of the University of Utah, No. 62. Salt Lake City.

AYRES, J. E.
1967 Prehistoric farm site near Cave Creek Arizona. Kiva, Vol. 32, pp. 106–11. Tucson.

BALDWIN, GORDON C.
1938 The excavation at Kinishba. American Antiquity, Vol. 4, pp. 11–21. Menasha.

———
1943 Archaeological survey in the Davis Dam Reservoir area. Unpublished manuscript. National Park Service.

———
1949 Archaeological survey in southeastern Utah. Southwestern Journal of Anthropology, Vol. 5, No. 4, pp. 393–404. Albuquerque.

BANDELIER, ADOLPH F.
1883 Report on the ruins of the pueblo of Pecos, second edition. Papers of the Archaeological Institute of America, American Series I, pp. 35–133. Cupples, Upham, and Company, Boston; N. Trübner and Company, London.

———
1890 Final report of investigations among the Indians of the southwestern United States, carried on mainly in the years from 1880 to 1885, part I. Papers of the Archaeological Institute of America, American Series III. John Wilson and Son, University Press. Cambridge.

———
1892 Final report of investigations among the Indians of the southwestern United States, carried on mainly in the years from 1880 to 1885, part II. Papers of the Archaeological Institute of America, American Series IV. John Wilson and Son, University Press. Cambridge.

———
1910 Documentary history of the Rio Grande pueblos of New Mexico, I. Bibliographic introduction. Papers of the School of American Archaeology, No. 13. Archaeological Institute of America. New York.

BANNISTER, BRYANT; DEAN, JEFFREY S., and GELL, ELIZABETH A. M.
1966 Tree-ring dates from Arizona E, Chinle-De Chelly-Red Rock area. Laboratory of Tree-Ring Research, The University of Arizona. Tucson.

———, ———, and ROBINSON, WILLIAM J.
1968 Tree-ring dates from Arizona C-D, eastern Grand Canyon-Tsegi Canyon-Kayenta area. Laboratory of Tree-Ring Research, The University of Arizona. Tucson.

———, ———, and ———
1969 Tree-ring dates from Utah S-W, southern Utah area. Laboratory of Tree-Ring Research, The University of Arizona. Tucson.

———, GELL, ELIZABETH A. M., and HANNAH, JOHN W.
1966 Tree-ring dates from Arizona N-Q, Verde-Show Low-St. Johns area. Laboratory of Tree-Ring Research, The University of Arizona. Tucson.

———, HANNAH, JOHN W., and ROBINSON, WILLIAM J.
1966 Tree-ring dates from Arizona K, Puerco-Wide Ruin-Ganado. Laboratory of Tree-Ring Research, The University of Arizona. Tucson.

———, ———, and ———

1970 Tree-ring dates from New Mexico M-N, S, Z. Laboratory of Tree-Ring Research, The University of Arizona. Tucson.

———, ROBINSON, WILLIAM J., and WARREN, RICHARD L.

1967 Tree-ring dates from Arizona J, Hopi Mesas area. Laboratory of Tree-Ring Research, The University of Arizona. Tucson.

BARTLETT, K.

1943 A primitive stone industry of the Little Colorado Valley, Arizona. American Antiquity, Vol. 8, pp. 266–88. Menasha.

BEAGLEHOLE, ERNEST

1937 Notes on Hopi economic life. Yale University Publications in Anthropology, No. 15. New Haven.

BEALS, RALPH L.

1943 Northern Mexico and the Southwest. In, El norte de Mexico y el sur de Estados Unidos. Tercera Reunion de Mesa Redonda sobre Problemas Anthropologicas de Mexico y Central America. Mexico, D. F.

———, BRAINERD, GEORGE W., and SMITH, WATSON

1945 Archaeological studies in northeast Arizona. University of California Publications in American Archaeology and Ethnology, Vol. 44, No. 1, pp. 1–171. Berkeley and Los Angeles.

BENNETT, JOHN W.

1943 Recent developments in the functional interpretation of archaeological data. American Antiquity, Vol. 9, No. 2, pp. 208–19. Menasha.

BINFORD, LEWIS R.

1968a Archaeological Perspectives. In, New perspectives in archaeology, edited by Sally R. Binford and Lewis R. Binford, pp. 5–32. Aldine. Chicago.

1968b Post-Pleistocene adaptations. In, New perspectives in archaeology, edited by Sally R. Binford and Lewis R. Binford, pp. 313–41. Aldine. Chicago.

BINFORD, SALLY R., and BINFORD, LEWIS R. (editors)

1968 New perspectives in archaeology. Aldine. Chicago.

BIRDSELL, JOSEPH

1966 Some predictions for the Pleistocene based upon equilibrium systems among recent hunters. In, Man the hunter, edited by Richard B. Lee and Irven deVore, pp. 229–40. Aldine. Chicago.

BLUHM, ELAINE A.

1957a Patterns of settlement in the southwestern United States A.D. 500–1250. Unpublished Ph.D. dissertation, Department of Anthropology, University of Chicago. Chicago.

1957b The Sawmill Site: a Reserve Phase village, Pine Lawn Valley, western New Mexico. Fieldiana: Anthropology, Vol. 47, No. 1. Chicago Natural History Museum. Chicago.

1960 Mogollon settlement patterns in Pine Lawn Valley, New Mexico. American Antiquity, Vol. 25, No. 4, pp. 538–46. Salt Lake City.

BOHRER, VORSILA L.

1967 Plant resources in a human ecosystem in southern Arizona, 100 B.C.–1100 A.D. Bioscience 17:12. Washington, D.C.

1968 Paleoecology of an archaeological site near Snowflake, Arizona. Unpublished Ph.D. dissertation, Department of Botany, University of Arizona. Tucson.

1970 Ethnobotanical aspects of Snaketown, a Hohokam village in southern Arizona. American Antiquity, Vol. 35, No. 4, pp. 413–30. Washington, D.C.

———, CUTLER, H. C., and SAUER, JONATHAN D.

1969 Carbonized plant remains from two Hohokam sites, Arizona. Kiva, Vol. 35, pp. 1–10. Tucson.

BOSERUP, ESTER
1965 The conditions of agricultural growth. Aldine. Chicago.

BRADFIELD, WESLEY
1931 Cameron Creek village. Monographs of the School of American Research, No. 1. Santa Fe.

BRAITHWAITE, R. B.
1960 Scientific explanations. Harper and Row. New York.

BRAND, DONALD D.; HAWLEY, FLORENCE M.; HIBBEN, FRANK C., *et al.*
1937 Tseh So, a small house ruin, Chaco Canyon, New Mexico (Preliminary Report). The University of New Mexico Bulletin, Whole No. 308. Anthropological Series, Vol. 2, No. 2. Albuquerque.

BRETERNITZ, DAVID A.
1957a 1956 excavations near Flagstaff, part I. Plateau, Vol. 30, pp. 22–30. Flagstaff.

———
1957b 1956 excavations near Flagstaff, part II. Plateau, Vol. 30, pp. 43–54. Flagstaff.

———
1957c Highway salvage archaeology by the Museum of Northern Arizona, 1956–1957. Kiva, Vol. 23, No. 2, pp. 8–17. Arizona State Museum, Tucson.

———
1959 Excavations at Nantack Village, Point of Pines, Arizona. Anthropological Papers of The University of Arizona, No. 1. Tucson.

———
1960 Excavations at three sites in the Verde Valley, Arizona. Museum of Northern Arizona, Bulletin No. 34. Flagstaff.

———
1966 An appraisal of tree-ring dated pottery in the Southwest. Anthropological Papers of the University of Arizona, No. 10. Tucson.

———
1969 Archaeological investigations in Turkey Cave (NA 2520), Navajo Na-

tional Monument, 1963. Museum of Northern Arizona Technical Series, No. 8. Flagstaff.

———, and SEBLEY, ROBERT A.
1962 Excavations at the New Leba 17 Site near Cameron, Arizona. Plateau, Vol. 35, No. 2, pp. 60–68. Museum of Northern Arizona. Flagstaff.

BREW, JOHN OTIS
1941 Preliminary report of the Peabody Museum Awatovi Expedition of 1939. Plateau, Vol. 13, No. 3, pp. 37–48. Flagstaff.

———
1946 Archaeology of Alkali Ridge, northeastern Utah, with a review of the prehistory of the Mesa Verde division of the San Juan and some observations of archaeological systematics. Papers of the Peabody Museum of American Archaeology and Ethnology, Vol. 21. Harvard University, Cambridge.

BRYAN, ALAN LYLE
1965 Paleo-American prehistory. Occasional Papers of the Idaho State University Museum, No. 16. Pocatello.

BRYAN, KIRK
1929 Flood-water farming. Geographical Review, Vol. 19, pp. 444–56. New York.

———
1941 Pre-Columbian agriculture in the Southwest, as conditioned by periods of alluviation. Annals of the Association of American Geographers, Vol. 31, No. 4, pp. 219–42.

———
1954 The geology of Chaco Canyon, New Mexico, in relation to the life and remains of the prehistoric peoples of Pueblo Bonito. Smithsonian Miscellaneous Collections, Vol. 122, No. 7. Washington, D.C.

BULLARD, WILLIAM, JR.
1962 The Cerro Colorado Site and pit house architecture in the southwestern United States prior to A.D. 900. Papers of the Peabody Museum of

Archaeology and Ethnology, Harvard University, Vol. 44, No. 2. Cambridge.

BURGH, ROBERT F.
1948   The archaeology of Castle Park. Colorado University Studies in Anthropology, No. 2. Boulder.

BURKENROAD, DAVID
1968   Population growth and economic change. Unpublished manuscript, Field Museum of Natural History. Chicago.

BURT, W. H.
1961   A fauna from an Indian site near Redington, Arizona. Journal of Mammology, Vol. 42, pp. 115–16.

BUTLER, B. ROBERT
1968   A guide to understanding Idaho archaeology, Second (Revised) Edition. The Idaho State University Museum. Pocatello.

BUTZER, KARL W.
1964   Environment and archaeology. Aldine. Chicago.

CAMPBELL, ELIZABETH CROZER
1931   An archaeological survey of the 29 Palms region. Southwestern Museum Papers, No. 7. Los Angeles.

CARNEIRO, ROBERT L.
1967   On the relationship between size of population and complexity of social organization. Southwestern Journal of Anthropology, Vol. 23, No. 3, pp. 234–43. Albuquerque.

CARTER, GEORGE F.
1945   Plant geography and culture history in the American Southwest. Viking Fund Publications in Anthropology, No. 5. New York.

CASTETTER, E. F., and BELL, W. H.
1942   Pima and Papago Indian agriculture. Inter-Americana Studies, No. 1. University of New Mexico Press, Albuquerque.
———, and ———
1951   Yuman Indian Agriculture, primitive

subsistence on the Lower Colorado and Gila Rivers. University of New Mexico Press. Albuquerque.

CHAMBERLIN, T. C.
1965   The method of multiple working hypotheses. Science, Vol. 148, pp. 754–59. Washington, D.C. (Reprinted from the original article published in Science [old series], Vol. 15, 1890).

CLARK, COLIN
1967   Population growth and land use. St. Martin's Press. New York.

CLARK, GEOFFREY A.
1969   Preliminary analysis of burial clusters at the Grasshopper Site, east-central Arizona. Kiva, Vol. 35, No. 2, pp. 57–90. Tucson.

CLARKE, DAVID L.
1968   Analytical archaeology. Methuen and Co. Ltd. London.

CLOWARD, RICHARD A., and PIVEN, FRANCES FOX
1965   Politics, the welfare system, and poverty. In, Poverty in America, edited by Louis A. Ferman, Joyce L. Kornbluh, and Alan Haber. University of Michigan Press. Ann Arbor.

COLTON, HAROLD S.
1932   A survey of prehistoric sites in the region of Flagstaff, Arizona. Smithsonian Institution, Bureau of American Ethnology, Bulletin 104. Washington, D.C.

———
1939a An archaeological survey of northwestern Arizona including the descriptions of fifteen new pottery types. Museum of Northern Arizona, Bulletin No. 16. Flagstaff.

———
1939b Prehistoric culture units and their relationship in northern Arizona. Museum of Northern Arizona, Bulletin No. 17. Flagstaff.

———
1945   The Patayan problem in the Colorado River Valley. Southwestern Journal of Anthropology, Vol. 1, No. 1, pp. 114–21. Albuquerque.

1946   The Sinagua, a summary of the archaeology of the region of Flagstaff, Arizona. Museum of Northern Arizona, Bulletin No. 22. Flagstaff.

——— (editor)

1955a   Pottery types of the Southwest. Museum of Northern Arizona, Ceramic Series No. 3A. Flagstaff.

——— (editor)

1955b   Pottery types of the Southwest. Museum of Northern Arizona, Ceramic Series No. 3B. Flagstaff.

——— (editor)

1956   Pottery types of the Southwest. Museum of Northern Arizona, Ceramic Series No. 3C. Flagstaff.

——— (editor)

1958   Pottery types of the Southwest. Museum of Northern Arizona, Ceramic Series No. 3D. Flagstaff.

———, and HARGRAVE, L. L.

1937   Handbook of northern Arizona pottery wares. Museum of Northern Arizona, Bulletin No. 11. Flagstaff.

CONNER, SYDNEY

1943   Excavations at Kinnikinnick, Arizona. American Antiquity, Vol. 8, No. 4, pp. 376–79. Menasha.

COOK, THOMAS GENN

1970   Social groups and settlement patterns in Basket Maker III. Unpublished Master's thesis, Department of Anthropology, University of Chicago. Chicago.

COSGROVE, C. B.

1947   Caves of the Upper Gila and Hueco areas. Papers of the Peabody Museum of American Archaeology and Ethnology, Harvard University, Vol. 24, No. 2. Cambridge.

COSGROVE, H. S., and C. B.

1932   The Swarts Ruin. Papers of the Peabody Museum of American Archaeology and Ethnology, Harvard University, Vol. 15, No. 1. Cambridge.

CRABTREE, DON E., and BUTLER, ROBERT

1964   Notes on experiments in flint knapping: I, Heat treatment of silica minerals. Tebiwa, Vol. 7, No. 1. Journal of the Idaho State University Museum. Pocatello.

CRESSMAN, LUTHER S.

1942   Archaeological researches in the northern Great Basin. Carnegie Institution of Washington, Publication No. 538. Washington, D.C.

———, WILLIAMS, HOWEL, and KRIEGER, ALEX D.

1940   Atlatls and associated artifacts from south-central Oregon. In, Early man in Oregon: archaeological studies in the northern Great Basin, edited by Luther S. Cressman, et al., pp. 16–52. University of Oregon Monographs, Studies in Anthropology, No. 3. Eugene.

CROSS, JACK L.; SHAW, ELIZABETH H., and SCHEIFELE, KATHLEEN (editors)

1960   Arizona, its people and resources. University of Arizona Press. Tucson.

CUMMINGS, BYRON

1935   Progress of the excavation at Kinishba. Kiva, Vol. 1, No. 3, pp. 1–4. Tucson.

———

1937   Excavation of Kinishba Pueblo. Kiva, Vol. 3, pp. 1–4. Tucson.

———

1941   Segazlin Mesa ruins. Kiva, Vol. 7, No. 1, pp. 1–4. Tucson.

CUSHING, FRANK H.

1890   Preliminary notes on the origin, working hypothesis and primary researches of the Hemenway Southwestern Archaeological Expedition. Congrès International des Américanistes. Compte-rendu de la septième session, Berlin, 1888, pp. 151–94.

CUTLER, H. C.

1966   Corn, cucurbits, and cotton from Glen Canyon. University of Utah Anthropological Papers, No. 8. Salt Lake City.

———, and WHITAKER, T. W.

1961   History and distribution of the cultivated cucurbits in the Americas. American Antiquity, Vol. 26, pp. 469–85. Salt Lake City.

DAIFUKU, HIROSHI
1952 A new conceptual scheme for prehistoric cultures in the southwestern United States. American Anthropologist, Vol. 54, No. 2, Part 1, pp. 191–200. Menasha.

———
1961 Jeddito 264: a report on the excavation of a Basket Maker III–Pueblo I Site in northeastern Arizona, with a review of some current theories in southwestern archaeology. Papers of the Peabody Museum, Harvard University, Vol. 33, No. 1. Cambridge.

DANSON, EDWARD B.
1957 An archaeological survey of west-central New Mexico and east-central Arizona. Papers of the Peabody Museum of Archaeology and Ethnology, Harvard University, Vol. 44, No. 1. Cambridge.

DAVIS, WILBUR A.
1966 Theoretical problems in western prehistory. In, The current status of anthropological research in the Great Basin: 1964, edited by Warren L. d'Azevedo, Wilbur A. Davis, Don D. Fowler, and Wayne Suttles, pp. 147–65. Desert Research Institute. Reno.

DEAN, J. S.
1970 Aspects of Tsegi Phase social organization. In, Reconstructing prehistoric pueblo societies, edited by William A. Longacre, pp. 140–74. University of New Mexico Press. Albuquerque.

DEETZ, JAMES, and DETHLEFSEN, EDWIN
1965 The Doppler effect and archaeology: a consideration of the spatial aspects of seriation. Southwestern Journal of Anthropology, Vol. 21, pp. 196–206. Albuquerque.

DeGARMO, G. D.
1970 Big game hunters: an alternative hypothesis. Paper presented at the 35th Annual Meeting, Society for American Archaeology. Mexico City.

DICK, HERBERT W.
1965 Bat Cave. Monographs of the School of American Research, No. 27. Santa Fe.

DI PESO, CHARLES C.
1951 The Babocomari Village Site on the Babocomari River, southeastern Arizona. The Amerind Foundation, No. 5. Dragoon, Arizona.

———
1953 The Sobaipuri Indians of the Upper San Pedro River Valley, southeastern Arizona. The Amerind Foundation, No. 6. Dragoon, Arizona.

———
1956 The Upper Pima of San Cayetano del Tumacacori: an archaeo-historical reconstruction of the Ootam of Pimeria Alta. The Amerind Foundation, No. 7. Dragoon, Arizona.

———
1958 The Reeve Ruin of southeastern Arizona: a study of a prehistoric western Pueblo migration into the Middle San Pedro Valley. The Amerind Foundation, No. 8. Dragoon, Arizona.

DOBYNS, H. F.
1956 Prehistoric Indian occupation within the eastern area of the Yuman Complex. Unpublished manuscript.

DOUGLASS, A. E.
1929 The secret of the Southwest solved by talkative tree rings. National Geographic Magazine, Vol. 56, No. 6, pp. 736–70. Washington, D.C.

DOWNS, JAMES F.
1966 The significance of environmental manipulation in Great Basin cultural development. In, The current status of anthropological research in the Great Basin: 1964, edited by Warren L. d'Azevedo, Wilbur A. Davis, Don D. Fowler, and Wayne Suttles, pp. 39–56. Desert Research Institute. Reno.

DUFFEN, WILLIAM
1937 Some notes on a summer's work near Bonita, Arizona. Kiva, Vol. 2, No. 3, pp. 13–16. Tucson.

DUTTON, BERTHA P.

1938 Leyit Kin, a small house ruin, Chaco Canyon, New Mexico, excavation report. A Monograph of the University of New Mexico, The School of American Research, Vol. 1, No. 6. Albuquerque.

EDDY, FRANK W.

1961 Excavations at Los Pinos Phase sites in the Navajo Reservoir district. Museum of New Mexico Papers, No. 4. Museum of New Mexico Press. Santa Fe.

————, HESTER, JAMES J., and DITTERT, ALFRED

1963 Pueblo Period sites in the Piedra River district. Museum of New Mexico Papers in Anthropology, No. 10. Santa Fe.

EGGAN, FRED

1950 Social organization of the western pueblos. University of Chicago Press. Chicago.

————, and d'AZEVEDO, WARREN L.

1966 Introduction. In, The current status of anthropological research in the Great Basin: 1964, edited by Warren L. d'Azevedo, Wilbur A. Davis, Don D. Fowler, and Wayne Suttles, pp. xiii–xx. Desert Research Institute. Reno.

ERDMAN, JAMES A.; DOUGLAS, CHARLES L., and MARR, JOHN W.

1969 Environment of Mesa Verde, Colorado. Wetherill Mesa Studies, Archaeological Research Series No. 7-B. National Park Service, U. S. Department of the Interior, Washington, D.C.

EULER, ROBERT C.

1958 Walapai culture-history. Unpublished Ph.D. dissertation. University of New Mexico. Albuquerque.

1963 Archaeological problems in western and northwestern Arizona, 1962. Plateau, Vol. 35, No. 3, pp. 78–85. Flagstaff.

FAIRBANKS, CHARLES H.

1968 The archaeological contribution to urban studies. In, Urban anthropology: research perspectives and strategies, edited by Elizabeth M. Eddy. Southern Anthropological Society Proceedings, No. 2. University of Georgia Press. Athens.

FERDON, EDWIN N., JR.

1955 A trial survey of Mexican-Southwestern architectural parallels. Monographs of the School of American Research, No. 21. Santa Fe.

1966 The prehistoric culture of Ecuador —a review. Science, Vol. 152, No. 3730, pp. 1731–32. Washington, D.C.

1967 The Hohokam "ball court": an alternative view of its function. Kiva, Vol. 33, No. 1, pp. 1–14. Tucson.

FERGUSON, C. W.

1969 A 7104-year annual tree-ring chronology for Bristlecone Pine, *Pinus aristata*, from the White Mountains, California. Tree-Ring Bulletin, Vol. 29, Nos. 3–4. Tree-Ring Society and the Laboratory of Tree-Ring Research, University of Arizona. Tucson.

FERMAN, LOUIS A.; KORNBLUH, JOYCE L., and HABER, ALAN (editors)

1965 Poverty in America. University of Michigan Press. Ann Arbor.

FEWKES, JESS W.

1891 Reconnaissance of ruins in or near the Zuni Reservation. Journal of American Ethnology and Archaeology, Vol. 1, pp. 93–132. Boston.

1896 Preliminary account of an expedition to the cliff villages of the Red Rock country, and the Tusayan ruins of Sikyatki and Awatobi, Arizona, in 1895. Smithsonian Institution, Bureau of American Ethnology, Annual Report, 1895, pp. 557–88. Washington, D.C.

1898   Preliminary account of an expedition to the pueblo ruins near Winslow, Arizona, in 1896. Smithsonian Institution, Bureau of American Ethnology, Annual Report, 1896, pp. 517–39. Washington, D.C.

1904   Two summers' work in pueblo ruins. Smithsonian Institution, Bureau of American Ethnology, 22nd Annual Report, 1900–1901, part 1. Washington, D.C.

1909   Antiquities of the Mesa Verde National Park: Spruce-Tree House. Smithsonian Institution, Bureau of American Ethnology, Bulletin No. 41. Washington, D.C.

1911a   Preliminary report on a visit to the Navaho National Monument, Arizona. Smithsonian Institution, Bureau of American Ethnology, Bulletin No. 50. Washington, D.C.

1911b   Antiquities of the Mesa Verde National Park, Cliff Palace. Smithsonian Institution, Bureau of American Ethnology, Bulletin No. 51. Washington, D.C.

1912   Casa Grande, Arizona. Smithsonian Institution, Bureau of American Ethnology, 28th Annual Report, pp. 25–179. Washington, D.C.

1916   Excavation and repair of Sun Temple, Mesa Verde National Park. Holmes Anniversary Volume. Washington, D.C.

1917   Far View House—a pure pueblo ruin. Art and Archaeology, Vol. 6, No. 3, pp. 133–41. Archaeological Institute of America. Washington, D.C.

1919   Prehistoric villages, castles and towers of southwestern Colorado. Smithsonian Institution, Bureau of American Ethnology, Bulletin No. 70. Washington, D.C.

FLANNERY, KENT V.

1965   The ecology of early food production in Mesopotamia. Science, Vol. 147, pp. 1247–56. Washington, D.C.

1968   Archaeological systems theory and early Mesoamerica. *In,* Anthropological archaeology in the Americas, edited by Betty J. Meggars, pp. 67–87. Anthropological Society of Washington. Washington, D.C.

1969   Origins and ecological effects of early domestication in Iran and the Near East. *In,* The domestication and exploitation of plants and animals, edited by P. J. Ucko and G. W. Dimbleby, pp. 73–100. Duckworth. London.

FOWLER, DON D.

1966   Great Basin social organization. *In,* The current status of anthropological research in the Great Basin: 1964, edited by Warren L. d'Azevedo, Wilbur A. Davis, Don D. Fowler, and Wayne Suttles, pp. 57–74. Desert Research Institute. Reno.

FRITTS, HAROLD C.

1963   Computer programs for tree-ring research. Tree-Ring Bulletin, Vol. 25, Nos. 3–4, pp. 2–8. Tree-Ring Society and the Laboratory of Tree-Ring Research, University of Arizona. Tucson.

1965   Tree-ring evidence for climatic changes in western North America. Monthly Weather Review, Vol. 93, pp. 421–43.

———, SMITH, D. G., and STOKES, M. A.

1965   The biological model for paleoclimatic interpretation of Mesa Verde tree-ring series. *In,* Contributions of the Wetherill Mesa Archaeological Project, edited by Douglas Osborne, pp. 101–21. Memoirs of the Society for American Archaeology, No. 19. Salt Lake City.

FULTON, WILLIAM S.

1934 Survey of Texas Canyon, Arizona. Heye Foundation Contributions, Vol. 12, Nos. 2 and 3. New York.

—— 1941 A ceremonial cave in the Winchester Mountains, Arizona. The Amerind Foundation, No. 2. Dragoon, Arizona.

——, and TUTHILL, CARR
1940 An archaeological site near Gleeson, Arizona. The Amerind Foundation, No. 1. Dragoon, Arizona.

GLADWIN, HAROLD S.
1928 Excavation at Casa Grande, Arizona. Southwest Museum Papers, No. 2. Los Angeles.

—— 1937 Excavations at Snaketown II: comparisons and theories. Medallion Papers, No. 26. Gila Pueblo. Globe, Arizona.

—— 1942 Excavation at Snaketown III: Revisions. Medallion Papers, No. 30. Gila Pueblo. Globe, Arizona.

—— 1945 The Chaco Branch excavations at White Mound and in the Red Mesa Valley. Medallion Papers, No. 33. Gila Pueblo. Globe, Arizona.

—— 1948 Excavation at Snaketown IV: Reviews and conclusions. Medallion Papers, No. 38. Gila Pueblo. Globe, Arizona.

——, HAURY, EMIL W.; SAYLES, E. B., and GLADWIN, NORA
1937 Excavations at Snaketown, material culture. Medallion Papers, No. 25. Gila Pueblo. Globe, Arizona.

GLADWIN, WINIFRED, and GLADWIN, HAROLD S.
1929a The red-on-buff culture of the Gila Basin. Medallion Papers, No. 3. Pasadena.

——, and ——
1929b The red-on-buff culture of the Papagueria. Medallion Papers, No. 4. Gila Pueblo. Globe, Arizona.

——, and ——
1930a The western range of the red-on-buff culture. Medallion Papers, No. 5. Gila Pueblo. Globe, Arizona.

——, and ——
1930b An archaeological survey of the Verde Valley. Medallion Papers, No. 6. Gila Pueblo. Globe, Arizona.

GLADWIN, THOMAS
1967 Poverty U.S.A. Little, Brown, and Company. Boston.

GOLDSCHMIDT, WALTER
1963 Man's way. Holt, Rinehart and Winston. New York.

GOODWIN, G.
1935 The social divisions and economic life of the Western Apache. American Anthropologist, Vol. 37, pp. 55–64. Menasha.

GORMAN, FREDERICK
1968 Archaeology as structural anthropology. Unpublished manuscript. Department of Anthropology. University of Arizona. Tucson.

—— 1969 The Clovis hunters: an alternate view of their environment and ecology. Kiva, Vol. 35, No. 2, pp. 91–102. Tucson.

GRAVES, T.; GRAVES, N., and KOBRIN, M.
1969 Historical inferences from Guttman Scales: the return of age-area magic? Current Anthropology, Vol. 10, pp. 317–38.

GREEN, CHRISTINE, and SELLERS, WILLIAM D.
1964 Arizona climate. University of Arizona Press. Tucson.

GREGORY, DAVID A.
1969 Test of an archaeological hypothesis and its possible implications for the definition and solution of the problems of urban poverty. Unpublished manuscript. Field Museum of Natural History. Chicago.

GRIFFIN, P. BION
1967 A high status burial from Grasshopper ruin, Arizona. Kiva, Vol. 33, No. 2, pp. 37–53. Tucson.

GUERNSEY, SAMUEL J.

1931 Explorations in northeastern Arizona. Papers of the Peabody Museum of American Archaeology and Ethnology, Harvard University, Vol. 12, No. 1. Cambridge.

————, and KIDDER, A.V.

1921 Basket Maker caves of northeastern Arizona, report on the explorations, 1916, 1917. Papers of the Peabody Museum of American Archaeology and Ethnology, Harvard University, Vol. 8, No. 2. Cambridge.

GUMERMAN, GEORGE J.

1966 Two Basket Maker II pithouse villages in eastern Arizona: a preliminary report. Plateau, Vol. 39, No. 2, pp. 80–87. Museum of Northern Arizona. Flagstaff.

————, and OLSON, ALAN P.

1968 Prehistory in the Puerco Valley, eastern Arizona. Plateau, Vol. 40, No. 4, pp. 113–27. Museum of Northern Arizona. Flagstaff.

————, and SKINNER, S. ALAN

1968 A synthesis of the prehistory of the central Little Colorado Valley, Arizona. American Antiquity, Vol. 33, No. 2, pp. 185–99. Salt Lake City.

GUNNERSON, JAMES H.

1969 The Fremont Culture. Papers of the Peabody Museum of American Archaeology and Ethnology, Harvard University, Vol. 59, No. 1. Cambridge.

GUTHE, CARL E.

1967 Reflections on the founding of the Society for American Archaeology. American Antiquity, Vol. 32, No. 4, pp. 433–40. Salt Lake City.

HACK, J. T.

1942 The changing physical environment of the Hopi Indians of Arizona. Papers of the Peabody Museum, Harvard University, Vol. 35, No. 1. Cambridge.

HACKENBERG, R.

1962 Economic alternatives in arid lands: a case study of Pima and Papago Indians. Ethnology, Vol. 1, pp. 186–96. Pittsburgh.

HALL, E. T., JR.

1942 Archaeological survey of the Walhalla Glades. Museum of Northern Arizona, Bulletin No. 20. Flagstaff.

HAMBIDGE, GOVE (editor)

1941 Climate and man. U. S. Department of Agriculture. Washington, D.C.

HAMMOND, E. H.

1963 Classes of land surface forms in the 48 states (map). Association of American Geographers. Washington, D.C.

HANDS, E. J.

1935 Tanque Verde ruins. Kiva, Vol. 1, No. 4, pp. 1–4. Tucson.

HANSON, N. R.

1965 Patterns of discovery. Cambridge University Press. London.

HARGRAVE, LYNDON L.

1931 Excavations of Kin Tiel and Kokopnyama. Smithsonian Miscellaneous Collections, Vol. 82, No. 11, pp. 80–120. Washington, D.C.

————

1933 Pueblo II houses of the San Francisco Mountains, Arizona. Museum of Northern Arizona, Bulletin No. 4, pp. 15–75. Flagstaff.

————

1935a Jeddito Valley and first pueblo towns in Arizona to be visited by Europeans. Museum Notes, Vol. 8, No. 4. Museum of Northern Arizona. Flagstaff.

————

1935b Report on archaeological reconnaissance in the Rainbow Plateau area of northern Arizona and southern Utah, based upon fieldwork by the Rainbow Bridge-Monument Valley Expedition of 1933. University of California Press. Berkeley.

HARRILL, BRUCE G.

1968 A small prehistoric rock shelter in northwestern Arizona. Plateau, Vol.

40, No. 4, pp. 157–65. Museum of Northern Arizona. Flagstaff.

HARRINGTON, JOHN P.; FRIERE-MARRECO, BARBARA, and ROBBINS, W. W.
1916   Ethnobotany of the Tewa Indians. Smithsonian Institution, Bureau of American Ethnology, Bulletin No. 55. Washington, D.C.

HARRINGTON, M. R.
1933   Gypsum Cave, Nevada. Southwest Museum Papers, No. 8. Los Angeles.

————, and SIMPSON, R. D.
1961   Tule Springs, Nevada: with other evidences of man in North America. Southwest Museum Papers, No. 18. Los Angeles.

HARRIS, MARVIN
1959   The economy has no surplus? American Anthropologist, Vol. 61, No. 2, pp. 185–99. Menasha.

1968   The Rise of Anthropological Theory. Thomas Y. Crowell. New York.

HAURY, EMIL W.
1932   Roosevelt 9:6, a Hohokam site of the colonial period. Medallion Papers, No. 16. Gila Pueblo. Globe, Arizona.

1934   The Canyon Creek ruin and the cliff dwellings of the Sierra Ancha. Medallion Papers, No. 14. Gila Pueblo. Globe, Arizona.

1936a   Some southwestern pottery types. Medallion Papers, No. 19. Gila Pueblo. Globe, Arizona.

1936b   The Mogollon culture of southwestern New Mexico. Medallion Papers, No. 20. Gila Pueblo. Globe, Arizona.

1936c   Vandal Cave. Kiva, Vol. 1, No. 6. Tucson.

1940a   Excavations at Forestdale, Arizona. Kiva, Vol. 6, pp. 6–8. Tucson.

1940b   Excavations in the Forestdale Valley, east-central Arizona. University of Arizona Bulletin, Vol. 11, No. 4. Social Science Bulletin, No. 12. Tucson.

1945   The excavation of Los Muertos and neighboring ruins in the Salt River Valley, southern Arizona. Papers of the Peabody Museum of American Archaeology and Ethnology, Harvard University, Vol. 24, No. 1. Cambridge.

1950   The stratigraphy and archaeology of Ventana Cave, Arizona. University of New Mexico Press. Albuquerque.

1956   Speculations on prehistoric settlement patterns in the Southwest. In, Prehistoric settlement patterns in the New World, edited by Gordon R. Willey, pp. 3–10. Viking Fund Publications in Anthropology, No. 23. New York.

1957   An alluvial site on the San Carlos Indian Reservation, Arizona. American Antiquity, Vol. 23, No. 1, pp. 2–27. Salt Lake City.

1965   Snaketown: 1964–1965. Kiva, Vol. 31, No. 1, pp. 1–13. Tucson.

1967   The Hohokam, first masters of the American desert. National Geographic, Vol. 131, pp. 670–95. Washington, D.C.

————, ANTEVS, ERNST, and LANCE, J. F.
1953   Artifacts with mammoth remains, Naco, Arizona. American Antiquity, Vol. 19, No. 1, pp. 1–24. Salt Lake City.

————, and FULTON, W.S.
1945   Painted Cave. The Amerind Foundation, No. 3. Dragoon, Arizona.

————, and HARGRAVE, LYNDON, L.
1931   Recently dated pueblo ruins in Arizona. Smithsonian Miscellaneous Collections, Vol. 82, No. 11. Washington, D.C.

————, and SAYLES, E. B.

1947 An early pit house village of the Mogollon culture, Forestdale Valley, Arizona. University of Arizona Bulletin, Vol. 18, No. 4. Social Science Bulletin, No. 16. Tucson.

————, ————, and WASLEY, WILLIAM W.

1959 The Lehner mammoth site, southeastern Arizona. American Antiquity, Vol. 25, No. 1, pp. 2–30. Salt Lake City.

HAWLEY, FLORENCE M.

1936 Field manual of Southwestern pottery types. University of New Mexico Bulletin, Whole No. 291. Anthropological Series, Vol. 1, No. 4. Albuquerque.

HAYDEN, JULIAN D.

1957 Excavations, 1940, at University Indian ruin. Southwestern Monuments Association, Technical Series, Vol. 5. Gila Pueblo. Globe, Arizona.

HAYES, ALDEN C.

1964 The archaeological survey of Mesa Verde National Park, Colorado. Archaeological Research Series, No. 7-A. National Park Service, U. S. Department of the Interior. Washington, D.C.

HAYNES, C. VANCE, and HEMMINGS, E. T.

1968 Mammoth-bone shaft wrench from Murray Springs, Arizona. Science, Vol. 159, pp. 186–87.

HEIZER, ROBERT F.

1966 General comments. In, The current status of anthropological Research in the Great Basin: 1964, edited by Warren L. d'Azevedo, Wilbur A. Davis, Don D. Fowler, and Wayne Suttles, pp. 239–47. Desert Research Institute. Reno.

————, and KRIEGER, ALEX D.

1956 The archaeology of Humboldt Cave, Churchill County, Nevada. University of California Publications in American Archaeology and Ethnology, Vol. 47, No. 1, pp. 1–190. Berkeley and Los Angeles.

HEMENWAY, MARY

1892 Catalogo objectos etnologicos y arqueologicos por la expedition Hemenway. Taramillo Impresor Val Verde. Madrid.

HEMPEL, CARL G.

1966 Philosophy of natural science. Prentice Hall, Inc. Englewood Cliffs, New Jersey.

HEVLY, RICHARD H.

1964 Pollen analysis of Quaternary archaeological and lacustrine sediments from the Colorado Plateau. Unpublished Ph.D. dissertation. University of Arizona. Tucson.

HEWETT, EDGAR LEE

1906 Antiquities of the Jemez Plateau, New Mexico. Smithsonian Institution, Bureau of American Ethnology, Bulletin No. 32. Washington, D.C. also: Archaeological Institute of America, School of American Archaeology, Paper No. 21.

————

1909a Excavations at El Rito de los Frijoles in 1909. American Anthropologist, Vol. 11, pp. 651–73. Lancaster.

————

1909b The excavation at Puye New Mexico. Archaeological Institute of America, School of American Archaeology, Paper No. 4. Santa Fe.

————

1934 The excavation of Chetro Ketl. Art and Archaeology, Vol. 35, No. 2. Washington, D.C.

HILL, JAMES N.

1970 Broken K Pueblo: Prehistoric social organization in the American Southwest. Anthropological Papers of the University of Arizona, No. 18. Tucson.

HOLE, FRANK, and HEIZER, ROBERT F.

1969 An introduction to prehistoric archaeology, second edition. Holt, Rinehart and Winston, New York.

HOUGH, WALTER

1903 Archaeological field work in northeastern Arizona, expedition of 1901, Museum-Gates Expedition. Report of the U. S. National Museum of 1901. Washington, D.C.

1914 Culture of the ancient pueblos of the Upper Gila. Smithsonian Institution, U. S. National Museum Bulletin, No. 87. Washington, D.C.

1920 Explorations of a pit house village at Luna, New Mexico. Proceedings of the U. S. National Museum, Vol. 55, pp. 409–31. Washington, D.C.

IRWIN-WILLIAMS, CYNTHIA
1967 Picosa: the elementary Southwestern culture. American Antiquity, Vol. 32, No. 4, pp. 441–57. Salt Lake City.

———, and C. V. HAYNES
1970 Climatic change and early population dynamics in the Southwestern United States. Quaternary Research, Vol. 1, pp. 59–71.

JEANCON, JEAN ALLARD
1922 Archaeological research in northeastern San Juan Basin, Colorado. University of Denver (Press of the Webb-Kennedy Publishing Company). Denver.

1923 Excavations in the Chama Valley, New Mexico. Smithsonian Institution, Bureau of American Ethnology, Bulletin 81. Washington, D.C.

JENNINGS, JESSE D.
1956 The American Southwest: a problem in cultural isolation. In, Seminars in archaeology: 1955, edited by Robert Wauchope, pp. 59–127. Memoirs of the Society for American Archaeology, No. 11. American Antiquity, Vol. 22, No. 2, Part 2. Salt Lake City.

1957 Danger Cave. University of Utah Anthropological Papers, No. 27. Salt Lake City.

1964 The desert West. In, Prehistoric man in the New World, edited by Jesse

D. Jennings and Edward Norbeck, pp. 149–74. University of Chicago Press. Chicago.

1966 Glen Canyon: a summary. University of Utah Anthropological Papers, No. 81 (Glen Canyon Series No. 31). Salt Lake City.

———, and NORBECK, EDWARD
1955 Great Basin prehistory: a review. American Antiquity, Vol. 21, No. 1, pp. 1–11. Salt Lake City.

———, and ——— (editors)
1964 Prehistoric man in the New World. University of Chicago Press. Chicago.

JETT, S. C.
1964 Pueblo Indian migrations: an evaluation of the possible physical and cultural determinants. American Antiquity, Vol. 29, pp. 281–300. Salt Lake City.

JOHNSON, ALFRED E., and THOMPSON, RAYMOND H.
1963 The Ringo Site, southeastern Arizona. American Antiquity, Vol. 28, No. 4, pp. 465–81. Salt Lake City.

JOHNSON, L., JR.
1968 Item seriation as an aid for elementary scale and cluster analysis. Museum of Natural History, University of Oregon, Bulletin No. 15. Eugene.

JUDD, NEIL M.
1916 Archaeological reconnaissance in western Utah. Smithsonian Miscellaneous Collections, Vol. 66, No. 3. Smithsonian Institution. Washington, D.C.

1917 Evidence of circular kivas in western Utah ruins. American Anthropologist, Vol. 19, pp. 34–40. Lancaster.

1930a Arizona sacrifices her prehistoric canals. Explorations and Field-Work of the Smithsonian Institution in 1929, pp. 177–82. Smithsonian Institution. Washington, D.C.

1930b Dating our prehistoric pueblo ruins. Explorations and Field-Work of the Smithsonian Institution in 1929, pp. 167–76. Smithsonian Institution. Washington, D.C.

1931a Arizona's prehistoric canals from the air. Explorations and Field-Work of the Smithsonian Institution in 1930, pp. 157–66. Smithsonian Institution. Washington, D.C.

1931b The excavation and repair of Betatakin. U. S. National Museum Proceedings, Vol. 77, Article 5. Washington, D.C.

1954 The material culture of Pueblo Bonito. Smithsonian Miscellaneous Collections, Vol. 124 (Whole Volume). Smithsonian Institution. Washington, D.C.

1959 Pueblo del Arroyo, Chaco Canyon, New Mexico. Smithsonian Miscellaneous Collections, Vol. 138, No. 1. Smithsonian Institution. Washington, D.C.

1964 The architecture of Pueblo Bonito. Smithsonian Miscellaneous Collections, Vol. 147, No. 1. Smithsonian Institution. Washington, D.C.

KAPLAN, LAWRENCE
1956 The cultivated beans of the prehistoric Southwest. Annals of the Missouri Botanical Garden, Vol. 43, pp. 189–251. St. Louis.

1963 Archeoethnobotany of Cordova Cave, New Mexico. Economic Botany, Vol. 17, No. 4, pp. 350–59. Lancaster.

KELLEY, J. CHARLES
1952 Factors involved in the abandonment of certain peripheral southwestern settlements. American Anthropologist, Vol. 54, pp. 356–87. Menasha.

1959 The Desert cultures and the Balcones Phase: Archaic manifestations in the Southwest and Texas. American Antiquity, Vol. 24, No. 3, pp. 276–88. Salt Lake City.

KIDDER, ALFRED VINCENT
1927 Southwestern archaeological conference. Science, Vol. 66, No. 1716, pp. 489–91.

1962 An introduction to the study of Southwestern archaeology, revised edition. Yale University Press. New Haven.

———, and GUERNSEY, SAMUEL J.
1919 Archaeological explorations in northeastern Arizona. Smithsonian Institution, Bureau of American Ethnology, Bulletin 65. Washington, D.C.

KIRCHHOFF, PAUL
1954 Gatherers and farmers in the greater Southwest. American Anthropologist, Vol. 56, No. 4, Part 1, pp. 529–50. Menasha.

KLUCKHOHN, CLYDE
1939 The place of theory in anthropological studies. Philosophy of Science, Vol. 6, pp. 328–44. Cambridge.

———, and REITER, PAUL (editors)
1939 Preliminary report on the 1937 excavations, Bc 50–51, Chaco Canyon, New Mexico. Anthropological Series, Vol. 3, No. 2. The University of New Mexico Bulletin, Whole Number 345. Albuquerque.

KROEBER, A. L.
1928 Native culture in the Southwest. University of California Publications in American Archaeology and Ethnology, Vol. 23, No. 9, pp. 375–98. Berkeley.

1939 Cultural and natural areas of native North America. University of California Publications in American Archaeology and Ethnology, Vol. 38. Berkeley.

KUCHLER, A. W.
1964 Potential natural vegetation of the

U. S. (map and explanatory text). American Geographical Society. New York.

KUHN, THOMAS
1964 The structure of scientific revolutions. University of Chicago Press. Chicago.

LANCASTER, JAMES A.; PINKLEY, JEAN M.; VAN CLEAVE, PHILIP F., and WATSON, DON
1954 Archaeological excavations in Mesa Verde National Park, Colorado, 1950. Archaeological Research Series No. 2. National Park Service, U. S. Department of the Interior. Washington, D.C.

LANCE, J. F.
1959 Faunal remains from the Lehner Mammoth Site. American Antiquity, Vol. 25, pp. 35–42. Salt Lake City.

LAWRENCE, BARBARA
1968 Antiquity of large dogs in North America. Tebiwa, The Journal of the Idaho State University Museum, Vol. 2, No. 2, pp. 43–49. Pocatello.

LEE, RICHARD B., and DEVORE, IRVEN
1968 Man the hunter. Aldine. Chicago.

LEE, THOMAS A., JR.

1966 An archaeological reconnaissance of the southeastern portion of the Navajo Reservation. Unpublished Master's thesis, Department of Anthropology. University of Arizona. Tucson.

LEONE, MARK P.
1968 Economic autonomy and social distance: archaeological evidence. Unpublished Doctoral dissertation. University of Arizona. Tucson.

LIEBOW, ELLIOT
1967 Tally's corner. Little, Brown, and Company. Boston.

LIFTON, ROBERT JAY
1969 The young and the old: notes on a new history, Part I. The Atlantic Monthly, Vol. 224, No. 3, p. 47–54.

LINDSAY, A. J., JR.
1961 The Beaver Creek agricultural community on the San Juan River, Utah. American Antiquity, Vol. 27, No. 2, pp. 174–87. Salt Lake City.

1969 The Tsegi Phase of Kayenta Cultural Tradition in northeastern Arizona. Unpublished Doctoral dissertation. University of Arizona. Tucson.

———, and AMBLER, J. RICHARD
1963 Recent contributions and research problems in Kayenta Anasazi prehistory. Plateau, Vol. 35, No. 3, pp. 86–92. Museum of Northern Arizona. Flagstaff. (Glen Canyon Project).

———, ———, STEIN, M. A., and HOBLER, P. M.
1968 Survey and excavations north and east of Navajo Mountain, Utah, 1959–1962. Museum of Northern Arizona, Bulletin No. 45. Flagstaff.

LISTER, FLORENCE C.
1964 Kaiparowits Plateau and Glen Canyon prehistory: an interpretation based on ceramics. University of Utah Anthropological Papers, No. 71 (Glen Canyon Series No. 23). Salt Lake City.

LISTER, ROBERT H.
1961 Twenty-five years of archaeology in the Greater Southwest. American Antiquity, Vol. 27, No. 1, pp. 39–45. Salt Lake City.

1965 Contributions to Mesa Verde archaeology: II, Site 875, Mesa Verde National Park, Colorado. University of Colorado Studies, Series in Anthropology, No. 11. Boulder.

1966 Contributions to Mesa Verde archaeology: III, Site 866, and the cultural sequence at four villages in the Far View group, Mesa Verde National Park, Colorado. University of Colorado Studies, Series in Anthropology, No. 12. Boulder.

1967 Contributions to Mesa Verde archaeology: IV, Site 1086, an isolated, above ground kiva in Mesa Verde

National Park, Colorado. University of Colorado Studies, Series in Anthropology, No. 13. Boulder.

———— (editor)

1968 Contributions to Mesa Verde archaeology: V, emergency archaeology in Mesa Verde National Park, Colorado, 1948–1966. University of Colorado Studies, Series in Anthropology, No. 15. Boulder.

————, and LISTER, FLORENCE

1964 Contributions to Mesa Verde archaeology: I, Site 499, Mesa Verde National Park, Colorado. University of Colorado Studies, Series in Anthropology, No. 9. Boulder.

LONG, PAUL V., JR.

1966 Archaeological excavations in Lower Glen Canyon, Utah, 1959–1960. Museum of Northern Arizona, Bulletin No. 42. (Glen Canyon Series No. 7). Flagstaff.

LONGACRE, WILLIAM A.

1970a Archaeology as anthropology: a case study. Anthropological Papers of the University of Arizona, No. 17. Tucson.

———— (editor)

1970b Reconstructing prehistoric pueblo societies. School of American Research, Advanced Seminar Series. University of New Mexico Press. Albuquerque.

LOWE, C. H.

1964 Arizona landscapes and habitats. In, The vertebrates of Arizona, edited by C. H. Lowe, pp. 1–132. University of Arizona Press. Tucson.

MacNEISH, RICHARD S.

1962 Second annual report of the Tehuacan Archaeological Botanical Project. Robert S. Peabody Foundation for Archaeology, Phillips Academy. Andover, Massachusetts.

MALOUF, CARLING

1966 Ethnohistory in the Great Basin. In, The current status of anthropological research in the Great Basin: 1964, edited by Warren L. d'Azevedo, Wil-

bur A. Davis, Don D. Fowler, and Wayne Suttles, pp. 1–38. Desert Research Institute. Reno.

MANGELSDORF, PAUL C.; MacNEISH, RICHARD S., and GALINAT, WALTON C.

1964 Domestication of corn. Science, Vol. 143, No. 3606, pp. 538–45. Washington.

————, ————, and ————

1967 Environment and subsistence. In, The prehistory of the Tehuacan Valley, Vol. 1, edited by Douglas S. Byers, pp. 178–201. Robert S. Peabody Foundation, Phillips Academy, Andover, Massachusetts. University of Texas Press, Austin.

————, ————, and WILLEY, GORDON R.

1965 Natural environment and early cultures. In, Handbook of Middle American Indians, edited by Robert C. West. University of Texas Press. Austin.

MARTIN, PAUL S.

1929 The 1928 archaeological expedition of the State Historical Society of Colorado. Colorado Magazine, Vol. 6, No. 1, pp. 1–35. Denver.

————

1936 Lowry Ruin in southwestern Colorado. Anthropological Series, Field Museum of Natural History, Vol. 23, No. 1. Chicago.

————

1943 The SU Site. Excavations at a Mogollon village, western New Mexico: second season 1941. Anthropological Series, Field Museum of Natural History, Vol. 32, No. 2. Chicago.

————, LLOYD, CARL, and SPOEHR, ALEXANDER

1938 Archaeological work in the Ackmen-Lowry area, southwestern Colorado, 1937. Anthropological Series, Field Museum of Natural History, Vol. 23, No. 2. Chicago.

————, LONGACRE, WILLIAM, and HILL, JAMES N.

1967 Chapters in the prehistory of eastern Arizona, III. Fieldiana: Anthropology, Vol. 57. Field Museum of Natural History. Chicago.

———, and RINALDO, JOHN B.

1939 Modified Basket-Maker Sites, Ack-men-Lowry area, southwestern Colorado, 1938. Anthropological Series, Field Museum of Natural History, Vol. 23, No. 3. Chicago.

———, and ———

1940 The SU Site. Excavations at a Mogollon Village, western New Mexico, 1939. Anthropological Series, Field Museum of Natural History, Vol. 32, No. 1. Chicago.

———, and ———

1947 The SU Site. Excavations at a Mogollon Village, western New Mexico: third season, 1946. Anthropological Series, Field Museum of Natural History, Vol. 32, No. 3. Chicago.

———, and ———

1950a Turkey Foot Ridge Site, A Mogollon Village, Pine Lawn Valley, western New Mexico. Fieldiana: Anthropology, Vol. 38, No. 2. Chicago Natural History Museum. Chicago.

———, and ———

1950b Sites of the Reserve Phase, Pine Lawn Valley, western New Mexico. Fieldiana: Anthropology, Vol. 38, No. 3. Chicago Natural History Museum. Chicago.

———, and ———

1951 The Southwestern co-tradition. Southwestern Journal of Anthropology, Vol. 7, No. 3, pp. 215–29. Albuquerque.

———, and ———

1960a Excavations in the upper Little Colorado Drainage, eastern Arizona. Fieldiana: Anthropology, Vol. 51, No. 1. Chicago Natural History Museum. Chicago.

———, and ———

1960b Table Rock Pueblo, Arizona. Fieldiana: Anthropology, Vol. 51, No. 2. Chicago Natural History Museum. Chicago.

———, ———, and ANTEVS, ERNST

1949 Cochise and Mogollon sites, Pine Lawn Valley, western New Mexico. Fieldiana: Anthropology, Vol. 38,

No. 1. Chicago Natural History Museum. Chicago.

———, ———, and BARTER, ELOISE R.

1957 Late Mogollon communities: four sites of the Tularosa Phase, western New Mexico. Fieldiana: Anthropology, Vol. 49, No. 1. Chicago Natural History Museum. Chicago.

———, ———, and BLUHM, ELAINE A.

1954 Caves of the Reserve area. Fieldiana: Anthropology, Vol. 42. Chicago Natural History Museum. Chicago.

———, ———, ———, and CUTLER, HUGH C.

1956 Higgins Flat Pueblo, western New Mexico. Fieldiana: Anthropology, Vol. 45. Chicago Natural History Museum. Chicago.

———, ———, ———, ———, and GRANGE, ROGER, JR.

1952 Mogollon cultural continuity and change: the stratigraphic analysis of Tularosa and Cordova Caves. Fieldiana: Anthropology, Vol. 40. Chicago Natural History Museum. Chicago.

———, ———, and LONGACRE, WILLIAM A.

1961 Mineral Creek Site and Hooper Ranch Pueblo, eastern Arizona. Fieldiana: Anthropology, Vol. 52. Chicago Natural History Museum. Chicago.

———, ———, ———, CRONIN, CONSTANCE, FREEMAN, LESLIE G., JR., and SCHOENWETTER, JAMES

1962 Chapters in the prehistory of eastern Arizona, I. Fieldiana: Anthropology, Vol. 53. Chicago Natural History Museum. Chicago.

———, ———, ———, FREEMAN, LESLIE G., JR., BROWN, JAMES A., HEVLY, RICHARD H., and COOLEY, M. E.

1964 Chapters in the prehistory of eastern Arizona, II. Fieldiana: Anthropology, Vol. 55. Chicago Natural History Museum. Chicago.

MARTIN, PAUL SCHULTZ (Arizona)

1963 The last 10,000 years: a fossil pollen record of the American Southwest. University of Arizona Press. Tucson.

————, and MEHRINGER, P. J., JR.

1965 Pleistocene pollen analysis and the biogeography of the Southwest. *In,* The Quaternary of the United States, edited by H. E. Wright and David G. Frey, pp. 433–51. Princeton University Press. Princeton.

————, and SCHOENWETTER, JAMES

1960 Arizona's oldest cornfield. Science, Vol. 132, pp. 33–34.

————, ————, and ARMS, B. C.

1961 Southwestern palynology and prehistory: the last 10,000 years. Program in Geochronology, Contribution No. 50. University of Arizona. Tucson.

MATTHEWS, W., WORTMAN, J. L., and BILLINGS, J. S.

1893 Human bones of the Hemenway Collection in the United States Army Medical Museum. Memoirs of the National Academy of Sciences, No. 7, Vol. 6, pp. 141–286. Washington. D.C.

MCGREGOR, JOHN C.

1943 Burial of an early American magician. Proceedings of the American Philosophical Society, Vol. 86, No. 2. Philadelphia.

1951 The Cohonina culture of northwestern Arizona. Contribution 178 from the Museum of Northern Arizona, Flagstaff. University of Illinois Press. Urbana.

1958 The Pershing Site. Plateau, Vol. 31, No. 2, pp. 33–36. Flagstaff.

1965 Southwestern archaeology. University of Illinois Press. Urbana.

1967 The Cohonina culture of Mount Floyd, Arizona. University of Kentucky Press. Lexington.

MCLELLAN, GEORGE EDWIN

1969 The origin, development, and typology of Anasazi kivas and great kivas. Unpublished Doctoral dissertation. University of Colorado. Boulder.

MEGGERS, BETTY J.; EVANS, CLIFFORD, and ESTRADA, EMIL

1965 Early Formative period of coastal Ecuador: The Valdivia and Machalilla phases. Smithsonian Contributions to Anthropology, Vol. 1. Smithsonian Institution. Washington, D.C.

MEHRINGER, P. J., JR.

1967 The environment of extinction of the late-Pleistocene megafauna in the arid southwestern United States. *In,* Pleistocene extinctions: the search for a cause, edited by Paul Schultz Martin (Arizona) and H. E. Wright, pp. 247–66. Yale University Press. New Haven.

MELLOR, JOHN W.

1969 The subsistence farmer in traditional economics. *In,* Subsistence agriculture and economic development, edited by Clifton R. Wharton. Aldine. Chicago.

MERA, HARRY P.

1934 Observations on the archaeology of the Petrified Forest National Monument. Laboratory of Anthropology Bulletin, Technical Series, No. 7. Santa Fe.

1938 Reconnaissance and excavation in southeastern New Mexico. American Anthropological Associatoin, Memoir No. 51. Menasha.

1944 Jaritas Rock Shelter, northeastern New Mexico. American Antiquity, Vol. 9, pp. 295–301. Menasha.

MIDVALE, F.

1965 Prehistoric irrigation of the Casa Grande ruins area. Kiva, Vol. 30, pp. 82–86. Tucson.

1968 Prehistoric irrigation in the Salt River Valley. Kiva, Vol. 34, pp. 28–32. Tucson.

MILLER, JAMES G.

1965 Living systems: cross-level hypotheses. Behavioral Science, Vol. 10, No. 4, pp. 380–411.

MILLER, R. R.

1955 Fish remains from archaeological sites in the lower Colorado River Basin, Arizona. Papers of the Michigan Academy of Science, Arts, and Letters, Vol. 40, pp. 125–45.

MILLON, RENE

1962 Variations in social responses to the practice of irrigation agriculture. *In,* Civilizations in desert lands, edited by Richard B. Woodbury, pp. 56–88. University of Utah Anthropological Papers, No. 62. Salt Lake City.

MINCKLEY, W. L., and ALGER N.

1968 Fish remains from an archaeological site along the Verde River, Yavapai County, Arizona. Plateau, Vol. 40, pp. 91–97. Flagstaff.

MINDELEFF, COSMOS

1895 Cliff ruins of Canyon de Chelly, Arizona. American Anthropologist, Vol. 8 (Old Series), pp. 153–74. Washington, D.C.

1896 Aboriginal remains in Verde Valley, Arizona. Smithsonian Institution, Bureau of American Ethnology, 13th Annual Report, pp. 179–261. Washington, D.C.

1897 Cliff ruins of Canyon de Chelly, Arizona. Smithsonian Institution, Bureau of American Ethnology, 16th Annual Report, pp. 73–198. Washington, D.C.

MINDELEFF, VICTOR

1891 A study of pueblo architecture: Tusayan and Cibola. Smithsonian Institution, Bureau of American Ethnology, 8th Annual Report, 1886–1887, pp. 3–228. Washington, D.C.

MORLEY, SYLVANUS G.

1908 The excavation of the Cannonball Ruins in southwestern Colorado. American Anthropologist, Vol. 10, pp. 596–610. Lancaster.

———, and KIDDER, ALFRED V.

1917 The archaeology of McElmo Canyon, Colorado. El Palacio, Vol. 4, No. 4, pp. 41–70. Santa Fe.

MORRIS, DONALD H.

1969 Red Mountain: an early Pioneer period Hohokam site in the Salt River Valley of central Arizona. American Antiquity, Vol. 34, No. 1, pp. 40–53. Salt Lake City.

MORRIS, EARL H.

1928 The Aztec ruin. Anthropological Papers of the American Museum of Natural History, Vol. 26. New York.

1936 Archaeological background of dates in early Arizona chronology. Tree-Ring Bulletin, Vol. 2, No. 4, pp. 34–36. Flagstaff.

1938 Mummy Cave. Natural History, Vol. 42, pp. 127–38. New York.

1939 Archaeological studies in the La Plata district, southwestern Colorado and northwestern New Mexico. Carnegie Institution of Washington, Publication 519. Washington, D.C.

———, and BURGH, ROBERT F.

1941 Anasazi basketry, Basket Maker II through Pueblo III—a study based on specimens from the San Juan River Country. Carnegie Institution of Washington, Publication 533. Washington, D.C.

———, and ———

1954 Basket Maker II sites near Durango, Colorado. Carnegie Institution of Washington, Publication 604. Washington, D.C.

MORRIS, ELIZABETH ANN

1959 Basketmaker caves in the Prayer Rock District, northeastern Arizona. Unpublished Ph.D. dissertation. University of Arizona. Tucson.

MORSS, NOEL

1931a Notes on the archaeology of the Kaibito and Rainbow Plateaus in Arizona. Papers of the Peabody Museum of American Archaeology and Ethnology, Harvard University, Vol. 12, No. 2. Cambridge.

———— 1931b Ancient culture of the Fremont River in Utah. Papers of the Peabody Museum of American Archaeology and Ethnology, Harvard University, Vol. 12, No. 3. Cambridge.

MURDOCK, GEORGE P.
1967 Ethnographic atlas. University of Pittsburgh Press. Pittsburgh.

NAROLL, RAOUL
1962 Floor area and settlement population. American Antiquity, Vol. 27, No. 4, pp. 587–89. Salt Lake City.

NELSON, NELS C.
1914 Pueblo ruins of the Galisteo Basin. Anthropological Papers of the American Museum of Natural History, Vol. 15, Part 1. New York.

———— 1916 Chronology of the Tano Ruins, New Mexico. American Anthropologist, Vol. 18, pp. 159–80. Lancaster.

NESBITT, P. H.
1938 Starkweather Ruin: a Mogollon-Pueblo Site in the Upper Gila area of New Mexico and affiliative aspects of the Mogollon Culture. Logan Museum Publications in Anthropology, Bulletin No. 6. Beloit.

NICHOL, A. A.
1952 The natural vegetation of Arizona. University of Arizona Agricultural Experimental Station, Bulletin 127. Tucson.

NICHOLS, ROBERT F., and HARLAN, THOMAS
1967 Archaeological Tree-Ring dates from Wetherill Mesa. Tree-Ring Bulletin, Vol. 28, Nos. 1–4, pp. 13–40. Tree Ring Society and the Laboratory of Tree-Ring Research, University of Arizona. Tucson.

NORDENSKIÖLD, G.
1893 The cliff dwellers of the Mesa Verde, southwestern Colorado, their pottery and implements, translated by D.

Lloyd Morgan. Royal Printing Office. Stockholm.

OLSON, ALAN P.
1963 Some archaeological problems of central and northeastern Arizona. Plateau, Vol. 35, No. 3, pp. 93–106. Flagstaff.

ORANS, MARTIN
1965 Surplus. Human Organization, Vol. 25, pp. 25–32.

OSBORNE, DOUGLAS, and NICHOLS, ROBERT F.
1967 Introduction. In, The dendrochronology of the Wetherill Mesa archaeological project. Tree-Ring Bulletin, Vol. 28, Nos. 1–4, pp. 1–6. Tree-Ring Society and the Laboratory of Tree-Ring Research, University of Arizona. Tucson.

PEPPER, GEORGE H.
1902 The ancient Basket Makers of southeastern Utah. Supplement to American Museum Journal, Vol. II, No. 4, April 1902, guide leaflet no. 6. New York.

———— 1920 Pueblo Bonito. Anthropological Papers of the American Museum of Natural History, Vol. 27. New York.

PETSCHE, JEROME E. (editor)
1968 Bibliography of salvage archaeology in the United States. Publications in Salvage Archaeology, No. 10. River Basin Surveys, Museum of Natural History. Smithsonian Institution. Lincoln.

PINKLEY, FRANK
1935 Seventeen years ago. Southwest Monuments Monthly, Report for November, p. 388. Casa Grande National Monument.

PLATEAU MUSEUM NOTES
1928– Vols. 1–4. Museum of Northern Ari-
1932 zona. Flagstaff.

PLOG, FRED T.
1969 An approach to the study of prehistoric change. Unpublished Ph.D. dissertation. University of Chicago. Chicago.

————, and GARRETT, C.

1970   Explaining variability in prehistoric southwestern water control systems. Paper presented at the 35th Annual Meeting of the Society for American Archaeology. Mexico City.

PLOG, STEPHEN

1969   Prehistoric population movements: measurement and explanation. Unpublished manuscript. Field Museum of Natural History. Chicago.

POLGE, HUBERT

1970   The use of X-ray densitometric methods in dendrochronology. Tree-Ring Bulletin, Vol. 30, Nos. 1–4, pp. 1–11. Tree-Ring Society and the Laboratory of Tree-Ring Research, University of Arizona. Tucson.

PRUDDEN, T. MITCHELL

1903   The prehistoric ruins of the San Juan watershed of Utah, Arizona, Colorado, and New Mexico. American Anthropologist, Vol. 5, pp. 224–28. Lancaster.

————

1914   The circular kivas of small ruins in the San Juan watershed. American Anthropologist, Vol. 16, pp. 33–58. Lancaster.

————

1918   A further study of prehistoric small house ruins. American Anthropological Association, Memoir No. 5, pp. 1–50. Lancaster.

RADIOCARBON

1963   Editorial statement. Vol. 5. Editors: Edward S. Deevey, Richard Foster Flint, and Irving Rouse. Yale University. New Haven.

RANERE, ANTHONY J.

1970   Prehistoric environments and cultural continuity in the western Great Basin. Tebiwa, The Journal of the Idaho State University Museum, Vol. 13, No. 2, pp. 52–73. Pocatello.

RAPAPORT, ANATOLE

1968   Foreword. In, Modern systems research for the behavioral scientist: a sourcebook, edited by Walter Buckley, pp. xiii–xxii. Aldine. Chicago.

REED, ERIK K.

1956   Types of village-plan layouts in the Southwest. In, Prehistoric settlement patterns in the New World, edited by Gordon R. Willey, pp. 11–17. Viking Fund Publications in Anthropology, No. 23. New York.

————

1958   Excavations in Mancos Canyon, Colorado. University of Utah Anthropological Papers, No. 35. Salt Lake City.

RENAUD, ÉTIENNE B.

1933   Archaeological survey of eastern Colorado, Third Report, season 1932. University of Denver, Department of Anthropology. Denver.

————

1942   Reconnaissance work in the Upper Rio Grande Valley, Colorado and New Mexico. University of Denver, Department of Anthropology, Archaeological Series, Third Paper. Denver.

————, and CHATIN, JANET

1943   Archaeological sites of the Cuchara Drainage, southern Colorado. University of Denver, Department of Anthropology, Archaeological Series, Fourth Paper. Denver.

RINALDO, JOHN B.

1959   Foote Canyon Pueblo, eastern Arizona. Fieldiana: Anthropology, Vol. 49, No. 2. Chicago Natural History Museum. Chicago.

————, and BLUHM, ELAINE A.

1956   Late Mogollon pottery types of the Reserve Area. Fieldiana: Anthropology, Vol. 36, No. 7. Chicago Natural History Museum. Chicago.

ROBERTS, FRANK H. H., JR.

1925   Report on archaeological reconnaissance in southwestern Colorado. Colorado Magazine, Vol. 2, No. 2. Denver.

————

1929   Shabik'eshchee Village, a Late Basketmaker site. Smithsonian Institution, Bureau of American Ethnology, Bulletin No. 92. Washington, D.C.

—— 1930 Early Pueblo ruins in the Piedra District, southwestern Colorado. Smithsonian Institution, Bureau of American Ethnology, Bulletin No. 96. Washington, D.C.

—— 1931 The ruins at Kiatuthlanna, eastern Arizona. Smithsonian Institution, Bureau of American Ethnology, Bulletin No. 100. Washington, D.C.

—— 1936a A survey of Southwestern archaeology. Smithsonian Annual Report for 1935, pp. 507–33. Government Printing Office. Washington, D.C.

—— 1936b Additional information on the Folsom Complex. Smithsonian Miscellaneous Collections, Vol. 95, No. 10. Washington, D.C.

—— 1939 Archaeological remains in the Whitewater District, eastern Arizona: Part I, house types. Smithsonian Institution, Bureau of American Ethnology, Bulletin No. 121. Washington, D.C.

—— 1940 Archaeological remains in the Whitewater District, eastern Arizona: Part II, artifacts and burials. Smithsonian Institution, Bureau of American Ethnology, Bulletin No. 126. Washington, D.C.

RODGERS, J. B.
1970 Prehistoric agricultural systems in the Vosberg locality, Arizona. Paper presented at the Pecos Conference. Santa Fe.

ROGERS, M. J.
1945 An outline of Yuman prehistory. Southwestern Journal of Anthropology, Vol. 1, pp. 167–98. Albuquerque.

ROHN, ARTHUR H.
1963a Prehistoric soil and water conservation on Chapin Mesa, southwestern Colorado. American Antiquity, Vol. 28, No. 4, pp. 441–55. Salt Lake City.

—— 1963b An ecological approach to the Great Pueblo occupation of the Mesa Verde, Colorado. Plateau, Vol. 36, No. 1, pp. 1–17. Flagstaff.

ROWE, CHANDLER
1947 The Wheatley Ridge Site. Unpublished Master's thesis. University of Chicago. Chicago.

RUDY, JACK R.
1955 Archaeological excavations in Beef Basin, Utah. University of Utah Anthropological Papers, No. 20. Salt Lake City.

RUPPÉ, REYNOLD J.
1966 The archaeological survey: a defense. American Antiquity, Vol. 31, No. 3, pp. 313–33. Salt Lake City.

——, and DITTERT, A. E., JR.
1952 The archaeology of Cebolleta Mesa and Acoma Pueblo: a preliminary report based on further investigation. El Palacio, Vol. 59, No. 7, pp. 191–217. Santa Fe.

——, and ——
1953 Acoma achaeology: a preliminary report of the first season in the Cebolleta Mesa region, New Mexico. El Palacio, Vol. 60, No. 7, pp. 259–73. Santa Fe.

SAHLINS, MARSHALL D., and SERVICE, ELMAN R. (editors)
1960 Evolution and culture. University of Michigan Press. Ann Arbor.

SAYLES, E. B.
1945 The San Simon Branch: excavations at Cave Creek and in the San Simon Valley I: material culture. Medallion Papers, No. 34. Gila Pueblo. Globe, Arizona.

——, and ANTEVS, ERNST
1941 The Cochise Culture. Medallion Papers, No. 29. Gila Pueblo. Globe, Arizona.

SCANTLING, FREDRICH H.
1939 Jack Rabbit Ruin. Kiva, Vol. 5, No. 3, pp. 9–12. Tucson.

SCHABER, G. G., and GUMERMAN, G. J.
1969 Infrared scanning images: an archae-

ological application. Science, Vol. 164, p. 712.

SCHIFFER, MICHAEL B.

1968 The relationship between economic diversity and population growth: the test of an hypothesis. Unpublished manuscript. Field Museum of Natural History. Chicago.

—— 1970 Cultural laws and reconstruction of past lifeways. Paper presented at the 35th Annual Meeting of the Society for American Archaeology. Mexico City.

—— n.d. Systemic context and archaeological context. American Antiquity. (In press.)

SCHOENWETTER, JAMES

1962 The pollen analysis of eighteen archaeological sites in Arizona and New Mexico. In, Chapters in the prehistory of eastern Arizona, I, by Paul S. Martin, et al., pp. 168–209. Fieldiana: Anthropology, Vol. 53. Chicago Natural History Museum. Chicago.

——, and DITTERT, A.

1968 An ecological interpretation of Anasazi settlement pattern. In, Anthropological archaeology in the Americas, edited by Betty J. Meggars, pp. 41–66. Anthropological Society of Washington. Washington, D.C.

SCHROEDER, ALBERT H.

1940 A stratigraphic survey of pre-Spanish trash mounds of the Salt River Valley, Arizona. Unpublished Master's thesis. University of Arizona. Tucson.

—— 1952 A brief survey of the Lower Colorado from Davis Dam to the international border. Unpublished manuscript. National Park Service. Copy in the Library of the Museum of Northern Arizona.

—— 1957 The Hakataya cultural tradition. American Antiquity, Vol. 23, No. 2, Part 1, pp. 176–78. Salt Lake City.

—— 1960 The Hohokam, Sinagua, and Hakataya. Archives of Archaeology, No. 5. Madison.

—— 1961a The archaeological excavations at Willow Beach, Arizona, 1950. University of Utah Anthropological Papers, No. 50. Salt Lake City.

—— 1961b An archaeological survey of the Painted Rocks Reservoir, western Arizona. Ziva, Vol. 27, pp. 1–28. Tucson.

SCHULMAN, ALBERT

1950 Pre-Columbian towers in the Southwest. American Antiquity, Vol. 15, No. 4, Part 1, pp. 288–97. Menasha.

SCHULMAN, E.

1951 Tree-ring indices of rainfall, temperature, and river flow. In, Compendium of meteorology, edited by T. F. Malone, pp. 1024–32. American Meteorological Society. Boston.

—— 1956 Dendroclimatic changes in semiarid America. University of Arizona Press. Tucson.

SCHWARTZ, DOUGLAS W.

1956 Demographic changes in early periods of Cohonina prehistory. In, Prehistoric settlement patterns in the New World, edited by Gordon R. Willey, pp. 26–31. Viking Fund Publications in Anthropology, No. 23. New York.

—— 1960 Archaeological investigations in the Shinumo area of Grand Canyon, Arizona. Plateau, Vol. 32, pp. 61–67. Flagstaff.

—— 1966 A historical analysis and synthesis of Grand Canyon archaeology. American Antiquity, Vol. 31, No. 4, pp. 469–84. Salt Lake City.

SERVICE, ELMAN R.

1960 The law of evolutionary potential.

In, Evolution and culture, edited by Marshall D. Sahlins and Elman R. Service, pp. 93–122. University of Michigan Press. Ann Arbor.

1962   Primitive social organization. Random House. New York.

SHARROCK, FLOYD W.; DAY, KENT C., and DIBBLE, DAVID S.

1963   1961 excavations, Glen Canyon area. University of Utah Anthropological Papers, No. 63 (Glen Canyon Series No. 18). Salt Lake City.

————, DIBBLE, DAVID S., and ANDERSON, KEITH M.

1961   The Creeping Dune irrigation site in Glen Canyon, Utah. American Antiquity, Vol. 27, No. 2, pp. 188–202. Salt Lake City.

————, *et al.*

1964   1962 excavations, Glen Canyon area. University of Utah Anthropological Papers, No. 73 (Glen Canyon Series No. 25). Salt Lake City.

SHELFORD, VICTOR E.

1963   The ecology of North America. University of Illinois Press. Urbana.

SHEPARD, ANNA O.

1956   Ceramics for the archaeologist. Carnegie Institution of Washington, Publication 609. Washington, D.C.

SHUTLER, RICHARD, JR.

1951   Excavation of a pithouse in Williamson Valley, Arizona. Plateau, Vol. 24, pp. 130–33. Flagstaff.

1965   Tule Springs expedition. Current Anthropology, Vol. 6, No. 1, pp. 110–11. Utrecht, Netherlands.

————, SHUTLER, M. E., and GRIFFITH, JAMES S.

1960   Stuart Rock Shelter, a stratified site in southern Nevada. Nevada State Museum Anthropological Papers, No. 3. Carson City.

SKOKES, M. A., and SMILEY, T. L.

1968   Tree-ring dating. University of Chicago Press. Chicago.

SMILEY, T. L.

1951   A summary of tree-ring dates from some southwestern archaeological sites. University of Arizona Bulletin, Vol. 22, No. 4, Laboratory of Tree-Ring Research, No. 5, Tucson.

SMITH, DAVID G., and NICHOLS, ROBERT F.

1967   A tree-ring chronology for climatic analysis. Tree-Ring Bulletin, Vol. 28, Nos. 1–4, pp. 7–12. Tree-Ring Society and the Laboratory of Tree-Ring Research, University of Arizona. Tucson.

SMITH, WATSON

1971   Painted ceramics of the western mound at Awatovi. Papers of the Peabody Museum of Archaeology and Ethnology, Harvard University, no. 38. Cambridge.

————, WOODBURY, RICHARD B., and WOODBURY, NATHALIE F. S.

1966   The excavation of Hawikuh by Frederick Webb Hodge: report of the Hendricks-Hodge Expedition, 1917–1923. Contributions from the Museum of the American Indian, Heye Foundation, Vol. 20. New York.

SPAULDING, ALBERT C.

1960a   Statistical description and comparison of artifact assemblages. *In,* The application of quantitative methods in archaeology, edited by Robert F. Heizer and Sherburne F. Cook, pp. 60–83. Viking Fund Publications in Anthropology, No. 28. New York.

1960b   The dimensions of archaeology. *In,* Essays in the science of culture: in honor of Leslie A. White, edited by Gertrude E. Dole and Robert L. Carneiro, pp. 437–56. Thomas Y. Crowell. New York.

SPICER, EDWARD H., and CAYWOOD, LOUIS R.

1936   Two Pueblo ruins in west central Arizona. University of Arizona Bulletin, Vol. 7, No. 1. Social Science Bulletin No. 10. Tucson.

SPIER, LESLIE

1919a   Notes on some Little Colorado ruins.

Anthropological Papers of the American Museum of Natural History, Vol. 18, Part 4, pp. 333–62. New York.

1919b Ruins in the White Mountains, Arizona. American Museum of Natural History, Vol. 18, Part 5, pp. 363–86. New York.

1921 The Sun Dance of the Plains Indians: its development and diffusion. Anthropological Papers of the American Museum of Natural History, Vol. 16, No. 7, pp. 451–527. New York.

1929 Problems arising from the cultural position of the Havasupai. American Anthropologist, Vol. 31, pp. 213–22. Menasha.

STEEN, CHARLES R.
1965 Excavations in Compound A, Casa Grande National Monument, 1963. Kiva, Vol. 31, No. 2, pp. 59–82. Tucson.

1966 Tse-Ta'a. National Park Service, Archaeological Research Series, No. 9. Washington, D.C.

————, PIERSON, L. M.; BOHRER, V. L., and PECK, K. K.
1962 Archaeological studies at Tonto National Monument. Southwestern Monuments Association, Technical Series, No. 2, Globe, Arizona.

STEPHEN, A. M.
1936 Hopi journal of A. M. Stephen, edited by E. C. Parsons. Columbia University Contributions to Anthropology, Vol. 23. New York.

STEWARD, JULIAN
1936 Economic and social basis for primitive bands. In, Essays in anthropology presented to A. L. Kroeber, edited by R. Lowie, pp. 359–70. University of California Press. Berkeley.

1937 Ancient caves of the Great Salt Lake region. Smithsonian Institution, Bureau of Amercian Ethnology, Bulletin No. 116. Washington, D.C.

1949 Cultural causality and law: a trial formulation of the development of early civilizations. American Anthropologist, Vol. 51, No. 1, pp. 1–27. Menasha.

1955 Theory of culture change. University of Illinois Press. Urbana.

————, and SETZLER, F. M.
1938 Function and configuration in archaeology. American Antiquity, Vol. 4, pp. 4–10. Menasha.

STEWART, G. R., and CONNELLY, MAURICE
1943 Soil and water economy in the pueblo southwest. Scientific Monthly, Vol. 56, No. 1.

STEWART, K. M.
1965 Mojave Indian gathering of wild plants. Kiva, Vol. 31, pp. 46–53. Tucson.

STEWART, T. D.
1940 Skeletal remains from the Whitewater District, eastern Arizona. Smithsonian Institution, Bureau of American Ethnology, Appendix to Bulletin No. 126. Washington, D.C.

STRONG, W. D.
1936 Anthropological theory and archaeological fact. In, Essays in anthropology presented to A. L. Kroeber, edited by R. Lowie, pp. 359–70. University of California Press. Berkeley.

STUBBS, STANLEY A.
1953 The excavation of Pindi Pueblo, New Mexico. Monographs of the School of American Research, No. 18. Santa Fe.

STUIVER, M.
1965 Carbon-14 content of 18th and 19th century wood: variations correlated with sunspot activity. Science, Vol. 149, pp. 533–35.

————, and SUESS, H.
1966 On the relationship between radiocarbon dates and true age samples. Radiocarbon, Vol. 8, pp. 534–40. New Haven.

SWANSON, EARL H., JR.
1966 The geographic foundations of the Desert Culture. *In*, The current status of anthropological research in the Great Basin: 1964, edited by Warren L. d'Azevedo, Wilbur A. Davis, Don D. Fowler, and Wayne Suttles, pp. 137–46. Desert Research Institute. Reno.

TANNER, CLARA LEE
1936 Blackstone Ruins. Kiva, Vol. 2, No. 3, pp. 1–12. Tucson.

TAX, SOL (editor)
1964 Horizons of anthropology. Aldine. Chicago.

TAYLOR, DEE CALDERWOOD
1954 The Garrison Site. University of Utah Anthropological Papers, No. 16. Salt Lake City.

TAYLOR, WALTER W.
1948 A study of archaeology. American Anthropological Association, Memoir No. 69. American Anthropologist, Vol. 50, No. 3, Part 2. Menasha.

————
1954a An early slabhouse, near Kayenta, Arizona. Plateau, Vol. 26, No. 4, pp. 109–16. Flagstaff.

————
1954b Southwestern archaeology, its history and theory. American Anthropologist, Vol. 56, No. 4, Part 1, pp. 561–69. Menasha.

THOMAS, TULLY H.
1952 The Concho Complex: a popular report. Plateau, Vol. 25, No. 1, pp. 1–9. Flagstaff.

THOMPSON, RAYMOND H. and LONGACRE, WILLIAM A.
1966 The University of Arizona archaeological field school at Grasshopper, east-central Arizona. Kiva, Vol. 31, No. 4, pp. 255–75. Tucson.

TRAUGOTT, JOSEPH
1968 The isolation and measurement of stylistic variation. Unpublished manuscript. Field Museum of Natural History. Chicago.

TRIGGER, BRUCE G.
1970 Aims in prehistoric archaeology. Antiquity, Vol. 44, No. 173, pp. 26–37. Cambridge, England.

TURNER, CHRISTY G., II
1963 Petrographs of the Glen Canyon region. Museum of Northern Arizona, Bulletin No. 38 (Glen Canyon Series No. 4). Flagstaff.

————, and MORRIS, N. T.
1970 A massacre at Hopi. American Antiquity, Vol. 35, pp. 320–32. Washington, D.C.

TURNEY, OMAR A.
1929 Prehistoric irrigation in Arizona. Arizona State Historian. Phoenix.

TUTHILL, CARR
1947 The Tres Alamos Site on the San Pedro River, southeastern Arizona. The Amerind Foundation, No. 4. Dragoon, Arizona.

UCKO, P. J., and DIMBLEBY, G. W. (editors)
1969 The domestication and exploitation of plants and animals. Duckworth. London.

VALENTINE, CHARLES A.
1968 Culture and poverty. University of Chicago Press. Chicago.

VAYDA, ANDREW P. (editor)
1969 Environment and cultural behavior. Natural History Press. New York.

VISHNER, STEPHEN S.
1966 Climatic atlas of the U. S. Harvard University Press. Cambridge.

VIVIAN, GORDON
1959 The Hubbard Site and other tri-wall structures in New Mexico and Colorado. Archaeological Research Series, No. 5. National Park Service, U. S. Department of the Interior. Washington, D.C.

1965   The Three-C Site, an Early Pueblo II ruin in Chaco Canyon, New Mexico. University of New Mexico Publications in Anthropology, No. 13. Albuquerque.

————, and MATHEWS, TOM W.
1966   Kin Kletso, a Pueblo III community in Chaco Canyon, New Mexico. Southwestern Monuments Association, Technical Series, Vol. 6, Parts 1 and 2. Globe, Arizona.

————, and REITER, PAUL
1960   The great kivas of Chaco Canyon and their relationships. Monographs of the School of American Research and the Museum of New Mexico, No. 22. Santa Fe.

VIVIAN, R. GWINN
1965   An archaeological survey of the Lower Gila River, Arizona. Kiva, Vol. 30, pp. 95–146. Tucson.

1970   An inquiry into prehistoric social organization in Chaco Canyon, New Mexico. In, Reconstructing prehistoric pueblo societies, edited by William A. Longacre, pp. 59–83. University of New Mexico Press. Albuquerque.

WADE, WILLIAM D., and KENT, KATE PECK
1968   An infant burial from the Verde Valley, central Arizona. Plateau, Vol. 40, No. 4, pp. 148–56. Flagstaff.

WARREN, CLAUDE N., and RANERE, ANTHONY J.
1968   Outside Danger Cave: a view of early man in the Great Basin. In, Early man in western North America, edited by C. Irwin-Williams, pp. 6–18. Eastern New Mexico University Contributions in Anthropology, Vol. 1, No. 4.

WASLEY, WILLIAM W.
1957a   Highway salvage archaeology by the Arizona State Museum, 1956–1957. Kiva, Vol. 23, No. 2, pp. 17–19. Tucson.

1957b   Highway salvage archaeology in Arizona. Kiva, Vol. 23, No. 2, pp. 4–9. Tucson.

1960a   A Hohokam platform mound at the Gatlin Site, Gila Bend, Arizona. American Antiquity, Vol. 26, No. 2, pp. 244–62. Salt Lake City.

1960b   Salvage archaeology on highway 66 in eastern Arizona. American Antiquity, Vol. 26, No. 1, pp. 30–42. Salt Lake City.

————, and JOHNSON, A. E.
1965   Salvage archaeology in Painted Rocks Reservoir, western Arizona. University of Arizona Anthropological Papers, No. 9. Tucson.

WATSON, PATTY JO; LeBLANC, STEVEN A., and REDMAN, CHARLES L.
n.d.   Explanation in archaeology. (In Press.)

WEAVER, KENNETH F.
1967   Magnetic clues help date the past. National Geographic, Vol. 131, pp. 696–701. Washington, D.C.

WENDORF, FRED
1953   Archaeological studies in the Petrified Forest National Monument, with sections by Kate Peck Kent, Earl H. Morris, and Anna G. Shepard. Museum of Northern Arizona, Bulletin No. 27. Flagstaff.

1956   Some distributions of settlement patterns in the pueblo Southwest. In, Prehistoric settlement patterns in the New World, edited by Gordon R. Willey, pp. 18–25. Viking Fund Publications in Anthropology, No. 23. New York.

————, FOX, NANCY, and LEWIS, ORIAN L. (editors)
1956   Pipeline archaeology, reports of salvage operations in the Southwest on El Paso Natural Gas Company projects, 1950–1953. Published jointly by the Laboratory of Anthropology and the Museum of Northern Arizona. Santa Fe and Flagstaff.

WHEAT, J. B.

1954   Crooked Ridge Village (Arizona W:10 15). University of Arizona Social Science Bulletin, No. 24. Tucson.

1955   Mogollon culture prior to A.D. 1000. Memoirs of the Society for American Archaeology, No. 10. Salt Lake City.

——, GIFFORD, J. C., and WASLEY, W. W.

1958   Ceramic variety, type cluster, and ceramic system in Southwestern pottery analysis. American Antiquity, Vol. 24, No. 1, pp. 34–47. Salt Lake City.

WHITE, LESLIE A.

1959a The evolution of culture. McGraw-Hill, New York.

1959b The concept of culture. American Anthropologist, Vol. 61, No. 2, pp. 227–51. Menasha.

WHITING, ALFRED F.

1939   Ethnobotany of the Hopi. Museum of Northern Arizona, Bulletin No. 15. Flagstaff.

WILLEY, GORDON R.

1956   Introduction. In, Prehistoric settlement patterns in the New World, edited by Gordon R. Willey, pp. 1–2. Viking Fund Publications in Anthropology, No. 23. New York.

1966   An introduction to American archaeology, Volume One, North and Middle America. Prentice-Hall. Englewood Cliffs, New Jersey.

——, and PHILLIPS, PHILLIP

1958   Method and theory in American archaeology. University of Chicago Press. Chicago.

WILMSEN, EDWIN N.

1970   Lithic analysis and cultural inference: a paleo-Indian case. Anthropological Papers of the University of Arizona, No. 6. Tucson.

WILSON, JOHN P.; WINSTON, JON H., and BERGER, ALLAN J.

1961   Burials at Kinnikinnick Pueblo. Plateau, Vol. 34, No. 1. Flagstaff.

WOODBURY, RICHARD B.

1954   Prehistoric stone implements of northeastern Arizona. Reports of the Awatovi Expedition, No. 6. Papers of the Peabody Museum of American Archaeology and Ethnology, Harvard University, Vol. 34. Cambridge.

1961   Prehistoric agriculture at Point of Pines, Arizona. Memoirs of the Society for American Archaeology, No. 17. American Antiquity, Vol. 26, No. 3, Part 2. Salt Lake City.

——, and RESSLER, JOHN Q.

1962   Effects of environmental and cultural limitations upon Hohokam agriculture, southern Arizona. In, Civilizations in Desert Sands, edited by Richard B. Woodbury. University of Utah Anthropological papers, No. 62. Salt Lake City.

WOODWARD, ARTHUR

1931   The Grewe Site. Los Angeles Museum of History, Science and Art, Occasional Papers, No. 1. Los Angeles.

WORMINGTON, H. M.

1947   Prehistoric Indians of the Southwest. Denver Museum of Natural History, Popular Series No. 7. Denver.

WRIGHT, B. A.

1954   Excavation of Catclaw Cave, Lower Colorado River. Unpublished Master's thesis. University of Arizona. Tucson.

ZAHNHISER, J. L.

1966   Late prehistoric villages southeast of Tucson, Arizona, and the archaeology of the Tanque Verde Phase. Kiva, Vol. 31, pp. 103–204. Tucson.

ZINGG, ROBERT MOWRY

1933   A reconstruction of Uto-Aztecan history. Unpublished Ph.D. dissertation. University of Chicago. Chicago.

ZUBROW, EZRA B. W.

1969a Carrying capacity as a dynamic equilibrium system in the Hay Hollow Valley. Paper presented at the Pecos Conference. Prescott, Arizona.

—————

1969b Population, contact, and climate in the New Mexico Pueblos. Unpublished Master's thesis. University of Arizona. Tucson.

—————

1970 Settlement pattern and the marginality hypothesis. Paper presented at the 35th Annual Meeting of the Society for American Archaeology. Mexico City.

—————

1971 A Southwestern test of an anthropological model of population dynamics. Unpublished Ph.D. dissertation. University of Arizona. Tucson.

Index

E

D

F